THIRD EDITION

STRATEGIC SPORT COMMUNICATION

Paul M. Pedersen, PhD
Indiana University

Pamela C. Laucella, PhD
Indiana University–Purdue University Indianapolis

Edward (Ted) M. Kian, PhD
Oklahoma State University

Andrea N. Geurin, PhD
Loughborough University

HUMAN KINETICS

Library of Congress Cataloging-in-Publication Data

Names: Pedersen, Paul Mark, author.
Title: Strategic sport communication / Paul M. Pedersen, PhD, Pamela C.
  Laucella, PhD, Edward (Ted) M. Kian, PhD, Andrea N. Geurin, PhD.
Description: Third edition. | Champaign, IL : Human Kinetics, [2021] |
  Includes bibliographical references and index:
Identifiers: LCCN 2019057316 (print) | LCCN 2019057317 (ebook) | ISBN
  9781492594499 (paperback) | ISBN 9781492594505 (epub) | ISBN
  9781492594512 (pdf)
Subjects: LCSH: Sports administration. | Communication in sports.
Classification: LCC GV713 .P43 2021 (print) | LCC GV713 (ebook) | DDC
  796.06/9--dc23
LC record available at https://lccn.loc.gov/2019057316
LC ebook record available at https://lccn.loc.gov/2019057317

ISBN: 978-1-4925-9449-9 (print)

The web addresses cited in this text were current as of February 2020, unless otherwise noted.

Acquisitions Editor: Andrew L. Tyler
Developmental Editor: Melissa J. Zavala
Copyeditor: Laura Stoffel
Proofreader: Shawn Donnelly
Indexer: Nan N. Badgett
Permissions Manager: Dalene Reeder
Graphic Designer: Denise Lowry
Cover Designer: Keri Evans
Cover Design Specialist: Susan Rothermel Allen
Photograph (cover): Mike Hewitt – FIFA / Getty Images
Photographs (interior): © Human Kinetics, unless otherwise noted
Photo Production Manager: Jason Allen
Senior Art Manager: Kelly Hendren
Illustrations: © Human Kinetics, unless otherwise noted
Printer: Sheridan Books

Printed in the United States of America   10 9 8 7 6 5 4 3

The paper in this book is certified under a sustainable forestry program.

Human Kinetics
1607 N. Market Street
Champaign, IL 61820
USA

United States and International
Website: **US.HumanKinetics.com**
Email: info@hkusa.com
Phone: 1-800-747-4457

Canada
Website: **Canada.HumanKinetics.com**
Email: info@hkcanada.com

E7983

Tell us what you think!
Human Kinetics would love to hear what we
can do to improve the customer experience.
Use this QR code to take our brief survey.

Contents

Part II   Examining the Strategic Sport Communication Model (SSCM)   77

Part III Addressing Issues in Sport Communication 335

Preface

Since the publication of the first two editions of *Strategic Sport Communication*, the field of sport communication continues to witness a massive transformation, which has brought changes of a profound and pervasive nature. These changes involve many facets of the field ranging from the financial (e.g., billion-dollar television rights deals), promotional (e.g., use of hashtags to generate interest and interaction), and technological (e.g., streaming services, cloud computing, artificial intelligence) to the personal (e.g., mediated interpersonal interactions, parasocial opportunities) and organizational (e.g., taking advantage of the opportunities offered in analytics and big data, responding to social media blunders by

stakeholders). The rapidity of such changes is emphasized by the fact that many aspects of sport communication now differ vastly from the form they took just a few years ago.

As a result, the changes transforming the field of sport communication over the last few years have introduced new and unique challenges, opportunities, issues, terms, activities, and even careers. Of course, many aspects of communication covered in the first two editions remain the same. For instance, the elements of the Strategic Sport Communication Model (SSCM) still represent the key communication components in the sport industry today: interpersonal communication, organizational communication, and

Professional golfers on the LPGA Tour talk with their caddies who are wearing bibs that include the golfers' names and Twitter handles.

mediated communication. However, although the SSCM components still apply, sport communication—which is situated within the multibillion-dollar sport industry—continues to witness such staggering changes and growth that a third edition of the textbook is needed to provide a current examination and overview of this evolving and exciting field.

The changes in the field have not only affected sport communication professionals, such as sportswriters, sports information directors, and sport broadcasters. They have also been felt throughout the sport industry, and the industry's growth and expansion have been accompanied by increased competition, which in turn has increased the need for individuals who are well versed in communication practices and management principles. More specifically, the ways in which organizations—particularly sport industry professionals—communicate with both internal and external publics has been reshaped by the development of new technologies and the demand for a diverse array of sport products.

These changes have increased the number of sport communication professionals and, more generally, increased the pressure felt by sport industry professionals to communicate effectively and make wise strategic communication decisions. As a result, courses and specializations in sport communication are now part of various curricula offered by academic units around the world. The students enrolled in these programs—whether they are considering a specific sport communication career or eyeing work in another area of the sport industry—can benefit from the expansive approach to sport communication that characterizes the third edition of this textbook. In each chapter, you will notice two profiles that highlight professionals using sport communication. Most of the profiles were written from interviews conducted by the authors. Sport Communication at Work profiles at the beginning of each chapter introduce readers to the concepts presented in the chapter. The Profile of a Sport Communicator profiles provide a taste of professional opportunities available after students complete their studies.

As with the earlier editions of *Strategic Sport Communication*, this third edition serves as a primary resource for academicians and students in sport communication and can also be used as

Aspects of sport communication are displayed in this photo of a coach interacting with an athlete.

Photo courtesy of Paul M. Pedersen.

an informational tool for sport industry professionals. In addition, although most students who read this book will major or take courses in sport-related areas of study (e.g., sport communication, sport management, sport media, sport journalism, sport studies), this third edition is also useful for students in interdisciplinary or indirectly related programs, such as new media studies, marketing, public relations, organizational communication, telecommunications, advertising, digital communication, photojournalism, and management. This edition is accompanied by an instructor guide, test package, and presentation package. The instructor guide includes chapter outlines, suggested lecture outlines, and student activities for the classroom to facilitate learning and engagement with the materials. The test package includes a variety of questions that instructors can use when creating or supplementing tests and quizzes. Instructors may use the presentation slides in the presentation package to customize lecture presentations. Instructor ancillaries are free to adoption instructors. Please contact your Sales Manager for details about how to access instructor resources.

Indeed, because of the multifaceted and inter-related aspects of sport communication, this introductory textbook focuses on the full scope, rather than on just one area, of the discipline. In other words, it covers the entire field of sport communication, which includes a wide range of endeavors—for example, mass media coverage of sporting events, marketing communication strategies of sport entities, interpersonal interactions between sport industry stakeholders, and use of social media by sport organizations. As a result, you will find coverage of topics as diverse as enhancing your communication skills, managing a website, and coordinating sport media relations. This macro analysis of sport communication is accomplished by examining the field from a wide variety of lenses, ranging from the personal to the organizational to the external and mass-mediated perspectives.

The organization of this book enables readers to build a knowledge base pertaining to current trends, industry demands, and professional opportunities upon which they can pursue a career in their chosen area of sport communication. The book's authors (Paul M. Pedersen, Pamela C. Laucella, Edward [Ted] M. Kian, and Andrea N. Geurin) aim for readers to become thoroughly familiar with—and excited about their aspirations in—the field of sport communication. For readers who do not plan to work in the field, the book provides an overview of sport communication's key aspects, its influence, and how knowledge of the field can position them to take advantage of opportunities in their own roles as stakeholders in the sport industry—for example, as consumers, managers, advertisers, or enthusiasts.

Part I (*Introducing Sport Communication*) includes the book's first three chapters, which familiarize readers with the field. Chapter 1 defines sport communication and illustrates changes and opportunities in the study and practice of sport communication. Chapter 2 provides readers with an extensive discussion of sport communication jobs and career-preparation strategies. Chapter 3 give an historical analysis of key eras, personalities, and activities in the field.

After this introduction to the field, the eight chapters of part II (*Examining the Strategic Sport Communication Model [SSCM]*) address the development, arrangement, and elements of the model (SSCM) upon which this textbook is configured. Built on communication theories and the unique structure of sport communication (chapter 4), this innovative model bridges theory and practice by detailing the three main components of the field. The first component consists of the personal (chapter 5) and organizational (chapter 6) processes and aspects of sport communication.

Photo courtesy of Dr. Antonio Williams.

The scene depicted in this photo of the filming of sport management professor Antonio Williams for a documentary on the Jordan Brand illustrates numerous aspects of the Strategic Sport Communication Model (SSCM), which provides the conceptual framework for this book.

The second component involves mediated communication in sport. The chapters covering this component emphasize multimedia and convergence and are particularly focused on sport-related mass media (chapter 7) and emerging and social media in sport (chapter 8). The third component is addressed by three chapters that cover sport communication services and support systems. This component includes integrated marketing communication in sport (chapter 9), sport public relations and crisis communication in sport (chapter 10), and sport communication research (chapter 11). The book closes with part III (*Addressing Issues in Sport Communication*), which examines critical sociological issues (chapter 12) and legal aspects (chapter 13) of the field.

Acknowledgments

Paul M. Pedersen, Pamela C. Laucella, Edward "Ted" M. Kian, and Andrea N. Geurin offer a special note of appreciation to several individuals who have contributed to this third edition of *Strategic Sport Communication*. In addition to once again acknowledging the original contributions of Kimberly S. Miloch (an original co-author of the first edition of this groundbreaking textbook) and the continued contribution of Barbara Osborne (the author of the legal chapter for both the second edition and now this third edition), the authorship team (i.e., Paul, Pam, Ted, and Andrea) expresses appreciation to Drew Tyler (our acquisitions editor). This third edition would not have happened without Drew's exceptional support and leadership. Furthermore, the authors truly consider themselves fortunate to have been able to work once again with Melissa Zavala (our developmental editor). We are indebted to Drew, Melissa, and the other dedicated editors and professionals at Human Kinetics (e.g., Dalene Reeder, Denise Lowry, Keri Evans, Aimee Minyard, and Jenny Lokshin).

In addition, Paul, Pam, Ted, and Andrea express gratitude for the time and contributions of numerous sport communication practitioners, leaders, and academics who were interviewed for this third edition. Their quotes and profiles can be found throughout the chapters. Thanks also to our colleagues and administrators at our respective universities—Indiana University, Indiana University–Purdue University Indianapolis, Oklahoma State University, and Loughborough University London—who provided us with the time, resources, and encouragement to complete this project. Finally, the following family members and friends deserve a special note of thanks for the sacrifices they made and for their patience and support during our work on this third edition: Elizabeth Brockelman, Patrick Geurin, Megan Grabowski, Martie Kian, David Kian, Christy Kian, Hayden Kian, Dave Koceja, the late Kenneth Laucella, the late Marie Laucella, Claudia Montgomery, Liam Murray, Brock Pedersen, Carlie Pedersen, Hallie Pedersen, Jennifer Pedersen, Zack Pedersen, Martyn Richards, Jeane Varone, and Mike Willett.

Photos courtesy of Paul M. Pedersen.

PART I

Introducing Sport Communication

Sport is a dynamic, multibillion-dollar industry whose popularity spans the globe. From neighborhood pickup games to intercollegiate athletics to the Olympic Games, sport captivates audiences and transcends borders. As a result, it is experiencing tremendous growth at all levels. This growth, in turn, has increased the need for individuals who are well versed in communication, and the discipline of sport communication has emerged as an integral area in the overall field of sport management. In that context, this textbook defines the evolving field of sport communication; its role in sport management, journalism, and communication; and its status as a stand-alone discipline. More specifically, the book outlines the nature and scope of the discipline as illustrated by the Strategic Sport Communication Model (SSCM).

Chapter 1 introduces you to the sport industry and the field of sport communication. It begins by examining the industry, the growth and segments of this broad field, and the specific places that sport management and sport communication occupy in the sport industry. Because sport-industry careers are founded on education, the chapter emphasizes the study of sport communication; it also addresses the content areas, programs, and options available to students who are interested in learning about the field.

The quest to understand and appreciate the complexity of sport communication begins with gaining knowledge of the field's career options. To this end, chapter 2 details careers in five distinct segments: management, mass media (e.g., print, electronic, visual), support services (e.g., advertising, public relations), entertainment (e.g., video gaming, movies, music), and ancillary opportunities. This chapter provides you with the keys for entering the field, including self-evaluation, education, networking, experiential learning, and the job search. With a clear understanding of the available opportunities and suggestions for pursuing them, you will have a strong foundation on which to expand your knowledge and your educational endeavors. The chapter concludes by describing steps that you can take to increase your marketability as a sport communicator, as well as listings of professional organizations that can help you do so.

Chapter 3 covers key historical developments and the growth of sport communication from the 19th century to the present. It discusses sport coverage in newspapers, magazines, radio, television, and emerging technologies, as well as the ways in which the sport media interact with other key entities in the field. Examining the field's historical development enables you to fully understand sport communication's skyrocketing growth, the full scope of how the key changes have occurred, and the opportunities in this expansive and still-burgeoning field. Therefore, this chapter explores how both technology and pioneers in sport communication—such as Grantland Rice, Mel Allen, Roone Arledge, Mary Garber, and Pete Rozelle—have contributed to the founding of the field as a powerful cultural force. By understanding sport communication's history, you can better understand current trends in the field, as well as the vast opportunities it offers to you.

Photo courtesy of Paul M. Pedersen.

CHAPTER 1

Study of Sport Communication: Revolutionary Change, Abundant Opportunities

LEARNING OBJECTIVES

- To become aware of the magnitude, finances, growth, and segments of the sport industry
- To learn about the role of sport communication in the sport industry
- To consider the academic aspects of sport management and sport communication
- To learn about the educational programs available in sport communication
- To understand the variety and prevalence of sport communication courses offered in both undergraduate and graduate settings

KEY TERMS

sport administration	sport journalism	sport management
sport communication	sport leadership	sport media

RISING TO THE TOP IN SPORT COMMUNICATION IN THE DIGITAL AGE

Nathan Ruiz

If you are reading this book, you likely aspire to work in or around professional sports. Reporting on or working within one of the three most popular professional sport leagues in North America (Major League Baseball [MLB], the National Basketball Association [NBA], and the National Football League [NFL]) often ranks near the pinnacle of such goals in the Western world. Accordingly, most of you would consider Nathan Ruiz's life ideal, especially for a 23-year-old.

In 2019, at the age of 23, Nathan Ruiz became one of the youngest full-time MLB beat reporters for a major media outlet when he was hired as an Orioles and general assignment reporter by the *Baltimore Sun.* "I've always wanted to be a baseball beat writer, so getting to do this is a dream," Ruiz said. "It's a grind with a long season and a lot of travel, but this is what I always wanted to do."

It would be a challenge to find many 23-year-olds with more exciting, high-profile jobs in **sport communication**, but it would be even more difficult to find someone so young in this industry who has worked as hard as Ruiz. A strong work ethic and a willingness to work one's way up from the bottom are common themes for all the sport communication professionals profiled in this textbook. In addition, U.S. students currently preparing for the profession can benefit from the availability of degrees and coursework (e.g., in **sport media**, sport communication, and **sport journalism**) not available at most American universities until recent years.

A native of Reno, Nevada, Ruiz chose his career early in his life. Ruiz knew he wanted to work around baseball; by the age of 15, he concluded that a career in sport journalism was his best path

As part of his job covering the Baltimore Orioles, Nathan Ruiz regularly travels to venues across North America to cover baseball games. However, he spends half of each regular season covering the Orioles in Baltimore's Camden Yards (pictured here).

Photo courtesy of Nathan Ruiz.

to reach that dream. "I wrote for my high school newspaper and literally pulled out my phone and Googled 'sports journalism degrees,' and Oklahoma State was the only university I found offering a full-time degree program in that area at that time. . . . I decided at 15 that's where I wanted to go and what I wanted to do, and I stuck with it."

As a double major in sports media and sports management who graduated summa cum laude from Oklahoma State with a perfect 4.0 grade point average, Ruiz took multiple courses that provided him with both theoretical and content knowledge about the sport communication and sport business industries. Incidentally, the largest of those courses (Intro to Sports Media) assigns this very textbook.

Even with his unwavering commitment to academics, Ruiz involved himself in as many activities as possible to gain more experience in pursuit of a career in sport communication. In addition to covering many sports, Ruiz held nearly every managerial role in his four years of working at the *O'Colly* (the Oklahoma State University student newspaper), including stints as sports editor and editor in chief. Ruiz also garnered student and professional experience in video production and editing, social media, photography, radio, and television.

Like most of the other industry professionals profiled in this book, of great importance to Ruiz's career ascension were the experiences that Ruiz created for himself outside of the classroom, in large part due to his work ethic and ability to excel in the classroom. He did his first summer internship with his hometown newspaper, the *Reno Gazette-Journal*, which was followed by internships with the *Oklahoman* and NewsOk. com in Oklahoma City; a copy-desk internship with the *Dallas Morning News*; and a position with MLB.com as an associate reporter covering the San Diego Padres and the MLB postseason. These internships and the local connections he built throughout Oklahoma helped Ruiz land his first full-time job shortly after graduating as Oklahoma State athletics' beat reporter for the *Oklahoman* and NewsOk.com.

In his first two full-time jobs, Ruiz wrote all types of articles, including game stories and previews, features, statistical analyses, breaking-news stories, player transaction reports, enterprise packages, and investigative reports. He also recorded podcasts, shot video with his phone at coaches' press conferences, discussed on camera the team he was covering—while also maintaining an active presence on social media, particularly Twitter. Ruiz initially learned all these skills as an undergraduate student. "My recommendation to students is to do anything you can outside of the classroom and find your niche," Ruiz said. "When I went to Oklahoma State, I wasn't sure if I wanted to do writing, play-by-play announcing, or another area of sports media. After doing a little of everything, I realized writing was my greatest strength, so I focused more in that area. Professors will help you, but what benefits you most is working outside events and meeting people in the profession who can hopefully help you down the line."

This chapter provides a brief examination of the sport industry as a whole, with a primary focus on the United States, where the financial and sociological effects of the sport industry cannot be overstated. More specifically, it analyzes the size and segments of the sport industry, as well as the role and importance of sport communication in the overall industry. The chapter then briefly examines the study of **sport management** before providing more detail about the emergence of sport communication as a stand-alone academic discipline. In particular, it examines the rationale for studying sport communication and highlights the processes and skills involved in studying the discipline. The chapter also addresses higher education programs, courses, and syllabi specific to sport communication as many colleges and universities continue to add offerings dedicated to the discipline.

GROWTH AND MAGNITUDE OF THE SPORT INDUSTRY

Although sport is already a major global industry, the business of sport continues to expand. Gray and McEvoy (2005) noted that sport "is intertwined with practically every aspect of the economy—from advertising and apparel, to computer technology and video games, to travel and tourism" (p. 230). Nearly 30 years ago, the U.S. gross national sport product—the sum total of value added with respect to sport over one year—was estimated at $50 billion (Sandomir, 1988). A decade later, Meek (1997) noted that the sport industry accounted for about $152 billion and supported another $259 billion in economic activity (also referred to as the *gross domestic sport product*).

Nearing the first decade of the 21st century, the size of the annual sport industry in the United States was estimated at $213 billion by *Sports Business Journal* (Broughton, Lee, & Nethery, 1999). In addition, Milano and Chelladurai (2011) used guidelines from the U.S. Department of Commerce's Bureau of Economic Analysis to estimate the size of the gross domestic U.S. sport product at between $168 billion and $207 billion for 2005. However, sport television rights deals have since exploded, and the sport industry escaped largely unscathed from the 2007-2008 financial crises that led to the 2008-2012 global economic recession. Most recently, Plunkett research estimated the total value of the annual global sport industry at $1.3 trillion USD in 2016, including $540 billion in the United States alone ("Sports Industry Overview," 2016). If that estimate is accurate, then the sport industry in the United States is seven times larger than the U.S. movie industry and twice the size of the U.S. auto industry (Masteralexis, Barr, & Hums, 2015).

More generally, a 2012 study of professional sport leagues and teams by global management consulting firm A.T. Kearney valued the overall sport industry at $480 billion to $620 billion and concluded that the global sport industry was growing faster than the gross domestic products of China, Brazil, India, and Russia (Borland, Kane, & Burton, 2014).

Moreover, sport finance professors Fried, DeSchriver, and Mondello (2013) pointed out that many estimates examine only *organized* sport for

Photo courtesy of Paul M. Pedersen.

U.S.-based companies realize the greatest potential for sport industry growth lies in foreign countries. For example, Oregon-based Nike has 1,182 official stores, 790 of which are located outside of the United States, including this Nike store in Seoul, South Korea (Pratap, 2018).

spectators and consumers, thus leaving out major areas of the sport industry (e.g., personal golf, fishing trips). Therefore, the actual size of the global sport industry may be even higher than indicated by the massive figures just noted.

The advent of legal sport gambling is a development likely to increase the overall size and impact of the U.S. sport industry in coming decades. According to the National Gambling Impact Study Commission (Asher, 2012), more than 99 percent of the estimated $380 billion wagered on sport in the United States in 2012 involved bets that were placed illegally. The prevalence of illegal and offshore sport gambling was largely because wagers on sport games could only legally be placed in Nevada. However, the Supreme Court overturned the Professional and Amateur Sports Protection

Act in 2018, thus opening the door for all U.S. states to potentially enact their own regulated systems for legal sport gambling. Within one year of that ruling, seven states had legalized sport gambling, and most states are expected to have a legal, regulated, and taxed system in place for sport gambling by 2024 (Purdum, 2019).

With such complications in mind, Plunkett Research ("Sports Industry Overview," 2014, para. 2) surmised that "the sports industry is so complex, including ticket sales, licensed products, sports video games, collectibles, sporting goods, sports-related advertising, endorsement income, stadium naming fees and facilities income, that it's difficult to put an all-encompassing figure on annual revenue."

It should not be surprising, then, that the sport industry offers ample job opportunities. In fact, according to the U.S. Bureau of Labor Statistics, career opportunities in sport are projected to increase by nearly 10 percent between 2016 and 2026 ("Entertainment and Sports Occupations," 2019). To meet this demand, the industry will need qualified professionals, which translates to opportunities for students who hold a degree from a good sport communication or sport management program.

TELEVISION CONTRACTS AND GROWTH IN SPORT FRANCHISE VALUES

Sport communication is a major reason for the rapid growth of the sport industry, as evidenced by the huge media rights contracts that reflect the popularity and value of the Olympic games, the most popular professional team-sport leagues, and revenue-producing intercollegiate sports. Since the advent of the World Wide Web in the late 20th century and the social media revolution of the early 21st century, sport media content has become available to consumers at all times through a variety of platforms. In the United States, for example, sport fans can

- stream live video of a lower-level sporting event halfway across the world;
- choose from dozens of all-sport stations available through high-definition television and streaming packages;
- listen to sports-talk programs and play-by-play sport coverage from across the country by means of satellite and Internet radio;
- read about any major sport or team anytime through traditional media (e.g., newspaper, magazine) or online sources;
- follow and occasionally interact with favorite athletes and teams, beat reporters, and other fans through social media; and
- do all of this while playing sport video games and receiving notifications of when to change fantasy-sport team lineups via their smartphones.

Despite this impressive array of changes, however, the growth in sport coverage is best indicated by the dramatic growth in sport television contracts, which have largely fueled the growth of the professional and major-college sport industries in the United States. Indeed, the highest levels of revenue-producing sport now command mind-boggling media rights fees. Nothing better exemplifies the popularity and financial magnitude of sport in the United States than the National Football League (NFL), which collected more than $8 billion in 2018 from CBS, DirecTV, ESPN, Fox, and NBC through new and ongoing television contracts (Badenhausen, 2018; Travis, 2017). The NFL's latest deal with DirecTV for its Sunday Ticket package, announced in 2014, was worth 50 percent more (rising to $1.5 billion annually) than the previous deal negotiated just five years earlier (Katowitz, 2014). Indeed, in a time of declining ratings for most television programs amid the vast array of media consumption choices, NFL ratings keep rising annually when compared with all other television programming. Through mid-2019, Super Bowls accounted for 26 of the 27 most-watched telecasts in U.S. history. Further, NFL games accounted for 7 of the 8 most-watched television broadcasts, and live sporting events accounted for 89 of the 100 most-watched television shows, in the United States in 2018 (Crupi, 2019).

Accordingly, the net values of NFL franchises (as well as other major sport teams) have risen considerably in recent years. In 2018, *Forbes* (Badenhausen, 2018) considered the Dallas Cowboys to be the most valuable sport franchise with an estimated worth of $4.8 billion, which marked a 50 percent increase in the Cowboys' overall value since 2015. The Cowboys were followed by European soccer clubs Manchester United ($4.12B), Real Madrid ($4.1B), and Barcelona ($4.064B) in *Forbes*' rankings of most valuable sport franchises (Badenhausen, 2018). In addition, an examination of sport franchise valuation reports by *Forbes* over the past two decades underlines the rapid and seemingly unending growth in the value of sport as a commodity.

The size of the sport industry is determined in large part by sport communication, whether in the form of a sport broadcaster's commentary, an advertiser's promotional message, the amount of social media posts on a trending sport topic, or a discussion at the water cooler about a heated rivalry game. Like the NFL, other U.S. professional sport leagues have reaped ample financial rewards from recent television rights deals and increases in general media exposure. The National Basketball Association (NBA), for example, renegotiated its television deals with ESPN and Turner Sports in 2014 for an annual total of $2.7 billion, which constituted an increase of 186 percent over the league's previous contracts with the same two partners. This deal followed the 2014 purchase of the NBA's Los Angeles Clippers franchise by former Microsoft CEO Steve Ballmer for $2 billion, which, along with the new television contracts, increased the average value of NBA teams by an estimated 72 percent in just one year (Rovell, 2015).

ESPN sport business expert Darren Rovell (2014) explained some of the reasons for increases in sport television rights deals: "While most other forms of television are commonly watched on demand or DVR'd, allowing viewers to fast-forward through commercials, sports programming is one of the few sectors remaining in which watching live is crucial for most audiences. Consider this: More than 99 percent of ESPN's content is consumed live. As we are starting to move away from television and on to other ways to watch—tablet, mobile—this equation hasn't changed. . . . [In contrast, the] rest of the TV world outside of sports is proving harder and harder to monetize" (para. 6). This distinction provides yet another rationale for students who seek a career in sport to study sport communication, as well as the economics of the sport industry.

Professional sport is not the only segment of the sport industry that is growing; intercollegiate sport is also increasing in size, influence, and revenue. The National Collegiate Athletic Association (NCAA) has grown into an institution that encompasses more than 460,000 students in athletic competition, 24 sports, and three major divisions. In recent years, the nonprofit NCAA has received as much as 90 percent of its revenue from contracts to televise its three-week Division I men's basketball tournament (i.e., March Madness). In 2010, the NCAA wisely pulled out of an existing 11-year, $6-billion deal with CBS to televise March Madness, quickly renegotiating with CBS and Time Warner to strike a deal worth $10.8 billion over 14 years (O'Toole, 2010).

The growth of the NCAA is a direct result of the outstanding expansion exhibited by many of its more than 1,200 members. At the top of the charts stands the athletics programs at in-state rivals the University of Texas at Austin and Texas A&M University, which generated $215 million and $212 million in total revenues, respectively, during the 2016-2017 academic year (Flaherty, 2018). The Texas football program alone—which had three different head coaches and averaged only seven total wins per season from 2010 to 2018—is still estimated to be worth more than $1.1 billion (Beaton, 2019).

According to a *USA Today* database, the following seven collegiate athletics programs generated at least $150 million in revenues during the 2016-2017 academic year (Flaherty, 2018):

1. University of Texas at Austin ($215 million)
2. Texas A&M University ($212 million)
3. The Ohio State University ($185 million)
4. University of Michigan ($175 million)
5. University of Alabama ($174 million)
6. University of Georgia ($158 million)
7. University of Oklahoma ($155 million)

More generally, 21 athletics programs generated revenues of at least $125 million during the 2016-2017 academic year, highlighted by 10 programs from the Southeastern Conference (SEC) and 6 from the Big Ten Conference. Furthermore, *all* athletics programs in the Power Five conferences of the NCAA's Division I Football Bowl Subdivision—that is, the Atlantic Coast, Big Ten, Big 12, Pac-12, and Southeastern Conferences—are expected to receive at least $40 million annually from their respective conferences by 2020. Most of that revenue comes from television contracts, which are negotiated primarily at the conference level for revenue-producing, major-college athletics programs (with the exception of Notre Dame, which has its own exclusive national television contract with NBC for football). The football programs alone at Texas A&M and the University of Texas at Austin each generated an average annual profit of $94 million and $92 million, respectively, over the 2015 to 2017 seasons (Smith, 2019).

It has been even more costly to obtain U.S. broadcast rights to the Olympic Games. NBCUniversal paid the International Olympic Committee (IOC) $4.4 billion for the right to televise four Olympic Games from 2014 through 2020, including two of the always-popular Summer Games and two of the lesser-watched Winter Games. Then, in just the first year of that deal, NBCUniversal agreed to pay the IOC an additional $7.8 billion for U.S. multimedia rights for the six Summer and Winter Games from 2022 to 2032 (Sandomir, 2014). As noted by the *New York Times* sport media reporter Richard Sandomir, NBC made the deal partly because it was unsure of what the future held regarding technological advances: "The agreement . . . captures just how technologically frenetic the media landscape is. Once, such deals had to contemplate only television, but smartphones and tablets have become an increasingly large segment of the viewing audience, and no one can guess how people will watch sports in 2032. The new Olympic contract acknowledges this, stipulating that NBC will have the exclusive rights to broadcast the Games on whatever technology emerges between now and then" (2014, para. 3).

When contemplating these huge financial figures, it is easy to forget that deals for sport media rights constitute just one part of sport communication, which, in turn, is just one segment of the greater sport industry. Let's now take a look at various ways of segmenting the industry.

SEGMENTATION OF THE SPORT INDUSTRY

Because of its enormous size and scope, the sport industry is best understood when its various components are categorized into segments. Sport communication has its own segmentation model

(Pedersen, 2013), which is discussed in detail in chapter 4, but we begin here by examining segmentation models used for the entire sport industry. Given the industry's complexity, it may come as no surprise that it has been segmented in multiple ways. For example, the Sport Management Program Standards and Review Protocol (2000) segmented the industry according to 10 areas of academic content: sociocultural dimensions, management and leadership in sport, ethics in sport management, sport marketing, communication in sport, budget and finance in sport, legal aspects of sport, sport economics, governance in sport, and field experiences in sport management.

Among other segmentation models, some of the most widely accepted were developed in part by sport management professors. For instance, Pitts, Fielding, and Miller (1994) authored one of the first—and still most used—segmentation models for sport. Their model segments the industry according to product and buyer type, which results in three main segments: sport performance (e.g., amateur and professional athletics, sport businesses, membership-supported sport organizations, fitness and sport firms), sport production (e.g., outfitting products, performance production products), and sport promotion (e.g., promotional merchandising and events, media relations, sponsorship, endorsement).

The next influential segmentation model came from Meek (1997), an economist who segmented the sport industry into three sectors consisting of sport entertainment (e.g., events, teams, participants, associated spending), sport products and services (e.g., design, testing, manufacturing, distribution), and sport support organizations (e.g., leagues, law firms, marketing organizations).

In another model, Mullin, Hardy, and Sutton (2014) noted that market segments are formed largely on the basis of consumer wants and desires and that the four bases commonly used to determine segmentation by marketers are consumers' state of being (e.g., their demographic characteristics), consumers' state of mind, product benefits, and product usage. Finally, the sport-activity model developed by Eschenfelder and Li (2007) is based on the concept that sport's uniqueness— as distinguished from other industries—lies in the games or events themselves. In this model, therefore, the sport-producing sector serves as the industry's core. In each of these segments, a vital role is played by communication, ranging from employee interactions in a sporting goods firm to broadcasts of a fishing tournament through the mass media.

ROLE OF COMMUNICATION IN THE SPORT INDUSTRY

Each segmentation model illustrates the vital role that sport communication plays in the sport industry. For example, Meek's (1997) model includes the media (e.g., television, radio, Internet, publications) in sport entertainment, his model's first primary sector, and Eschenfelder and Li's (2007) sport-activity model addresses sport media (e.g., television, radio and cable networks, magazines and other periodicals) as one of its six subsectors. Beyond sport media, sport communication also includes interpersonal and small-group communication; organizational communication in sport; sport public relations; and other components of the field not categorized in the models, such as sport advertising and the newer realm of sport social media.

This attention to communication is appropriate because sport communication plays a vital role in the management of sport. Without it, professionals would be unable to set strategy, advertisers would be unable to promote products and services, and members of the media would be unable to cover sport. Sport communication is vital to the continued health and growth of the sport industry, and, for the most part, vital skills in this realm are learned through academic study and training.

STUDY OF SPORT MANAGEMENT

Before examining the study of sport communication, we look first at the academic field of sport management. This discipline, which is also an academic major, is often referred to by multiple interchangeable names: *sport management*, **sport administration**, and occasionally **sport leadership** (Kian, Pedersen, & Vincent, 2008). *Sport management* has also been defined in different ways. For example, DeSensi, Kelley, Blanton, and Beitel (1990) described it as "any combination of

skills related to planning, organizing, directing, controlling, budgeting, leading, and evaluating within the context of an organization or department whose primary product or service is related to sport and/or physical activity" (p. 33). In another example, Pitts and Stotlar (2013) defined *sport management* as "the study and practice of all people, activities, businesses, or organizations involved in producing, facilitating, promoting, or organizing any sport-related business or product" (p. 3). This definition incorporates the aspect of sport management education.

The rapid expansion of the sport industry over the past three decades has increased the demand for trained and educated individuals to manage and promote the increasingly sophisticated operations that characterize the field (Pedersen & Thibault, 2019; Stier, 2001). Today, this training and education are found most often in sport management programs. Before the explosion of such programs in the late 1980s, there were few opportunities to pursue a major in sport management or sport administration: "Early on, sport managers learned from hands-on experiences gained in the industry. However, as the sport industry became more complex, there was a need to train sport managers in a more formal fashion. From this need emerged the formal study of sport management" (Crosset & Hums, 2005, pp. 15-16). After higher education administrators realized the demand for trained individuals and recognized sport management as a valid career path, they worked to put together academic majors and degrees in sport management to keep up with the phenomenal growth of the sport industry (Pedersen & Schneider, 2003).

The first sport management program was initiated in 1966 at Ohio University (Mason & Paul, 1988). Additional programs began to emerge in the late 1960s; over the next 15 years, the number of programs approached 100. However, as noted by sport management scholars Parkhouse and Pitts (2001), "The significant proliferation in curricular development was not observed until the mid-1980s" (p. 5). Since then, sport management offerings have exploded. By 2019, according to the North American Society for Sport Management website, there were 506 different institutions of higher learning in the United States alone offering a sport management (or related) program at some level, including 439 undergraduate sport management (or related) programs, 246 master's programs, and 37 doctoral programs ("Sport Management Programs: United States," 2019). Sport management programs and courses are also now offered around the world in such places as Australia, Canada, China, France, Greece, Italy, Japan, New Zealand, Portugal, South Africa, Switzerland, and the United Kingdom. Some programs are quite small, with only a few students and a professor or two; others are very large, with hundreds of students and many professors. Amid this variety, there appears to be nearly infinite potential for growth in sport management degree offerings at the undergraduate, master's, and doctoral levels.

In addition to traditional undergraduate and graduate sport management programs, students can also gain an introduction to the sport industry through other programs. For example, the Massachusetts Institute of Technology (MIT) takes an interdisciplinary approach to the study of sport. MIT's Center for Sports Innovation was launched in 1999 as an opportunity for undergraduate and graduate students to learn about the development of sport technology and products; it has since grown and been renamed as Sports Technology and Education @ MIT (STE@M). In addition, dozens of sport management programs are now offered at two-year institutions, and some basic sport management courses are even offered at the high school level. Furthermore, many traditional and online universities now allow students to earn a degree in sport management at the undergraduate or master's level either partially or entirely through the Internet (i.e., through distance learning).

STUDY OF SPORT COMMUNICATION

The study of sport management includes many content areas. Sport management programs are structured in various ways but typically include courses in sport marketing, sport finance, legal aspects of sport, management and organizational behavior of sport, sport governance, sport facility management, event management, sociocultural aspects of sport, and a variety of other topics. The careers associated with these courses are discussed in chapter 2, and they all involve aspects of sport communication. As covered in chapter 4, sport communication is a process by which people—in sport, in a sport setting, or through a sport endeavor—share symbols as they create meaning through interaction. Therefore, sport communication plays a role in all areas of sport management.

As Brad Schultz wrote in *Sports Media: Reporting, Producing, and Planning* (2005, p. xvi), "the study of sports media is important, both in a theoretical and [a] practical perspective." Although Schultz's focus is specific to the sport media (e.g., television, radio, newspaper, Internet), his statement also applies to sport communication more generally. Studying this field helps people understand and appreciate the vital role that sport communication plays in all sport organizations. If you are a sport management or sport business major, then you are likely required to take at least one sport communication class. If you are pursuing another major, you can still take sport communication classes in programs that specialize in sport media and sport journalism. Furthermore, many communication, journalism, and media programs offer at least one sport-focused communication class, and some offer entire programs in this area; in fact, sport communication courses and programs may be housed in various departments, such as business, education, kinesiology, journalism, or telecommunications.

Overall, courses and programs in sport communication have increased along with the growth in the study of sport management. The expansion of sport communication studies can be attributed both to the increase in sport coverage and to the demand for skilled sport management professionals. As noted by Gillentine and Crow (2014), sport organizations and teams need communication to survive. In turn, the growth of the sport communication segment of the industry has naturally prompted an increase in sport communication offerings in higher education.

PREPARING FOR A CAREER IN SPORT COMMUNICATION

The study of sport communication has long been affiliated (and often intertwined) with the academic aspects of sport management. In addition, as with the terms *sport management* and *sport administration*, course and degree names in sport communication often make interchangeable use of the terms *sport communication, sport journalism*, and *sport media*. However, the term *sport communication* is a more encompassing title for both this specific field of the sport industry and the associated academic discipline. Moreover, *sport communication* is the most commonly used term for the field in the discipline of sport management.

As a field of study, sport communication is built on (and requires) interdisciplinary knowledge, which can be obtained through disciplines and courses including advertising, broadcasting, communication, cinema, electronic media, journalism (including electronic journalism), film, finance, informatics, information services, law, management, marketing, mass communication, media production, public relations, social media, speech, and writing. Students who aspire to work in any part of sport communication need to take a variety of courses and gain experience in multiple areas. In their skills-focused textbook, *Multimedia Sports Journalism: A Practitioner's Guide for the Digital Age*, Kian, Schultz, Clavio, and Sheffer (2019) wrote, "The ability to produce multimedia content in a variety of forms has also become the norm for those working in all types of sports media, including television, radio, and team and league media relations. . . . In the digital era, there are very few jobs in sports media that focus on just one medium and almost none of those jobs are entry-level positions" (p. 3).

This flexibility is exemplified by the best sport communication professionals, even if they were trained to focus on just one medium. For example, you may know former ESPN personality Jemele Hill from her stint as co-host of the television show *His & Hers* and for her frequent appearances on ESPN's *First Take*. Hill's background and initial training, however, focused almost entirely on print journalism, beginning with her time as an undergraduate student at Michigan State University and extending well into her career in reporting positions for the *Raleigh News & Observer, Detroit Free Press*, and *Orlando Sentinel*. These days, however, ESPN does not hire top reporters only to write. Although she has returned to writing and now works for *The Atlantic*, as Hill sees it, this demand for adaptability has been a good thing for her:

I have been able to pick up a variety of skills that I will be able to use for the future. My dream was to be a sportswriter. When I was growing up, the only thing a newspaper sportswriter needed to know was how to be a reporter and write. But if you are going to be a reporter today, you must be able to do a lot of things or you aren't going to make it. ESPN does a very good job of working with you on those skills (e.g., on-air appearances, videography, social media use), but you also have to be willing to change your routines and adapt to a changing media environment. (personal communication)

Accordingly, students now have increasing options for studying sport communication, and the development of this academic area has been both rapid and multidisciplinary. An excellent example of this growth can be found at Pennsylvania State University, which launched the John Curley Center for Sports Journalism in 2003. Just two years later, the center had attracted 174 enrolled undergraduates and received a $1.5 million Knight Foundation Grant to create the Knight Chair in Sports Journalism and Society. As noted by Knight Foundation President Alberto Ibargüen, the foundation began supporting such work when its leaders "realized that sports and sports journalism . . . [constitute] one of the major reasons that people watch TV, read newspapers, and go online" (Penn State News online, 2005).

The development of the Penn State program also demonstrates that support from institutional leaders can help grow sport communication offerings. One key figure in the creation of the Curley Center was Doug Anderson, former dean of the Penn State College of Communications and a former newspaper sports editor. In addition, the college's current dean, Marie Hardin, directed research for the Curley Center and is among the world's most prolific sport communication scholars. With support from these two individuals and others, the success of sport journalism at Penn State refutes the negative stigma sometimes attached to sport journalism or sport communication as a "toy department" of the newsroom or of higher education (Billings, 2011; Wanta, 2006).

In the same year that Penn State launched the Curley Center, the University of Maryland created the Shirley Povich Chair in Sports Journalism, which is named after the late *Washington Post* sport columnist. More generally, over the last 15 years, sport communication programs, majors, and courses have been steadily introduced at institutions of higher learning. As Wordsman (2014) surmised in the *American Journalism Review*, "Thanks to a boom in the business of sports, sports journalism is one of the fastest-growing areas of media today, bucking a general downsizing trend prevalent in much of the news industry. . . . Schools have been responding by adding all kinds of courses" (para. 18).

In the United States, current offerings allow many students either to take sport communication classes in a sport management program or to major in a specific sport communication program. The path chosen is not as important as the fact that one takes sport communication courses and—most importantly—acquires practical experience. In the words of sport broadcaster and educator Ted Hedrick, "Absorb all the education possible, and be aggressive in pursuit of on-the-job training along the way" (2000, p. 22).

Options at the Undergraduate Level

Undergraduate students can take any of three distinct avenues to learn more about sport communication: (1) majoring in sport communication or completing a sport communication track (concentration) while majoring in a closely related field; (2) enrolling in individual sport communication courses; and (3) developing skills through experiential classes and practical experiences. These approaches are detailed in the following subsections.

Majoring in Sport Communication

An academic program focused on sport communication usually provides the most courses and opportunities for practical experiences that help students learn about and enter the field. "I believe sport communication deserves its own program because the positions it entails are becoming more expansive," noted John Koluder, director of public relations for the Indy Eleven professional soccer team (personal communication). At institutions that offer such opportunities, majoring in a discipline such as sport communication, sport media, or sport journalism is an obvious choice

for students who wish to pursue academic studies in sport communication.

A few sport management programs offer an undergraduate major or a distinct track in sport communication, including those at Elizabeth City State University, Kennesaw State University, Miami University in Ohio, Mississippi State University, New York University, University of Southern Indiana, and Winston-Salem State University. Although most sport management programs do not offer a major or specialized track in sport communication, nationally approved sport management programs (and those seeking such standing) must still emphasize communication skills and offer sport communication courses. As a result, nearly every large undergraduate program in sport management offers at least one course in sport communication (e.g., sport communication, sport media, sport public relations). For example, the sport management program at Indiana University includes a number of sport communication offerings, such as introductory, issues-based, and sport public relations courses. In addition, students who wish to focus exclusively on sport media can pursue their interests through courses offered by the university's media school.

The standards for sport management programs were developed by two academic associations—the National Association for Sport and Physical Education (NASPE) and the North American Society for Sport Management (NASSM)—which worked together to launch the Commission on Sport Management Accreditation (COSMA) in 2008. The COSMA accreditation guide, *Accreditation Principles and Self-Study Preparation* (2010), lists sport communication as an essential content area in sport industry. In addition, some sport management programs (e.g., those at George Mason University and West Virginia University) offer a minor in sport communication; more often, however, such minors are offered in conjunction with a journalism or communication school.

Indeed, over the past decade, the greatest growth in sport communication programs and similar offerings (e.g., sport journalism, sport media) has occurred in schools and colleges of communication and journalism (Wenner, 2015).

Universities that offer an undergraduate major, track, or concentration in sport communication or a related area include the University of Alabama,

Arizona State University, Ashland University, Clemson University, Columbia College Chicago, Ferris State University, University of Florida, University of Kansas, Lasell College, Montclair State University, Morehouse College, Oklahoma State University, Penn State University, Quinnipiac University, Springfield College, and Syracuse University, among others. In addition, in 2015, a gift from an alumnus and famed former ESPN broadcaster enabled Bradley University to create the Charley Steiner School of Sports Communication, which is the first school dedicated fully to the study of sport communication in the United States.

Other ways to secure an education in sport communication include studying the field in a sport management, journalism, broadcasting, or telecommunication program. The greatest recent growth in sport communication certificates and minors has occurred in journalism and mass communication schools.

The growth of programs related to sport communication is not limited to the United States. In the last two decades, multiple programs have been launched internationally, including programs at the University of the Arts London, the University of Brighton, and the University of Sunderland—all in the United Kingdom—as well as La Trobe University and the University of Queensland in Australia. In addition, many more universities around the globe are adding sport communication courses to meet both student interest and demand from the burgeoning sport industry.

Photo courtesy of Paul M. Pedersen.

The University of Alabama is best known for its football program, led by legendary coach Nick Saban, who is depicted by this statue outside of Bryant-Denny Stadium. However, Alabama is also home to a growing undergraduate sport communication program and multiple top scholars on campus with a research focus on sport communication.

Spotlight on an Undergraduate Sport Communication Program

One of the developing programs in the United States—and an example of the rapid growth in this area throughout academia—is the sports and media specialization at the University of Florida. Since its launch in 2016, the Florida program has grown from 15 initial students to an average of more than 100 students. This program is a specialization offered by the journalism department, but it regularly includes courses and initiatives through the entire UF College of Journalism and Communications and the acclaimed sport management program in the Florida College of Health and Human Performance. The Florida sports and media curriculum offers overview courses (e.g., Introduction to Sports and Media, Sports Media and Society, Sports Media Law and Ethics), practitioner-focused skills courses (e.g., Multimedia Sports Reporting, Sports Production), and internship and practicum opportunities for credit.

The program's faculty possess academic and professional backgrounds in sport and journalism, thus positioning students to enter the profession. However, the program's uniqueness, and perhaps its greatest strength, lies in the opportunities it provides to students outside of the classroom. For example, students in the Florida sports and media specialization have opportunities to work for a variety of award-winning student and professional media outlets on campus, which include an ESPN radio station, GatorVision (the video production arm of UF athletics), ESPNU Campus Connection, and other work opportunities throughout the UF athletics department. Florida students can also get involved with a variety of student organizations, including an on-campus chapter of the Association for Women in Sports Media (AWSM@UF) and a Sports Media Society club. "The strength in our program lies within the experiential opportunities afforded to our students working in our Innovation News Center and working with a top-class athletic department," said Eric Esterline, director of sports journalism and communication at the University of Florida. "I think the growth for our program over the last few years is attributed to our unique experiential opportunities, dedicated faculty and staff, as well as our strong Gator alumni working in the sports industry across the country and globe" (personal communication).

Eric Esterline, UF Director of Sports Journalism and Communication

University of Florida Sports and Media students deliver a segment on the NFL Draft for ESPN 98.1/850 WRUF in Gainesville.

Taking Individual Sport Communication Courses

For students whose institutions of higher education do not offer sport communication or sport management programs, another option is to take individual sport communication courses. Some of these courses are offered as electives, whereas others can lead to either a certification or a minor in sport communication. For example, the University of North Carolina at Chapel Hill offers a certificate in sport communication for students who complete the following three courses: sport communication, ethical issues and sport communication, and sport marketing and advertising. The breakout box provides other examples of individual sport communication courses.

Examples of Sport Communication Courses

Whether a university offers a program complete with numerous sport communication courses or just one or two classes in the field, a wide variety of sport communication courses are available in higher education today.

Undergraduate Courses

Typical sport communication course topics include the following: sportswriting and reporting (George Mason University); sport communication (Ferris State University, Slippery Rock University, University of Massachusetts at Amherst); sport journalism (Suffolk Community College); public relations in sport (Clemson University); sport media relations (Rice University); sport, media, and society (Penn State University); ethical issues and sport communication (University of North Carolina at Chapel Hill); sport video production (Ithaca College); sport media and public relations (Old Dominion University); sport reporting (Ashland University); introduction to integrated communication for sports (University of Texas at Austin); sports information management (Waynesburg College); introduction to sport communication (Indiana University); sport public relations (Wichita State University); sport, gambling, and the media (Springfield College); sport broadcasting (University of North Texas); public and media relations (York College); sport communication internship (Mississippi State University); sport, communication, and culture (University of Southern California); business of sport communication (University of Iowa); sport media literacy (Indiana University); management, leadership, and communication in sport (San Jose State University); sport enterprise reporting and writing (University of Georgia); sport media criticism (Clemson University); social media in sport (University of Georgia); contemporary sport media (Oklahoma State University); sport journalism in the Internet age (Tufts University); and, arguably the most distinctive title, Super Bowl reporting (Arizona State University).

Graduate Courses

Sport communication courses at the master's level, although less common, include such topics as the following: advanced issues in 21st-century sports and media (Arizona State University); public relations in sport (Baylor University); reporting and writing about sport (University of California, Berkeley); sport public relations and information systems (University of Northern Colorado); sport marketing and public relations (East Carolina University); sport and the media (Florida State University); public and media relations (Neumann College); sport communication (Indiana University); studio sport broadcasting (Sacred Heart University); advanced sport reporting (Northwestern University); marketing and public relations in sport and recreation (Temple University); sport publicity and promotion (University of Louisville); sport and media issues (University of Tennessee); public relations for sport organizations (Western Illinois University); sport media, social networking, and brand communication (Seattle University); sport media and society (University of Florida); sport media formats (Valparaiso University); sport studio anchoring, writing, and editing (Iona University); and diversity in sport media (Oklahoma State University).

Additional Courses and Practical Experience

Although students can learn about sport communication through a variety of majors, it is also vital for them to engage in other "coursework or volunteer or work experience that helps in understanding the fundamentals of public relations, communications, marketing, advertising, and journalism. Public speaking skills, writing skills, and knowledge of TV/video production and computer technology are a must for all future sport communications professionals" (McGowan & Bouris, 2005, p. 355). "If you are a beat writer anywhere, you are essentially a multimedia reporter, because that's where the industry has gone at any major paper or Internet site," said Anthony Slater, a reporter who covers the Golden State Warriors and the NBA for The Athletic. "My advice to students who want to break into this field is to do anything and everything. Accept any assignment. Do as much work as you can, even if the direct payoff isn't obvious" (personal communication). More specifically, a 2014 survey found that newspaper sports editors and television sports directors were both most likely to rank writing as the number one skill needed for a career in either medium (Ketterer, McGuire, & Murray, 2014). This finding indicates the continued relevance of advice given a bit earlier in the field's history by Anderson (1994), who emphasized the importance of learning how to write and describe events with correct grammar and accuracy: "Students interested in careers in sports reporting must realize that masterful use of the language and knowledge of style are as important on sports pages as on page one" (p. 13).

Anderson (1994) added that a sport journalist also needs "a working knowledge of the sport being covered" (p. 14). Similarly, veteran sportswriter and current professor Joe Gisondi (2010) emphasized that "good writing comes from solid reporting. . . . If writing about a game were as simple as showing up and watching, anybody could do it. You need to understand the context of the event, know the key participants, and have some idea of what makes today's game unique—all before you even arrive" (pp. 9-10). High-quality writing is also of paramount importance for a successful career in sport public relations (Stoldt, Dittmore, Ross, & Branvold, 2021).

In addition to taking multiple writing courses, many industry professionals recommend that sport communication students learn another language and gain knowledge of other fields related to the sport industry. One professional who regularly gave such advice was legendary sport columnist and television commentator Bud Collins, who passed away at the age of 86 in 2016. Collins' route to the top was anything but direct. His first jobs in the field included positions as sports editor of a small-town weekly newspaper in Ohio and with his college newspaper. He was pursuing a graduate degree in public relations from Boston University when he joined the staff of the *Boston Herald* newspaper for $60 per week. Collins, who was one of the first journalists to successfully

Caleb Surly, a graduate of the Sports Media program at Oklahoma State University, used industry contacts made during a class tour of the ESPN College GameDay set to help land a summer internship with ESPN in Bristol, Connecticut, which led to Surly eventually being hired as a full-time social media specialist for ESPN.

Photo courtesy of Caleb Surly.

transition from a top print-focused reporter to a television commentator, offered sound advice for people wanting to break into the business: "Learn Spanish. . . . [It is] helpful in communicating comfortably with the growing number of Hispanic athletes. Study business/finance and some law. Writing sports is much more than covering games" (quoted in Glatzer, 2006, para. 9). Collins' sentiments were seconded by veteran sportswriter Joanne C. Gerstner, who has taught sport communication at multiple universities and currently serves as sport journalist in residence at Michigan State University: "Some of the athletes on your team may not speak English, so knowing another language or two is very helpful" (Joanne C. Gerstner, personal communication).

Any educational program in sport communication must provide opportunities for skill development. The chapters that follow address skills in such areas as interpersonal relationships, organizational communication, and oral and written communication. Although formal education and textbooks provide the framework for developing skills and expertise, effective education for sport communication must also involve internship, practicum, and volunteer experiences that collectively can be dubbed *professional development*. As McGowan and Bouris (2005) explained, "It is no longer acceptable to enter the sports communications field, even as an intern, without some practical, first-hand experience" (p. 355).

Options at the Graduate Level

Although fewer programs are available in sport management or sport communication at the graduate level than at the undergraduate level, prospective graduate students still have options. The first option is to pursue a master's degree or doctorate in sport communication; at this point, however, the United States is home to few master's programs and no doctoral programs in the field. The second option—and one that is currently more available—is to pursue a concentration or emphasis in sport communication within the study of another discipline (e.g., journalism, sport management). The third option is to take sport communication courses as electives while pursuing a degree in another field or concentration. For example, it would be difficult to find a high-quality master's program in sport manage-

ment that did not offer at least one sport communication course.

Master's Programs

Over the last two decades, the study of sport management and the study of sport communication at the graduate level have increased, although not as quickly with regard to programs devoted specifically to sport communication. As noted earlier, most sport management programs include at least one sport communication course, and several programs offer multiple courses. In addition, some are one-year programs, whereas others require a two-year commitment. Some require a thesis, but others do not. Most are traditional programs featuring in-class lectures, but a few are delivered either partially or fully online. Some require at least one internship experience, while others do not. Finally, some serve full-time students, whereas others are geared toward working students.

One example of a graduate program focused on sport communication is the MA in sports communication and media at Iona College. Iona graduate students can take a variety of theoretical or content-based courses (e.g., sport history and culture, sport media and public relations). However, most of the Iona curriculum is focused on teaching and enhancing the development of skills needed to work in 21st-century sport communication (e.g., sport video and field production, sport imaging, sport radio hosting and producing, sport studio anchoring, writing and editing, creative content in sport communication and media, etc.). The few other U.S. schools now offering graduate degrees in sport communication or a related area include Arizona State University, DePaul University, Indiana University–Purdue University Indianapolis, Oklahoma State University, Quinnipiac University, Sacred Heart University, and Valparaiso University. In addition, an increasing number of journalism programs now offer graduate courses in sport communication to better prepare their students for careers in the sport communication industry.

Doctoral Programs

The number of universities in the United States offering doctoral programs in sport management has increased dramatically, from 12 to 37, since the early 2000s, according to the NASSM website ("Sport Management Programs: United States"). Most of the top sport management doctoral programs include sport communication courses; some, such as those at Florida State University and the University of Tennessee, offer an optional concentration or emphasis in sport communication. The sport management doctoral program at Indiana University, in particular, has produced many top young sport communication scholars over the past decade. At this point, such programs are offered largely in traditional settings rather than online. In fact, as of 2014, none of the 206 U.S. universities classified in 2015 as Research-I (i.e., the highest possible rating to be considered a research-intensive university) by the Carnegie Institute offered fully online doctoral programs in sport management or sport communication. However, a few other U.S. schools—such as the United States Sports Academy in Daphne, Alabama—do offer students the chance to earn a doctorate in sport management entirely online.

Historically, more top sport communication scholars came from sport management and sport sociology programs than from schools of journalism and communication, many of which largely ignored sport communication as a viable research field for doctoral students. That pattern has changed, however, in recent years, and prominent institutions (e.g., Penn State University, University of Alabama) now produce top sport communication scholars. Regardless of your particular field, it is important to choose a doctoral program that features faculty whose research interests are similar to yours and who express a willingness to advise you.

Familiarity with communication in sport is important for all doctoral students in sport communication, sport management, and sport sociology programs. Pursuing a doctorate in sport management or sport communication prepares an individual for leadership positions in academics and athletics. Regardless of which track one takes—academician or practitioner—communication is a major requirement of the work. To exercise leadership in academics, professors must be able to write (research, writing for the industry) and speak (present, lecture) effectively. For leadership in athletics, communication skills are needed all the more. This kind of leadership,

according to Carla Green Williams, director of athletics at the University of Virginia and the first female African American athletics director at an NCAA Division I Power Five conference member school, requires "the ability to share a vision and get the right people to follow . . . [as well as] the ability to serve all in the organization. . . . If I am an effective communicator, people will follow my vision" (personal communication).

Williams, who concentrated in sport management for her doctoral studies at Florida State University, is now a groundbreaking sport leader in many areas. Williams notes that her work requires constant communication: "My day is spent communicating with senior administrators within the university's leadership, as well as with coaches in every sport and most staff members," including academic counselors and compliance officers. She also speaks frequently with staff members of her athletic conference. Her example demonstrates that anyone who plans to pursue a doctorate in sport management or sport communication should prioritize the development of strong communication skills in his or her studies.

Courtesy of UVA Media Relations.

In her leadership position, Carla Green Williams, athletics director at the University of Virginia, hugs basketball star Mamadi Diakite shortly after the Cavaliers defeated Texas Tech in overtime to claim the 2019 NCAA men's Division I national title.

TENNIS: A PASSION TURNED INTO A CAREER

Jeff Sikes
Marketing and communications manager
United States Tennis Association Southwest Section

Tennis has always been Jeff Sikes' passion. He grew up playing on hard courts in the sweltering heat of Galveston, Texas, and watching the sport's top professionals on television. Now 40 years old, Sikes holds a perfect job for his interests: handling marketing and communication for the United States Tennis Association (USTA) Southwest Section, based in Scottsdale, Arizona. He has held his current position since 2008; he started with the USTA in 2005 and spent his initial three years as senior communication coordinator for the USTA Missouri Valley Section, headquartered in Overland Park, Kansas. The earlier parts of his career journey, however, were much more typical of most 21st-century sport communication professionals than the rapid ascension of Nathan Ruiz as an MLB team beat reporter, as profiled at the beginning of this chapter.

After serving as editor of his high school newspaper, Sikes enrolled at the University of Texas at Austin in the fall of 1992 with the intention of becoming a top sportswriter. Since the university then offered no undergraduate courses in sport communication or sport management, he majored in journalism and began acquiring sport media experience outside of class by writing regularly for the student newspaper (the *Daily Texan*), the Associated Press, and *Horns Illustrated* magazine while also freelancing for other newspapers.

After graduating from college, Sikes took a part-time position that included sportswriting and desk duties for the *San Antonio Express-News*. He served as the primary tennis columnist for the *Express-News* and covered a variety of other professional and college sports, although most of his assignments involved high school and amateur sport. Overall, he spent four years working 30 to 35 hours per week in the same roles for the same newspaper without earning a promotion

Jeff Sikes gets a courtside view of tennis legend Rafael Nadal while working an event for the USTA.

Photo courtesy of Jeff Sikes.

or even being eligible for health benefits. "I felt like I was on a track to moving up," he said, "but it never materialized, and [finally] I just had to go elsewhere."

Sikes eventually went to a smaller media market to land his first full-time position as prep sports editor for the *High Point Enterprise* newspaper in the Triad area of North Carolina, where covering high school sports accounted for a large part of his job duties. Sikes, however, also regularly covered Atlantic Coast Conference football and men's basketball, as well as the National Football League's Carolina Panthers. However, after less than two years in North Carolina, he began to grow weary of the lifestyle of a newspaper sportswriter, which allows few weekends off and requires frequent evening hours and travel.

In search of a new job—and possibly a new profession—Sikes kept coming back to the sport he had always loved most, and he eventually decided to pursue a career in the tennis industry. There are few full-time, traditional reporting jobs for journalists exclusively covering tennis, but his reporting experience and writing samples helped him quickly land a communication job in one of the USTA's 17 regional offices, even though he had no experience in public relations. The job gave Sikes the opportunity to gain new experiences and develop new skills. In his newspaper work, his skill set had been somewhat limited—he had written, reported, copyedited, and done a little page design. With the USTA, in contrast, his job duties and skill set encompass a much wider range, as seen in the following list:

- Sport reporting and sportswriting
- Public and media relations
- Membership promotions
- Press releases
- Website design, content creation, and maintenance
- Graphic design
- Social media management (e.g., Twitter, Instagram, YouTube, Facebook)
- Creative marketing operations
- Brochures, flyers, collateral pieces
- Photography
- Video filming, editing, and production
- Blogging
- Obtaining sponsorships (in-kind and cash)
- Serving as a spokesperson for the organization

Depending on the event and the level of participants (e.g., youth, adult amateurs, professionals), Sikes may also help with event planning, event management, and facility operations. "I was strictly a reporter and writer before joining the USTA," Sikes said. "Since then, I've added and continue to add new skills. You have to keep up with changing technology and trends, not only because it happens so fast but even more so because you'll quickly become a dinosaur in your job if you don't. The social media thing hadn't even exploded yet when I began with the USTA, and now it's a large part of what I do. I'd still say writing—both AP style and creative—

would be the number one skill you'd need in a communications gig, and that newspaper background has always served me well. Most of the other skills, though—website design, Photoshop, marketing—I learned on my own and adapted, or I just couldn't do my job. I sometimes miss working for newspapers because I enjoyed the intensity and the deadline-driven environment. The goal of finishing what felt like this big group project each and every day was fun, and the time in those newsrooms taught me a lot about writing and reporting, what news value is, and to look at all sides objectively. Those things are still essential to what I do."

Like many probable readers of this book, Sikes grew up a huge fan of most sports and many athletes. His fandom ebbed while he worked in traditional media but has since returned in a more mature form now that he works in marketing, communication, and media relations. "When you are a newspaper sportswriter, you just can't be a fan . . . [because you] have to always remain objective and impartial," he said. "Now, I can still be a fan of and enthusiastic about my subjects, although I'd never exhibit that when working in a media or event setting. As a reporter, you have to suppress that feeling and learn to look at all sides. It's a bit different now with my job, as I can actively root for American players doing well. Their success is integral to what we try to promote at the USTA."

As an example of this shift, Sikes mentions his enduring friendship with three-time Grand Slam doubles champion Jack Sock and Sock's family. Sikes first started writing about Sock, then 12 years old, shortly after Sikes began working with the USTA, which roughly correlated with Sock's relocation from Nebraska to Kansas City for better training. Sikes quickly became good friends with the Sock family, particularly Jack Sock's parents, and that friendship continues today. "I was invited to social settings with the Sock family that I certainly would not have felt comfortable doing when I was a reporter," Sikes said. "All of this started because I was writing features and covering this 12-year-old and then promoting his success on our website. I've known their family for a while, and it's really cool to see him move up the ranks in the pros after seeing him start at such a young age. That friendship would have probably never happened had I remained a reporter."

Whether pursuing an undergraduate, master's, or doctoral degree, all sport management students are expected to finish with a strong background in sport communication. All the sport communication content areas that have been presented here are relevant to any position at any level of the sport industry. Therefore, any academic preparation in sport communication— whether one course or an entire major—will provide you with useful education, background, skill development, confidence, and networking opportunities. Regardless of the specific sport communication career you decide to pursue (see chapter 2 for more on career options), a good education in the field makes you more attractive to potential employers.

CHAPTER WRAP-UP

Summary

This chapter outlines basic issues related to the study and practice of sport communication, which has spurred much of the growth in the sport industry as a whole. No other media segment is growing as fast as sport media (Andrews, 2013), and the increased mass media coverage and financial backing have tremendously affected the sport industry, particularly the most popular professional team sports and the revenue-producing intercollegiate sports in the United States. Without effective communication in, between, and about sport organizations, the sport industry would not be as large and influential as it is today. Indeed, much of the reason for the enormity of the sport industry can be traced to some aspect of sport communication—whether interpersonal, organization, mass mediated, or involving support services.

In keeping with these realities, this chapter emphasizes the need for future sport industry leaders to obtain strong academic preparation, both in sport management generally and in sport communication in particular. The chapter concludes with suggestions to make sport communication students as marketable and knowledgeable as possible through reading outside materials and participating in academic and professional activities.

Review Questions

1. What are the size and scope of the sport industry?
2. How is the sport industry segmented?
3. What are examples of some sport leagues or organizations that currently hold lucrative television rights deals in the United States?
4. Why are communication skills important in any position in the sport industry?
5. Why is professional development important when preparing for a career in sport communication?

Individual Exercises

1. Choose a sport, sport entity, or segment of the sport industry. Write a one- or two-page summary statement describing how your chosen subject has contributed to the growth of the sport industry. Share your findings with the class.
2. Write a description of an ideal job that you would like to pursue in the field of sport communication. List five courses offered at your university that can best prepare you for this profession, and provide your rationales for your selected courses.

Photo courtesy of Paul M. Pedersen.

CHAPTER 2

Careers in Sport Communication

LEARNING OBJECTIVES

- To recognize the breadth of professional opportunities in the communication segment of the sport industry
- To learn about the five key career areas and many career options in sport communication
- To become acquainted with the trends in—and current status of—the sport communication job market, particularly in relation to the Internet and social media
- To understand the importance of learning and professional development through sport communication publications, associations, conferences, and conventions
- To comprehend the integral components, resources, techniques, and skill development necessary to prepare for a position in sport communication

KEY TERMS

leaders

sport media buying

sports information directors

web development

WORKING AT HOME: THE ATHLETIC MAY BE THE FUTURE OF SPORTSWRITING

Lisa Wilson

The newspaper industry continues to struggle as increasingly more Americans expect to get their news for free, often from websites. Layoffs, smaller staffs, less coverage of local and national sport teams, and fewer pages in the sports section have unfortunately become commonplace in modern newspapers.

The Athletic, an advertisement-free and subscription-based website, believes that sport fans still want to read great writing and print reporting and that many are willing to pay for such content. Since its launch in early 2016, The Athletic has hired experienced reporters to cover nearly every major professional sport league and team in the United States and Canada and has recently started hiring beat reporters to cover major college teams.

Early results were positive as The Athletic raised more than $70 million in venture capital from investors over its first three years to increase the company's estimated value to $200 million (Fischer, 2018). Accordingly, The Athletic is expanding its coverage to include podcasts and videos, as well as many more teams and cities. As of August 2019, The Athletic employed more than 300 full-time writers and editors. After surpassing 500,000 paid subscribers in early 2019, The Athletic CEO Alex Mather said he expected to see that number increase to nearly one million by the end of 2019 (Boudway, 2019).

The Athletic's strategy is clear—hire established and top-tier reporters and editors, often poaching from newspapers. One of those hires was Lisa Wilson, who spent 26 years working for daily newspapers as a reporter; copy editor; and in a variety of managerial positions, including 7 years as the executive sports editor of her hometown paper, the *Buffalo News*.

Photo courtesy of James P. McCoy Photography.

After 26 years in the newspaper industry, Lisa Wilson has settled into her role as a managing editor for The Athletic, an online site that features many of the top writers in the industry.

Wilson, who is slated to ascend to president of the Associated Press Sports Editors (APSE) in 2020, initially left the newspaper industry in 2017 for a senior editor position with The Undefeated, a sport and popular culture website owned and operated by ESPN.

"When The Undefeated launched, I really loved the work they were doing," Wilson said. "I found myself reading the site and enjoying it because it looked at sports through a different lens. When I saw that they needed a senior editor, I just applied—even though I really loved my job at the *Buffalo News*. It was a hard choice."

But after 1.5 years at The Undefeated, Wilson accepted a position with The Athletic, which enabled her family to return to her native Buffalo. Wilson serves as a managing editor who oversees NFL coverage for The Athletic. For the first time in her long media career, she no longer has to work from an office, which is common for The Athletic employees.

"I work from my house or Panera or Starbucks," Wilson said. "I thought it was going to be a huge adjustment because you are used to the camaraderie of the office, but I am in touch with people so much that it really isn't that big of a change. Of course, when there's a snowstorm, I just have to get up and go down to the kitchen now to work, so that's an advantage."

Although the sport communication field is perpetually changing, Wilson is confident she will be at The Athletic for many years and that the site will continue to grow. "People will pay for good journalism, good stories, and journalism that differentiates itself, and I think that's what we do at The Athletic," Wilson said. "One of the best things about The Athletic is that writers are given time to write really good stories, and you see that in our content."

Wilson's four-fold advice to students seeking sport communication careers is to (1) garner experience, (2) commit yourself to the field, (3) network, and (4) join professional organizations, with the latter two often intertwined. "Find a mentor, and join professional organizations; I can't stress those enough," Wilson said. "Those you meet can help you, not only with networking but with feedback and constructive criticism."

This chapter describes the five major career segments of sport communication (see figure 2.1): management, media, support services, entertainment, and other opportunities. As you will see throughout this chapter, many 21st-century jobs in sport communication require individuals to handle a convergence of job roles and use a variety of skills, many of which involve the Internet and social media.

The multibillion-dollar sport industry is full of exciting and challenging career opportunities. One estimate credited the industry with accounting for nearly five million jobs (Pedersen, Whisenant, & Schneider, 2005). In another analysis, Career-Builder and Economic Modeling Specialists International (EMSI) found that jobs in U.S. sport-related industries increased by nearly 13 percent between 2010 and 2014; in contrast, the overall national job market grew about 6 percent over the same period (CareerBuilder, 2014). Not only do the vast majority of jobs in the sport industry involve communication (e.g., writing, speaking, social media), but the sport communication segment of the industry is also particularly vibrant. This chapter introduces you to the broad range of careers available in this field. More specifically, it answers questions such as, "What kinds of jobs are available in sport communication?" and "How do I prepare myself for a position in sport communication?"

The various occupations that make up the field of sport communication typically involve some aspect of covering, delivering, publicizing, financing, or even shaping sport. Professionals in sport communication craft and send messages in various ways, and they may alter their modes of communication depending on the nature of their position as well as audience needs and desires. Although positions in sport communication vary in both nature (e.g., management, publicity, writing) and scope (e.g., traditional print, television, radio, online, social media), the various career paths in the field all hinge on the ability to communicate with key audiences. These audiences also vary, depending on the type of sport entity in question, but they generally consist of the constituencies deemed most valuable to the organization. Key audiences may include fans, members of the public, politicians, owners and investors, athletes, and even members of the media.

The development of sport communication professionals has also been affected by the growth of sport communication as a discipline. For example, as discussed in chapter 1, recent years have brought an increase in academic publications, courses, and programs of study in sport communication. This, in turn, has produced more versatile and prepared students entering the sport communication profession.

Management	Media	Support services	Entertainment	Miscellaneous
• VP of communication for team • Associate AD for communication • CEO of sports broadcasting network	• Sports broadcaster • Executive sports editor • Sportswriter • Sport social media expert	• Sports information director • Media relations coordinator • Director of public and community relations • Social media coordinator	• Video game designer • Sports filmmaker • Software developer	• Media researcher • Sport media buyer • Sport communication educator

Figure 2.1   Careers in sport communication can fall under one or more of five major areas.

In addition, career opportunities in sport communication have been greatly influenced by the convergence of the mass media—that is, the increasingly overlapping relationships between media entities—and, as a result, the variety of multimedia skills increasingly required of nearly all individuals who work in any aspect of the sport industry. Media convergence provides a wide array of opportunities for professionals who possess a strong skill set and an adaptable attitude toward change and new technology. For example, today's newspaper editors often work with both the print and the online versions of their publications; in recent years, the most successful newspapers have added in-house video production units or television studios. Similarly, it has become common, and even expected, for prominent sportswriters to cross over into sport broadcasting while continuing their writing careers. This is the case, for example, with longtime columnists Christine Brennan of *USA Today* and Mike Lupica of the *New York Daily News*, who, like many other print reporters (particularly columnists), serve as regulars on ESPN television and sports-talk radio programs.

Another example is former ESPN television personality and current *Atlantic* reporter Jemele Hill, who has said that one reason she left her position as a sport columnist at the *Orlando Sentinel* in 2006 was ESPN's promise that she would appear as a guest on a few of its television shows while continuing to focus most of her efforts on writing. "I made the jump because I looked around the landscape and saw that a lot of columnists were beginning to get larger platforms on television," Hill said. "It was just a matter of kind of following where the market was going. I watched shows like *Around the Horn* and *PTI*, and most of the shows' guests and hosts are former newspaper columnists. I saw going to ESPN as a way to brand myself and take advantage of the enormous media platform" (Kian & Zimmerman, 2012, p. 293).

As it turned out, Hill's guest appearances on ESPN television shows, particularly *First Take*, increased steadily, and in 2013 she replaced Jalen Rose as co-host of the network's afternoon talk show *Numbers Never Lie*, rebranded as *His & Hers* in 2014. "I will always credit newspapers for making me into the journalist that I am because I learned basically everything in an old-school way that serves me very well in the new medium," Hill

said. "I don't feel like I abandoned newspapers. Instead, I feel like they were my foundation, and I used that foundation in another medium to still perform many of the same job duties" (Kian & Zimmerman, 2012, p. 293).

The next portion of this chapter examines the five major segments of sport communication, beginning with the various management, leadership, and administrative positions found in the field. The chapter then covers the many careers available in sport mass media, which fall into the broad categories of print media, electronic and visual media, and new and emerging media—although, as mentioned earlier, work in the field is now marked by the ongoing convergence of media companies and job roles in the digital age. Next, the chapter describes the professions involved with the support services of advertising and public relations. Sport communication professionals who work in support services have long used a variety of techniques to disseminate messages through the media, but currently they increasingly bypass traditional media to deliver messages and content directly to audiences via websites and social media (Stoldt, Noble, Ross, Richardson, & Bonsall, 2013). The next section illustrates the many sport communication opportunities found in entertainment, as well as some nontraditional positions now available in the field.

The chapter then takes a step back to detail the components necessary for entering into a sport communication career. It also examines sport management and sport communication publications, with particular focus on sport communication textbooks, journals, and books. The chapter concludes by addressing relevant academic affiliations, professional associations, and conferences and conventions.

CAREERS IN MANAGEMENT

Managers and administrators serve as **leaders** in the field of sport communication. Many have worked in sport communication for decades and have worked their way up the ranks, just as young professional athletes climb their way through the minor or developmental leagues and into the majors. In addition, most high-ranking sport executives in major communication companies, sport organizations, and intercollegiate athletics departments have earned an advanced degree, usually in business or sport management (Bower & Hums, 2014; Wong, 2014). In fact, from 2009 through 2014, nearly 90 percent of athletics directors hired at National Collegiate Athletic Association (NCAA) Division I programs held at least one graduate or terminal degree (Wong, 2014).

Leaders in sport communication include owners, publishers, producers, presidents, vice presidents, and entrepreneurs. Most oversee the day-to-day sport communication operations of a sport-focused organization; in doing so, they must perform a variety of functions. As the former ESPN president, George Bodenheimer, stated, "While corporate leaders certainly have to know every aspect of their business, they also better pay extra-close attention to things that are important to employees" (Bodenheimer & Phillips, 2015, p. 151). For example, sport communication leaders manage employees; plan strategies; organize campaigns; and handle budgetary, staffing, policy, legal, and ethical issues.

Leaders must also foster mutually beneficial partnerships with stakeholders, such as advertisers, other sport organizations, media outlets, clients, and fans. "Part of business leadership is maintaining the personal relationships you've built with your customers," noted Bodenheimer. "If you make it a habit to deliver the tough news as well as the good news, and if you do so honestly, straightforwardly, and with respect, more often than not you'll maintain your relationships and keep your customers" (Bodenheimer & Phillips, 2015, p. 141). To work with a variety of stakeholders, leaders must possess a wide range of skills. In the 21st century, they increasingly spend time addressing issues or opportunities that arise through social media. This burgeoning area of technology allows fans, athletes, coaches, and organizational representatives to communicate directly with each other; at the same time, it can lead to problems not encountered in previous eras, when communication processes were more structured and predictable.

Individuals who hope for a career in sport leadership can pursue numerous managerial and administrative tracks. In sport organizations, these positions range from vice president of communication to corporate communication specialist to sport media manager. For example, the sport management leaders of the National

Football League's Pittsburgh Steelers, as listed on the club's official website, include the team's president (Art Rooney II), vice president (Art Rooney Jr.), vice president and general manager (Kevin Colbert), and vice president of football and business administration (Omar Khan). Managers serving under these top management professionals include Burt Lauten, the team's communication coordinator, who oversees all aspects of the Steelers' public relations efforts, both directly to the public and through the media. Lauten and members of his communication staff also work closely with directors and staff members from other departments, particularly information technology, photography, and marketing.

As compared with professional sport teams, major college athletics departments usually include fewer divisions for their communication staff. For example, Claude Felton serves as senior associate athletics director for sport communication at the University of Georgia. He has headed the sports information department since 1979, and his responsibilities have expanded regularly over that period. He currently manages all the athletics department's communication functions: radio, television, public relations, sports information, social media, and written website content. This work includes overseeing eight associate and assistant sport communication directors, interns, and other staff personnel. Felton's department has been continually recognized for excellence by the Football Writers Association of America, which dubbed Felton "collegiate sports' premier publicist," and by the College Sports Information Directors of America, which inducted him into its Hall of Fame in 2001 (Gardner, 2014, para. 1).

Sport communication leaders such as Lauten and Felton shoulder numerous duties that may include broadcast rights negotiations, strategic planning for communication, and a host of other typical managerial and leadership responsibilities. Moreover, they are continually taking on more work with other departments in their organization or institution due to the convergence of media and the emphasis on digital and social media as a way to reach fans, alumni, and key stakeholders. "The advances in technology over a relatively short period of time represent the most significant change and impact in our communications mission," Felton said. "The speed and efficiency of

Photo courtesy of UGA Sports Communications–Claude Felton.

University of Georgia associate athletics director for sport communications Claude Felton speaks with former Bulldog football coach Mark Richt after a victory over Florida Atlantic.

communications tools are overwhelming along with continuing technology advancement. At the same time, I'm still convinced the development and maintenance of interpersonal communications is still the formula for getting important things done" (personal communication).

Similar executive positions and opportunities can be found in sport media enterprises. For example, *Sports Illustrated*—the most popular sport magazine in the United States—is led by its new publisher Ross Levinsohn and longtime editorial director Chris Stone but depends on numerous managerial and administrative professionals who, in turn, lead other employees. These leaders hold titles such as publishing director, editorial projects director, advertising revenue manager, director of positioning, director of book makeup, director of plant operations, regional director, advertising director, sales manager, account manager, and production staffer. In 2018, according to *Sports Business Journal*, television and digital sport media executives were prevalent among the 50 most influential people in sport business. For example, Eric Shanks (CEO & executive producer of Fox Sports) ranked fourth, David Levy (president of

Turner Broadcasting System) ranked sixth, Mark Lazarus (chairman of NBC Broadcasting and Sports) ranked eleventh, and Sean McManus and David Berson (chairman and president of CBS Sports) tied for seventeenth ("50 Most Influential," 2018).

Steve Bornstein, who retired in 2014 from his position as the inaugural CEO of the NFL Network, is another example of a successful executive who worked in high-profile positions for some of the biggest companies in the U.S. sport communication industry. Before joining the NFL, Bornstein served as president of ABC Entertainment and chairman of ESPN. He climbed the ranks at ESPN after joining the start-up company in 1980, just four months after it had gone on the air. With the NFL, Bornstein led multiple negotiations regarding the NFL Sunday Ticket, which culminated in a massive increase in the annual rights fees paid to the league by DirecTV—from $144 million in 2002 to $1.5 billion per year under the 2014 renewal deal (Moritz, 2014). In Bornstein's initial renegotiation, DirecTV had also agreed to carry the NFL Network, which was then in its infancy.

Known for his strategic-thinking ability and tough negotiating tactics, Bornstein began his career by working at two local television stations while attending the University of Wisconsin. After graduation, he worked as a remote crew chief for a television station in Milwaukee and as a freelance camera operator for the Marquette Warriors, Milwaukee Bucks, and Milwaukee Brewers. He later served as an executive producer at an Ohio television station before beginning a two-decade stint at ESPN and ABC Sports, where he was instrumental in establishing ABC as a premier network for college football. "If you want to talk about what's on my tombstone, which I hope is far away, both the NFL Network and ESPN would have to be mentioned," Bornstein told the *New York Times* in 2013 after his announcement that he would be leaving the NFL of his own volition. "The difference is, the N.F.L. was going to thrive with or without me. At ESPN, we were faced with a touch-and-go situation. There were no guarantees that business was going to survive" (Miller, 2013, para. 12).

Although sport communication managers and administrators hail from varying backgrounds and positions, they move into executive and other leadership positions by honing their skills and building relationships at lower levels of organizations. They then rely on the experience gained by working their way through various positions to prepare them for managerial and administrative opportunities at higher levels. For both sport media entities and sport teams, the rapid growth of the sport industry has resulted in an increase in sport communication professionals—and a growing need for people to lead them.

CAREERS IN MEDIA

Where do sport fans find news and updates about their favorite teams and players? For the most part, these enthusiasts get their information through media sources. They turn on the television and tune in to one of the many ESPN channels offered through their cable or satellite package, pick up a smartphone to get information about their favorite team through websites and social media, or grab a daily newspaper or sport-focused magazine to read on the treadmill. Although sport action takes place on the field, rink, or court, the produc-

tion and transmission of sport information to the public typically comes from the efforts of sport communication professionals working in the mass media. The mass media constitute the segment of the sport communication field that houses the major outlets for the transmission of ideas. This segment—which informs, educates, persuades, and entertains masses of sport viewers, listeners, and readers—employs thousands of professionals.

In the past, the primary sport occupation in the mass media was sport journalism, and the majority of sport journalists were housed in newspaper sports departments through the end of the 20th century. Although newspapers still represent a sizable portion of the mass media, people interested in a career in the sport mass media today have a myriad of additional options from which to choose, and most of them require some expertise in working with websites and social media (Finberg & Klinger, 2014). Professionals in this segment of the industry work for numerous and varied mass media, and the diverse positions in the sport media involve gathering, selecting, processing, and presenting sport news to the masses. Careers include such possibilities as designing and maintaining sport websites; coordinating a team, organization, or media outlet's social media efforts; writing sport books; taking photographs for various publications or websites; handling sport radio programming; delivering sport news on television; and writing scripts for sport movies. This section of the chapter examines some of the unique sport communication careers available in the mass media.

Traditional Print Media

The traditional print component of the sport mass media encompasses several broad areas. For individuals interested in a sport communication career, the most prominent and attractive print options include newspapers (e.g., *New York Times, USA Today*), wire services (e.g., Associated Press), magazines (e.g., *Golf Digest, Runner's World*), and books (e.g., *Friday Night Lights* by H.G. Bissinger, *A Season on the Brink: A Year with Bob Knight and the Indiana Hoosiers* by John Feinstein, *Moneyball: The Art of Winning an Unfair Game* by Michael Lewis). Each print sport medium offers numerous and varied careers ranging from business and production occupations to editorial professions.

Sport coverage in the print media serves as a major information source for fans. Even though the increase in new technology has been accompanied by a reduction in the number of daily newspapers, exciting and abundant careers can still be found in writing for newspapers, wire services, magazines, and books. Furthermore, many newspaper and magazine writers now work exclusively for—or have their print articles placed on—a website associated with a print-based publication (Kian & Murray, 2014). In addition, a few print publications have moved mostly online, and that trend will continue until nearly all newspapers and most magazines are electronic-only publications (Benton, 2018). However, the trend away from print publications is not limited to newspapers. For example, the *Sporting News*, which began publishing a regular sport magazine in 1886, still publishes profitable preview magazines for many sports (e.g., pro and college football, pro and college basketball, Major League Baseball), but it no longer publishes a weekly print magazine, having ended that practice at the end of 2012 to focus on digital media (Price & Howard, 2012).

In terms of business operations and production, the print sport media include jobs in publishing, accounting, administration, finance, sales, marketing, human resources, promotions, corporate communication, business development, and strategic planning. For instance, all areas of the sport mass media include sales representatives. These professionals contact prospective clients to sell advertising slots for print and web-based media, as well as radio and television time for broadcast media. They also work with copywriters to create advertisements for sport publications and broadcasts.

On the journalistic side of the print sport media, many full-time and freelance positions are available in writing, reporting, editing, designing, and photography. Working for print media or wire services, these journalists research and gather information and then communicate their work to the public through words, photographs, and other creative endeavors. Many of these print media activities are also performed in different ways for radio and television broadcasts, as well as web-based publications. The leader of a sport magazine or newspaper sports department is often referred to as the *sports editor*, although the exact wording may vary (e.g., executive sports editor, managing editor for sports). By any name, this professional is responsible for addressing both planned coverage and breaking news, deciding what gets covered, juggling deadlines, handling assignments and special projects, dispatching reporters, supervising coverage and production, and setting and upholding the standard for sports department practices.

Does the sports section cover everything deemed newsworthy? What about an event that drew thousands of spectators but received only limited coverage buried near the back of the publication? The mere fact that an event was not covered does not necessarily mean that it is any less important than another event that did receive coverage. The discrepancy does, however, illustrate the power of the sports editor, the media's "gatekeeper," in sport communication (Hardin, 2005; Shoemaker & Vos, 2009). This key decision maker determines what gets covered by a given magazine or newspaper—whether national, regional, or local and whether tabloid, broadsheet, daily, weekly, or specialized—and what does not make the cut. Some events receive additional coverage (e.g., longer articles, more photos) on the publication's website, which generally is not subject to space restrictions. However, even online print sources cannot cover everything because they, too, face limitations in staffing, resources, and time.

With respect to writing for print sport media, sport columnists lead the way. These professionals provide subjective opinions and analyses, and their headshots regularly appear with their columns, thus making them more recognizable to readers, particularly in newspapers that cater to small-town audiences. Other jobs in sportswriting include beat writer, feature writer, general assignment reporter, agate clerk, and photographer, as well as regular part-time correspondent and freelance reporter. Sportswriters and photojournalists cover events, issues, and personalities. The events they cover range from youth leagues to interscholastic athletics to college and professional sport, depending on the market of the publication or wire service. Their work includes attending games, interviewing subjects, and providing information and expert analysis for fans and readers.

In addition to employing staff reporters and photographers, many print publications are relying more often on correspondents and freelancers to meet their sport coverage needs. Freelancing is a good choice for someone who wants to be a sportswriter or photographer but does not want the demands of a full-time position with a newspaper, wire service, or magazine. Most full-time freelancers accumulate years of experience before deciding to become an independent professional, but any prospective sportswriter or photographer can embark on a career as a freelancer. Although writing for a college newspaper is usually the best path for students interested in a sportswriting career, many have garnered experience, made industry contacts, and acquired extra income while in school by serving as a freelance stringer or regular correspondent for a professional newspaper or magazine. Regardless of experience, working as a freelancer requires developing contacts with web-based publications, newspapers, magazines, and other media.

In addition to storied sport publications such as *Sports Illustrated*, there are also magazines dedicated specifically to just about every sport, such as *Mountain Biking*, *Black Belt*, and *American Snowmobiler*. Indeed, most sport magazines—whether they are sponsored magazines, trade journals, or news-rack publications—cater to narrow audience segments. Even so, they offer countless opportunities. Depending on your interests, ability, and experience, you can find professional opportunities in sport magazine publishing in such areas as management, production, editing (e.g., editor in chief, editorial director, executive editor, managing editor, senior editor), writing (mostly on a freelance basis), design, advertising sales, promotion, marketing, public relations, circulation, art, and photography.

Finally, no analysis of print sport media is complete without including what is often considered the first and most respected mass medium—books. Each year brings the release of hundreds of sport-related novels, biographies, commentaries, histories, trade books, and textbooks. A small number are even made into movies—for example, Michael Lewis' *The Blind Side*, Norman Maclean's *A River Runs Through It*, Bernard Malamud's *The Natural*, and Peter Gent's *North Dallas Forty*. Individuals who choose this profession can emulate plenty of writers of classic sport books, including Roger Kahn (*The Boys of Summer*), Jim Bouton (*Ball Four*), Dan Jenkins (*Semi-Tough*), George Plimpton (*Paper Lion*), Terry Pluto (*Loose Balls*), Rick Telander (*Heaven Is a Playground*), David Halberstam (*The Breaks of the Game*), and Roger Angell (*The Summer Game*).

The publishing of a sport book involves many occupations in addition to that of author, biographer, or chronicler. Publishing positions for sport communication professionals include acquisitions, press agentry, sales, promotion, editing, layout, and design, both at large, well-known publishing houses and at thousands of smaller publishing ventures. Additional opportunities may arise as publishers of sport books move increasingly into digital and web-only publications.

Electronic and Visual Media

Rapid changes are happening in sport broadcasting, and this dynamic field needs management, production, and news professionals. The opportunities—whether for 24-hour sport ventures or sports departments and productions—can be found in a variety of areas, such as local television and radio stations, nonprofit and federally funded noncommercial enterprises, in-house video production units in professional sport franchises and college athletics departments, independent production facilities, sole proprietorships, networks, and satellite and cable companies.

It is not uncommon for a career in sport broadcasting to begin in radio, which is considered the first broadcast medium. Sport radio broadcasts—ranging from campus and local endeavors to regional and national networks—reach people in various markets and, in some cases, throughout the United States with sport-related opinions, news, entertainment, business, and advertising. Each sport station and sport program offers job possibilities in management, on-air talent, production, sales, marketing, engineering, research, and programming. In addition, the delivery of this sport content via the web creates opportunities for sport communication professionals with technical expertise.

Television—long recognized as the most influential form of media (Bandura, 2002)—offers similar career offerings, both on the air and behind the scenes. The most competitive opportunities are found at cable and other multichannel sport services. For instance, ESPN has become by far the most dominant force not only in U.S. sport communication but also in all of U.S. sport because its channels own the rights to televise most major sporting events and leagues (Sandomir, Miller, & Eder, 2013). Along the way, ESPN has created a generation of sport enthusiasts who want to become the next Chris Berman or emulate the late, great Stuart Scott. However, due to the mass of people who dream of careers where they essentially talk about sports on television, the odds of finding employment with this sport conglomerate are far greater for individuals interested in working in areas *other* than sportscasting—for example, business affairs, video production, engineering, facilities, operations, research, web design, information services, new media, graphics, and fact checking.

The demand for sport communication professionals has also been increased by the growth of digital cable companies and satellite radio and television programming. One example is Sirius Satellite Radio, which offers commercial-free programming for numerous sports in addition to 14 all-sport talk channels. Sport broadcasting opportunities are also available in producing sport training materials, sport videos, commercials for sport organizations or commercials about sport from nonsport organizations, and sport education materials.

Countless managerial positions are available in electronic and visual media related to sport. Management areas include production, programming, sales, administration, research, marketing, and promotions in the broadcast, cable, and satellite industries. Positions include sports director, director of sport broadcasting, tape librarian, film editor, news writer, engineer, corporate officer, advertising sales coordinator, media buyer, market researcher, business manager, account executive, general manager, station manager, operations staff, and operations manager. Other off-air options include sports producer, technical director, video technician, media production assistant, and audio consultant. Much like the sports editor at a newspaper or sport magazine, a sports producer is the leader of the radio or television sports department. This person sets

assignments; coordinates programming; keeps stories and programs on schedule and on budget; finds new sources for stories; sets and upholds the department's standards of operation; and works to keep the show entertaining, profitable, and organized.

There are also plenty of opportunities for those who wish to go into the performance side of the sport broadcasting, cable, and satellite industry. The options include on-air positions in sport radio, sport television, and sport programming—for example, an anchor, broadcaster, reporter, sideline reporter, and talk-show host. Although the average annual salary for radio reporters is relatively low ($36,000), these positions are highly competitive because of how many individuals desire a career in this area ("RTNDA Survey," 2016). For sport television reporters and anchors, the pay ranges from somewhat to considerably higher, averaging $37,500 for reporters and $60,400 for anchors (Papper, 2017).

Sport Internet and Sport Social Media

The amount of Internet-based sport information continues to increase exponentially. The Internet has become an accepted method for presenting and retrieving sport information through websites and social media services. It has also become necessary for staff members at most newspapers, magazines, and radio and television stations to generate content for their own websites and to promote themselves and their organizations through social media. As a result of these developments, the web now includes an abundance of high-traffic, sport-oriented sites that address topics ranging from general sport news (e.g., ESPN, Yahoo! Sports) to specific teams and athletes. As a whole, the advent of the Internet and social media have transformed the field of sport communication more than any other medium since the rise of television in U.S. households in the 1950s (Owen, 2009).

As you might expect, the rise of social media tools (e.g., Facebook, Twitter, Snapchat, Instagram) has created many career opportunities in sport communication, most of which are being filled by recent college graduates who use these platforms in their daily lives. "College athletics programs are hiring people to run their social media, and college students today have an advantage when applying for these jobs, because they use . . . [them] as part of their daily lives," said Kevin DeShazo (personal communication), founder and CEO of Fieldhouse Media, which addresses social media education, monitoring, and strategy and has contracted with more than 120 NCAA athletics departments. "Social media can be tremendous tools to advance your career. But you can also end . . . [your career] by doing or saying something stupid on social media, because it's a mistake you'll never be able to erase completely."

The global social media phenomenon has opened up career opportunities for many individuals who might never have found a position in traditional sportswriting or sport broadcasting—for example, Kevin DeShazo. One such career is that of **web development**, which involves planning, creating, and updating sport sites for intercollegiate athletics departments, newspapers, television stations, sport teams, and other sport media outlets and sport organizations. Professionals in this realm of sport communication must have expertise both in web-based technology—for example, mastery of scripting languages—and in the needs and interests of web users to create appropriate and effective messages. Typical job focuses in this area include website design, multimedia project management, marketing, business development, online and off-line promotions, sales, web-content writing, organizational web maintenance and management, web animation, Internet content coordination, and search engine optimization.

Careers focused on communication systems technology and computer networking careers include e-commerce, network design, analysis, and administration. Support services in this field include computer-assisted design, consulting, graphics and animation, operations, database administration, desktop publishing, management, sales, technical support, technical writing, web page design and maintenance, and word processing. Emerging jobs in sport social media include social media strategist, social media coordinator, social media engagement specialist, social media marketing specialist, social media manager, and social media copy editor.

CAREERS IN SUPPORT SERVICES

Few organizations could operate effectively without support services, and sport-related entities are no exception. Support services are vital to the overall mission of an organization, and they offer many career opportunities. This section of the chapter highlights the main support services in the sport communication industry. Professionals in each of the main areas must be creative and possess a keen ability to communicate persuasively—both orally and in writing—with supervisors, co-workers, and key publics. In addition, as with nearly all other realms of professional sport communication, careers in support services increasingly require skills in digital and social media.

Sport Advertising

As the number of sport-focused organizations has increased, so has the need for professionals who are well trained in the principles of advertising. Many sport organizations, teams, and athletes now outsource their advertising efforts or at least consult with advertising firms that specialize in sport or have a sport division. Jobs in sport advertising are abundant; in 2016, roughly 250,000 U.S. jobs were filled by advertising, promotions, and marketing managers in advertising-related fields, with an increasing number involving work with sport or recreational endeavors. Even that sizable figure may underrepresent the number of individuals who spend at least part of their work time in this area, especially given the fact that multitasking has become the norm in many white-collar vocations in the Internet era (Bureau of Labor Statistics, 2019). Advertisers carefully craft and communicate messages regarding their products to key audiences for the specific purpose of convincing them to purchase products. In sport, these products range from sports sections in daily newspapers to sporting event tickets. The exact manner in which a message is crafted and communicated varies based on the nature of the product and the profile of the key audience.

Sport advertising professionals should expect to travel frequently, work under deadline pressure, and work long hours that may include evenings

Photo courtesy of Paul M. Pedersen.

The field of sport communication includes marketing professionals, such as the sport executives who launched the tennis advertising campaign appearing on this London taxi.

and weekends. Students preparing for a career in sport advertising should possess knowledge of advertising trends; strong visual communication skills; and an ability to generate creative content for print, broadcast, and electronic media. Advertising positions in sport may involve crafting campaigns for a sport organization or selling sponsorships in which a sport organization or professional athlete is used as a vehicle for advertising by a company or corporation. Examples of specific positions include advertising sales, advertising management, advertising placement, **sport media buying**, and sponsorship sales.

Sport Public Relations

Sport public relations is related to both marketing and advertising in that its goal is to generate awareness of an organization's products. The key focus of sport public relations is to manage information flow between the organization and its key publics—both internal and external. In managing information flow, sport public relations professionals are most concerned with crafting positive images that present the organization and its stakeholders in the most favorable manner possible. They accomplish this task by fostering mutually beneficial relationships with the general public, the media, and the local community. In

part, this work involves identifying the concerns and expectations of the organization's publics and explaining those concerns to the organization's management team. Thus, even though the term *sport public relations* is often considered synonymous with *sport media relations*, the nature and scope of sport public relations are broader and encompass a myriad of functions. These functions include message development, community relations, internal collaboration with various departments, and communication with the organization's key constituents (e.g., stockholders, boosters, season-ticket holders, fans, others in the local community, sport media consumers).

Sport-focused organizations are growing in number and are becoming more sophisticated in the manner in which they communicate with their key internal and external publics. As these communication efforts have become more refined, sport public relations professionals have adapted by changing the nature and scope of their positions. Traditionally, these professionals were considered glorified statisticians who provided information to the media and tried to get the media members who covered their teams to disseminate a positive message to fans and consumers. Even today, such tasks as keeping statistics, writing press releases, and doing basic print reporting remain key duties for most sport public relations professionals. This is particularly true for those who work at the entry level or for a lower-level sport organization, such as a professional minor league team or the sports information department at a small college athletics program.

In recent years, however, top professionals in sport public relations have become integral to the process of shaping their organizations' messages and images. What's more, they often present this content directly to fans by updating the organization's (or team's) official website, livestreaming media conferences, generating in-house video productions, and maintaining social media channels. These approaches allow public relations professionals either to bypass traditional media altogether or at least to influence the ways in which the sport media reframe the messages that an organization is trying to send (Stoldt et al., 2013). In summary, sport public relations professionals play a key role both in managing the complex issues that face sport-focused organizations and in helping management understand and gain support from key constituents.

Many public relations positions in sport-focused organizations now include community relations, particularly with the higher-profile professional sport teams and organizations (Stoldt, Dittmore, Ross, & Branvold, 2021). Community relations managers usually work under the direction of public and media relations directors and are responsible for planning and initiating active participation in the organization's community. This participation is intended to maintain and

Sports Information Director: Public Relations at the Collegiate Level

Like their counterparts in the major leagues, collegiate **sports information directors** (SIDs) must meet the demands of an ever-changing environment. The collegiate SID profession has been examined in several research articles. Hardin and McClung (2002) found that it is considered one of the best jobs in the sport industry, although it is also a fast-paced and stressful vocation (Battenfield & Kent, 2007). In particular, the commercialization of collegiate athletics has forced sport public relations professionals at this level to respond to demands from various parties: their athletics department; their educational institution; and their external publics, including fans and boosters (Hardin & McClung, 2002; Hardin, Whiteside, & Ash, 2014; Whiteside & Hardin, 2010). In addition, the profession at this level is often characterized by long hours and requires exceptional writing skills, excellent technological skills (including web mark-up and video streaming), and experience gained either as a student or as an intern.

Typical duties of college SIDs include drafting media releases; coordinating media conferences; scheduling interviews with student-athletes, coaches, and athletics directors; developing and producing game notes and media guides; and working with colleagues at other institutions to share information when their teams face each other in competition. For the most part, SIDs find their relationships and interactions with traditional mass media to be mutually beneficial (Miloch & Pedersen, 2006). Local journalists who work with SIDs in requesting access to college athletes and coaches believe SIDs are more likely to give better access to major and national media organizations such as ESPN (Suggs, 2016). However, the majority of SIDs and reporters both agree that journalists generally continue to receive the same access to college athletes and coaches even if they produce media reports that are critical of those teams and athletes (Suggs, 2016). Increasingly, SIDs also promote their teams through social media and provide social media training for—and occasional monitoring of—their teams' coaches and athletes. A 2014 member survey of the College Sports Information Directors of America found that the average college SID earned $37,000 annually; however, individuals at the top of the profession at major college athletics programs often hold different titles (e.g., associate athletics director) and earn considerably more.

enhance the local environment in ways that benefit both the community and the sport-focused organization. To initiate and develop community-based programs, community relations managers work closely with colleagues in public and media relations, marketing, and advertising. Often, they also work with marketing and promotions executives at various charitable organizations, such as the United Way, the Children's Miracle Network Hospitals, and the American Red Cross. A sport-focused organization may partner with charitable organizations to combine resources and enhance overall efforts to establish a mutually beneficial environment for the community, the charity, and the sport-focused organization. Sport-focused organizations are increasingly community minded, in part because they recognize the value of establishing a favorable image of exhibiting strong corporate social responsibility.

Professionals in sport public relations use research—often obtained through surveys or from an in-house marketing department—to determine the attitudes and behaviors of key publics. Survey results enable these professionals to plan and implement strategies for influencing, and measuring changes in, their key publics' attitudes and behaviors. Public relations professionals must also develop skills in relationship building, both within and outside of their own organization. They often serve as key advisors to management regarding the image and perceptions of the organization; in many cases, they make recommendations to managers about how to craft messages consistent with the organization's mission and values. This role requires that public relations professionals work with various units within the organization, as well as with management staff at other corporations and charitable organizations.

CAREERS IN ENTERTAINMENT

Sport consumers have become technologically savvy, which poses a challenge to sport communication professionals as technology continues to evolve rapidly in the 21st century. The benefit is that technology provides sport communication professionals with a direct link to loyal, casual, and potential fans. Still, as sport consumers have increased their technological demands, sport communication professionals have been forced to become more creative in how they communicate messages to their publics. This communication is often manifested as some form of entertainment, such as video games, music, or movies. Sport consumers not only want access to a variety of sport information, but they also want it to be readily accessible. In this way, sport and entertainment can be combined to send powerful messages to sport consumers. This technological trend has created a demand for sport communicators who possess skills in areas such as software development, technological support, video editing, sound recording, and web programming.

Video Gaming

The driving force in the sport video game market is EA Sports, which produces popular and profitable video games for major professional sport leagues, including the Fédération Internationale de Football Association (FIFA), National Football League (NFL), National Basketball Association (NBA), National Hockey League (NHL), Professional Golf Association (PGA), and Ultimate Fighting Championship (UFC). In addition to games based on professional leagues, profitable video games based on NCAA football were produced beginning in 1993 by Sega Games. The rights were later acquired by EA Sports, which halted its production of games based on NCAA football in 2014 due to court cases.

EA Sports eventually reached a legal settlement with a group representing former NCAA football and men's basketball players who were depicted in such games (Farrey, 2014). However, legal disputes persisted between the NCAA and groups attempting to professionalize certain college sports—or at least provide more monetary compensation (beyond scholarships) for major college football and men's basketball players. As a result, several major conferences (e.g., Southeastern, Big Ten, Pac-12) announced that they would no longer license their trademarks to EA Sports. NCAA basketball games had already been discontinued by EA Sports in 2009 due to a lack of interest as compared with the popularity of its games based on professional leagues and NCAA football (Brennan, 2013).

Positions in sport video gaming include graphic artists, designers, and quality-assurance game testers. Graphic artists and designers should be familiar with the latest software design programs. These professionals often collaborate with colleagues (e.g., engineering staff) in other areas of video game production. They must also understand trends in the sport industry, as well as texturing and modeling techniques and the best ways to communicate clearly and openly with all parties involved in the development process. Game testers working in quality assurance must possess advanced troubleshooting skills to identify software defects in games. Sport communication professionals in this field must also possess strong verbal and written communication skills.

Movies and Music

The increase in sport films—both fictional stories and documentaries (e.g., ESPN's *30 for 30* series)—has generated a growing need for sport communication professionals with the ability to write, direct, produce, and serve as technical directors in film and movie production. Sport communication professionals are also needed in various aspects of nontraditional sporting events. These careers can be found in the sport management aspects of certain music tours, entertainment districts that offer sport-related activities, and ancillary activities.

OTHER CAREER OPPORTUNITIES

Most professional careers in sport communication are found in management, mass media, support services, and entertainment. Beyond those major areas, however, numerous other positions are available in nontraditional aspects of the field. In fact, some of the best opportunities in sport communication involve behind-the-scenes occupations, many of which exist in the production and operation sides of the industry. Examples include equipment technician, audio engineer, sport videographer, and technical writer. Many other sport communication positions can be found at sport arenas and stadiums—for example, electronic technician, master control operator, public address announcer, and video engineer.

Another often-ignored sport communication career—and one of the most lucrative—is sport media buyer. This area includes professionals in

sport sales and sport marketing who either secure media purchases for sport teams and organizations or work with a private enterprise to secure media purchases through sport media outlets (e.g., sport broadcasts, sport websites). Media buyers work to ensure that every media investment—whether in or through sport—works well for the organization. For example, a buyer might pay the Ladies Professional Golf Association a certain amount based on the number of ad views generated for his or her company through the association's website. To ensure effective media buys, buyers also create media plans—a process that involves researching distribution, setting goals, media mixing (combining media that can be used to achieve goals), and creating and monitoring schedules—to ensure effective media buys.

For those interested in pursuing an advanced degree in sport communication, another career possibility is teaching. Instructors can teach in a variety of sport communication areas, including sport journalism, communication, sport public relations, telecommunication, sport media, and sport radio and television, as well as in sport management and sport studies programs (most of which offer at least one class dedicated to sport communication). Sport communication teachers also guide students through internships, practicums, and other practical experiences that provide students with opportunities to build their résumé by working for a sport organization or sport media outlet.

Other educational careers in sport communication can be found in technical or trade schools, nontraditional four-year colleges (e.g., Full Sail University, which offers online degrees in sport marketing and media and another in sportscasting), some community colleges, and an increasing number of high schools. For example, one might teach a sportswriting course or oversee a student-run video production unit that films high school football games. Other education-related careers can be found in corporate consulting and training (e.g., organizational communication), as well as motivational speaking (e.g., oral communication). Sport-related speakers bureaus and talent agencies provide speakers for personal, motivational, and endorsement appearances.

Sport communication research takes two forms—theoretical (found in academia) and applied. For the most part, sport media organizations are more interested in applied research. As noted in *Profiles of Sport Industry Professionals*, sport media research involves developing "knowledge of advertising and broadcasting business principles such as market share, Nielsen ratings, designated market areas (DMAs), cost per thousand (CPM), cumulative audience over time, and return on investment (ROI)" (Robinson, Hums, Crow, & Phillips, 2001, p. 241). Applied sport

Spotlight on Practical Experience in Sport Communication

James Poling graduated in 2013 from the Oklahoma State University sport media program, which, with more than 250 annual majors and premajors, is one of the largest sport communication programs in the world. However, Poling's career prospects were also aided by experiences that he pursued outside the classroom through a variety of student media (newspaper as well as radio and television stations) and through professional freelance opportunities and internships with newspapers and websites. Poling's education helped him gain admittance to the MBA program in sport management at Florida Atlantic University (FAU), and his practical experiences both in and beyond the classroom helped him land a graduate assistantship with the FAU college of business, as well as paid positions with the Miami Dolphins as a communication assistant in media relations and then as a football administrative assistant.

"Majoring in sport media helped me understand not only how sports operate but how the general public—who are the paying customers of the industry—view these events and react," Poling said. "As I transitioned away from the newspaper industry and into my role within the communication department at the Miami Dolphins, I felt [that] adjusting to the other side of the journalist–PR relationship was seamless because of all that I was taught through my sport media classes at Oklahoma State. The biggest thing that really helped was that I was always confident in my writing, and that is so important no matter what you do in this profession."

After his time with the Dolphins, Poling returned to Oklahoma to work as a digital sport producer, sport reporter, and sport copy editor for the *Oklahoman*, the state's largest newspaper based out of Oklahoma City. However, his dream was to work in professional soccer. Poling jumped on an opportunity in 2017 to become communication director of the Women's Premier Soccer League (WPSL), where he currently oversees communication and media relations for an organization that includes 119 teams in the United States, Canada, and Puerto Rico.

Whether working in the fast-paced realm of NFL communication, executing multiple responsibilities for a daily newspaper and website, or trying to grow women's soccer in North America as a communication coordinator, Poling regularly falls back on lessons learned in the classroom, as well as through the many experiential experiences he garnered as a student. "Working in soccer, especially at a time of unprecedented growth for women's soccer, has been a dream come true," he said. "I am glad I get to be a part of this development, and can help provide the opportunities and exposure that these talented athletes deserve."

Communication coordinator James Poling speaks at an owners' meeting for the Women's Premier Soccer League in Las Vegas in 2019.

media research professionals work with the latest technology and software to provide crucial information for sport organizations, sport media entities, and sport media buyers. Research about sport markets and news (e.g., surveys, interviews, focus groups, sales figures, press runs) informs sport organizations about their consumers and informs sport media entities about their audiences. Therefore, practical sport communication research can involve working both with sport media organizations and with nonsport organizations that do research about sport organizations.

INCREASING YOUR MARKETABILITY THROUGH ANCILLARY ACTIVITIES

To make the most of your courses and practical experiences in sport communication, take a proactive approach. Specifically, you can take two crucial steps to make yourself more knowledgeable in your desired field and thus more marketable. First, read sport communication literature (books, academic journals, and trade publications); second, become affiliated with and involved in professional organizations.

Reading Sport Communication Literature

During their studies, sport communication students should read a variety of sources: textbooks; trade publications; and academic, popular, and industry journals and magazines.

Books Focused on Niche Segments

Supplement your reading of this textbook by looking at other academic publications that address specific areas likely to be discussed in various courses in your academic major. This textbook's broad communication perspective gives you a taste of the entire field—thus providing insight into the sport communication discipline as a whole—whereas other texts focus on certain segments of the field. Therefore, you can use other textbooks and book chapters to gain further understanding of specific topics. For example, although we introduce you to sport public relations in chapter 10, you can find additional information in various other publications. For a full

analysis of sport public relations, we recommend *Sport Public Relations* (Stoldt et al., 2021). Other high-quality texts in this area include *Media Relations in Sport* (Schultz, Caskey, & Esherick, 2014); *Sport Public Relations and Communication* (Hopwood, Kitchin, & Skinner, 2010); *Sports Publicity: A Practical Approach* (Favorito, 2012); *Media Relations in Sport* (Hall, Nichols, Moynahan, & Taylor, 2006); *Sports Public Relations* (L'Etang, 2013); and *The Dream Job: Sports Publicity, Promotion, and Marketing* (Helitzer, 2001).

Similarly, this text discusses (in chapter 7) the convergence of various types of media and the effect of this convergence on the modern field of sport communication. One book that tries to cover all convergent skills needed for modern sport communication professionals is *Multimedia Sports Journalism: A Practitioner's Guide for the Digital Age* (Kian, Schultz, Clavio, & Sheffer, 2018). Other quality skills-focused textbooks in this realm include *Sports Media: Reporting, Producing, and Planning* (Schultz & Arke, 2015); *Sports Journalism: A Multimedia Primer* (Steen, 2014); and *Sports Journalism: A Practical Introduction* (Andrews, 2013). For a scholarly examination of convergence, see *Sports Beyond Television: The Internet, Digital Media, and Rise of Networked Media Sport* (Hutchins & Rowe, 2012). The relatively few textbooks that specifically address social media in sport communication include *Developing Successful Social Media Plans in Sport Organizations* (Sanderson & Yandle, 2015) and *Social Media in Sport Marketing* (Newman, Peck, Harris, & Wilhide, 2013).

In contrast, numerous books are available to help you learn more about sport broadcasting. Two excellent and encompassing texts are *Total Sportscasting: Performance, Production, and Career Development* (Zumoff & Negin, 2014) and *Sports on Television: The How and Why Behind What You See* (Deninger, 2012), which cover both sport broadcasting and electronic sport media production. For a nice overview of the profession, see *Sportscasters/Sportscasting: Principles and Practices* (Fuller, 2008). Another popular and helpful book is *The Art of Sportscasting: How to Build a Successful Career* by Tom Hedrick (2000), a legendary broadcaster with more than four decades of experience as the voice of various teams, including the Kansas City Chiefs, Cincinnati Reds, Texas Rangers, Dallas Cowboys, University of Kansas Jayhawks, and

University of Nebraska Cornhuskers. If you are interested in sport radio, pick up a book such as *Sports Talk: A Journey Inside the World of Sports Talk Radio* (Eisenstock, 2007).

In addition to these practical sport broadcasting books, you can also choose from a host of biographies and autobiographies of past and present sport television and radio broadcast personalities (e.g., Howard Cosell, Linda Cohn, Dick Enberg, Marv Albert, Gary Bender, Curt Gowdy, Red Barber). *Television Sports Production* (Owens, 2015) is an excellent resource for those interested in careers in sport video production or sport television show production, while *Digital Sports Journalism* (Lambert, 2018) provides guidelines on producing sport media content on smartphones.

Students interested in print media (e.g., newspapers, magazines, online journalism), sport reporting, or sportswriting can turn to numerous exceptional books that go beyond the scope of this textbook (which addresses these areas of sport communication in chapters 7 and 8). *Field Guide to Covering Sports* (Gisondi, 2017) provides insight into the terminology common in covering a variety of sports that would be helpful in all sport communication careers, including sport broadcasting and public relations. Other high-quality books that focus largely on print sport reporting and sportswriting include *The Essentials of Sports Reporting and Writing* (Reinardy & Wanta, 2015); *Sports Journalism: An Introduction to Reporting and Writing* (Stofer, Schaffer, & Rosenthal, 2019); *No Time Outs: What It's Really Like to Be a Sportswriter Today* (Walsh, 2006); *Inside the Sports Pages* (Lowes, 2000); *Contemporary Sports Reporting* (Anderson, 1994); *Sports Writing: A Beginner's Guide* (Craig, 2002); *Sports Reporting* (Garrison & Sabljak, 1993); *Associated Press Sportswriting Handbook* (Wilstein, 2002); *Writing Sports Stories That Sell* (Butler, 1999); *Real Sports Reporting* (Aamidor, 2003); *The Coverage of Interscholastic Sports* (Hawthorne, 2001); as well as self-analyses from inside the profession by famed sportswriters, including Christine Brennan (*Best Seat in the House*, 2006), Leonard Koppett (*Sports Illusion, Sports Reality*, 1994), and Jim Murray (*Jim Murray: The Autobiography of the Pulitzer Prize Winning Sports Columnist*, 1995).

Beyond these practical and biographical examinations of sport communication, one can also learn more about the field by reading relevant books with a cultural, sociological, or critical focus. We introduce you to the sociological aspects of sport communication in chapter 12, but if you have an interest in studying this subject in more detail, you can choose from a number of useful books. Good examples include *Changing Sports Journalism Practice in the Age of Digital Media* (Boyle, 2019); *Sports Journalism: Context and Issues* (Boyle, 2006); *Critical Readings: Sport, Culture, and the Media* (Rowe, 2004a); *Playing Ball With the Boys: The Rise of Women in the World of Men's Sports* (Ross, 2010); *Representing Sport* (Brookes, 2002); *Power Play: Sport, the Media, and Popular Culture* (Boyle & Haynes, 2009); *The Meaning of Nolan Ryan* (Trujillo, 1994); and *Sport, Culture, and the Media: The Unruly Trinity* (Rowe, 2004b).

If you are interested in upper-level critical analyses or economic analyses of sport media, you will find the following books very useful for discussions of global sport, rhetoric, and gender: *Historical Perspectives and Media Representations* (Fuller, 2006); *The Business of Sports: A Primer for Journalists* (Conrad, 2011); *Communication and Sport: Surveying the Field* (Billings, Butterworth, & Turman, 2017); *Sports and the Media: Managing the Nexus* (Nicholson, Kerr, & Sherwood, 2015); *Olympic Media: Inside the Biggest Show on Television* (Billings, 2008); *Exploring Media Culture: A Guide* (Real, 1996); *Case Studies in Sport Communication* (Brown & O'Rourke, 2003); *Women, Media, and Sport: Challenging Gender Values* (Creedon, 1994); *MediaSport* (Wenner, 1998); *Sport, Media, Culture: Global and Local Dimension* (Bernstein & Blain, 2003); *The Economics of Sport and the Media* (Jeanrenaud & Kesenne, 2006); and *The Fantasy Sport Industry: Games Within Games* (Billings & Ruihley, 2014).

The maturation of sport communication as a scholarly field is reflected in the recent publication of multiple edited volumes of work by top scholars on a variety of topics. Examples include *Routledge Handbook of Sport Communication* (Pedersen, 2013); *Handbook of Sports and Media* (Raney & Bryant, 2006); *Routledge Handbook of Sport and New Media* (Billings & Hardin, 2014); *Sports Media: Transformation, Integration, Consumption* (Billings, 2011); *Digital Media Sport: Technology, Power and Culture in the Network Society* (Hutchins & Rowe, 2013); *Evolution of the Modern Sports Fan: Communicative Approach* (Billings & Brown, 2017); and *Examin-*

ing Identity in Sports Media (Hundley & Billings, 2010). Finally, *Casing Sport Communication* (Tucker & Wrench, 2015) provides a wide variety of hypothetical cases that students can work through to develop their grasp of best practices in sport communication.

Academic and Trade Journals

Further reading in sport communication can also be found in academic journals, which provide research and theory that support, enhance, and advance the work of practitioners. Many fields of study do not have a dedicated journal; therefore, when a discipline does produce its own journal, this development "can be interpreted as a sign that the demand for and supply of research . . . is now large enough to necessitate a field journal" (Jewell, 2006, p. 16). Although sport communication articles have long been published in academic journals covering various fields (e.g., journalism, communication, sport management, sociology), it was not until 2006 that a journal was dedicated solely to advancing the body of knowledge in sport communication. That publication, the *Journal of Sports Media*, received its impetus during a conversation between sport communication professors and researchers at a scholarly convention in 2004. One of the participants, Brad Schultz (2005), explained the vision at the time: "The journal would fill a niche in the academic and research community by focusing on all areas of sports media, including broadcasting, print, and the Internet" (p. xvi). The journal was published annually for two years before becoming a semiannual publication in 2008.

That year also brought publication of the first issue of the *International Journal of Sport Communication* (IJSC). Edited by Paul M. Pedersen (lead author of this textbook), IJSC is published four times per year by Human Kinetics. The scholarly work published in IJSC is the most cited among the three current sport communication journals (Abeza, O'Reilly, & Nadeau, 2014). The mission of IJSC "is to provide a platform for academics and practitioners to disseminate research and information on the unique aspects and divergent activities associated with any communication in sport, through sport, or in a sport setting" (Pedersen, 2013, p. 3). Both the *Journal of Sports Media* and IJSC regularly publish research articles on the sport communication industry, and each issue of IJSC includes at least one industry interview with a sport communication pro. The newest journal in the field is *Communication & Sport*, which appeared in 2012. Published bimonthly by Sage and edited by Lawrence Wenner, *Communication & Sport* is the official journal of the International Association for Communication and Sport (IACS).

Beyond these three journals dedicated to sport communication, many other journals publish special issues dedicated to sport communication topics. These academic publications have included the *International Journal of Sport Management and Marketing*, the *Journal of Sport Management*, the *Journal of Sport and Social Issues*, and the *Western Journal of Communication*. In addition, numerous other academic journals, both broad and segmented, publish articles about sport communication. Some of these publications average several sport communication articles per year, whereas others publish on the topic only now and then. Most journals related to sport management publish at least an occasional article about sport communication. Journals that publish sport communication articles frequently include *Entertainment and Sports Law Journal*; *European Sport Management Quarterly*; *ICHPER-SD Journal of Research*; *International Journal of Sports Marketing and Sponsorship*; *Journal of Applied Sport Management*; *Journal of Contemporary Athletics*; *Journal of Legal Aspects of Sport*; *Journal of Physical Education, Recreation, and Dance*; *Journal of Quantitative Analysis in Sports*; *Journal of Sports Economics*; *Quest*; *Research Quarterly for Exercise and Sport*; *Sport Journal*; *Sport Management Review*; *Sport Marketing Quarterly*; *Sport, Education, and Society*; *The Physical Educator*; and *Women in Sport and Physical Activity Journal*.

Sport communication articles are also published in numerous journals dedicated to history, sociology, and communication. For example, published research on topics covered in the remaining chapters of this textbook can often be found in such journals as *Communication Teacher*; *Critical Studies in Mass Communication*; *European Journal for Sport and Society*; *International Journal of the History of Sport*; *International Review for the Sociology of Sport*; *Journal of Advertising*; *Journal of Broadcasting and Electronic Media*; *Journal of Communication*; *Journal of International Communication*; *Journal of Homosexuality*; *Journal of Sport History*; *Journalism*;

Journalism Quarterly; Journalism: Theory, Practice and Criticism; Mass Communication and Society; Men and Masculinities; New Media and Society; Newspaper Research Journal; Public Relations Quarterly; Quarterly Journal of Speech; Sex Roles: A Journal of Research; Sexualities; Soccer and Society; Sociology of Sport Journal; Sport History Review; Sport in History; Sport in Society: Culture, Commerce, Media, Politics; and *Women's Studies in Communication.*

In addition to reading academic journals—as well as popular print publications (e.g., *Sports Illustrated*) and mainstream sport websites (e.g., ESPN, CBS Sports, The Athletic, Yahoo! Sports)—a well-rounded sport communication student should also keep up with practitioners in the field of sport communication. You can do so by reading trade journals and professional publications in the areas of media, communication, journalism, and sport management. Publications that frequently cover sport topics include *Sports Business Journal, NCAA News, Coach and Athletic Director, Columbia Journalism Review, Broadcasting and Cable, Amusement Today, Editor and Publisher, SportsTravel, Advertising Age, SportBusiness International, Adbusters, Athletic Business, American Photo, Migala Report, Sports Forum, PRWeek, RTNDA Communicator, Athletic Management, Quill and Scroll, Athletics Administration, Team Marketing Report,* and *Media Ethics.*

You would also do well to read about sport and the sport industry in the popular general media, including newspapers and magazines. These days, you can also use Twitter as a way to hear from top sport communication professionals and individuals who write about the sport media industry (e.g., Richard Deitsch of The Athletic, John Ourand of *Sports Business Journal*, and the staff writers at Awful Announcing). Another option is to subscribe to academic and professional email lists that cover sport management and sport communication. The bottom line is this: Read as much as possible about your chosen profession!

Joining Academic and Professional Organizations

To give yourself the best opportunity for entering the field of sport communication, join academic and professional organizations dedicated to sport communication, sport management, sport marketing, journalism, communication, or the media. Membership provides you with various educational and networking opportunities. For example, most associations hold conferences, seminars, and workshops at least once a year in which participants discuss key topics in sport communication. In addition, some universities now hold conferences or other gatherings focused on sport communication, such as the annual Steiner Symposium on Sport Communication at Bradley University. Examples of *practitioner-based* associations include the College Sports Information Directors of America, Associated Press Sports Editors, Association for Women in Sports Media, National Sportscasters and Sportswriters Association, Sportscasters Talent Agency of America, American Sportscasters Association, United States Basketball Writers Association, Football Writers Association of America, Baseball Writers' Association of America, and National Collegiate Baseball Writers Association. Examples of *academic* associations for future sport communication professionals include the North American Society for Sport Management, North American Society for the Sociology of Sport, and the Sport Marketing Association.

In an exciting recent development, sport communication now has its own academic association, thanks to the launch of the International Association for Communication and Sport (IACS) in 2012. IACS, which offers discounted student memberships, hosts an annual academic conference (the Summit on Communication and Sport), which increasingly features industry professionals as speakers. Most of the founders of IACS began gathering for sport summits every other year in 2002 before creating the annual conference with the official formation of IACS. In addition, since the first edition of this textbook was published in 2007, large journalism and communication conferences have created divisions specifically for sport communication. For example, the Association for Education in Journalism and Mass Communication created a sport communication interest group, and the International Communication Association's sport communication interest group officially accepted papers for the first time in 2015. In addition, the National Communication Association's Division for Communication and Sport was approved in 2014 and issued its first call for submissions in 2016.

YOUR KEYS TO ENTERING THE FIELD

The preceding sections of this chapter examine numerous career opportunities available to sport communication students. However, to fully prepare for and eventually enter one of these professions, you need not only to understand the nature and scope of the available options but also to take certain key steps. Therefore, this section details key elements of career preparation (i.e., skill development, knowledge, experience, and distinction) that will help you enter and succeed in this competitive field (see figure 2.2).

Self-Evaluation

The first step in career preparation is evaluation. If you are considering a career in sport communication, assess your potential by examining your skill set and your passion for the field. Self-assessment involves exploring and evaluating one's needs, interests, personality, skills, values, work style, and expectations. This process can be accomplished through a variety of means (e.g., personal reflection, reading, consulting with a friend), but

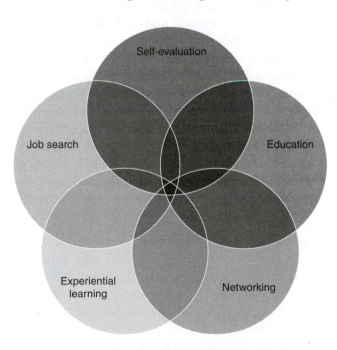

Figure 2.2 Keys to successful entry into a sport communication career.

they are most often carried out through career counseling. This counseling may include completing surveys, such as the Strong Interest Inventory, Knowdell Career Values Card Sort, Campbell Interest and Skill Survey, and Myers-Briggs Type Indicator—all of which can be done online. Individuals preparing to enter sport communication should know their interests and determine which aspect of the field appeals most to them.

As discussed earlier, many career options are available in management, mass media, and support services, and entries into many of these careers are detailed in this chapter and throughout this text. However, people who have a passion for any of the career options in sport communication may reveal this passion in actions that go unseen by others and cannot be included in a résumé. For example, when college students and young professionals attend sporting events today, they often perform mock broadcasts as a way to develop their craft. In one particularly striking example, NFL draft expert Mel Kiper Jr. essentially launched the entire phenomenon of media coverage of the Draft when he produced his first prospect guide as a high school senior. Before then, the draft had never even been televised. At first, Kiper sent his guide off to NFL teams, but he soon began selling copies to other people by mail order (Peter, 2014). Such endeavors originate from a passion for communication and reveal a deep interest in a career in sport communication.

Because of the diverse career options available in sport communication, professionals in this field require varied abilities and skill sets—for example, attention to detail, openness to change, strategic thinking, goal setting, and self-motivation. Above all, as noted by the authors of *Profiles of Sport Industry Professionals*, "Whereas excellent oral and written communication skills are important in most segments of the [sport] industry, they are the foundation of communications in sport. . . . [Professionals also need] skills in computer and electronic technologies, news and feature reporting and writing, the ability to work well with diverse populations, statistical expertise, creativity in a variety of publications, and a thorough knowledge of a wide range of sports" (Robinson et al., 2001, p. 241). After you perform a self-assessment and evaluate your knowledge, skills, interests, and abilities, you can begin strengthening yourself in the areas that need improvement by refining certain skills, developing needed abilities, and increasing your knowledge.

Education

Individuals who pursue full-time employment in sport communication usually need a college degree of some sort. Most positions also require professional preparation, which can be achieved in part by earning a college degree specifically in sport communication, sport management, sport studies, communication, journalism, broadcasting, public relations, advertising, telecommunication, or another closely related discipline. As discussed in chapter 1, the field of sport communication has seen considerable growth in academic offerings over the last two decades. Even so, your education should not be limited to the classroom. Regularly read sport communication publications. Observe best practices by sport communication professionals. Volunteer in sport communication activities with sport organizations and media outlets. Such activities enable you to network and gain experience, which are essential to becoming a successful professional in sport communication.

Networking

To advance in sport communication, professionals must be willing to build relationships and network with colleagues, both within the field and in separate but related fields. As noted by University of Miami sport management professor Warren Whisenant, "Working in the sport industry requires an individual to establish a web of intersecting relationships that reach across industries and business segments (operations, marketing, sales, finance) within both the public and the private sector. Although an individual's career path will influence his or her level of position power in the sport industry, a continually evolving and growing network of personal relationships will enable the individual to amass a significant level of personal power and loyalty, which can ensure a successful and fulfilling career in sport" (personal communication).

The adage "it's not *what* you know but *who* you know" is true in sport communication. "Meet people," ESPN *SportsCenter* anchor Linda Cohn told Oklahoma State sport media students in a guest lecture on campus in 2013, when asked to provide advice for aspiring sport media professionals. "Do not be afraid to walk up to those in the industry and ask for a business card, and then send them an email afterward." Indeed, top-level positions often go unadvertised because the people who fill them are recruited through existing relationships. Moreover, the field of sport communication is highly competitive, and building a sound network of relationships can help you advance your career. Be persistent in meeting colleagues and individuals who hold decision-making positions in various organizations. Remember the names of people you meet, and maintain enough communication with them to establish a favorable relationship, which may generate positive word of mouth for you.

More generally, be flexible and remain open minded, especially before you land your first full-time job. Do not discount any potential employment in sport communication. Being versatile increases your chances of finding opportunities. Be willing to conduct informational interviews, attend conferences and meetings of professional associations, and read articles and publications pertinent to the field. In addition, becoming a student member of a professional association allows you to make contacts and build a solid knowledge base in the field. Consider the Association for Women in Sports Media, the Associated Press Sports Editors, College Sports Information Directors of America, Sport Marketing Association, National Sportscasters and Sportswriters Association, Sportscasters Talent Agency of America, and other organizations listed in chapter 1.

Experiential Learning

Anyone desiring a career in sport communication should make every effort to cultivate opportunities to volunteer or work in the field in an applied capacity. Real-world experience enhances your chance of landing that all-important first job and gives you the chance to acquire new skills. Indeed, the amount and quality of your practical experience help determine the quality of your first position in the field, which in turn can set up opportunities throughout the remainder of your career. There are many ways to get involved. Because sporting events rely heavily on volunteers, they provide excellent opportunities to gain valuable practical experience that complements your educational training. Sport franchises and event managers need volunteers to assist in all aspects of operations, including sport communication. Volunteers may help with media relations and public relations for professional teams, event managers, and school media (e.g., campus newspapers). Other opportunities exist in sport radio and television broadcasting and in web-based aspects of a team or media organization's operations.

Another way to advance your career in sport communication is to do an internship. The value of internships has been described as follows by John K. Koluder, senior director of communication and marketing for the Indy Eleven professional soccer team:

> An internship truly is the best way to get a foot in the door, because it allows you to trumpet your work ethic and skills in a professional setting. Make friends with your academic and internship advisors as soon as you can. Whether students are seeking a job with a professional team or in the media, my advice would be to take an internship as an undergraduate as early as possible. Although networking with professors and guest lecturers at classes can prove valuable, I don't think they can match the contacts that can be made during a successful internship in your chosen field. I also highly advise students looking to break into the media to seek opportunities with as many media outlets on campus as possible, whether it be in television, radio, or print. (personal communication)

An internship may be paid or unpaid, and college credit may also be granted, either in lieu of or in addition to any monetary compensation. Interns typically perform a variety of tasks for an agreed-upon period of time. Because the field of sport communication is quite broad, an internship can help a student determine which aspect of the field to pursue. Competition for sport communication internships is quite fierce—possibly even more so than for full-time jobs in the same field. Therefore, you should approach the process as you would approach a full-scale job search, complete with résumé and interview preparation.

Job Search

Searching for a job is similar to the process of finding an internship. Select positions for which you are qualified, and craft your résumé and cover letter to highlight your experiences, abilities, and key strengths as they relate to the specific position. Typically, a résumé should not exceed two pages (ideally one page for college students); a cover letter should also be limited to no more than two pages. A cover letter allows you to draw attention to key skills and explain how they would benefit the hiring organization. Create a résumé that is professionally presented and graphically pleasing and concisely describes your accomplishments and past job responsibilities. An increasing number of sport communication students also create online portfolios to present both their résumés and their creative works. Arguably most important, clean up your social media, and use it for professional purposes; most prospective employers will search your name for everything they can find online and scroll through all of your social media posts before hiring or offering an internship (Kian et al., 2018).

You should also prepare purposefully for the interviewing process. First, research the hiring organization to obtain as much information as possible. Next, research the backgrounds of the people who will conduct the interview; doing so helps you get a feel for questions you might be asked. When the interview day arrives, dress conservatively and professionally, arrive on time, and be ready to market your skills and a positive attitude to the potential employer. Remember, too, that the interview gives you a chance to gauge the culture of the organization and determine whether it is indeed a place where you would like to work.

DEVELOPING SKILLS FOR AN EVOLVING WORKPLACE

Tyler Dimich
Senior social media manager
ESPN

If you are among the hundreds of millions of combined followers of ESPN platforms on social media apps such as Facebook, Instagram, or Twitter, there is a good chance that you have viewed a post created by Tyler Dimich or by someone on a team of content producers working under his leadership.

Dimich works as a senior social media manager for the "Worldwide Leader in Sports" media conglomerate. He began his ESPN career in 2011 as a production assistant who focused primarily on editing video content but quickly rose in the company hierarchy as social media evolved. Beginning as a production assistant in Bristol, Connecticut, he was promoted to content associate for SportsCenter in Los Angeles and then social media content associate for SportsNation and NBA on ESPN before moving to a larger team that produces content across various brands, first as an associate editor, then as manager, and now in his present position as senior manager.

"Fortunately, I was young enough to intuitively understand the (social media) platforms because I was using them on a daily basis," Dimich said. "But to be successful in this business, you have to think about the platforms differently; you need to learn how to create social media content that people want to engage with and share."

Dimich or employees he assigns regularly attend marquee sporting events to produce social media content for ESPN. The majority of his team, however, produces content out of their offices based in Bristol or Los Angeles, where weekends and long nights on the job are commonplace because that is when most games are scheduled. While he now assigns employees to attend and work some of the biggest sporting events, Dimich attended and worked the last three NBA Finals, the last two NFL Pro Bowls, and six ESPY Awards shows, among other events.

He also regularly works with ESPN television personalities and reporters to help build

Photo courtesy of Tyler Dimich.

ESPN social media senior manager Tyler Dimich annually attends the ESPY Awards show to produce social media content for a variety of ESPN brands.

their social media audiences and brands. For example, Dimich and others helped ESPN NBA Insider Adrian Wojnarowski (a.k.a. "Woj") start his Instagram account and pick up more than 1.5 million Instagram followers in less than two years. Woj's dominance of being the first to report so many major NBA news stories and transactions was a key part of that growth, but Dimich and others worked with the veteran NBA journalist to produce Instagram stories, videos, and graphics based on his reporting that helped build and engage his audience.

Ironically, less than a decade ago, the now-29-year-old Dimich had less sport communication professional experience than many students reading this book. After a two-year stint playing junior college football at West Valley Community College in California, Dimich enrolled at the University of California, Los Angeles (UCLA), where he became an honor student and earned a bachelor's degree in communication studies with a 3.9 grade point average.

In his very first week on the Westwood campus as a student, Dimich attended an ESPN info session that forever changed his life. There he listened to and learned from Joe Franco, a veteran in productions operations who had worked at ESPN headquarters in Bristol since 1979.

Although he was two years away from graduating, Dimich interviewed with Franco the next day to find out what he needed to do to one day work for ESPN. Franco advised that he gain as much experience in video editing as he could.

"The moment I left that info session and interview with Joe Franco, working for EPSN became my goal," Dimich said. "I knew that I wanted a job that I am driven by and not one that I have to begrudgingly drag myself to every day."

From that point forward, Dimich applied the dogged work ethic he learned as an athlete to build and diversify his sport communication résumé and skill set. He was a sport reporter and videographer for the UCLA campus newspaper, the *Daily Bruin*. Dimich also did internships with the Golden State Warriors marketing department, but he could not land an internship with ESPN during his time at UCLA.

Ultimately, Dimich was hired by ESPN and moved to Bristol in 2011, just a few months after graduating from UCLA. He continuously advanced and was eventually able to move back to his native California after ESPN expanded its operations on the West Coast.

Dimich now meets regularly with students and interviews prospective interns and job applicants. Previous industry experience and a strong work ethic are required for almost any sport communication full-time job, especially at ESPN, but the social media content producers Dimich has hired likely have less cumulative years of professional experience than those hired for any other ESPN division. "If we could hire people who are experts in social media but also have 15 to 20 years of experience in the sport media industry, then we would," he said. "But that kind of person does not really exist because of how long social media has been around and who is truly immersed in it."

Among the skills needed to work for ESPN social media are expertise in graphic design, video editing, and Adobe Photoshop, although Dimich notes that those will change and expand as social media grows and shifts. Not surprisingly, many of Dimich's hires have experience working for major sport organization or media outlets, often specializing in social media. But the candidates who impress him most are those who showcase individual creativity at the highest level. "Some of the candidates who have impressed me most are those who have built up their own social media accounts and are swimming in the same stream I am," Dimich said. "Some of my best leads are those whose content pops up on my Instagram feed. I'll say, 'Oh, that's a really cool graphic on Stephen Curry. Let me see who did this, look at their other work, and then see if they have a job.' The key is to show your creativity and knack for content in social space because that's what we look for at ESPN."

CHAPTER WRAP-UP

Summary

Sport communication is involved in countless professions. Sport communication professionals are in demand thanks to the growth of the multifaceted sport industry combined with sport consumers' increased demand for sport-related information. Within the vast and diverse field of sport communication, this chapter highlights a number of key career paths, including traditional, nontraditional, and emerging positions.

This chapter helps you assess your interests and abilities and evaluate your potential for a satisfying and successful career in sport communication. The chapter concludes with suggestions for making yourself as marketable and knowledgeable as possible by reading a variety of relevant materials and participating in academic and professional activities. The activities and references provided at the end of this chapter can help you further examine your interests, abilities, and career options.

Review Questions

1. What has driven the demand in the sport industry for professionals who are well versed in sport communication?

2. Throughout the 20th century, what was the primary sport media occupation?

3. Identify some of the new sport-related jobs available in web-based communication and social media.

4. What academic and professional associations exist to further the advancement of sport communication?

5. What are the keys to entering the field of sport communication?

Individual Exercises

1. Arrange to spend a day or an event with a sport communication professional. Afterward, reflect on the experience, and write a three-page paper detailing it. Specifically, describe the professional's duties and responsibilities, organizational role, work environment, and interactions with other staff members.

2. Search online job postings in sport communication. Find a posting that might be of interest to you, then prepare a cover letter and one-page résumé for submission to the hiring organization. Tailor your cover letter for the specific position, and ensure that your résumé includes an objective, along with key information about your education, work experience, and extracurricular activities. If the section addressing your work experience turns out to be sparse, now is the time to volunteer in some facet of sport communication.

3. Follow on Twitter at least 10 sport communication professionals from a segment of the industry in which you might like to work. Observe the content of their tweets and their interactions with others. Write a two-page paper on the practices and tactics they used on Twitter.

Photo courtesy of Paul M. Pedersen.

CHAPTER 3

History and Growth of Sport Communication

LEARNING OBJECTIVES

- To understand the historical, technological, and cultural development of sport communication
- To learn about sport coverage in newspapers, magazines, radio, television, cable, new media, and emerging technologies
- To recognize the effect of the 1920s golden age of sport on sport coverage
- To learn about key pioneers in sport communication while considering the evolution of sport coverage
- To understand the significance of sport coverage from its agrarian roots to today's multimedia world and the differences in content, distribution channels, and fans' experiences

KEY TERMS

Agricultural Age	Industrial Age	network television
cable television	Information Age	sport journalism
digital age		

THE FIRST INFLUENTIAL U.S. SPORTSWRITER

Grantland Rice

The SEC Network's documentary *By Grantland Rice* traces one of the most famous and prolific sportswriters of all time. It focuses on Rice's years at Vanderbilt University, where he graduated with a degree in classics in 1901. At Vanderbilt, he began to develop his heroic prose and unique writing style (Furlong, 2018). Today's media universe differs greatly from that of Rice's era, but Rice's memory lives on.

Touted as "the first important American sportswriter," Rice wrote more than 67 million words; 22,000 columns; 7,000 sets of verse; 1,000 magazine articles, and a number of books—all of which helped set the agenda of U.S. popular culture before the advent of television (Fountain, 1993, p. 4; Rice 1954). Charles Fountain (1993), whose biography of Rice provides the framework for this vignette, noted that as many as 100 newspapers published Rice's daily "Sportlight" column, which enjoyed a circulation of more than 10 million. His legacy endures today through verses such as the following: "For when the One Great Scorer comes to mark against your name, He writes—not that you won or lost—but how you played the game" (Rice, p. 169). Rice's most famous lede about the Four Horsemen, which opened his story on the 1924 football game between Notre Dame and Army, is discussed later in this chapter.

Rice was the epitome of a Renaissance man. After graduating Phi Beta Kappa in 1901 at the age of 20 from Vanderbilt University with a Bachelor of Arts in Greek and Latin, he worked for the *Nashville Daily News*, *Atlanta Journal*, *New York Sun*, *New York Tribune*, *New York Herald Tribune*, *Nashville Tennessean*, and *New York Mail*. He also wrote more than 500 articles for *Collier's* magazine over a span of 35 years, including the "All-America" football articles from 1925 through 1947. In addition, in 1921, he provided the play-by-play announcing for the first World Series game

The Fighting Irish maintain a stellar record here at Notre Dame Stadium. Grantland Rice helped solidify the power and prestige of the football program through his coverage of Knute Rockne's teams, including the Four Horsemen.

Photo courtesy of Paul M. Pedersen.

covered live on radio (Ham, 2011). He continued his work in radio by hosting a weekly National Broadcasting Company (NBC) show in the 1920s and 1930s, reporting at major sporting events, and appearing as a guest on other radio shows (Harper, 1999).

Rice was also credited with popularizing the game of golf and, with Bobby Jones, helped create the Masters Tournament in 1938. In addition to his journalistic pursuits, Rice dabbled in more creative ventures, receiving two Academy Awards for short-subject features for his Sportlight Films and even writing a play titled *The Kick Off*.

On July 13, 1954, Rice died of a stroke in his Sportlight office at the age of 73. Fountain (1993) called him the "Matthew, Mark, Luke, and John of American sport" (p. 4). Rice not only captivated a public weary from World War I and later the Great Depression but also contributed to the rising popularity of sport during this era. Until Howard Cosell came along in the latter half of the 20th century, no one rivaled Rice's effect on sport coverage.

This chapter traces the development of sport communication in the United States from the 19th century to the present. Along the way, it addresses Grantland Rice and golden age pioneers who made an indelible mark on sport. It also discusses the profession of **sport journalism** and specific practitioners and academics, such as former reporter and columnist Malcolm Moran, who is profiled at the end of the chapter. In addition, it explores how technology and cultural changes have affected the growth of sport communication over decades and even centuries. By studying sport communication's history, we can see how it has evolved and gain insight into how it may continue to develop as an important industry in the economic and social fabric of the United States and beyond.

Technology has long influenced sport's expansion in U.S. society and altered the ways in which reporters and organizations work and how they report sport news and information (Laucella, 2014). As addressed further in chapter 7, sport, media, technology, and culture have shared a symbiotic relationship that began with early sport in the United States. As part of that relationship, sport communication has exercised considerable influence on the gathering, processing, and transmitting of information, especially in the arenas of sport media and public responsibility (Laucella, 2014). At the same time, sport communication itself has evolved in response to cultural changes and the expansion of technology during the industrialization, urbanization, and modernization of the United States. As a result, although sport communication scholars may emphasize different eras and categories of development, all devote considerable attention to the evolution of technology and cultural values.

In terms of historical development, Garrison and Sabljak (1993) suggested that sport journalism developed over the course of six distinct periods: the pioneer era (up to 1830), the period of acceptance (1830 to 1865), the era of consolidation and growth (1865 to 1920), the golden age (1920 to 1930), the perspective period (1930 to 1950), and the transition years (1950 to 1970). In a different model, Bryant and Holt (2006) divided development into what they termed the **Agricultural Age** (the late 18th century through most of the 19th century), the **Industrial Age** (late 19th century through the 1980s), and the

Information Age (1990s), which then morphed into the current **digital age**. Regardless of which model one subscribes to, sport has functioned in all eras as a "conduit or medium through which feelings, values, and priorities are communicated" (Wenner, 1998, p. xiii).

After covering key historical periods and technological growth, the chapter examines leaders in this expansive field, then concludes with an exploration of today's sport communication arena. Figure 3.1 shows key events in the development of sport communication in the 20th and 21st centuries. It includes cultural and technological changes, which have influenced how fans consume and experience both sport and sport communication.

EARLY ERAS OF SPORT JOURNALISM

Although individuals have participated in sport since the beginning of humanity, the activities focused on recreation and leisure in past centuries (Garrison & Sabljak, 1993). For example, as recently as the pioneer era in the colonial United States (that is, before about 1830), many individuals participated in a variety of leisure activities—including fishing, hunting, boat racing, cricket, horse racing, cockfighting, swimming, skating, billiards, and wrestling—but these activities received only limited newspaper coverage.

Early Coverage of Leisure Activities

As the 19th century wore on, however, daily newspapers and weekly papers dedicated to leisure life began appearing in the United States. For example, William Trotter Porter's *Spirit of the Times* was launched in 1831 and reportedly had 40,000 subscribers nationwide by the middle of the century. Other sporting sheets (e.g., *New York Clipper*, *Sporting News*) appeared in the latter part of the century, and the *National Police Gazette*, which covered all areas of entertainment and leisure activity, was the highest-selling weekly newspaper. Thanks to technological developments and increasing literacy rates, more and more newspapers arose (Rader, 2004). The first sporting journal, the *American Turf Register and Sporting Magazine*, appeared in 1829 and covered

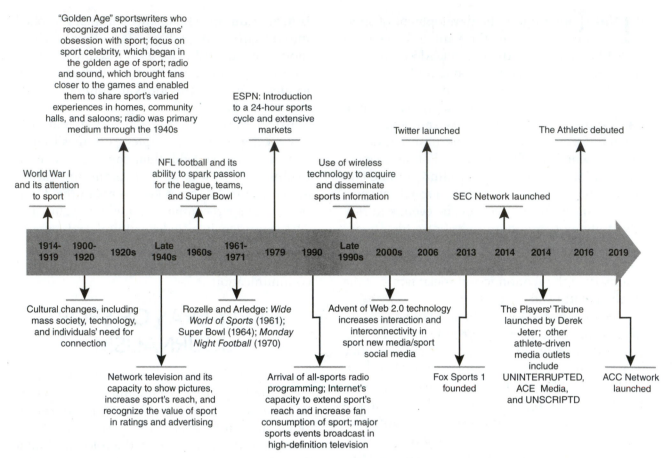

Figure 3.1   Key events in the development of sport communication.

horse racing. Many of the journals covered outdoor activities as well.

When newspapers reported on sport, they typically addressed horse racing, boxing, and wrestling (Garrison & Sabljak, 1993). New York-based "penny" newspapers initiated their coverage of sport in the 1830s, thus making sport news more accessible to the mass public, and they generally exuded a partisan and sensational tone (Blanchard, 1998). Advertisers valued the newspapers' extensive reach, and the revenue gave editors and publishers the freedom to experiment with printing equipment and news-gathering techniques (Laucella, 2014). By the mid-19th century, both Porter's *Spirit of the Times* and the *New York Clipper*, founded by Frank Queen, had become popular sport journals (Betts, 1953a). By then, the *Spirit of the Times* had taken over the *Turf Register* (in 1839) and was covering such sports as cricket, baseball, rowing, and yachting (Harper, 1999).

By the 1840s, James Gordon Bennett and his *New York Herald* were offering front-page coverage of such sporting events as trotting matches, thoroughbred racing, and boxing bouts (Betts, 1953a). With the advent of the electric telegraph in 1844, sport news featured instantaneous reports of games, horse races, boxing bouts, and other events (Betts, 1953b). Sport's popularity developed further after the Civil War, propelled especially by the popularity of baseball (Fountain, 1993). The game not only entertained the Union and Confederate armies but also bypassed class and geographic lines after the war was ended. Baseball clubs expanded in the 1870s, and the National League was formed in 1876. A key pioneer in baseball's popularity and development was the *New York Herald's* Henry Chadwick, who is often referred to as the *father of baseball*. Accordingly, his Hall of Fame plaque reads: "Henry Chadwick: Baseball's preeminent pioneer writer for half a century. Inventor of the box score. Author of the first rule book. In 1858 Chairman of rules committee in first nation-wide baseball organization" (National Baseball Hall of Fame, n.d.).

Importance of Sport Recognized by Newspapers

As baseball gained popularity, sport became a daily feature of the larger newspapers in the 1870s, and the press increasingly realized the importance of recurrent and innovative sport reporting (Betts, 1953a; Fountain, 1993). As a result, the first regular sports pages were created by Charles A. Dana of the *New York Sun*, Joseph Pulitzer of the *New York World*, and William Randolph Hearst of the *New York Journal* (Betts, 1953a; Garrison & Sabljak, 1993). By the 1880s, sports pages were covering football, boxing, baseball, horse racing, cricket, croquet, yacht racing, homing pigeon racing, bicycle racing, and lacrosse. Along the way, the growth of sport journalism was also propelled by the development of the web printing press (in 1865), improvements in the typewriter (1869), and the invention of the telephone (1876).

The Industrial Age

The steam engine drove the Industrial Revolution in late 18th-century Britain; by the mid-19th century, it had reached the United States (Laucella, 2014). As a result, American life became more industrial, urban, and modern, which resulted in a relatively detached society based more on efficiency than on relationships (Lowery & DeFleur, 1995). By the 20th century, journalists and writers were attending to a mode of life marked by transition in the midst of modern advancements and individuals' problems (Emery, Emery, & Roberts, 2000, p. 213). This type of journalism and reporting was referred to by the terms *New Journalism* and *muckraking*. New Journalism sought social reform—a fact evidenced by the articles it inspired in mass-produced, sensationalized newspapers. Journalists depicted, for example, the lives of immigrants, outcasts, and those deemed "degenerate" while describing systemic societal problems. Muckraking sustained this focus with investigative reporting focused on prompting reforms in an increasingly modern and technological society. The dramatic flair of muckraking exposed societal problems with a critical yet optimistic tone (Blanchard, 1998).

Although crusading muckrakers depicted political and economic injustices in American life, newspapers viewed sport as performance. Only a handful of sport periodicals existed—mainly trade papers such as *Sporting News* and *Sporting Life* in St. Louis and Philadelphia, respectively (Halberstam & Stout, 1999). Their stories were succinct and offered readers the bare minimum of information about the games and athletes. Whereas trade papers stuck to presenting facts, magazines such as *Harper's Weekly*, *Illustrated American*, and *Leslie's Illustrated Weekly* included photographs of athletes and sportspeople (Betts, 1953b). As sport coverage continued to describe events, more individuals sought to participate.

Moreover, according to sport historian Michael Oriard, "sport accommodated participants' desire to play, while at the same time enabling the advocates of sport to harness the play impulse to the new industrial order" (Oriard, 1991, p. 11). In the first three decades of the 20th century, the growth of efficient transportation and communication triggered an expansion of city life, as well as wealth and leisure time (Noverr & Ziewacz, 1983). By the 1920s, mass production brought about a more rigid and structured work environment, and technological developments (e.g., railroad, telegraph, electric lighting, streetcar) led to a reduced work week of 48 to 60 hours (Inabinett, 1994). Living standards improved, work laws dissipated, and Sunday blue laws disintegrated, thus offering Americans more time, money, and opportunity for leisure activities. As a result, Sundays were no longer off-limits for games, competitions, and other activities. Previously, these laws restricted activities and promoted Sunday as a day of rest or worship.

Turning to Sport for a Sense of Cohesion

Although technology freed many workers from grueling hours, it also increased urbanization and dehumanization. Meanwhile, between 1870 and 1920, the U.S. population increased by 44 million people, and individuals increasingly turned to sport as an escape from the complexities of a bustling world (Hardy, 1997). In this climate, sport offered an outlet both for celebrating individual achievement and for creating a sense of community and social cohesion (Inabinett, 1994).

Cities and their inhabitants became a central focus, and interplay between cities' infrastructures, groups, organizations, and systems created much of sport's historical narratives (Riess, 1990). The millions of Europeans who migrated to U.S. cities came with diverse faiths, customs, and rituals, and community building took the form of sport clubs, jockey clubs, yachting associations, baseball leagues, and athletic conferences. This melting-pot ideology followed a vision in which sport and games promoted unification and provided a means for overpowering racial, ethnic, and class divisions (Hardy, 1997). The resulting organizations not only facilitated the transition but also unified cultures and identities, created heroes, and evoked pride among ethnic team members and fans (Riess, 1990).

Military Legitimation of Interest in Sport

From 1900 to 1920, the United States developed both as an industrial nation and as a formidable world power as American imperialism and military power escalated under Presidents William McKinley and Theodore Roosevelt (Noverr & Ziewacz, 1983). Given the sense that the United States needed to protect its interests, physical strength and conditioning came to the forefront of the nation's priorities. In this context, sport was viewed as a means for achieving physical fitness and gaining an advantage in life. Progressive supporters of athleticism touted sport's function in readying both individuals and nations for life's tasks, and this legitimizing of sport was bolstered by communication and journalism (Dyreson, 1989).

The U.S. military also helped legitimize sport's utility in World War I as the armed services made sport central to military life by advancing a "national sport culture" (Pope, 1995, p. 436). More than four million men and women participated in intercamp competitions in football, baseball, basketball, soccer, boxing, and track and field. In 1918 and 1919, soldiers read the *Stars and Stripes* and *Sporting News* for information about service sports. In addition, the *New York Herald*, *Chicago Tribune*, and *London Daily Mail* published 190 items on the Inter-Allied Games of 1919, which featured 1,500 competitors from 18 Allied countries (Pope, 1995).

Before World War I, national heroes had come from the ranks of business, industry, and science; after the war, athletes also soared to celebrity status (Inabinett, 1994). The rise of sport celebrities and mass-mediated hero worship represented both a generation's quest for meaning during a turbulent time in U.S. history and a response to an increasingly complicated and bureaucratic society (Evensen, 1993; Inabinett, 1994). Sport represented a postwar optimism, an escape, and a means for exalting the human spirit (Noverr & Ziewacz, 1983). "Sport had become an opiate", noted Dyreson (1989). "It offered an arena in which the masses could turn their eyes away, if only briefly, from the grim political and economic realities of the modern world" (p. 269).

GOLDEN AGE OF SPORT

Throughout history, sport has reflected cultural values, and this was especially true in the early 20th century, when individuals sought to assimilate into modern mass society while escaping postwar struggles. Sport offered one means of doing so, either through participation or through spectatorship, and its popularity increased rapidly, especially in the 1920s. The golden age of sport was an appropriate title for this decade because it was a time when athletes, coaches, and sportswriters all gained iconic status. Household names included those of athletes such as Babe Ruth, Ty Cobb, Red Grange, Bill Tilden, and Bobby Jones, along with writers such as Grantland Rice, Paul Gallico, Ring Lardner, Westbrook Pegler, and Damon Runyon. The writers set the agenda for sport coverage by documenting coaches' and athletes' unique stories and achievements. As a result, for the first time in history, people became obsessed with sport and its many participants.

During this period, sportswriting appeared in newspapers and in both general interest and sport magazines (Halberstam, 1999). Golden age sportswriters created champions by constructing images that elevated athletes to celebrity status (Inabinett, 1994). Indeed, because few sport fans regularly saw their heroes in action, the athletes described by sportswriters became "bigger than life" and were viewed as icons (Starr, 1999). In addition, sport journalists no longer just reported from the playing field but also analyzed strategy, provided background, and illuminated the character of such athletes as Babe Ruth and Bobby Jones (Inabinett, 1994). Other famous sport figures in the golden age included Joe DiMaggio, Knute Rockne, Babe Didrikson Zaharias, Red Grange, Jack Dempsey, Suzanne Lenglen, Gertrude Ederle, Walter Hagen, and Helen Wills. According to Rice (1954), "Sport—games, hard competition played under the rules, is the greatest thing a country can know. Sport offered the greatest fund of national entertainment. It offered relief from the drabness and dullness of making a living. It was a cure for lonesomeness, the dark spectre so many people face" (p. 349).

Sportswriters' Development of Unique, Descriptive Prose

During sport's golden age, the most magnificent athletes prompted sport journalists to use vivid descriptive and imaginative language (Danzig & Brandwein, 1948). This writing style was not unrelated to the fact that the 1920s saw a restructuring of sport ideology in American culture, during which the newspaper sports section was established as an indispensable part of the daily newspaper (Dyreson, 1989; McChesney, 1989). The amount of space devoted to sport coverage had expanded from less than 2 percent of total news

Photo courtesy of Paul M. Pedersen.

Notre Dame Stadium, one of the most famous stadiums in all of sport. Coach Knute Rockne was a celebrated football coach in the golden age and beyond due to his impact on Notre Dame's historic football program. Notre Dame had two national championships during the golden age of sport.

Sport Communication in the Golden Age of Sport

- Sporting events made front-page headlines.
- Writers embellished prose with metaphors, analogies, and other literary devices.
- Top athletes became the subject of hero worship; examples include baseball player Babe Ruth, boxer Jack Dempsey, and Notre Dame football coach Knute Rockne.
- Writers used emotional and gripping language with vivid imagery.
- Meticulous detail was used to describe events and define sport and cultural agendas.
- Article ledes were written with high drama and low factual content.
- Writers used few quotations.

- Stories were written in a conversational tone.
- Columns focused on frivolity in sport and merely hinted at the deeper implications of issues such as politics and race relations.
- Writers used war and mythological references and "rags to riches" stories.
- Writers used humor, slang, romance, and drama.
- Storytelling was considered paramount.
- Stories relied on expert description and commentary for the pretelevision audience.
- Writers made extensive use of nicknames, many of which were created by Grantland Rice—for example, the "Sultan of Swat" for Babe Ruth.

space in 1875 to more than 20 percent in 1927, by which time the popularity of sport depended on the daily sports section (Jordan, 1927). Overall newspaper circulation rose to 36 million by 1926, and one of four readers purchased a newspaper solely for the sports section—the single most significant catalyst to circulation (Evensen, 1993; Inabinett, 1994).

As circulation increased, so did the number of writers covering sport. For instance, when the Boston Braves ventured south in 1922 for their first spring training in St. Petersburg, six New England sportswriters traveled with the team on the train to Florida (Pedersen, 1997). This level of coverage for a mediocre team—Boston had posted a losing record in four of the previous five years—reflected the increased attention devoted to sport by newspapers, as well as the importance of sportswriters. "Their unique prose delighted readers, sold more copies, [and] appealed to more advertising agencies with products to sell" (Susman, 1984, p. 143). Sportswriters used their imagination to develop stories through hyperbole, similes, metaphors, and other literary devices that illuminated the cultural era (Lipsyte & Levine, 1995). Along the way, these writers became nearly as famous as the heroes personified in their texts, based on how they covered the "dope" (analysis and inside information) (Fountain, 1993).

This pattern persisted and remains evident in the style and content of today's sportswriting, including its celebration of celebrity athletes. As a result, sportswriters still look back to the golden age and its importance:

> After World War I, a gorgeous flowering burst forth in American newspapers: Heywood Broun, Paul Gallico, Ring Lardner, W.O. McGeehan, Westbrook Pegler, Grantland Rice, Damon Runyon. The general approach was tough-guy romantic, as "when Homer smote his bloomin' lyre," and their best work is belletristic—writing that is not merely informative but also beautiful to read. (Kahn, 1999, p. 443)

There were two classifications of sport journalist during this era. Grantland Rice and Paul Gallico epitomized the "Gee Whiz!" style with florid prose that venerated athletes and reveled in their heroic attributes and feats (Inabinett,

1994, p. 21). Other "Gee-Whizzers" were Heywood Broun, Damon Runyon, Joe Vila, and William B. Hanna (Fountain, 1993, p. 133). The other category—"Aw-Nuts!" sportswriters such as W.O. McGeehan—were skeptics who wrote with a "how-can-you-let-these-guys-break-your-heart-they're-scarcely-worth-the-bother attitude" (Fountain, p. 133). They wrote in a coarser and less glorious style, often using sarcasm and irony to debunk or humanize athletes and events (Fountain, 1993). Most of the writers, however, were Gee-Whizzers who characterized a postwar period full of hope.

During the 1920s and into the 1930s, sporting events made front-page newspaper headlines. Writers sought to instill excitement in their readers, and Rice and Gallico embodied the era's obsession with romance, heroes, war references, and an unwavering human spirit. Rice is most remembered for a column written about the 1924 football game between Army and Notre Dame (won 13-7 by Notre Dame), in which he famously referenced Vicente Blasco Ibáñez's novel *The Four Horsemen of the Apocalypse* in detailing the moves of Notre Dame backfielders Harry Stuhldreher, Jim Crowley, Don Miller, and Elmer Layden (Fountain, 1993). As was characteristic for the time, Rice used story ledes that were high in embellishment and low in factual detail, and his eloquent words about the Notre Dame quartet still resonate with fans today:

> Outlined against a blue gray October sky, the Four Horsemen rode again. In dramatic lore they are known as Famine, Pestilence, Destruction, and Death. They are only aliases. Their real names are Stuhldreher, Miller, Crowley, and Layden. They formed the crest of the South Bend cyclone before which another fighting Army football team was swept over the precipice at the Polo Grounds yesterday afternoon as 55,000 spectators peered down on a bewildering panorama spread on the green plain below (1924, p. 1).

Notre Dame still includes Rice's full article on its athletics website, Notre Dame Fighting Irish (2019).

For his part, Gallico gained a reputation as the "Hemingway of the sports page" (Tuite, 1995, p. 9). The ex-Columbia University oarsman wrote for the *New York Daily News* before devoting his career to writing fiction (Harper, 1999). After working

Photo courtesy of Jerry McKenna, Sculptor; Michael & Susan Bennett, Photographers.

Statue commemorating Grantland Rice's legendary Four Horsemen, the backfield of Notre Dame's 1924 championship team.

as a sports editor, he wrote freelance articles for *Vanity Fair* and the *Saturday Evening Post*; served as a World War II correspondent; and wrote books while living in England, Mexico, Lichtenstein, Monaco, and Antibes (Gallico, 1946). A few of his books include *The Snow Goose*, *The Poseidon Adventure* (which was also made into a movie), and *Mrs. 'Arris Goes to Paris*. Like many of the era's writers, he viewed athletes as legends and recounted the fairy-tale nature of their "rags to riches" stories (Gallico, 1965, p. 26). Gallico, Rice, and other journalists of this era served as catalysts, both in propelling the growth of sport's popularity and in changing perceptions of their own profession. Their names and verses are remembered and quoted today, and their enthusiastic and praising tone instilled athletes with heroic status and sparked excitement in the war-weary public. For the first time, sportswriters enjoyed celebrity status akin to that of their subjects. For example, in 1925, Rice signed a contract to serve as associate editor of the *New York Herald Tribune* for the yearly sum of $52,000—an amount equal to Babe Ruth's salary (Fountain, 1993).

The narratives produced by golden age sportswriters sparked interest in sport overall and in particular athletes even as they helped restore and energize Americans in an era that preceded the commercialization of sport and television. These writers engaged readers in their stories and offered renewed hope in the American dream and in the sport hero. They also exhibited the mythologizing power of journalism in their war metaphors, literary devices, and descriptive prose about baseball and other sports. Jack Lule (2001) defined *myths* as "archetypal stories that play crucial social roles" (p. 15). Myths draw on archetypal figures—for example, heroes, scapegoats, victims, and tricksters—to tell real stories of humanity (Lule, 2001), thus enabling members of society to express and share ideals, values, perceptions, and ideologies. This approach to sportswriting marked the beginning of mass-mediated hero worship and celebrity treatment of athletes. As a result, the golden age of sport remains an important era for sport, journalism, and American culture (Laucella, 2004).

Whereas the golden age of sport celebrated athletes and heroes in a joyous and romantic tone, the ensuing "perspective period" reflected changing perceptions of both American culture and journalism.

PERSPECTIVE PERIOD

In the perspective period of 1930 to 1950, the "giddiness and devil-may-care attitude" in the United States changed dramatically during the Depression and World War II (Harper, 1999, p. 474). Although Americans revered the writers of the golden age of sport, they began to question the profession's ethics and importance. Also during this period, the staff members of sports sections began editing their own copy, and professional sport gained more popularity than college sport. In addition, newspapers as a whole had to adjust their content and style in the face of new competition from radio.

Change in Public Perception

The first trend of the perspective period was that, in the 1930s, some people began to view sportswriting as a trivial and sometimes crooked occupation. According to Harper (1999), readers came to question sportswriters' professionalism, objectivity, and ethics in light of their laudatory coverage of such athletes as Babe Ruth. They also questioned the liaisons between journalists, promoters, and owners; as the Great Depression drastically affected newspaper revenues and therefore writers' salaries, sport team owners paid for writers' expenses on the road in return for positive publicity. The resulting charges of graft and "tainted sportswriters" warranted discussion at the 1926 American Society of Newspaper Editors' annual meeting, where editors debated key topics (Towers, 1981, p. 16) such as the mutually beneficial relationships between journalists, owners, and promoters. Journalists needed owners and promoters for stories, and owners and promoters rewarded journalists with gifts based on their coverage (Harper, 1999). Emotional graft also existed due to the camaraderie that journalists developed with athletes and coaches when sharing train rides and social outings (Towers, 1981). The resulting friendships between journalists and sources potentially eroded writers' objectivity, neutrality, professionalism, and ethics.

Reorganization of Newspaper Structure

In another trend of the perspective period, newspapers reorganized in such a way that sport departments began to edit their own copy and were thus freed from their papers' general editorial structures (Towers, 1981). For syndicated columnists such as Grantland Rice, work routines were also changed to minimize newspapers' expenses. For example, when Rice left the Tribune syndicate for the North American Newspaper Alliance in 1930, he began to "batch" his columns, writing seven at once, thus restricting the timeliness of his work (Harper, 1999).

Expansion of Coverage

The third trend of this period involved a shift in popularity from college sport to professional sport. In addition, whereas golden age newspaper coverage had been dominated by baseball, boxing, and horse racing, coverage now branched out to include football and basketball (Garrison & Sabljak, 1993).

Today, interscholastic sporting events are often given plenty of space in newspaper sports sections, but this has not always been the case. Furthermore, football—which often dominates sport coverage today—was often ignored in newspapers until the arrival of the golden age of sport. In 1938, though, the year's top newsmaker was "an undersized, crooked-legged racehorse named Seabiscuit" (Hillenbrand, 2001, p. xvii). This horse was a cultural phenomenon that became the subject of stories in major U.S. newspapers and magazines during the Great Depression. In 1938, at Pimlico, he overcame adversity and defeated the heavily favored War Admiral, a Triple Crown winner. In 1940, Seabiscuit and his hard-luck jockey Red Pollard won the "Hundred Grander" race at Santa Anita with 78,000 people in attendance and millions more listening by radio.

Development of Radio

The fourth trend of the perspective period was the development of radio as a medium, which led to increased realism and objectivity in reporting, as well as a flair for verbal commentary. As detailed by Covil (2005), sporting events were covered on the radio by Westinghouse, General Electric, American Telephone and Telegraph, and Radio Corporation of America. Frank Conrad, a Westinghouse engineer, built KDKA in Pittsburgh—the first licensed radio station that was not considered an experiment. Its first sport broadcast covered the Johnny Ray–Johnny Dundee fight in 1921. Other stations followed suit. For example, in the same year, RCA's WJY broadcast the Jack Dempsey–Georges Carpentier title fight. Also that year, Westinghouse's Newark station WJZ broadcast the 1921 World Series with Tommy Cowan narrating games between the New York Yankees and New York Giants. In 1922, WJZ broadcast the Series with Grantland Rice as the lead announcer. In addition, the Chicago Cubs broadcast baseball games as early as 1924, and the *Chicago Tribune* experimented with baseball coverage on a "bare news basis" (Towers, 1981, p. 18).

Coverage Influenced by National Mood

Although sport coverage was changed by the four trends just discussed, perhaps the greatest influence on sportswriters' work during the 1930s involved the sheer gravity of the era as a whole. As life and priorities continued changing for many people, the Olympics—and especially the 1936 Games—brought a transformation of political proportions, which resulted in simpler and more serious writing (Harper, 1999). The most memorable moments of the 1936 Berlin Olympics involved African American track-and-field athletes. Even as they excelled at the pinnacle of athletics competition and shattered world records, prejudice precluded them from receiving equitable treatment in both Europe and the United States (Laucella, 2016). Most notably, Jesse Owens won four gold medals and was the star of the Games. He set a world record of 10.3 seconds for 100 meters and an Olympic record of 20.7 seconds for 200 meters. He also covered 8.06 meters in the long jump and helped his teammates set another world record in the 400-meter relay (Guttmann, 2002). Owens later said that his life had been "wrapped up, summed up—and stopped up by a single incident"—the "clash with Adolf Hitler in the 1936 Olympics" (Owens with Neimark, 1972, pp. 17-18).

The 1936 Games also featured other compelling athletes and stories. In a group effort, the University of Washington men's rowing team captured gold in Berlin as documented in Daniel James Brown's book *The Boys in the Boat: Nine Americans and Their Epic Quest for Gold at the 1936 Olympics*. On the individual level, 5,000-meter runner Louis Zamperini became the focus of two books and a film. The late airman's heroic story of survival is told in Laura Hillenbrand's award-winning book *Unbroken: A World War II Story of Survival, Resilience, and Redemption*, which was made into a Hollywood film directed by Angelina Jolie. Earlier, Zamperini had co-written his autobiography with David Rensin, *Devil at My Heels: A Heroic Olympian's Astonishing Story of Survival as a Japanese POW in World War II*. Zamperini's indefatigable human spirit epitomized the heroic qualities associated with an Olympian.

Equality, teamwork, and perseverance are just a few of the requisite attributes of athletes and nations seeking Olympic victory. This was especially true during the Depression, a tumultuous period of world dissension that had tremendous psychological and financial effects (Towers, 1981).

Impact of the Depression

The U.S. stock market crash in 1929 caused the national income to plummet from $81 billion to $41 billion by 1932; in addition, 85,000 businesses declared bankruptcy, and nearly 5,800 banks failed to survive (Tallack, 1991). Even with the economic recovery efforts of President Franklin Delano Roosevelt's New Deal, 10 percent of Americans were still unemployed in 1940 (Hunnicutt, 1996; Tallack, 1991). At newspapers, advertising revenue fell, leading to substantial reductions in stories, narrower columns, and larger fonts. Tabloid formats and pictures took the forefront; by 1938, some city newspapers devoted as much as 38 percent of their space to pictures. At the same time, technological developments in radio, photography, and film changed communication and created cohesion in an evolving environment of reform. In this era, sport and good sporting behavior gained prominence, both mirroring and influencing U.S. culture, and sport also became more democratized (Harper, 1999; Susman, 1984; Towers, 1981).

Influential newspaper sportswriters of the time included Westbrook Pegler of the *New York World-Telegram*, Arthur Daley of the *New York Times*, Red Smith of the *Philadelphia Record* and the *New York Times*, John Kieran of the *New York Times*, and Shirley Povich of the *Washington Post*. Radio sportscasters during the period included the NBC's Graham McNamee, CBS's Ted Husing, baseball announcer Mel Allen, Jack Buck at St. Louis' KMOX-AM, and the Dodgers' Vin Scully.

In addition to newspapers and radio, sport magazines (e.g., *Sport, Sporting News, Sports Digest*) gained prominence with their attention to facts, statistics, and literary writing. The 1940s also saw the emergence of specialized magazines (e.g., *World Tennis, Golf Digest, Yachting, Football Annual, Daily Racing Form*) as the market for niche writing took shape (Garrison & Sabljak, 1993). These magazines covered events such as the Joe Louis–Max Schmeling fights and Jackie Robinson's integration of baseball as he took the field for the Brooklyn Dodgers from 1947 through 1956. The

Vin Scully's Contributions to the Dodgers and Sport Broadcasting

For a record 67 years, Vin Scully was voice of the Dodgers and was known for his "keen insight and subtle humor" (Enders, 2016). To date, it's the longest any broadcaster has worked for one team. Scully is the last broadcaster who can say he saw Babe Ruth play. He called his first game for the Dodgers in 1950 at Philadelphia's Shibe Park when he was 22 years old. The Dodgers lost 9 to 1 to the Phillies. The beloved broadcaster retired in October 2016 (Shaikin, 2018), and according to Jon Weisman, Dodgers' director of digital and print content, "He's a force that transcends demographics, generations, geography. It's something that unites 99.9 percent of this area. The entire population has lived their lives through Vin Scully and relished it. Even people who aren't baseball fans value him" (Enders, 2016).

alternative press also gained momentum in covering sporting events, and its origins and ideologies are detailed in the following discussion.

Impact of the Alternative Press

Throughout history, the media have both reported on and sometimes reflected friction between mainstream culture and diverse subcultures in the United States (Folkerts, Lacy, & Davenport, 1998). For example, by 1900, nearly 200 African American newspapers were being published in the United States (Blanchard, 1998), and these papers offered diverse viewpoints and published articles on (as it was sometimes called at the time) the "Negro cause" (Strother, 1978). The first newspaper produced by black Americans, *Freedom's Journal*, began in 1827 and was edited by Samuel Cornish and John B. Russwurm (Wilson, 2017). Other more recent examples include the *Chicago Defender, Baltimore Afro-American, Pittsburgh Courier, Boston Guardian, Indianapolis Freeman*, and *New York Amsterdam News*. After World War I, the black press redoubled its efforts as a crusader, and circulation grew to more than a million copies per week as it fought for racial integration, equality, and national black consciousness (Carroll, 2007). Today, the legacy is carried on through the Black Press of America, a trade association with more than 200 black newspapers in the U.S. and Virgin Islands, an electronic news service, and the BlackPressUSA website. The combined readership is 15 million, and they provide real-time news that continues to support Cornish and Russwurm's proclamation: "Too long have others spoken for us. . . . We wish to plead our own cause" (Wilson, 2007).

The situation of black Americans was also taken up by various groups such as the National Association for Colored Women, the National Association for the Advancement of Colored People, the National Urban League, the United Negro Improvement Association, and the Brotherhood of Sleeping Car Porters. In the arts, the Harlem Renaissance produced artistic contributions from writers such as Langston Hughes, James Weldon Johnson, Nella Larsen, Jean Toomer, and Countee Cullen; musicians such as Duke Ellington, Count Basie, and Fats Waller; and magazines such as *Crisis, Messenger*, and *Opportunity* (Baker, 1998; Laucella, 2015). For the first time, there was a concerted, collaborative effort to challenge stereotypical images of black Americans (Baker, 1998).

Alternative voices and social activism were also promoted by the American Communist press. By the late 1930s, the *Daily Worker* in New York had a circulation of 100,000 (Emery et al., 2000). Founded in 1924, the *Daily Worker* had unusual journalistic freedom since it was supported by workers rather than corporations (Lamb, 2012). In the face of increasing apprehension about fascism and the Depression, Communists advocated equity between races, genders, and classes in U.S. society (Rusinack, 1998). Leftist newspapers and pamphlets appeared at U.S. universities, highlighting societal and economic problems and promoting radical solutions during the Great Depression (Silber, 2003). New York University student Lester Rodney received his first copy of the *Daily Worker* in the mid-1930s, soon became its sports editor, and went on to influence U.S. sport coverage for more than two decades (Silber, 2003).

Although the Communist press and the black press held disparate ideologies, both fought for equality and integration regardless of race, sex, ethnicity, and socioeconomic background (Laucella, 2016). As part of this effort, the black press, especially the *Pittsburgh Courier*, pressured baseball to end discrimination and helped hasten the racial integration that eventually occurred with Jackie Robinson's inaugural game as a Brooklyn Dodger on April 15, 1947. Particularly influential was the *Courier's* Wendell Smith, who mentioned Robinson's name to Brooklyn's president, Branch Rickey. Other vocal proponents of integration included Sam Lacy, writer for the *Defender* and sports editor of the *Baltimore Afro-American*, and Joe Bostic of the *People's Voice* (Roberts & Klibanoff, 2006). These and other black sportswriters and editors remained resolute in their principles while promoting equality, yet many denounced confrontation and militancy (Lamb, 2012).

Regardless of differences in their overarching ideologies, the black and Communist presses both acted as "primary promoters and catalysts for baseball's integration" (Laucella, 2005, p. 209). In the case of Jackie Robinson, the alternative press played a role in "progress, equality, and justice" even as the mainstream press failed to illuminate the significance of Robinson's accomplishment. As Lamb wrote in *Conspiracy of Silence: Sportswriters and the Long Campaign to Desegregate Baseball* (2012), "Sportswriters did not merely ignore the color line; they defended it. They did not merely ignore racial discrimination; they practiced it. . . . They were willful conspirators in the perpetration of the color line" (p. 24). In contrast, alternative publications worked actively to integrate baseball and portrayed athletes fairly rather than using stereotypes and racially marked language. The historic significance of Robinson joining the Brooklyn Dodgers was crucial in reintegrating both professional and amateur sport in the United States. The NFL and NBA followed MLB and in the early 1970s, the Southeastern Conference in NCAA football became the last major sport league to integrate (Nauright & Wiggins, 2010).

TRANSITION YEARS

Whereas newspapers devoted much attention to sport, a new medium enabled fans to experience sport instantly and visually. With World War II

in the past, nearly 100 television stations operating in the United States, and more discretionary money in the pockets of the working class, the transition years brought a spike in the purchase of televisions. According to sport historian Benjamin G. Rader (2004), "Nothing was more central to the history of organized sports during the second half of the twentieth century than television" (p. 249).

Sport Coverage Increased by Network Television

From 1950 to 1970, print journalists modified both the style and the content of their offerings to compete with sport coverage provided by the new medium of television. National broadcasting was made possible by the development of coaxial cable lines, and television was mostly live during this era (Emery et al., 2000). In terms of sport, television brought live events to fans and visually captured key moments and plays. As a result, print journalists searched for different angles and wrote more features, human-interest stories, and articles about sport's overarching significance (Garrison & Sabljak, 1993). Meanwhile, television was making sport a national and global phenomenon by transporting viewers to events instantly (Rader, 2004, p. 249). Boxing was broadcast throughout the 1950s, and increasing attention was also given to basketball, bowling, and baseball (Garrison & Sabljak, 1993). Broadcasters also covered the World Series and the Olympic Games, and teleprinters (e.g., Teletype) enhanced communication from reporters in the field to workers in the newsroom (Garrison & Sabljak, 1993).

By 1952, more than 15 million U.S. homes had a television (Emery et al., 2000). The major networks—National Broadcasting Company (NBC), Columbia Broadcasting System (CBS), and American Broadcasting Company (ABC)—sought to expand their reach further through affiliates, with NBC leading the way at 64 (Emery et al., 2000). Network executives also realized that sport fans could be viewed as commodities with which to lure advertisers (e.g., Coca-Cola, McDonald's) to sponsor events and promote their products. ABC, which ranked third in ratings in the 1950s, used sport as a vehicle for network exposure and rose to the top of the rankings by the 1970s (Rader, 2004). The effects of television and other electronic media on sport communication are covered extensively in chapter 7.

In the 1960s, sport journalism gained even more momentum and higher status as it increased the diversity of the stories it told, which resulted in increased numbers for participation, attendance, and circulation. The new breadth of topics included legal, political, economic, and social issues in sport, as well as stories aimed at satisfying fans' obsession with athletes' and coaches' lives, both on and off the field. One example was writer Gay Talese's (1966) intimate portrait of Joe DiMaggio for *Esquire*, "The Silent Season of a Hero." Talese, hailed by the late author Tom Wolfe as the founder of New Journalism (Boynton, n.d.), enjoyed a journalism career that spanned decades of writing for such publications as the *New York Times*, *The New Yorker*, *Newsweek*, and *Harper's*; he also produced 14 books. Other areas that gained in importance during this period included in-depth analysis, international stories, and women's sport (Garrison & Sabljak, 1993).

Women's Entry Into the Field

Female reporters entered the scene with Dorothy Lindsay of the *Boston Herald*, Janet Valborg Owen of the *New York Evening World*, and Olympic skater Maribel Vinson of the *New York Times* (Creedon, 1994). One of the first women to be a full-time sport reporter was Mary Garber of the *Twin Cities Sentinel* (later the *Winston-Salem Journal*). She was a key precursor to Lesley Visser, Melissa Ludtke, Jane Gross, Michele Himmelberg, Lisa Olson, and other female sport journalists.

Launch of *Sports Illustrated*

In 1954, Henry Luce created the weekly magazine *Sports Illustrated*. Although aides scoffed at his idea—calling it "expensive, misguided, and inherently trivial folly" (MacCambridge, 1997, p. 4)—the publication satisfied fans' fascination with spectator sport. During the transition years, sport was more "compartmentalized, regionalized, [and] marginalized" (MacCambridge, 1997, p. 4) as attendance plummeted after World War II and game shows captured viewers' attention. RCA began manufacturing color televisions, and networks broadcast more games. Teams expanded to smaller cities, and *Sports Illustrated* gained popularity among middle-class subscribers of the postwar period. *Sports Illustrated* legitimized sport with its sophisticated and colorful journalism, captivating readers and influencing the skyrocketing growth of sport in the 1950s and 1960s. Although historians credited the state of the economy and the invention of television as crucial contributors to sport's growth, *Sports Illustrated* also influenced its expansion, according to MacCambridge (1997):

> It made an art out of in-depth reporting on those games, and thereby made the games themselves more important to more Americans. By setting the agenda of just what sports were important, [Sports Illustrated] pointed the way for much of the television revolution that would follow. (p. 6)

PIONEERING VISIONS: PETE ROZELLE AND ROONE ARLEDGE

The advent of a new medium in the form of television, coupled with specific technological advancements in televised sport coverage, influenced sport's development as part of the social fabric in the United States and beyond. Two men were crucial to the development of both sport and television. Former National Football League (NFL) commissioner Pete Rozelle and former ABC president Roone Arledge were pioneers whose visions shaped televised coverage of sport. Along the way, they contributed to the development of sport marketing, communication, and broadcasting—both singularly and collaboratively—as ways to promote and use sport as a powerful and lucrative business vehicle in television and U.S. culture.

The *Sporting News* named Rozelle the 20th century's most powerful person in sport (Carter, 2000). When Rozelle took over as commissioner of the fledgling NFL in 1960, the 12 football franchises competed against each other for profit and garnered less than $20 million in total revenues (Lewis, 1998). Today, the NFL is the most popular sport in the United States (Rovell, 2014); it is also the "most valuable sports league in the world," according to *Forbes*, with an average team value over $2 billion (Ozanian, 2015). This success can be attributed to Rozelle, who imagined the role that television could play in sport's popularity and growth, especially during the prime-time viewing hours (Shapiro & Maske, 2005).

Rozelle also saw the importance of combining the teams' broadcast rights into one bidding package for the television networks, which tightened the teams into a single cohesive entity rather than a fragmented set of stand-alone franchises. With this "league think" approach, NFL team owners considered the league's welfare over their teams' individual needs while increasing the value of the NFL brand as a whole. Rozelle used this philosophy to develop a business strategy centered on a national television package (DeGaris, 2003). By persuading the U.S. Congress to legalize single-network contracts for professional leagues, he forced networks to compete for the league's pooled rights (Carter, 2000). The Sports Broadcasting Act of 1961 enabled professional leagues to bundle their rights for sale in a combined package ("Sports Law," 2005).

Under Rozelle, NFL Properties became the league's independent marketer in 1963 (Lefton, 2002). In addition to laying the foundation for today's NFL business model, Rozelle merged the NFL and the American Football League (AFL) in 1970, which led to the AFL–NFL World Championship Game and ultimately the Super Bowl, which has become "the most lucrative annual spectacle in American mass culture" (Real, 1975, p. 31). Not only does the Super Bowl unite electronic media and sport in a "ritualized mass activity," but it also propagates American cultural values and ideologies in a "mythic spectacle" (Real, 1975, p. 31). As a result, corporations use Super Bowl ads to vie for viewers in the "most-watched television event of the year" ("Super Bowl," 2015). In 2020's Super Bowl LIV, the Kansas City Chiefs defeated the San Francisco 49ers 31-20. Fox, Fox Deportes, NFL, and Verizon's digital properties drew 102 million total viewers. This was up slightly from 2019's cumulative number of 100.7 million. The audience on Fox alone was 99.9 million, the first year-to-year increase since 2015 and up 1.5 percent over 2019's championship game between the New England Patriots and Los Angeles Rams (Battaglio, 2020). Ratings have consistently surpassed 100 million viewers since 2010, with 2015 having the highest at 114.4 million viewers, and the Super Bowl remains by far the year's most-watched program. Events that rival Super Bowl viewership include the Apollo moon landing, the start of Operation Desert Storm, Richard Nixon's resignation, and the final episode of *M*A*S*H* (Korman, 2019). Some explanations for the ratings drop in 2019 included Patriots fatigue. At that point, New England had won six titles and played in nine of the last 18 Super Bowls. Additionally, Los Angeles ratings were the second worst in history (to St. Louis) for a television market with a team playing in the game. The NFL booked Maroon 5, a controversial choice, for the halftime show. Another controversy included former St. Louis Rams fans, who may not have watched because the team left St. Louis and moved to Los Angeles in 2016 (Caron, 2019). And finally, New Orleans and Louisiana tuned out the game after officials blew a crucial pass interference call in the NFC championship game between the Saints and Rams. The overnight rating in New Orleans was a mere 26.1 rating, down from 53.0 in 2018 (Korman, 2019).

Still, since 2010, advertising prices for the Super Bowl nearly doubled. CBS charged, on average, a record $5.25 million per 30-second spot during Super Bowl LIII (McCarriston, 2019). All of this happened in an era when NFL commissioner Roger Goodell dealt with off-field headlines that included domestic violence scandals involving LeSean McCoy, Josh Brown, Kareem Hunt, and others (Clark, 2018). In response, crisis communicators at the league and team levels crafted messages to reinforce the league's power, influence, and averred commitment to fighting domestic violence. Time will tell how scandals will affect the league's (and Goodell's) brand as it continues to evolve from the form originally envisioned by Rozelle.

In 1970, Arledge and Rozelle worked together to mastermind *Monday Night Football*, which "created a national pastime" (Boss, 2002, para. 15). Trailing only CBS's *60 Minutes* news program, *Monday Night Football* is the second-longest-running prime-time show on U.S. television (Lewis, 1998). In its first season, *Monday Night Football* featured the legendary Howard Cosell, as well as Keith Jackson and former Dallas Cowboys quarterback Don Meredith; in the show's second season, Jackson was replaced by Frank Gifford. According to Al Michaels (2014), "Roone Arledge's decision to go with a three-announcer booth—

Photo courtesy of Paul M. Pedersen.

NFL teams, such as the Cleveland Browns, and their actions (e.g., the on-field brawl involving Myles Garrett, the signing of Kareem Hunt) are often criticized. Even as the NFL faces various crises (e.g., domestic violence issues, head trauma debates), it continues to dominate the media landscape, and the cost of Super Bowl advertising sets new records every year.

including the polarizing Cosell—had made the show more than just a football game. It made it a national communal sports experience" (p. 93). More than two decades later, in 1993, the Fox network acquired broadcast rights to the National Football Conference (NFC) package, thus establishing itself as a fourth major television network (Sweet, 2002).

The price of televising football has grown exponentially over the years. In 1962, CBS paid $9.3 million to televise NFL games for two years. In 2014, *Thursday Night Football* debuted on CBS and pulled in strong ratings with Jim Nantz and Phil Simms in the broadcast booth ("NFL Expands," 2016). Former Dallas Cowboys quarterback Tony Romo replaced Simms and started calling games with Nantz on CBS after he retired. The NFL and Fox partnered together in 2018 for *Thursday Night Football* after a number of "short-term marriages over the years" (Deitsch, 2018). The five-year rights agreement is for $550 million yearly and includes 11 games between weeks 4 and 15 (except Thanksgiving night). The NFL Network will simulcast these games, and Fox Deportes will distribute them in Spanish.

In the NFL's latest television deal, the league was paid more than $5.5 billion by Fox, NBC, ESPN, and DirecTV for television rights in 2014—a 22 percent increase over 2013 (James, 2014). ESPN's commitment of close to $1.7 billion for 17 Monday night games (24 percent more than the 2013 price) is the highest price paid and includes game highlights and digital rights. ESPN had already acquired *Monday Night Football* in 2006, with Al Michaels and Joe Theismann broadcasting the games. Today, Michaels (2014) still calls NFL games but has moved to the Sunday night broadcast on NBC. Even so, he views *Monday Night Football* as his "calling card at ABC Sports" (p. 183). As for the Monday broadcast, it still adheres to Rozelle and Arledge's three-pronged plan: to showcase the league and its players and coaches, to present sport reporters as experts and celebrities, and to use up-to-date technological advancements in sport broadcasting.

In 2015, ESPN broadcast its first NFL playoff game. As part of its eight-year extension with the NFL, ESPN can now broadcast one wild card game per season (Finn, 2015). Meanwhile, Fox paid over $925 million for its NFC games on Sundays, and that price will cross the billion-dollar line during the life of Fox's current nine-year contract (James, 2014). NBC continues to broadcast *Sunday Night Football*, and satellite broadcaster DirecTV offers its Sunday Ticket package. While NFL's Sunday Ticket has spent all of its existence on DirecTV, NFL commissioner Roger Goodell seeks to modernize it and change its delivery to several different platforms. After the 2019 season, the league had the option to find a new partner, but decided to stay with the satellite TV carrier at least through the 2020 season (Frankel, 2019). All told, the NFL's current broadcast contracts are worth $27 billion and run through the 2022 season (Badenhausen, 2011). The networks realize the scarcity of "must-see" live programming, and the NFL delivers some of their highest-rated content (Kondolojy, 2014). The networks also use their football programming as a vehicle for promoting other shows to young male viewers during prime time (Sweet, 2002). In addition, female viewership represents 45 percent of the league's overall audience, and they account for about half of the Super Bowl audience (de la Cretaz, 2019). Companies and brands are targeting women, as was evident in the 2019 Super Bowl where Olay and Bumble advertised for the first time during the megaevent, using Sarah Michelle Gellar and Serena Williams, respectively. Women are 27 percent more likely to pay attention to ads, according to TVision Insights (de la Cretaz, 2019).

Like Rozelle, Arledge was a visionary in sport broadcasting who contributed to the NFL's growth. *Life* named Arledge as one of the most important Americans of the 20th century (Boss, 2002). Al Michaels worked under Arledge for his first 10 years at ABC and credits Arledge's philosophy for everything that was achieved at ABC Sports during that time—and for a great deal of what is still done today. "Storytelling was the tool he used to transform coverage of sports on television" (Michaels, 2014, p. 152). ABC was the third network but rose to prominence thanks to Arledge's risk-taking attitude (Michaels, 2014). That approach was evident in Arledge's introduction of technological innovations, such as instant replay, slow motion, handheld cameras, split-screen coverage, and end zone cameras.

In 1961, Arledge also created the longstanding show *Wide World of Sports*, which showcased every sport imaginable—from football to bobsledding and luge. The program featured international events broadcast via satellite and enabled viewers to connect with athletes through in-depth human interest stories. In addition, Arledge made the Olympics a "television event," and ABC's coverage of the Israeli hostage tragedy during the 1972 Munich Games not only won multiple Emmy Awards but also created a foundation for how breaking news would and should be covered (Michaels, 2014). After Arledge's death in 2002, ESPN columnist Ralph Wiley (2002) lauded his contributions to sport as president of ABC Sports and ABC News:

"The thrill of victory and the agony of defeat." His. "Up close and personal." His. "Wide World of Sports." His. Epic Olympic coverage. His. Breaking spot news on terrorism. His, really. "Monday Night Football." His. Howard Cosell. His. Dandy Don Meredith (TV version). His. Frank Gifford. His. "American Sportsman." His. "Nightline." His. "20/20." His. Isolated camera. His. Instant replay. His. All totally his. Sports as storytelling. His, in a big way. (para. 5)

As the "Mark Twain of TV sports" (Wiley, 2002), Arledge recognized that "stars sell" (Harris, 2002, p. 11). He captured the entertainment element in sport and transported it to a different level, setting the standard for the technological innovation we now experience and expect in sport communication and broadcasting.

CONTEMPORARY SPORT COMMUNICATION AND DIGITAL SPORT COMMUNICATION

Lawrence A. Wenner (1998) coined the term *MediaSport* to refer to the "mediation of sport" in culture and the "broader public sphere" (p. xiii). According to Real (1998), "No force has played a more central role in the MediaSport complex than commercial television and its institutionalized value system—profit seeking, sponsorship, expanded markets, commodification, and competition" (p. 17). Sport appeared across many platforms, as newspapers, magazines, film, radio, and television; all covered sport by the end of the Industrial Age (Bryant & Holt, 2006).

Influence of Sport Increased by Cable Television

Whereas sport was influenced primarily by **network television** in the 1950s through the 1970s, its reach was expanded exponentially in the late 1970s and 1980s by **cable television**, especially by the Entertainment and Sports Programming Network (ESPN). Ironically, when ESPN co-founder Bill Rasmussen thought of broadcasting sport 24 hours a day via cable television, network and newspaper executives downplayed the idea's potential impact, never envisioning the potential of cable's reach and fans' obsession with the nonstop sport approach (Freeman, 2001). Rasmussen was vindicated, of course, and, as the "worldwide leader in sports," ESPN now sets the agenda for sport and entertainment coverage on its multiple platforms worldwide (Smith & Hollihan, 2009, p. xiv).

Since its first broadcast on September 7, 1979, ESPN has featured many talented anchors and reporters: Keith Olbermann, Chris Berman, Bob Ley, Dick Vitale, Dan Patrick, Chris Fowler, the late Stuart Scott, Linda Cohn, Sage Steele, Chris McKendry, and Robin Roberts, to name just a few (Freeman, 2001). These individuals and others have offered provocative commentary, wit, keen writing and reporting, and charismatic personalities both on and off the field. It has done so through various longtime shows, including *The Sports Reporters*; *Pardon the Interruption (PTI)*; *Outside the Lines*; *Mike and Mike*; and, particularly, *SportsCenter*, which delivered its 50,000th episode on September 13, 2012 (Fay, 2012). In 2015, when much-loved ESPN star Stuart Scott passed away from cancer at age 49, journalists across the platforms expressed grief for the popular anchor with a "transformational personality" (Ourand, 2015, p. 12). In his memory, the NFL, NBA, and college basketball games all held moments of silence (Ourand, 2015).

Today, ESPN reaches sport fans in over 200 countries and territories, across all seven continents in five languages. It has dubbed itself the "leading multinational, multimedia sports entertainment company" with over 50 business entities ("ESPN About," 2019). These include 32 television networks; 13 websites; more than 90 broadband networks; seven radio properties; print, mobile, and consumer products; and event management. Its sport rights include over 130 leagues and sports. The network's majority (80 percent) owner is ABC, which is an indirect subsidiary of Walt Disney; the other 20 percent is owned by Hearst. From domestic cable networks to radio, print, broadband, wireless, and on-demand offerings, ESPN provides programming and entertainment for sport enthusiasts and fanatics alike. The network pursues an expansive mission of serving "sports fans wherever sports are watched, listened to, discussed, debated, read about, or played" (Badenhausen, 2014; "ESPN, about," 2019). Even with the rising rights fee costs and the loss of cable subscribers, ESPN still earned more than $3 billion in operating earnings. *Forbes* ranked ESPN No. 47 among the "World's Most Valuable Brands" in 2019 (Badenhausen, 2019b). The network owns broadcast rights to the NFL, MLB, NBA, major college football conferences, Major League Soccer (MLS), Grand Slam tennis tournaments, NASCAR, and major golf tournaments. ESPN also secured the coveted broadcast rights for the College Football Playoff, which began in 2015, for about $470 million per year ("ESPN Lands," 2012). ESPN continues to expand partnerships with leagues, too; the ACC Network launched in August 2019 and has a 20-year contract with ESPN (Hale, 2018).

ESPN delivers its content through multiple platforms, including mobile applications, social platforms, and game consoles (Greenfield, 2012; Rob King, personal communication; Laucella, 2014). In 2018, ESPN+, a subscription service with thousands of live sport content options, launched and creates a personalized viewing experience for fans (Spangler, 2018). In addition, ESPN.com has been the leading sport website each month since its launch as ESPNet SportsZone in 1995 (King, 2005; Fischer, 2019).

Bob Ley, One of ESPN's Founding Anchors

Bob Ley's 40-year career at ESPN ended when he announced his retirement in June 2019 as he appeared with his longtime *Outside the Lines* colleague Jeremy Schaap. Ley, ESPN's longest-tenured anchor, had been on a leave of absence since the prior October and stressed it was entirely his decision ("Bob Ley Retires," 2019). Ley became a *SportsCenter* anchor the third day of ESPN's operation, Sept. 9, 1979. He hosted the first NCAA selection show in 1980 as well as the live broadcast of the NFL Draft that year. He hosted *Outside the Lines* since its inception in May 1990 and also hosted ESPN's weekly *E:60* on Sunday mornings. During Ley's tenure, he won 11 Sports Emmy Awards, including an Emmy for outstanding studio host in 2018. Other awards include the 2014 DuPont Award for reporting on issues in football at the youth level and four Edward R. Murrow Awards ("Bob Ley Retires," 2019).

As noted by ESPN's Rob King, senior vice president and editor-at-large for original content, the ongoing evolution of technology means that live sport content is no longer the "exclusive domain of radio and television"; instead, it is now "disseminated in myriad forms: instant messaging, tweets, live blogging, real-time data," and so forth (personal communication). As a result, every sport journalist now has the ability—and responsibility—to participate in real-time relationships with audiences. Of course, the same technology is also available to amateur journalists, players, agents, teams, and leagues. "In the realm of real-time journalism, every second becomes a potential deadline, and every fact has the feel of breaking news," said King. "But immediacy does not equal authenticity, and it can imperil accuracy" (personal communication). These statements epitomize sport communication's opportunities and challenges in today's 24-7, data-driven, multimedia arena.

Communication Strategies Altered by Technology

In the Information Age, sport's focus has shifted to that of a "spectator-centered technology and business" (Real, 1998, p. 18). As described by Bryant and Holt, the Information Age began in the 1990s and merged into the digital age as technology and media increasingly influenced interactions, communication experiences, and global perspectives (Bryant & Holt, 2006; Laucella, 2014). Amidst a combination of technological, economic, demographic, and social changes, traditional media (e.g., newspapers, radio) have matured, and new and emerging media have transformed the way we experience and consume sport (Laucella, 2014). These innovations affect the coverage of sport, the norms and practices of professionals, and the transmission of values and ethics to audiences. Technology can also join, split, or segment audiences as consumers both tailor their experiences privately and interact with others in the public arena (Dizard, 2000; Laucella, 2014; Putnam, 2000).

In the fragmented media environment—including television, broadband, satellite radio, Internet, and mobile technologies—media entities fight to reach and retain audiences. In this environment, in 2014, 70 percent of U.S. adults claimed to follow sport, and media executives believe that they must reach these 170 million fans who consume an average of nearly eight hours of sport per week (*Know the Fan*, 2014). To participate actively in this scene, sport entities of all types use digital technologies; in addition, teams, leagues, and sport media outlets are altering their strategies. The media are trying to tap into the power of esports since the fanbase has grown quickly (Nielsen sports, 2018). Examples of this include Formula 1 team McLaren, which hired a new simulator driver in 2017. Formula I had more than 60,000 gamers enter its Esports Series that year (Nielsen sports, 2018). The NFL's Pittsburgh Steelers work alongside a 12-person esports operation. The Pittsburgh Knights receive assistance from Steelers staff on marketing, ticketing, merchandising, and sponsorship sales. The Steelers have a minority stake in the Knights and see the relationship as a way to understand potential fans while building an esports scene in Pittsburgh (Fischer, 2019). In esports media, there's competition for Twitch, the market-leading platform owned by Amazon. Twitch had the rights for the Overwatch League in 2018 and 2019 as well as the inaugural 2018 season of NBA 2K League. YouTube, Facebook, Twitter have all moved into esports and the lucrative streaming space.

Another example can be seen in Dallas Mavericks owner Mark Cuban, who regularly uses his blog (Blog Maverick), as well as Twitter, Instagram, and other outlets. The former computer consultant sold CompuServe for millions in 1992, then sold Broadcast.com to Yahoo! for $5.6 billion (Scola, 2014). He sets precedents and takes risks. In 2019, his team also became the first NBA team to host a combine for elite teen players. The Mavs Youth Combine featured 40 athletes from Dallas and the nearby area and followed the NBA's initiative to increase involvement in youth basketball (Jolee, 2019; Townsend, 2014).

In summary, technology has transformed sport communication with speed, accessibility, interactivity, and multimedia strategies. Technology is discussed more extensively in chapter 8.

Expansion of Sport in the Digital Age

Continuity and change are part and parcel of the digital age (Boyle, 2006), which is characterized by rapid transmission of information across multiple platforms, synergy between discrete media entities and the resulting effects on news values, and elite sport's reliance on the media (Boyle, 2007; Laucella, 2014). At this point, nearly all forms of media, information, entertainment, and commerce have expanded to the web and to mobile technologies (Boyle, 2006; Giuliano, 2011). As a result, the arena of sport has become increasingly diverse, fragmented, and competitive. Sport organizations break and report news, as well as blog, tweet, and provide game and story updates (Andrews, 2011). Anyone can publish in today's digital world—teams, leagues, organizations, athletes, coaches, agents, fans, and others (Laucella, 2014). In addition, social and technological changes have led to redesigned routines (Fry, 2011a), and reporters' and sport organizations' responsibilities have expanded and evolved. Sport journalism is still as relevant and important today as it was in the last century (Solomon, 2018).

In the golden age of sport, journalists focused tightly on the games and on athletes' on-field heroics. Today, journalists carry expanded responsibilities, and convergence and synergy abound in a world where digital media are transforming and reshaping journalists' roles and norms (Boyle, 2006). According to Tim Franklin, senior associate dean and professor at Northwestern's Medill School, "New digital platforms not only are changing the industry; they're redefining how journalists work and report the news. Every millisecond counts to readers and viewers who have an insatiable appetite for the latest information" (personal communication).

According to Mike Butterworth, director of the Center for Sports Communication & Media, "We're at a transitional moment, not just in terms of what's happening in the industry and digital platforms—the nature of how we think about great writing is evolving with that. People can not only distribute stories in different ways, but they are accessible to different kinds of audiences" (Solomon, 2018, para. Para. 5). These changes bring both challenges and, increasingly, opportunities—to publish, drive traffic, draw readers, and expand one's brand (Kindred, 2010; Laucella, 2014). In this environment, writers such as Jon Wertheim, Sally Jenkins, Christine Brennan, Dana O'Neil, and Mike Lupica possess unique styles with which they can detail the action and spark people's interest in developments both on and off the field. Butterworth believes that "what distinguishes competent work from important work is the ability to contextualize the choices that we make, and the understanding of the historical background, the recognition of critical identity positions that are at stake, being able to make those kinds of interpretations" (Solomon, 2018, para. 8). Those trained in both the vocabulary and specific skills in sport can ask good questions, make solid language choices, and exhibit versatility.

Due to role convergence, journalists now perform multiple roles in a variety of media forms (Huang et al., 2006). For example, they write stories and columns for newspapers, appear on broadcast outlets (e.g., ESPN, local affiliates), write for digital entities (e.g., newspaper websites, blogs), and write books. In addition, all these media forms feature more in-depth analyses, interviews, and opinions, as well as an avoidance of the celebratory tone that characterized the golden age of sport.

A primary challenge today for sport journalists is access (Solomon, 2018). According

Student and aspiring journalists need to be multifaceted as they navigate the expansive field of sport communication and coverage.

Photo courtesy of Malcolm Moran.

to the Nieman Reports' J. Brady McCollough, "In an age of social platforms and celebrity athletes, Bleacher Report, The Players' Tribune, and The Athletic are challenging legacy sports media" (2018, para. 1). For example, in 2017, the *Washington Post*'s Kent Babb was brushed off by former NFL running back Marshawn Lynch after a training camp practice, yet earlier that day Lynch was accommodating with a Bleacher Report crew. Bleacher Report, with more than 14 million combined followers, landed Lynch. It used the self-professed "Beast Mode" to launch into longform documentary production in the eight-episode "No Script With Marshawn Lynch," which aired on Facebook Watch. At the time, Dave Finocchio, Bleacher Reports' founder and CEO, said, "He appreciates that B/R is a little bit more celebratory in nature and has less 'gotcha' content on athletes" (McCollough, 2018, para. 3). Bleacher Report never revealed whether it paid Lynch to participate. In the end, Facebook bought the rights from Bleacher Report to stream the documentary, and Babb wrote a profile that did not have a proper interview with Lynch yet still received praise for his work.

This shows how the journalist–source relationship has changed. Unlike the 1920s and 1930s, today's sport journalism is marked by a more detached relationship between reporters and sources. The relationship can even become evasive or contentious, as it has, for instance, in media incidents involving Cam Newton and Kevin Durant. In other examples, as documented in ESPN's *Nine for IX* episode "Let Them Wear Towels," pioneering sport reporters Lisa Olson and Melissa Ludtke went to court to fight for gender equality in their respective cases against the New England Patriots and Major League Baseball (Baranauckas, 2013). For now, old and new sport media coexist, but long term, how will serious sport journalism survive when "entertainment dressed up as journalism is the only proven way to subsidize work that matters?" asked McCollough (2018, para. 7). Investigative journalism still has significance today, as evident in the time and resources some outlets devote to it. As The Athletic's Richard Deitsch noted, *Indianapolis Star* reporters broke the Larry Nassar sex abuse scandal, and CNN's Sara Ganim broke the sex abuse investigation into Penn State assistant football coach Jerry Sandusky when she worked at the *Harrisburg Patriot-News* (McCollough, 2018). Her coverage won her a Pulitzer prize, reinforcing the power of investigative journalism. ESPN's *Outside the Lines* covers investigative issues daily, and its reporters have discussed such issues as the NFL's handling of concussions, national anthem controversies, and the Larry Nassar sex abuse scandal (McCollough, 2018).

Media organizations also grapple with boundaries in a 24-7 news arena. For example, ESPN's journalistic integrity, ethics, and objectivity have been questioned in regard to its slow response to stories involving business colleagues and partners. Examples include *The Decision*, a live television special in which Cleveland Cavaliers star LeBron James announced his departure for the Miami Heat, and ESPN's decision not to collaborate with PBS on the award-winning documentary *League of Denial*, which investigated the NFL's concussion crisis (Lipsyte, 2014). In addition, *SportsCenter* anchors have been criticized for advertising products, thus compromising their role as journalists (Boyle, 2006).

With such issues in mind, it was surprising when ESPN ended its public editor position and regular ombudsman column (Yoder, 2018). It was a valuable resource for the network and outside media since its inception in 2005 (Yoder, 2018). An ombudsman fosters transparency within the media organization by promoting journalistic values like accuracy, accountability, and fairness. *Washington Post* editor George Solomon was ESPN's first ombudsman, and the late *New York Times* sports editor Le Anne Schreiber, discussed later in Malcolm Moran's profile, followed Solomon (Yoder, 2018). ESPN's fifth ombudsman, Robert Lipsyte, analyzed the "empire" and emphasized the need to cut through speculation and the "overgrowth of faux news sources—league- and team-sponsored blogs, player tweets, fanboy sites, rumor mills" (2014, para. 9). This challenge has also been addressed by others. For instance, according to Boyle (2006), "Television . . . frames sport within a paradigm that is predominantly entertainment-driven, with journalism always invariably second in this hierarchy of values" (p. 130). Similarly, the Poynter Institute's Kelly McBride holds that sport media corporations are "more enmeshed in the entertainment business than in promoting the public interest" (personal communication).

The Poynter Institute and other such organizations stress professionalism, accuracy, and ethics in the digital age. Journalists delve deeper because television, the Internet, and emerging technologies bring coverage to fans in real time. As observed in the Pew Research Center's *State of the News Media* reports, news organizations must keep pace with mobile platforms and social media; in fact, the study found that approximately 13,000 worked as editors, reporters, photographers, and videographers at digital-native outlets as reported by the Bureau of Labor Statistics Occupational Employment Statistics ("Digital News Fact Sheet," 2018). Some digital sites (e.g., BuzzFeed, Mashable, Vox Media) now employ large staffs and have lured away former print media professionals, such as Pulitzer Prize winner Mark Schoofs, former *New York Times* assistant managing editor Jim Roberts, and former *Washington Post* staffer Ezra Klein (Mitchell, 2014).

SB Nation, part of Vox Media, touted itself as "the fastest-growing online sports media brand and the largest network of fan-centric sports communities" ("SB Nation," 2015). Digital sport content is also provided by Yahoo! Sports, The Ringer, Deadspin, Bleacher Report, The Big Lead, RantSports, FanSided, and many others. As a result, traditional sport outlets, such as *Sports Illustrated*, have had to "reboot for the mobile world" (Moses, 2014, para. 1), especially with TMZ and other entertainment sites entering the sport arena with racy and entertainment-driven content. Therefore, the *Sports Illustrated* website competes with many sites for its audience. The site was previously housed at Turner Sports but built its own platform (Moses, 2014), which went live in June 2014 and is designed for the smaller screens of mobile phones and tablets. It was also designed to keep people on the site longer; for example, additional articles are promoted to the left and bottom of each screen. The site featured bigger buttons for social sharing as a way of promoting and embracing socially driven traffic. In addition, SI.com created a video streaming site (120 Sports), as well as second screen viewing options and a daily fantasy game app (Fan Nation) that can be played while watching games live on television

(Moses, 2014). While the *SI* website finished in the top 10 of digital sport media sites in early 2019 (as of January), the print publication was reduced to biweekly in 2018 after editor Chris Stone alerted subscribers of the change in a letter (Edmonds, 2018; Fisher, 2019). *Sports Illustrated*'s parent company, Time Inc., was sold to Meredith in 2018, and Meredith later sold *Sports Illustrated* to Authentic Brands Group for $110 million (Steinberg, 2019). The brand development company markets, develops, and licenses *Sports Illustrated*, *Sports Illustrated Kids*, the swimsuit issue, and "Sportsperson of the Year" franchises and photo archive. Meredith paid to operate the editorial operations of *SI* in print and digital for a minimum of two years. Chris Stone and publisher Danny Lee will lead *SI* and Meredith (Steinberg, 2019).

These and all decisions are backed by finances, analytics, and research. Pew's study (Mitchell, 2015) found that social and mobile developments are not only bringing consumers into the process of news gathering and acquisition but also transforming the process. In describing the state of the news media, Pew Research's State of the News Media study found that a vast majority of consumers get news online, with nearly six in ten (57 percent) getting news on a mobile device ("Digital News Fact Sheet," 2018; Walker, 2019). In addition, the *Global Sports Media Consumption Report* found that 19 percent of social sport fans share short clips of games on social networks (*Know the Fan*, 2014). Among sport fans, the report found that 68 percent of fans consume sport online and 45 percent use a second screen while watching sport on television. In other findings, 42 percent of fans consume sport through mobile devices, 70 percent follow sport on Facebook, 40 percent watch on YouTube, 24 percent on Twitter, and 16 percent on Google+ (*Know the Fan*, 2014).

In one striking example, the 2019 World Cup prompted more than 670 million tweets worldwide. As the United States defeated the Netherlands to win its historic fourth title (Litman, 2019), Twitter and Facebook competed to win users. After the American women's victory, Twitter reported a five-time increase in tweets mentioning "pay" (Butler, 2019). Fox Sports' telecast had 14.2 million viewers, third to 1999 and 2015 World Cup finals in terms of U.S. women's team telecasts (Quillen, 2019). In March 2019, all 28 members of the U.S. women's soccer team filed a suit against the U.S. Soccer Federation to gain equal pay to the men's team. The parties agreed to mediate the suit; if it is not settled, there could be a trial in 2020. From 2016 through 2018, women's games garnered $50.8 million compared to $49.9 million dollars earned by the men (Butler, 2019).

Networks, leagues, teams, and individual athletes are also using technology to promote their brands. For example, Ken Rosenthal broke the Boston Red Sox's signing of left fielder Hanley Ramirez on Fox Sports in the late-night hours via Twitter. Rosenthal admits that he checks his phone "every waking minute" for texts and Twitter news ("Red Sox' Free Agent Signings," 2014). According to Brian Hendrickson, former NCAA director of membership communications and executive editor of *NCAA Champion* magazine, "This is the first time that the number of Twitter followers someone has can impact hiring. In the past, it was about writing, breaking news, and working with people" (personal communication). Now, by tracking page views and the number of Twitter followers, an organization can measure the audience drawn by a particular sport communication professional.

Broadcasting networks and outlets also use technology to cross-promote their programming. For example, after Super Bowl LIV, Fox's season 3 premiere of *The Masked Singer* averaged 23.7 million viewers at 10:40 PM ET, up from CBS' *The World's Best* with a start time of 10:36 PM (Andreeva & Hipes, 2020). Streaming continues to expand each year. The 2020 Super Bowl streamed live on FoxSports.com and the Fox Sports app, and NFL digital properties including the NFL app, NFL Fantasy, and NFL.com mobile websites, as well as on Yahoo! Sports and other Verizon Media properties. Fox Deportes' exclusive Spanish-language rights drew 757, 000 total viewers as reported by Nielsen (Andreeva & Hines, 2020).

More generally, the big four professional U.S. sport leagues now offer a variety of mobile applications, including MLB At Bat, NHL GameCenter, NBA Game Time, and NFL Mobile (Sheridan, 2014). The NBA, NHL, and various college teams have also tested ways to sell game tickets through texts. To this end, tech firm ReplyBuy made deals with more than 100 teams across the major sport leagues and universities, including all four men's

Final Four teams in 2019 ("ReplyBuy, the Technology," 2019). As these examples show, all sport organizations are using technology to reach and connect with fans, showcase their brands and products, and improve the mediation and expansiveness of sport.

Of course, athletes themselves also reach fans directly through social media and other outlets. According to Hookit, Real Madrid's Cristiano Ronaldo was the first athlete to reach 200 million combined followers across Twitter, Instagram, and Facebook (Badenhausen, 2016). Primetag also develops technology to measure online influence. In 2018, for example, Brazil lost the World Cup trophy to France; however, Primetag found that Brazil's players still had nearly 194 million interactions on Instagram, which nearly matched the country's population (Kidd, 2018). Ronaldo had 110 million Instagram interactions (he is the most followed athlete on social media with nearly 400 million total followers), Brazil's Neymar had 97.9 million followers, and France's Paul Pogba came in third with 35.9 million (Kidd, 2018). Cristiano Ronaldo came in second in Forbes' 2019 "World's Highest-Paid Athletes" ranking with $109 million, second to footballer Lionel Messi with $127 million in earnings (Badenhausen, 2019a).

As *USA Today* journalist Christine Brennan wrote (2019), "Sometimes, journalism and social media work together in the most interesting way" (para. 1). After Serena Williams lost in the Wimbledon final to Simona Halep in 2019, a reporter approached her by saying, "There have been a few comments made in the last couple of weeks from people like Billie Jean King that maybe you should stop being a celebrity for a year and stop fighting for equality and just focus on tennis. How do you respond to that?" (para. 3). Williams responded, "Well, the day I stop fighting for equality and for people that look like you and me will be the day I'm in my grave" (para. 5). Her response took off on social media, even prompting a reply by Senator Kamala Harris, one of the 2020 Democratic presidential candidates (Brennan, 2019). This shows the influence top athletes have in both legacy and social media outlets.

Athletes also reach fans through websites, such as Derek Jeter's The Players' Tribune, which started out with the NBA's Blake Griffin, the NFL's Russell Wilson, and NASCAR's Danica Patrick listed

BECOMING A CROSS-PLATFORMED COMMUNICATOR

Malcolm Moran
Director, Sports Capital Journalism Program
at Indiana University–Purdue University Indianapolis
Former New York Times, USA Today, *and* Newsday *reporter and columnist*

Malcolm Moran is an award-winning reporter and columnist who has worked over four decades at *Newsday*, the *New York Times*, *Chicago Tribune*, and *USA Today*. He has covered 21 Final Fours, 11 Super Bowls, 15 World Series, and two Olympics to name just a few events. He was the inaugural Knight Chair in sport journalism and society at Penn State and director of the John Curley Center for Sports Journalism. Currently, he is the director of the Sports Capital Journalism Program at Indiana University–Purdue University Indianapolis and president of the U.S. Basketball Writers Association. His career has spanned different eras and outlets, and he realized early on the importance of convergence and cross-platform reporting.

At Fordham, long before anyone talked about crossing platforms, Moran worked at the school's radio station and newspaper, WFUV and the *Ram*, respectively. "I wasn't a math major, but if I could learn how to do two things reasonably well, that would increase my chance of getting hired," he said. And that it did. Moran started as an intern at *Newsday* in 1975. At the time, a sports editor there said, "Look, there's virtually zero chance that anything full-time will ever develop here and we need to make sure you're aware of that and plan accordingly." Yet when the *Long Island Press* suddenly folded and the *Daily News* and *Post* started a daily Queens edition, *Newsday* did, too, and needed someone who knew Queens quickly. Moran said, "All of a sudden the switch

Malcolm Moran (left) with student journalists Frank Bonner, Ryan Gregory, and Hall of Fame sport columnist Dick "Hoops" Weiss (right). They covered the FIBA Women's Basketball World Cup in Tenerife, Spain.

Photo courtesy of Malcolm Moran.

was flipped, and I was working there full-time," covering Queens high school sports and occasionally the Yankees, Mets, and the MLB All-Star Game.

Moran's next set of self-professed "bizarre circumstances" happened after newly hired *New York Times* sports editor Le Anne Schreiber read his stories in *Newsday* while the New York newspaper guild was on strike. "From March 1977 to Thanksgiving 1978, I went from being a part-timer making less than $3 an hour to interviewing at the *New York Times*," Moran said. "What I've told students is that's how random the process is. I wasn't that much better—I was better just through repetition."

After being offered a job at the *Times*, Moran remembers thinking, "a director will come out and say cut! It was a surreal moment . . . it was all Le Anne that orchestrated it. She picked me out of the chorus line." She wanted to hire young, moldable people that would tell stories differently. "She really changed my life," Moran said. "It was her faith in me that I could do things that I hadn't done yet that opened the door."

Moran was a general assignment reporter and columnist who covered the Los Angeles and Atlanta Olympics (he was the *Times*' Olympic writer for 16 hours in July 1993) and then focused on college football and basketball. Moran was teammates for three years with the legendary Red Smith and remembers covering the 1981 Eagles–Raiders Super Bowl with him in New Orleans. That was Smith's last Super Bowl. Other colleagues included Dave Anderson and Tony Kornheiser.

Moran remembers sitting on a couch in September 1979 in the late Alabama coach Bear Bryant's office that is now on display at the Paul W. Bryant Museum on campus. When he sat down on the sofa, he kept sinking down and down until he looked over the edge of the desk at Bryant's face. "I remember thinking, this must have been like what it was to go see the Wizard of Oz," said Moran. Bryant volunteered compelling stories; however, Moran did not understand a word due to his gravelly voice. "I could feel myself perspiring," he said. "All I'm thinking is here's the greatest story ever, and I can't understand a word he's saying." Moran had the presence of mind, though, to ask if he could follow up later with any questions his editors may have. When Moran called Bryant back, he asked the same questions and received the same animated answers; this time, Moran understood everything Bryant said.

Another part of the Bryant interviews "eerily foreshadowed things." Bryant told Moran, "as long as they have me, I will coach until they fire me or until I die." Bryant announced his retirement Dec. 15, 1982, and the Crimson Tide played in the Liberty Bowl against Illinois on December 29. The following month, Bryant passed away. Similarly, Moran had also talked to the late Penn State coach Joe Paterno in a story for *USA Today* in 2005. Paterno said he did not want to have the same thing happen to him. Paterno's last game was on October 29, 2011, also against Illinois. He was fired on November 9 and died in January 2012.

Moran has been fortunate to cover many historic events. One that stands out is the 1984 Los Angeles Olympics, which included the first women's marathon; in years prior, there was "silly rhetoric" about how women weren't capable of running the distance. Moran never understood this misperception. He had covered Joan Benoit, who won the gold medal, in the 1979 Boston Marathon. He had covered Norway's Grete Waitz, who won the silver medal, in the 1979 and 1980 New York Marathons. "To be sitting there in the Coli-seum—to see Joanie running in and she emerged into the sunlight in front of a full house, and then to see Grete not too far behind and having dealt with both of them, that was probably the most memorable thing I've covered in terms of historical relevance," Moran said.

When discussing sport journalism, Moran believes the biggest question now is whether there will be a sustainable business model, specifically a subscription-based model that can salvage regional operations. "To a large degree the outcome of The Athletic will answer that question. Are people willing to pay for quality information that is not going to torment them with popup ads to an extent that makes it sustainable?" he asked.

As sports editors grapple with reinventing game stories, in part due to perceptions that people already know what happened and have limited attention spans, Moran believes words are being devalued. Reporters can still explain, analyze, and interpret. "Why was this game won or lost? What's going on with this team? Is the coach down on the superstar because he's not playing enough defense?" he asked. "Deliver information and insight and not rote play by play. I don't think that's old-school. I think that's timeless."

As far as advice, Moran stresses the importance of clean copy and attention to detail. "There is no small stuff. The small stuff becomes the big stuff, especially when people are filing on deadline," he said. According to Moran, "the safety net is gone. . . . It's not unthinkable that there's content where the only set of eyeballs is the person who wrote it."

As an educator, he is committed to helping students reach their career goals. He has given students the opportunities to cover major title games, the Olympics, FIBA Women's Basketball World Cup, the Pan American Games, and other global and national events. According to Moran, "As the journalism industry becomes more fragmented and the needs of outlets continue to evolve, it becomes even more important for us to make sure that students understand the requirements and expectations they will face."

as "senior editors" (Ourand, 2014). While the athlete-centric publisher continues to make its mark in the digital space, it, too, has challenges. In January 2019, CEO Jeff Levick confirmed that eight employees were laid off (Patel, 2019). Vice Sports also features content from athletes, such as the NBA's Carmelo Anthony, who discussed free agency on the site. Vice Sports sees itself as a way to examine culture and the sport-celebrity lifestyle. As it moved more toward video and away from original reporting, Vice laid off staff in 2017 as well (Fang, 2017). While the impact remains to be seen, such sites offer new avenues for athletes to interact with fans, and, unlike ESPN (which pays nearly $2 billion per year to cover NFL games), they are not burdened with team or league relationships (Ourand, 2014).

In summary, sport communication has evolved into a potent force in contemporary U.S. culture thanks in part to technological advancements in sport coverage and the development of new kinds of sport content. Fans continue to want more and more information on their favorite teams, athletes, coaches, and events, but a balance must be kept between data and information and the real story: human beings (Solomon, 2018). By analyzing the origins of sport communication and tracing its development from the 19th century to the present, we can identify pioneers and key trends that have contributed to the growing possibilities in all facets of sport communication—print journalism, electronic media, public relations, marketing, advertising, interpersonal communication, research, and emerging technologies.

CHAPTER WRAP-UP

Summary

This chapter concludes the book's first part (Introducing Sport Communication). It sets the context and outlines the development of sport communication and provides an overview of sport coverage by newspapers, magazines, radio, television, cable, and emerging technologies. It discusses the importance of the golden age of sport in the 1920s, when journalists focused on chronicling athletes' and coaches' heroic feats, thus setting the agenda for readers through their dramatic and vivid prose. Although sport communication was transformed by the introduction of radio in the 1920s and television in the 1950s, the golden age of sport set the foundation and profoundly affected both sport and the coverage of sport. Since then, radio, television, cable, and electronic media have contributed to sport's growth by adding sounds and pictures to stories and bringing events to fans in real time. From early radio announcers such as Mel Allen and Vin Scully to television pioneers Pete Rozelle and Roone Arledge to ESPN founder Bill Rasmussen, talented people have combined vision and technology to promote sport's value and maximize fans' experiences.

Today, the field of sport communication integrates the sport media with other entities that are crucial for the sport enterprise. As a result, professionals must embrace technology and focus on developing transferable skills and knowledge. Digital technology is used by media organizations, teams, athletics departments, leagues, and other sport-related organizations to enable new kinds of interactivity, productivity, and efficacy. Accordingly, sport organizations have embraced new social media and enacted new policies, and they no longer rely solely on journalists to communicate with fans and set agendas. Parasocial interactions (PSI) signify media users' relationships and rapport with media figures and the ensuing bonds that evolve over time. Users' relationships with journalists and professionals are no longer insular or restrictive. Instead, fans can maintain their own parasocial and social relationships with athletes, coaches, journalists, and other fans, eliminating gatekeepers (Auter & Palmgreen, 2000; Horton & Wohl, 1956; Kassing & Sanderson, 2010; Laucella, 2014). This "disintermediation"—that is, elimination of intermediaries—forces sport journalists to focus on statistical analysis, investigative reporting, scouting, minor league reports, and historical perspective, among other topics, to provide fresh and innovative content (Fry, 2011b; Laucella, 2014).

As history shows, technological and cultural changes have fostered evolution, progress, and innovation. Looking ahead, sport communication in the 21st century offers virtually infinite potential as ideas, information, and data are dispersed instantaneously and powerfully through both legacy media outlets and digital technologies. Professionals continue to create and use technologies that improve and expand job functions and performance to continually serve sport consumers and publics. Still, even though the field of sport communication is subject to change, the fundamental values of fairness, ethics, professionalism, accuracy, and diligence remain precious in today's vibrant, digital-first environment.

Review Questions

1. What cultural changes have influenced the ascent of sport, and how has that ascent affected sport journalism?

2. What are the characteristics of the golden age of sport, and how did this era affect the development both of sport and sport communication?

3. What changes did radio and television bring about in sport coverage?

4. In what ways were Pete Rozelle and Roone Arledge pioneers in sport communication?

5. How have cable and emerging technologies changed the playing field of sport communication?

Individual Exercises

1. Write a one- or two-page summary about the importance of media rights deals for the major U.S. sport leagues. Why are they so important to major corporations? Consider consolidation, convergence, conglomeration, and how corporations use sport to promote other holdings.

2. Follow some of your favorite sport journalists and reporters on social media. How would you rate their posts, videos, and interactions? Think about how convergence has affected sport journalists' jobs and how their roles and responsibilities have changed from the golden age of sport to today.

PART II

Examining the Strategic Sport Communication Model (SSCM)

Part II contains eight chapters examining the conceptual and practical aspects of sport communication, which is defined in this book as the process by which people share symbols to create meaning through interaction in sport, in a sport setting, or through a sport endeavor. This part of the book opens with chapter 4, which explores the concepts of communication, and sport communication, from a broad perspective that leads to the framework on which the textbook is structured: the Strategic Sport Communication Model (SSCM). Sport communication involves the general process of communication, its various components, and the ways in which sport-industry professionals and organizations communicate with both internal and external stakeholders. The SSCM illustrates the sport communication process and categorizes the varied aspects of communication in the sport industry into three major components. Thus, the model details the complex nature and tremendous breadth of sport communication. The process portion provides a *micro* view of the field, whereas the rest of the model presents a *macro* view. The model was developed to provide the first conception of sport communication as a formal discipline. Chapter 4 concludes with a discussion of sport communication's effects and its consumption communities—that is, its audiences and consumers.

The SSCM divides sport communication into the following three components: personal and organizational communication in sport (component 1), mediated communication in sport (component 2), and sport communication services and support (component 3). The first component is covered in chapters 5 and 6. Chapter 5 examines the three segments of personal communication in sport: intrapersonal communication (inward communication, or speech inside one's mind), interpersonal communication (two-way flow of information between two or three individuals), and small-group communication (communication between individuals in small gatherings). Communicators in sport participate in one of these three forms of personal communication when they interact in an intimate and direct manner.

Chapter 6 covers sport communication both within and between organizations. Organizational sport communication is the process by which messages are created, exchanged, interpreted, and stored within a system of human relationships in sport. This chapter introduces the theoretical, conceptual, and practical aspects of communication that occurs either within a sport organization or between a sport organization and another organization. Intraorganizational sport communication involves communication with internal publics, whereas interorganizational sport communication involves communication between a sport organization and one or more external publics.

The second component of the SSCM—mediated communication in sport—includes aspects of sport communication such as sport reporting, sport commentary, the various associated media (e.g., mass media, social media) activities surrounding sport, and the media influences that shape sport. In addition to covering the sport industry, the sport media often reinforce and reflect the institution of sport and, increasingly, help to shape it. Mediated communication in sport can be grouped into two major segments: (1) sport mass media and (2) emerging and social media in sport. Chapter 7 covers the sport mass media, including everything from sport publishing and print sport communication to electronic and visual sport communication. Sport publishing is the business or profession of the commercial production and dissemination of information related to sport (e.g., sport books, newspaper sports sections, sport magazines, sport websites, sport annuals, team newsletters, fan magazines, media guides, game programs, fact sheets). Print sport communication involves any medium that disseminates printed matter related to sport. This segment also includes wire services and web sport media in addition to electronic and visual sport communication involving such areas as radio, television, cable, and films. Chapter 8 covers the digital, mobile, and social media aspects of sport communication. It provides an analysis of the Model for Online Sport Communication (MOSC) and of the various new (e.g., emerging, social) sport media and communication methods. The online sport communication framework includes the areas of content, design, performance, usability, commerce, and consumer motivations and needs.

The third component of sport communication includes services and support, which are covered in chapters 9 through 11. This component consists of the following three segments: integrated sport marketing communication, public relations and crisis communication in sport, and sport communication research. Integrated marketing communication, covered in chapter 9, takes many forms and includes the advertising of both sport products and the advertising of nonsport-related products through sport (e.g., a company promoting its product through the use of a sport endorser such as an athlete, team, facility, or league). This chapter addresses the history of sport advertising and provides an analysis of sport sponsorship and endorsements.

Chapter 10 examines public relations and crisis communication in sport. It begins with a discussion of sport public relations, which is the management of sport information flow between a sport entity and its key publics to present the organization in the most favorable manner possible and establish mutually beneficial relationships. The chapter also examines crisis communication for sport organizations and outlines strategies for managing crisis situations both internally and externally.

Chapter 11 addresses sport communication research from both the practical (e.g., research in the sport industry) and scholarly or theoretical (e.g., research in academic settings) perspectives. The chapter begins with a discussion of how both the media and sport industries use research, then examines the uses of research in academia and the specifics of writing research and choosing methodologies in sport communication.

Photo courtesy of Paul M. Pedersen.

CHAPTER 4

Sport Communication and the SSCM

LEARNING OBJECTIVES

- To learn what sport communication is and how it has developed
- To comprehend the elements, process, and theoretical components of sport communication
- To get acquainted with the Strategic Sport Communication Model (SSCM)
- To recognize the segments and convergent aspects of personal and organizational sport communication, as well as mediated communication in sport
- To understand the relationship between the SSCM and integrated marketing communication, public relations, crisis communication, and sport communication research

KEY TERMS

context
emerging and social media in sport
genre
integrated marketing communication in sport
interorganizational sport communication
interpersonal sport communication
intraorganizational sport communication

intrapersonal sport communication
process of sport communication
public relations and crisis communication in sport
small-group sport communication
sport communication research
sport mass media

COMMUNICATION STRATEGIES
OF THE GREAT WHITE SHARK

Greg Norman

A social media search of #AttackLife reveals a variety of posts, photos, and tweets either by Greg Norman or by stakeholders (e.g., fans, business associates) interacting with the legendary golfer and entrepreneur. The hashtag is appropriate because Norman, often referred to as the Shark (or the Great White Shark), has been known for decades for his adventurous and hard-charging approach to both golf and life. The mention of his name conjures images of a swashbuckling style, a competitive spirit, and (Norman's trademark) a wide-brimmed black hat. Aside from his thrill-seeking attitude and charismatic personality, Norman is also one of the greatest golfers of all time, having amassed more than 90 victories—including two British Open championships—and a place in the World Golf Hall of Fame. Beyond his iconic status in golf, the former top-ranked golfer has transcended the sport through his ability to communicate with various publics, and his actions outside the competitive arena of golf provide a perfect illustration of the connection between communication theory and practice.

The Shark has engaged in sport communication throughout his career. Even his nickname was given by a media scribe looking for a way to describe the golf legend's aggressive style. Although Norman's professional playing days are over, he is still involved with golf through many avenues, including communication (e.g., granting interviews, writing books and columns, appearing on shows). His media involvement also includes his work with Greg Norman Interactive. This company runs his website (www. shark.com), which provides information about golf news, biographical and statistical material, and a photo gallery.

Norman is also active on social media, using platforms such as Facebook (TheGreatWhiteShark), Twitter (@SharkGregNorman), and Instagram (@ shark_gregnorman) to inform and interact with stakeholders about his various adventures (e.g., golfing, bungee jumping, hiking, fishing), as well as his family and business activities. "It is a luxury to be a living brand, but the older I've become, the more I am aware of public perception," Norman notes. "With social media all around, I have to be aware of what I do, what I say."

Beyond Norman's engagement with media and social media, the Australia native communicates most often with business colleagues, employees, financial strategists, public relations officers, and a host of other sport professionals. As the leader of the Greg Norman Company, Norman has become one of the wealthiest golfers by building his business into a multinational corporate empire valued at more than $300 million. His numerous business ventures—the majority of which bear his image—are wholly owned, partially owned, or licensed under the Greg Norman Company. They include such enterprises as the Greg Norman Collection (apparel), Greg Norman Golf Course Design, Greg Norman

Greg Norman (left) on the NBC/Golf Channel set with golf analyst David Feherty and sportscaster Steve Sands.

Photo courtesy of Greg Norman Company.

Australian Prime (Wagyu beef), Greg Norman Real Estate, Greg Norman Eyewear, and Greg Norman Estates (wine).

Although Norman has talented employees in each business entity, he takes a proactive approach to communication, and this involvement demands that he communicate effectively across several levels. These levels—which are called *contexts of sport communication*—involve all aspects of sport communication. For instance, in his role as the leader of Greg Norman Golf Course Design, he communicates with developers, architects, designers, salespeople, and a host of other stakeholders. Norman is involved in each step of the design, construction, and opening of his golf courses, which requires him to be constantly engaged in communication. Even when he is alone—as when fishing, one of his favorite hobbies—Norman cannot escape communication. When he talks to himself or brainstorms on his own about a new business venture, he is engaged in what is referred to as **intrapersonal sport communication**. When he interacts with individuals within any of his businesses, he is engaged in **intraorganizational sport communication**.

The Greg Norman Company maintains a complete staff of professionals, including numerous individuals who work in communication. For instance, Jane MacNeille serves as director of communications. "My role is all encompassing," MacNeille explains. "My job is to manage the communications and relationships not only for each business that falls under the Greg Norman Company umbrella but also for Mr. Norman himself. Every day, I interact with media, fans, and partners that are all crucial to the image and success of the company."

MacNeille is a sport communication professional, and her various activities fit the model of communication presented in this chapter. Whether she is communicating with fans (inter-

Greg Norman, who was selected for *ESPN The Magazine*'s 10th Anniversary Body Issue, with Jane MacNeille, director of communications for the Greg Norman Company.

Photo courtesy of Greg Norman Company.

personal and small-group communication), employees (interorganizational and intraorganizational communication), social media followers or sport reporters (sport media), designers (sport communication services and support), or any other message sender or receiver, her work embodies the sport communication definition, process, elements, and theoretical framework on which this and the following chapters are based.

In examining the educational, professional, and historical aspects of sport communication, part I of this book illustrates that the field continues to evolve in terms of opportunities (e.g., growth of esports participation and broadcasts, expansion of college conference cable television networks, increase in mediated international contests), technology (e.g., 5G, VR, AI), and influence (e.g., financial, sociological, political). Much of the growth and expansion of the sport industry relates directly to sport communication. A recent estimate by one research firm—which includes media rights (in addition to merchandise sales, sponsorships, etc.) as part of its segmentation of sport market revenues—puts the value of the global sport industry at just over $488 billion, with the firm projecting that esports will "drive the global sports market" ("2022 Global," 2019, para. 3). While the nearly $500 billion sport industry estimate is quite significant, an Internet search will reveal even higher estimations. Regardless of the multibillion-dollar estimate used, the sport industry makes a significant economic impact on the global community, and "the key facilitator of sport is sport communication" (Pedersen, 2013, p. 1).

Communication is necessary for the sport industry, whether it takes the form of mediated interpersonal communication (e.g., social media interactions between fans and team personnel), mass media broadcasts of hallmark sporting events, or skyrocketing participation rates in esports games and fantasy sport sites. Indeed, as illustrated by this book's chapter titles, communication in sport encompasses a striking diversity of activities, including (to name a few) interpersonal engagements, integrated marketing endeavors, public relations functions, theoretical work, research, social media platforms, and the various mass media affiliated with sport.

One example of the growing significance of sport communication in the sport industry can be seen in the $24 billion television rights deal signed in 2016 by the National Basketball Association (NBA) with ESPN and Turner Sports. A significant part of the National Football League's (NFL) growing overall league revenues—which appear to be increasing at a rate by which they would reach NFL commissioner Roger Goodell's goal of $25 billion by 2027—is the money that comes from broadcasting rights contracts "with ESPN and network partners Fox, CBS and NBC, and those deals contain accelerators to increase payments annually" (Kaplan, 2016, p. 33). The fact that some of these NFL television rights deals expire in 2021 and 2022 "means another round of negotiations in the years to come, likely contributing even more toward the $25 billion goal" (p. 33). Similar growth in sport communication has been witnessed around the globe. "Sports will remain one of the most valuable parts of the media and entertainment industry globally for years to come,"

notes Collignon and Sultan (2014, p. 10). They add that, "For media companies, leagues, clubs, and sponsors, tackling strategic and operational challenges will help extract the most value and build a sustainable industry going forward" (p. 10).

The global sport media is a highly visible and major component of sport communication, but the field consists of much more than the media. Although a few individuals may still take a narrow view of sport communication (as dealing only with sport journalism), practitioners and scholars are increasingly endorsing a broader perspective of the discipline. As in the first two editions of this textbook, the first three chapters of this edition reveal that we advocate the broader approach because, in reality, sport communication includes everything from watercooler conversations between front-office colleagues in sport organizations to NBC's Olympic broadcasts, which are watched by millions of viewers.

This expansive view of the field necessitates segmentation, and one of the best ways to segment the industry is through modeling, which creates a theoretical framework for expressing a concept. This chapter explains a framework—which we refer to as the *Strategic Sport Communication Model* (SSCM)—that encompasses the field of sport communication and its unique components. Sport communication involves the sport communication process, its components, and how sport industry professionals and organizations communicate with both internal and external stakeholders. The SSCM both illustrates the sport communication process and categorizes the varied aspects of communication in the sport industry; in this way, the model details the complex nature and tremendous breadth of the sport communication segment of the sport industry. The process portion of the model provides a micro view of sport communication, whereas the rest of the model presents a macro view of the field.

The original SSCM, developed over a dozen years ago, provided an initial model and overview of the field and its interrelated components, categories, processes, and activities. The updated model, as it appears in this third edition, remains within this sport communication framework. The remainder of this chapter explains the SSCM, and the following chapters provide more detail regarding the model's various components. However,

Although the media (e.g., mass media, social media) receive the most visibility, sport communication includes many additional components, activities, and professionals. For example, this exchange—involving Swin Cash (right), the former WNBA star and 2020 Women's Basketball Hall of Fame inductee who was hired in 2019 as the vice president of basketball operations and team development for the New Orleans Pelicans—illustrates **interpersonal sport communication**.

before exploring the SSCM, let's first examine the concepts of communication and sport communication from a broad perspective. This examination of communication theories will lead us naturally to the framework—the SSCM—upon which the rest of the book is structured.

DEFINITION OF SPORT COMMUNICATION

Studying sport communication involves more than simply looking at sport-related messages. That is, it must go beyond the end product, whether that be a social media post, the sports section of a newspaper, or a sport radio broadcast. Sport communication involves both texts (i.e., materials produced through sport communication) and representations (i.e., versions of subject matter that appear in sport texts). However, in applying to the sport industry the work of Burton (2002, 2010) and other communication scholars, there are many additional aspects of sport communication and media, and many of these facets are quite distinct from a specific sport message or end product. They include, for example, institutions (e.g., organizations that own, finance, and operate sport media and sport communication departments), production systems (e.g., activities involved in generating a sport message), and conditions (e.g., the environment in which an instance of sport communication takes place). They also include meanings, audiences, content, and **context**.

There is more to sport communication than the sport media or sport communication product itself; still, arriving at a definition of sport communication is quite difficult. Fred Battenfield (2013), a former college sports information director who now studies the culture of communication in the sport industry, puts it this way: "Because the process of communication is so complex, a precise definition is arguably impossible to put forward" (p. 443). We agree with this expert, just as we concur with other scholars (Thomas & Stephens, 2015) who explain the challenges of developing a definition for a related area of study: "Several definitions of strategic communication have surfaced, and like the myriad of definitions associated with the terms 'strategy' and 'communication,' we do not expect that a singular definition of strategic communication will ever be agreed on" (p. 4). Most likely, any definition offered for communication, strategic communication, or sport communication can be challenged by someone. With that said, and although it is seemingly impossible to put forth a universally accepted definition of sport communication, we believe that the best definition to date is the one depicted in figure 4.1.

At its basic level, *sport communication* could be defined as the exchange of information by or through sport. We prefer, however, a more integrated, detailed, expansive, and interrelated definition. Sport communication is a process by

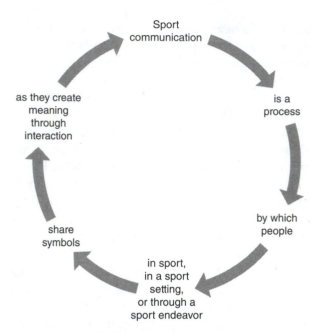

Figure 4.1 The definitional components of sport communication.

which people—in sport, in a sport setting, or through a sport endeavor—share symbols as they create meaning through interaction (Pedersen, Laucella, Miloch, & Fielding, 2009). In addition to embracing the ritual or cultural approach (Subtil, 2014) to communication, this definition integrates the communication aspects involved in and through sport.

To illustrate, let's imagine a hypothetical scenario in the sport industry. Say that Big East Conference commissioner Val Ackerman wants to motivate her front-office personnel by calling a meeting at the conference's New York City headquarters and giving a rousing pep talk. In attendance are the conference's executive associate commissioner (Stu Jackson), deputy commissioner and chief operating officer (Vince Nicastro), senior associate commissioners (for broadcasting, media relations, etc.), and other top members of the managerial team. Could this action be viewed as sport communication? Absolutely. Through Ackerman's expressive talk with executive administrators, she is sharing verbal and nonverbal messages in a sport setting. Her interaction with conference executives creates meaning; specifically, in this case, the managerial team appreciates her visit and feels motivated.

By extension, the definition of sport communication encompasses any example that involves communication in or through sport. Thus, the definition is broad enough to include interpersonal sport communication, group and organizational sport communication, mediated sport communication, and any other type of communication that occurs in or through the sport industry.

THEORETICAL FRAMEWORK OF SPORT COMMUNICATION

Before analyzing the Strategic Sport Communication Model (SSCM), let's examine how it was developed. The study of communication theory provides insight into the study of sport communication. The theories used in the field of communication can be thought of as systematic generalizations and plausible explanations of phenomena, and they can be arrived at through the linkage of certain variables (Heath & Bryant, 2000). These theories consist of either "abstract or concrete concepts or constructs that function as representations or means by which we are able to understand and handle the complex reality" (Cobley & Schulz, 2013, p. 8).

The SSCM is built on numerous theories and models of communication, media, and information that have been proposed across various disciplines over the years. "The diversity of theories in communication research has been influenced by recent interdisciplinary trends," notes Craig (2013), who adds, "however, it is not only a product of recent developments." In fact, the communication scholar explains that various theories "sprang up independently across the humanities and social sciences before a distinct field of communication research took shape in the second half of the twentieth century." Craig adds that scholarly work in the area of communication "developed lines of inquiry from many sources, and even now the field continues to grow, in part, by incorporating new interdisciplinary areas with their sometimes distinct theoretical approaches" (p. 39).

Theoretical and conceptual advancements across academia have worked (and continue to work) in varying degrees to illustrate communication concepts; detail relationships; and explain occurrences, aspects, and experiences in and around communication. These conceptualizations of communication range from social-scientific theories that have been refined by researchers to the normative theory that has been proposed to improve human communication. They also include working theories that are under development and commonsense theories focused on just that—common sense. What these diverse theories hold in common is the fact that, as Cobley and Schulz (2013) note, "theorizing or modelling includes the conceptualization of phenomena in terms of a set of concepts or constructs and relationships among them." They add that "learning what a discipline is about and what is the common wisdom in this field means studying its major theories and models" (p. 8). To embrace as many theories and models as possible, the broad approach of the SSCM is based on research into the **genres**, contexts, and processes of communication.

Genres

The genres of communication are addressed by theories that come in various shapes and sizes. Some are valid, applicable, and accurate, whereas others may be criticized for coming up short in one area or another. The process of explaining and categorizing these theories has been a years-long focus for communication scholars Stephen W. Littlejohn, Karen A. Foss, and John G. Oetzel. In the latest edition of their work in this area (2017), they integrate various communication theories by using a framework based on seven traditions (i.e., rhetorical, semiotic, phenomenological, cybernetic, sociopsychological, sociocultural, and critical) established by the now-retired communication scholar Robert T. Craig. Building on these traditions, Littlejohn and colleagues then organized communication theories around contexts (e.g., relationships, groups, organizations, culture, society) and communication model elements (e.g., communicators, messages, medium).

The work of Littlejohn and colleagues, as well as that of other communication scholars,

points to various groups of theories. Structural theories focus on language and social systems; functional theories focus on how organized systems function; cognitive and behavioral theories focus on individuals; interactional and conventional theories focus on the processes and effects of interaction; interpretive theories focus on the discovery of meaning in actions and texts; and critical theories focus on specific issues, such as domination, inequality, and oppression.

The study of sport communication involves all the main groups of communication theory. In this text, for instance, critical communication theories are applied in chapter 12 (Sociological Aspects of Sport Communication), cognitive and behavior theories can be found in chapter 5 (Personal Sport Communication), and structural and functional theories are evident in chapter 6 (Organizational and Leadership Communication in Sport). In such ways, the many communication theories put forth by scholars over the years have influenced sport communication, and they provide foundational aspects of the SSCM.

Contexts

Regardless of one's theoretical approach, communication involves contexts (or levels); indeed, it is impossible to analyze sport communication

Photo courtesy of Paul M. Pedersen.

Sport communication is interactive and multidimensional and involves a multilateral flow of communication. For example, football coaches send and receive many messages, even though their direct communication is focused on their players.

without examining contexts of communication (e.g., interpersonal, group, organizational, mediated). As an extension of work done by others (e.g., Heath & Bryant, 2000), the dominant communication contexts or levels can be associated with any given theory. Sport communication involves all these contexts, and they are each represented, at least to some degree, in one of the SSCM's three components. Component 1 includes intrapersonal, interpersonal, small-group, intraorganizational, and interorganizational communication in sport. Component 2 includes mediated sport communication, and component 3 includes sport communication services and support.

The categorization of sport communication into three main components closely resembles the segmentation approach often taken in other fields (e.g., segmentation models in sport marketing). In this text, all the components (entities) of sport communication are contained in the sport communication levels (contexts) just mentioned. The specific levels or contexts of sport communication are discussed in greater detail later in this chapter and in subsequent chapters.

Process

Sport communication is a dynamic process, and a process approach is often used in sport studies (e.g., sport management, sport marketing). In the process approach used in this textbook, sport communication includes active, interactive, and reactive processes involving institutions, texts, and audiences. The sport communication process—whether it results in profits or individual gratification—is vibrant, interactive, multidimensional, and limitless.

In taking a process approach to any aspect of communication, we must engage in theoretical analysis using tools that range from information theories to communication theories (Lanigan, 2013). The process approach to information and communication has been used for decades but remains valid and applicable today because "communication is still commonly understood as a process" (Craig, 2013, p. 40). Although sport communication is interactive, multidimensional, and marked by multilateral flows of communication, the foundation for processes and communicative actions consists of simple, linear communication models (e.g., sender-message-channel-receiver).

Early communication pioneers possessed educational backgrounds in sociology or psychology (Greenberg & Salwen, 2009). For example, by asking a famous question about media effects—"Who says what in which channel to whom with what effect?"—sociologist Harold Lasswell developed a formula in the late 1940s that is viewed as the first transmission model of communication. As Lasswell's question indicates, this model studies the elements of who (the communicator) says what (the content) through which channel (the medium) to whom (the audience) and with what effect (Shoemaker & Reese, 2014). Although the Lasswell formula was created to explain mass communication, it can be applied to all forms of communication, including (as discussed later) sport communication. His formula and other early communication models viewed communication as a persuasive process in which a message sender seeks to influence a receiver; these models made no mention of feedback in the process. Today's audiences, of course, often possess considerable power, as seen, for example, in fans' engagement with social media and sometimes as sport content producers.

Around the same time that Lasswell posed his question, media scientists Claude Shannon and Warren Weaver developed the influential general model of communication. The Shannon–Weaver model—a linear creation similar to the Lasswell formula—proposes six elements in the communication process: a source, an encoder, a message, a channel, a decoder, and a receiver. Again, like other early models, this one reduced communication to a one-way process of transmitting information. These linear models also failed to allow for the fact that senders and receivers often fail to handle messages smoothly. When someone (a communicator) sends a message to an audience, the channel affects how the message is conveyed; for example, the process may be affected by noise or interference. In addition, the context, or environment, may either impede or promote effective communication or feedback (Griffin, 2018). Examples in sport communication include technical difficulties during a broadcast such as the loss of video during part of NBCSN's coverage of the first race in the 2019 NTT IndyCar Series, fan noise produced by capacity crowds in facilities such as Duke University's Cameron

Indoor Stadium, or spectators at outdoor events such as some boisterous attendees at the 2019 PGA Championship at Bethpage Black.

Early models of communication have limitations; for example, the transmission models fail to consider context, the effect of the communication channel, and the relationship between sender and receiver. Even so, they laid the foundation for the more accepted communication model developed by communication researcher Wilbur Schramm. His simplified communication model (like the ensuing Schramm–Osgood model that he developed with Charles Osgood) allows both for the factor of understanding in the communication process and the involvement of feedback and two-way communication (Greenberg & Salwen, 2009). Specifically, Schramm's model involved the elements of a source who encodes, a message or signal that is transmitted either through interpersonal communication or through a medium, and a destination where the receiver decodes the message or signal (Pavlik & McIntosh, 2019). Unlike the earlier linear models, this model illustrates a circular communication process and accounts for behavioral aspects of the communicators and environmental circumstances (McQuail & Windahl, 1993).

In sport communication, one example of this process can be found in ESPN's broadcasts of Ultimate Fighting Championship (UFC) events. Let's break it down: The images from the cameras and the words of the commentators are broadcast to viewers. Those who tune in to the broadcasts interpret and process the messages. They then exercise power in the process by either staying tuned, switching to another channel, turning off the television, surfing the web (perhaps at a site affiliated with ESPN or UFC), or interacting with other viewers and UFC stakeholders through various social media platforms (e.g., Facebook, Twitter). For instance, the nearly seven million subscribers to the UFC's YouTube channel can watch pay-per-view events, interact with others, etc.

The early communication models—although groundbreaking and useful—have been criticized and updated over the decades. Some criticisms have focused on the need to include a broader social component and the movement toward more critical and cultural analyses (Pavlik & McIntosh, 2019). One such approach is the ritual model of communication. Whereas transmission models view communication as a linear process from communicator to audience with control as the main goal, the ritual model takes a more interactive, meaningful, and interpretive approach to communication (McQuail & Windahl, 1993). The impetus for viewing communication as a ritual can be traced to the words of a philosopher from over a century ago. "Society not only continues to exist by transmission, by communication, but it may fairly be said to exist in transmission, in communication. There is more than a verbal tie between the words common, community, and communication," noted John Dewey (1916). He added that individuals in a society "live in a community in virtue of the things which they have in common; and communication is the way in which they come to possess things in common" (para. 10). Cultural communication scholars (e.g., James W. Carey) note that the ritual view of communication includes the perspectives of conversing, sharing, participating, associating, and fellowshipping (Subtil, 2014).

Both the process models and the ritual models of communication can be used to explain how sport communication works and to develop a critical perspective on the field. "All acts of communication are a process. This process includes a source, a message, and a receiver of the message," explains Burton (2002), and "any one of these factors within any communication process will affect the content and treatment of its messages" (p. 30). As shown in figure 4.2, sport communication—whether face to face or mediated—can be conceptualized as the process of producing and delivering messages to an audience of one person, a few colleagues, or a massive group (e.g., sport enthusiasts around the country downloading and listening to a sport podcast such as *Pardon My Take*, *Evolve Women's MMA Podcast*, or *The Bill Simmons Podcast*). It is a system comprised of many components. It can be intentional, unintentional, complex, circular, irreversible, transactional, unrepeatable, dynamic, and interactive. Although effective communication in sport is often difficult to accomplish because of interference and poor listening skills, it is, at its foundation, quite simple.

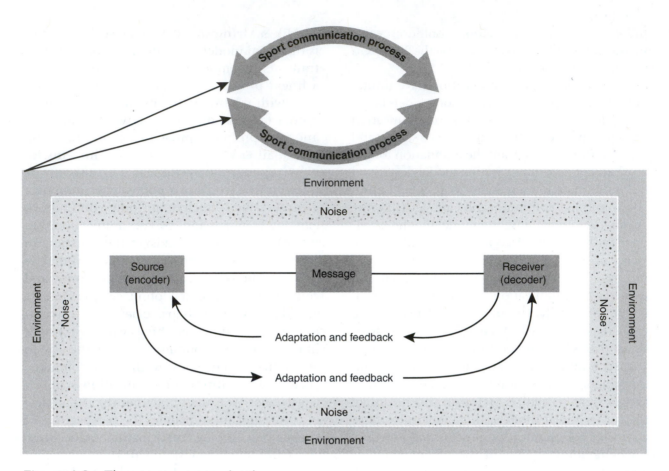

Figure 4.2   The sport communication process.

ELEMENTS OF SPORT COMMUNICATION

As discussed earlier, sport communication is a process by which people in sport, in a sport setting, or through a sport endeavor share symbols as they create meaning through interaction. In addition to providing the various fields of communication (e.g., communicator, message, medium, audience, effect, noise, feedback, context), we can also trace every action, aspect, and activity of sport communication to at least one of the unique components of this process definition. Therefore, this definition of the **process of sport communication** provides—through the cumulative grouping of the components—the framework for the Strategic Sport Communication Model (SSCM).

Sport Communication as Process

Sport communication is a dynamic process that is active and interactive. Whether the com-

munication is face to face or mediated, sport communication can be conceptualized as the process of producing and delivering messages to an audience. This audience can range from one dedicated sport fan receiving a Snapchat ephemeral (i.e., self-destructing) message to a few front-office employees of a professional team listening to a recap of last night's sporting event to the millions of television viewers (in addition to the hundreds of thousands streaming the event) who watched the 2019 FIFA Women's World Cup Final between the United States and the Netherlands. As with communication in general, each of these sport communication examples involves a process that can be characterized in terms of whether it is intentional or unintentional, verbal or nonverbal, and a variety of other characteristics (e.g., complex, circular, transactional, dynamic, multidimensional, continuous).

Within the communication process, receivers of sport communication messages can accept or reject a message and its intensity, direction, duration, or effect. For instance, sport journalists constantly communicate with sources, editors, managers, and readers through conversations, gestures, text messages, emails, letters, articles, columns, and various social media platforms. Similarly, fans communicate with organizations through various avenues, such as social media messages, emails, letters, and ticket-sale transactions; they also communicate with other fans through phone calls, messaging systems, social media platforms, chat rooms, video game and esports participation, fantasy leagues, and in-person discussions about the progress of their teams. A front-office employee for a sport franchise communicates with the media, colleagues, other managers, and fans as part of his or her daily job routines and responsibilities.

The communication process in and through sport includes interdependent communication. It also allows for feedback through actions such as retweets, eye contact, verbal responses, phone calls, email messages, sport podcasts and talk shows, social media emojis, or simply expressing frustration with how a game is going by turning off the television. Communication has many effect. For example, communication within a sport organization may have the effect of motivating, instructing, facilitating, encouraging, or serving any number of other purposes. Communication involving the **sport mass media** may have effects such as increased ratings, fan support, and purchases of advertised goods and services. The process involves many variables, such as the communicator's personality, status, expertise, trustworthiness, prestige, physical attributes, relationship to a group or individual, and psychological attributes. For example, Nike signed Zion Williamson as an endorser of the Jordan Brand because the company believes the young basketball star communicates a certain image that will have an effect (e.g., company image, shoe purchases) on fans and other consumers. Key variables can exert influence before, during, or after communication. Before-communication variables include, for example, knowledge levels, opinions, needs, expectations, motivation, and participation. During-communication variables may include situation, filters, physical constitution, psychological constitution, evaluation of content, evaluation of the communicator,

agreement, and disagreement. And after-communication variables may include selectivity and capability of memory.

Another key aspect of the process of sport communication is the concept of the gatekeeper. It was identified by White (1950), who defined the *gatekeeper* as an editor who—through subjectivity and value-based judgments—selected the news stories for newspapers. In this model, gatekeepers include or exclude stories based on what they consider to be important. They decide, according to Shoemaker and Reese (2014), what becomes news based on the information they select, the production of that information, and the platform(s) upon which the information is delivered. Therefore, their decisions affect both the content and the process of mass communication. Gatekeepers' decisions themselves may be affected by the space available to a given media outlet, which can range from media outlets that have space restrictions (e.g., only so much information can fit on a printed page in the sports section of a newspaper) to media platforms that have no limitations in terms of space (e.g., a sport website such as Yahoo! Sports or Bleacher Report).

The power and influence of traditional sport media gatekeepers have been challenged because various parties (e.g., fans, athletes, sport organizations) now have more options for bypassing the traditional mass media. As a result, these parties may serve as their own gatekeepers and decide for themselves how to get their own messages out to stakeholders through such avenues as blogs, posts, personal media channels, social media platforms, podcasts, and websites. For instance, The Players' Tribune publishes articles written by sport industry stakeholders, allowing them to bypass the traditional mass media and speak directly to their fans. Some of the recent first-person accounts published on the website range from Sabrina Ionescu, Kemba Walker, Ali Krieger, Christian Yelich, and Luka Jovic to Hailie Deegan, Nick Foles, Carli Lloyd, and Sue Bird.

Although athletes and sport industry personnel can use various platforms to craft and deliver their own messages, gatekeepers—such as sports editors, sports producers, and sport media managers—still function as message filters. Consider, for instance, televised sport media content in which certain sports are covered and broadcast while others are ignored. In the print media, some sporting events receive front-page articles, whereas others receive only a mention on the agate page or none at all. In all these cases, someone—the gatekeeper—is deciding what will be broadcast or printed and what will receive little (if any) coverage. These are just some of the subjective decisions that are part of the sport communication process. This kind of decision making, as Greenberg and Salwen (2009) note, includes activities of selection (e.g., determining message content), creation (e.g., developing message content), dissemination (e.g., diffusing information), and reception (e.g., decoding and using content) in all communication processes.

Senders and Recipients

Sport communication requires senders (communicators) and recipients (receivers, or an audience). These people can be individuals, small groups, mass audience members, private discussion participants, public discussants, bystanders, lurkers (e.g., individuals who read a website or social networking site but rarely or never comment), or any other type of sport communication participant. In many cases, sport media professionals and social media participants play both roles—that is, sender and receiver (audience). For example, the broadcast professionals associated with a telecast send messages to the audience even as they receive messages from other stakeholders (e.g., superiors, producers, engineers) and audience members (e.g., through social media responses and feedback in the form of ratings or subscriptions).

Let's look now at the specific people involved in the communication process in sport organizations and sport media outlets. In sport organizations, potential senders include any stakeholders (e.g., fans, owners, media members, employees, supervisors, colleagues, consumers, subscribers, social media followers) who are engaged in communication in, with, or about the sport entity. For example, a team's general manager communicates (sends a message) to consumers when she greets season-ticket holders during a fan appreciation day. Potential recipients in sport organizations include the same stakeholders just identified as

potential senders, but in this case, they take on the role of receiver or audience. For example, that same general manager acts as a recipient when she listens to her assistant general manager. In sport media outlets, the potential senders are the personnel engaged as communicators—for example, book authors, sport magazine editors, sideline reporters, production engineers, and social media managers. The receivers in sport media outlets include readers, television viewers, social media followers and subscribers, podcast listeners, fans, corporate sponsors, and any other audience member or media stakeholder engaged as a receiver of communication—that is, as a decoder of a sport-related message.

Communication in a Sport Context

Any communication that involves sport can be found in our definition of sport communication. For instance, consider the context or environment in which communication takes place. As revealed in figure 4.3, our definition includes any sport-related place (e.g., context, setting, environment) because sport communication can involve communication in sport (e.g., teammates supporting each other with words of encouragement), in a sport setting (e.g., athletics apparel executives exchanging ideas during a brainstorming session), or through sport (e.g., salespeople using a sporting event to entertain prospective clients).

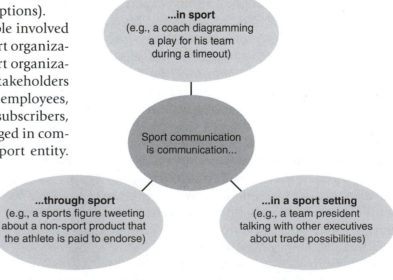

Figure 4.3   Places where sport communication occurs.

The medium through which an instance of sport communication takes place is known as the *communication channel*. In sport organizations, for example, typical channels of communication include email, phone, and social media; channels may also be categorized as either verbal or nonverbal. Often, multiple channels are used in the delivery of a message to an intended audience in the sport industry. Take, for instance, the communication efforts of the NBA G League's Aqua Caliente Clippers. "We may get a new player," notes the team's former director of business operations, Cara Wright, "or we will have an assignment player joining our roster for a game from the LA Clippers team and we have to be able to adjust internally and communicate that information externally through our channels and to our season-ticket holders, as well" (personal communication). At sport media outlets, the communication channels used for management and production are often similar to those used in sport organizations; however, the mediated communication often involves other visual and auditory channels, such as radio and satellite signals, fiber-optic cables, and the web. Examples of the specific means of communication used in sport media include social media platforms, websites, podcasts, documentaries, email systems, blogs, satellite signals, internal repositories, cable lines, forums, radio stations, news aggregators, and printed materials. The proliferation of technological devices affiliated with innovative areas such as augmented reality, predictive analytics, blockchain, artificial intelligence, cloud computing, and so forth continues to increase the number and types of available communication channels. Society is increasingly interconnected through the proliferation of devices and channels. This interconnectedness will only continue with the ongoing development of the Internet of Things (IoT), in which devices—such as home appliances, business machines, etc. connected to the Internet—communicate with each other.

Transmission of Shared Symbols

Sharing symbols is the transmission of messages in and through sport. These messages can be posts, tweets, sport columns, signs, sport programs, texts, images, sounds, advertisements, or any other shared symbols that are communicated.

The shared symbols in sport organizations include communicative acts, such as a message or offer of advice or support. Communicative acts are also the shared symbols in sport media outlets, but they add the components of mediated communicative activities such as sport reports and game stories. The sharing of symbols in the sport industry is affected by many variables, ranging from sense, content, size, style, and language to trustworthiness, type of argument, intelligence, and clarity.

In the sport industry, the sharing of symbols consists of the way in which communicators use language to create symbolism in and through sport. The language used to share a symbol may create or reinforce certain beliefs and values held by sport participants, sport entities, external stakeholders, or various publics. The symbolism created by a sender conveys meaning that is influenced both by its content and by its context as the receiver assigns multiple (and sometimes contradictory) meanings to it. In the sport industry, entities use symbols as part of their efforts to create organizational identity and reinforce organizational culture. Scholars have differed in their characterizations of the functions of symbols (i.e., illustrators of reality, preservers of calmness during challenging or transitional times, and protectors of self-esteem and self-worth). Regardless of how symbols are characterized, Vaughn (1995) notes that most scholars agree that symbols are "stories, ritualized events, specialized language, and material manifestations" (p. 222). In other words, in addition to storytelling, the use of a symbol may involve a formalized, repeated event sustained by a sport entity; specialized or unique language; or tangible manifestations specific to the organization. Let's look a bit closer at each of these four possibilities.

A symbol in a sport organization might be as simple as a story passed along through the years. Stories such as event narratives, histories, and myths can help a sport organization create, sustain, and reinforce its desired images. For example, the NFL's Green Bay Packers have long used stories to enhance the team's general perception and brand image. Stories of Vince Lombardi, Cheesehead fans, legendary players, a sense of team ownership by the community, and Lambeau Field are just a few of the ways in which the

Photo courtesy of UVA Media Relations.

Symbolism, such as the gold shovels used by athletics department stakeholders for the ceremonial groundbreaking of the new University of Virginia (UVA) softball stadium and training facility, is often part of communication in the sport industry. The university's athletics director, Carla Williams (left), has led a major initiative to upgrade UVA's athletics facilities or build new ones such as the softball complex that opened at this site in 2020.

organization uses symbols to construct and convey its meaning, history, and culture.

The use of symbols in the sport industry can also involve ritualized events—that is, formalized and repeated activities—such as the opening and closing ceremonies of the Olympic Games, the seventh-inning stretch during baseball games, and the singing of the national anthem at many sporting events. It is also common practice in the sport industry to create symbolism and reinforce culture through the use of specialized language. Examples include the humorous and at times irreverent approach that is strategically used by some teams (e.g., NHL's Los Angeles Kings) in their social media engagement. "In the football world, we're beginning to see professional clubs utilize their accounts beyond the standard team news and game score updates, instead injecting their posts with personality and gaining thousands of followers along the way," notes Vote (2018). "This effortless communication allows clubs to use social media,

more specifically Twitter, as a marketing tool to capture and retain a larger audience. In order to engage these online fans, savvy clubs hire Twitter administrators and essentially give them free reign over the account, which makes for some hilarious moments." Vote then highlights five specific soccer clubs whose Twitter content and language are particularly engaging and unique: Sampdoria, Sevilla, Bayern Munich, Bayer Leverkusen, and AS Roma.

More generally, words and phrases such as *cutting edge, slam dunk, due diligence, focus, cheap shot, Protect This House, Just Do It,* and *Impossible Is Nothing* all work symbolically to communicate identity and reinforce perceptions and values. Another form of symbolism used in the sport industry is material manifestation. For example, the Gatorade lightning bolt and the iconic Olympic rings each express what the organization stands for and how it is marketed. Such material manifestations can communicate brand image (including personal brand image in the case of athletes who have their own logo) and reinforce a sport organization's values and culture.

In summary, symbolism is used in sport to create, maintain, and reinforce the values, beliefs, and culture of sport entities and sporting publics. It does so by helping sport entities convey and assign meanings to messages. In this way, it is a key element in sport communication, and it is widely used in the industry to communicate with both internal and external audiences.

Meaning Created Through Interaction

For sport communication to create meanings, there must be action and interaction between communicators and recipients. One central element of this relationship is language, which involves a system of verbalizations and gestures used in a community to facilitate communication (Griffin, 2018). Language is ambiguous and varies across cultures, yet individuals still seek to create meaning through the communication process amidst their varied experiences. In the process of sport communication, meaning is created through the actions, interactions, and reactions of the participants (e.g., sport communicators, subordinates, recipients, colleagues, fans, viewers, listeners, friends, subscribers, followers). The communicators (or encoders) are the individuals, groups, and organizations that send messages; for example, in sport broadcasting, encoding can involve everything from reporting to production and editing. The recipients (e.g., readers, viewers) must decode and interpret messages, as well as the ideologies and cultural meanings they carry. Receivers also provide responses or feedback, either verbally (e.g., cheering) or nonverbally (e.g., retweeting), thus advancing the interactive process.

POPULAR THEORIES IN SPORT COMMUNICATION

Let's now look at some of the theories that have been used by communication scholars over the years. Research in sport communication has been classified into various areas, ranging from the interpersonal and public to the sociological and cultural. It has embraced everything from

disposition-based and self-categorization theories to social identity and excellence theories (Abeza, O'Reilly, & Nadeau, 2014; Yoo, Smith, & Kim, 2013). General communication research has often focused on how the media send (encode) and how their audiences interpret (decode) communication. As a result, communication scholars have long studied the media audience, which both receives messages (e.g., sport broadcasts) and provides feedback (e.g., tweeting about the broadcast, continuing to watch, switching the channel, turning off the television).

This audience-oriented research in general communication studies has often focused on media effects. The same can be said for **sport communication research**, in which numerous studies have focused "on motivation for consumption and the effects of that consumption," note Yoo and colleagues (2013). They add that theories of media effects have "become increasingly popular as theoretical groundings for research," and they posit that "media effects theories will retain their popularity in the field of sport communication research" (p. 10). The following subsections address some of the early communication theories, as well as some of the more popular communication theories used in sport communication research today.

Powerful Effects

This model or theory of media effects arose during the first half of the 20th century, when the media were considered by some researchers as having unlimited power (Moy & Bosch, 2013). It has been described in many ways (e.g., hypodermic needle, magic bullet). The fundamental assumption behind the theory of powerful effects was that audiences were overwhelmed by the power and persuasiveness of messages delivered by the mass media (Bryant, Thompson, & Finklea, 2013). The model prompted increased research into media effects, some of which led to certain limited-effects theories detailed in following sections of this discussion.

Uses and Gratifications

Whereas the hypodermic needle model theorized that mass media messages carried overwhelming power, limited-effects theories challenged such assumptions. For instance, the uses and gratifications theory (UGT) noted that audience members reacted to mass media and sought to use it for specific purposes based on their own individual characteristics, social categories, and relationships. "The theoretical conceptualization of the audience in active terms is undoubtedly most closely associated with the" UGT, note Oliver, Woolley, and Limperos (2013). They add that from the time the UGT originated, research related to this theoretical perspective "has provided much insight into how people use media and communication technologies by linking individual differences with motivations and selection of media, as well as outcomes of media use" (p. 416). UGT focuses on audience members' psychological attributes as reasons that they select certain content and avoid other content. This approach has been used increasingly in sport communication research with the rise in social media studies. For example, Moore (2018) applies the UGT to examine audience retention of sport news depending on consumption patterns, sport fandom, and the medium (e.g., print media, broadcast media, social media) involved.

Two-Step Flow

Two other limited-effects conceptualizations are the diffusion-of-innovation theory and the associated diffusion-of-information theory. The diffusion-of-innovation theory posits a two-step flow of communication in which consumers (e.g., subscribers to sporting message boards) or audience members (e.g., television viewers) are receptive to and adopt a new innovation. This theory is relevant in all facets of consumption because information about new inventions is often delivered by way of mediated messages (Lowery & DeFleur, 1995). This diffusion-of-innovation conceptualization can be applied to the sport industry by examining new ideologies, approaches, and concerns in the sport world (e.g., media coverage of head trauma and resulting demands for better concussion protocols); new design trends (e.g., fashionable monitors for tracking personal fitness); new sport technologies (e.g., drones for filming practice sessions, ultra-high-definition TV sets); and new communication platforms (e.g., a new social networking site). Of course, people sometimes get information about such developments from personal contacts (e.g., friends, associates, and family, as noted in the

diffusion-of-information theory), but in many cases the source is the media—whether traditional mass media, new media, or social media.

The two-step model postulates that the media exert "their influence on individuals by virtue of influencing key members of the public identified as opinion leaders, people viewed by others to be influential" (Moy & Bosch, 2013, p. 293). The closely affiliated diffusion-of-information theory proposes that we all have personal contacts who often act as sources of information. Therefore, the concept of a two-step flow of communication considers the fact that audiences often acquire media messages (e.g., information from media, posts, tweets) from friends, colleagues, family, and so forth. In fact, these days, due to the ongoing overload of information and media messages, information is often spread (diffused) through opinion leaders or personal contacts. For example, when sport enthusiasts are unable to watch a certain sporting event (or must choose between two occurring at the same time), they often rely on friends and family to provide them with information—by means of interpersonal communication, text messages, interactions on social networking sites, and so forth—about what they missed.

Parasocial and Circumsocial Interaction

Given the proliferation of social media, scholars have increasingly examined parasocial relationships and identifications by using the parasocial theoretical framework as the foundation for their research endeavors. In the world of sport, "social media has become the predominant choice for athletes and fans to engage in parasocial interactions" (Pegoraro, 2013, p. 253). Sport-related parasocial investigations often involve studies of social media interactions but have also examined topics ranging from the communication in television shows such as *The Biggest Loser* (Tian & Yoo, 2015) to the media coverage of athletes' perceptions and reactions at the Olympic Games (Kastrinos, Damiani, & Treise, 2018). The thrust of the parasocial-interaction conceptualization is that "media users develop a sense of relationships with media personae. As viewers continue to view media personalities, they develop bonds of intimacy, which resemble interpersonal social interaction but differ as is mediated" (Abeza et al., 2014, p. 304). Some scholars (e.g., Kassing & Sanderson, 2015) suggest that some interactions between social media participants (rather than just a perceived relationship by one side) could be considered circumsocial interactions rather than parasocial interactions. This would be evident if a fan not only believes there is a relationship with an athlete but also if the athlete interacts in some capacity with the fan's communication (e.g., retweeting a fan's message directed toward the athlete, liking a fan's photo in which the athlete is tagged, commenting on a fan's post that mentions the athlete).

Agenda Setting and Framing

The agenda-setting theory resulted from seminal work by McCombs and Shaw (1972), who theorized that although mass media outlets may not have the power to tell audiences what to think (as posited by the hypodermic needle model), they do have the power to tell audiences what to think *about*. In the study of sport communication, the "agenda-setting theory is used to explain how the media's agenda affects the public's attitudes and behaviors and makes them fans of certain sports" (Yoo et al., 2013, p. 11).

The media influence audiences' perceptions of reality in part by the sheer fact that gatekeepers (e.g., editors, producers) decide what to cover and then rank possible news stories in order of priority. This is particularly true in the sport industry, where certain topics or sports are emphasized and covered while others are trivialized or ignored. Sport media consumers (e.g., readers, viewers, listeners) often have their own perceptions regarding agenda setting. For instance, a *Sports Illustrated* reader contacted the magazine regarding its coverage of an incident involving former NFL quarterback Peyton Manning while he was at the University of Tennessee. "I thought the story on the harassment allegations… should have been on the cover," notes the reader. "By not giving it more attention, you gave the appearance that you were reluctant to push a story about the misbehavior of universities that prioritize sports success at all costs" ("Inbox," 2016, p. 10). Along this line, many studies have addressed the media's coverage—or lack thereof—of women in sport (e.g., Godoy-Pressland, 2014). When gatekeepers give female athletes less coverage than men (or none at all) or subject them to sexualized and trivializing portrayals, their decisions help shape audiences'

Photo courtesy of Paul M. Pedersen.

The agenda-setting theory proposes that although the media may not have the power to tell the audience what to think, they do have the power to tell the audience what to think *about*. In other words, the sport media may not be able to tell viewers and readers what to think, but their coverage decisions—what is covered and how—can set the agenda for the next day's watercooler conversations.

perceptions of female athletes and women in sport in negative ways. Take, for instance, the limited media coverage of the WNBA. "There would be more corporate support if there was more coverage in mainstream media," notes Kelly Krauskopf (2016), the former president of the WNBA's Indiana Fever who is now the assistant general manager of the NBA's Indiana Pacers. "Let's face it: The media tell people what is important. We have seen it in our own market" (p. 13).

Agenda-setting theories include framing, cueing, and priming. The framing theory has been featured in the content-analysis work of Abeza and colleagues (2014) examining common theories in sport communication research. As they note, the framing theory "proposes that not only do the media determine issue saliency, but also, by selecting themes, phrases, and images of a story, they determine the salience of specific attributes attached to an issue and thus determine how it is perceived" (p. 304).

Modeling and Cultivation

The modeling theory and cultivation theory are media effects theories that often come up when the discussion centers on children or young adults. According to the modeling theory, audience members model their behavior on actions viewed on television, heard on the radio, read in a printed publication, or consumed in another way of receiving messages from the mass media. For example, after many instances of seeing Kyrie Irving play in NBA television broadcasts, star in the movie *Uncle Drew*, and appear in numerous commercials on YouTube, children might be inclined to ask their parents to purchase Nike Kyrie basketball shoes, Pepsi Max soda, Skullcandy headphones, and other products endorsed by Irving.

The cultivation theory explores the mechanics of how those children—or members of any sport communication audience—might be persuaded to purchase certain products. This model, which is "arguably one of the most widely referenced and researched theories in the discipline, argues that television programming in general tells consistent and repetitive stories across different types of content" (Oliver et al., 2013, p. 413). For instance, cultivation theory posited that because of the prevalence of violence on television, individuals who watched a lot of television might view the world as more violent than those who did not (Lowery & DeFleur, 1995). To put it in terms of sport, individuals who repeatedly watch programming that features violent sporting events (e.g., hockey brawls, MMA fights) might be more likely to view the world as more violent than those who do not watch them.

Some of the theories covered in the preceding paragraphs involve short-term effects, whereas others involve long-term effects. Regardless of the duration of a given effect, however, we need to identify and examine how mass media messages convey information, shape values, unite people, and lead them to action or inaction. While effects theories have often been examined and used in sport communication studies, scholars have also used a variety of other conceptualizations in their research. To survey this variety, sport communication and marketing researchers Gashaw Abeza, Norm O'Reilly, and John Nadeau (2014) conducted a content analysis of one of the field's leading journals, the *International Journal of Sport Communication* (IJSC). The study revealed that the theories most commonly used in IJSC were agenda setting, framing, parasocial interaction, disposition, uses and gratifications, cultivation, social identity, self-categorization, and excellence. The following year, Abeza, O'Reilly, Seguin, and Nzindukiyimana (2015) found 26 theories and conceptual frameworks in their review of social media research within sport management. The most common theories and models were uses and gratifications, relationship marketing, parasocial interaction, agenda setting, image or reputation repair, media framing, and social identity. Several of the theories revealed in the two studies above are touched on elsewhere in this textbook, including in chapter 11 (Sport Communication Research).

STRATEGIC SPORT COMMUNICATION MODEL

The preceding pages in this chapter lead to the formulation of a unified and dynamic model of sport communication. In our effort to represent the big picture while also detailing interrelationships between various components, we propose a conceptual analysis that presents (and integrates) both the process of sport communication and the micro and macro perspectives on the discipline. This unique model—the Strategic Sport Communication Model (SSCM)—illustrates the uniqueness of sport communication. It is built on the elements—theory (i.e., communication genres), context (i.e., levels and segmentation), and the communication process—outlined in the preceding parts of the chapter. As revealed in figure 4.4, the SSCM explains, systematically and rationally, the relationships between the key variables in sport communication. The model's framework bridges theory and practice by combining the process of sport communication and the main elements (categories) of the field. Therefore, it is both a process-based and a structurally based approach.

The SSCM encompasses—and is highly influenced by—the many areas and perspectives associated with communication, as well as other sport-related segments of the communication field, such as marketing and management. For example, the major influence from marketing is segmentation. By segmenting sport communication, the model includes all the major levels, contexts, and content areas of the field (e.g., advertising, broadcasting, communication studies, communication technology, social media, journalism, public relations). The context or levels of sport communication consist of three components. Component 1 includes personal and organizational communication in sport, component 2 includes mediated communication in sport, and component 3 includes sport communication services and support systems. The use of models is nothing new in sport-related disciplines; for example, areas such as sport public relations and sport marketing using numerous theories, models, processes, concepts, and strategic approaches for both research and practice.

The major influence on the model from the field of communication consists of the processes used in communication, including sport communication. The SSCM, which uses modeling to illustrate both the process and the components of sport

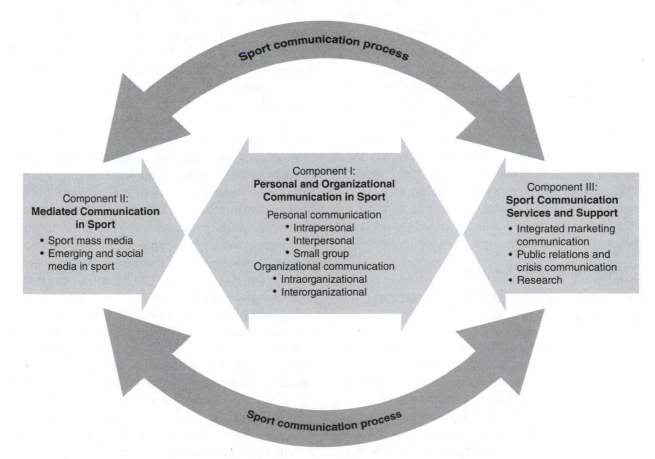

Figure 4.4   The Strategic Sport Communication Model (SSCM).

communication, is also influenced by the areas of applied communication (e.g., communication needs of sport organizations, ways to improve communication between sport supervisors and employees); public address, speech education, and communication education (e.g., speech communication, pedagogical contexts); communication theory (e.g., analyses of communication in social interactions); gender and communication (e.g., differences and similarities in styles and characteristics); international communication; intercultural communication; legal communication; performance communication; political communication; and a host of other communication perspectives.

In short, the SSCM requires the perspectives of a variety of academic disciplines. One must understand communication theory and the process of communication to look at the entire field of sport communication. In all facets of sport communication, the communication process is evident. Sport communication is a process, and that process does not take place in a vacuum—it must be played out in a context. That context, or level, can involve personal settings (e.g., face to face, small group), organizational settings (e.g., between two sport organizations), mediated sport communication (e.g., social media postings and tweets), or sport communication support services (e.g., sport public relations podcasts). Beyond the process, the other components of the model provide a comprehensive segmentation of the entire field of sport communication. In other words, the process and components included in the model account for every activity and career, as well as every attribute and aspect, of sport communication. In this way, the model combines the process view with structural analysis of sport entities.

Component 1: Personal and Organizational Communication in Sport

Component 1 involves two segments: personal communication in sport (i.e., intrapersonal, interpersonal, and small-group communication) and organizational communication in sport (i.e., intraorganizational and interorganizational). This component of the SSCM is an understudied area in the field, as personal communication and organizational communication accounted for just over 7 percent of the published articles in the *International Journal of Sport Communication* (Abeza et al., 2014). Even so, the personal and organizational segments make up the first component of the SSCM because they are foundational and critical areas in sport communication. The following subsections provide an overview of this first component, which is explored in much greater detail in the next two chapters (personal communication in chapter 5 and organizational communication in chapter 6).

Personal Sport Communication

The most basic, and most often used, communicative act among sport professionals or sport media professionals is intrapersonal sport communication—that is, communicating with oneself, or internal communication. Although this is the most common type of communication in sport, it is nearly impossible to examine because it is performed individually and is generally kept private. The exception is *mediated* intrapersonal communication, which is internal communication revealed through some form of media—for example, a sport industry executive typing out a Facebook post that reveals his or her thoughts. Instances of mediated intrapersonal communication abound and are often revealed on social media platforms.

In sport organizations, the second most common form of daily communication takes place between sport professionals in either interpersonal or small-group settings. Interpersonal sport communication involves a two-way flow of information between individuals. While interpersonal sport communication would typically involve communication between two people, it can involve more than that as long as the communication between the individuals is, as Wood (2020) notes, personal, selective, and systemic (i.e., in a certain context). Thus, in applying the work of Wood to the sport industry, interpersonal sport communication is a process that allows sport industry stakeholders "to reflect and build personal knowledge of one another and create shared meanings" (p. 21). On the other hand, **small-group sport communication** involves the flow of information within a small group (typically three or more people) who are either in a sport environment or involved with a sport-related subject.

The interpersonal communication process is both contextual and developmental and involves specific applications in sport communication and in the sport industry. Interpersonal sport communication involves a few participants who are in close proximity, use many sensory channels, and provide immediate feedback. It can occur in all stakeholder relationships that are conducted in sport, in a sport setting, or through a sport endeavor. For instance, in an organizational setting in the sport industry, interpersonal communication can involve communication between any of the stakeholders—both inside (intraorganizational) and outside (interorganizational) the organization. It can also include both unmediated interactions (e.g., face-to-face encounters) and mediated communicative endeavors (e.g., an email sent to a sport industry stakeholder, a text message sent to a colleague, a social media activity such as an ephemeral selfie sent via Snapchat to a co-worker). In DeVito's (2019) examination of interpersonal communication, the communication scholar integrates face-to-face and mediated (which he refers to as "online/social media") communication. DeVito explains that this integration is appropriate for a number of reasons (e.g., off-line and mediated interpersonal communication research and theory inform each other; employees are expected to possess skills in both forms of communication; off-line and mediated communication is how interpersonal communication occurs in our technologically advanced society).

While email and text messages are still often used in interpersonal sport communication, engagement in various social media platforms is increasing a significant part of our interpersonal communication interactions. "Social media has transformed the way we make, maintain, and dissolve relationships," note communication scholars Beebe, Beebe, and Redmond (2020). "We frequently use technology to make and keep friends; to share information; and to listen and respond to, confirm, and support others . . . people often seamlessly and easily switch" (p. 16) between unmediated and mediated interpersonal communication. Overall, interpersonal communication can be either verbal or nonverbal and can be conducted either face to face, in writing, or through any other mediated or unmediated avenue of communication.

Mediated interpersonal communication is increasingly prevalent in the sport industry, as evidenced by the social and parasocial interactions facilitated by social networking sites, the mass media, and other communication channels. In fact, as Pavlik and McIntosh (2019) detail (and as covered in chapter 5 of this textbook), the increase in interpersonal communication revealed to mass audiences (e.g., interpersonal interactions occurring on publicly visible social media accounts; interpersonal interactions such as text messages being displayed through the mass media) has created a blurring of the lines between interpersonal communication and mediated communication (e.g., mass media, social media). Therefore, although we have located social media in the second component of the SSCM (mediated sport communication), we could just as easily have included it in this first component (personal and organizational communication in sport).

Interpersonal sport communication is usually not anonymous; in fact, it is most often thought of as one-on-one communication. This basic type of communication in sport involves communication behaviors in dyads (pairs) and their effect on personal relationships and activities in sport. Small-group sport communication, which is closely affiliated with interpersonal sport communication, involves communication between individuals (typically three or more) who interact with respect to a common purpose and who influence one another. Furthermore, the components of interpersonal communication are often found in public speaking, even though that type of interaction may involve one-way communication with many audience members. Interpersonal sport communication is discussed in more detail in chapter 5, which examines the functions, patterns, and conflicts related to this form of personal sport communication. Chapter 5 also discusses how face-to-face communication in sport is similar to, dissimilar from, and interconnected with other forms of sport communication, such as the use of social media and mass media.

Organizational Sport Communication

Sport communication can take place outside of organizational environments. For instance, a freelance sport reporter might interview a retired professional golfer; in this case, neither participant has a direct organizational affiliation, but they are involved in interpersonal sport communication. For the most part, however, communication in sport occurs either within a sport entity (e.g., sport organization, sport media outlet) or between a sport entity and another entity. The latter case—communication between a sport stakeholder in one entity and a stakeholder in another entity—is referred to as *interorganizational sport communication*. This, of course, is the type of communication that takes place between a sport organization and its external organizational publics, such as boosters, media entities, consumers, and leagues. For example, Joe Sargent, the director of brand marketing for the Kansas City Chiefs (and the sport communicator featured at the beginning of Chapter 6), explains that externally he often works with the team's retail partners (e.g., pro shop, online shop vendors), media partners (e.g., TV, radio), community partners, and various vendors. "I communicate with these external stakeholders primarily by email," notes Sargent. "With all of these partners, I'm either working through previously negotiated deal points, or developing custom plans that can push our business further. For retail partners, that could include our existing merchandise deal, custom merchandise, jersey sales, or placement of merchandise at an event. This varies greatly depending on the project" (personal communication). Even more specifically, mediated interorganizational sport communication involves activities such as a sport organization (e.g., team) using email or social media to communicate with another entity (e.g., sponsorship group).

Whereas interorganizational communication involves communication between organizations, intraorganizational sport communication involves communication within a sport-affiliated organization. The prefix *intra* simply means "within," and this type of communication occurs between a sport organization's internal publics. This category includes communication between employees and colleagues of an organization, as well as the organizational culture, staff rituals, traditions, and other organizational influences that affect communication. Take, for instance, how ESPN's culture influenced communication within the organization. George Bodenheimer, whose lengthy ESPN career included advancing

from the mailroom to becoming the longest-serving president of the network, notes in his biographical and leadership text (Bodenheimer & Phillips, 2015), "The first thing I did to amplify ESPN's culture was to start talking about it both casually and in more formal settings" (p. 155). Some of his actions resulted in unforeseen influences on communication and culture within his organization. This was evident when he pushed for and built the first cafeteria at ESPN. He admits that he "had not anticipated that ESPNs's first cafeteria would play such a large role in enhancing our culture. Suddenly at lunch, everybody was bumping into other employees" (p. 153). He adds that with the new cafeteria, "People from different departments started mixing. On-air talent ate with technicians. Managers chatted with mailroom guys. It seemed like everyone was swapping stories, sharing information, and talking about new developments where they worked. . . . The next thing you knew, people were holding on-the-spot informal meetings that led to new ideas. Without ever planning for it to happen, our new cafeteria immediately began facilitating communication and collaboration among all departments" (p. 153). Our detailed analysis of intraorganizational sport communication is provided in chapter 6, which examines the structure, management, production, activities, and role of communication in sport organizations. It then applies leadership concepts to the field of sport communication by addressing topics such as leadership traits, followership, transformational leadership, power and influence, leadership and diversity, and leadership development.

Component 2: Mediated Communication in Sport

This component of the Strategic Sport Communication Model (SSCM) includes the most readily apparent segments of sport communication—the discrete elements of the sport media. It is through the media that communication influences the sport industry most obviously—for example, through "newspaper sports sections, sports television and radio broadcasts, sports websites and social media platforms, and sports magazines" (Pedersen, 2013, p. 1). Mediated communication in sport is conducted through myriad mass media

Last Chance U and the SSCM

In 2020, Netflix shifted its focus to California (Laney College in Oakland) for the fifth installment of its popular junior college football documentary, *Last Chance U*. In each season of this series, a viewer can see—typically through the act of binge watching (viewing several or all episodes in one setting)—aspects of sport communication that fit into various parts of the SSCM. For example, each episode reveals interpersonal communication (e.g., the athletics director interacting with the coaching staff, the players consoling one another) and organizational communication (e.g., intraorganizational interactions between stakeholders within the athletics department, interorganizational interactions between stakeholders of competing athletics departments). Sport communication involving verbal (e.g., an instructor talking to a student-athlete, a coach yelling at his or her assistants), nonverbal (e.g., a player expressing displeasure by the look on his or her face, a local fan making a gesture during a game), symbolic (e.g., the school logo, a tattoo), mediated (e.g., radio broadcast), and the remaining parts of the SSCM are evident throughout the series. Even crisis communication was evident numerous times, such as when—in the fourth season (focused on Independence Community College of Kansas) of the series—the overseers of the university were confronted with an inci-

dent that became a career- and organization-changing incident.

The event became what could be considered an international story, as the head coach used offensive communication when dealing with a student who had come from another country to play football at the Kansas college. The reference used in the text eventually brought about the end of the coach's tenure at the college. Text messages—a form of mediated interpersonal sport communication—from the coach were released to the media. Thus, mediated (text messages), interpersonal (player and coach) communication became mass-mediated communication when the personal texts were revealed to the world through television broadcasts, social media platforms, etc. After the fourth season was released and the coach had moved back to California, communication continued (in person, over social media, through the mass media, etc.) regarding the series and coach (who released his biography, *Hate Me Now, Love Me Later*, the same month the fourth season was released by Netflix). There was also legal activity surrounding some of the alleged communication, with a local county attorney's office proceeding with charges against one of the stakeholders in the series, alleging blackmail, identity theft, and false communication in his interactions with a local newspaper.

and social media endeavors, ranging from social media interactions by sport teams to fantasy sport apps and from sport television programs broadcast around the world to sports sections of local newspapers.

This component of the SSCM is also particularly visible and important due to the sheer amount of time that many individuals devote to mediated sport consumption. Consider, for instance, the viewing preferences of a group sometimes referred to as Gen Z—those born after the mid-1990s—which likely includes most readers of this book. In a recent survey ("How Gen Z," 2019) of the content that Gen Z is watching, the findings revealed that 73 percent of those classified as Gen

Z watch video content on their smartphones while only 33 percent watch content on TV and only 18 percent watch cable TV. Furthermore, the survey found that YouTube (76 percent) is the top source for media content consumption; 35 percent and 27 percent of Gen Z report that they watch video content each week on social media platforms Instagram and Snapchat, respectively. "Gen Z didn't cut the cord—they never connected it in the first place," notes those who conducted the survey. "Gen Z is a video-first generation. They're more likely than Millennials to prefer video over text, and are attracted to social platforms that put video front and center (see: YouTube, Snapchat, Instagram, and TikTok)" (para. 1-2).

The media consumption (and cord cutting) of Gen Z is different than the previous generation (millennials), who reported spending an average of about 18 hours per day using various media, such as surfing the web, seeing a movie, listening to the radio, reading print material, watching television, playing a video game, engaging in social networking, texting, and emailing (Fitzgerald, 2014). Although these activities are not mutually exclusive—and therefore can (and often do) occur at the same time (e.g., tweeting about a sporting event while watching it on television)—the surveys of both Gen Z and millennials still indicate that media consumption is prevalent in society, both as a whole and in the sport industry in particular.

The word *media* is the plural form of *medium*, and each medium helps to make up the various segments of the mediated communication component of the SSCM. As noted in the earlier discussion of personal communication in sport, the blending of the various forms of communication makes it more challenging to articulate distinct components in sport communication. "Our engagement with media has also changed, becoming more active as mass and interpersonal communications converge," note John Pavlik and Shawn McIntosh (2019, p. xxiv), who go into detail regarding the convergence of mass communication and interpersonal communication, even going so far as to call it *intermass* communication and noting the blurred line between interpersonal communication and mass communication. The communication scholars add that "social media represent a convergence of mass communication and interpersonal communication," (p. 188) and, thus, they would hold that sport industry professionals participate in interpersonal or mass communication convergence when they engage in online social networking (e.g., Instagram, Snapchat, Facebook, LinkedIn, Twitter), personal blog or website creating or interacting, reading a book on a tablet, participating in music or video file sharing sites, and so forth. Mass media convergence involves much more than one medium and thus brings about crossover and connections between various segments and components. This intersecting and interacting is particularly evident as interpersonal communication is often delivered or is visible through some type of media—such as through a social media platform or some

type of mass media—and could be categorized as mediated interpersonal communication. However, to create a model that best categorizes the components of sport communication, we have separated interpersonal communication in sport (placing it in the first component of the SSCM) and defined *mediated communication in sport* as including a segment for sport mass media (e.g., print, broadcast) and a segment for **emerging and social media in sport**.

The segment devoted to sport mass media consists of the traditional areas of mass communication, such as print and broadcast media. Print sport communication and sport publishing include various communication channels, such as sport magazines and books and newspaper sports sections. The professionals who work in these areas include sport journalists, such as sportswriters, columnists, photographers, and editors. The broadcast media (e.g., electronic and visual sport communication) include sport radio, sport films, sport television networks, satellite providers, and cable companies. In the media activity survey mentioned a bit earlier (Fitzgerald, 2014), millennials reported spending about seven hours per day consuming mass media products that fit into this segment of the component (e.g., radio, television, film, newspaper). It is not a stretch to suppose that a majority of these general consumption hours are devoted to sport, especially given the popularity and proliferation of sport mass media outlets such as all-sport television channels (e.g., ACC Network, Fox Sports 1, SEC Network). The sport mass media are examined in detail in chapter 7, which provides an exhaustive examination covering everything from historical developments and business aspects to production functions and media rights fees. Chapter 7 focuses, however, on convergence and on how the sport mass media work and interact in light of changes (e.g., technological developments) that the industry has witnessed over the past decade.

Chapter 8, in turn, examines emerging and social media in sport, which constitute the other half of the SSCM component referred to as *mediated communication in sport*. This segment also reflects the media convergence discussed earlier in this chapter (and in chapter 7); in addition, it addresses cutting-edge elements, activities, and innovations in sport communication (e.g.,

Photo courtesy of Hallie S. Pedersen.

The television coverage and sponsorship signage are examples of aspects of sport communication that fit into the second (Mediated Communication in Sport) and third (Sport Communication Services and Support) components of the SSCM.

the usage of virtual reality by sport consumers, athletes, and teams). Consider, for instance, how emerging and social media have affected sport journalists, who "are expected to use new media technologies and adjust their newsgathering, dissemination, and readership and source interaction activities accordingly," (Pedersen, 2014). "New media influences, digital interactivity and participatory elements, and the overall technological impact have significantly shifted the landscape in newspaper sports reporting, and the surviving print sportswriters have embraced—or been forced into—their new role as digital sports journalists" (p. 101). Beyond these effects on sport communication professionals, "social media is now the primary means that many people get their sports news" (Evans, 2015, p. 17).

More generally, digital, mobile, and social media are increasing in both their pervasiveness and their importance to sport and media organizations and sport stakeholders (e.g., bloggers, columnists, consumers, executives, fans, entrepreneurs). As a result, this segment of mediated

sport communication is covered throughout this book and is given detailed treatment in chapter 8. In addition, this segment and the other (sport mass media) that make up this component of the SSCM are also the most studied areas of sport communication. As reported in a content analysis of the *International Journal of Sport Communication* (Abeza et al., 2014), three-quarters of research articles published in the journal were coded as addressing either mass media (half) or social media (one quarter).

Component 3: Sport Communication Services and Support

The last area of the Strategic Sport Communication Model is the critical component referred to as *sport communication services and support*. Segments in this component include sport-related integrated marketing communication, public relations and crisis communication, and communication research. Of these segments, **integrated marketing**

communication in sport encompasses technological advancements in sport industry marketing (e.g., mobile payment options at sporting events), innovative and traditional methods in the advertising of sport (e.g., connecting with potential consumers via their smartwatches), and advertising through sport (e.g., marketing a product through a popular sport media app). To be effective, integrated marketing communication requires "a strategy that manages communication exchanges between a marketer and its target customer segments" while serving "the overarching objective of building and maintaining a brand's identity" (Fetchko, Roy, & Clow, 2013, p. 207). This way of managing brand communication involves coordinating the aspects of a brand (e.g., image, identity) with opportunities presented through various channels of communication (e.g., digital and social media, email, direct marketing, personal selling, advertising, publicity, sponsorship). The marketing segment of sport communication is covered chapter 9. In addition to that chapter, you can learn more about this segment by reading the opening profile in chapter 6, which features Joe Sargent, the director of brand marketing of the Kansas City Chiefs.

It is increasingly difficult for companies and products to stand out in a sport industry marked by traditional advertising as well as email campaigns and promotions conducted through social media platforms (e.g., TikTok, Pinterest, Twitter, Snapchat, Facebook). On Instagram, for example, companies often spend a significant amount of money just for one sponsored mentioned by a sport industry celebrity such as Cristiano Ronaldo, Lionel Messi, LeBron James, Floyd Mayweather, and Serena Williams (see table 4.1 for a listing of the cost per sponsored Instagram post). Through social media platforms, the Internet, and traditional advertising channels, consumers are "bombarded with messages" as the marketing "landscape is saturated with media messages from every conceivable angle," note Dittmore and McCarthy (2014). The scholars add that "From television commercials to in-show and stadium advertising to billboards and signs, media marketing is impossible to avoid" (p. 165). Because of the saturation and competition in this area of the sport industry, this textbook takes an integrated approach to examining the aspects presented under the umbrella of marketing communication. This approach, pursued in detail in chapter 9,

Table 4.1 Cost for a Sponsored Instagram Post With Celebrity Sport Industry Stakeholder

Athlete	Athlete's Instagram handle	Approximate number of followers	Cost per sponsored post
Cristiano Ronaldo	@cristiano	173 million	$975,000
Neymar da Silva Santos, Jr.	@neymarjr	122 million	$722,000
Lionel Messi	@leomessi	124 million	$648,000
David Beckham	@davidbeckham	56.6 million	$357,000
LeBron James	@kingjames	50.2 million	$272,000
Ronaldo de Assis Moreira	@ronaldinho	47 million	$256,000
Gareth Bale	@garethbale11	40.2 million	$218,000
Zlatan Ibrahimović	@iamzlatanibrahimovic	36.8 million	$200,000
Virat Kohli	@virat.kohli	36.2 million	$196,000
Luis Suarez	@luissuarez9	34 million	$184,000
Conor McGregor	@thenotoriousmma	31 million	$169,000
Mohamed Salah	@mosalah	30.4 million	$165,000
Stephen Curry	@stephencurry30	26.1 million	$142,000
Floyd Mayweather	@floydmayweather	22.8 million	$124,000
Ronda Rousey	@rondarousey	12.5 million	$67,700
Serena Williams	@serenawilliams	11.2 million	$60,500

Data from Hopper HQ's "Instagram Rich List 2019": https://www.hopperhq.com/blog/instagram-rich-list/niche/sport/

INTERCOLLEGIATE COMMUNICATION SUCCESS: ENGAGING INTERNAL AND EXTERNAL STAKEHOLDERS

Chevonne M. Mansfield
Deputy athletics director and senior woman administrator
Florida Memorial University (FMU)

Intercollegiate athletics programs need highly skilled professionals, such as Chevonne Mansfield, to provide leadership and facilitate communication with both internal and external publics. In 2019, Mansfield transitioned to her current intercollegiate athletics leadership position after working her entire career in various sport communication capacities and positions. "Growing up as a sports information director (SID) helped shape my career," notes Mansfield. "If you can be an SID, you can do anything." Mansfield brings into her college leadership role a proven track record of building communication and public relations programs, excellent written and verbal communication skills, expertise in utilizing social media platforms, and an understanding of and experience in college sports. While her executive position with the Florida Memorial University Lions does not include an official sport communication role or title, Mansfield is still very much involved with the communication segment of the sport industry. "My role encompasses executive communications, public relations, and assistance with special events," states Mansfield.

Mansfield shoulders numerous duties and responsibilities. Her daily and near-daily work includes responsibility for external areas including communication, marketing, promotions, and development. She has direct oversight of several athletics programs and employees, as well as providing vision and leadership to advance the athletics department's fundraising efforts, including annual and major gift planning with a concerted focus on building the Lions' donor base and engaging contributors.

Arriving at her leadership position in intercollegiate athletics has not been easy; in fact, it has required many years of dedication, strategic decisions, and sacrifices. "I got to where I am today from my work ethic, experience, and relationships," notes Mansfield. "I put the time in and was not afraid to go the extra mile. Some people shy away from grunt work, but you need to start somewhere. Many times when you do an internship or volunteer work, you're tasked with grunt work, like answering phones, running copies, etc. How you do that work (and any work you're given) goes a long way."

As a student at St. John's University, Mansfield initially set out to become an interpreter for the United Nations. Her plans changed (as did her major—from Spanish to communication) during her first year when she found out how much she enjoyed working in the university's athletics communication office. Throughout her undergraduate years, she was active in a variety of ways: interning (e.g., New York Liberty, New York Jets, National Invitational Tournament, ESPN); volunteering (e.g., NBA Draft, Heisman Trophy presentation, MLB playoffs with the New York Yankees, NCAA basketball tournaments); and gaining experience with the New York Knicks (public relations), New York Rangers (marketing), and even the University of Leicester in England (local basketball team, campus television).

Photo courtesy of Chevonne M. Mansfield.

Chevonne M. Mansfield, deputy athletics director and senior woman administrator (SWA), Florida Memorial University.

(continued)

(continued)

After securing her undergraduate degree, Mansfield spent three years as a graduate sports information assistant at the University of Maryland Eastern Shore, where she earned a master's degree in criminology while gaining valuable experience in sport communication. Mansfield then took her first full-time position, at the age of 25, when she became assistant sports information director at Howard University. Later, she moved on to positions with the Southwestern Athletic Conference (SWAC), the Southeastern Conference (SEC), the American Athletic Conference (The American), and the LEAD1 Association (a sport organization, through its representation of the athletics directors and programs of the 130 member universities of the NCAA Division I Football Bowl Subdivision, that seeks to influence how the rules of college sports are enacted and implemented, advocates for the future of college athletics, and provides services to member schools).

Mansfield has also served on the board of directors for the Association for Women in Sports Media (AWSM) and the College Sports Information Directors of America (CoSIDA). CoSIDA, a national organization that started in 1957, now has over 3,000 members of "sports public relations, media relations and communications/information professionals throughout all levels of collegiate athletics in the United States and Canada" ("Our Organization," 2020, para. 1). In addition to assisting professionals in the field, CoSIDA plays an integral role in terms of providing leadership and resources "within the overall collegiate athletics enterprise, thus helping other management groups and their respective memberships deal with the set of communications-based issues that is the most complex and challenging in history" (para. 6). Mansfield readily acknowledges the role this organization has played in her professional advancement, and she can connect the dots regarding her various experiences and positions in the field, describing her growth and skill development along the way. "I had increasing responsibility at my various jobs on my way to FMU, and those skills helped me get to where I am today," notes Mansfield. "All of my related experience had a hand in shaping me as a professional. When I was in college, I got acclimated to different work environments in pro and college sports by doing internships. In grad school, I learned the technical things like writing, game operations, and what it meant to be a media relations contact for a team." Mansfield explains what she learned at each of her career stops. For instance, at Howard she developed skills in multitasking and building a network. At the SWAC, she took on her first supervision position "and interacted with coaches from the administrative side." At the SEC, Mansfield notes that she "firmed" her "soft skills" and was able to witness "the inner workings of a major FBS conference." From there, while at The American, Mansfield explains that she "learned a great deal about revenue generation, the structure of college sports," as well as other aspects of hosting and working media operations at major events. Overall, she notes, "We are always learning at every stage of our career."

At this point in her career, Mansfield can provide outstanding suggestions for individuals who are thinking about pursuing a leadership career in sport communication. She has built a successful leadership career and offers sound advice for those seeking similar success: "Get as much experience as you can and continue being a sponge at each step of your career. Be active in professional organizations and pick up another language. The world is changing, and it helps to be well versed in other languages. Build meaningful relationships. Don't be the person that collects a thousand business cards at a networking event. Focus on connecting with a few folks and follow up the contact from there. With relationship building, it's important to give something first before making an ask. Utilize social media in a good way; that is another way to build relationships and your personal brand. Work on your soft skills, they are often more important than the technical skills you will learn. Don't be afraid to move for a position. Take breaks at work and while you're studying, when needed; you'll be more effective that way instead of plowing through everything with no break. Finally, make time for yourself and your family. Life is short, and time with family and loved ones is precious and important."

includes the traditional areas of sport marketing, as well as the more innovative and sometimes controversial opportunities (e.g., native advertising) found in this initial segment of the last component of the SSCM.

The component's second segment—**public relations and crisis communication in sport**—involves message development and image building through effective management of sport media. Sport public relations, according to Stoldt, Dittmore, Ross, and Branvold (2021), "is a brand-centric communication function designed to manage and advance relationships between a sport organization and its key publics" (p. 2). Therefore, this segment of the SSCM's third component includes both internal and external communication endeavors, ranging from involvement in community relations efforts to managing the media through media relations techniques (e.g., social media posts, media releases, website updates, credentialing, fact sheets, game notes, media kits, news conferences).

Beyond public relations endeavors, this second segment of the SSCM's third component includes crisis communication. More generally, sport communication crises range from an inappropriate tweet sent out by a sport organization stakeholder to announcements regarding a natural disaster affecting a sporting event or facility. Such situations demand effectiveness in terms of both internal and external communication. An effective crisis communication plan "specifies what roles people in the organization will play in responding to the crisis; sources of information that will support timely actions; and key steps to take in engaging with external publics such as the mass media, donors, and customers" (p. 165).

The last segment of the third SSCM component is sport communication research. On the academic side, this research includes scholarship disseminated at academic gatherings (e.g., the International Sports Events Broadcasting Forum held in Beijing, China) and through various publications (e.g., journals, textbooks, edited volumes). In the content analysis of research published in the *International Journal of Sport Communication*, Abeza and colleagues (2014) found that the most common methodologies used were survey, experimental, phenomenological, case study, interview, and analytic approaches (related to content, text, and themes). Two other examples of relevant academic outlets are *Communication & Sport* and the *Journal of Sports Media*.

Sport communication research is also conducted outside of academia, where it is used for evaluative and practical purposes in the sport industry. Those purposes range from publishing media reports (e.g., *TV Sports Markets*) to measuring media exposure in sport sponsorship arrangements to using analytics and big data in sport. For example, Nielsen Sports provides market research and intelligence, media evaluation and auditing, digital media services, and consulting to brands, sponsors, clubs, colleges, events, federations, teams, venues, and agencies. Therefore, the sport communication research segment involves both academic and practical research in sport public relations, sport mass media, integrated marketing, sport social media, and any other activity or aspect of the field as it is captured by the sport communication process and components that make up the Strategic Sport Communication Model (SSCM).

CHAPTER WRAP-UP

Summary

This chapter explores the concepts of communication and explains our broad perspective on the field of sport communication. As noted at the beginning of this chapter, sport communication is broader and more complex than one might gather from a mere glance at any of its individual elements. For example, some might view the sport mass media as synonymous with the field of sport communication; however, we view the sport mass media as only one of many segments that make up the field of sport communication. Similarly, some might think that sport communication consists only of public relations aspects of professional sport and the sports information activities of intercollegiate athletics. In our view, however, although media relations does constitute a significant segment, it is only one part of the overall field, which encompasses work in a variety of segments, as well as the various ways in which sport industry professionals and organizations communicate with both internal and external stakeholders.

To help you understand this broad and complex field, this chapter begins with a foundational definition for both this textbook and the field in general: Sport communication is a process by which people in sport, in a sport setting, or through a sport endeavor share symbols as they create meaning through interaction. The chapter then examines the theoretical framework of sport communication by discussing genres, contexts, process, and the elements of sport communication.

Identifying these aspects of the field allows us to fully understand the Strategic Sport Communication Model (SSCM). This model, represented in figure 4.4, provides a conceptual framework for addressing communication in the sport industry; it also provides the structure on which the upcoming chapters are based. The SSCM breaks the sport communication process into its constituent elements and covers the major components of the field. As a result, all sport communication processes, careers, and activities can be situated within the model. The SSCM's three major components are as follows: personal and organizational communication in sport (i.e., intrapersonal, interpersonal, and small group), mediated communication in sport (i.e., mass media and emerging and social media), and sport communication services and support (i.e., integrated marketing communication, public relations, crisis communication, and communication research). Personal communication in sport, which makes up half of the SSCM's first component, is explored in the next chapter.

Review Questions

1. What are the genres (or the main groups of communication theory) on which sport communication is based?

2. What are the major contexts (or levels) of sport communication?

3. In what way is sport communication a process, and what are the elements of the sport communication process?

4. In the field of sport communication, how do people create meaning through interaction?

5. What are the major components of the Strategic Sport Communication Model, and how does it relate to the sport communication process?

Individual Exercises

1. List five career opportunities in each of the three main components of the Strategic Sport Communication Model (SSCM). Select one of these careers, and list how job opportunities associated with it may have shifted over the past decade as a result of changes (e.g., technological developments) in the field of sport communication.

2. Interview a local sport communication professional (e.g., sport radio broadcaster, sport communication executive or entrepreneur, sport blogger, sports information director for a university athletics department, media relations assistant for a professional team, television sportscaster). Focus on finding out which aspect of communication the sport communication professional uses most often, and least often, in a typical workday.

Photo courtesy of Paul M. Pedersen.

Personal Sport Communication

KEY TERMS

chronemics

environmental factors

haptics

interaction management

kinesics

metacommunication

other-orientedness

proxemics

small-group communication in sport

source–receiver

speech act

PERSONAL COMMUNICATION IN TEAM MANAGEMENT

Cara Wright

It should come as no surprise that effective sport industry leaders are those who are skilled communicators. This is especially true for front-office executives, such as Cara Wright, who up until recently was the director of business operations for the Agua Caliente Clippers (in 2020 Wright moved across the country to New York and became the Senior Associate Athletic Director of External Operations at Columbia University). While in her leadership role with the Agua Caliente Clippers—an NBA (National Basketball Association) G League-affiliated team of the Los Angeles Clippers (both teams are owned by former Microsoft CEO Steve Ballmer)—Wright managed a host of areas, including the team's efforts related to public relations, game operations, marketing, community relations, programming, social media, broadcasts, social responsibility, and media relations. In addition to her leadership in basketball operations and her liaison work to the team's venue, she was also engaged in sales (e.g., ticket packages, group sales, sponsorships). Wright notes that in terms of game operations, most of her focus was on "how we can provide the best product from when the doors open at the arena to the end of the game, every home game."

Wright explains that in terms of her communication, half of her time while in the G-League was spent in face-to-face meetings and half was spent "on email correspondence, conference calls, phone calls, and reporting." On game days during the season, her face-to-face meetings increased due to "working with our venue and basketball operations and game night staff. But I would continue to get emails at any time and would respond accordingly whether it was within my regular office hours or after hours." To be effective in her leadership role, Wright is constantly engaged in the various forms of personal communication covered in this chapter. Take, for instance, her engagement in intrapersonal communication during the Clippers' games: "I would be thinking about how entry went for our fans and what needed to happen to make it better at the next game, how smoothly we were able to get a giveaway out to fans, and how to improve that process. I would internally process our processes and how successful they were each game. I would also go through the things that needed to be completed prior, during, and after a game to myself each home game." Beyond the communication going on in her head (intrapersonal communication in sport) on game days, Wright was heavily invested in personal interactions with others. "Being in

Photo courtesy of Felisha Carrasco.

Cara Wright, a senior associate athletic director at Columbia University and the former director of business operations for the Agua Caliente Clippers, an NBA G League-affiliated team of the Los Angeles Clippers.

sports and a developmental professional team, interpersonal communication happens all the time," states Wright, who was one of the four front-office executives who comprise the sport organization's management team. Her interpersonal communication involved, for example, her interactions with the team's communication professionals (e.g., preparing social media strategies, planning for media days) or with her fellow front-office executives (e.g., discussing the upcoming season, strategizing for certain events).

Wright's effectiveness as a leader is related to her ability to observe and react to all types of personal communication, even if not spoken. "Nonverbal cues are very important. In manage-ment you have to be able to work with all different kinds of people and you can tell how they respond to verbal communication sometimes through their nonverbal response," notes Wright. "It's important to be able to pick up on the body language of your staff." She adds that effective interpersonal communication in the sport industry involves "being able to read what kind of communication others are comfortable with and being able to adjust your interaction accordingly." The personal communication activities in which Wright engages are examples of intrapersonal, interpersonal, and **small-group communication in sport**. These three forms of sport communication are examined in this chapter.

Careers in the sport industry involve a considerable amount of communication. "A great deal of my work and time revolves around written communication," states Chevonne Mansfield, the intercollegiate athletics administrator who is profiled in chapter 4. "About 60 percent of what I do is written (content creation, publications, emails, reports), and 40 percent requires oral communication, usually in the form of presentations and face-to-face meetings" (personal communication). Although not all jobs require as much communication as Mansfield's leadership position does, communication—in particular, personal communication—is integral to the sport industry and its various stakeholders. Thus, in this chapter, we introduce you to three closely related forms of intimate communication in sport: intrapersonal, interpersonal, and small-group sport communication.

Your success in a sport industry job—whether as an intern for an English Premier League (EPL) club, a social media manager for an intercollegiate athletics department, an employee with a sportswear manufacturer, a professional in the front office of a Formula One (F1) team, a supervisor for a sport commission, or a broadcaster for a National Women's Soccer League (NWSL) franchise—depends largely on the effectiveness of your personal interactions with others. Therefore, this chapter introduces you to the concepts behind, and the skills needed in, the personal aspect of sport communication. The chapter first addresses what is involved in intrapersonal sport communication, interpersonal sport communication, and small-group sport communication. After illustrating the distinctiveness of these types of communication, the chapter examines their characteristics, functions, and contextual and developmental processes. After reading this chapter, you will be familiar with the activities, components, and workings of personal communication in sport—and be able to start refining your skills in this area.

FORMS OF PERSONAL COMMUNICATION IN SPORT

As illustrated in the chapter 4 discussion of the Strategic Sport Communication Model (SSCM), sport communication takes various forms, ranging from a simple shrug or sigh by a disgruntled assistant ticket manager to a deeply revealing memoir, such as the recent autobiographies by Rachael Denhollander (2019, *What Is a Girl Worth?*) and Rachel Haines (2019, *Abused*) in which they speak out about sexual abuse in the sport of gymnastics. Sport communication audiences also vary greatly and involve anything from a single sport organization employee (e.g., reading an email message from a colleague) to an audience of millions watching an international broadcast of the Paralympic Games. Regardless of the form or audience, however, sport communicators interact with one another by sharing meaning; therefore, at its basic level, sport communication is personal in nature. Consequently, although this chapter focuses on personal interaction in sport, the concepts and issues examined here touch all forms of sport communication and all components of the SSCM.

The specific form of sport communication is also determined by the number of communicators involved and the situation in which they communicate. Fundamentally, communication can be reduced to three forms; in the context of sport, these three direct communication forms are intrapersonal, interpersonal, and small-group sport communication. As shown in figure 5.1, these three forms make up one part—referred to as *personal communication in sport*—of the first component of the SSCM. The other part of this first SSCM component—organizational communication in sport—is covered in chapter 6. While we separate personal and organizational communication within the SSCM, keep in mind that

personal communication in sport is involved in each aspect of the SSCM and can (and often does) occur across organizations. For instance, entrepreneur and sport organization owner Mark Cuban engaged in both personal (e.g., interpersonal) and organizational communication when, during the 2019 offseason, he communicated with a reporter about a decision that was made at an NBA Board of Governors meeting. Although the owner of the Dallas Mavericks was effective in getting his message across to the intended audience (as the reporter published the insider information), the league fined Cuban $50,000 because the NBA considered his communication a leak of confidential information. In 2020 Cuban used both traditional organizational communication (e.g., press release) and mediated personal communication (e.g., social media) to express his personal feelings regarding team issues (e.g., his usage of a press release to announce that in honor of Kobe Bryant the Mavericks would retire the number 24) and league issues (e.g., his usage of social media to criticize the officiating in the NBA).

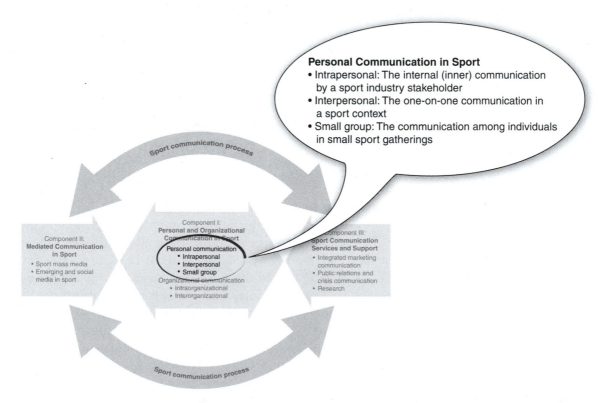

Figure 5.1   Intrapersonal, interpersonal, and small-group sport communication make up the first half of the personal and organizational communication component—that is, the personal communication segment of the component—in the Strategic Sport Communication Model (SSCM).

Intrapersonal Communication in Sport

The most commonly used form of communication in the field is intrapersonal communication in sport. This type of communication occurs when a person turns his or her communication inward; in other words, it is the speech inside one's own mind, where one is both the sender and the receiver of the message. In other examples, when a meeting gets too boring and daydreaming takes over an attendee's mind, he is engaged in intrapersonal communication. When an executive rehearses in her mind the presentation she is about to deliver, she, too, is involved in intrapersonal communication. In fact, this form of personal communication occurs anytime you engage in an internal dialogue or brainstorm ideas, such as thinking about creative ways to solve a risk management issue in your facility.

Because everyone engages in self-talk, all sport professionals are involved in intrapersonal communication at various times. However, although it accounts for the majority of sport communication, it is mostly done individually and is therefore private. The exception to this generalization involves mediated intrapersonal communication—that is, internal communication revealed through some medium, such as through a social media platform, an online diary, or a sport blog.

Interpersonal Communication in Sport

Beyond intrapersonal communication, the most common form of daily communication in sport organizations occurs between sport professionals; in other words, most communication between people in sport occurs in interpersonal settings. According to Wood (2020), interpersonal communication is a selective and "systemic process that allows people to reflect and build personal knowledge of one another and create shared meanings" (p. 21). By extension, interpersonal communication in sport is the two-way flow of information between individuals (typically two people) in a sport setting or regarding a sport issue. That is, whenever two people communicate in the sport industry, they are involved in interpersonal sport communication. For example, this type of communication might take the form of a dialogue between individuals in a hallway or a meeting between executives. The communicators might be interns, athletes, executives, agents, sponsors, colleague, owners, or any other stakeholder involved in an interpersonal communicative interaction, whether mediated or unmediated.

Interpersonal communication typically involves one-on-one or face-to-face interaction. Many scholars refer to this type of communication as *dyadic* because it consists of behavior in dyads (pairs), as well as that behavior's effect on personal relationships and activities in sport. Even when communication includes more than two individuals—for example, a triad, a small group, or even a large group—it is often marked by a dyadic primacy because many of the interactions happen face to face between two people. Typically, this form of communication is spontaneous, informal, and unstructured and involves close (e.g., intimate) proximity of participants and immediate feedback. Interpersonal sport communication is usually *not* anonymous, although there are exceptions, such as debates among and trolling by anonymous sport fans interacting on online message boards, newspaper website comment sections, and social media platforms. There are even anonymous social media smartphone apps such as Yolo and Whisper. Because the interactants are both senders and receivers, the roles in the interpersonal communication process are flexible.

Small-Group Communication in Sport

Closely affiliated with interpersonal sport communication, *small-group communication in sport* involves communication between individuals in small gatherings (typically three or more people) who interact for a common purpose and influence one another. This definition separates small groups from mere collections of people (e.g., fans gathering outside the ticket office for postseason tickets).

The characteristics of small groups involve such aspects as interaction (members act and react), perception (members view the group as real), norms (members have an idea of what others expect), roles (members have certain formal and informal positions), affective relationships (members are not indifferent), and goals (members share purposes and objectives) (Hartley, 1999). Although these characteristics can describe most of the mediated and unmediated interpersonal communication noted in the previous section, there are a few differences between small-group (intragroup or intergroup) communication and interpersonal communication. These differences can stem from issues related to pressure, conformity (i.e., groupthink), and leadership. Regardless, small-group communication is included in the discussion of interpersonal communication because most small groups, as Hartley notes, involve dyadic relationships and possess many of the components found in interpersonal communication.

Small groups in sport range from office gatherings (e.g., watercooler conversations) to conference calls to pack interviews (e.g., a group of sport journalists interviewing an athlete in the locker room) and media days. Small-group communication takes place when information flows between a few interactants who are either in a sport environment or involved with a sport-related subject. As Trenholm and Jensen (2013) explain, interpersonal communication becomes small-group communication when a third party enters the interaction. They note that while small groups vary in size, the small groups need to "be small enough that everyone can interact freely" (p. 24); if a specific dyadic communication link between two of the small-group members is broken, the members can still communicate with fellow members of the group.

Overall, whether small-group communication in sport is mediated or unmediated—and whether the messages are verbal or nonverbal—it occurs in a wide variety of settings. Examples include "war rooms" on National Football League (NFL) Draft days, broadcast programming sessions at the Chicago Cubs' new Marquee Sports Network, and editorial meetings for the sports section of the *Los Angeles Daily News*.

INTERPERSONAL SPORT COMMUNICATION

Despite the distinctions between the basic forms of communication, there are also strong similarities in the characteristics, practices, conflicts, and issues involved in all forms of personal communication. Although this section of the chapter focuses on interpersonal sport communication, many of the aspects examined can also be applied to other areas of communication. We can distinguish interpersonal communication by noting that, according to Pavlik and McIntosh (2019), interpersonal communication "is communication between two or more persons . . . is usually interactive, or flowing at least two ways, and tends not to be anonymous" (p. 22). They add that interpersonal communication occurs in face-to-face interactions but "can also take place through a medium, or communication channel, such as the telephone, when texting or talking, or the Internet, when participating in a chat room or on a discussion board, for example," thus blurring the lines "between interpersonal and mass communication, as a private email or text can be forwarded to many other people" (p. 23). In addition, its form and content are shaped by the personal qualities of the interactants, as well as their social roles and relationships (Hartley, 1999). This definition allows for the inclusion of most forms of mediated and unmediated personal communication—two-person (dyadic), three-person (triadic), and small-group communication—and provides the grounding for our use of the phrase *interpersonal sport communication*. Here are some examples of interpersonal sport communication:

- Two colleagues direct messaging each other to explain their ideas for a sport marketing campaign
- A face-to-face discussion between partners of a sport agency over whether their client should accept an endorsement opportunity that will be financially rewarding but involve a controversial company or product
- A dialogue between a panelist at an Association for Women in Sports Media (AWSM) convention and three attendees who came forward after the session to pursue a networking opportunity

Having established this functional definition, we can also emphasize the importance of interpersonal communication in sport. Because sport communicators often blend forms and contexts (especially when using new technologies, such as social media, email, chat rooms,

Photo courtesy of Paul M. Pedersen.

The interaction exhibited here between legendary basketball player Dr. J (Julius Erving) and the Big3 basketball league event staff member is an example of interpersonal sport communication.

municate directly with our fans on a daily basis (often one-to-one but more often via a mass tweet or Instagram post, etc.)" (personal communication).

Based on the work of numerous communication scholars, we propose that interpersonal sport communication occurs whenever individuals in sport, in a sport setting, or through a sport endeavor share the roles of sender and receiver and create meaning through their mediated or unmediated personal interactions. In addition to its various mediated forms (e.g., text, email, social media, phone), interpersonal sport communication also includes the face-to-face encounters that sport professionals and communicators have with each other and with colleagues, advisors, sales managers, media relations professionals, interns, employees, and other stakeholders.

Interactants engage in interpersonal sport communication for a range of reasons. Sometimes they do so to provide advice, such as discussing with an intern the best way to approach a supervisor for a letter of recommendation. On other occasions, they do so to learn something new, such as learning from a colleague about a new position in the sales department. Thus, as DeVito (2019) explains, "Interpersonal communication, whether face-to-face or online, is purposeful and serves a variety of purposes" (p. 19). The myriad reasons for which people in the sport industry engage in interpersonal communication—which can range from conscious and intentional to subconscious and unintentional—can be reduced to five primary reasons: to relate, to learn, to play, to help, and to influence. These reasons, which are illustrated by DeVito (2019) and examined in the following paragraphs, all stem from various motivations and often produce unique results.

The first reason that people engage in interpersonal communication is to relate; they feel a need to establish and maintain relationships. Even the most ruthless negotiator in the sport industry is likely to feel at least a small desire to love and like and to be loved and liked. On social media sites such as LinkedIn, a sport industry stakeholder

instant messages, and other computer-mediated interpersonal communication)—and because many interactions in sport are interpersonal to a certain degree—we join Trenholm and Jensen (2013) in preferring to "think of all communication as having an interpersonal element. While the clearest instance of interpersonal communication takes place when two people interact directly and personally, many other interactions are partially interpersonal." These scholars note, for example, that "situations overlap, and when they do communication may take on the characteristics of both situations" (p. 26), such as when the interpersonal sport communication occurs through some type of technology (e.g., a social media platform) and thus becomes mediated interpersonal sport communication. One example of such communication can be found in the mediated interactions between Josh Rawitch of the Arizona Diamondbacks (featured in the chapter-ending profile) and his stakeholders. "Through social media," states Rawitch, "I com-

exhibits a desire to relate by liking a comment (or clicking on another reaction such celebrate, love, insightful, and curious) that a colleague posted.

The second reason for interpersonal communication is to learn. Participants in interpersonal communication learn about the world, other people, themselves, etiquette, feelings, and perceptions; they also learn about specific desires, needs, behaviors, thoughts, feelings, and likes of others. Interpersonal sport communication can help sport industry stakeholders learn about themselves. "By talking about yourself with others, you gain valuable feedback on your feelings, thoughts, and behaviors . . . you also learn how you appear to others—who likes you, who dislikes you, and why," notes DeVito (2019). He adds that such a function "is written into the very fabric of Facebook, Twitter, and blogs, where commenting, recommending, and liking for a post can be indicated so easily" (p. 19).

The third reason is to play, which involves more than simply participating in games. It also includes the social media interactions we have with friends about our activities, jokes, stories, and sports.

The fourth reason for interpersonal communication is to help others. This purpose might involve, for example, guiding, consoling, comforting, or advising. "Social media websites such as LinkedIn and Plaxo and even Facebook and Twitter are used extensively for securing the help of others and giving help to others," notes DeVito (2019). "Success in accomplishing this helping function, professionally or otherwise, depends on your knowledge and skill in interpersonal communication" (p. 20).

The fifth reason is to influence—to persuade others in terms of attitudes, perceptions, purchases, or other behaviors. For example, a person might decide to make a particular sporting goods purchase based on a recommendation received from a friend through a mediated interpersonal interaction—in other words, through electronic word of mouth (eWOM).

Each of these five reasons for participating in interpersonal communication relates to activity in the sport industry. Such interaction is used on a daily basis by all sport communication and sport management stakeholders to relate, learn, play, help, and persuade.

ELEMENTS OF THE INTERPERSONAL SPORT COMMUNICATION PROCESS

The interpersonal communication process in sport is similar to the communication process outlined in chapter 4. To thoroughly understand interpersonal sport communication, one needs to understand the developmental and contextual processes involved. Whenever there are at least two interactants involved, the process of interpersonal communication in sport is active and multifaceted (e.g., sender, receiver, feedback, verbal, nonverbal, mediated). For instance, imagine that a recent sport management graduate is invited for an interview with a sport franchise. We might be tempted to view the interpersonal communication process as beginning with an event (i.e., the first question of the interview). However, the process was actually initiated as soon as one interactant communicated the first message to the other. This beginning might have occurred when their eyes met after an administrative assistant ushered the interviewee into the office, or perhaps it happened when the interviewer noticed the interviewee's confident posture upon entering the room. However it started, the process continued in an ongoing fashion through verbal and nonverbal messages until the two communicators stopped sending and receiving messages.

Regardless of the forms of interpersonal sport communication (e.g., mediated, unmediated, verbal, nonverbal), several key elements or variables are involved in this ongoing process. The major elements— presented here in modified form based on the work of various communication scholars (e.g., DeVito, 2019; Trenholm, 1986; Trenholm & Jensen, 2013)—include the following: **source–receiver** (encoder–decoder), message, feedback, channel, noise, and context.

Source–Receiver

The first element, source–receiver, consists of the individuals (generally two) who are involved in an instance of interpersonal communication. Interpersonal sport communication typically involves few interactants (or participants)—

generally either two or a few. Each interactant sends messages (as source) and receives messages (as receiver); thus, as noted by Trenholm and Jensen (2013), the individuals involved share the roles of sender and receiver. The interactants both encode the messages they send (i.e., produce messages, as by speaking or writing) and decode the messages they receive (i.e., understand them). For interpersonal communication to occur, there must be both a sender and receiver; without one or the other, the process is lost. For instance, when a sport supervisor jumps up and down while yelling to his or her subordinate who is outside of hearing range, no interpersonal communication is involved because the intended receiver does not receive (and thus cannot decode) the verbal and nonverbal messages.

Messages

A message in interpersonal communication is an expression of thoughts or feelings by the communicator. As DeVito (2019) notes, messages come in various types: metamessages (e.g., a coach winks to his or her team when jokingly evaluating a particular player after a big win), feedback messages (e.g., an athlete receives thousands of "likes" for a Facebook post), and feedforward messages (e.g., a fantasy football participant warns another person in the league to brace himself for some bad news regarding one of his players). In addition, messages sent as part of interpersonal communication in a sport organization can be grouped according to the following categories: upward (e.g., message sent from sportswriter to sports editor expressing frustration with workload), downward (e.g., message sent from athletics director to ticket manager regarding ticketing procedure), lateral (e.g., message sent by account representative to colleague in same position), and grapevine (e.g., message sent within the organization to a colleague regarding rumors about a front-office shake-up).

As Adler and Proctor (2017) explain, messages used as part of interpersonal communication generally have both content and relational dimensions. The content dimension contains the subject that the communicators are discussing. For example, the content dimension of a message in a ticket sales meeting might contain verbal suggestions by the ticket manager about how account representatives can improve their cold-

call techniques. A message's relational dimension, on the other hand, "expresses how you feel about the other person: whether you like or dislike the other person, feel in control or subordinate, feel comfortable or anxious, and so on" (p. 10).

Relational messages generally deal with social needs (e.g., affection, respect, control) and are usually communicated through nonverbal channels. Most relational messages fit into four categories:

1. Affinity—for example, a smile from the ticket manager revealing the degree to which she or he likes one of the salespeople
2. Immediacy—for example, a salesperson moves into close proximity and leans in when the ticket manager starts to talk
3. Respect—for example, a motivational talk that inspires a salesperson who holds the ticket manager in high esteem
4. Control—for example, the ticket manager reveals his or her influence over the salespeople, whether through a conversational (e.g., dominating conversation) or decision-making (i.e., determining what will happen) approach

Interpersonal messages can be verbal, nonverbal, or a combination of the two. Words, gestures, photos, videos, and emoticons (DeVito, 2017) are used when sport industry stakeholders engage in interpersonal communication. Whether the communication is conducted face to face, through a smartphone, on a tablet, or via a computer keyboard, as DeVito notes, "everything about you has the potential to send interpersonal messages, and every message has an effect, or outcome" (p. 9). For example, people often communicate interpersonally through their choice of clothing, such as league- or team-sponsored apparel, which, along with other sport merchandise, accounts for a considerable portion of the licensing segment of the sport industry.

Feedback

Feedback consists of information that we receive both from ourselves (e.g., hearing what we say, seeing what we write, feeling the way we move) and from others (e.g., hearing an affirmation, seeing a frown). Interactants, who play informally defined communication roles, have the ability to adapt messages to the specific needs of others. Legendary sport agent Ron Shapiro explains the importance of feedback—as well as preparation and practice—when selling and negotiating in the sport industry. "If a deal is big enough, I can't stress enough how impactful scripting can be," notes Shapiro (2015), who is the special advisor to Baltimore Ravens owner Steve Bisciotti. "Write down a script for your important meetings, run it by a devil's advocate, and fine-tune it based on that feedback. Include possible objections you might face and your response to questions you expect. Keep practicing until you're satisfied you can confidently deliver the message" (p. 14). Such an approach was taken by Cal Ripken Jr. when Shapiro helped the Hall of Famer secure a sizable corporate sponsorship package.

Channels

The medium through which the message is sent is referred to as a *channel*, which connects the source and the receiver (DeVito, 2017). Types of channels include vocal–auditory (carrying speech), visual (facilitating nonverbal communication, as in gestures), chemical (accommodating smell), and tactile (involving touch). Thus, interactants can use multiple sensory channels and can deliver and receive feedback immediately. In interpersonal communication, the various channels are typically used simultaneously (Hargie, 2011). For instance, when the vice president of sales gives a pep talk to her sales team, she speaks to them through the vocal–auditory channel, they see her excitement through the visual channel, they smell the crisp dollar bills laid out as an incentive through the chemical channel, and they slap high fives using the tactile channel.

Interpersonal communication channels, also referred to as *means of communication*, can be either unmediated (face to face) or mediated—that is, involving some type of medium (e.g., webcam, text-messaging system, online chat room) through which the communication is facilitated (Pavlik & McIntosh, 2019). Mediated interpersonal

Photo courtesy of Hallie S. Pedersen.

Fans in Paris watch the giant screen and celebrate together as France wins the FIFA World Cup. The temporary video board broadcasting the event and the raised cellphones videoing the celebration are examples of channels in sport communication—in this case, each is a visual medium facilitating mediated verbal (e.g., celebratory noises) and nonverbal (e.g., waves, smiles) communication.

communication—which is distinct from mass communication or mass-mediated communication—typically does not allow for complete interaction; instead, various aspects of interpersonal communication are often limited by the mediation because, for instance, visual cues are often missing when sport industry stakeholders interact using their smartphone to talk, text, or email each other. While there are limitations with various forms of mediated communication, such channels make "it possible for people to develop interpersonal relationships with others, whether they are miles away or in the next room" (Beebe, Beebe, & Redmond, 2020, p. 24).

Pavlik and McIntosh (2019) state that "the interplay between mediated interpersonal communication and mass communication" is changing as "interpersonal communication is capable of adopting some characteristics of mass communication, and mass communication is trying to adopt certain characteristics of interpersonal communication in an attempt to remain relevant to audiences" (p. 24). Email and social media were two of the examples they provide for this interplay. While they note that email is categorized as an example of mediated interpersonal communication, "it can also be broadcast to many recipients, following the one-to-many model typical of mass communication" (p. 24). They add that "Twitter also follows a blended mass-communication and mediated interpersonal-communication model, as people broadcast their tweets to thousands or even millions of followers, yet the followers can retweet and interact with each other and their followers in a way that more closely emulates mediated interpersonal communication than it does mass communication" (p. 25).

There are many communication channels used in the sport industry, as Chevonne Mansfield explains when she talks about her director of communications position that she had with the LEAD1 Association, which represents NCAA Division I FBS athletics directors. "I frequently liaised with the NCAA, conference commissioners, policymakers, and other LEAD1 stakeholders through various aspects of communication," notes Mansfield, who is now the deputy athletics director and senior woman administrator at Florida Memorial University. "Most of my communication was via email, but I also made good old-fashioned phone calls if I needed a quick response or if more insight/clarification was needed." Through such explanations, Mansfield is providing examples of unmediated (e.g., her face-to-face interactions with external stakeholders) and mediated (e.g., her emails, phone calls) interpersonal communication channels.

Noise

Interpersonal communication also involves message distortions and interferences, which are referred to as *noise*. The noise in the communication process can originate from various types of sources: physical, psychological, physiological (biological), and semantic. Physical interference occurs, for example, when crowd noise prevents sport administrators from hearing each other at a basketball game. One example of psychological noise would be a sport reporter accepting responsibilities grudgingly due to a personal bias or prejudice against an editor or producer. Examples of physiological or biological noise include illness and exhaustion. Last, semantic noise occurs when, for example, an employee fails to understand a message sent by a boss or when participants struggle to understand each other due to language differences; semantic noise is also more likely to occur when a message is very technical or uses complex terms. All these types of noise can occur in sport management and communication.

Context

The context in interpersonal communication involves the location of the communication and any relevant surroundings. The interactants in interpersonal sport communication are typically in close proximity to each other. Context can influence both the form and the content of interpersonal communication. Look, for instance, at how context affects the communication approach used by Joe Sargent, the director of brand marketing for the Kansas City Chiefs. When his NFL team is not playing, he notes that he communicates "primarily by email as it is the most efficient way to get information across." When schedules allow for an in-person meeting, Sargent states that he likes to take advantage of such an opportunity "because an in-person meeting is sometimes faster than email and encourages departments to work together and avoid silos within the organization."

He adds that "texting is the most effective form of communication on game days. Usually plans are set well ahead of game day, so texts are a good way to confirm plans or share changes as things change quickly." Thus, a brand activation activity at a football game influences the form and content of the communication in a different way than a front-office board meeting would. Interacting with a senior official is different than interacting with a young fan. The reason for these differences is the difference in context. The contexts in sport settings can range from official (e.g., formal dinners) to unofficial (e.g., casual golf outings). The three dimensions of context are the physical (e.g., the tangible environment), the social–psychological (e.g., status relationships between interactants), and the temporal (e.g., the time dimension or sequence of communication events). These three dimensions interact with and influence each other.

In addition to possessing a contextual element, the process of interpersonal sport communication involves a developmental (or continuous) element. This part of the interpersonal sport communication process is evident in every interaction between communicators in sport, and anyone in sport who communicates with another individual (dyadic communication) or a few individuals (triadic or small-group communication) is a participant in interpersonal communication. This continuous interpersonal communication is a part of the communication between any stakeholders in a sport organization or sport media outlet, either inside (intra) or outside (inter) the organization. The communication can be face to face, verbal, nonverbal, written, spoken, electronic, or handled through any other mediated or unmediated channel. For example, Sargent states, "I would estimate that 70% of my communication is written, whether that is through writing emails, compiling reports, or sending text messages." The sport industry executive adds, "I spend the rest of my communication time contributing in meetings or participating in impromptu conversations with internal counterparts." Overall, the developmental process of interpersonal communication occurs in the context of the communication culture of the sport organization and its personnel, their interactions, and their daily work.

NONVERBAL COMMUNICATION IN SPORT

Interactants communicate both verbally and nonverbally; generally, these two forms are used in combination with one another, but we separate them here for the purposes of inquiry. Let's first examine nonverbal communication, which is a component of emotional intelligence. Although often overlooked in the workplace, nonverbal communication is generally an expected, if not required, component of one's image or brand; it is also a key to functioning effectively and efficiently. "Nonverbal communication is a primary source of relationship cues," explain communication scholars Beebe, Beebe, and Redmond (2020). "A person's tone of voice, eye contact, facial expressions, posture, movement, general appearance, use of personal space, manipulation of the communication environment, and a host of other nonverbal clues reveal how that person feels about others" (p. 181).

In addition to "reading" nonverbal communication from others, one must also be able to use it to convey meaning to others. "Interpreting others' unspoken messages and appropriately expressing your own feelings through nonverbal communication are key components of being other-oriented," note Beebe and colleagues (2020). Sport industry professionals need to be able to express—as well as interpret—messages that are nonverbal in nature because "nonverbal communication is important in establishing interpersonal relationships" (p. 181). The need to be able to express and interpret nonverbals may be obvious in some cases—for instance, sport media personalities who work the sidelines and are expected to be expressive in their gestures and delivery. But it is just as important in the office of a sport organization. For example, showing an excited facial expression after hearing about the closing of a new luxury-suite deal can motivate your sales team. In addition, sport management and sport communication professionals are often required to use nonverbal communication to show that they are empathic, sympathetic, understanding, and sensitive. A ticket manager, for instance, expresses sensitivity by showing respect for a colleague's personal space in a crowded ticket office. The president of a sport team must be able to end a conversation with a disgruntled fan in a timely and positive manner, which often requires the use of effective nonverbal communication tactics.

Clearly, communication involves more than talking. In fact, psychology researcher Albert Mehrabian made estimates regarding the frequency and effect of nonverbal communication among individuals. As Beebe, Beebe, and Redmond (2020) note, Mehrabian found that 93 percent of a message is communicated through nonverbal channels (i.e., 55 percent of a message's effect involves facial expressions, and another 38 percent involves vocal inflections and other aspects of vocalics), while only 7 percent is communicated through the words themselves. Although the percentages may vary across studies and situations, it is clear that nonverbal communication is a significant part of interpersonal interaction.

Nonverbal communication is often used to practice what is called *impression management* and to project a desired personal and social identity. "The potency of the nonverbal aspects of interaction must be recognized by professionals, who should be sensitive to the kind of atmosphere they are creating, the scene they are setting, and the parameters they are placing on an interaction, often before they even begin to speak" (Hargie, 2011, p. 82). With this in mind, sport industry practitioners can greatly enhance their interactions with all stakeholders by recognizing, learning, and mastering the functions and elements of nonverbal communication.

Based on work by Hargie (2011)—and without getting into the semantics of the definition—we define *verbal communication* as the content (e.g., words, language) used in sport communication and *nonverbal communication* as all other aspects of communication. This view of nonverbal communication in sport encompasses the ways in which individuals in the sport industry communicate by using their body movements (e.g., posture, facial expression, physical appearance, gestures, movements), nonverbal aspects of speech (e.g., tone of voice, speed, volume, intonation), and **environmental factors** (e.g., noise, decorations, architecture, texture, furniture, color). This dimension of communication is not lost on Duke

University's Mike Krzyzewski: "People talk to you in different ways—through facial expressions, moods, mannerisms, body language, the tone of their voice, the look in their eyes," notes the legendary coach, who is 2019 became the all-time wins leader in college basketball. He adds that while it is a challenge, he believes it is necessary for him as a leader "to figure out what the members of my team are thinking, to determine who they are at one particular moment in time." He concludes by noting that "Sometimes, I may be wrong in my interpretation, but if I have built strong relationships and spent quite a bit of time observing and listening, I'll usually be pretty close to the truth" (Krzyzewski & Phillips, 2000, p. 107). Krzyzewski's approach to nonverbal communication as a crucial part of interpersonal relationships has helped him build a remarkable and impactful career.

Functions of Nonverbal Communication in Sport

Sport communicators and other industry professionals use nonverbal communication for a variety of reasons, ranging from the simple (e.g., to enhance verbal communication) to the complex (e.g., to express dominance). Hargie (2011) illustrates nine primary purposes for nonverbal communication, which can be applied to all sport communication: substituting, complementing, modifying, contradicting, regulating, expressing, negotiating, conveying, and contextualizing.

One of the main functions of nonverbal communication is to serve as a substitute for verbal communication. For example, communicators may use nonverbals (e.g., gestures) to replace words when they are unable to speak effectively (e.g., using hand signals due to crowd noise) or unwilling to do so (e.g., communicating secretly with a colleague about a possible trade or draft pick). Other examples include a racecourse bookmaker using the ticktack system of signaling and a baseball manager giving signals from the dugout or notifying umpires of a pitching change.

Nonverbal communication is also used often as a complement to verbal communication. Specifically, the verbal message can be enhanced or clarified through the use of nonverbal actions. When the message is hard to convey in words alone, the overlapping of gestures, illustrators, or other nonverbal movements can facilitate speech. For example, a sport executive might increase her effectiveness in a motivational speech by not simply reading the prepared speech but also using enthusiastic gestures and facial expressions.

Another key function of nonverbal communication is to modify a spoken message. This usage involves such actions as stressing certain words in a speech, pausing at crucial intervals in a conversation, and smiling while providing a stern warning to a subordinate.

Nonverbal communication can also contradict what is said, either intentionally or unintentionally. The contradiction between the verbal and nonverbal signals is often quite subtle—for example, when someone expresses sarcasm or has a dry sense of humor. In situations involving deception (i.e., lying), nonverbal cues can be quite revealing—for example, nervous sweating, conspicuous attempts to control one's performance (e.g., appearing wooden), or displays of emotion (e.g., anxiety, guilt). Even in acts of deception, however, Machiavellian individuals often master the ability to present consistent verbal and nonverbal signals.

Another common use of nonverbal communication is to regulate or manage a conversation. For example, to prevent talking over one another, individuals involved in interpersonal communication can use nonverbal cues to mark speech turns. Specifically, cues such as gestures, tone of voice (e.g., downward vocal inflexion), and eye contact can give interactants information about acceptable times to speak.

Another purpose of nonverbal communication is to express emotional states and attitudinal conditions. A professional basketball scout gives an example of this in evaluating potential players for an NBA team: "You've got to look at his body language. Ninety percent of that is nonverbal communication," notes the veteran scout. "Is he paying attention when he gets back to the huddle down by 15 points, listening to the coach? What is he doing when (the team is) down by 25 points or up by 25 points? What is his behavior? Those are the things right there" (Benbow, 2019, para. 16). Emotions expressed as nonverbal communication can be revealed in facial expressions (e.g., frowning, smiling, sneering), body movements, and gestures. Attitudes expressed as nonverbal communication

can be revealed in smiles, gazes, proximity, touching, and more heightened behaviors that reveal relationships. Both emotional and attitudinal nonverbal communication are frequently—and often unprofessionally and regretfully—expressed over social media. Sport industry professionals often receive social media training and are increasingly aware of the fallout that can happen from a hastily created and posted social media message, but hardly a week goes by when there is not a new example—from athletes to executives—of a post on a social media platform that goes viral and requires an apology or deletion (or both).

In addition to the verbal text of social media posts, individuals often use emoticons as a way to express emotions and attitudes nonverbally. "Emoticons have a mixed reputation in the workplace," notes Bradberry (2015). Some believe that such mediated symbolic representations of emotions "are unprofessional, undignified, and have no place outside of a high school hallway." However, he adds that with nonverbal communication conveying the vast majority of a message's meaning in our face-to-face interactions, "it's time to ditch the stigma attached to emoticons in the business setting" (para. 9). Although emoticons are still not always viewed as an acceptable form of nonverbal communication, they often provide a way for communicators in the sport industry to express emotions.

Nonverbal communication is also used to negotiate interpersonal relationships. This function may involve issues of dominance and control—for example, using a louder voice, interrupting, talking longer, or assuming a focal position (e.g., on a raised platform, behind a desk, at the head of a table, in an impressive chair). It can also be used to express affiliation and liking—for example, through immediacy, interpersonal distance, gaze, and posture.

The final two uses of nonverbal communication serve conveyance and contextual purposes. Nonverbal communication is often used to convey identification (e.g., personal identity, social identity). Individuals send messages about who they are and what group they belong to by their choice of attire and adornments, their accent, their office size and furnishings, and other identifiers. Nonverbal communication is also used often to contextualize interactions by creating a particu-

Photo courtesy of UVA Media Relations.

Interpersonal sport communication is on display in this interaction between an athletics director (Carla Williams, University of Virginia) and university stakeholders.

lar social setting in which people are expected to comply with certain codes of communication conduct. Examples of different settings include an informal watercooler gathering, a formal staff meeting, the funeral of a colleague, and an opulent dinner with an international contingent.

These nine purposes encompass the ways nonverbal communication is used in interpersonal sport communication. They can be applied independently or simultaneously, depending on the complexity of the communication and the situation. Overall, the ability to use and interpret nonverbal communication can assist sport industry personnel in their interpersonal interactions. Take, for instance, Josh Rawitch, the executive profiled at the end of the chapter. "You can often tell whether your message is sinking in with your audience by watching nonverbal cues," notes Rawitch. "This is often the case when I am presenting to our players (about social media, etc.) or in a staff meeting (if people are on their phones or are truly engaged in the conversation)."

Forms of Nonverbal Communication in Sport

There are several codes, or forms, of nonverbal communication. What follows are nine nonverbal forms of communication applied to sport from the work of Wood (2020) and Hargie (2011): **haptics**, **kinesics**, **proxemics**, physical characteristics, artifacts, environmental factors, vocalics, silence, and **chronemics**.

Haptics

The first form of nonverbal communication is haptics. This form involves physical touching, or the sense of touch, which can be used to comfort, calm, offer support, or nurture. Some of the possible beneficial outcomes of touching another person include positive evaluations and increased compliance with requests. Despite its benefits, however, touch is a rule-based behavior; that is, it can be used only at certain times, with certain people, and in certain places. Touching affects both context and relationships, as well as the power relations involved. For instance, in sport, handshakes and embraces are common in social or polite contexts. In a friendship or other warm context, behaviors of touch often include pats, soft touches on the hand, expressions of interest, positive feelings, encouragement, expressions of care, shows of concern, demonstrations of understanding, and provisions of support. In some cases, of course, touch can reveal negative feelings; it can also be used to manage interaction or gain control through symbolic, ritualistic, or accidental methods.

Kinesics

The second form of nonverbal communication—performed through body motion—is known as *kinesics*. This type of communication includes hand and arm gestures (e.g., pointing, scratching, rubbing), head movements (e.g., turning, nodding, dropping), facial expressions, and gaze (e.g., eye contact, gaze omission, gaze avoidance, and staring—all of which can be used to express personal information, regulate conversation, and monitor feedback). It also includes posture—for example, standing, sitting, relaxing, leaning forward, slumping, and showing rigidity, all of which can be used to reveal status, emotions, and interpersonal attitudes. In particular, communicators who supplement their words with gesture cues "usually arouse and maintain the attention of their listeners, indicate their interest and enthusiasm, and tend to make the interaction sequence a stimulating and enjoyable experience for all participants" (Hargie, 2011, p. 61). Gesture cues also help people more readily identify objects, recall stories, and increase comprehension.

Facial expressions allow people to reveal and recognize emotional states, such as sadness, anger, disgust, fear, surprise, happiness, contempt, shame, guilt, pride, embarrassment, and amusement. In fact, the human face can make more than a thousand expressions, which is why facial signaling is the most studied and debated nonverbal information source. The use of facial expressions is regulated by display rules addressing when it is acceptable to show certain expressions. Facial expressions are sometimes subject to emotional contagion in which a person's facial expression is adopted by another person—for example, an infectious smile. By the way, the smile is the most common form of human facial expression.

Proxemics

The third type of nonverbal communication is proxemics, which is constituted by our perceptions and the ways in which we use space in personal and social settings. Four categories of proxemics affect the interpersonal communication process: territoriality, distance, orientation, and interpersonal communication. The first category—territoriality—involves claims to certain spaces: primary territory (involving exclusivity by the occupier), secondary territory (held by habit rather than ownership), public territory (open to anyone), and interaction territory (temporary space where interactants are meeting).

The second category is distance, which involves both personal space and interpersonal distance. Personal space is the area that immediately surrounds and envelops us. The exact size of the space depends on one's personality (e.g., introverted, extroverted), situational variables, and the relationship between the interactants. Personal space violations disturb individuals and affect how they function in interpersonal relationships. Interpersonal distance is the distance that communicators keep from each other during an interaction; interactants can be as close as a handshake or as far as a noise heard in the distance. Interpersonal distance is affected by numerous factors, such as culture, gender, age, status, and communication topic. It affects the interactants' comfort levels, reflects the relationship, and regulates interaction. The four categories of physical closeness are as follows:

1. Intimate: touch to 18 inches (0.5 meter); for close friends and family
2. Casual–personal: 18 inches to 4 feet (1.2 meters); for informal interactions between friends and acquaintances
3. Visual–consultative: 4 to 12 feet (3.5 meters); for professional interaction
4. Public: 12 feet to the limits of sound and vision; for speeches and public addresses

The third category is orientation, which involves the angling of the body (e.g., directly facing, shoulder to shoulder, side by side). This angling can be used to reflect intimacy, inclusion, or exclusion; the position most conducive to communication is that of participants sitting at a 90-degree angle to each other. The fourth category—interpersonal communication—is affected by seating arrangements. More specifically, interaction can be encouraged through what are referred to as *sociopetal* layouts, in which seating is arranged to facilitate seeing and interacting with one another (e.g., a semicircle), and discouraged through *sociofugal* layouts, in which seating is arranged to afford some degree of privacy (e.g., a conventional classroom setup). Therefore, the seating arrangement depends on whether the speaker wants to facilitate interaction or take up a central position, which in turn affects the interpersonal communication process.

Physical Characteristics

The fourth form of nonverbal communication involves physical characteristics. Used by communicators to make judgments, they include height, dress, body shape and size, adornments (e.g., jewelry, false nails), and hair color and style. People form impressions of others based on how they look. "Before we even know what people sound like or what they have to say, we begin to form impressions based on physical appearance. At the centre of most of these will be evaluations of physical attractiveness" (Hargie, 2011, p. 74). Attire is important enough that *Fortune* magazine published a list of the best-dressed U.S. CEOs, one of whom was Kevin Plank of Under Armour. Similarly, in 2019, *Sports Illustrated* unveiled its fourth annual "Fashionable 50," which included names such as Serena Williams, Cam Newton, Megan Rapinoe, LeBron James, Ashlyn Harris, and Bryce Harper. Many athletes embrace the fashion world because, according to Steven Kolb (who leads the Council of Fashion Designers of America), their involvement "can be a statement, it can be a way to start a conversation or change a tradition" (Lisanti, 2019, para. 1).

Sport industry executives and many athletes recognize the value of a favorable image and therefore devote the necessary effort to being well dressed and carefully groomed before a media conference. They do so because they know they gain certain advantages through their ability to present themselves in an attractive and stylish light. When individuals are perceived as attractive, they are also viewed as possessing charisma, popularity, persuasiveness, and confidence. These nonverbal perceptions are important in professional settings because they can affect work relationships and evaluations. People make assumptions about other people, their occupations, and their status by looking at physical characteristics, such as body size (e.g., weight, shape), baldness, height, and dress. Professionals who dress impressively (e.g., dark suits, corporate attire) often increase their credibility and command respect and compliance from others.

Artifacts

A fifth form of nonverbal communication is artifacts—when a team prominently displays a piece of vintage memorabilia from a historic event or season. Such objects displayed by a sport organization (through the use of a particular sculpture, painting, photo, flag, banner, etc.) or by a sport industry stakeholder (through the use of a particular hairstyle, tattoo, attire, uniform, jewelry, hat, luggage, online avatar, social media image, etc.) are used to announce "identities and heritage and to personalize our environments" (Wood, 2020, p. 153).

Environmental Factors

The sixth type of nonverbal communication in sport involves environmental factors. Physical settings can shape interpersonal interactions either by enhancing them or by impeding them. Is the locker room open and inviting for players and for members of the media, or is it crowded and restrictive? Is the office layout at team headquarters dominated by partitions and privacy, or is it warm, expansive, and inviting? Impressions and judgments are often heavily influenced by the organization of both the fixed environmental elements (e.g., architecture, size, shape, material) and the semifixed elements (i.e., movable or modifiable materials). Office-space arrangements communicate information about status, authority, position, and personality; the same is true of the presence (or absence) of openness, elevation, barriers, and separation from others by means of a desk or administrative assistant (gatekeeper). Typically, a sport organization's space includes more than one arrangement, thus allowing for a variety of options (e.g., an enclosed private room where a confidential discussion can be held, an open break area where casual conversations can take place) from which to choose, depending on the interpersonal interaction needed.

Vocalics

The seventh form of nonverbal communication is vocalics. When you interview for a sport industry position, you'll use various inflections in your vocal delivery to influence the prospective employer by sounding enthusiastic and confident. Even when a sport industry leader doesn't use words or language, his or her nonverbal communication can still include some aspects of speech. Such nonverbal communication is what Wood (2020) refers to as *paralanguage*. For instance, paralanguage or vocalics is involved in the way that an executive pronounces words, uses complex sentences, talks with an accent, talks quietly when providing inside information, or indicates by tone of voice that she is being sarcastic or derisive. Thus, paralinguistics addresses the components of speaking related to tone of voice, talking speed, speech volume, intonation, articulation, pitch, quality of voice, rhythm, rate, sighs, and fillers (e.g., *uh, er*). Vocalics also involves changing the meaning of words through vocal variations (prosody) and variations in accent (extralinguistics).

People often make judgments about a speaker and message based in part on vocalics; specifically, they form impressions about age, gender, personality, occupation, temperament, and emotional state (e.g., someone who is angry may talk fast). People also make decisions about messages based on vocalics—for example, an excited delivery, a monotone reading, or clues about how certain content should be received (e.g., with humor or seriousness). Indeed, as Hargie (2011) notes, the way in which "information is delivered paralinguistically has important consequences for how much of the message is understood, received, and acted on" (p. 81).

Silence

The eighth form of nonverbal communication is silence. This form can be used to "communicate different meanings" (e.g., intimacy, awkwardness, respect, thoughtfulness) as well as to "communicate powerful messages" (Wood, 2020, p. 158). For example, a sport industry executive might speak volumes by using silence to convey frustration or might ignore a certain text message to convey irritation. A powerful message is communicated through the use of silence in both instances. Furthermore, silence can be used to set the tone or get a meeting back on track, such as when a sport sales executive does not say anything at the beginning of—or takes long pauses during—her speech to make sure everyone in sales is listening and on the same page regarding a certain issue.

Chronemics

The ninth form of nonverbal communication is chronemics, which involves how individuals perceive and use time. For example, one standard practice in sport (and in most other industries in the United States) is for subordinates to be punctual; the expectation is that they will be on time to meetings, assignments, and sporting events. At the same time, although showing up on time is a sign of respect, it is often accepted that those who hold a high rank or status can keep others waiting. Doing so conveys the message that the leader's time is more valuable than the subordinates' time. Chronemics also involves how much time people spend with one another, and such decisions can reveal interpersonal priorities in daily interactions. For example, what does it say when an athletics director spends more time with wealthy boosters than with everyday folks who are "just" season-ticket holders?

Overall, the forms of nonverbal communication just described—haptics, kinesics, proxemics, physical characteristics, artifacts, environmental factors, vocalics, silence, and chronemics—illustrate both the complexity and importance of the nonverbal messages that individuals send and receive.

VERBAL COMMUNICATION IN SPORT

We also interact with others through verbal messages. Although we may not often think about it, language is symbolic. This is because, according to Adler and Proctor (2017), "words and the ideas or things to which they refer" are only arbitrarily connected. The communication scholars add that the symbolic nature of language enables human beings "to communicate in ways that wouldn't otherwise be possible about ideas, reasons, the past, the future, and things not present. Without symbolic language, none of this would be possible" (p. 179).

Functions of Language

In sport, as in life, language is used for countless purposes—for example, talking with sport organization colleagues about a new marketing scheme, detailing the advantages and disadvantages of a potential player trade, telling the event production staff about the script for that evening's game, or generating a strategic plan for a minor league hockey franchise. This virtually infinite variety can be categorized into eight distinct functions (Trenholm & Jensen, 2013), all of which apply to sport settings:

1. To break the silence and conquer the unknown (e.g., talking just to make noise when in a quiet or dark setting)

2. To vent and control emotions (e.g., shouting at a game, cursing in a meeting)

3. To express or conceal true motives and thoughts (e.g., purposefully, accidently, or unknowingly revealing or camouflaging inner feelings)

4. To either engage in or avoid contact with another person (e.g., connecting with others by just talking, talking compulsively, or using exclusionary language to hold others off)

5. To express either individuality or identification with a group (e.g., creating a personal image through language, using jargon to fit in with others, using impression management or personal brand management)

6. To facilitate the exchange of information (e.g., using language to seek or provide information)

7. To influence, control, or persuade—or to *be* influenced, controlled, or persuaded (e.g., using language to impress or "brainwash" others, having one's perceptions influenced by language)

8. To engage in **metacommunication** (i.e., communicating about and monitoring the communication process)

Levels of Meaning

To analyze and understand language and its structure, scholars typically look at three levels of meaning (Trenholm & Jensen, 2013): word, sentence, and **speech act**.

First Level: Word

In our examination of language in sport, the first level (or unit) of meaning is the word, and this type of study is known as *semantics*. Word meanings can be either denotative or connotative. Denotation is the generally accepted meaning of a word, whereas

In the sport industry, language can be used for a variety of functions, such as to vent emotions, express thoughts, engage in conflict, persuade others, etc.

Photo courtesy of Paul M. Pedersen.

connotation involves a subjective dimension by which an individual gives his or her own meaning to a word. Similarly, words can also be viewed as carrying both content meaning and relationship meaning. Whereas content meaning is the explicit or literal meaning, relationship meaning is "what communication expresses about relationships between communicators" (Wood, 2020, p. 25).

Along these lines, the term *networking* carries a unique meaning in the sport industry. The denotative (i.e., content, or literal) meaning of the term is, according to sport management professor Warren Whisenant, "the development and maintenance of formal and informal relationships with individuals both internal and external to one's own organization." The University of Miami (UM) scholar elaborates on that meaning as follows: "Effective networks—which require strong social and political interpersonal skills—allow individuals to become well informed; sustain levels of loyalty among colleagues; leverage cross-functional alliances to assist the individual and his or her workgroup in securing the necessary resources to be successful; and provide access to those who may have the power to influence an individual's job, career, and even social relationships" (personal communication).

Connotative (or relationship) meanings of networking, on the other hand, range from a simple greeting to aggressive pursuit and follow-up activities conducted by job seekers and professional decision makers. For instance, sport management students are constantly told to network to learn, make contacts, and obtain a competitive edge. What this means to individual students, however, can vary greatly. To some students, it means going beyond traditional networking activities by engaging in virtual networking. Those who engage in this practice use the web to develop relationships, exchange information, and sustain contact with sport management and communication professionals.

In any given instance of communication, regardless of whether communicators in the sport industry are networking or simply performing their job duties, they must have semantic competence to communicate effectively, feel that they are a vital part of their group or organization, and avoid arguments over connotations and semantic differences.

Second Level: Sentence

The second unit of meaning is the sentence—that is, words grouped together—and the study of this level of meaning is referred to as *syntactics*. Words must be combined in an orderly fashion for message recipients to make sense of a phrase or sentence. Therefore, syntactic competence (or lack thereof) affects the judgments passed and the impressions made by one's communication. Indeed, grammatical mistakes and violations of accepted rules of sentence construction have kept many otherwise qualified candidates from securing a desired position in sport or advancing within the industry.

Third Level: Speech Act

The third level of meaning is the speech act—the use of words and sentences in interactions—and the study of this level is referred to as *pragmatics*. As Trenholm and Jensen (2013) note, "Having a good vocabulary and knowing the rules of sentence construction will not guarantee adequate communication. We have to know how to use sentences in actual conversation" (p. 87). To be competent, a communicator "must be able to choose the best way to express him- or herself in order to achieve what he or she wants to achieve" (p. 91). Of course, what one wants to achieve with words and sentences can vary greatly—for instance, to criticize, promise, warn, question, compliment, threaten, or simply request.

With so many possible meanings, we must make a point to clearly communicate our intentions and accurately perceive the intentions of others. Interpersonal interaction in sport requires pragmatic competence. "Communication is a cognitively complex, rule-bound process," explain Trenholm and Jensen (2013, p. 92), who add that mastering the pragmatics of communication will result in rewarding and easy relationships. "If we have trouble with pragmatics, however, the world can be a hostile place. In fact, it's been argued that many interpersonal problems result from differences in pragmatics" (p. 92). Therefore, for those wishing to enter and succeed in the sport industry, the ability to read, write, and speak effectively is a basic requirement.

EFFECTIVE INTERPERSONAL SPORT COMMUNICATION: SKILL DEVELOPMENT

Learning about interpersonal communication in sport would not be complete without learning what it takes to be effective in interpersonal interactions. Success in interpersonal communication involves many variables, some of which are out of your control, and some of the most successful people in sport have many detractors. Because you cannot please everyone, some of your effectiveness in interpersonal communication simply does not lie within your power to determine. Furthermore, certain characteristics produce effective interpersonal interactions in some cases yet at other times produce ineffective interactions. For example, speaking candidly and openly might be judged with favor when the team owner specifically asks for it, but doing so on a regular basis will most likely cause problems. Therefore, sport communicators need to be able to judge and decide when it is appropriate to use each particular interpersonal skill. "Because no single set of skills composes interpersonal communication competence, we need to learn a range of communicative abilities" (Wood, 2020, p. 37).

Although there is no definitive approach to effectiveness, effective communicators in the sport industry often exhibit certain general skills. Therefore, by developing and refining these skills, a sport communication professional can increase his or her odds of success in the field. The following paragraphs apply to the various interpersonal communication skills necessary in the sport industry, as covered by scholars such as Beebe, Beebe, and Redmond (2020); DeVito (2017, 2019); Hargie (2011); Trenholm and Jensen (2013); and Wood (2020). Your competence in—and mastery of—these skills will go a long way toward determining your success in the sport industry. "From the initial interview at a college job fair to interning, to participating in and then leading meetings, your skills at interpersonal communication will largely determine your success," notes communication scholar Joseph DeVito (2019, p. 2). He adds, "The importance of interpersonal communication skills extends over the entire spectrum of professions. Clearly, interpersonal skills are vital to both personal and professional success" (p. 2).

The interpersonal communication skills covered here can help you at any stage of your career, whether you are educating yourself about the field (e.g., interacting with your peers and professor in a sport communication class), exploring sport industry options (e.g., interning with a sport network), beginning your sport industry career (e.g., working as an entry-level employee), advancing and maturing in your career (e.g., being promoted from assistant to associate athletics director), or leading employees as a sport industry executive or entrepreneur. The skills covered here also share certain characteristics: They involve actions that are under your control and learned behaviors that you can improve through repetition and outside input; they are interrelated and integrate verbal and nonverbal interactions; they are best used to serve a purpose or goal in a way that is situationally or contextually appropriate; and, when executed properly, they involve no awkwardness (Hargie, 2011).

As noted earlier, communicating effectively in interpersonal relationships requires you to possess a wide variety of general skills. Although the following paragraphs cover 14 essential interpersonal communication skills, the list is not exhaustive; mastering these skills, however, will help you maximize your own interpersonal abilities. Scholars have compiled various and somewhat differing lists of interpersonal communication skills, but the differences often involve semantics, and many of the skills are interrelated. Therefore, although some skills identified by other scholars may not be listed here, you will most likely find those skills, or features of them, integrated in the general categories we examine. For instance, in our examination of the skill of exhibiting equality in your interpersonal communication, we include listening as an aspect of this skill, whereas some scholars refer to listening as a skill of its own. However, whether you view equality and listening as two different skills or view one as a subset of the other, they are both important areas of competence for sport industry professionals.

Our list of 14 essential skills includes many of the key interpersonal communication skills that should be developed by anyone looking to enter or advance a career in the sport industry. The skills covered here are as follows: mindfulness, flexibility, sensitivity, self-disclosure, empathy, supportiveness, positiveness, equality, immediacy, **interaction management**, expressiveness, **other-orientedness**, assertiveness, and metacommunication.

Building skills in interpersonal communication requires "becoming aware of what's going on when you communicate, and beginning to recognize how the underlying processes involved in communication manifest themselves in everyday performance. Too often people communicate in a mindless way" (Trenholm & Jensen, 2013, p. 18). In other words, the first skill you should develop is mindfulness, or attentiveness, which "is a state of awareness; in a mindful state, you're conscious of the reasons for thinking or communicating in a particular way" (DeVito, 2019, p. 14). As a future sport industry professional, you should learn to be cognizant of your communication situation and your options in it. Only then can you develop the ability to shape the climate through effective communication techniques.

Knowing your communication situation and options is a key, but being able to communicate effectively after possessing that knowledge is just as important. Thus, flexibility is another critical skill for effective interpersonal communication in sport. This is the ability to vary your responses according to the stakeholders and situation involved. Because of the uniqueness of the sport industry, successful professionals in this field exhibit adaptability in their interpersonal communication activities.

The sport industry is a diverse area in which you must be sensitive in your interactions with others. Thus, sensitivity is another interpersonal communication skill that should be embraced and refined by those working in sport communication and sport management. In all interactions, "competent communicators must be sensitive to the context, to their own self-presentations, and to the target's needs and vulnerabilities" (Trenholm & Jensen, 2013, p. 223). Being aware of differences, and accommodating them, is vital to your success in the sport industry. In addition, in the increasingly global sporting environment, you must use sensitivity to various cultures: "Success in interpersonal communication—at your job and in your social and personal life—depends in great part on your understanding of, and your ability to communicate effectively with, persons who are culturally different from yourself" (DeVito, 2019, p. 35). DeVito adds, "Without cultural sensitivity, there can be no effective interpersonal communication between people who are different in gender or race or nationality or affectional orientation. So be mindful of the cultural differences between yourself and the other person" (p. 37). Sensitivity to diversity involves awareness and accommodation not only of differences related to cultures and individuals but also of differences involving communication choices and relationships.

Effective interpersonal communicators in sport are also skilled at providing appropriate self-disclosure. Appropriate openness must be embraced by sport communication professionals, especially those in leadership positions. After trust has been established, they must be willing to disclose information about themselves, such as their fears and feelings, and to listen to disclosures made by others. Once a disclosure has been made to them, they must be willing and able to respond honestly and spontaneously. Such openness also requires accepting responsibility for one's own feelings and thoughts.

The ability to express empathy is another skill that increases your effectiveness in interpersonal communication in sport. Empathy is the ability to sense or experience what another person is feeling or experiencing. For example, an executive empathizes with an employee when he puts himself in the place of a subordinate who just lost a relative and, to a certain degree, feels what the employee is feeling. Empathy differs from sympathy, which involves feeling *for* a person; empathy, on the other hand, involves feeling the feelings that the other is experiencing. As Wood (2020) notes, "empathic communication confirms the worth of others and our concern for them." Wood offers the following examples: "'It's an entirely reasonable way to feel in your situation,' and 'Wow, it must have really stung when your supervisor said that to you'" (p. 242). Wood adds that it is especially important to communicate that we value others as people when we don't agree with them.

Empathic (also referred to as *empathetic*) communication allows us to understand at an emotional and intellectual level what another person is experiencing. Effective communicators must be able to both experience empathy and communicate this understanding. Empathetic communicative expressions reveal concern for others and their worth as individuals; such is not the case with expressions of detachment and neutrality. "Neutral communication is often interpreted as a lack of regard and caring for others. Consequently, it does not feel validating to most of us" (Wood, 2020, p. 241). For example, a chief executive of a sport organization engages in neutral or detached communication if she appears distant or withdrawn from her subordinates.

Another key skill in effective interpersonal communication in sport is supportiveness. Working relationships require acknowledgement, acceptance, and confirmation of others. To be supportive, we can describe rather than evaluate or judge; those with whom we communicate tend to feel less threatened when they hear a request or a description rather than a judgmental statement or evaluation. Supportive interactions lead to a supportive communication culture; in contrast, people immediately erect barriers when they experience nonsupportive communication. For example, using a critical, evaluative, judgmental approach when communicating with a young sales associate will not be as effective as using a supportive and descriptive approach that instructs in a nonthreatening way. In this way, supportive communication can help people improve their skills. Another part of being supportive in communication is to be provisional rather than fixed in our views. This means being open-minded in our approach to situations, open to others' points of view, and willing to change our own positions when given good reason to do so. Once we understand that we do not know everything or always have the answer, we can develop a supportive approach to communication.

Supportiveness and reinforcement are interrelated with the ability to express positiveness. Having a positive attitude involves being uplifting and encouraging in our communication and interaction with others. More concretely, positiveness involves "positive attitudes and the use of positive messages expressing these attitudes (as in complimenting others), along with acceptance and approval" (DeVito, 2017, p. 267). Positive attitudes often come from those who are optimistic and confident, and the ability to express these

attributes is a key to effective interpersonal communication. Uplifting others involves acknowledging your satisfaction with them, as well as their inherent importance and significance; you are not merely indifferent to their existence and contributions. Uplifting others can be done either verbally (e.g., a word of encouragement) or nonverbally (e.g., a smile or hug). It can also be delivered through social media, as explained in the sidebar entitled "Expressing Emotions in Social Media Through Interpersonal Interactions."

Exhibiting equality is another key skill that you can develop to increase your interpersonal communication effectiveness in the sport industry. This quality is the opposite of superiority, which takes a condescending and patronizing approach to interactions. Equality, in contrast, is the ability to be accepting and approving. "Communication that conveys equality fosters a confirming communication climate. We feel more relaxed and comfortable with people who treat us as equals . . . expressed equality communicates respect and equivalent status" (Wood, 2020, p. 242-243). Of course, there is usually some inequality in job positions; that is, some people hold higher positions and make more money than others. Even so, the work atmosphere can still be one of equality in which everyone is viewed as a key contributor and a valuable and worthwhile member. Establishing this sense of equality takes work because it must permeate all listening and speaking.

Effective listening is the key to developing your skill in exhibiting equality in your interpersonal communication. According to Adler and Proctor (2017), listening "easily qualifies as the most important kind of communication" if we are measuring communication in terms of frequency. These communication scholars add that human beings "spend more time listening to others than in any other type of communication. . . . Besides being the most frequent form of communication, listening is at least as important as speaking in terms of making relationships work" (p. 244). Therefore, listening is one of the best skills to hone to facilitate both effective interpersonal communication and career advancement. As Adler and Proctor illustrate, the process of listening includes the elements of hearing, attending, understanding, responding, and remembering. Hearing is the element of

Expressing Emotions in Social Media Through Interpersonal Interactions

While social media platforms are often used for negative behavior (e.g., bullying, trolling), sport industry stakeholders (e.g., employees, sponsors, athletes, fans) can use social media in a positive way to uplift, encourage, and connect with one another at an interpersonal level. Such positiveness is seen, for example, when a fan likes a sportswriter's Instagram photo of a team's mascot or an athlete retweets a colleague's encouraging post. Such compliments on social media function as "a kind of interpersonal glue," notes DeVito (2017, p. 187). Engagement in such activities, as DeVito explains, can allow people to relate in positive and immediate ways with one another. He adds that when people interact on social media (e.g., by tagging people in a photo, by reposting and retweeting a message), they are reminding others that they are thinking of them by engaging in complimentary behaviors. The uplifting and encouraging interpersonal interactions on social media often involve emojis. While the standard positive social media icons are still effective for conveying positive feelings (e.g., a smiley face), new emojis are frequently released by various social media platforms and technology companies (e.g., Apple and Google each rolled out over 50 new emojis in 2019). Similarly, social media platforms and sport organizations and leagues create and unveil specific emojis and hashtag-triggered emojis for special occasions (e.g., Australian Open, NBA All-Star Game). Using the new emojis allows sport industry stakeholders to express their emotions in more detail in their interpersonal interactions on social media.

listening that involves the physiological (i.e., sound waves striking the ear), whereas attending is the element that involves the psychological (i.e., what one chooses to attend to). Of the remaining elements, understanding involves making sense of what is heard, responding involves providing visible and verbal feedback, and remembering means the ability and desire to recall what was heard.

Without effective listening, one cannot manifest equality in interpersonal communication; in other words, to improve one's communication, one must reduce ineffective listening. Adler and Proctor (2017) detail types of ineffective listening, which include pseudo-listening (giving the appearance of listening), stage hogging (turning conversation to oneself), selective listening (responding only to content of particular interest), insulated listening (ignoring or avoiding a topic), defensive listening (taking comments personally), ambushing (listening only to collect information for an attack), and insensitive listening (taking comments at face value without understanding hidden meanings or nonverbal cues). A viewer of the Fox Sports 1 show *Skip and Shannon: Undis-*

puted may perceive aspects of ineffective listening when the hosts, Skip Bayless and Shannon Sharpe, get into a heated debate.

Effective interpersonal communication also requires the ability to establish immediacy, which brings the speaker and receiver together through an expression of interest. In other words, the communicator shows a liking of or attraction to the topic being discussed, and this immediacy joins the interactants. It can be achieved by staying physically close (i.e., maintaining an effective interpersonal distance), using the name of the person with whom you are interacting, providing relevant feedback, reinforcing, rewarding, complimenting, and being attentive to the other person's remarks.

Another skill to develop for effective interpersonal communication in sport is interaction management, or competence in controlling an interaction. This skill takes work because it involves making sure that one's communication partner does not feel ignored. Interaction management includes maintaining roles (both speaking and listening), keeping the conversation flowing, and helping interactants feel that they are valued as contributors. Effective interaction management involves self-monitoring skills.

Expressiveness is another skill that can improve your effectiveness in interpersonal communication. Similar to openness, it conveys a sense of involvement—that you are active rather than passive in the process. Being appropriately expressive in interpersonal communication requires you to provide honest and direct feedback, encourage others to be expressive and open, state disagreements directly, and accept responsibility. Therefore, it involves the ability to respond in a nondefensive and constructive way when others offer criticism. Positive ways to embrace constructive criticism include seriously contemplating the validity of the criticism and requesting more information for clarity.

Another key skill is the ability to focus on others, which is sometimes referred to as *other-orientedness*. This skill involves watching, listening, and talking in a way that is not self-focused. "The more you focus on the other person, the more accurately you're likely to understand this person and the more effectively you'll be able to adapt your own messages to them," notes DeVito (2019). The renowned communication scholar adds that, "Other-orientation involves communicating attentiveness to and interest in the other person and in what the person says" (p. 68). Techniques for doing so include eye contact, facial expressions, and other cues (both verbal and nonverbal) that communicate an interest in what the other person says.

You should also develop assertiveness, which can be a challenging skill to master because to be effective requires striking a delicate balance; the goal is to come across as assertive without seeming aggressive. Closely associated with assertiveness is confidence, both in yourself and in those with whom you interact. For example, Josh Rawitch, the senior baseball executive profiled at the end of this chapter, discusses the importance of assertiveness in his work: "This job requires that your communication skills build others' confidence in you. You are an advisor to people who are extremely successful [e.g., Tony La Russa, Joe Torre, Randy Johnson, Derrick Hall, Paul Goldschmidt], and they can tell if you are confident in what you are saying or if you are in over your head. It takes time to build that confidence and to get past the fact that at times, you may be advising someone that you grew up idolizing, but it's a very important part of this role" (personal communication).

For interpersonal communication in sport to be effective, the communicators must express social confidence. This is done through being relaxed, flexible, controlled, and comfortable with other individuals and situations. Although you may often feel some apprehension and shyness, these variables should not be allowed to interfere with your communication. Taking deep breaths, imagining successful interactions, and thoroughly preparing your argument are all ways in which you can combat apprehension and shyness. Along with confidence comes the ability to assert oneself through honest, respectful, and direct communication. Assertive communication is simply stating one's feelings, needs, or wants with clarity and without judgment.

The final critical skill for effective interpersonal communication is metacommunication, which involves proficiency in conveying and understanding messages by communicating about the communication. "Your interpersonal effectiveness will often hinge on your competence in metacommunication" (DeVito, 2017, p. 9). DeVito describes instances of metacommunication, such as communicating about how someone argues during times of conflict, raises his or her voice during confrontations, delegates assignments, or expresses criticism. For example, an assistant general manager who is criticized by his or her general manager in front of the office staff could use metacommunication skills to talk with his or her boss about such public communication.

Overall, success in the sport industry often follows those who have developed the interpersonal communication skills just examined. You can study more about this topic by reading general interpersonal communication books or specific textbooks in this area, such as Dariela Rodriguez's (2016) *Sport Communication: An Interpersonal Approach*. Through your reading and application of the knowledge gained, you can develop, refine, and master your interpersonal communication skills to advance your career in the sport industry.

EXECUTIVE EFFECTIVENESS: INTEGRATING AND NAVIGATING PERSONAL COMMUNICATION IN SPORT

Josh Rawitch
Senior vice president of content and communications
Arizona Diamondbacks (Major League Baseball)

Over the course of his distinguished career, Josh Rawitch, senior vice president of content and communications for the Arizona Diamondbacks of Major League Baseball (MLB), has fulfilled the words of his mother, who told him when he was a teenager that if he could write, he could do anything. "I have absolutely found that to be true," states Rawitch, "but would amend it slightly to say, 'If you can communicate well, you can do anything.' It is easily the most important part of my job—being able to speak publicly, in meetings, with high-profile athletes and executives, and so on. And it's a challenge because each of these types of communication can require a different approach."

Given that communication is the most important part of Rawitch's job, it should come as no surprise that it occupies the majority of his work schedule. He estimates that he spends nearly 75 percent of his time engaged in some type of communication. The following list provides a few examples of his communicative activities:

- Pitching a story to a media outlet (in person or by email or phone)
- Serving as team spokesperson in an interview in both English and Spanish
- Making a baseball presentation to hundreds of students in Hermosillo, Mexico
- Lecturing three dozen students in his strategic sport communication class at Arizona State University

- Writing or proofreading any of the 200-plus news releases that his team produces each year
- Participating in internal meetings
- Brainstorming creative video content or working to perfect a caption on a tweet or Instagram or Facebook post
- Responding to more than 100 emails per day

Rawitch, whose excellence in MLB public relations was recognized in 2018 when he won the

Photo courtesy of the Arizona Diamondbacks.

Josh Rawitch, second from left, is the senior vice president of content and communications for the Arizona Diamondbacks (Major League Baseball). Here, Rawitch, Mike Hazen (general manager of the Diamondbacks), and NBC reporter Jeff Schneider share a laugh with star pitcher Zack Greinke.

Robert O. Fishel Award, is responsible for the internal and external communication efforts of the Diamondbacks. Such efforts include player and media relations, broadcasting, corporate communication, social media, creative services, photography, publications, in-game entertainment, and multimedia production.

In his leadership position with this MLB franchise, Rawitch oversees a staff of more than two dozen individuals who facilitate the club's communication endeavors. Those activities can be grouped broadly into two categories:

1. Internal communication (e.g., player relations, daily front-office briefing, photography, corporate communication)
2. External communication (e.g., media relations, social media, fan feedback, publications)

Despite the division into internal and external communication, the two are often intertwined in actual practice. For example, a media relations activity might involve a player who is an internal stakeholder being interviewed by a reporter who is an external stakeholder. In both internal and external communication, Rawitch has excelled in his sport management career largely due to his personal communication skills (i.e., intrapersonal communication, interpersonal communication, and small-group communication) across various platforms and with all types of individuals, including more than 300 colleagues in the team's front office.

As the club's senior communication executive, Rawitch communicates with a wide range of stakeholders, including external audiences (e.g., television network executives, international celebrities, sport reporters), internal audiences (e.g., club president Derrick Hall, general manager Mike Hazen), the leadership team (made up of vice presidents from around the company), staffers in his own department, other colleagues, players, college interns, and so on. "In my role, the most important internal groups to communicate with would be our staff and my bosses (the president and chief executive officer and the executive VP of business operations)," notes Rawitch. "The media is our biggest external stakeholder, and there isn't a day that goes by in the last 20 years where I haven't had a conversation of some sort with a media member. Usually it's via email or telephone, but I've also pitched stories (successfully and not) via social media."

Over his years with the Diamondbacks, the team—which has been recognized with the Copper Anvil Award for its public relations work—has garnered local, national, and international attention, with features on programs ranging from *The Today Show* and FOX News to *Good Morning America* and *CBS This Morning*. Increasingly, Rawitch finds that his department's success can be measured by the reach of the team's message on social media.

Rawitch has worked in the sport industry for more than 25 years. His background—beyond his undergraduate degree in sport marketing and management—includes 15 years with the Los Angeles Dodgers, where he advanced to the position of vice president of communications. He also worked for MLB Advanced Media, where he was part of a groundbreaking project that transformed MLB's official website (www.MLB.com) from an independent operation into a fully integrated and highly profitable league venture.

Throughout his career, Rawitch has engaged in countless interactions with groups and individuals. In addition to his intrapersonal communication (e.g., inner speech), he is frequently involved in one-on-one communication, both mediated and unmediated, such as hallway or on-field chats, email and social media interactions, phone conversations, and other forms of interaction. "I'm probably most proficient in email and would say that a lot of my communication is done in that fashion, but there's also truth in the idea that nothing beats an old-school, face-to-face conversation, so I try to do that whenever it's an important topic. Social media has certainly become another valuable way for me to communicate—usually with media members as opposed to co-workers, although occasionally I will reply to a player who has tweeted."

Beyond the individual encounters, Rawitch also engages in interpersonal interactions in small-group settings. As Rawitch notes, "My weekly staff meetings are one example where I need to make sure that everyone hears what I have to say while also providing opportunities for them to share their own thoughts or topics. The same goes for our weekly business operations meeting and weekly leadership meetings with those at the VP level and above. In terms of a little larger group, each year, I put together a presentation for the major

(continued)

(continued)

league team and another for our minor league players where I go over the benefits and pitfalls of social media and try to help them understand the best ways to utilize that medium as a means of communicating with fans. It has to be humorous (to keep their attention) but direct (to make sure they understand the severity of a misstep)."

Any effective professional who works in sport must possess strong interpersonal and communication skills to work with colleagues, fans, corporate partners, athletes, supervisors, and a host of other individuals in the industry. Rawitch is one such communicator, and he appreciates the doors that this skill has opened for him: "The game of baseball has given me endless opportunities, for which I'm extremely grateful and humbled, and almost all of them have come from my ability to communicate."

CHAPTER WRAP-UP

Summary

The first component of the Strategic Sport Communication Model (SSCM) includes personal and organizational communication in sport. This chapter focuses on the first segment of this component: personal communication in sport. All individuals who work in the sport industry should seek to master the key skills of personal communication because most instances of communication in sport are of the personal variety. That is, they are conducted with oneself (intrapersonal communication), another individual (interpersonal communication), or a few interactants (small-group communication).

We define *interpersonal sport communication* as occurring whenever individuals in sport, sharing the roles of sender and receiver, create meaning through unmediated (i.e., face-to-face) or mediated (e.g., online) personal interactions. This type of communication frequently involves face-to-face and mediated encounters between sport professionals, such as advisors, sales managers, media relations professionals, interns, employees, fans, readers, viewers, and any other sport industry stakeholders.

After analyzing the reasons for which people engage in interpersonal communication, the chapter examines the process of interpersonal sport communication, including the major elements of source, receiver, message, feedback, channel, noise, and context. The chapter next covers the topic of nonverbal communication in sport, including analyses of communicative body movements, nonverbal aspects of speech, and environmental factors. It also addresses the purposes and forms of nonverbal communication in sport. Next, the chapter details verbal communication in sport by examining the functions of language and the levels of meaning in the use of language in sport-related settings. The chapter concludes by discussing how to develop competence in 14 interpersonal communication skills and apply those skills to the interpersonal communication that occurs in sport settings.

The individuals who wield influence in the sport industry are often the ones who can integrate and master the various interpersonal communication skills covered in this chapter. Such individuals "are generally the people with whom you find it interesting and comfortable to talk. They seem to know what to say and how and when to say it," notes DeVito (2019). He adds that their competency in this area was most likely developed "by observing others, by explicit instruction, and by trial and error." Overall, competence includes "knowledge that, in certain contexts and with certain listeners, one topic is appropriate and another isn't" and "knowledge about the rules of nonverbal behavior—for example, the appropriateness of touching, vocal volume, and physical closeness." Overall, DeVito explains that "interpersonal competence includes knowing how to adjust your communication according to the context of the interaction, the person with whom you're interacting, and a host of other factors" (p. 6) examined in the previous pages. Regardless of where you find yourself in your career preparation, remember that success in the sport industry often depends on your overall competence in this area—and that you can enhance this competence by developing and refining your specific interpersonal communication skills.

Review Questions

1. Beyond intrapersonal communication, what form of communication is used most often in sport? What is the definition of that form of communication?

2. What are the differences between mediated and unmediated interpersonal communication in sport? As part of your answer, provide an example of each.

3. What are the characteristics of small-group communication in sport? Why is it included in the discussion of interpersonal sport communication?

4. What are the essential elements in the process of interpersonal sport communication? How do they relate to each other?

5. What skills or qualities are necessary for effective interpersonal sport communication?

Individual Exercises

1. Suppose that you have just accepted an entry-level position in the sales department of a professional sport franchise. With this position in mind, rank the key skills of interpersonal sport communication from 1 to 14 in order of importance. Then explain why you believe the top two are the skills you should most focus on to be an effective salesperson. What behaviors should you use in demonstrating these two qualities?

2. Select a sport-related article about a topic that has been in the news over the past month. The topic should involve an aspect of either mediated or unmediated interpersonal communication, and the article can come from an online or print publication (e.g., local newspaper, ESPN.com, *Sports Business Journal*). While reading the story, think about the elements of the interpersonal communication process. After you finish the story, write down the source, receiver, message, feedback, channel, noise, and context involved. Share the story and your findings with the class.

Photo courtesy of Paul M. Pedersen.

CHAPTER 6

Organizational and Leadership Communication in Sport

LEARNING OBJECTIVES

- To learn about the components and features of sport organizations that both influence and are influenced by communication
- To consider formal, informal, and cultural communication in sport organizations
- To recognize the various forms of organizational sport communication
- To understand sport leadership and the importance of effective communication as a leader
- To become aware of leadership communication styles and the variables that affect them in sport organizations

KEY TERMS

autocratic communication style
change-oriented communication
consultative communication style
interorganizational sport communication
interpersonal-oriented communication
intraorganizational sport communication

laissez-faire communication style
organizational communication in sport
participative communication style
situational supervisory style
sport leadership communication style
task-oriented communication

SUCCESSFUL SPORT LEADERSHIP, COMMUNICATION, AND ORGANIZATION

Joe Sargent

Effective communication is vital for the success of any sport organization, and successful **organizational communication in sport** depends in part on effective leadership. "I think the best leaders promote communication and accountability, and that is what I try to represent as a leader," says Joe Sargent, who over the past decade has exemplified leadership as he advanced from assistant and associate brand manager titles to brand manager (e.g., Beam Suntory, Wilson Sporting Goods) and then to his current role as director of brand marketing with the Kansas City Chiefs, who in 2020 won the Super Bowl. Within this sport organization, Sargent works across departments to align all activities under the Chiefs' brand umbrella. He is primarily responsible for stewarding all aspects of the team's brand, including the look and feel across all forms of media, event activation, game day themes, and merchandise. He is also in charge of segmenting the team's fans by their behaviors and psychographic profiles and creating unique communication strategies to reach them in the most efficient way.

In his leadership position, Sargent owns the relationship with the Chiefs' media and merchandising partners and works with them on the most effective presentation of the team's brand. He also works with various departments (e.g., content, ticket sales, sponsorship, community) to align activation efforts, culminating with game days. "In doing all of this," notes Sargent, "I support the organization's broader goals of driving revenue, elevating the Hunt Family (team ownership) legacy, engaging with fans, and developing

Joe Sargent, director of brand marketing for the Kansas City Chiefs, the 2020 Super Bowl champions of the National Football League (NFL).

Photo courtesy of Joe Sargent.

my staff." As a director, most of his days are spent aligning with other departments on campaign activation efforts affiliated with game days, season-ticket member events, training camp, hall of fame inductions, youth-focused gatherings, and so on. "Ensuring that all of our departments are in lockstep behind an overarching theme that supports the Chiefs brand is the most important aspect of my job," states Sargent, a Cornell University alum who also has two graduate degrees (including one in sport management).

Sargent's activities within the sport organization illustrate the communication types detailed in this chapter. Take, for instance, his participation in directional communication. His upward communication involves formal requests (e.g., a new creative design, a new game day activation element) that require approval from the organization's ownership or executive team. Sargent states that because the designs, logos, and activations all affect "how the Chiefs brand is perceived by large swaths of fans, we need buy-in from the ownership and executives to move forward. We also want to make sure they feel involved with the process, and so I will share plans in progress or options with my recommendation based on what I believe best expresses our brand for the target audience." In contrast, his downward communication often involves "in-person meetings with my staff to share direction from above that impacts their responsibilities. In these cases, I'll often need a deliverable, and I'll outline that to my staff with any context and direction," which can be seen through his leadership regarding the creation of a line of merchandise to celebrate the team's 60th season in 2019. "I shared the key asks from leadership with my creative lead to guide the direction of the designs," notes Sargent. "That team created designs with my input and direction, and I shared the final designs with ownership to get final approval. There was much more communication downward as we went through rounds of development. I communicated upward as needed to keep ownership aware of the process and to make sure that their direction and priorities didn't change." Sargent's views of organizational communication and leadership are highlighted throughout the following pages. His comments and experiences illustrate the thrust of this chapter, which is to show the importance of communication in sport organizations and the role that leaders play in facilitating an effective communication culture.

Effective organizational communication is a prerequisite for success regardless of whether the sport entity is a local youth soccer team or a highly visible football club such as Bayern Munich. "Whether it is between two teammates on a sports team or two managers in a corporate office, communication is vital to success," observes Alan Bass (2018, para. 1), a writer whose work has been published in *Hockey News*, *Inside Hockey*, and *HockeyBuzz*. Bass also stresses that "communication is crucial between all members, regardless of what role each person plays" (para. 1). This is true both for individuals (from leaders to front-line employees) and for the various levels of the sport organization; in other words, individuals in the sport industry interact with one another through both personal communication and organizational communication.

As discussed in chapter 5, personal communication in sport involves intrapersonal, interpersonal, and small-group forms of communication. The emphasis here in chapter 6 shifts to organizational communication, whose formats and aspects are intertwined with those of personal communication (remember, communication is both situational and personal). The intertwining of the personal and the organizational is revealed in the work of Lussier (2019), who refers to organizational communication as "the compounded interpersonal communication process across an organization" (p. 102). Therefore, chapter 5 (personal) and chapter 6 (organizational) are distinct from each other yet still so tightly connected that when combined they make up the first component of the Strategic Sport Communication Model (SSCM).

Our definition of *communication in* and *with sport organizations* is a slightly modified version of the definition of organizational communication offered by Modaff, Butler, and DeWine (2017). In this view, organizational communication in sport is the process in which messages are created, exchanged, interpreted, and stored within a system of human relationships in sport. As sport management scholars Jeremy Jordan, Aubrey Kent, and Matt Walker (2015) note, "communication is critical for coordination. Without effective communication, people in the organization would not know what to do or what others were doing" (p. 68). Although both casual observers and scholars often pay more attention to aspects of sport communication related to social media and mass media, the importance of organizational communication cannot be overstated. "Without communication, there is no team, groups or organization itself," notes Saxtorff (2018) in his discussion of the importance of building organizations in the rising esports segment of the sport industry. As the chapter you are reading covers both organizational and leadership communication in sport, it is particularly relevant that Saxtorff adds that "the most important factor you can act upon as a leader is to further the communication within an organization" (para. 22).

Organizational communication in sport includes both **interorganizational sport communication** (between organizations) and **intraorganizational sport communication** (within an organization) elements. This chapter introduces both kinds of elements in their theoretical, conceptual, and practical aspects. It also defines both terms (*interorganizational* and *intraorganizational*), illustrates their unique aspects, and examines their elements and functions. After reading this chapter, you will be familiar with the activities,

Organizational Communication in Sport

While the various aspects of organizational communication in sport do not receive as much attention as social media and mass media, scholars research organizational communication in sport by focusing on a mediated aspect (e.g., social media, new media, mass media). The textbook *Sport Communication Case Studies* (Pedersen, 2020) contains case studies placed in categories that align with the components of the Strategic Sport Communication Model (SSCM). In the organizational communication in sport section, all seven of the sport organization case studies are focused on social media, new media, or mass media topics. For instance, case studies focusing on social media within an organizational context include the following: Marion Hambrick and Per Svensson's case on how a nonprofit sport organization (Gainline Africa) engaged in relationship building through the use of social media; Glynn McGehee, Armin Marquez, Beth Cianfrone, and Tim Kellison's case on the dissemination of social media messages regarding a redeveloped stadium (Georgia State University); and Brody Ruihley, Jason Simmons, Andy Billings, and Rich Calabrese's case examining organizational crisis communication by focusing on the social media messages that the organization (ESPN) and the consumers posted regarding the failure of a fantasy sport product. Regarding new media and organizational communication in sport, Dichter's case examines a university website (MGoBlue.com) and the adoption and usage of a content-management system by the athletics department (University of Michigan), and Jimmy Sanderson's case analyzes three incidents in which information and communication technologies helped sport organizations monitor professional athletes. Lastly, two case studies in the section focus on mass media and organizational communication in sport: Laura Richardson Walton and Kevin Williams' case of how an organization (World Wrestling Entertainment) engaged in crisis communication by using the mass media as well as press releases and Richard Southall and Mark Nagel's case examining the broadcasts of women's basketball games and how the mediated production represent the affiliated educational institutions and the National Collegiate Athletic Association (NCAA). Thus, while there are many aspects of organizational communication in sport, mediated (e.g., social, new, mass) communication receives the majority of the attention by sport management scholars.

components, and workings of communication in sport organizations; ultimately, similar to the work by Modaff and colleagues (2017), this study will help you become aware of and appreciate how embedded and influential communication is in all aspects of each organization within the sport industry.

ORGANIZATIONAL SPORT COMMUNICATION

The importance of communication to organizational success has been noted for decades. Communication scholar Pam Shockley-Zalabak (2016), who as senior advisor sits on the board of directors of the United States Olympic Museum, has noted that general communication research has linked organizational communication to effectiveness (e.g., effective leaders, supervisors, organizations), innovation, job satisfaction, creativity, integration of organizational aspects (e.g., units, levels), and organizational performance. The same benefits can be found in the sport industry in particular, where effective organizational communication is a prerequisite for a successful sport organization and, more specifically, for productive and satisfied employees.

This section of the chapter examines the definitions and elements of *organizational sport communication*. The discussion uses an organizational-behavior approach—that is, examining the collective behavior of groups and individuals in a sport organization—to analyze the organization, management, and production of the collective communication performed by individuals and groups in sport organizations. As part of this discussion, we explain how organizational structure, culture, and climate affect the formality and complexity of communication.

The framework for this chapter is provided through theories of organizational communication. These perspectives include the mechanistic approach (focused on transmission of messages through channels), the psychological approach (focused on interpretation of messages by receivers), the interpretive–symbolic approach (focused on how shared meaning both shapes and is shaped by organizational communication), and the systems–interactive approach (focused on how communication sequence patterns predict organizational outcomes). These organizational communication theories (which are not themselves analyzed here) provide the conceptual foundation for any discussion of communication in sport organizations.

Definition of Sport Organization

A *sport organization* is a group of individuals working in or through sport to accomplish a certain objective (or objectives). This definition, which is a modified version of Lussier's (2019) definition of an organization, encompasses local high school athletics departments, multinational sport management firms (e.g., IMG), and everything in between. When a group of stakeholders (e.g., publicists, employees, volunteers, marketers, advertisers, lawyers) work together toward a sport-related purpose, goal, or objective, they are part of a sport organization. The organization could be a nonprofit enterprise or a for-profit business, and its status as a sport organization is not affected by its size or its focus (e.g., goods, services).

Just as there are various organizational designs in traditional business organizations (e.g., simple structure, bureaucracy, matrix structure, virtual structure, team structure, circular structure [Robbins & Judge, 2019]), sport organizations exist in a variety of forms. For instance, in knowledge-based or learning organizations, knowledge is shared throughout the sport organization. Another form involves cross-functional teams, where work is accomplished across the sport organization's departments. Yet another form, which is increasingly being used in the sport industry, is the virtual or network organization; in this organizational form, the major business functions are outsourced to allow for a focus on core competencies. Numerous sport entities also exist in the form of an e-organization in which the entity uses the Internet, intranets, and extranets to handle sales (i.e., e-commerce), connect with suppliers (i.e., business to business [B2B]), and run a business (i.e., e-business).

Another form often used in the sport industry is the membership organization. Consider, for instance, the Professional Association of Athlete Development Specialists (PAADS). This nonprofit membership organization—which has individual memberships as well as organizational memberships such as global partners (e.g., National Rugby League), educational partners (e.g., University of Florida's MS in sport management with a PAADS certificate), institutional partners (e.g., U.S. Anti-Doping Agency), and associate partners (e.g., New Orleans Pelicans)—advises sport organizations on how best to develop, mentor, and train athletes.

Yet another form is the boundaryless organization, which combines outsourcing, participative decision making, cross-functional teams, and computers networked between the organization and its suppliers and customers. A boundaryless sport organization exists on the opposite end of the spectrum from what many would view as a traditional, bureaucratic, and structured sport organization. As Robbins and Judge (2019) illustrate it, on one end of this spectrum lies the mechanistic organizational design model which is "generally synonymous with the bureaucracy in that it has highly standardized processes for work, high formalization, and more managerial hierarchy"; on the other end lies the organic organizational design model (which resembles a boundaryless sport organization), which is "flat, has fewer formal procedures for making decisions, has multiple decision makers, and favors flexible practices" (p. 526). Their detailed examples of the differences between the mechanistic model (e.g., high specialization, rigid departmentalization, clear chain of command, narrow spans of control, centralization, high formalization) and the organic model (e.g., cross-functional and cross-hierarchical teams, free flow of information, wide spans of control, decentralization, low formalization) can be applied to the various organizational designs of today's divergent sport organizations.

Regardless of its form or design, an organization can exist only if its foundation includes three major elements (Barnard, 1938): cooperation, common purpose, and communication. First put forward nearly eight decades ago, these elements still apply to all organizations today, and we apply them here to sport organizations. The first essential element is that the organization's members must be willing to contribute and cooperate. Some individualism and dissension will arise from time to time, but, as a whole, a sport organization cannot exist without a certain level of cooperation and contribution from its members. Take, for instance, the Toronto Raptors, whose 2019 NBA championship was celebrated by the rapper Drake and millions of fans during a parade after the team defeated the Golden State Warriors. This sport organization cannot exist without contributions from, and cooperation between, its various units—ranging from the personnel, finance, marketing, ticket, and arena operations to the corporate partnerships, human resources, hospitality solutions, information technology, and media relations departments.

The second essential element of a sport organization is that it pursues a common purpose or objective that focuses the efforts of its members. Purposes and objectives vary widely in the sport industry. Some focus more on the bottom line or on winning, whereas others focus on other objectives—for example, an NCAA Division III athletics department. The mission statement of the athletics program at the Pratt Institute in Brooklyn, New York, explains that "Pratt Athletics instills habits that will lead students to better, healthier and successful lives" ("Athletics," 2020, para. 2). The values outlined within the statement include "the pursuit of excellence through personal development and teamwork; ethical and responsible behavior on the field and off; adherence to the spirit of rules as well as to their letter; leadership and strength of character; sportsmanship, respect for one's opponents, acceptance of victory with humility, acknowledgment of defeat with grace, respect for the value of cross-cultural understanding and acceptance" (para. 2). Thus, this athletics program seeks to cultivate students and future leaders by providing them with competitive athletic opportunities in an academic environment. The department's employees are most likely aware

of—and committed to—the common athletics purpose and focused on working to provide such an environment.

The third essential element of an organization is communication, which is necessary for the organization's survival. Without it, the purpose of the organization could never be communicated, and there could be no interaction between the organization's members. It has even been argued that this element—communication—makes an organization what it is. Indeed, many scholars have suggested "that organizations are essentially complex communication processes that create and change events" (Shockley-Zalabak, 2016, p. 5). Regardless of the degree to which communication "makes" the organization, "there is broad agreement about the centrality of organizational communication and that organizational communication plays a significant part in contributing to or detracting from organizational excellence" (p. 5). Thus, even for those who do not consider communication to be synonymous with the organization itself, communication is one of the three essential and intertwined elements of a sport organization.

Communication in and Between Organizations

Organizational communication in sport includes both communication *in* a sport organization and communication *between* a sport organization and another organization. The *communication in* aspect is referred to as *intraorganizational sport communication*—that is, communication with internal publics. Communicating internally involves exchanging information within the sport organization. As Deborah Barrett (2014) notes, "organizations exemplifying internal communication best practices have an open flow of communication with communication considered everyone's responsibility." Barrett adds that "effective communication has become even more essential and intertwined with the organization itself" (p. 316). In other words, communication is a competency that must be embraced and developed to deal effectively with organizational stakeholders.

Consider, for instance, the following insights provided by Joe Sargent, the world champion NFL executive profiled at the beginning of this chapter:

"Depending on the project in which I am involved, some of the internal stakeholders with whom I communicate the most are the team's ownership, executive team, and cross-department heads." Sargent explains that when he communicates upward to leadership or executive team members, he usually does so "via email as directly as possible. I understand these individuals have very limited time given the scope of their responsibilities, so I want to provide appropriate context and answer questions in as pointed a way as possible." He adds that when he communicates across the organization with other department heads, "I tend toward email or in-person meetings because we are usually working together to build a campaign or presentation, so I spend more time with them to make sure we're on the same page before sharing our plans, presentation, and information more broadly" (personal communication).

In these descriptions, of course, Sargent is discussing his organization's intraorganizational communication. As shown in figure 6.1, organizational sport communication (consisting of intraorganizational and interorganizational communication) is the second segment of the first component of the Strategic Sport Communication Model.

The *communication between* aspect of organizational communication is referred to as *interorganizational communication*—that is, communication with external publics (i.e., between organizations in the sport environment [e.g., B2B communication]). When an individual in a sport organization interacts with someone outside of the organization (e.g., nonaffiliated blogger, media member, sales client, prospective sponsor), she is communicating with an external public. "While there are key external stakeholders for most brands, Gatorade is a bit unique in the range of critical folks" with whom the company looks to engage, noted former Gatorade executive Lauren Burns, who was featured in the second edition of this textbook. When she was still with Gatorade, she listed among the company's critical audiences "those within the sports media space; the science influencer as well as the athletics influencer space; food and beverage and consumer packaged goods (CPG) top media mavens; and business, trade, and industry reporters" (personal communication).

Whether a baseball bat salesperson interacts with a college baseball representative or the agent of a prospective bat client, the communication is interorganizational because it involves two

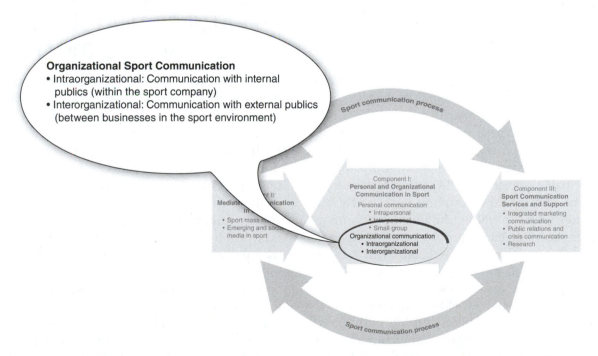

Figure 6.1   Organizational sport communication is the second segment of the first component of the Strategic Sport Communication Model.

Photo courtesy of Paul M. Pedersen.

Within the Indianapolis Motor Speedway (IMS) administrative building, there is both intraorganizational (e.g., between IMS staff members) and interorganizational (e.g., between staffers and media members requesting credentials for the Indy 500) communication.

organizations (i.e., bat company and either athletics department or sport agent firm). For sport teams who belong to the same league, the distinctions between internal and external communication can sometimes be challenging to navigate. For instance, when Kelly Krauskopf was the president and general manager of the Indiana Fever, she noted that "There is a real sense of togetherness among the WNBA teams." When Krauskopf, who in 2019 became the first female assistant general manager in the National Basketball Association (NBA), was interviewed in the first edition of this textbook and talked about her work with the WNBA, she added that teams in the league "often communicate ways to help each other with our business growth, but when it comes to players or any part of the game that involves the competitive aspects on the floor, we often keep that to ourselves—like true competitors" (personal communication). In addition, communication between organizations often results in career opportunities and upward mobility for individuals who choose to interact with others outside of their own organization.

THREE ORGANIZATIONAL FEATURES THAT AFFECT COMMUNICATION

Just as effective communication is the predominant factor in a team's success (Kaser & Oelkers, 2016), it is also crucial to the success of a sport organization. This fact is well recognized by Bob Williams, senior vice president of communications for the National Collegiate Athletic Association (NCAA), who leads a communication staff of more than 50 professionals ("Chat," 2015). "Communicating to a variety of key stakeholders is critical to the NCAA's success," said Williams, who arrived at the NCAA after an extensive career in leadership communication in the armed forces and is a McLendon Minority Athletics Administrators Hall of Fame inductee. One of his top goals is to communicate about "the NCAA's goals and priorities with student-athletes and their families, the membership, and the public" (Barrett, 2005, para. 3). Communication is vital to the success of a sport organization regardless of whether we view organization in sport as a process (of organizing by a group of individuals in sport) or as an entity (i.e., the result of organizing efforts). "Communicating and organizing are two sides of the same coin," explained Pepper (1995). "The process of communicating is the act of organizing, and efforts to organize are communication bound" (p. 7). In other words, a sport organization is created, developed, and maintained through the communicative actions of its stakeholders.

The forms that make up organizational structure involve transactions at the individual, dyadic, small-group, intergroup, and technological levels. Therefore, as noted earlier, communication in a sport organization occurs in both the interpersonal and the contextual dimensions. Interpersonal dimensions are examined in chapter 5, whereas here in chapter 6 we focus on the fact that communicators use their skills in a certain context or setting—the sport organization. The skills needed for effective organizational communication in sport derive from awareness of the relationships found in sport organizations and knowledge of how to communicate within these relationships. This knowledge is essential to sustained organizational success because, as sport management scholar David Scott (2014) notes, "Leaders whose organization produces extraordinary results are still not likely to be effective in the long term unless they attend to the demand for high-quality and trusting relationships" (p. 34). Thus, to succeed over the long haul, communicators—and leaders, in particular—need to be effective in their relationship building and interactions within the organization.

The vital importance of communication to organizations has been described in detail by Modaff and colleagues (2017). Just as the creation and sustaining of a sport organization are accomplished through communication, it is also "the prime coordinating mechanism for activity designed to attain personal and organizational goals. Hence, communication and organization are intimately interrelated." They add that, "Communication is central to the existence of the organization; it creates and re-creates the structure that constitutes the organization. That structure, in turn, affects the nature and flow of communication within it" (p. 2). Thus, communication is integral to the creation (and re-creation)

of the structure that makes a sport organization. However, although communication creates that structure, what is created then has an effect on the communication activities within that structure. Therefore, a sport organization both shapes and is shaped by the communication activities of its stakeholders. In particular, as illustrated in figure 6.2, communication flow influences, and is influenced by, three features of a sport organization: its formal structure, its informal networks, and its culture. Overall, the work of Lussier (2019) and Kelly, Lederman, and Phillips (1989) provides the basis for our analysis of organizational influence.

Formal Structure in Sport Organizations

The structure of an organization is often viewed as essentially physical (e.g., building, walls, hallways, desks) or conceptual (e.g., charts, titles, positions, levels, bureaucracies). In reality, however, organizational structure goes beyond both physical and conceptual aspects to include "working relationships, experiences and interpretations, and power relationships" (Pepper, 1995, p. 10). These factors bear consideration as we discuss how organizational communication is shaped by formal, informal, and cultural influences. The formal structure of a sport organization refers to the design or arrangement of its divisions, departments, and units; in applying the work of Bovee and Thill (2018) to the sport industry, a formal communication network within the sport entity reflects this formal organizational structure. The relationships between the various organizational titles and positions define the sport organization's formal communication network as the messages within the sport organization flow from lower-level to higher-level employees (i.e., upward organizational communication), from higher-level to lower-level employees (i.e., downward organizational communication), and from employees holding similar positions or levels in the sport organization (i.e., horizontal organizational communication).

With these considerations in mind, a sport manager works to design her organization's structure in a way that best achieves the organization's goals and objectives. The design of a sport organization's structure is revealed, developed,

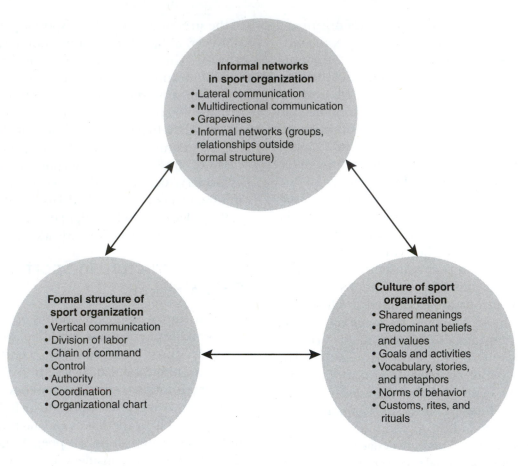

Figure 6.2   Features that influence—and are influenced by—communication activities in and between sport organizations.

and accomplished through an understanding of the five organizational principles (Lussier, 2019): division of labor and departmentalization, chain of command, span of control, authority, and coordination. First, the sport manager must understand the organization's division of labor and departmentalization. This aspect involves how the work (i.e., tasks) of the sport organization is subdivided (i.e., jobs) and how related activities are grouped into units (e.g., marketing, ticketing, sales personnel).

Second, the sport manager must understand the chain of command. An organizational chart illustrates an organization's formal structure and line of authority from top to bottom. The chart is not static because "just as people change jobs (through hirings, firings, promotions, etc.), an organization often revises job duties and responsibilities (and sometimes job titles) to capitalize on the strengths of its employees. This ultimately results in changes to the entity's orga-

nizational chart" (Wong, 2013, p. 357). Despite its sometimes-changing nature, an organizational chart represents the organization's reporting structures (i.e., the people to whom departments and individuals should report) and overall chain of command. "Generally, you should follow the line of hierarchy in your department," notes Chevonne Mansfield, the senior woman administrator (SWA) in intercollegiate athletics who is profiled in chapter 4. "That is very important, and every place I've worked at emphasizes the proper chain of command" (personal communication).

Third, the sport manager must understand the span of control (span of management). This factor involves the number of individuals and departments that report to each manager within the sport organization. Fourth, the manager needs to be aware of the centralization or decentralization of authority in the organization. If top leaders make the important decisions, then the sport organization uses centralized authority. If middle and front-line managers make decisions where the action occurs, then the authority is decentralized.

Fifth, the sport manager needs to be aware of the specific roles and coordination of work in the organization. This aspect involves getting employees and departments to work together. Although decentralization encourages greater participation among employees, it also adds to the difficulty of coordination. Whether or not the entity is decentralized, for effective management there must be effective and efficient coordination of job duties, hierarchy of positions, relationships between members, and other components of the formal structure of the sport organization. As Lussier (2019) notes, coordination involves "implementing the other four principles to achieve organizational mission and goals" (p. 101).

Decentralization Versus Centralization

The formal structure found in sport organizations has evolved over the years. The changes have resulted from efforts to create a healthier bottom line (e.g., downsizing) while increasing the satisfaction and production of an organization's members (e.g., encouraging more communication and input through decentralization). Thus, sport organizations have increasingly moved from hierarchical structures to more decentralized or flat structures. In "tall" (hierarchical, traditional) formal structures, communication (e.g., instructions) has to go through multiple levels as opposed to the fewer reporting levels of flat formal structures. With that said, whether the sport organization is tall or flat, an acknowledgment of "the central role of communication in the production and reproduction of organizational structures is also an acknowledgement that misunderstandings will occur as well" (Modaff et al., 2017, p. 9).

Communication challenges will arise in any structure. For instance, in a flatter structure with fewer reporting levels, the span of management is wider because sport managers have more individuals and departments reporting to them. As a result, they must now direct—and communicate with—more people. Abe Madkour (2015), who in 2019 was named the publisher of *Sports Business Journal*, once interviewed John McDonough, the president and CEO of the Chicago Blackhawks. "I try to make sure that I stay in touch with everybody," noted McDonough. "I want to make sure

everybody has a voice. I don't like the cascading effect that all the ideas come from the top. I love a lot of organic decisions. I want to make sure that everybody in the organization has a pulse. They know they matter" (p. 20). The increase in communication and complexity consumes considerably more time for sport managers, but it also allows individuals to have more input and power in the decision-making process.

This participative decision making is reflected in the changing climate of sport organizations from more authoritarian to more empowerment oriented (e.g., managers act less like authoritarians and more like coaches). These changes are discussed later in this chapter in the analysis of sport leadership in organizations. Overall, communication in many sport organizations has been changed by decentralization as managers have moved from a more top-down (centralized) approach to a more multidirectional (and often more complicated) approach.

Chain of Command

Communication in a sport organization generally follows the reporting structures illustrated in the organizational chart. For instance, if a corporate account manager for FC Cincinnati (one of the most recent expansion teams, with its inaugural Major League Soccer [MLS] season in 2019) faces an ethical dilemma, she is not likely to seek clarification directly from the team's general manager or the senior vice president of sales and marketing. Rather, she will probably run the scenario by her immediate supervisor (e.g., director of ticket sales) or one of her ticket sales colleagues. This chain-of-command type of communication—that is, following the organizational chart—is not always used but is the generally accepted process for communication in sport organizations. The formal organizational structure in a sport organization generally influences the way in which employees proceed in their communication within the organization.

As Lussier (2019) notes, the direction in which formal communication flows in an organizational chart is categorized as vertical. This formal communication (or intraorganizational communication) is the official communication of the organization because it flows upward and downward according to the organization's chain of command. Downward communication in sport organizations occurs when subordinates receive communication (e.g., job instructions, results of decisions, procedural information, feedback, job rationales, indoctrination efforts) from those who hold superior positions. For example, downward communication is used when an assistant ticket manager receives instructions about her job or an evaluation from her ticket manager or another individual higher in the chain of command. Sport organization leaders use this type of communication throughout the day; sometimes it is effective and in other cases has unforeseen effects. This is old news to Josh Rawitch, the Arizona Diamondbacks communication executive profiled in chapter 5: "I'm far from perfect at communication as I can still say the wrong thing sometimes or say the right thing in the wrong way and it will have unintended consequences" (personal communication).

Upward communication in sport organizations occurs when subordinates send messages up the organizational chart—for example, information about a subordinate, communication about a policy, or questions or comments about work. Upward communication occurs in sport organizations when an employee makes a suggestion, airs dissatisfaction, seeks information, attempts to impress a superior, or does any number of other actions meant to communicate with someone higher in the chain of command. Sport leaders should value and encourage this type of communication because it provides them with information they can use in decision making and helps them understand how their followers are doing and to what degree they understand their roles, duties, and activities.

Upward communication can be hindered in various ways, such as when subordinates hide thoughts and feelings, view superiors as uncaring or inaccessible, offer misleading information just to please superiors or to make themselves look better, or use information to subvert the position of the superior (Pepper, 1995). Communication between superiors and subordinates is affected by several major factors: trust, a subordinate's desire to move up, a superior's upward influence, openness, overloaded or underloaded channels (e.g., too much information coming to superiors, not enough information coming to subordinates),

gender, power dynamics (e.g., unequal relationships), and message clarity (e.g., gaps between the message sender's intention and the receiver's understanding).

Top-level sport managers can increase the flow of upward communication by remaining cognizant of the factors that affect communication and taking steps to reduce the barriers noted here. They can do so by implementing an open-door policy, facilitating employee meetings, conducting attitude surveys, and initiating suggestion systems. Former ESPN president George Bodenheimer sought to exhibit availability and visibility by making it "easy for people to talk" to him: "I met with anybody who ever asked to see me" (Bodenheimer & Phillips, 2015, p. 154).

Suggestions for Formal Communication

Sport managers can communicate more effectively, both within the organization and between organizations, if they respect the formal structures of the organizations involved (Kelly et al., 1989). To do so, they can begin by obtaining a prepared organization chart that shows the formal chains of command and lines of communication. They can then follow the proper channels (i.e., formal lines) of communication in the organization. Bypassing such channels often results in alienation and anger, so it is best to stay within the formal lines of communication until the informal lines are understood.

Informal Structure in Sport Organizations

In addition to the communication that occurs through an organization's formal channels, some communication is done informally or unofficially. This type of communication can take the form of lateral communication, multidirectional communication, grapevines, and informal networks. "Some of this informal communication takes place naturally as a result of employee interaction on the job and in social settings, and some of it takes place when the formal network doesn't provide information that employees want. In fact, the inherent limitations of formal communication networks helped spur the growth of social media in the business environment" (Bovee & Thill, 2018, p. 9). Thus, in addition to the use of social media for business purposes, organizational stakeholders today often find themselves interacting with each other via social networking sites. The majority of this communication can be categorized as grapevine or informal network communication.

Lateral Communication

Horizontal (lateral) communication occurs when information flows between individuals at the same level (Lussier, 2019). In a sport organization, for example, this type of communication might involve messages between peers, such as two assistant sports information directors or two managers. Lateral communication often involves informal interactions and typically does not constitute formal or official communication in the sport organization because it does not follow the chain of command. Even so, it is essential for coordinating tasks, solving problems, sharing information, resolving conflicts, establishing support systems, and facilitating cooperation both by individuals and by departments.

Multidirectional Communication

As its name indicates, multidirectional communication involves communication in a variety of directions. Consider, for instance, a new sport marketing initiative. Downward communication would involve supervisors communicating the initiative's goals to the sales staff. Horizontal communication would involve salespeople communicating with each other in to reach goals. At the conclusion of the campaign, upward communication would involve salespeople communicating the success (or failure) of their efforts to supervisors and upper management. As this example illustrates, an organization's members sometimes need to use the multidirectional approach to share information, efficiently coordinate activities, solve problems, and resolve conflicts. "Issues are bound to arise with your boss, co-workers, subordinates, and people outside the organization," notes Adler and Proctor (2017). "Your career success and peace of mind will depend on when and how you deal with those conflicts—and when you choose to keep quiet. Deciding when to speak up is the first step in managing conflicts successfully. Staying silent about important issues can damage your career and leave you feeling like a doormat. But

asserting yourself too often or in the wrong way can earn you a reputation as a whiner or hothead" (p. 386). Whether dealing with conflicts, sharing information, or coordinating tasks, individuals in the sport industry must thoughtfully determine when it is appropriate to use the multidirectional approach and then follow through as needed with superiors, subordinates, and colleagues.

Grapevines

Grapevine communication, which is the unofficial and informal method of moving messages in all directions throughout a sport organization, is an often-overlooked avenue of sport communication. Unofficial information, including rumors, is often passed through text messages, emails, and social networking sites. Social media postings and interactions play an important role in grapevine communication both in and beyond the sport organization itself. "With the rise in usage of social media, the grapevine is now more powerful and faster and . . . [possesses] greater reach" (Potter, 2013). "Using Twitter and Facebook, among others, employees often discuss ostensibly taboo subjects with much wider audiences than just co-workers" (para. 4). Although scholars debate the accuracy and effects of rumors within an organization (whether spread via traditional correspondence or social media), the importance of this form of communication should not be overlooked. "Rather than ignore or try to repress the grapevine, tune in to it," suggests Lussier (2019). "Identify the key people in the organization's grapevine and feed them information. To help prevent incorrect rumors, keep the information flowing through the grapevines as accurate and rumor-free as possible. Share all nonconfidential information with employees; tell them of changes as far in advance as possible. Encourage employees to ask questions about rumors they hear" (p. 103).

Informal Networks

Groups and relationships are also formed outside the formal structure of a sport organization—for example, a group of colleagues participating in a weekly golf outing or watching games together. These informal networks are established and maintained through proximity (e.g., working in the same office suite), the development of friendships and political alliances, social networking, and other relationships. Within these networks, individuals must make decisions about what information should be shared and with whom. This informal communication often takes the form of interpersonal sport communication (examined in chapter 5), but it can also involve several individuals. These information networks often involve social networking interactions through a sport organization's chat apps (e.g., Chanty, ChatWork, Facebook Workplace, Google Hangouts Chat, Microsoft Teams, Slack) and traditional social media platforms such as Facebook, Twitter, Snapchat, and Pinterest. Other common channels include meetings after work and during lunch. The functions of such communication include supporting the formal structure (e.g., interacting and coordinating with others without the chain of command), developing emotional and support networks, increasing the willingness of individuals to work toward organizational objectives, and increasing job and communication satisfaction.

Suggestions for Communicating Informally

Numerous websites and scholarly sources offer suggestions about how to engage properly in informal communication. For instance, in today's active and engaged communication environment, texting is frequently—and at times excessively or inappropriately—used by most sport organization stakeholders. "While you might be comfortable texting in your personal life, not everyone is open to using it for workplace communications," notes Vasel (2019). "Managers should set expectations of how they prefer to communicate in and out of the office. Some workers might find texting easier than emails or phone calls, while others might find it too invasive." Vasel's tips regarding texting are applicable to any sport organization: Employees should determine if the sport organization has a texting policy; evaluate if, for legal or record-keeping reasons, the sport organization needs to keep a record of the texts; only send short texts if a sport organization leader entrusts you with a personal phone number; respond to texts within an appropriate time period; proofread texts; and don't use emojis in work-related texting as

they can be misinterpreted. Those in leadership positions in the sport industry should be careful regarding their usage of texting. "Texting at all hours can also violate an employee's personal time and lead to burnout," states Vasel. Another suggestion for communicating comes from Bradberry (2014), who refers to a study that found that more than 80 percent of the working professionals surveyed found it inappropriate to answer phone calls or write text or email messages during a meeting: "The more money people make the less they approve of smartphone use [during meetings]." Bradberry notes that it is typically inappropriate to use a smartphone during a meeting because it is viewed as indicating a lack of respect, attention, listening, power, self-awareness, and social awareness. More generally, Kelly and colleagues (1989) offer suggestions for communicating informally overall. Their suggestions include cultivating informal relationships (e.g., establishing mentors), exercising restraint (e.g., being aware of hidden agendas), and being discreet (e.g., keeping confidences, not flaunting your informal network).

Culture of the Sport Organization

As with formal structure and informal networks, the culture of a sport organization both influences and is influenced by communication. In fact, some scholars postulate that "culture *is* communication, or, to be more precise, a cultural approach to organizations . . . focus[es] on the everyday ordinary and extraordinary communication of organization members" (Pepper, 1995, p. 3). Sport organizations have their own unique culture or way of life. Each organization is home to shared meanings and predominant beliefs, goals, activities, values, rites, vocabulary, stories, metaphors, norms for behavior, customs, rituals, and other indicators of organizational culture. This culture is created, shared, and altered through both verbal and nonverbal communication. For example, Carla Williams, the University of Virginia's athletics director (and one of only five current female ADs at a Power 5 school), notes that the culture of her department is conveyed to its various stakeholders through "a number of means, including communications from leadership, staff meetings, departmental policies, and intentional messaging" (personal communication).

Nonverbal and verbal communication influence the culture of a sport organization or team.

Photo courtesy of Paul M. Pedersen.

Furthermore, just as communication influences the culture of the organization, the organization influences the communication. "Not only do organizations *have* their own cultures, organizations *are* cultures—systems of values, beliefs, artifacts—that are constituted through the process of communication" (Witherspoon, 1997, p. 74). In a similar vein, ESPN's longest-serving president, George Bodenheimer, notes, "The importance of culture to a company cannot be overstated—and it becomes even more valuable as the organization prospers and grows" (Bodenheimer & Phillips, 2015, p. 154). In addition, the 33-year veteran of ESPN provides three particular reasons for the importance of culture in businesses: "First, it is the only thing leaders can truly control" (p. 154). He adds that "culture is all about people and the environment where they work. And because people take their cues from their top executives, setting the culture is 'job one' for a business leader. Second, culture supports everything a business is trying to do. It drives quality, profit, and employer passion. . . . Third, a great corporate culture attracts an industry's best people—and that results in more action, superior products, and better efficiency" (p. 155).

The following subsections use the work of Witherspoon (1997) to apply the factors, functions, and forms of organizational culture to the sport industry.

Cultural Factors in Sport Organizations

The factors that help shape the culture of a sport organization include its environment, mission, various tasks, leadership, structure, resources, and climate. Such factors are prominent in the thinking of sport industry executive Joe Sargent and his reflections regarding the Kansas City Chiefs: "We are evolving our culture to be more inclusive and less siloed. I appreciate this change, and I find that departments are encouraged and empowered to share their plans and seek feedback across departments." The sport marketing veteran adds that "the end result will be an organization that's on the same page where everyone feels connected to and accountable for their portion of the business' success. Communication is a key part of that because the more we share news and activation plans, the more people can weigh in and see their contributions in the final output."

For one Major League Baseball (MLB) team in particular, its organizational culture has made the team one of the best sport organizations to work for. "There is no better example of the importance of positive organizational culture than the Arizona Diamondbacks" (Belzer, 2015, para. 6). Team president and CEO Derrick Hall postulated that the team's "competitive advantage" lies in its culture: "We're in an industry where early-entry jobs are extremely difficult, the turnover is devastating, and so you have to create a culture where your employees, not the customers, come first. If the employee feels respected, developed, and promoted, he or she will in return treat the customer the same way" (para. 7).

Cultural Functions in Sport Organizations

One of the key functions of organizational culture is to provide knowledge about the organization so employees know how to act; for example, rules, procedures, and rumors may all provide information about issues such as dress code, interactions with superiors, and prescribed working hours. Organizational culture also provides a shared sense of emotional involvement in, and commitment to, organizational values; helps members identify and affiliate with the organization; assists members in processing (collecting, disseminating, using) information; helps members solve problems; defines the organization's boundaries that distinguish members from nonmembers (e.g., physical boundaries, identification badges); and provides a system of control (e.g., rules, behaviors). While the culture of a sport organization often influences the internal stakeholders, it can also influence internal and external stakeholder interactions. Take, for instance, the communication and relational dynamics that existed a few years ago between some members of the media and some of the Oklahoma City Thunder (NBA) players and team officials. In a detailed analysis of this relationship, Curtis (2015) explains the challenges of covering the team and getting access to players. He notes that "in the Thunder locker room, there's a watchfulness that prevents all but the most formal interactions. Reporters said that nearly every time they approach a player, even with tape recorders holstered, a Thunder PR rep sidles up to listen." Reporter Darnell Mayberry told Curtis that "If you have a conversation with a player about parenting, someone is going to be standing right there hovering and trying to steer it whichever way they think it should go." He added, "That's the kind of culture they've created here. No one has a personal relationship with any of these guys" (para. 45). Organizational culture can also function to enhance organizational performance because, as Witherspoon (1997) notes, "A strong culture is characterized by a continuity in leadership, stable group membership, numerous commonly held values and shared behavior patterns among organizational levels, and organization-wide success" (p. 81).

Culture, leadership, and success are often intertwined. As Lussier (2019) notes, the organizational culture—and the challenges of either fitting into or trying to change that culture—can affect individuals and the effectiveness of leadership. For example, the operational, stylistic, competitive, communication, and other challenges a sport organization might face during a transitionary time both influence and are influenced by the culture of the particular sport organization.

Cultural Forms in Sport Organizations

A sport organization has three predominant forms of culture—that is, ways in which it creates its culture through information processing. The three forms are symbols (e.g., logo, slogan, metaphor), schemas (i.e., stored representations of knowledge that help the organization's members make sense of information), and scripts (i.e., typical behavior or sequence of events in a given situation). For example, the culture of a professional soccer team is created, developed, and sustained through the interaction of symbols such as shirts bearing the team logo, schemas such as soccer knowledge, and scripts such as how employees are expected to treat superiors or season-ticket holders. The team's employees and internal stakeholders use these forms to develop common interpretations (shared meanings) of activities and events within the franchise.

Consider, for instance, the office opened in New York City by FC Bayern Munich. The office "helps Bayern Munich further its reach with fans in America, and provides a showcase to corporate sponsors of what the club means to those back in Germany and millions more around the world". Rudolf Vidal, the club's managing director in the United States, describes the club's ethos: "When we talk to potential partners about soccer and what it means to Bayern Munich, it's about emotion and passion for the sport" ("In the Office," 2015, p. 30) . The objects in the office that reveal this passion and emotion include championship photos, the team mascot, trophies and awards, signed soccer balls, framed jerseys, and pennants. These objects are examples of the forms that organizational culture takes for Bayern Munich.

The forms of communication in a sport organization's culture also include language (i.e., common words, terms, and phrases), myths (i.e., repeated stories), and ceremonies and rites (e.g., elaborate activities, planned functions, dramatic endeavors, regularly scheduled rituals, special ceremonies). The rites in a sport organization might include rites of passage (e.g., training sessions), rites of enhancement (e.g., awarding performance), and rites of integration (e.g., picnics, parties).

In sport organizations, employees participate in the various forms of communication (e.g., language, myths, rituals). These forms not only create the organizational culture but also reflect and reinforce it.

Summary: Organizational Features That Affect Communication

The culture of a sport entity can be viewed as the manifestation of the organization's internal operational influences, practices, beliefs, norms, and values. This inner self of the sport organization is reflected both in interactions between internal stakeholders and in their communication with external stakeholders. Effective communication in an organizational culture can be accomplished if stakeholders listen carefully, observe others (e.g., model effective communication, realize inappropriate behavior), and fulfill their roles (Kelly et al., 1989). Ineffective communication in an organizational culture can be detrimental to a sport organization and its stakeholders. Take, for instance, Pat Riley's views on the leadership controversies (resignation of team president Magic Johnson and the rise of general manager Rob Pelinka) surrounding the Los Angeles Lakers: "The organization gets too big, there are too many people who have been around a long time, and they start voicing their opinion about things, and that's when the culture starts to crack," (MacMullan, 2019, para. 10). In part, the culture of the Lakers was affected by the informal communication (e.g., grapevine) within the organization. Johnson told ESPN sportscasters that "I started hearing, 'Magic, you're not working hard enough. Magic's not in the office.'" He added that, "People around the Lakers office were telling me Rob was saying things, and I didn't like hearing those things being said behind my back" (para. 2). Whether individuals are working for an NBA franchise or a youth sport program, the three features of sport organizations that affect communication—formal structure, informal networks, and organizational culture—need to be understood and appreciated for an organization to be characterized by effective communicative interactions. In addition, information must flow between the various levels of the organization; leaders must facilitate that movement, both through formal channels (i.e., up, down, and across hierarchical levels) and informal channels, as well as through the organizational culture.

We noted earlier that one type of sport organization is the learning organization. A learning sport organization makes changes based on information and feedback that it receives through systematic inquiry. It can do so because of its culture of communication. As Torres, Preskill, and Piontek (2005) explain, an organization creates a culture of learning through activities. These activities might include implementing the organization's findings from systemic inquiry, establishing feedback loops so the entity's members can learn from past activities, developing a mind-set that reframes problems as opportunities, and encouraging collaboration.

The learning culture of a sport organization can be discerned by communicative actions, such as simply asking and being receptive to questions. This point was made by movie producer Brian Grazer, whose credits include the boxing film *Cinderella Man*:

> If you're the boss and you manage by asking questions, you're laying the foundation for the culture of your company or your group. You're letting people know that the boss is willing to listen. This isn't about being "warm" or "friendly." It's about understanding how complicated the modern business world is, how indispensable diversity of perspective is, and how hard creative work is. Here's why it's hard: because often there is no right answer. That's why asking questions at work, instead of giving orders, is so valuable. . . . Questions create both authority in people to come up with ideas and take action and the responsibility for moving things forward. Questions create the space for all kinds of ideas. Most important, questions send a very clear message: We're willing to listen, even to ideas or suggestions or problems we weren't expecting. (Grazer & Fishman, 2015, p. 44)

In addition to the curiosity mentioned by Grazer, communicative activities also help create a culture of learning by enhancing individual learning and the development of team knowledge, appreciating conflict as an aspect of the process of changing and growing, reevaluating the reward structure to include both productivity and new learning measures, and creating a structure that increases and enhances communication within the organization. Furthermore, in applying the work of Torres and colleagues (2005) to the sport industry, a sport organization can work to create a culture of learning by establishing a mechanism for easy storage and retrieval of information; implementing new technology to improve the transfer of information; and examining the perceptions, norms, values, assumptions, activities, and policies surrounding the organization and its internal stakeholders.

FORMS OF COMMUNICATION IN SPORT ORGANIZATIONS

Communication in sport organizations involves numerous interaction levels, audience types, and channels. It might involve, to give just a few examples, posting a comment on a social media site, texting with subordinates while planning an event, talking with colleagues at team headquarters, making a presentation at an awards banquet, holding a strategic meeting with upper management, sending a written evaluation to a subordinate, soliciting advice from a mentor in a different organization, making a training video for employees, training salespeople in effective presentation skills, establishing an e-commerce website, or preparing a Heisman Trophy campaign. Timely and effective communication in the sport industry typically demands the use of various communication channels. For example, Carla Williams, the University of Virginia's athletics director (and the first African American female AD at an NCAA Power 5 school), states that she engages in many forms of communication, including meetings, interviews, presentations, emails, letters, memos, and reports: "About 50 percent of my time spent communicating is face to face, 30 percent is email, and everything else falls in the remaining 20 percent" (personal communication).

The communication channels in sport organizations—that is, the forms in which messages are transmitted—include both the verbal and nonverbal forms of discourse. They encompass all forms—whether formal or informal, mediated or unmediated, spoken or written. The most effec-

tive way to illustrate the forms of communication in sport organizations is to arrange the channels into categories. Here, we use the three categories created by Torres and colleagues (2005)—least interactive, potentially interactive, and most interactive—to arrange communication according to the degree of audience interaction. While channels that fit into the most interactive category are often the preferred choice for effective communication, not all situations allow for such personal and responsive interactions. Such would be the case when, for example, an executive at a large sport organization (e.g., Reebok, the National Football League, ESPN) communicates with dozens or hundreds of stakeholders at the same time (e.g., in a mass email message). Regardless of the channel used, those making hiring decisions continue to stress the importance of developing communication skills. One recent study—the Job Outlook 2019—found that employers rated written communication (82 percent) as the attribute they most want to see represented on a résumé (NACE, 2018). Other highly rated attributes include ability to work on a team (78 percent), leadership (67 percent), oral communication (67 percent), and interpersonal skills (53 percent).

Least Interactive Formats

The least interactive formats involve written forms that can be delivered to an audience without face-to-face or oral interaction. Thus, the written word, when delivered by itself without any accompaniment (e.g., gestures, emoticons) or feedback, is the least interactive format. This type of text-based communication can be delivered through such formats as email, social media platforms (e.g., tweeting), the web (e.g., blogging), smartphones (e.g., texting), traditional mail services (e.g., postal, intraorganizational, overnight), the sport media (e.g., newspaper sports section), and various other written documents (e.g., annual reports, memos, executive summaries, letters, agendas, bulletin board announcements, brochures, newsletters). As this list indicates, written communication options include both mediated forms (e.g., social media, email) and unmediated forms of written communication.

In sport organizations, email is the most commonly used form of communication—and one of the most abused. Even for those who may prefer other means of communication, email is still a significant part of their work interactions. While some may prefer other forms of communication, email is a preferred form for many because of its unique uses. For example, when a sport manager receives an email, she can read it and respond at her own pace; she can also use email as she works on other tasks. Other advantages include speed, immediacy, efficiency, cost-effectiveness, and easy distribution to a broad range of stakeholders; in addition, it creates a communication trail.

Josh Rawitch, the sport communication executive profiled in chapter 5, commented on the volume and importance of email communication in his role with the Arizona Diamondbacks: "On a daily basis, I usually receive somewhere in the range of 100 to 150 emails (more than 200 when I was with the Los Angeles Dodgers and served as the daily media contact), and it's important that I respond to each in a timely and professional manner. Nothing makes an organization look worse than an email filled with typos, or a delayed response" (personal communication).

Thus, as illustrated by Rawitch in the previous quote, while email has many positive uses, it also brings challenges (e.g., a lighthearted email might be taken the wrong way, a confidential email might get forwarded, an email not related to work might get intercepted). With these and numerous other pitfalls in mind, sport leaders and organizations should set guidelines for when and how to use email, who gets copied on messages, how long messages should be, how responses should be formulated, and what level of formality to use.

In a similar vein, Lussier (2019) provides suggestions for the proper use of both email and smartphones in organizational communication. For email, use complete sentences; keep responses short; proofread messages; and attend to subject-line information, greetings with the recipient's name, and sign-offs. Lussier also suggests not sending emails that are not needed, not copying others on an email when not needed, not pressing send when emotions (e.g., anger) are in play, being careful with confidential information, and assuming that the email may get forwarded.

Photo courtesy of the Arizona Diamondbacks.

Josh Rawitch (right) talks with Olympic legend Michael Phelps in the dugout of the Arizona Diamondbacks. As the team's senior vice president of content and communications, Rawitch uses various other forms of communication—including responding to more than 100 emails each day.

"Don't forget the need for human contact through conversation," states Lussier. "E-mail should be business formal, with texting and instant messaging (IM) less so. Don't send a text/IM unless it has immediate job relevance to the person—email instead" (p. 468). A sport organization employee who takes heed of Lussier's suggestions regarding smartphones focuses on returning calls in a timely manner, not letting a smartphone call interrupt a conversation or meeting, not disrupting people nearby when talking on a smartphone, not taking multiple calls at the same time, leaving only brief voicemail messages, speaking clearly, putting the smartphone down or not constantly checking it when interacting with others, and not disrupting people nearby when talking on the smartphone.

One should also remember that in many cases, the best way to send an important message, resolve a conflict, convey a confidential matter, or make the best impact is to arrange a face-to-face meeting or another more personal approach. For example, the value of the personal approach to communication is clear to Josh Furlow, the former president and CEO of Competitor Group, a sport organization that oversees triathlons (e.g., TriRock) and marathon series (e.g., Rock 'n' Roll Marathon). "The events business is a relationship game," Furlow noted, adding that he traveled the majority of the time during his leadership of the sport organization, "making personal relationships with the city partners, sponsor reps, and other executives" and having a lot "of face time with them" (qtd. in Dreier, 2015, p. 3).

Beyond mastering the skill of email correspondence, you should also develop your overall writing skills to maximize your success in the sport industry. Whether you want to be a sport agent, a social media manager, a sport reporter, or a sports information director, you will frequently rely on your writing skills to be effective and efficient in your communication and interactions. "With the increased reliance on social media as a primary form of communication, there is an old-school skill that is being lost amongst many of today's job applicants—the ability to write clearly and with purpose," notes Brian Clapp, host of the WorkInSports.com podcast and director of content marketing for the sport industry job and internship website. "*Writing* sounds boring in a world of quick-witted retorts and anecdotes, com-

pressed into 140 characters or broken down into acronyms, but the truth is, writing with skill is a big part of every sports jobs you will ever have" (Clapp, 2015, paras. 1-2).

Although we often use quick-and-easy texts, emails, and social media messages, most positions in a sport organization carry the expectation of—and in some cases the demand for—strong writing skills in longer formats. "Although the channels through which information is carried vary from news releases to publications to blogs, the core competency remains constant—being able to write effectively. Writing skills cannot be developed simply by accessing educational resources. They must be honed through practice" (Stoldt, Dittmore, Ross, & Branvold, 2021, p. 12). Without writing skills, individuals in the sport industry risk losing both opportunities and influence. "The inability to create clear and coherent written communication has hindered countless careers. Even something as apparently innocuous as an internal e-mail can hurt us and our organization," notes Barrett (2014, p. 85). "By recognizing the importance of every written communication we create, we begin to appreciate the importance of making sure we approach the writing of all of it with utmost care, from the simplest text messages and e-mails to the most complicated reports" (p. 86).

As noted earlier, this discussion categorizes the forms of communication in sport organizations according to the level of interactivity they involve. Although social media (e.g., tweets, posts) is addressed in the "least interactive" category, it could just as easily be placed in the "potentially interactive" or even the "most interactive" category, depending on the degree to which the user interacts with his or her audience (e.g., through Twitter follows and Facebook likes). Even employment decisions can be affected by individuals' profiles and engagement on social media (e.g., a decision to not hire an entry-level employee based on something that shows up in his digital footprint, a decision to hire a sport media member based in part on her social media presence and following). Social media are covered in more detail in upcoming chapters.

Potentially Interactive Formats

The category of potentially interactive formats—which can be delivered to an audience either with or without interaction—includes activities such as verbal and video presentations. Especially for those in management and leadership positions, oral communication is the overwhelming communication preference. "The skills of a leader are most visible when he or she is speaking—whether informally, with a few people around a conference room table or in a virtual meeting, or formally, standing before a large group or sitting in a Webcast delivering a presentation," notes Barrett (2014). "Much of the 70 to 90 percent of the time that managers engage in communicating is spent in conversations or in presenting, either talking to others one-on-one or speaking in groups or to groups" (pp. 144-145). In the sport industry, as one advances within the organization, one typically discovers that his or her communication is much more visible (e.g., internal meetings secretly recorded and released, external actions caught on video) and that his or her speaking engagements are much more frequent with both internal and external publics.

Oral communication in sport organizations comes in a variety of formats. The most frequently used type of oral communication is one-on-one delivery (and receipt) of messages. As with all forms of oral communication, this form can be either one-way or two-way (i.e., interactive) communication. Personal oral communication is generally conducted face to face via smartphone, the web (e.g., a team's decision maker using Skype to interview a potential summer intern), and social media platforms. Although talking via telephone or smartphone is useful for getting information quickly or checking on progress, phone calls (like texting and social media) should not be used for disciplining employees or other such personal matters in the workplace. Such situations are best handled in a face-to-face setting. For more information on interpersonal communication, see chapter 5.

Other common forms of oral communication in sport organizations include meetings (e.g., committee, departmental, executive), interviews (e.g., hiring, performance appraisal, counseling), training sessions, and both internal (e.g., to employees) and external (e.g., to audiences at trade shows, conventions, media) presentations and speeches. Just as Barrett (2014) notes for traditional businesses, the common types of presentation in sport organizations are round-tables, stand-up impromptu or extemporaneous presentations, and webcasts and webinars. A roundtable presentation involves sitting at a table—or connecting remotely (e.g., via phone or videoconference)—to interact with audience members rather than standing in front of the audience. Although roundtable presentations can be delivered with minimal interaction, they are more likely to range from somewhat interactive (e.g., soliciting feedback) to very interactive (e.g., brainstorming ideas).

A stand-up presentation, in contrast, involves an in-person or online delivery that is either extemporaneous or impromptu. An extemporaneous presentation involves presenting prepared information without reliance on notecards or another means of prompting, thus allowing the presenter to establish a rapport with an audience. An impromptu presentation involves presenting on the spur of the moment, as is the case when someone is called on to talk without warning. An extemporaneous presentation occurs, for example, when the CEO of a sport organization informs the various department heads that they will each provide an assessment of their areas of oversight at an upcoming meeting. Thus, they have time to jot down a few notes and maybe even put together a few quick PowerPoint slides, but for the most part their presentations will involve simply talking about key points with the meeting's attendees. One example of an impromptu presentation, on the other hand, would be when that same CEO attends a charity function and, on the spur of the moment, the host asks the CEO to say a few words about her company.

Sport industry professionals should know that they may be called on—for example, by their bosses, peers, boosters, or sponsors—to deliver a presentation at any time. Therefore, you should always be prepared with talking points, even for an impromptu delivery. You should also practice giving presentations and be as knowledgeable as possible about your organization and its personnel, activities, strategies, and stakeholders. This preparation helps you be ready to give any form of presentation, whether it be roundtable, extemporaneous, impromptu, or any online version of these forms, such as live-streaming webinars and webcasts (via a service such as EverWebinar, WebinarJam, Webex, Zoom, etc.).

Presentations in large-group and small-group meetings can be either very interactive or one-sided, depending on the meeting's setting and purpose. Meetings can also range from the informal get-togethers to more formal meetings that involve coordinating activities, delegating tasks, and resolving conflicts. Therefore, a leader must be able to communicate in a variety of settings to run an effective sport organization.

Of course, oral communication in sport organizations can also take any of various mediated forms—for example, smartphone apps, social networking platforms, telephone calls, and videoconferencing. Many of these forms (e.g., videos, apps) allow the audience to see the presenter. As a result, as with video presentations and social media postings, apps such as Snapchat allows communicators to convey immediacy through live broadcasts.

To use oral communication effectively in sport, communicators must prepare for speaking opportunities. Consider, for instance, Michele Roberts, a defense attorney who in 2018 was elected for another four-year term as executive director of the National Basketball Players Association (NBPA). "Before interviewing for the job, Roberts spent hours online, educating herself about the NBPA," notes Schwartzberg (2015). Roberts told her that, "As a fan, you watch the game, but you don't think about it in terms of the business"

Immediacy in Organizational Communication

Immediacy can also be established via social media through live-streaming platforms, and fans and sport industry personnel increasingly use apps such as Periscope, Livestream, and Facebook Live to communicate live with their various stakeholders and audiences. For example, WNBA center Liz Cambage, who has the single-game league scoring record with 53 points in one game, requested a trade in 2019 from the Dallas Wings. During the trade negotiations, she disclosed in an Instagram story (posted on her @ecambage Instagram account) the stress that the extended delays and uncertainty had caused (Spruill, 2019): "I'm sick of being patient and quiet. I'm sick of not eating and not sleeping. I'm sick of being stuck in limbo. I see all your [fans'] messages and it really does mean the world to me." While wearing her endorsed Adidas apparel, she appeared to direct a finger at the team's organization and management, noting that she was "this close to running my mouth" and stating that "you never cared about me, you just care about owning me. I'm a human and I deserve to be treated that way." Soon after, it was announced that Cambage had been traded to the Las Vegas Aces and in her first season with the team she was named a WNBA All-Star for the third time in her career.

Photo courtesy of Paul M. Pedersen.

WNBA officials communicate with each other at a game between the Chicago Sky and the New York Liberty.

(p. 60). Roberts prepared purposefully, and her efforts were rewarded when she was hired into her current prestigious and influential position. In addition to being fully prepared, sport industry communicators must work on overcoming any fear they may have of public speaking. It should be noted, however, that while it is important to work steadily to improve your oration skills, failure to become a great orator is not a fatal blow in the sport industry.

Most Interactive Formats

The most interactive formats include working sessions, synchronous electronic communication (e.g., chat rooms, teleconferences, videoconferences, Web conferences), and personal discussions (e.g., over the telephone, via the web, in person). This approach was taken when former ESPN president George Bodenheimer addressed more than 700 on-air professionals in his organization after sex scandals and accusations involving a few of his employees made national news. Because of the large number of attendees, he noted that "we had to schedule it in two back-to-back sessions and include videoconference for those who could not be there in person. . . . I needed to get it across that if people acted this way, they were going to be fired—although I conveyed the message more diplomatically" (Bodenheimer & Phillips, 2015, p. 249). An interactive approach that includes approachability and visibility, combined with trustworthy and supportive actions, helps maintain open communication lines and a culture of fairness and equity.

Individuals in organizations are often put into working sessions that encourage collaboration, discussion, and decision making. At the same time, they often find that geographical separation makes it impractical or impossible to hold a face-to-face meeting with certain stakeholders. For instance, when the general manager of the San Diego Seals (National Lacrosse League) attends a business meeting in New York, he may still need to disseminate information, seek input, or participate in communication with his subordinates based in California. This communication often involves the fully interactive format of synchronous electronic communication, which allows the general manager and other participants to communicate in real time without being in the same place.

Such technologies allow us to "routinely communicate across both geography and organizational levels" (Shockley-Zalabak, 2016, p. 4). As a result, they enable individuals to collaborate and get work accomplished "without ever leaving their homes as they 'telecommute' from automated home workstations to offices around the globe" (p. 4). At the same time, as Shockley-Zalabak describes, "Workers in the communications era of microelectronics, computers, and telecommunications have an abundance of information for decision making and a growing concern for information overload. Research suggests virtually all knowledge workers use e-mail and voicemail, with use of mobile phones, conference calls, corporate intranets, IM and text messaging, corporate Web sides, information portals, and corporate extranets commonplace. Social media have become a cultural phenomenon in all aspects of our lives. We are connected around the clock as work and personal time merge for many" (p. 4).

Interactive tools and platforms allow sport industry personnel to use technological innovations (e.g., social media platforms, the cloud) to work on projects, brainstorm ideas, edit files, collaborate on electronic whiteboards, and negotiate with clients via tablet, smartphone, or laptop. As technological advances continue to make their way into the sport industry, highly interactive formats will improve productivity and increase efficiency in all areas of communication. In addition to working sessions and synchronous electronic communication, personal discussions between two individuals fit into the "most interactive" category because they are interactive by nature.

Regardless of the form or platform one uses, communicating effectively is essential for success in any sport-related occupation and in any area of the sport industry. "You can have the greatest ideas in the world, but they're no good to your company or your career if you can't express them clearly and persuasively. Some jobs, such as sales and customer support, are primarily about communicating," note Bovee and Thill (2018, p. 4). They add that "improving your communication skills may be the single most important step you can take in your career" and that by learning to write, speak, listen well, and "recognize the appropriate way to communicate in any situation, you'll gain a major advantage that will serve you throughout your career" (p. 5).

LEADERSHIP COMMUNICATION IN SPORT

Leadership is an integral component of effective communication in sport organizations. More than 75 years ago, scholar Chester Barnard (1938) noted that leaders were responsible for developing and maintaining a communication system. The same holds true today, and this section of the chapter covers sport leadership, leadership communication in sport, and sport leadership communication styles. As O'Boyle, Cummins, and Murray (2015) note in their book *Leadership in Sport*, there are "everyday practical examples within the sport industry where leaders are required to plan, organise, control, delegate, and empower others to achieve organisational objectives as effectively and efficiently as possible" (p. 2). Effective communication by leaders in sport organizations must include several fundamental elements and meet certain competency requirements. For instance, ESPN's George Bodenheimer (Bodenheimer & Phillips, 2015, p. 240) notes that his company's leadership training program published a set of competencies related to leadership in the organization; one of them was "effective communication" (the others were "vision, strategic thinking, a drive for results, entrepreneurial spirit, embracing diversity, . . . teamwork, passion, integrity, trust, and courage"). Another example of this leadership comes from the WNBA. Just a few days before the 2019 regular season tipoff, Cathy Engelbert was named the league's first commissioner. The WNBA's press release ("Cathy," 2019) delivered the news regarding NBA commissioner Adam Silver's announcement of the appointment of the former Deloitte CEO. Silver noted that Engelbert "is a world-class business leader with a deep connection to women's basketball, which makes her the ideal person to lead the WNBA into its next phase of growth." He added, "The WNBA will benefit significantly from her more than 30 years of business and operational experience including revenue generation, sharp entrepreneurial instincts and proven management

abilities." Within the press release, Engelbert is quoted as stating that in leading the WNBA she sees "tremendous opportunity to bolster visibility for the sport of women's basketball, empower the players, and enhance fan engagement." She added that she looked to use her "business expertise and passion for basketball to promote women in the game and beyond, and to working with the teams and world-class athletes to help grow this league into a thriving business."

The fundamental elements and competency requirements of effective communication are crucial to both organizational performance and career success in the sport industry. They include leadership attitudes, behaviors, styles, and strategies that help sport industry professionals communicate effectively. The goal of this section is to help readers—many of whom will become sport industry leaders—understand the importance of leadership communication and appreciate and develop the necessary skills to share, persuade, and present their ideas to others. "Once we are in leadership positions, our communication can be far-reaching and public, with the power to affect the reputation of ourselves and our organization and potentially even change the entire direction of our organization" (Barrett, 2014, pp. 85-86).

Certain key organizational and interpersonal communication skills can support and enhance effective leadership in sport organizations. It is particularly important to be able to use these skills to create a commitment to organizational vision, goals, and workplace culture. Regardless of the many manifest and latent reasons for a successful sport organization, the importance of leadership communication in sport cannot be overstated. This section of the chapter—which relies heavily on the work of Johnson and Hackman (2018)—covers the theory and application of leadership communication in sport organizations.

Definition of Sport Leadership

Thousands of articles and books have been published on the subject of leadership, and the sport industry has its share of leadership publications. Scholars engaged in sport management research have "been enamored with the concept of leadership, whether it concerns how coaches deal with their athletes, how athletic directors motivate their employees, or how people create successful sport companies" (Jordan et al., 2015, p. 62). The multitude of both sport and nonsport studies and publications on leadership has generated hundreds of definitions of the word. "Most definitions of leadership," observe Yukl and Gardner (2020), have little in common except for reflecting the assumption that leadership "involves a process whereby intentional influence is exerted over other people to guide, structure, and facilitate activities and relationships in a group or organization" (p. 2). Yukl and Gardner add that the multitude of leadership definitions "differ in many respects, including who exerts influence, the intended purpose of the influence, the manner in which influence is exerted, and the outcome of the influence attempt" (p. 2). Thus, as leadership is defined in myriad ways across the various disciplines of study, it is not surprising that scholars and practitioners in the sport industry would have their own definitions of leadership.

If you go to a sport organization and ask a dozen of its employees to define leadership, you will probably receive a dozen unique definitions. Some might say that leadership is an act that brings about a response or is the art of influencing or persuading. Others might think that leadership is simply the way one motivates subordinates, how one coordinates people and activities, or the approach that one takes to guiding and directing the behavior of people or groups. What the many definitions reveal is that there are many types, attributes, and perceptions of effective leadership. The hundreds of leadership definitions are a result of the fact that there is not just one standard type of leader. Even so, Yukl and Gardner (2020) offer a comprehensive definition: "Leadership is the process of influencing others to understand and agree about what needs to be done and how to do it, and the process of facilitating individual and collective efforts to accomplish shared objectives" (p. 6).

Regardless of one's particular definition of leadership, communication must play an integral role. In their overview of sport industry leadership and management, Jordan and colleagues (2015) observe, "The vast majority of a leader's time is spent communicating with others, whether it is speaking or listening to others, emailing, text messaging, writing personal notes, or reading material transmitted from others" (p. 68). There-fore, effective leadership requires the leader to be effective at speaking, listening, writing, and reading. The leader first needs to develop his or her leadership message, whether it be a vision statement, mission statement, or call for change or action. In this step, the leader determines what to say or do and selects the proper communication channel. The leader then needs to deliver the leadership message. In this step, the leader proclaims the message to an audience; if the leader does not understand the audience and its perceptions, the leader will fail. Last, the leader must sustain the leadership message, which means keeping it alive and meaningful through feedback, reiteration, and coaching.

Because of their symbiotic nature, the words *leadership* and *communication* have been combined into one phrase by some scholars. "Leadership communication," according to Barrett (2014), "is the controlled, purposeful transfer of meaning by which individuals influence a single person, a group, an organization, or a community by using the full range of their communication abilities and resources to connect positively with their audiences, overcome interferences, and create and deliver messages that guide, direct, motivate, or inspire others to action" (p. 7). This connectedness is reflected in the definition of sport leadership that we propose, which is a slightly modified version of the communication-driven definition of leadership offered by Johnson and Hackman (2018). Thus, we believe that *sport leadership* is communication in and through sport that influences others' actions and attitudes, thus resulting in the fulfillment of a shared purpose or need. This definition makes clear that communication lies at the core of sport leadership.

As Barrett (2015, p. 5) argues, "Effective leadership depends on effective communication, that ability to connect to others and, through that connection, guide, direct, motivate, and inspire. Good communication skills enable, foster, and create the understanding and trust necessary to encourage others to follow a leader." Travis Bradberry (2019), the author of *Emotional Intelligence 2.0*, further explains the connection between effective leadership and communication. He notes that great communicators are authentic, honest, proactive, active listeners, and knowledgeable of their audience; they are able to admit mistakes, solicit feedback, read body language, and speak with authority, and convey a message directly to an individual even in a group setting. "Great communicators stand out from the crowd," adds Bradberry. "They excel in communication because they value it, and that's the critical first step to becoming a great leader" (para. 14). Although most would agree that successful leadership is connected to effective communication, there is no standard, universal communication approach for leaders. Therefore, various communication styles of leadership are examined in the next section.

Styles of Sport Leadership Communication

You can take advantage of opportunities to advance in sport leadership positions by knowing and applying what effective leaders do when they communicate with followers. "Leadership and management communication affect nearly all aspects of organizational life," notes Shockley-Zalabak (2016, p. 193). "In fact, leadership communication can come from virtually anyone in the organization, with the effectiveness of leadership and management communication directly relating to organizational success and work satisfaction" (p. 193). Thus, it is crucial to understand the behavioral approaches or communication styles that leaders exhibit toward those they lead. The ways in which a leader behaves toward and interacts and communicates with followers constitute her **sport leadership communication style**. This subject matters because, as Johnson and Hackman (2018) explain, a leader's communication style influences the effectiveness of the leadership: "Leadership communication style is a relatively enduring set of communicative behaviors in which a leader engages when interacting with followers. The communication style a leader selects contributes to the success or failure of any attempt to exert influence" (p. 40).

The most effective communication style for a sport leader depends on the organizational context, the specific situation, and the followers' capabilities and perceptions. As Jordan and colleagues (2015) point out, "To be a good leader you must understand that *how* you communicate sends messages equally as strong as *what* you communicate. It therefore stands to reason that

employees must also be satisfied not only with the leader's communication but also with the more general communication lines that exist within the organization. As a leader, the established communication patterns will be important in crafting a leadership image" (p. 68, emphasis added). Aware of this need for flexibility, Chevonne Mansfield, the deputy athletics director at Florida Memorial University, notes that her communication approach depends on the individual with whom she is interacting: "I think it's all about your approach. Everyone is different, so you have to flex and communicate on his or her terms. For example, if you're communicating with someone that is direct in their communications style, it's best to get straight to the point without lots of minutia." Mansfield further explains her leadership communication style and its effectiveness: "I am even-keel and calm, but very candid, frank, and straightforward. That is my preferred style of communication inside and outside of work. It has proven beneficial at various stops in my career" (personal communication).

In summary, the degree to which sport leaders provide supportive and directive behaviors varies depending on contextual, situational, and subordinate influences.

Task-Oriented and Interpersonal-Oriented Communication

Sport leadership communication styles are typically viewed as consisting of two dimensions: **task-oriented communication** and **interpersonal-oriented communication**. In their discussion of dimensions, Johnson and Hackman (2018) note the emergence over the last couple of decades of a third leadership dimension—consisting of change-oriented leadership behaviors. Yukl and Gardner (2020) explain that the types of behaviors associated with this third leadership dimension "include communicating an appealing vision of what could be changed, proposing specific changes, implementing a change, and encouraging innovation" (p. 25). Johnson and Hackman add that change- oriented (or development-oriented) communication "fosters innovation and change" (p. 68) and involves encouraging "creativity, experimentation, risk taking, and the adoption of innovations" (p. 52). Although the **change-oriented communication** dimension has received some attention, the two sport leadership communication styles that have been most examined are those involving task-oriented communication and interpersonal-oriented (or relationship-oriented or relations-oriented) communication.

When a sport leader closely supervises a performance and tells a subordinate what to do, she is exhibiting task-oriented communication. Other labels for this type of communication include *task behavior, production-oriented communication, initiating structure, theory X management,* and *concern for production.* In applying the work of Yukl and Gardner (2020) to the sport industry, when a sport industry leader plans, clarifies, and monitors, she is typically exhibiting behaviors that can be classified as task-oriented communication. With this type of communication, the leader "is primarily concerned with accomplishing the task in an efficient and reliable way" (p. 23), and the associated behaviors include actions such as "clarifying work roles and task objectives, assigning specific tasks to subordinates, planning activities and tasks for the work group, and monitoring performance by subordinates" (p. 24). This type of communication can also involve such activities as taking a greater interest in getting a task completed than in the people completing it, disseminating information while ignoring feelings, exhibiting rigid communication, interrupting others, being demanding, and focusing on information relevant to task and productivity.

When a sport leader is *not* closely supervising the performance of subordinates but works instead to listen and provide a supportive, trusting, and respectful working environment, he is exhibiting interpersonal-oriented communication. An example of this approach is Becky Hammon, the first female full-time assistant coach in the National Basketball Association (NBA). She notes that in her position with the San Antonio Spurs, she connects by "getting to know these guys as people, and as players. You have to develop a rapport. They give me a lot of respect" (Battan, 2015, para. 6). Other labels for this type of communication include *relationship behavior, concern for people, employee-oriented communication, theory Y management,* and *consideration.* Again applying the work of Yukl and Gardner (2020) to sport organizations, when a leader in

the sport industry supports, develops, and recognizes his subordinates, he is typically exhibiting behaviors that can be classified as interpersonal-oriented communication. With this type of communication, the leader "is primarily concerned with increasing mutual trust, cooperation, job satisfaction, and identification with the team or organization" (p. 23). This type of communication can also involve such activities as being concerned with relationships, soliciting opinions, recognizing feelings, engaging in open communication, listening to others, and making requests.

The daily interactions engaged in by leaders of sport organizations "may occur internally as a part of formal work meetings, in individual consultations and employee evaluations, or in informal conversations," notes sport management scholar David Scott (2014). He adds that most of these leaders must also "interact with numerous external stakeholders, both in one-to-one situations and as a part of larger group events. In all instances, these interactions demand that leaders be highly cognizant of interpersonal relationship skills" (p. 34). The importance of such relationships became clear to former ESPN executive George Bodenheimer as he rose through the ranks: "As president, I began to realize that the higher a leader rises in an organization, the more important it is to build and maintain interpersonal relationships—both inside and outside the company" (Bodenheimer & Phillips, 2015, p. 159).

Depending on the communicator's emphasis, his or her task-orientedness and interpersonal-orientedness can be described as either high or low. These variations mean that there are various leadership communication styles, just as there are various leader types in the sport industry. "They come in all varieties," notes Wertheim (2015, p. 15). "There are micromanagers and bloviators. There are delegators and relegators. Kiss-ups and kick-downs. Name a workforce and, almost by definition, there is a boss. In sports, bosses cut a wide swath." Wertheim then offers a couple of prominent examples from the National Football League and the National Basketball Association, respectively: "Armed with talking points, projecting defiance as he defends the often indefensible, Roger Goodell is one kind of boss. Adam Silver, self-deprecating yet decisive, is another" (p. 15). The following descriptions combine the work done on communication, leadership, and organizations by Johnson and Hackman (2018) and Lussier (2019) to present four **situational supervisory styles** in the communication process in the sport industry: autocratic, consultative, participative, and laissez-faire.

Autocratic Communication Style

In the summer of 2015, a report surfaced regarding frustrations felt by some stakeholders about the perceived management style used by Steve Patterson, who was then the athletics director at the University of Texas. One report indicated Patterson had "been told to change his personal style" (Carlton, 2015, para. 1). Although he had been praised by some for his business acumen, Patterson was facing backlash due to perceived ineffectiveness on the interpersonal side of his leadership communication style. As the frustrations reached a tipping point, the university's president informed Patterson "of the need to change an approach" seen by some "as impersonal or even arrogant" (Carlton, 2015, para. 2).

It is not clear whether the perceptions of Patterson—who has had a long and distinguished career in the sport industry, including leadership stints with Arizona State University as well as the Arizona Coyotes of the National Hockey League (NHL)—were accurate and relatively consistent over time. Regardless, in more general terms, if a sport leader exhibits a high level of task-oriented communication (i.e., directive behavior) and a low level of relationship-oriented communication (i.e., supportive behavior), then he or she is demonstrating an **autocratic communication style**. As explained by Lussier (2019), if you use the autocratic communication style in a presentation, you are assuming that you are dealing with audience members who "know that they are expected to comply with your message" (p. 118) and have low capability as well as limited or no information.

The autocratic—or authoritarian—communication style is evident when a leader regulates policy, procedures, and behavior to maintain strict control over followers. Communication patterns of this leadership style include setting goals individually, engaging in one-way or downward communication, controlling discussions, setting policy and procedures unilaterally, dominating interactions, directing tasks personally, providing infrequent positive feedback, rewarding obedience and punishing mistakes, using conflict for personal gain, and exhibiting poor listening skills (Johnson & Hackman, 2018).

Regarding this last pattern—poor listening—LPGA commissioner Mike Whan takes just the opposite approach. This sport industry leader remembers being told somewhere along the line that an individual should first listen, then learn, and *then* lead. He followed this advice when he became commissioner of the LPGA: "My first agreement with the board was to have 100 days where I could just listen and learn" ("Whan's World," 2015, p. 96). Clearly, Whan's approach is not aligned with the autocratic communication style, in which input and responses from subordinates are neither solicited nor valued. As noted earlier, and as Lussier (2019) details, autocratic communication generally carries an expectation of compliance from those on the receiving end. Thus, the authoritarian or autocratic communication style is generally one sided and is often associated with detailed instructions given to—and close supervision of (but only limited input received from)—those to whom the message is directed.

Consultative Communication Style

When sport leaders exhibit a combination of high task-oriented communication (i.e., high directive) and high relationship-oriented communication (i.e., high supportive), they are demonstrating a **consultative communication style**. A leader who uses this style wants to determine whether the subordinate is interested in the message and accepts the leader's influence; therefore, he or she does such things as explaining why the task should be completed, answering questions, and showing empathy. However, there is little openness on the leader's part to any question of the subordinate accepting the task itself; in other words, the leader has the final say. Therefore, throughout the project, the leader gives specific instructions, explains tasks, and oversees performance. Or, as Lussier (2019) put it more bluntly, "You initiate the communication by letting the other party know that you want him or her to buy into your influence. You are closed to having your message accepted (task), but open to the person's feelings (relationship)" (p. 118).

Participative Communication Style

When sport leaders exhibit a combination of low task-oriented communication (i.e., low directive) and high relationship-oriented communication (i.e., high supportive behavior), they are demonstrating a **participative communication style**. The participative (or democratic) style is evident when interaction between the leader and followers is both encouraged and achieved through supportive communication. Communication patterns of this style of leadership include involving followers in setting goals, engaging in two-way and open communication, facilitating discussion, soliciting input in determining policies and procedures, focusing on interactions, providing suggestions and positive feedback, rewarding good work while punishing colleagues only after exhausting all other options, engaging in effective listening, and mediating conflicts (Johnson & Hackman, 2018). "The lesson for people striving to be exceptional is not to try to do it completely alone," advises consultant Bob Rotella in *How Champions Think*. "You're going to need other people on board with you. You need to select those people carefully, and you need to treat them right" (Rotella & Cullen, 2015, p. 229). Take, for instance, Joe Sargent. As the director of brand marketing for the Kansas City Chiefs, Sargent engages in participative leadership through communication and accountability. "It's important to me that my marketing unit has an understanding of everything going on with the Chiefs, even if it doesn't touch marketing specifically," explains Sargent. He adds that by doing this, those under his leadership understand what the team values and how their work can affect the team. "I want my staff to understand how their work is connected to the organization's priorities so that they feel valued," notes Sargent. "Promoting accountability is important because it encourages everyone to want to participate and get the credit for what they have done to drive the business" (personal communication).

In *Wooden on Leadership*, legendary basketball coach John Wooden argued that cooperation is part of the foundation for organizational success. "Sharing ideas, information, responsibilities, creativity, and tasks is a priority of good leadership and great teams" is one of the legendary coach's popular quotes ("John Wooden," 2020, para.

27). This cooperation approach helped Wooden lead the UCLA Bruins to four perfect seasons, 88 consecutive victories, and 10 national championships. Wooden embraced this cooperation approach with his talented athletes, and sport industry leaders can use such a participative or democratic style of communication effectively with subordinates who are highly capable and can provide information. Such subordinates are consulted to determine how to solve a problem or reach an objective, and they are encouraged and supported throughout the process. In this approach, communication is open (two-way), directions are general, and the relationship between the communicators is helpful and supportive.

Laissez-Faire Communication Style

When sport leaders exhibit a combination of low task-oriented communication (low directive) and low relationship-oriented communication (low supportive), they are demonstrating a **laissez-faire communication style**. This style, also referred to as *nonleadership* or *avoiding leadership*, is used when a sport leader accepts messages and decisions from subordinates and conveys the message to them that they are in charge. After informing subordinates of the task and answering any questions, the leader provides little direction because the followers are highly motivated and highly capable. Communication patterns of this style of leadership include allowing followers total freedom in setting their goals and procedures, engaging in superficial and noncommittal communication, avoiding discussions and interactions with followers, providing input regarding alternatives or suggestions only when asked, providing infrequent and limited feedback, not punishing but also not offering rewards, exhibiting poor listening skills, and avoiding conflict (Johnson & Hackman, 2018).

It can be challenging for some individuals to work under a leader who uses a laissez-faire communication style. This style can be especially difficult when the feedback is infrequent or nonexistent. This reality is familiar to intercollegiate athletics administrator Chevonne Mansfield, who observes, "Sometimes it's hard to gauge success if you're not getting constant feedback from your supervisor or team leader." However, she also points out that this situation does not render one helpless. "If you find yourself in that position, don't fret. I think there are other ways to gauge success outside of receiving feedback from colleagues. The kind of projects/work you get is also a good indicator of success," notes Mansfield, who is featured in chapter 4. She adds, "From my experience, executive staff connect with trusted team members they can count on, so if you're handpicked to work on a big project, consider that kudos for you." Mansfield explains that she gauges her success "by the opportunities that come my way and how I transitioned over the years in college athletics and higher education working in all three subdivisions of NCAA Division I" (personal communication).

Leadership Grid

Robert Blake and Anne Adams McCanse (1991) created the leadership grid, which plots five communication styles based on the degree to which leaders exhibit task-oriented behaviors (i.e., concern for production) and relationship-oriented behaviors (i.e., concern for people). The five styles are as follows: impoverished, authority–compliance, middle of the road, country club, and team oriented. Impoverished leaders exhibit low concern for both task and relationship. In this laissez-faire approach, a leader "does not actively attempt to influence others but rather assigns responsibilities and leaves followers to complete tasks on their own" (Johnson & Hackman, 2018, p. 55). In contrast, authority–compliance leaders exhibit high concern for task but little concern for relationship. The next type, middle-of-the-road leaders, demonstrate adequate concern for both task and relationship; these leaders "do not rock the boat—they push enough to achieve adequate productivity but yield if they believe increasing the workload will strain interpersonal relationships" (Jp. 55). Country club leaders tip to the other side, exhibiting low concern for task but high concern for relationship.

The last category—team leadership—is characterized by high concern for both task and relationship. This approach is considered the most effective because it enables work to be accomplished through relationships built on the trust

A leader in the sport industry exemplifies team leadership when she exhibits both task-oriented and relationship-oriented behaviors.

Photo courtesy of Paul M. Pedersen.

and respect that derive from interdependence and a push to achieve a common objective. This style results in increased productivity, increased profitability, effective communication, and positive relationships. When Kelly Krauskopf was the president and general manager of the Indiana Fever, she made a statement that could be used as an example of what team leadership is all about: "Since we operate as a small unit, I need to have strong people, and I urge them to take a proactive approach in their respective areas. It is less of an 'org' chart approach, although we have reporting structures for clarity. I try to give staff members leadership roles in their areas so that they feel ownership of the goals we are trying to achieve. I think it is important to empower your staff to be the best they can be" (personal communication). According to Johnson and Hackman (2018), followers are nurtured "so that they are able to achieve excellence in both personal and team goals" and followers and leaders "work together to achieve the highest level of productivity and personal achievement" (p. 55).

In applying to the sport industry the work of Johnson and Hackman (2018) and Blake and McCanse (1991), most sport leaders embrace and exhibit one or another of these leadership communication styles. Any given leader uses his or her dominant style in most interactions. Most sport leaders also have a backup style, or second orientation. For instance, Jim Harbaugh, head football coach at the University of Michigan, appears to embrace an autocratic style. For instance, in a discussing Winston Churchill's quote "You have enemies? Good," Harbaugh notes, "That means you've stood for something some time in your life" (Rosenberg, 2015, p. 36). At the same time, many of Harbaugh's associates, subordinates, and players would probably argue that he also has a strong relationship-oriented approach to leadership that many outsiders do not see. Regardless of the style that a leader exhibits, leadership is a requirement for success in sport organizations. More specifically, to accomplish both individual and organizational goals, sport industry leaders need to find the right balance between task-oriented communication and interpersonal-oriented communication. As Yukl and Gardner (2020) conclude in their overview of research that has been conducted related to specific types of task-oriented (e.g., planning, clarifying, monitoring) and relation-oriented (e.g., supporting, developing, recognizing) leadership behaviors, "The overall pattern of results suggests that effective leaders have a high concern for task objectives and interpersonal relationships, but they use specific types of behavior that are relevant for their leadership situation" (p. 43).

Variables That Affect Leadership Communication Styles

In addition to understanding the styles of leadership communication, people in sport organizations should be familiar with the general conceptual categories of leadership characteristics and the variables that affect one's selection of a leadership communication style. First, any examination of leadership communication should include an analysis of key characteristics. Yukl and Gardner (2020) note three basic categories—leader, follower, and situation—as well as various aspects of each category in which leadership theories have been grouped:

- Leader characteristics, such as motives, personality, values, integrity, moral development, confidence, optimism, skills, expertise, behavior, tactics, attributions, affective displays, beliefs, and assumptions
- Follower characteristics, such as needs, values, self-concepts, confidence, optimism, skills, expertise, attributions, identification, affective displays, commitment, effort, satisfaction, cooperation, and trust
- Situation characteristics, such as type and size of organizational unit, power and authority of leader, structure and complexity of task, organizational culture, environment, external constraints, and cultural values

For an example, consider Masai Ujiri, the president of the 2019 NBA world champion Toronto Raptors. As described by *Sports Illustrated*, this sport leader "has, through sheer force of personality, engineered a culture change" for his sport organization (Shipnuck, 2015, p. 110).

Second, practical application of the three characteristics—leader, follower, and situation—involves examining how the selection of a leadership communication style is affected by

LEADING SPORT ORGANIZATIONS THROUGH EFFECTIVE COMMUNICATION

Ildiko Buranits
Chief executive officer of Belváros-Lipótváros Sportközpont Kft (Budapest, Hungary)
Vice president of MTK Budapest Futball Club
Publisher, Pump & Flex

Throughout her career, Ildiko Buranits has used her communication skills to take on and excel in leadership positions in numerous sport organizations. In 2019, Buranits did it again when she was elected as only the second female vice president of MTK Budapest, a highly successful Hungarian soccer club founded in 1888. "One of my strengths is communication," observes Buranits, who has developed and leveraged that strength into phenomenal success in sport organizations and her own business entities. Born in the Hungarian town of Sopron and given a name that means "warrior" and "victorious woman," Buranits first wanted to be an archeologist then thought about becoming a newspaper writer. Instead, she became a multitalented leader as a business entrepreneur, international sport event director and promoter, sport magazine publisher, and general manager of a large and profitable sport venue in Budapest, Hungary.

Before obtaining her degree in directing and promotions, Buranits began her highly successful sport event management career, which included directing more than 50 sport competitions with independent prize money. In fact, her career dates back to the time when, as a 15-year-old, she organized an amateur rally-sport race. She hoped to eventually be an Olympian but had to choose between sport participation and a business career: "I gave up my dream of being in the Olympics in order to pursue entrepreneurial and business opportunities, because you cannot dream of the Olympics with an empty stomach."

Her two-decade career in business, however, has been remarkable; for instance, by age 23, she was Hungary's youngest factory owner.

Buranits is a legend in gym sports and a leader in executive positions for sport organizations, including the European Bodybuilding and Physique Sports Federation, World Bodybuilding and Physique Sports Federation, and the World Strongman Federation. She also helped establish the International Federation of Bodybuilding and Fitness Pro League in Hungary in 1999 and served as its president. Recognition for her work in the sport industry includes being named promoter of the year by the sport media, being honored for her sport diplomacy work by the Hungarian ministry of

Ildiko Buranits, center, is the vice president of the Hungarian soccer club MTK Budapest. Buranits is pictured with Peter Deutsch (left), the executive chair of MTK Budapest, and Tamas Deutsch, president of MTK as well as European Parliament delegate and vice president of NOC.

Photo courtesy of Ildiko Buranits.

sport, and having her sport strategies presented in Hungarian Parliament in 2002.

Buranits also owns and operates an independent and world-famous multisport festival known as Fitparade, an international annual convention featuring more than 50 sporting events, performances, and competitions. In addition to her oversight of Fitparade, a contracted partner with the IFBB (International Federation of Bodybuilding and Fitness) Pro League, Buranits became the CEO of a major sports and entertainment center (Belváros-Lipótváros Sportközpont Kft) in Budapest with its grand opening in 2020. Before her CEO position she was the general manager of MoM Sport, a government-owned entity that operates one of the largest sport complexes in Budapest.

As a highly successful sport industry executive, Buranits explains her leadership approach as follows: "I can only work with diligent and talented people whom I can trust and who subscribe to a work philosophy of teamwork built upon strategy and fair play." Buranits adds, for example, that "while the various area leaders who report to me are separate and have independence in terms of decision making and responsibility, they have a duty to help and support each other, and they are pleased to do so as they see this is good for the atmosphere and success of the company." Buranits' leadership approach could be classified as embodying a consultative communication style. For instance, she notes that while she has an open-door policy (e.g., relationship-oriented communication), it is "obligatory" that her colleagues answer her phone calls or call her back (e.g., task-oriented communication).

While at MoM Sport, Buranits' internal stakeholders included, among others, a public relations and communication officer, as well as directors (e.g., financial, technical), organizers (e.g., event, sport), coordinators (e.g., facility, cleaning, training), and managers (e.g., office, front desk, pool). In addition to their day-to-day activities, her employees organized events and facilitated a variety of sports, including soccer, water polo, basketball, and handball. Buranits herself is an international athlete at the masters level who has been a member of the Hungarian judo team, as well as a national champion. She explains that she and her staff would coordinate their work through "weekly meetings, email, phone, and personal dialogues as the basic tools for the internal communication in MoM Sport. In our weekly meetings, we evaluated the results of the previous week (e.g., accidents, complaints) and then prepared for the upcoming week's tasks." Buranits notes that complaints were rare, but she answered them "personally" whenever they arose.

Over the years the external stakeholders with whom she has communicated include tenants, journalists who cover her sport organization and events, services business (e.g., security, cleaning), various professionals (e.g., accountant, lawyer, bookkeeper), and other clients (e.g., guests, customers). "Regarding our customers, we respond immediately to all questions or requests, as such interactions take us closer to them." Buranits adds that "the basic—obligatory—rule is that consumers have to be informed properly in a kind and polite way all the time."

Beyond her various previous sport industry roles (e.g., general manager) and her current positions (e.g., festival owner, club VP, facility CEO), Buranits—who typically puts in more than 12 hours of work each day—also focuses on introducing her sport publication, *Pump & Flex* magazine, into international markets. When traveling abroad, she often communicates with her stakeholders via email, as well as the mobile messaging platforms Viber and WhatsApp. In the office, although her sport organization continues to use traditional media (e.g., newspaper, television) to communicate with and inform the general public, she also works to stay on top of social media: "I can see all the messages on our various social media sites, and I make sure we are communicating according to my guidelines. We engage ourselves in special training by media professionals from time to time so that we keep track of the changes, developments, and opportunities in social media." In addition to her sport organizations' usage of social media, Buranits' frequent professional postings and interactions on LinkedIn and Facebook are examples of how a sport industry leader embraces engagement on social media platforms.

certain key variables. As sport leaders adjust their communication style based on organizational demands (e.g., context), situational demands, and individual demands (e.g., listeners) (Witherspoon, 1997), they should consider four key variables: time, information, acceptance, and capability (Lussier, 2019). First, the sport leader must determine whether there is time for two-way communicative interactions. If so, the leader can use the consultative communication style, participative style, or laissez-faire style; if not, he must use the autocratic style.

The sport leader must also determine whether she has enough information for communicating, making a decision, or taking action. The leader can use the autocratic approach if there is no need for information, the consultative approach if some of the information is known, and the participative or laissez-faire style if she has little information. Regarding acceptance, the sport leader must determine whether the follower will simply accept the message (in which case, the autocratic approach can be used), will accept it with some reluctance (which calls for the consultative approach), or will reject it (which calls for the participative approach or laissez-faire approach to gain acceptance).

In terms of capability, the sport leader needs to determine both the ability and the willingness (i.e., motivation) of the follower. The leader can use the autocratic style if there is low capability (inability, unwillingness), the consultative style if there is moderate capability (moderate ability and motivation), the participative style if there is high capability (high ability but low confidence and motivation), and the laissez-faire style if there is outstanding capability (very capable and highly motivated). The leader must also be aware that capability can vary based on the task (Lussier, 2019). That is, a subordinate might be highly capable—possessing the ability and motivation—to engage in certain tasks (e.g., writing a blog entry, taking photographs) but less capable in other tasks (e.g., facilitating a press conference, hosting boosters at an event).

The work required to learn these various styles and be able to adapt accordingly is well worth it. As Lussier (2019) observes, "The better you match your supervisory style to employees' capabilities, the greater the chances of being successful" (p. 198). Therefore, sport managers should decide their approach to communication by first diagnosing the situation (in terms of time, information, acceptance, and capability), then selecting the appropriate leadership communication style (autocratic, consultative, participative, or laissez-faire) for that situation. The process of selecting a communication style has been complicated for sport leaders by the proliferation of social media. The various social media platforms and options require "leaders to adapt their communication strategies in response to the growth within this form of communication where stakeholders expect almost instant, accurate, and up-to-date information to be constantly forthcoming" (O'Boyle et al., 2015, p. 3). Regardless of the specific channels (e.g., social media, face to face, email, phone) through which they communicate, most effective sport industry leaders adapt to the situation and use flexibility in selecting communication styles.

CHAPTER WRAP-UP

Summary

A sport organization is a group of people working in or through sport to accomplish a certain objective (or objectives). This chapter starts by laying out the three essential elements of a sport organization: cooperation, common purpose, and communication. Organizational communication is the process through which messages are created, exchanged, interpreted, and stored within a system of human relationships. Communication both influences and is influenced by three features of a sport organization: formal structure, informal networks, and culture. Formal communication in sport organizations consists of intraorganizational or official communication that flows upward and downward according to the organization's chain of command. Informal communication in sport organizations consists of unofficial, lateral, multidirectional, and grapevine communication. The culture of a sport organization consists of its way of life and its predominant beliefs, goals, behaviors, and customs. A sport organization creates, shares, and alters its culture through both verbal and nonverbal communication.

The chapter also examines the forms of communication in sport organizations. To aid understanding, we categorize the forms into least interactive, potentially interactive, and most interactive formats. The chapter concludes by examining leadership, which is crucial to effective communication in sport organizations. Leadership and communication are often intertwined. Thus, in our analysis of sport leadership communication, we first define *sport leadership* as communication in and through sport that influences others' actions and attitudes, thus resulting in fulfillment of shared purpose or need. We then examine sport leadership communication styles—including dominant and backup styles of leadership communication. The chapter concludes with an examination of the four variables—time, information, acceptance, and capability—that should guide the selection of a leadership communication style.

Review Questions

1. What are the three major elements and the three key features of a sport organization?
2. What are the five organizational principles on which sport organizations are designed and structured?
3. How does the culture of a sport organization affect—and how is it affected by—communication in the organization?
4. What are the three categories of communication forms in sport organizations?
5. What variables affect leadership communication styles, and how are these variables manifested in sport organizations?

Individual Exercises

1. Select a sport organization, and determine its organizational chart. What is the organization's chain of command? Choose a couple of departments in the organization, and identify the span of management for each departmental manager. Is authority in the organization centralized or decentralized?
2. Reflect on your career ambitions. Where do you hope to be in the next decade? Then list five people who hold jobs similar to what you hope to do. Contact these five people, and ask them to define the term *sport leadership*. What are the similarities and differences in their definitions? How is communication intertwined with their definitions?
3. Describe your sport leadership communication style. How do you lead? Which style do you like to experience when you're a follower? What about when you're a leader?

Photo courtesy of Paul M. Pedersen.

CHAPTER 7

Sport Mass Media: Convergence and Shifting Roles

LEARNING OBJECTIVES

- To consider the types of sport publishing and print-communication entities
- To understand the media convergence permeating sport journalism in the digital age
- To understand the global trend of corporate media consolidation and its effect on sport journalism professionals and the content they produce
- To become aware of the history, issues, and challenges for newspaper sports sections
- To recognize the activities associated with sport books, wire services, and sport magazines and the affiliation between print publishing and the Internet
- To learn about diverse types of electronic mass media and their coverage of sport
- To become aware of key pioneers and media practitioners in electronic media
- To consider the growth of radio, television, cable, visual, and emerging technologies and their effects on sport communication
- To trace and evaluate convergence and multiplatform approaches to sport media content
- To analyze shifting roles and responsibilities of electronic media and the effects on practitioners, content, and coverage

KEY TERMS

actuality sound	media	premium channel	toy department
demassification	multimedia	publishing	wire services
mass media	convergence	sport mass media	

KEEPING UP WITH INDUSTRY CHANGES

Hannah Withiam

Chapter 11 of this text introduces you to sport communication research, and chapter 12 explains the most examined topic by sport communication scholars—sport media coverage of men's sport versus women's sport. The vast majority of published research on this topic dates back more than 40 years and overwhelmingly and consistently shows that men's sport and male athletes generally receive far more coverage than women's sport and female athletes regardless of the level of competition, age of participants, or the type of media providing coverage (e.g., Internet sites, newspapers, television). For example, the Women's National Basketball Association (WNBA) has received scant media coverage since it began play in 1997, while National Basketball Association (NBA) games are marquee media events. Even NBA off-season free agency garners lead stories on ESPN SportsCenter and headlines on sport websites across the United States.

Editor Hannah Withiam oversees all WNBA coverage for The Athletic and also serves as the associate editor for The Athletic New York.

Hannah Withiam hopes to chip away at those disparities by providing far more coverage of the WNBA, both in terms of quantity and quality of content. Withiam, just 25 years old, is the associate editor for The Athletic *New York*, where she works with reporters and edits articles covering all major sport teams in New York City and Buffalo.

However, Withiam's other passion lies in her newest duty for The Athletic, which is to oversee all WNBA coverage published on the website. After providing minimal coverage of the WNBA on a city-by-city basis during its first three years of existence, The Athletic changed course in 2019, hiring beat reporters to cover each of the 12 WNBA franchises, employing a pair of writers to cover the league from a national perspective, and delegating the responsibility of overseeing all this expanded coverage to Withiam.

"I think I've never been more proud of working for something than I am right now with our [The Athletic] coverage of the WNBA," Withiam said. "I grew up playing sports; I'm an athlete myself. I always believed in women getting equal coverage and support. Now that I am part of such an increase in the coverage of these athletes, it is powerful to me."

But The Athletic was not alone in expanding its WNBA coverage in 2019. Broadcast partners ESPN and CBS televised more WNBA games, while Bleacher Report and *Slam* magazine were among major media outlets that joined The Athletic in significantly expanding their WNBA coverage before the 2019 season started (Underwood, 2019). "I can't speak for other media outlets, but we [at The Athletic] thought it was the right time as a company to expand our WNBA coverage," Withiam said. "We have the resources to cover the WNBA as we wanted and have a writer for each team. It's great to see other outlets taking similar initiatives."

Withiam was a two-sport varsity athlete at Hamilton College in upstate New York, playing soccer and lacrosse while also serving as the editor of *Change* magazine, a national student outlet. She completed multiple internships in college, but her big break came from a post-undergraduate internship with the *New York Post*. Withiam was then hired by the *Post* as a full-time sport reporter and digital producer for the website.

This chapter covers the second component of the Strategic Sport Communication Model (SSCM)—**sport mass media**. At its basic level, the word *media* refers to a variety of means through which communication takes place. The term *mass media* denotes the segment of media focused on reaching the masses—that is, large numbers of people. Mass media come in various types (e.g., newspaper, radio, television, the web, other new media platforms) and use various modes of delivery (e.g., print, radio signals, the Internet, various social media tools). Increasingly, however, most media companies are converging these modes of delivery; for example, a television broadcaster also writes for his station's website, just as a newspaper reporter shoots video from a media conference with her smartphone.

The primary roles and functions of mass media often include the following:

- Informing (e.g., presenting newsworthy stories)
- Creating (e.g., producing a story or event)
- Influencing (e.g., reporting information that changes mindsets and actions)
- Entertaining (e.g., providing diversion for people to hear, see, read, or experience)
- Telling (e.g., publishing commentary and opinions)
- Delivering (e.g., bringing messages to an audience)
- Reinforcing (e.g., supporting cultural values)

In attempting to perform these functions, the mass media cover a multitude of areas and beats—for example, national and local news, politics and religion, science and entertainment, and business and finance. One of their major roles has been to cover sport, which is given a dedicated section in nearly every major U.S. newspaper and is one of three major segments (along with news and weather) on local television newscasts.

The term *sport mass media* encompasses reporting and commentary on sport and the various associated activities that surround and influence sport. In addition to covering sporting events and the sport industry, the sport mass media often reinforce and reflect the institution of sport. Furthermore, the sport mass media can even help shape sport, as noted earlier in the discussions of the agenda-setting theory and the roles of media gatekeepers. Although the vast majority of sports do not depend on the media for their survival—especially at the lower levels of organized sport—most profit-driven sports that lack media attention struggle to attract fans or achieve financial success. A sport's inability to make it as a mediated sport—or as a nationally televised mediated sport—directly affects consumers' awareness of it. A lack of media coverage results in a lack of awareness, which makes it hard for a sport entity to build or sustain success.

When it comes to popular, revenue-producing sport teams, both professional and at the major college level in the United States, the sport entity and the sport media are interdependent. In other words, it is truly a symbiotic relationship. This intertwining of sport and the mass media occurs across the United States and around the world. The sport media rely on sport to help fill programming schedules and newspaper columns, to sell advertising, to increase profits through higher ratings, to improve circulation figures, and to increase web traffic. Meanwhile, the sport industry depends on the media to provide visibility (e.g., coverage of a track meet), promotion and marketing (e.g., preview of a high school baseball tournament that increases community interest and attendance), credibility (coverage helps legitimize an event), information (e.g., analysis of trade rumors), advertising and publicity (e.g., coverage without having to pay for space or time), and revenue (e.g., broadcast rights fees).

In fact, one of the predominant reasons for the growth of the sport industry is the influence of the sport media. This industry segment—which ranges from newspaper sports sections to all-sport cable channels to satellite sports-talk radio stations and stand-alone sport websites—has had a profound effect on sport through its myriad activities associated with covering, delivering, publicizing, financing, and shaping sport. In response to this expansion of sport media, sport entities' communication departments face increasing demands. For example, for each of its home football games, the University of Alabama athletics department credentials more than 350 media members, including newspaper reporters and columnists, website reporters and analysts, national and local television and radio broadcasters, technicians, announcers, photojournalists, videographers, television production staff, and support staff. For big games, the demand is even higher; for example, 600 media credentials were issued for the second-ranked Crimson Tide's showdown versus top-ranked LSU in 2011 (Kausler, 2011).

Along with their growth in numbers, the sport mass media have grown in influence. Indeed, they are now pervasive in everyday life, play a key role in Western society, and are viewed by some as the most influential form of sport communication. The sport mass media reach audiences through various types of media, which consist of numerous channels and programming arrangements. These options include mediating sport through movies, photography, videography (much of which is now posted on YouTube), live transmissions (e.g., sporting event broadcasts on radio, web, local or network television, cable or satellite television), delayed and rebroadcast transmissions, magazines (e.g., sport news, interviews, reportage, documentary journalism), activity programming (e.g., active participation by the audience), made-for-television events (e.g., organizing and broadcasting of events such as the X Games), paid programming (i.e., time-buys, or programs for which event organizers buy broadcast time), the Internet (e.g., websites, blogs, news services, updates, broadcasts, games,

chat rooms), social media (e.g., Twitter, Facebook, Instagram, Snapchat), and print (e.g., newspapers, team newsletters). As a result, sport fans can now watch, read, and listen to sport-related content 24 hours a day, 365 days per year.

This chapter focuses on the first two segments of the sport mass media: sport **publishing** and print sport communication, as well as electronic and visual communication; chapter 8, in turn, delves into online communication, social media, and other emerging technologies (see figure 7.1). However, it is paramount to remember that many of these realms have converged. For example, instead of just being shown on television, video is increasingly streamed or cut into highlights to be shown exclusively on websites, including sites operated by television stations.

TWENTY-FIRST-CENTURY MEDIA CONVERGENCE AND CORPORATE CONSOLIDATION

New media have introduced multiple platforms and services for delivering sport content. The evolving sport media landscape hinges on such

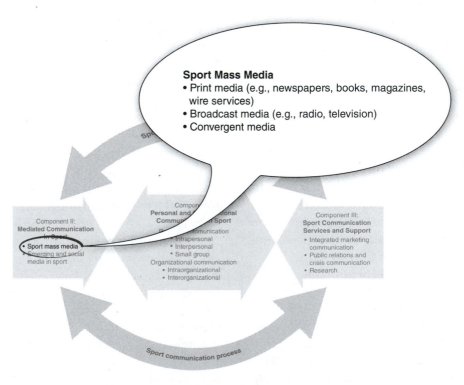

Figure 7.1 Sport mass media segment of the SSCM.

processes as digitization, convergence, and inter-activity. The seemingly infinite availability of and access to sport content has transformed the way in which breaking news is obtained, chosen, and distributed. Sport now merges audiences from traditional and new media platforms and delivery systems (Boyle & Haynes, 2003). **Multimedia convergence** is also evident in sport reporters' expanding routines and responsibilities; words, pictures, videos, audio recordings, and other interactions now exist across both legacy and digital platforms (Pedersen, 2014). As a result, since the turn of the 21st century, sport reporters have increasingly crossed over into multiple kinds of media and are now heavily involved in digital media convergence. Storytelling is still important, but stories now often involve not only text but also audio, video, data, photos, links, and other multimedia elements, with an increasing trend toward publishing more videos and graphics instead of traditional print or broadcast commentary (Madrigal & Meyer, 2018; Pedersen, 2014).

Due to the increase of convergence—that is, partnerships across various mass media—and advances in electronic and digital communication, many sport media entities are now involved in more than one genre of sport communication. This convergence in sport communication is best exemplified by media superpower ESPN, as can be seen in the various platforms used by Mark Fainaru-Wada, the prolific ESPN investigative reporter profiled at the end of this chapter. ESPN is most known for its television programming (e.g., *SportsCenter*, *Outside the Lines*, *Baseball Tonight*, and the *30 for 30* films), live broadcasts of sporting events (e.g., NBA playoffs, College Football Playoff), domestic television networks (e.g., ESPN, ESPN2, ESPN Classic, ESPNEWS, ESPN Deportes, SEC Network, Longhorn Network), and other electronic and digital media (e.g., ESPN HD, ESPN Radio, ESPN.com, ESPN Broadband, ESPN Wireless, ESPN Video On Demand, ESPN Interactive, ESPN PPV). However, this multinational and multimedia corporation is also heavily involved in sport publishing and was in print sport communication until 2018. In addition to operating the most-trafficked sport website in the United States, ESPN also published one of the two leading U.S. sport magazines, *ESPN The Magazine*, for 21 years, although ESPN decided to stop producing a print version of the magazine after September 2019 and instead plans to have more magazine-type content appear on its various web pages (Tracy & Draper, 2019).

Until his departure from ESPN, Grantland founder Bill Simmons was arguably the company's most well-known sport media personality. He is also an example of a sport media professional who rose to stardom in part because of his ability to adapt to modern media convergence. Simmons, who said he could not land a full-time job as a sport reporter for a newspaper after earning a master's in journalism from Boston University, launched the Grantland blog on June 8, 2011. As editor in chief, he initially hired well-known writers (e.g., Malcolm Gladwell, Wright Thompson, Dave Eggers, Chris Jones, Chuck Klosterman) then opted for younger writers (e.g., Zach Lowe, Bill Barnwell, Brian Phillips, Molly Lambert, Rembert Browne, Jason Concepcion).

In 2015, ESPN opted not to renew Simmons' contract, and speculation swirled about why. Simmons' relationship with top management, including ESPN president John Skipper, was shaky after his criticisms of ESPN's *First Take* and NFL commissioner Roger Goodell, which was viewed as the "last straw for ESPN" (Biasotti, 2015; "Simmons' Goodell Barb," 2015). In September 2014, the network suspended him for calling Goodell a liar during the Ray Rice domestic violence scandal. Then, in May 2015, Simmons said Goodell lacked "testicular fortitude" on *The Dan Patrick Show* ("Simmons' Goodell Barb," 2015). Skipper insisted that the split was a business decision, highlighted by philosophical differences between Simmons' goals and those of the network ("ESPN's Skipper," 2015).

Regardless of exactly what happened to cause the split, Simmons left an indelible mark that affected the entire sport media industry. In March 2015, comScore data indicated that Grantland had six million unique visitors, doubling its total from two years earlier. In addition, Simmons' impact on ESPN's overall sport media content was not limited to Grantland. He also served as executive producer of ESPN Films' popular and award-winning *30 for 30* series and hosted *The B.S. Report* podcast ("Theories Swirling," 2015). Indeed, no one had a bigger effect on the current boom of sport documentaries or was more influential in the mainstream popularizing of sport podcasts than Bill Simmons during his tenure at ESPN.

Major media corporations increasingly own more than one medium in a metropolitan area—for example, a city's daily newspaper, a major network television affiliate, and multiple radio stations. As of 2012, 90 percent of the media in the United States were owned by just 6 corporations, down from more than 50 major media companies in 1983 (Lutz, 2012). This consolidation of corporate media often requires convergence among media outlets and professionals. Consider: If the same company owns a television station and a newspaper in one city, it would be illogical and financially wasteful to assign both a television videographer and a newspaper photojournalist to shoot a high school football game when one person can do the job for both outlets.

However, even though most new hires are expected to use a variety of media, the sport media profession can still be broken down into primary sectors. In other words, journalists who work for newspapers still have a primary duty of writing and editing articles, whereas most reporters working for sport television and radio still take on broadcasting and production as their main tasks. Therefore, it remains important to examine print sport communication and electronic sport communication as different media even in this era of media convergence.

SPORT PUBLISHING AND PRINT SPORT COMMUNICATION

As shown in figure 7.1, the Strategic Sport Communication Model includes three major segments of sport media, the first of which consists of publishing and print communication. What exactly are sport publishing and print sport communication? This chapter addresses these questions in much detail, but here we provide short answers to set a foundation for the rest of this section. *Sport publishing* is the business or profession involving the commercial production and dissemination of information related to sport. This definition, which is a sport-related spin-off from the dictionary definition of *publishing*, is broad enough to include nearly all forms of sport-related publishing—for instance, sport books, newspaper sports sections, sport magazines, sport websites,

annuals, team newsletters, fan magazines, media guides, and game programs.

Although print sport communication is similar to sport publishing, there is a slight difference. Print sport communication involves any medium that disseminates printed matter related to sport. Therefore, all print sport communication is sport publishing, but not all sport publishing is print sport communication. For instance, electronic sport publishing—the distribution of sport information by means of a computer network—is sport publishing but not print sport communication. Because electronic sport publishing involves both sport publishing and the Internet, this aspect of sport communication is discussed in both this chapter and the chapter on new media (chapter 8).

NEWSPAPER SPORT COVERAGE

The mass media influence and are influenced by sport, but television is generally considered the most powerful of the media, and it has exerted major influence on the growth of U.S. sport over the past six decades. At the same time, sports and sport organizations that receive consistent coverage by local dailies know that their bottom line is also bolstered through the coverage and hype provided by newspapers and their affiliated websites. Many sporting events have press boxes that are full of print journalists who cover the action. This was not always the case; even after the first daily newspaper arrived in the 1780s, sport articles did not begin regularly appearing for nearly a century (Sowell, 2008). Today, however, sport coverage is a sizable component of newspapers. Indeed, it is rare to find a publication that does not have a sports section or at least give some attention to the sport industry. The smaller the newspaper, the more likely it is to emphasize sport, particularly in the form of high school and community sport coverage, in large part because the families and friends of athletes and coaches tend to buy and save the papers that mention them.

Background of Sport Coverage in Newspapers

Sport has not always received coverage in newspapers, which have a history in the United States that goes back four centuries. In 2016, fewer than 1,300 daily print newspapers were published in the United States, although that figure has been declining in recent years (it was nearly 1,800 in 1950) largely due to a drop in readership among younger generations, who prefer to obtain their news online (Benedetto, 2018; "Newspaper Circulation," 2012). This number, however, does not include the weekly and biweekly newspapers that are common in small towns across the country, nor does it include community newspapers, online services, and **wire services**.

Daily newspapers are categorized by circulation, although that has become more difficult to tally in the digital age because all major newspapers in North America now have both print and digital circulations. In 2014, according to the Alliance for Audited Media, the three most circulated daily U.S. newspapers (combining both print and digital editions) were, in order, *USA Today*, the *Wall Street Journal*, and the *New York Times*, which were also the only three U.S. newspapers still distributed nationally in print form (Malcolm, 2014). The *New York Times* has the largest annual Sunday circulation by far because the other two national papers do not publish Sunday editions (Edmonds, Gasking, Mitchell, & Jurkowitz, 2013).

For the vast majority of the history of U.S. newspapers, most dailies were owned and operated by individuals, families, and private groups. However, the 20th century brought about a concentration of ownership, which has continued in the present, as most papers are now owned by newspaper chains or groups. Leading chains include Digital First Media; Community Newspapers Holdings, Inc. (CHNI); Lee; and Tribune Publishing Tronc/Tribune, some of which also own other media entities (e.g., television and radio stations). As detailed by Pavlik and McIntosh (2015), newspaper chains bring some benefits, such as shared resources and freedom from relying on—and possibly being influenced by—one major advertiser or industry. But there are also many problems with chains, including reduced connection with local communities, reduced local reporting in favor of material from wire services or the chain's other papers, and increased pressures to be profitable by reducing staff and quality control. Nevertheless, the trend toward more corporate consolidation of the newspaper industry will continue, evident by

the two largest newspaper chains in the United States merging in 2019 when GateHouse Media purchased *USA Today* owner Gannett for $1.4 billion, giving the combined company more than 260 U.S. daily newspapers (Arbel, 2019).

Newspapers in the Digital Age

In recent years, the newspaper industry has faced a daunting set of challenges: competition (e.g., competition for advertising dollars by Craigslist and niche websites that can better reach potential consumers with specific interests), changes in readership and consumption patterns (e.g., readers gravitating toward the immediacy of the web and social media), and layoffs and downsizing (Kian & Zimmerman, 2012). Historically, newspapers struggled financially during recessions but fared much better in strong economies when potential readers had more discretionary income, but that is no longer the case, evident by 2019 being one of the worst years ever for newspaper layoffs despite a strong U.S. economy (Smith, 2019a). In response to these challenges, newspapers are continually shifting more resources to their websites while asking their reporters and columnists to both promote their work and engage readers through social media (Butler, Zimmerman, & Hutton, 2013). "I keep hearing that I am going to lose my job because of the Internet," said Mark Purdy, a longtime sport columnist for the *San Jose Mercury News*. "Yet more people are reading my columns than ever before, and my readership is coming from more different places because of the Internet. I'm getting people reading my columns from all over the world, and that's something that was unimaginable before the Internet" (personal communication).

Early in newspaper history, sport was not a regular feature, and sports editors often had to fight with news editors who did not see much value in sport. In 1733, the *Boston Gazette* published an article on a boxing match, which has been referred to as the first sport story printed in a U.S. newspaper (Sowell, 2008). Throughout the 1700s and most of the 1800s, newspapers covered sport but only in a sporadic and isolated manner (Sowell, 2008). That began to change in the last two decades of the 19th century. The initiator of this change was Joseph Pulitzer, who, in 1883, created the first newspaper sports department

Although most newspapers are owned by newspaper chains or groups, the *Seattle Times* is an exception as it is a family-owned daily that provides a variety of content—including extensive sport coverage (Seattle Reign, Seattle Storm, Seattle Seahawks, Seattle Mariners, Seattle Sounders, University of Washington, local high schools, and so forth)—across a wide range of platforms (e.g., print, website, mobile app).

for his *New York World* (Brian, 2001). Pulitzer's sports pages covered boxing, baseball, football, and many types of races (e.g., horse, bicycle, roller skating).

Twelve years later, sport began to be covered to an even greater degree when William Randolph Hearst established the first sports section in a U.S. newspaper (Belts, 1953). Hearst, who realized that the attention he gave to sport helped increase his circulation figures, created this innovative section in his *New York Journal*. Sport received increasing coverage in newspapers over the next few decades, and sports sections became more common and specialized in the 1920s, with expanded pages, extended coverage, improved sportswriting, and the arrival of the "golden age of sports" (McChesney, 1989). This was an era when people had more leisure time, higher literacy rates, economic prosperity, and a desire to put World War I behind them, so they turned to their newspapers to read about their favorite sports and the sporting heroes that newspaper reporters helped create

(Laucella, 2014). Sport coverage has remained a major component of newspapers throughout the ensuing decades.

The staff of a sports department can be as small as a lone part-time journalist assigned as the writer, photographer, layout artist, and editor of the sports pages while also being assigned to another section of the newspaper. A sports staff can also be as large as three dozen employees, although the largest newspaper sports staffs have seen significant layoffs over the last 20 years— more so than smaller and more community-oriented newspapers (Kian & Zimmerman, 2012). In an extension of the quip about sport being the **toy department** of life (found in chapter 1), some individuals have referred to newspaper sports departments as the toy departments of journalism (Creedon, 1994). This labeling comes about because sportswriting is often very different from other journalistic endeavors. After all, the primary duty of most newspaper sportswriters is to cover games (Gisondi, 2010).

WIRE SERVICES AND TECHNOLOGICAL ADVANCEMENTS

Numerous wire services supply sport news to both print and nonprint media organizations and customers. This content includes text (i.e., articles), graphics, audio, video, and photographs. It is provided by sport journalists to the wire services, which distribute it to print publications, websites, and multimedia companies. The most popular wire services are Reuters, the Associated Press (AP), and United Press International (UPI). Reuters is the largest international multimedia news agency thanks to its associated information services (e.g., financial information). Among organizations focused primarily on news, the AP is the oldest (started in 1846) and the largest in the world, with 3,200 editorial, communication, and administrative employees and 263 bureaus in 106 countries. It covers most major sporting events in the United States. UPI turned 100 years old in 2007, but this news agency, which provided an alternative to the monopoly that the AP had long enjoyed in the United States, has struggled financially since the 1980s. It now concentrates on smaller information-market niches and remains a distant third to the AP and Reuters.

WEB SPORT MEDIA

For the past two decades, print sport reporters have used the Internet to find background information for stories, search for sources, and interview sources via email. Now they are also required to use social media platforms, such as Twitter and Facebook, for similar purposes and to help market their own work and interact with media consumers. In these ways, the advent of the Internet has made print sport reporters' jobs easier, helped them save time on research and following their beats, and enabled them to increase the quality of their content (Kian & Murray, 2014). Need to know who played on an all-state volleyball team in 2017? You can probably find the answer in seconds via a web search engine (e.g., Google, Yahoo!, Bing) instead of having to spend hours going through old newspapers or even microfiche as reporters regularly used to do.

Most top newspaper sport journalists across the world now spend much of their time on Twitter, either looking for or posting information (Schultz & Sheffer, 2007; Sheffer & Schultz, 2010; Sherwood & Nicholson, 2013). Twitter, an asynchronous form of social communication that is similar to cell phone text messaging but allows tens of millions of individuals to tweet simultaneously, is discussed in depth in chapter 8. For now, suffice it to say that Twitter has had a huge effect on print sport journalism (Clavio & Kian, 2010; Sanderson, 2011). As ESPN college football and college basketball reporter Mark Schlabach put it, "No one sits on news anymore. You can't, because it's all broken on Twitter" (personal communication).

The increased national competition in sport journalism sparked by the advent of new media has also reignited investigative sport journalism. Given the increasing number of media outlets and options, journalists have focused more on the "why" of events and on interpreting their significance for fans. Television provides pictures, so writers offer more opinion pieces and in-depth reporting to differentiate their stories from the content of broadcast packages. As competition has stiffened due to websites, 24-hour sports-talk radio, cable sport stations (e.g., ESPN), and social media outlets, newspaper sportswriters have been forced to focus more on "enterprise, feature, and investigative pieces" rather than typical game stories (Strupp, 2001, p. 10). Therefore, whereas the "golden age of sport" created hero worship, sport journalists and reporters today delve into scandals, such as the Ray Rice domestic violence case, the International Federation of Association Football scandal of 2015, and the NCAA's Division I men's basketball recruiting scandal largely uncovered by the Federal Bureau of Investigation (FBI). Journalists continually create new angles to compete with nonstop sport coverage and reinvent content by integrating trends, novel subjects, and local stories.

Most large and midsize U.S. newspapers have maneuvered many of their resources to their websites in response to declining readership for print editions, reductions in classified advertising due largely to the popularity of Craigslist, and an increase in the cost of paper. In March 2015, U.S. newspaper websites combined for a record 176 million adult unique visitors, including a higher percentage of readers under 45 than over 45 (Conaghan, 2015). In other words, younger generations are reading newspaper content; they are simply doing so on their home computer, laptop, tablet, or phone. As a result, some newspapers (e.g., the *Times-Picayune* in New Orleans) have either reduced the number of days per week on which they print and circulate hard copies or gone entirely online, and most major U.S. newspapers have reduced the number of pages in their daily editions (Edmonds et al., 2013).

As of 2015, 78 percent of U.S. newspapers with circulations over 50,000 had implemented some sort of paywall for its websites, which require readers to subscribe for access, pay to read individual stories, or limit themselves to only a certain number of free articles per month (Williams, 2016). However, in addition to proving largely unsuccessful, newspaper paywalls have come with the adverse effect of precipitously dropping a newspaper's digital readership, which in turn deters online advertisers (Edmonds, 2014). The only major U.S. newspapers to successfully implement paywalls for significant financial gain are the *New York Times* and the *Wall Street Journal*, which together accounted for more paid digital subscribers than the next 16 newspapers combined in 2013 (Edmonds et al., 2013). Furthermore, 56 percent of people who regularly read newspaper content still do so in the printed format, thus indicating that there remains a place for traditional newspapers in the sport media industry (Mitchell, 2015).

As the web has grown, web-only sport journalists have emerged. The vast majority of those who work for major web-based sport outlets (e.g., ESPN.com, Yahoo! Sports, CBSSports.com) are former newspaper sport reporters who moved to the web for higher salaries, more stable jobs, and a national platform for their work (Kian & Zimmerman, 2012). Similarly, most of the beat reporters who cover college athletics teams and professional sport franchises for popular websites (e.g., Rivals, 247Sports, etc.) also have traditional print media backgrounds.

In contrast, many of the top writers and bloggers who have emerged at nontraditional sites (e.g., Deadspin, SB Nation) did not come through the newspaper ranks (Kian, Burden, & Shaw, 2011). Although many of these individuals are professional and credible journalists who value strict editing, accuracy, and strong reporting, some who call themselves sport journalists (e.g., some sport bloggers, sport website owners and operators, and sport podcasters) are seemingly more interested in speed and sensationalism than in upholding high journalistic standards. Without the controls imposed in traditional sport journalism, much sensationalism and gossip are available on the web. In fact, many stories and commentaries are published on the web that never would have been published by more traditional avenues.

SPORT MAGAZINES

Changing media consumption patterns and increased competition have eroded much of the influence of sport magazines over the past two decades. Like newspapers, magazines have struggled to retain subscribers, and most of the ones that have survived and flourished have done so by adjusting to this era of sport media **demassification** (i.e., specialization) and digitization. Sport magazines began to appear in the latter part of the 19th century; over the years, two all-sport publications stood the test of time: the *Sporting News* (started in 1886) and *Sports Illustrated* (the preeminent U.S. sport magazine, which dates back to the 1950s). The sport magazine industry was dealt a major blow when the *Sporting News* (*TSN*) stopped publishing its regular print magazine at the end of 2012 (Mullis, 2012). The last cover of a regular issue of *TSN* featured football players from the Universities of Alabama and Notre Dame, which were set to square off in the national championship game. Ironically, neither Alabama nor Notre Dame—arguably the two most storied programs in college football history—fielded a football team when the first issue of *TSN* was published (Mullis, 2012). *TSN*, however, still publishes regularly through a digital-only format while also producing annual preview magazines for major professional and college team sports, as well as for fantasy sports and the NFL Draft.

According to a 2017 report by the Alliance for Audited Media, *Sports Illustrated* (*SI*) ranked 12th among all U.S. magazines with a paid and verified weekly circulation of more than three million ("Total Circ," 2017). According to Megargee (2004), *SI* received its impetus in 1950, when Time Inc. employee Bob Cowin sent a three-page memo to the company's founder, Henry Luce. "My wife likes to say I was the founder of *Sports Illustrated*," Cowin once told a reporter. "That makes me squirm. I had the idea, yes. But somebody else would have come up with the idea sooner or later. Ideas are often a dime a dozen" (p. 3C). Cowin had done some door-to-door research in Ohio earlier that year and discovered an interest in more sport publications. In August 1954, the first issue of *SI* was published, and it has since become not only the premier U.S. sport magazine but also the nation's standard for long-form, investigative sport journalism.

Sports Illustrated, however, is also facing challenges in the digital era. *SI* published its print edition 50 times in 2015, but that was reduced to 38 in 2017; the magazine is now published biweekly (MacCambridge, 2018). Moreover, a sale in ownership led to a significant reduction of *SI* reporting and editorial positions in 2019, bringing into question the quality and depth of reporting that made *SI* a gold-standard for quality print sport journalism in the United States (James, 2019; MacCambridge, 2018).

ESPN The Magazine was the only other general U.S. sport magazine with a large, national readership, evident by a regular circulation of more than two million (Battaglio, 2019). However, despite its success, ESPN elected to stop publishing the magazine in late 2019 after 21 years, citing internal research that most *ESPN The Magazine* readers

While some sport magazines have moved fully online or ceased publication altogether, other general and specialized sport magazines have survived in the face of changing media consumption patterns and increased competition.

were already accessing content on ESPN web platforms and thus the same content could just be published online (Battaglio, 2019).

Overall, paid subscriptions to U.S. magazines have been declining, whereas revenues from digital content account for a small but growing share of the magazine industry's finances ("Total Circ," 2017). After *Sports Illustrated*, the most popular sporting magazines in the United States are niche and single-sport publications, such as *Golf Digest*, *Golf Magazine*, *Field & Stream*, *Runner's World*, and *Tennis*. Consumers access these popular magazines, referred to as *consumer titles*, either by subscribing or by purchasing single issues at retail outlets. The majority of magazines, however, are trade or business-to-business publications that are unknown to the general public and are almost never sold at bookstores or newsstands. These magazines have limited circulation to specific readers within a given profession. Examples of sport trade publications of this type include *American Football Monthly* and *Tennis Industry Magazine*.

SPORT BOOKS

Sport books are forgotten in most discussions about print sport media delivery systems. The writing and publishing of sport books, however, are major aspects of sport communication. Each year, thousands of sport books are published covering a wide variety of topics, including commentaries, novels, self-help books, biographies, histories, and a host of others. In addition, the web has made it easier to publish books, and many appear in e-book format.

According to Pavlik and McIntosh (2015), major functions of books in society include transmitting culture; providing entertainment; and diffusing information, ideas, and knowledge. Although sport books play a key role in entertaining readers through escapism and diversion, they also can inform (e.g., about sport history or business), transmit, reinforce, question, and challenge culture (e.g., socially acceptable behaviors, rules, norms, morals, values). According to the Association of American Publishers, the book-publishing industry in the United States had net sales of just under $28 billion in 2014, representing nearly a 5 percent increase over 2013 ("U.S. Publishing Industry's Annual Survey," 2015).

ELECTRONIC AND VISUAL COMMUNICATION

Whereas print is the oldest type of sport media, the most influential type throughout history has been electronic media. This form of media began with the advent of radio in the early 20th century, which was followed by the spread of television sets in U.S. homes after World War II and now the digital age dominated by the Internet and social media.

Experiencing Sport Through Radio

As the first electronic medium, radio had an effect that was powerful and immediate. According to Brinson (2005), "Since 1920, broadcasting has been one of the defining features of modern American sociocultural, political, and economic life" (p. 1). We cannot ignore or escape its pervasive and forceful influence on American culture because it directly affects every element of our lives. Although many forms of electronic media are available today, radio was first among national mass media and gave people the chance to connect via programs, music, drama, sport, and political messages. Radio united people in the early 20th century as they listened to boxing bouts and other sporting events either in their homes or in public spaces.

On November 2, 1920, U.S. election results were broadcast live for the first time with news of Senator Warren G. Harding's victory over Governor James M. Cox from a 100-watt transmitter in a dilapidated shack. Thanks to this coverage, Pittsburgh's KDKA became known as the Pioneer Broadcasting Station of the World (Harbord, 1929, p. 61). Soon after, the Jack Dempsey–Georges Carpentier boxing bout of 1921 drew thousands of listeners to shops, halls, and other spaces where they could share a communal experience. By the beginning of 1922, 30 stations were broadcasting music and messages to 60,000 receivers in the United States (Ackerman, 1945). Westinghouse was the first company in the radio business, first with KDKA and then with WBZ in Springfield, Massachusetts, and later Boston.

History of Radio and Sport

In the 1920s and 1930s, sport was important for radio networks—such as the National Broadcasting Company (NBC) with its Red and Blue networks, the Columbia Broadcasting System (CBS), and the Mutual Broadcasting System—which helped establish radio as a primary medium. Listeners wanted to hear about boxing bouts, their favorite horses, football teams, and baseball teams. Thus, "fandom" was one element of radio's ability to connect the nation and help overcome differences in race, gender, age, and location (Blanchard, 1998; Harper, 1999; Vaillant, 2002).

The "golden age of radio" began in the 1930s and continued through the 1940s, when the medium reached maturity as more listeners tuned in for entertainment, news, and sport information. As mentioned in chapter 3, individuals had more leisure time than before, and people relied on radio and the movies for entertainment and enjoyment. During the 1930s, the number of homes with radios increased from 12 million to 30 million, and advertising revenue expanded from $40 million to $155 million (Blanchard, 1998). Although the Great Depression affected all aspects of life in the United States, radio recovered quickly and sustained its place in American life. In fact, it "became the one widely available distraction from the awful daily struggle" (Blanchard, 1998, p. 239).

Radio appealed to individuals for various reasons. For one thing, it adds sound to listeners' experiences while still using words as the primary means for communicating messages. Although newspaper journalists in the early 20th century used imagery and stylistic devices to transport readers to the events they described, radio incorporated the sounds fans would hear if they were at a game, bout, or match—cheers and boos, for instance, as well as referees' whistles, bats hitting baseballs, basketballs hitting the floor, car engines, tennis rackets striking balls, and so on. The term *actuality sound* (Andrews, 2013) refers to the sounds that you would hear if you were live at an event; by providing such sounds, radio helps listeners imagine the event, the players, the fans, and the stadium or arena.

Of course, radio also incorporates music, as well as the voice of the journalist, interviewee, or commentator. Key play-by-play sportscasters on radio included Mel Allen, who started broadcasting New York Yankees games in 1939. He was baseball's first nationally recognized voice and was known for his catchphrase "How about that!"

Emergence of All-Sport Radio Format

Today, as in the 20th century, fans still catch games on the radio, but now sport radio has its own dedicated space. Sport radio caters to the much-coveted male demographic through sharp-edged and often off-color dialogue and commentary. Fans tune in daily to hear their favorite programs, which range from edgy, irreverent shows to more straitlaced offerings. Listeners can also call in to debate topics of the day and engage in lively discussions.

In 1987, Emmis Communications introduced New York's WFAN, the first all-sport radio station in the United States. Initially, it lost money and was nearly shut down (Adgate, 2013); however, after its dial position was changed and its signal strengthened, it became part of the CBS network. In 2012, it earned $41 million in revenue and ranked first among all-sport stations across the country (Adgate, 2013). Once WFAN got started, other sport stations and networks quickly joined the airwaves. ESPN Radio debuted in 1992, and One-on-One Sports Network appeared in 1993.

The current mass media landscape is consumed with digital technology, live streaming, interactive apps, and audio and video podcasts. All are part of 21st-century sport radio. Accordingly, *Sports Business Journal*'s John Ourand (2012) wrote that sports-talk radio is going through a "renaissance" (p. 17). In 2002, there were 413 sports-talk stations; a decade later, there were 677. Today, ESPN Radio, Fox Sports Radio, Yahoo! Sports Radio, NBC Sports Radio, CBS Sports Radio, and others have stations and programs in the largest radio metro markets nationwide (Adgate, 2013).

NBC Sports Radio, which launched in 2012, expanded its coverage to include all three Triple Crown horse races, which are also televised by NBC. NBC Sports Radio content is distributed by Westwood One, and affiliates across the country carry its programming. Its content is also live streamed on NBCSportsRadio.com and can be accessed through other NBC sites. According to NBC Sports Ventures senior VP Rob Simmelkjaer, "NBC and these races are pretty synonymous in a lot of people's minds. So I think having the races on radio under the NBC brand will increase the exposure of the radio broadcast. . . . And I think it will strengthen racing as an audio product" (Mullen, 2015). NBC Sports Radio also has programs such as *Pro Football Talk Live* with Mike Florio and *The Daily Line* with Tim Murray and Michael Jenkins, as well as *Safety Blitz* with Rodney Harrison and Dan Schwartzman.

Radio is still a powerful medium in the United States. Nielsen Media Research data published by the Radio Advertising Bureau found that 89 percent of American radio stations garnered a total revenue of more than $14 billion in 2018. Of this, $920 million came from online radio streaming (Watson, 2019). "The Infinite Dial," a report by Edison Research and Triton Digital, found 67 percent of Americans 12 years old or older had listened to online radio in the past month, showing online radio's further growth and expansion ("Audio and Podcasting Fact Sheet," 2019). Although radio broadcast rights fees and advertising revenue are lower than those for television, media companies still compete for listeners, content, and advertising dollars in today's "era of audience fractionalization with entertainment and news programs" (Adgate, 2013). Furthermore, the skyrocketing costs of rights fees will bolster sports-talk shows, which is radio's primary strength.

All-sport radio stations appear to be supported by industry power ratios, which, as explained by Stark and Schiffman (2000), "measure the sales strength of individual formats by showing how many cents on a hypothetical dollar each format returns in ad revenue" (p. 116). For instance, if sports-talk radio had a power ratio of 1.82 in a market where each audience share was valued at $1 million in ad revenue, then a sports-talk station would bill $1.82 million per share. According to these ratios, it is not unusual for any type of sport radio to be the top-billed format. Advertisers are drawn to sport radio's affluent and focused audience, as well as its local nature. According to Nielsen, of the 23 million Americans who listen to sport radio weekly, 8 of 10 are employed and overindexed on incomes of more than $75,000 annually and college education levels ("Nielsen: Sports Radio Listeners," 2018). In 2017, the median age of listeners was 44 years old. According to Traug Keller, ESPN senior vice president who oversees ESPN Audio and Talent, between 80 percent and 90 percent of ESPN Radio's audience across its more than 400 U.S. affiliate stations are male (Notte, 2018).

Although men form a coveted demographic in sport radio, the target audience includes people with various interests and levels of interest in sport. The first segment, or main target, consists of sport nuts who thrive on scores, news of trades and suspensions, and playoff information. This audience accounts for the bulk of listeners to any all-sport format, but it is not the only target audience. Another group consists of fans interested in just one sport; these fans will not tune in 24 hours a day, but they will listen when their favorite sport is being played or discussed. The last target consists of those who like sport but are not devoted faithfully or fanatically to any particular team or sporting event. This group just tunes in to catch up on sporting news and be generally aware of the sport scene. These three target audiences all have one thing in common: They all have at least some interest (whether passive or active) in sport.

In 1994, Nanci Donnellan, known as the "Fabulous Sports Babe," became the first woman to host a national sports-talk radio show; she was also the first to run her own program. From 1994 to 2001, Donnellan was heard nationally on ESPN Radio and Sports Fan Radio Network until she took time off because of breast cancer. Her experiences are detailed in her autobiographical book, *The Babe in Boyland*. Despite Donnellan's success— and although women such as Andrea Kremer, Hannah Storm, Doris Burke, Allie LaForce, and Samantha Ponder work as sport reporters and anchors on network or cable—most sport radio stations across the United States are dominated by male (and white) employees. In fact, sport radio is considered by some to be "the last bastion of the old-boys club," featuring "shock jock" hosts and comments that "marginalize and objectify women, statements that offend the LGBT community, and jokes that border on or are openly racist" (Spain, 2015).

In contrast, Sarah Spain, host of "Spain and Company" on ESPN Radio and host of ESPN's *That's What She Said* podcast and many other roles at ESPN, believes that hosts can be inclusive and create positive conversations about race, gender, and other social issues ("Sarah Spain About," 2019). "By introducing progressive ideas into a traditionally masculine space, hosts can show that the two are not at odds," she wrote in a 2015 espnW column. "The best sports radio shows elevate the conversation, are smart, funny, insightful and irreverent and do not leave a significant portion of the listeners feeling insulted or marginalized" (Spain, 2015).

Radio is also used as part of cross-platform deals at Fox Sports Media Group and ESPN, which strengthens the brand and taps into an underestimated and authentic medium that appeals to average listeners and fans. As with other mass media, radio programmers use new technologies and stream programs via the Internet, televise their radio programs on television stations, and offer apps for mobile devices; for example, ESPN Radio made World Cup games available on multiple platforms. Podcasts are another way in which new media extends the reach of audio content, and many people use them to make programs available on demand. "The digital world of sports radio is infinity," said former CBS Radio executive Tom Bigby. "There's so much more that we can do" (Ourand, 2012, p. 17). From its early sport programming to today's sport radio shows, radio has shown both strength and versatility.

Radio's Popularity and Ability to Adapt

RCA founder David Sarnoff set up a boxing bout to promote radio on July 2, 1921. For the following 30 years, radio was stable, steady, and solid. In the 1950s, television took advertising revenue away from radio, but radio adapted by seeking local sport fans who were interested in high school and college sports. Two benefits of radio are its low costs and simple technology. In terms of technology, larger stations use microwave signals or Cellcast, which uses cellular phone technology to transmit signals. All stations use mixers, thus allowing talent to mix their voices with other audio. And, of course, reporters and producers use microphones for interviews with athletes and coaches and to pick up environmental sounds such as crowd cheers and boos (Schultz & Arke, 2015).

Although radio does not offer visuals, it has adapted with new technology and targets of its own. High-definition (HD) and satellite radio, local audiences, and an emphasis on sports-talk stations and programs have enabled the medium to thrive, in part by catering to diehard sport enthusiasts and fanatics. In addition, radio is often used to supplement other media. For example, a fan might watch a game on television then either go online to discuss the outcome with other fans on social media or call a sports-talk radio show to share ideas or debate issues. Radio's adaptability and commitment to progress and change are evident in its continued evolution and expansion. In addition to listening to traditional radio, listening is now done through mobile devices and web-based devices in cars. Advances in technology have also helped podcasts' popularity (Vogt, 2015a).

According to Pew's "State of the News Media," increasingly more Americans have listened to podcasts over the last decade. Edison Research and Triton Digital survey data indicate that as of 2019, 51 percent of people 12 years of age and older have listened to a podcast, with 32 percent having listened to one in the past month, marking an increase from 26 percent in 2018 and 9 percent in 2008 ("Audio and Podcasting Fact Sheet," 2019). Some top podcasts, according to *Esquire* magazine, include *Moneyball* author Michael Lewis' *Against the Rules*; *First Take* with Stephen A. Smith, Max Kellerman, and Molly Qerim; *Pull Up* with CJ McCollum; *The Mina Kimes Show* featuring Lenny; Dave Zirin's *Edge of Sports*; *View From the Cheap Seats*; NPR's *Only a Game*; *RCC2* hosted by CC Sabathia and Ryan Ruocco; *Sports Wars*; *The Bill Simmons Podcast*; *30 for 30* podcasts; *Men in Blazers*; and *Outside Podcast* ("The 15 Best Sports Podcasts of 2019," 2019). Bill Simmons' The Ringer celebrated its third anniversary in 2019; its 30 podcasts had 53.5 million downloads in May that year. Ad sales for his sports, technology, and pop culture site exceeded $15 million in 2018. Former ESPN talent Ryen Russillo joined The Ringer for his *Dual Threat* podcasts and to team up exclusively with Simmons ("The Ringer's Bill Simmons," 2019).

Barstool Sports has also used podcasts as a growing part of its business. In 2016, it had 3 podcasts, but that number increased to more than 30 in 2019. Its CEO, Erika Nardini, said that more than 35 percent of Barstool Sports' new revenue comes from podcasting, which she views as far more cost-effective than video production ("Podcasts Quickly Become," 2019).

In other podcasts, The Athletic expanded and launched a multimillion-dollar podcasting service with more than 20 exclusive, ad-free podcasts.

Most range from 15 to 40 minutes long, and the site hopes to distinguish itself by offering hyper-localized podcasts behind a paywall. It hopes to attract new sport fans who consume and engage with sport in different ways ("The Athletic Grows Business Model," 2019).

From HD radio (digital) to satellite radio, the medium has adapted to changes in technology and addressed its competition. Although its strength is specific to sound, its reach and power are infinite. It enables sport fans to interact on issues with other sport fans; to hear their favorite games in their car, home, or office; and to gain insider information about teams, players, and coaches (Grossman, 2005a, 2005b).

Experiencing Sport Through Television

Print journalism and radio have clearly influenced the development of sport and of sport communication; however, the most powerful and significant of all media is television (Bandura, 2002). According to Kellner, U.S. television is "one of the most far-reaching communication apparatuses and information and entertainment transmitters that has ever existed" (1981, p. 31). This view was reinforced by Garrison and Sabljak (1993): "Television's love affair with sports, especially major professional sports and college football and basketball, was the most important factor in creating a sports-oriented American society" (p. 235). Although many agree that the media have transformed sport, it is also true that sport has transformed the media.

History of Television and Sport

Sport has dominated U.S. television since soon after the medium's inception in the 1930s (Vogan, 2014). In the late 1940s, broadcasters used sport as a vehicle to increase demand for television, which in turn boosted advertising revenues. As noted earlier, networks sought first and foremost to sell television sets; by 1950, around 10.5 million had been sold in the United States alone (Vogan, 2014). Because they used heavy camera equipment that needed bright light for maximum efficacy, early broadcasters restricted telecasts to certain events, types of sport, and locations. It was easiest to broadcast boxing, wrestling, baseball, and

football because the first two took place in small, lighted gyms and the latter two were played outside. On the positive side, sport programming was inexpensive because it required no writers, actors, props, or sets. In addition, sporting contests are dramatic events, and, like sport radio, sport television enabled viewers to watch events live without having to attend in person (Vogan, 2014).

In 1939, a single camera on the third-base line transmitted the first televised sporting event to fans—a college baseball contest between Columbia and Princeton. The first network broadcast of sport came in 1944 in the form of NBC's *Gillette Cavalcade of Sports*, which stayed on the air for 20 years. In 1945, NBC also mounted the first broadcast of a college football game as Columbia defeated Lafayette, 40 to 14. That same year, NBC's new image-orthicon camera brought viewers the annual Army–Navy football rivalry game. In 1947, George Halas, founder of the Chicago Bears, received only $900 per game for the broadcasts of his team's efforts. Although television programming began as a prime-time event, it expanded in the 1950s to include weekend programming. One example was college football, which was broadcast by NBC on Saturday afternoons with its "game of the week" (Baran, 2006; Bernstein & Blain, 2002; Castleman & Podrazik, 2003; Garrison & Sabljak, 1993).

By the late 1950s, televised sporting events were a vital part of network television and were also important for sport leagues' financial stability. Networks sought to improve sport coverage and expand their audience reach. As a result, they highlighted drama and created more stylistic productions through increased numbers of cameras, enhanced editing, and the use of graphics. Storytelling also augmented drama through the creation of heroes, villains, and compelling plot lines (Vogan, 2014). In the 1960s, the sport audience increased as advertisers continued to value sport despite its rising expense. Television, and specifically the camera, could tell each sport's unique story in a visually aesthetic way.

ABC sought to broaden its sport coverage in 1960 by contracting to broadcast the Winter Olympics (held in Squaw Valley, California), which had never before been shown live on U.S. television. ABC paid $167,000 for the broadcast rights and tried to purchase the rights for the

Summer Games in Rome as well. When CBS outbid ABC, however, ABC canceled its contract for the Winter Games. CBS broadcast the games instead, without sponsors, and it ended up enjoying high ratings for both the Winter and Summer games. Jim McKay broadcast from Rome, and the network's use of videotape enabled viewers to see events from the same day for the first time (Baran, 2006; Castleman & Podrazik, 2003).

In 1963, the Army–Navy football rivalry broadcast featured instant replay, thus improving fans' at-home viewing experience of the game. As discussed in chapter 3, ABC executive Roone Arledge revolutionized sport broadcasting and the way consumers experience sport. He not only recognized fans' desire to learn more about the human-interest side of athletes through "up close and personal segments" but also revolutionized the technical elements of broadcasting to capture sport's most dramatic moments, both on the field and off. His vision was to create "immersive viewing experiences"; he wanted to ensure that viewers felt as if they were at the games by focusing on the totality and grandeur of the events (Vogan, 2014, p. 132).

Arledge's *Wide World of Sports* debuted in 1961 with Jim McKay as host. It showcased many sports from numerous venues using both live and taped segments. It highlighted popular mainstream sports as well as lesser-known sports, such as bowling and racing. To broadcast the Summer Olympics of 1972, Arledge, McKay, and Howard Cosell used satellite transmissions; they averaged a 52 percent share for prime time during their coverage. During the 1976 Olympics, Arledge's crew of Frank Gifford, Cosell, and Chris Schenkel presented "up close and personal" segments and emotional human-interest stories that garnered top ratings in most time slots (Hilliard & Keith, 2005). Over time, this approach "established the network's reputation as an effective and innovative source for sports" (Castleman & Podrazik, 2003, p. 137).

Around the same time, made-for-television documentaries about professional football appeared, including CBS's *The Violent World of Sam Huff*, which focused on the New York Giants' middle linebacker named in the title. Walter Cronkite hosted and narrated the film, which was part of the network's *The Twentieth Century*

documentary series. Huff wore a wireless microphone in his shoulder pads to give viewers access to the game's action and audio, thus amplifying the viewing experience. It also helped promote Sunday afternoon football broadcasts on CBS, which was the National Football League's main network partner in 1960 (Vogan, 2014). Other television documentaries of the time included *Run to Daylight* (1964) about legendary Green Bay Packers coach Vince Lombardi and *Pro Football: Mayhem on a Sunday Afternoon* (1965) about the sport's place in U.S. culture. The latter program used montage editing, sideline sounds, color film, and narration to portray "pro football as an epic and violent spectacle that reflects 1960s America" (Vogan, 2014, p. 136). More sport documentaries are discussed later in this chapter.

In 1970, Arledge and NFL commissioner Pete Rozelle brought *Monday Night Football* to prime time on a weekly basis; since that time, it has been "an institution of historical significance for broadcasting and for American popular culture as well as sport" (Crepeau, 2005, para. 1). Arledge's ABC network paid $8.5 million for the rights to broadcast 14 games. In the first of the weekly Monday night games, the Cleveland Browns defeated the New York Jets, with Cosell and Keith Jackson offering play-by-play narration and Don Meredith providing color commentary. When asked about Arledge, CBS Sports chairman Sean McManus (son of Jim McKay) said, "He understood the importance of on-air talent and building stars, whether it was Peter Jennings, David Brinkley, Ted Koppel, Jim McKay, or Howard Cosell. He understood how much of your identity really is placed in the people who are in front of the camera. No. 2, he understood that all good television basically comes down to storytelling" ("CBS's McManus," 2006). *Monday Night Football* offered both of these elements through charismatic and witty announcers and state-of-the-art technology that captured emotion and intimate stories.

Arledge also wanted to add show business to sport and attract women to football. To that end, he created a media spectacle by using story lines to frame contests; using three commentators rather than two; increasing the number of cameras; and including graphics, slow motion, split-screen visuals, and reverse-angle replays (Vogan, 2014). Arledge used nine cameras on the field and two production units for the beginning shows. As the number of cameras increased, the "sport as soap opera" method of showing athletes' emotions with tight camera shots and angles enabled fans to see firsthand the struggle and conviction of their favorite athletes and teams. By 1977, *Monday Night Football* helped ABC become America's highest-rated network (Vogan, 2014).

At that time, the NFL's broadcast rights package was worth $50 million, which dwarfed Major League Baseball's $18 million and the NBA's $2 million. This was the first time the networks realized that "major league sports meant major league broadcasting" (Baran, 2006). As Crepeau (2005) pointed out about *Monday Night Football* (MNF), "The amazing thing is how much the habits of the nation were transformed. The football weekend was extended, reducing some of the gloom that is Monday. The ratings exceeded everyone's wildest expectations. MNF became the king of the Monday night television. The other networks could not compete and sometimes gave up trying. People gathered in bars and homes in groups to watch these games and see what outrageous thing would happen next" (para. 7). In 2005, after 36 years, *Monday Night Football* ended on ABC, but ESPN (ABC's partner in the Walt Disney Company) moved into the Monday slot in 2006 (Baran, 2006; Castleman & Podrazik, 2003; Schoenherr, 1999).

ABC also pioneered the celebrity sport announcer in the form of Howard Cosell on *Monday Night Football*. Although some considered him arrogant and overly dominant in his approach, this lawyer-turned-announcer is considered one of the legends of sport broadcasting. In the words of *Washington Post* sportswriter Shirley Povich, written after Cosell's death in 1995, "Cosell was identified as the foremost sports television journalist of his time. He would have accepted it all with his trademark comment, 'That's telling it like it is'" (Povich, 1995, p. E2). Cosell entertained, and he recognized the importance of communication skills. He considered himself a "communicator with a human perspective," someone who would "bridge the gap between entertainment and journalism" (Schultz, 2005, p. 128). Robert Lipsyte called Cosell the "most valuable property in American sports" (Lipsyte, 1975).

Cosell was controversial and sometimes caustic, but he stood up for his beliefs regardless of the consequences. He supported legendary boxer Muhammad Ali's refusal to join the U.S. Army during the Vietnam War, which cost Ali his heavyweight title, and he idolized Jackie Robinson for integrating professional baseball in the 20th century. Cosell was also outspoken about baseball's reserve clause, the commercialization of major collegiate athletics, and the Olympic Games. Fans loved Cosell's unique style. After his controversial departure from *Monday Night Football* in the mid-1980s, he had two radio shows on ABC, *Speaking of Sports* and *Speaking of Everything* (Shapiro, 1995, p. A1).

In other sporting events, ABC's broadcast of the 1973 "Battle of the Sexes" between tennis stars Bobby Riggs and Billie Jean King in the Houston Astrodome gained high ratings during prime time. King defeated the 1939 Wimbledon champ 6-4, 6-3, 6-3, thus helping make it acceptable and fashionable for women to be athletes. She also started the Women's Tennis Association, *womenSports* magazine, and the Women's Sports Foundation (Billings, Butterworth, & Turman, 2015; Castleman & Podrazik, 2003; Schwartz, 2000). ABC also broadcast the Montreal Olympic Games in 1976 after paying $25 million for the rights and charging sponsors (e.g., Sears, Schlitz, Chevrolet) $72,000 per minute for advertising spots. In 74 prime-time hours, with Jim McKay as the host, the network used 25 color cameras, including four electronic sport gatherer (ESG) minicameras. In the late 1970s, sport coverage expanded into cable shows on WTBS, WGN, HBO, and ESPN. In addition, college football and basketball games were either syndicated nationwide or broadcast through conference- or school-related networks. Broadcast networks recognized that amateur sport evokes a special kind of loyalty and found ways to help fans identify with their favorite teams, players, and fan bases (Schoenherr, 1999).

Emergence of ESPN

As noted in chapter 3, ESPN changed sport, and *SportsCenter* arose as a cultural phenomenon through its charismatic and witty anchors, flashy technical tricks, and nonstop sport coverage. ESPN is still the best-known television sport franchise in the world. Originated by founder Bill

Rasmussen's initiative and inaugural ESPN president Chet Simmons' vision, ESPN no longer offers only the major leagues and NCAA sport but also presents original series, films, reality shows, and even game shows to appeal to a wide audience. From its foundation, ESPN has stood apart thanks to creativity and innovative uses of technology. For example, ESPN's electronic cut-ins during the 1980 NCAA Tournament interspersed clips of games in progress within a featured game's broadcast. In 1983, ESPN broadcast in stereo for the first time; in 1985, ESPN Sports Update offered on-screen, in-game scores from other games. Since then, the network's SportsTicker and BottomLine have kept fans updated with scores and information. Thus, it is no surprise that ESPN won six Sports Emmy Awards in 2019, tying it with NBC for the most trophies that year (Pedersen, 2019). ESPN is also part of Statista's top 10 list of most valuable sport business brands worldwide, as sourced from *Forbes*. Even with its high-profile layoffs, increased rights fees, and a decrease in cable subscribers (Lisa, 2019), *Forbes* still considers ESPN, which has an estimated value of $13.1 billion, the most profitable media brand in the world ("#47 ESPN," 2019).

In addition to taking advantage of technical innovations, ESPN continues to expand and evolve its programming as it offers cross-platform options for advertisers through its varied networks. ESPN has always targeted young males, but when college football became a foundation for the network in the 1980s, it was clear that ESPN sought to widen its audience. This continues to hold true with such long-term shows as *PTI*, *SportsCenter*, and the *ESPY Awards*, which moved to sister network ABC in 2015. ESPN offers sport-based programs as well as political coverage, news, social issues, and pop-culture pieces through a wide variety of anchors, reporters, and other talent (Hill, 2004; Reynolds, 2004; Whitney, 2004). It consistently taps into fans' passion for sport and recognizes the global power of leagues, teams, and athletes. In 2018, ESPN launched its streaming service, ESPN+. In 2019, it partnered with the Atlantic Coast Conference to launch the ACC Network; the deal includes media, digital, marketing, and sponsorship for the Power 5 conference's 15 schools (Smith, 2019c). Of note is the ACC Network's female leadership, which built the network and prioritizes female viewership ("ACC Network's Female Leadership," 2019).

Other recent initiatives include acquiring the rights to the Bundesliga league from Fox Sports, a six-year deal worth more than $30 million each year (Ourand, 2019c). In the inaugural year following its launch, ESPN+ produced eight episodes on Duke men's basketball. and followed up with the University of Memphis in 2019 when the Tigers had the number one recruiting class in the country that year ("Memphis Latest College Hoops Program," 2019). ESPN also extended its broadcast deal for eight years with the Special Olympics ("ESPN Extends," 2019).

Despite its continued expansion, ESPN still has its share of challenges. It shut down ESPN Deportes radio in 2019 and laid off its employees. ESPN now focuses more on mobile and audio podcasts rather than Spanish-language radio. Some of the radio programs were turned into podcasts (Ourand, 2019a).

Jimmy Pitaro took over as president of ESPN in 2018 after running Disney's digital and consumer product divisions. He moved the network away from politics and controversy and toward sport and ESPN's core business and digital efforts. One move Pitaro made was acquiring the rights to UFC and boxing (after carrying fights for 45 years, HBO gave up boxing in 2018 due to viewership decline ["HBO Planning," 2019]) as a way to increase ESPN+ subscribers. "When I think about a future where we're sitting down with the major leagues to negotiate renewals of our existing deals and potentially acquire additional rights, I really like the situation that we're in," Pitaro told Vox. ESPN has the power of its platforms—a broadcast network, several cable channels, the Walt Disney synergy, and a talented production team. According to Pitaro, the network wants more access to athletes. One place this access is granted is on *Detail*, which includes in-depth game analysis from players and athletes across leagues and sports. Both Kobe Bryant and Peyton Manning have participated. While *Detail* is currently on ESPN+, parts also appear on the regular ESPN television networks which tease for viewers to go to ESPN+ for more detail, which drives fans back to ESPN+ (Kafka, 2019). Manning's *Peyton's Places* also appears exclusively on ESPN+.

Photo courtesy of Paul M. Pedersen.

Over the past decade, ESPN has made significant adjustments and strategic decisions regarding its offerings and divisions. For instance, in September of 2019, the company shut down both ESPN Deportes Radio and *ESPN The Magazine*. In its statement regarding ceasing its Spanish terrestrial radio, ESPN noted that "It's no secret Hispanic fans skew heavily on digital and social which is why we made the decision to discontinue ESPN Deportes terrestrial radio (ESPN Deportes Radio) in September."

Mutually Beneficial Relationship Between Sport and Television

Sport became an integral part of local television in the medium's early days. In the 1970s, local television was a popular source of news for Americans (Schultz & Sheffer, 2014). At the national level, networks recognized the importance of sport to their ratings in the 1980s, and the three major networks at the time broadcast 1,500 hours of sport programming in 1985. In 1989, CBS paid $1 billion for the right to broadcast the NCAA basketball tournament for seven years. That same year, Major League Baseball received $500 million from television and radio broadcasters for one season. In 1990, NBC paid $150 million per year for four years of NBA broadcasts. CBS then carried the rights for Major League Baseball for four seasons at a price tag of $1 billion, and ESPN paid $400 million for the rights to 175 games during that same time period. Networks paid these huge amounts of money to keep sporting events away from their competition, solidify their audiences, and differentiate their network from others. For the first time, sport was part of the overall promotional effort for an entire network.

As the Internet became a newsroom tool in the late 1990s and beyond and digital technology created more options and faster communication, local sport coverage struggled to survive. Some stations, like WTEN in Albany and WDSU in New Orleans, eliminated their anchored sport segments. Others used the Internet to expand their reach and interact with viewers through blogging and social media. As fans and athletes also used both of these technologies, they began to assume roles traditionally held by local sport broadcasters. Along the way, the sport-news cycle went from days to seconds. Stories would no longer be heard first on the six-o'clock news; instead, they were broken on Twitter and Facebook.

Change in television sport has tended to happen incrementally, as evidenced in the evolution from black-and-white to color images, film to videotape, and analog to digital transmission. Even though the transition to digital took decades, television broadcasters endured challenges in adjusting to it, especially in relation to the Internet. Still, sport remains lucrative and maintains dominant viewership. In the 2018 calendar year, for example, 88 of the top 100 broadcasts were in sport, up from 81 in 2017. Within that ranking, 63 NFL telecasts made the list (Karp, 2019a). Sport journalists tried to maximize their work efforts and incorporate digital technology into their traditional roles. Local sport reporters depend on access for compelling content; as the Internet

Photo courtesy of Larra Overton.

Larra Overton is a producer, host, and reporter for the Indianapolis Colts. Her many roles with the NFL team show the importance of versatility in sport industry jobs and careers.

shifted control from reporters to newsmakers, local television stations and newspapers lost power in the gatekeeping process.

TV and Football

By 1991, a 30-second advertising spot during the Super Bowl broadcast drew $800,000. In 1993, Fox gained NFL rights, paying $1.58 billion for four years, and used professional football as a means to gain exposure for its upstart network. With anchors John Madden and Pat Summerall, the network used innovative graphics and introduced cutting-edge technology. By the late 1990s, the networks as a group paid $17.6 billion for eight years to cover NFL games. Since then, NFL television rights deals have continued to grow much larger. Brian Rolapp, the NFL's executive vice president of media, negotiated a $275 million deal with CBS in 2014 and a $1.5 billion annual deal for DirecTV's Sunday Ticket package, which were in addition to the NFL's existing lucrative television deals with ESPN, Fox, and NBC ("50 Most Influential," 2014). As of 2019, there was an antitrust lawsuit against the NFL and DirecTV over their Sunday Ticket package. The case had been dismissed by a fed-

eral judge in 2017, but the Ninth Circuit Court of Appeals reversed the decision two years later. According to plaintiffs, if the NFL did not pool games' out-of-market telecasts, there would be multiple telecasts of games as teams would compete against one another, distributing telecasts through cable, satellite, and Internet channels. Antitrust law makes sure that competing businesses actually compete rather than conspire (McCann, 2019). This continues the debate about the NFL's power over individual teams' distribution rights ("Antitrust Lawsuit Revived," 2019).

Football is the most popular sport in the United States and has been since 1972 (Norman, 2018). In 2018, Gallup found that 37 percent of respondents picked football as their favorite sport followed by basketball (11 percent), baseball (9 percent), and soccer (7 percent). Football's popularity peaked in 2006 when 43 percent listed it as their favorite sport. It should be noted, though, that there was a decline in the percentage of Americans who said they were fans of professional football, which could be due to the physical and mental impact on players, anthem protests, domestic violence cases, or other factors (Norman, 2019).

The NFL launched its own broadcasting venture, the NFL Network cable channel, in 2003. NFL Media now includes the NFL Network, NFL.com, NFL Films, and other entities (Vogan, 2014). NFL Films also offers off-season programming such as HBO's *Hard Knocks* series, which frequently wins Sports Emmy Awards, including in 2019 for its preceding season's coverage of the Cleveland Browns' training camp. The NFL Network also broadcasts *A Football Life*, which provides player and coach profiles; *NFL Total Access*, a television news program; *Good Morning Football*, which covers breaking news and other sports, news, and entertainment weekday mornings; *Thursday Night Football*; and *NFL Top 10*. In 2019, HBO's fictional drama *Ballers* aired its final episode after five seasons ("Ballers," 2019).

Stars of the Gridiron: Super Bowl Ads

The Super Bowl is consistently one of the highest-rated television programs. In 2019, viewership for the New England Patriots' victory over the Los Angeles Rams in Super Bowl LIII was the lowest in 11 years, at 98.2 million; however, there were 32.3 million social media interactions across Facebook, Instagram, and Twitter ("Super Bowl LIII Draws," 2019). In 2020, Super Bowl LIV scored 99.9 TV viewers and averaged 102 million viewers across channels and streaming outlets (Pallotta, 2020). The viewership record was set in 2015 when a record 114.4 million viewers tuned in to see the Patriots defeat the Seattle Seahawks in Super Bowl XLIX (Gough, 2019)

Although sport fans want to see the game itself, some Super Bowl viewers watch the event exclusively for the ads. The ad market is challenging, but Super Bowl ads have a long life because some are released early and many generate attention afterward through the annual *USA Today* Ad Meter rankings and other postgame coverage. As a result, the value of Super Bowl ads has skyrocketed since 1967, when NBC charged $37,500 for a 30-second spot. In 2020, Fox sold 30-second commercials for $5.6 million, nearly double the cost charged in 2011 (Yang, 2020). The Super Bowl's television audience may have waned in the last few years; however, it is still the most-watched U.S. television event of the year (Smith, 2019b). Tim Calkins, marketing professor at Northwestern's Kellogg School of Management, has studied Super Bowl commercials over time and still believes the megaevent is the best way to reach large numbers of people at once. In an interview with CNN, he said, "There's a symbolic nature of Super Bowl advertising that just isn't the same as other platforms," he said. "A Super Bowl ad used to be a Super Bowl ad, but over the past decade, it's really become a two-week extravaganza" (Calkins as quoted in Disis, 2019). More and more companies are releasing ads ahead of time on YouTube to generate buzz prior to the big event. An example is Volkswagen's 2011 Passat commercial, "The Force," which showed a child dressed up in a Stars War costume trying to use special powers on his dog, a washing machine, and his parents' new car. It was popular on YouTube, and *Time* magazine called it "the ad that changed Super Bowl commercials forever" (as quoted in Disis, 2019). Increased brand awareness, immediate boosts in sales, and a surge in stock price all make the Super Bowl a top ad platform (Smith, 2015).

Rob Siltanen, founder and chief creative officer of the Los Angeles firm Siltanen and Partners, compares Super Bowl ads to "must have guests that keep a party rockin'" (2014, para. 2). He considers the Super Bowl one of the "safest bets" (para. 6) for good marketers with smart and creative advertising agencies due to the PR and "replay value" (para. 8). In 2012 and 2013, Siltanen's agency created spots to help introduce a new line of running shoes for Skechers. He believes that the value of the ads "easily quadrupled" (para. 9) the cost thanks to PR gained through features on *Good Morning America*, the *Colbert Report*, and the *Tonight Show*, as well as hundreds of news stations, newspapers, blogs, radio programs, and You Tube. Viewers watch these ads for entertainment and for discussion rather than tuning them out or changing the station (Mandese, 2005, p. 14), and this viewer engagement lures advertisers.

TV and the Olympic Games

The NFL anticipates earning $6 billion to $7 billion per year in television revenue from its broadcast partners under its current contracts: ESPN ($1.9 billion yearly), satellite operator DirecTV ($1.5 billion), CBS ($1 billion), Fox ($1.1 billion), and NBC ($950 million) (Chemi, 2014). For 2015, the NFL projected a profit of more than $12 billion—$1 billion more than in 2014—making the league the most lucrative and robust of sport properties (Kaplan, 2015). Even so, the Olympic Games rival the NFL in both prestige and power. Over the years, television has brought us some spectacular Olympic moments, such as Al Michaels' famous call—"Do you believe in miracles? Yes!"—to capture the U.S. men's hockey team's thrilling victory over the heavily favored Soviet team in the 1980 Winter Olympics in Lake Placid (Michaels, 2014, p. 117). The lasting effect of Michaels' six words is still discussed today, and it shows the power of Olympic broadcasts.

In 1984, ABC paid $92 million for the rights to broadcast the Sarajevo Winter Games and $225 million for the Los Angeles Summer Games. As the Olympics became increasingly profitable, the cost of broadcast rights fees rose as well. In 1992, the broadcast rights (for the Barcelona Olympics) reached $610 million. In the current broadcast rights agreement, NBCUniversal (NBCU) secured winter and summer rights through 2032 for a price of nearly $7.7 billion. It includes rights across all platforms and an additional $100 million signing bonus paid by NBCUniversal to assist in the promotion of the Olympics and Olympic values between 2015 and 2020 (Crupi, 2014). The International Olympic Committee (IOC) did not invite other networks to bid for the package this time around; previously, NBCU had offered nearly $4.4 billion to outbid ESPN and Fox Sports by about $1 billion for the 2014 Sochi Winter Games, the 2016 Rio de Janeiro Summer Games, the 2018 PyeongChang Games, and the 2020 Tokyo Games, which were postponed to 2021 (Crupi, 2014).

NBC executive Dick Ebersol cultivated the network's relationship with the IOC decades ago and sustained it through his retirement in 2011. The sport icon was a visionary when it came to broadcasting sport and entertainment on television and is considered one of the "most accomplished executives in U.S. television history" (Ourand, 2015b). Early on, as a researcher for Roone Arledge, he learned the power of storytelling, which characterized his Olympic broadcasts (Ourand, 2015b). Over the years, he secured numerous rights deals for events such as the Olympics, *Sunday Night Football*, and the Super Bowl. When Muhammad Ali presented Ebersol with the *Sports Business Journal* Lifetime Achievement Award in 2015, six sport commissioners (from the NFL, NBA, MLB, NHL, NASCAR, and PGA Tour) all delivered their praise.

NBCU lost $223 million on the 2010 Vancouver Olympics but made money on the 2012 London Games and brought in nearly $850 million in revenue

from the 2014 Sochi Games (cable networks earned $257 million). Taken as a whole, the London Olympics were the "most-watched event in U.S. television history" at that time (Crupi, 2012). According to Nielsen, the London Games drew nearly 220 million total viewers, which was 2 percent higher than the 2008 Beijing Games (215 million viewers). The network garnered a 17.5 rating and more than 31 million viewers for its prime-time coverage, the best audience for a Summer Olympics since the Atlanta Games in 1996. Moreover, the average viewership for 17 nights was up 8 percent and 12 percent, respectively, from a 16.2 rating and just under 28 million viewers for the Beijing Games (Karp, 2012). The network also enjoyed improved ratings across various platforms (NBC, NBC Sports Network, MSNBC, CNBC, Bravo, and Telemundo). Cable audiences increased by 2 percent over Beijing (Karp, 2012), and 70 percent of all Americans watched part of the Games (Crupi, 2012).

For the 2014 Sochi Games, NBC offered more than 1,500 hours of content across platforms and more than doubled its total programming hours

Photo courtesy of Paul M. Pedersen.

As this chapter details, the television packages paid by media entities for the rights to broadcast the Olympic Games are some of the highest-priced deals in sport broadcasting. NBCUniversal has an agreement with the International Olympic Committee (IOC) to broadcast Youth Olympic Games (YOG) through 2032. In addition to watching highlights of the 2016 YOG Winter Olympic Games on the NBC Sports Network, viewers were able to watch on-demand coverage as well as live coverage of certain events on the IOC's YouTube channel.

from the 2010 Vancouver Games. Sochi coverage averaged more than 21.4 million viewers and a 12.3 household rating. Although this result was 11 percent lower than the 24.4 million viewers and 13.8 household rating for the Vancouver Games (Crupi, 2014), the total number of exposures for all NBCUniversal platforms was 242 million, which was 3.5 million more than for Vancouver (*Nielsen*, 2014).

In 2014, NBCUniversal paid $7.75 billion to secure Olympic rights through 2032. Despite controversies leading up to the Rio Games over the Zika virus, polluted air and water concerns, and athletes' safety, coverage averaged 27.5 million viewers across all platforms, including digital streaming. Traditional television ratings were 10 percent to 15 percent lower than what NBCU had expected, but the growth of streaming exceeded expectations. Roughly 10 percent of NBCUniversal's ad revenue came from digital streaming, and viewers streamed more than 2.71 billion minutes of coverage—nearly double the combined number for the two prior Olympic Games (Holloway, 2016).

In 2018, PyeongChang hosted the first Winter Olympics where prime-time coverage was available simultaneously on broadcast, cable, and streaming. Nevertheless, it was the least-watched Olympics on record. Prime-time coverage averaged 19.8 million viewers nightly on NBC, NBC Sports Network, and NBC Sports Digital's streaming platforms, which was down 7 percent from the 2014 Sochi Olympics. Important to note is that the 2014 Olympics did not air on NBC Sports Network and did not have simultaneous streaming. Some of the prime-time coverage was tape-delayed in PyeongChang, but NBC did live stream some events. Despite the 7 percent drop from 2014, NBC still dominated coverage during the 18 days of competition and were top-rated programs during that time span. Mark Lazarus, chairman of NBC Broadcasting and Sports, said, "In today's media environment, to average approximately 20 million viewers over 18 nights—which is essentially the number of hours for a full season of three prime-time shows—is a tremendous accomplishment" (as quoted in Otterson, 2018). NBC Sports Digital live streamed 1.85 billion minutes of coverage, 2.17 billion being streamed total, which more than tripled the streaming from 2014. The Games brought NBC $378 million in the first quarter

of 2018 (Hayes, 2019a). Whereas consumption habits change and evolve with Netflix, Hulu, and other streaming services, the Olympics still remain a "ratings juggernaut," according to *Forbes* (Barr, 2018).

Ad sales continue to be strong for the Olympics, evident by NBC's ad sales generating $900 million from the 2018 Olympics (Settimi, 2018). NBCUniversal expects the 2020 Tokyo Games to bring in more than the 2016 Rio Games' record $1.2 billion in national ad sales. The 2020 Olympics is the first time NBCUniversal is selling the Games as a unified offer that combines broadcast, cable, digital, and social reach and expanse for its advertisers. In its second Olympics (the 2018 Winter Olympics was the first), NBCUniversal will guarantee audiences with its Total Audience Delivery metric (TAD) and measures across linear, out-of-home, digital, and streaming. Advertisers will be able to buy against audience demos, which helps brands that may need demo guarantees. NBCUniversal's ad-supported streaming search, Peacock, launched in 2020. The opening ceremony for Tokyo will take place in 2021; however, advertising sales began in 2018 (Sutton, 2019).

In 2016, the IOC launched its own digital Olympic TV channel before the Summer Games in Rio. Olympic Broadcast Services CEO Yiannis Exarchos expects that in 10 years the channel will see a profitable return on the $600 million investment ("Media Notes," 2015). The Olympic Channel calls itself a "multi-platform, global media destination where fans can discover, engage and share in the power of sport and the excitement of the Olympic Games all year round" ("About the Olympic Channel," n.d.). It has original programs as well as live sporting events and highlights such as Simone Biles' fifth all-around world title in gymnastics in 2019. By providing coverage of sports and athletes 24 hours a day, 365 days a year, fans can relive Olympic moments and stay connected to their favorite athletes and sports.

World Cup Soccer and Television

The World Cup rivals the Olympics in both stature and global audience. In 2019, around 14.3 million American viewers watched the U.S. women's national team win its fourth World Cup title on Fox Sports. Fox TV's broadcast additionally had

289,000 viewers streaming the game (Atkinson, 2019). In the last three cycles, the women's World Cup ratings have surpassed the men's final. Around 11.3 million viewers watched the men's 2018 final won by France over Croatia, 4 to 2. Experts believe the 2019 Women's World Cup did well due to the U.S. team's historical dominance. The women's gender discrimination lawsuit with the U.S. Soccer Federation also garnered media attention and interest (Mullin, 2019). After the U.S. women prevailed, Nike aired a 60-second black-and-white ad, "Never Stop Winning," that featured a female narrator and feminist message about support, equality, and empowerment (Mullin, 2019).

Fox Sports now owns the U.S. media rights to both the men's and women's World Cup events through 2026. Fox began its coverage with the 2015 Women's World Cup, televising all 52 games live on either Fox or Fox Sports 1. Fox heavily promoted the event by broadcasting *Women's World Cup Today* before most matches and *Women's World Cup Tonight* after matches on Fox Sports 1. In its telecasts, Fox used 28 on-air broadcasters, many of whom had extensive World Cup playing and coaching experience (Deitsch, 2015). The 2015 Women's World Cup ended up being a ratings bonanza, shattered expectations, and was followed by much of the country. The United States' World Cup championship game victory over Japan was the most-watched soccer match (female or male) in U.S. television history and drew more viewers than the previous final games of the World Series or NBA Finals (Yoder, 2015). There were 22.3 million viewers on Fox Sports (Mullin, 2019).

While networks struggle to engage U.S. soccer fans beyond World Cup or Olympic matches, networks view it as an important part of their broadcasting properties. Univision has found success in its soccer telecasts broadcasted to the United States regardless of language or fans' teams. In 2019, Univision had 7 of the 14 most-watched soccer broadcasts in the 18 to 49 age group and also outpaced the English-language competition from the MLS ("Univison Finds Success," 2019).

In 2019, the Football Federation Australia signed a joint broadcast deal with ABC and Fox Sports. They will broadcast A-League, W-League, and men's and women's national team soccer matches. This is ABC's first time broadcasting the A-League; under this agreement, 29 live matches will be broadcast on ABC TV and iview on Saturdays throughout the 2019-2020 season. Additionally, ABC will broadcast all Socceroos matches that Fox Sports broadcasts ("Football Federation Australia," 2019).

In other sports, the 2019 FIBA World Cup enjoyed a record-breaking TV audience of over three billion on over 70 broadcast partners in 190 territories. The basketball tournament also generated 1.5 billion video views on social media. The total cumulative TV audience increase was over 80 percent compared to the 2014 World Cup ("2019 FIBA World Cup," 2019). Basketball games, overall, have been some of the most-watched sports telecasts, especially in 2019. Following the Super Bowl through April 2019, 20 of the top 25 sports telecasts were basketball games. The number one spot was CBS' telecast of the NCAA Men's Basketball Division I Championship; 19.7 million viewers watched the University of Virginia defeat Texas Tech ("Basketball Dominates," 2019b).

NBC Sports' first exclusive season with the NTT IndyCar Series saw an increase in its audience from 2018, according to *Sports Business Daily*. The total audience delivery was 1.11 million viewers for 16 races, up from 1.01 million viewers the prior season when ABC and NBCSN aired the races. Indianapolis led all markets with a 3.8 local rating ("Audience Analysis," 2019).

As this section has illustrated, sport and television share a mutually beneficial relationship. Networks seek high ratings and advertising revenue, and sport fans' loyalty and zeal make it a perfect fit. From monumental global events (e.g., Super Bowl, Olympic Games, World Cup) to regional and local team coverage, television captures dramatic victories and defeats; tells athletes' and coaches' human-interest stories; and offers vital scores, statistics, and other sport information. From television's inception to the current day, it has changed the ways in which Americans experience sport.

Recognizing the Influence of Cable Television

Cable television, particularly the launch of ESPN in 1979, brought about the opportunity for sport fans to consume sport media at all hours of every day. However, cable television is facing new challenges as consumers now have endless and instantaneous options in consuming media. As such, it is all about choices in today's information-rich media society. Sport has no boundaries in a technologically advanced society; indeed, it is a 24-7 passion. Fans tune in to radios, televisions, tablets, mobile screens, and computers to satisfy their passion for sports. According to Nielsen Sports' *Year in Sports Media Report*, U.S. residents 18 or older consume an average of over 79 hours of content weekly, 28 more hours per week than in 2002. Access to sports content is at a 15-year high across television, according to the report, with more than 134,000 hours of news, events, and commentary. The increase can be attributed to the use of tablets, smartphones, and personal computers, and this trend shows the number of opportunities for consuming sport across media (Stainer & Master, 2018).

As is evident in these statistics, fans use multiple means and screens to consume sport, and many enjoy on-the-go portability and convenience. However, although most people recognize that newspapers, radio, and television have covered sport for some time, not as many realize that cable has existed for more than 40 years or understand how it has greatly influenced the prevalence of sport media over that span ("How We See It," 2005; King, 2005).

History of Cable and Sport

Cable television was originally pursued to sharpen reception for television viewers. It began in the late 1940s, when it was known as *community antenna television*, and spread to small areas throughout the United States. It provided customers with network affiliates, educational television, and independent stations. In the 1970s, two developments helped propel its growth and secure its acceptance as a modern medium. First, the Federal Communications Commission's Cable Television Report and Order of 1972 laid the foundation for rules and regulations in the industry. Second, satellites began to be used in the mid-1970s to allocate services to cable systems and networks. Subsequently, the Cable Communications Policy Act of 1984 eradicated the regulation of cable rates, but the Cable Television Consumer Protection and Competition Act

of 1992 reinstated regulation for basic cable and allowed cable companies to set prices for their premium stations (Blanchard, 1998).

In 1972, HBO became the first **premium channel**; by 1980, it was joined by CNN and ESPN. Although CNN is now a staple of 24-hour news coverage, it lost $2 million per month in its early stages. Founder Ted Turner kept it on the air with profits from television superstation WTBS. Although ESPN also struggled in the beginning, it is now the most powerful and prominent sport media property (Smith & Hollihan, 2009). When the U.S. Congress passed the Cable Communications Policy Act of 1984, cable was enabled to compete with broadcast television; by 1987, more than 50 percent of U.S. households had cable.

The industry expanded in the 1990s in the form of original content and additional networks. Multimedia communication was now the new medium. In the mid-1990s, cable offered more specialized content with the advent of the History Channel and Home and Garden; by 1997, cable's overall share of prime-time television had grown to more than 30 percent. As was also the case in radio and broadcast television, the industry became rife with mergers, monopolies, and consolidation. By the late 1990s, the 10 largest multiple-system operators accounted for 74 percent of cable subscriptions. By 2000, cable reached 66 million of the 100 million U.S. homes reached by television (Blanchard, 1998; "Exit Interview," 2005; Folkerts & Lacy, 2004; Hilliard & Keith, 2005).

Growth of Cable Television and Diversity of Programming

Despite increased competition from other media, sport cable rights deals and offerings of sport on cable television continue to grow and expand in the new millennium. For example, Comcast completed its acquisition of AT&T Broadband in 2002, which brought together cable assets serving more than 21 million U.S. cable subscribers. Having since acquired NBCUniversal, Comcast has three operating segments: Comcast Cable; NBCUniversal; and Sky, which operates video, high-speed Internet, voice, and wireless phone services and runs Sky News broadcast network and Sky Sports networks. Comcast Cable provides high-speed Internet, video, and voice services in the United States. Comcast's total revenue increased from

$81 billion in 2016 to $95 billion in 2018 and is expected to hit $115 billion by 2021 (Team, 2019). NBCUniversal includes media, cable networks, broadcast television, film, and theme parks.

There are other big players in the industry. In 2015, Charter Communications purchased Time Warner Cable (owner of HBO, CNN, Turner Broadcasting, AOL, Time Warner Cable, and Time Inc.) for $55 million; in 2018, AT&T purchased Time Warner for $85 billion. In 2019, the merger took place after a victory in federal court, upheld on appeal by the D.C. Court of Appeals, that rejected the U.S. Department of Justice's assertion that the merger would violate antitrust law (Teitelman, 2019). Meanwhile, Rupert Murdoch's News Corporation and 21st Century Fox hold key assets in Fox, FX, Fox Sports Network, the National Geographic Channel, 20th Century Fox (film and television), and Shine Group. In December 2018, News Corporation announced the split into two corporate entities: News Corp and 21st Century Fox would separate. The former includes the publishing divisions and the *New York Post*, *Wall Street Journal*, the *Times of London*, and HarperCollins Publishing. Meanwhile, the latter includes 20th Century Studios and television studio, Fox Sports, Fox News Channel, and FX. The Walt Disney Company acquired 20tth Century Studios from News Corporation and also owns the ESPN Networks, ABC, Disney Television Group, Disney Interactive, Lucas Film, and Marvel Entertainment, as well as theme parks and resorts (Carpenter, 2019). Additionally, large tech companies such as Google, Amazon, and Apple are getting more involved. Apple TV+ launched in November 2019 (Fleenor, 2019).

Synergies also grew between disparate media outlets. One example was the partnership between HBO and Showtime to co-produce the 2015 Floyd Mayweather Jr.–Manny Pacquiao boxing match. The rival networks joined together to hype "the Fight of the Century" (Dirs, 2015; "Rival Networks," 2015), and the fight defied recent downward trends in boxing with an astonishing 4.4 million pay-per-view (PPV) buys, which shattered the preview PPV record of 2.48 million buys for Mayweather–Oscar De La Hoya in 2007 (Gaines, 2015).

The proliferation of sport on more networks and outlets gives viewers many choices; however, ESPN still covers more sport programming than any other network. Former president Barack Obama watched ESPN's *SportsCenter* from the White House and annually filled out his March Madness bracket as part of the network's programming (Miller & Shales, 2011). ESPN has also won recognition for its efforts. For instance, along with the NBA, ESPN won the "Best in Digital Sports Media" award for ESPN+ at the 2019 Sports Business Awards. The "Sports Event of the Year," the U.S. Open Tennis Championships, also was broadcast on ESPN ("2019 Sports Business Awards," 2019). Fox Sports won "Best in Sports Media" for 2019; however, ESPN regularly tops comScore sport rankings for multiplatform digital reach with its millions of unique visitors (Adler, 2019). It averages 115 million users a month, making it number one in sports in average number of minutes each visitor spends on the site, in both total minutes of usage and total visits (Nagle, 2019). In other areas, ESPN Fantasy was the top provider of fantasy sports in 2018 with more than 20 million fans. ESPN Radio is home to half of all sport radio listenership with its more than 600 stations and 32 million listeners weekly (Nagle, 2019).

In 2002, ESPN became the first network to televise four major professional leagues in one year. This trend of broad involvement in the sport world continues with ESPN's broadcasts of the NFL, MLB, and NBA. It has covered the NFL Draft since 1980, and the early years of this coverage enabled ESPN to gain credibility in the sport media industry. Now, ESPN and the NFL Network broadcast the draft, which has become a multiday media event ("Sweet Home," 2015). In 2015, ESPN broadcast the inaugural College Football Playoff championship game with a "Super Bowl-like" approach (Ourand & Smith, 2015). The game set cable TV viewership records and became the first cable show to surpass 30 million viewers (Ourand, 2015e). Advertisers paid an average of $800,000 to $1 million per 30-second spot (Ourand, 2015e).

In other rights deals and partnerships, ESPN is part of Dish Network's web TV service, Sling TV, which offers streamed channels including ESPN, ESPN2, TNT, TBS, and many others (Ourand, 2015d). Dish Network pays ESPN a monthly fee to be included in its service. At the same time, however, cable and satellite distributors have created smaller tiers that do not include ESPN. As a result, according to Nielsen, ESPN subscriber numbers have dropped from more than 100 million U.S. homes in 2012 to a projected 80 million subscribers in 2019, with future declines likely (Travis, 2019). However, ESPN has signed lucrative long-term contracts for league broadcast rights and still earns more than $3 billion annually in operating earnings (its brand value is $13.1 billion) from cable, satellite, and telephone carriage fees (Badenhausen, 2019). ESPN launched ESPN+ in 2018, and it reached one million subscribers in under six months.

Also in 2018, ESPN announced a five-year, $1.5 billion deal with UFC to stream its fights on ESPN+ and show them on cable channels. ESPN carries 30 "Fight Night Events" annually on broadcast and ESPN+. In 2019, it extended the contract two years and also signed a pay-per-view partnership. This seven-year pact enables ESPN to sell and stream pay-per-view fights exclusively on ESPN+. This strengthens parent company Walt Disney's business strategy to increase direct-to-consumer streaming opportunities (Mullin, 2019a).

ESPN has recognized and embraced technological innovation since its inception in 1979, and it continues to do so with web and mobile technology. Its recent website redesign, which focused on in-depth reporting, coincided with the site's 20th anniversary and was the first large overhaul since 2009 ("ESPN's First," 2015).

Beyond ESPN, of course, other networks and outlets give viewers additional choices for consuming sport content. AOL, for example, seeks to add to the public discourse on sport with original content through partnerships with Relativity Media and Derek Jeter's The Players' Tribune. AOL may not have the ability to compete for rights to stream events, but it offers the expanse of its AOL On Network, where it can run both exclusive and nonexclusive content. For example, it has launched a series with The Players' Tribune that shows Ben Lyons' experiences with star athletes and sport figures called *Real Fan Life With Ben Lyons* ("AOL Using," 2015; "Real Fan Life," n.d.).

Regional Sport Networks and Other Outlets

Given the increasing interest in niche markets, regional sport networks (RSNs) such as Fox Sports (FS) Network have continued to expand and have

in fact caused a "conundrum" (King & Ourand, 2014, p. 1). For instance, the Arizona Diamondbacks' $250 million rights fee from Fox Sports Net in 2007 quadrupled to about $1 billion in the follow-up deal in 2015 (Piecoro, 2015). As a result of such deals, teams wield leverage and negotiating power. They can launch regional networks, partner with distributors on new RSNs, or sign a rights deal with existing RSNs such as FS Arizona (King & Ourand, 2014).

In other baseball examples, we consider four teams that have handled their rights differently in nontraditional content deals. In 2018, the YES Network was the most-watched regional sport network in both prime-time and total day slots, making it the most-watched RSN in the United States for 14 of the last 16 years (SVG staff, 2019). The New York Yankees sold 80 percent of ownership of the YES Network (launched with Goldman Sachs in 2002) to 21st Century Fox. In 2019, the U.S. Department of Justice forced Disney to sell its RSNs as part of its acquisition of 21st Century Fox. YES Network, the regional sport network that houses both the New York Yankees and the Brooklyn Nets, was sold for $3.5 billion to a group that includes Amazon, the Yankees, and Sinclair Broadcast Group (Hayes, 2019b). Under the new ownership structure, the Yankees own 26 percent of YES; Sinclair will own 20 percent; Amazon will own 15 percent; and the other 39 percent will be split between Redbird Capital (financial partner for Yankees' Yankee Global Enterprises), Blackstone, and Mubadala Capital (Weprin, 2019). The 21 other regional sport networks are owned by Sinclair and Byron Allen. According to Sinclair CEO Chris Ripley, "While consumer viewing habits have shifted, the tradition of watching live sports and news remains ingrained in our culture" (as quoted in Szalai, 2019). As a result of sport rights and high-value sport organizations, RSNs have had rate increases and are perceived as "top financial earners" (Friedman, 2019). YES has been the most-watched RSN since its launch in 2002 (Hayes, 2019b). Sinclair is the largest owner of local television stations in the United States and has made a splash in the regional sport business. In addition to acquiring Fox RSNs, it partnered with the Chicago Cubs to launch a new RSN in 2020 (Hayes, 2019b). The new network, called

Marquee Sports Network, is run by general manager Michael McCarthy, former president of MSG Network (Lafayette, 2019). In 2019, NBC Sports Chicago announced a multiyear media rights deal with three Chicago teams—the White Sox, Bulls, and Blackhawks. It will broadcast regular season games, preseason and spring training games, and the first rounds of the postseasons for the Bulls and Hawks. Previously, all four Chicago professional sport teams partnered with NBC Sports Chicago and then Comcast SportsNet Chicago for 15 years (Greenstein, 2019).

In contrast, the Philadelphia Phillies relinquished rights fees revenue for a 25 percent stake in CSN Philadelphia; in other words, the Phillies chose equity over rights to share in the profits. Meanwhile, the Seattle Mariners increased their stake in Root Sports Northwest (owned and operated by DirecTV) from minority to majority status. And the Los Angeles Dodgers created SportsNet LA, which is owned by the team but operated by Time Warner Cable. This 25-year, $8.35 billion rights deal protects the team from potential financial burdens (King & Ourand, 2014).

For professional teams, regional sport networks fit into three distinct categories. First, a team can own or share the majority of the network, as is the case with CSN Chicago and the White Sox, Bulls, Cubs, and Blackhawks; SportsNet LA and the Dodgers; Root Sports Northwest and the Mariners; SNY and the Mets; and NESN and the Boston Red Sox and Bruins. Second, a team can hold a minority stake in a network owned by FSN, Comcast, or DirecTV. These deals range from 10 percent to 33 percent and include the Yankees, Phillies, San Francisco Giants, San Diego Padres, Los Angeles Angels, Texas Rangers, and Boston Celtics. Third, a team can be fully owned by one of those distributors (King & Ourand, 2014).

While MLB saw overall attendance drop for a fourth straight year to 68.5 million in 2019, games on RSNs were first in prime time on cable in 24 of the 25 U.S. markets where MLB teams played. Additionally, the league's three national TV partners—Fox, ESPN, and TBS—all saw viewership increases during the regular season (Prisbell, 2019b). Fox debuted new technology that year in the MLB postseason, including 4K HDR (Prisbell, 2019a).

As these various deals and partnerships indicate, the diverse options available in today's sport media universe create choices and expanded content for leagues, teams, and fans. This is especially true with the Longhorn Network (LHN), a joint partnership between ESPN and the University of Texas launched in 2011. The 20-year deal brings Texas $300 million, which averages $15 million annually. The deal happened shortly after Texas opted to remain in the Big 12 Conference rather than join the Pac-10 (now Pac-12). Debate by those who work in and follow the industry will likely continue on issues related to objectivity and impartiality when journalists are assigned to cover and report on sports, teams, and leagues that have entered into partnerships with the media outlets covering them, such as the Longhorn Network and ESPN. Meanwhile, in at least one critic's view, the network is "the farthest thing from must-see television in cable sports history" (Travis, 2015b, para. 8). The network's nonrevenue sport coverage and its limited number of football games do not necessarily increase demand for the network's content.

This view is disputed, however, by SB Nation's Steven Godfrey, who built on analyses from market-intelligence analyst SNL Kagan. In addition to its guaranteed LHN money, Texas also receives the Big 12's standard distribution of $26 million for all member schools (except its newest universities, West Virginia and TCU). ESPN senior vice president of programming acquisitions Burke Magnus concurs: "A comparison of LHN to a conference network is apples and oranges, although Longhorn does stack up from a distribution perspective pretty favorably compared to some conference networks" (Godfrey, 2015). LHN is offered by various providers, including Time Warner, DirecTV, and nine of Texas' 10 biggest carriers.

In 2019, the ACC Network launched, and potential carriers similarly have disparate views about the network providers and the ESPN partnership. As of October 2019, Comcast Xfinity customers still did not have access to the network. According to ESPN's Jimmy Pitaro, "It's incorrect to look at the ACC Network as just a linear, traditional television network. This is a cross-platform, multi-platform experience," he said. "We're in a good place. We're checking the box in terms of linear distribution but we're also taking the experience to new fans" (as quoted in Hayes, 2019c).

Networks and Major Media Rights Deals

The sport TV business is in an "unprecedented period of stability" (Ourand, 2014b, p. 1). ESPN and Turner signed NBA broadcast deals worth $24 billion to showcase the NBA through 2025, and many major television sport rights are locked up beyond 2020 (see table 7.1). As streaming companies pursue live sports, rights fees will continue to rise. In Verizon's five-year deal with the NFL, it pays $500 million annually to live stream games on mobile and digital platforms. Amazon Prime live streamed *Thursday Night Football* in 2018 and 37 ATP global tennis matches in the United Kingdom and Ireland in 2019. It also bought the rights to 20 matches of English Premier League soccer matches per season from 2019 to 2022 (White, 2019).

In 2019, the NFL renewed its deal with Facebook through the 2020 season. The deal includes highlights and will also have fan Facebook groups as well as a weekly "Watch Party" around a game recap. The league also will offer clips of news and analysis from the NFL Network, *Around the NFL*, and *Move the Sticks* (Fischer, 2019). Facebook and the NFL have had deals in place since 2017, and the social media outlet believes the NFL will help its growth as a video streaming site. In turn, the NFL has benefited by growing its fandom in new markets in Germany, the United Kingdom, and other international markets (Fischer, 2019).

These are just a few examples of how tech companies are entering the lucrative arena of sport rights. In addition, as the television landscape evolves, network executives are taking different approaches to revenue outlets in the sport media industry. Digital has been a top initiative, and the cable industry has been promoting TV Everywhere (wherein subscribers can stream channels on multiple devices) since 2010. Consumers can also stream events by means of apps such as WatchESPN and Fox Sports Go. Digital advertising is still growing and has vast untapped potential. Still, much of ESPN's revenue will continue to come from cable due to its long-term contracts with major distributors.

Other networks also value digital while continuing to recognize the importance of traditional outlets. As CBS Sports president David Berson said, "Digital is important because you want to make sure that your content is available to fans wherever they want. We're obviously always looking at expanding distribution and utilizing new technologies. But to be clear, the lion's share of consumption is still on television" (qtd. in Ourand, 2014b, p. 1). CBS Sports remains committed to its broadcast channel, as Fox Sports does to FS1 and FS2, both launched in 2013 (Ourand, 2014b, p. 1). FS1 and FS2's revenue comes from distribution and affiliate fees, and its MLB postseason coverage, NASCAR races, U.S. Open golf, and World Cup will all help expand its content. FS1 also featured *Garbage Time With Katie Nolan*, a witty show featuring guests and field segments ("People & Personalities," 2015). NBC has also focused on marketing its current portfolio of coverage and league partners. Examples include *NASCAR America* and the *Sunday Night Sports Report*, which centers on the specific sports that NBC broadcasts. NBC also markets the Triple Crown horse races, the Olympics, and other major events.

New technologies have created a sport media landscape in which "the games, the stats, the players, the other fans—they're everywhere," said *Sports Business Journal* writer Bill King (2005, p. 23). "Thanks to the proliferation of niche TV channels and sports talk radio, the popularity of the Internet and the evolution of wireless devices . . . content is available anytime, anywhere in almost any way you want it." In this environment, fans both crave and expect content, and content providers use technology to satiate that desire; as a result, today's sport fan truly is a "24-7 fan" (p. 23). Technology is especially necessary in reaching the 18- to 34-year-old demographic. This group has always been the most coveted, especially to advertisers, but network executives admit that times are changing. As described by Fox Sports president Eric Shanks, "The 18–34s—that demographic that TV ratings have been based on for decades—make absolutely no sense anymore" (Ourand, 2015f, p. 12). The reason? Millennials have made different life choices about working, getting married, and having children. As a result, they tend to have less disposable income, and younger millennials (under age 25) are viewed more as adolescents than as adults in terms of their media consumption habits (Ourand, 2015f).

Networks also recognize that certain sports, such as soccer and mixed martial arts, do better with younger audiences because they do not require a lengthy time commitment. "The more

Table 7.1   Media Contracts and Properties

Property	Network(s)	Terms	Final season
Mountain West*	CBS, ESPN	$116 million, 7 years**	2019-20
NHL	NBC	$2 billion, 10 years	2020-21
PGA Tour	CBS, NBC	N/A, 9 years	2020-21
NFL	ESPN	$15.2 billion, 8 years	2021
MLB	ESPN	$5.6 billion, 8 years	2021
MLB	Fox	$5.1 billion, 7 years	2028
MLB	Turner	$2.6 billion, 8 years	2021
Australian Open	ESPN	N/A, 10 years	2021
NFL	DirecTV	$12 billion, 8 years	2022
NFL	Fox (Sunday)	$9.9 billion, 9 years	2022
NFL	Fox (Thursday)	$3 billion, 5 years	2022
NFL	CBS	$9 billion, 9 years	2022
Pac-12**	ESPN, ABC, Fox, FSN, FX	$3 billion, 12 years**	2022-23
MLS**	ESPN, Fox	$600 million, 9 years***	2026
World Cup***	Fox	$950 million-$1 billion, 12 years	2026
World Cup***	Telemundo	$600 million, 8 years (extended; terms undisclosed)	2022 (2026)
MLS	Univision	$120 million, 8 years	2022
WNBA	ESPN	$72 million, 6 years (extended; terms undisclosed)	2022 (2025)
WNBA	CBS	N/A	N/A
Wimbledon	ESPN	$480 million, 12 years	2023
NASCAR***	NBC	$4.4 billion, 10 years	2024
NASCAR***	Fox	$3.8 billion, 10 years	2024
NCAA D-I basketball	CBS, Turner	$19.6 billion, 22 years**	2032
SEC	CBS	$825 million, 15 years	2023-24
French Open	NBC	N/A, 12 years	2024
NBA***	ESPN	$12.6 billion, 9 years	2024-25
NBA***	Turner	$10.8 billion, 9 years	2024-25
College Football Playoff****	ESPN	$7.3 billion, 12 years	2025
Big 12	Fox, FSN, FX	$1.2 billion, 13 years	2024-25
Big 12	ESPN, ABC	$1.34 billion, 13 years***	2024-25
U.S. Open tennis	ESPN	$825 million, 11 years	2025
Big East	Fox	$500 million, 12 years	2024-25
Notre Dame	NBC	N/A, 10 years	2025
U.S. Open golf***	Fox	$1.12 billion, 12 years	2026
ACC	ESPN	$4.2 billion, 15 years	2026-27
Big Ten	Big Ten Network	$2.8 billion, 25 years	2031-32
Olympics U.S. rights	NBC	$7.65 billion, 12 years	2032
SEC	ESPN, ABC	$6 billion, 20 years	2033-34

N/A = not available

Note: Some contracts may share rights with related networks.

*CBS Sports Network and ESPN will alternate game selections in football and men's basketball. ESPN will control rights to Boise State home football games, and CBS Sports has the rights to their away football games.

**Combined total for both networks.

***Includes two separate deals, with the second an extension.

****Figure takes into account $215 million payout committed by ESPN to the Rose Bowl, Champions Bowl, and Orange Bowl, along with a playoff package.

Adapted by permission from J. Ourand, "With Major Media Rights Deals Done, How Will Networks Grow Revenue?" *Street & Smith's SportsBusiness Journal* (2014): 1. Retrieved from http://www.sportsbusinessdaily.com/Journal/Issues/2014/11/03/In-Depth/Networks-main.aspx

important issue with the millennials is that they spend less than a third of their time watching video [by] watching it on traditional television," observed former ESPN president John Skipper. "This is why it has to be about mobile, other kinds of devices, and authenticated television" (Ourand, 2015f, p. 12). In today's fragmented media environment with its niche markets, sport communication organizations must use technology purposefully to reach fans and fully exploit marketing potential and profits.

In addition to new technology, networks focus on local and regional appeal, including efforts to tap into underdeveloped markets. This is especially true of the Latino market. In 1996, when Fox created Fox Sports en Español (now called Fox Deportes), it became the first U.S. network to create a Spanish-language option. The NBA also recognizes the importance of Hispanic fans and has a deal with Univision to produce two weekly Spanish-language shows for UniMás and Univision Deportes. Univision also runs the NBA's Spanish-language website. This partnership shows that the NBA seeks to expand its Hispanic outreach, with league executives noting that Hispanics and Latinos already accounted for 18 percent of its fan base in 2015 (Ourand, 2015c).

Cable television and emerging technologies have made sport into a 24-7 passion. The number of media outlets has skyrocketed over the last 50 years, leading to more shows and programs, more diversity, and more choices for sport fans. From newspapers and magazines to radio, network television, cable, satellite, web-based choices, and the rise of social media, technology has created a world of opportunities for sport communication and its practitioners (Powell, 2003).

Sport Photojournalism

Whereas television brings us live images, magazines such as *Sports Illustrated* capture still shots of athletes, coaches, and fans, thus portraying unique moments in time. The work of photographers is often used to enhance and supplement printed work, but it can also stand alone. Like reporters and broadcasters, photojournalists have seen changes in their roles due to emerg-

Photo courtesy of Andrea N. Geurin.

The cameras were on Leo Manzano as he celebrated winning the men's 1,500-meter race at the U.S. Olympic Trials (and as some of his competitors struggled with the agony of defeat). Manzano went on to win a silver medal in the event at the London Olympics.

ing technologies and different outlets for posting their images to a wide audience (e.g., social media). In 2015, for example, *Sports Illustrated* laid off all six of its full-time staff photographers. In 2013, the *Chicago Sun-Times* laid off all of its 28 full-time photographers. The newspaper noted that it planned to use readily available freelance photographers and also urged reporters to start shooting pictures—before eventually rehiring 4 of the 28 photographers after much criticism was received from those who report on the media industry, a union grievance was filed against the paper directly related to these layoffs, and some subscribers publicly complained or expressed concerns about a drop in quality (Beaujon, 2014).

Such cost-cutting efforts derive in part from the fact that global travel expenses have increased exponentially. At the same time, entities such as *Sports Illustrated* can now hire local photographers around the world on a freelance basis to upload their pictures to the magazine's servers. In addition, many younger photographers now have technological expertise and access to affordable cameras, lenses, and other equipment. Such advances allow magazines and publications to pull digital stills from videos for use on blogs and websites. Traditional photography is still valuable, but technology and economics have affected photography and visual media just as they have in other areas of the sport media.

In addition to radio, television, and cable, films also use powerful pictures to showcase the emotion of sport and the commitment of athletes and coaches to competition and to their sports. Motion pictures developed from photography, peep shows, and vaudeville acts. In the 1920s, the film industry was located in California; by 1930, the industry was controlled by Warner Brothers, Lowe's, Metro-Goldwyn-Mayer, Paramount, RKO, and 20th Century Fox. When television gained popularity in the 1950s, the film industry responded to the new competition by adding color; larger theater screens; and technical advancements, such as Cinerama (wide screens), 3-D (image depth), and Panavision (natural-looking depth). Hollywood also released older movies for network broadcasting in the 1950s (Folkerts & Lacy, 2004).

Documentaries began in the late 1890s with "actualities," which were short pieces of nonfiction. Inventor Thomas Edison produced sporting actualities about boxing bouts before the turn of the 20th century. Although fiction gained prominence in the 20th century, social documentaries and propaganda appeared during the World Wars. The decades from the 1950s through the 1970s brought television documentaries, direct cinema, and cinema verité. ESPN's *SportsCentury*, which began in 1999; *Outside the Lines*, from 1990 to present; and E:60 (2007 to the present) have taken a different approach to sport. *SportsCentury* provides historical analysis and narrative insight on people and events who have defined and played large roles in 20th- and 21st-century

Photo courtesy of Paul M. Pedersen.

Sport documentaries have been around for over a century and are popular offerings by media entities ranging from cable networks (e.g., HBO Documentaries, ESPN *30 for 30*) to subscription streaming services. Pictured here is a billboard (across the street of the Santiago Bernabéu Stadium, home of Real Madrid) promoting the Amazon Prime documentary of Sergio Ramos, the captain of Real Madrid and the Spanish National Team.

sport. *Outside the Lines*, in contrast, provides a critical look and in-depth news investigations on current issues in sport. *E:60* features investigative sport journalism, often uncovering scandals and criminal acts. Some of these are uncomfortable for sport viewers to watch due to their serious nature, such as reports on sexual assault against women by NFL players.

In other examples, the Tennis Channel aired the documentary series *No Strings* about Pete Sampras and *Net Films* about past tennis greats. These and other programs resemble ABC's syndicated series *Greatest Sports Legends*, which was televised from 1973 to 1993. Many of these documentaries and other shows have dealt with strong and compelling content, affirming that sport transcends the playing field and both humanizing and celebrating athletes, coaches, and their feats. For instance, Showtime's 2015 documentary *Dean Smith* explored the legendary UNC men's basketball coach ("Relatively Cheap Sports Documentaries," 2015). There is now even a Tribeca/ESPN Sports Film Festival ("Tribeca," 2015).

In 2009, ESPN created the *30 for 30* documentary series to celebrate the network's 30th anniversary with 30 films. It was a "thunderclap in the industry" (Sandomir, 2015), and the network has since expanded the genre with *30 for 30 Shorts*, which were shown online at Grantland and SEC Storied (Sandomir, 2015). The success of the *30 for 30* series has created a growing industry and "quickly brought a niche market into the mainstream" (Sandomir, 2015).

HBO continues its longstanding tradition of important documentaries, including *Diego Maradona* about one of the most legendary soccer players in the world; *Lindsey Vonn, The Final Season*; *Belichick & Saban: The Art of Coaching*; and *At the Heart of Gold* about the Larry Nassar sex abuse scandal.

Director Jonathan Hock considers today "a golden age for sports documentaries" ("Relatively Cheap Sports Documentaries," 2015). This is largely because documentaries fit well in the current media landscape of changing viewing habits and choices. For example, the *30 for 30* films are available on ESPN platforms, as well as iTunes, Netflix, and DVD sets. The genre was once dominated by ESPN and HBO, but other players now include Showtime, Epix, DBS, and Fox Sports 1. The genre is popular in part because of the low production costs. ESPN, for instance, spends about $500,000 for each documentary, which can be repeated for years to come.

Garnering practical experiences is vital for students. Here, Mark Travis, a former Oklahoma State University sport media major, interviews superstar Kyrie Irving at a USA Basketball training camp.

Photo courtesy of Mark Travis.

KEYS TO SUCCESS FROM AN AWARD-WINNING INVESTIGATIVE REPORTER

Mark Fainaru-Wada
Investigative reporter
ESPN

Mark Fainaru-Wada's investigative reporting and its effect on two major sport leagues—MLB and the NFL—show the transcendent power of reporting in sport communication and society. Fainaru-Wada is a member of ESPN's investigations and enterprise unit, which produces work for the award-winning program *Outside the Lines* and other ESPN platforms. He is best known, however, for coauthoring two award-winning books that have promoted changes in both perception and policy.

Fainaru-Wada and former *San Francisco Chronicle* colleague Lance Williams wrote *Game of Shadows: Barry Bonds, BALCO, and the Steroids Scandal That Rocked Professional Sports* (2006). For his second book, he partnered with his Pulit-

zer Prize–winning brother Steve Fainaru to write *League of Denial: The NFL, Concussions, and the Battle for Truth* (2013). The first book induced MLB to investigate steroid use and implicated top athletes, such as Barry Bonds and track-and-field star Marion Jones. The second book elucidated the NFL's deception in hiding key information about professional football's health effects, especially chronic traumatic encephalopathy (CTE), on its players. The book, along with the accompanying PBS *Frontline* documentary, sparked discussions about the sport's safety among NFL owners, coaches, players, fans, parents, and their children. It also pushed the NFL to begin taking responsibility for past negligence and denial.

Official White House Photograph.

Mark Fainaru-Wada (left) and *Game of Shadows* coauthor Lance Williams receive a White House Correspondents' Association award from President George W. Bush.

(continued)

(continued)

Fainaru-Wada's love for journalism started at a young age. As he grew up in California's Marin County, two things prompted him to pursue journalism—his older brother Steve and the book *All the President's Men*, which, in Fainaru-Wada's words, depicted the "heroic nature of investigative journalism." Steve and Mark both wrote for the *Bark*, Redwood High School's student newspaper. From there, Fainaru-Wada graduated from Northwestern University's prestigious Medill School of Journalism before working at a series of newspapers.

Fainaru-Wada credits his success to his bosses at the *Knoxville News-Sentinel*, the *Los Angeles Daily News*, and the *San Francisco Chronicle*, where he worked until 2007. Fainaru-Wada's big break came in covering the BALCO scandal. "You're doing work that's drawing widespread attention and eliciting change, which I think is every reporter's dream," he explained. "At the same time it had some really troubling elements that weren't pleasant." He is referring here to the legal battle associated with the scandal. U.S. prosecutors pressured Fainaru-Wada and Williams to disclose the names of sources who provided them with the grand jury testimony of Barry Bonds and other athletes covered in the book. Both refused to violate their pledges of confidentiality to sources, even in the face of threatened prison time, which neither ultimately received.

Based on the book's reporting, MLB launched an investigation that resulted in the Mitchell Report and a stricter MLB policy regarding the use of performance-enhancing drugs. "We knew it was a big story," Fainaru-Wada said. "But I don't think we anticipated it would generate the kind of discussion it did and create the kind of awareness around the extensive use of performance-enhancing drugs in sports."

The work on steroids also affected Fainaru-Wada's career path. His current job at ESPN "grew out of BALCO work." Fainaru-Wada and T.J. Quinn, then an investigative reporter at the *Daily News*, reached out to ESPN about joint freelance projects. When they found out about the new investigative unit for *Outside the Lines*, they both had the same initial reaction: "We're newspaper guys. We're not going to TV." After further consideration, though, Fainaru-Wada admitted, "It seemed like too good of an opportunity to pass up. Total commitment to investigative reporting. Financially supportive.

Making a lot more money than we ever made in newspapers. Being able to live where we wanted to live. It seemed like a perfect situation."

Now, Fainaru-Wada's work appears in television, digital, magazine, radio, and on all major ESPN platforms. He signed another contract in November 2018, and his ESPN executive editor, Chris Buckle, considers him a unique reporter and colleague. "Mark shares the traits of the nation's best investigative reporters who like to solve complex puzzles and who are insanely curious, stubborn, skeptical, tireless, and dedicated to finding and exposing the truth," Buckle said. "He's all of that but also has such an approachable personality that he can get most anyone to talk. Toss in that he is obsessed with accuracy, objectivity and fairness—and that he is as respectful to someone he is systematically dismantling in an interview as he is to his friends and colleagues in casual conversation and you get a really special reporter and human being."

Fainaru-Wada believes his second book, *League of Denial*, and the ensuing *Frontline* documentary based on the book raise two issues—the NFL and youth sport. Since the book came out in 2013, the NFL agreed to a concussion settlement with retired players that could cost the league more than $1 billion. The problem was the NFL's concealment of information. "The disservice was for 20 years, players were told that there wasn't an issue and they didn't have to worry about their brains," said Fainaru-Wada. Football at the youth level involves a different dynamic. "There's more focus on health and safety, as there should be, and there are real questions about when you want to let your kids play [tackle football]," he said. Fainaru-Wada doubts, however, whether the sport can, or will, be changed: "It is inherently built around contact. It's a collision sport. When you collide, your head is going to get rocked."

In more recent work, Fainaru-Wada wrote about why Bob Costas was dropped from covering the Super Bowl after speaking out on head trauma and brain injuries in the NFL (Fainaru-Wada, 2019). Nobody at NBC wanted to discuss it; however, "in the end, the people who matter and were most supportive of it, made sure it got published and aired," said Fainaru-Wada, "And Jimmy Pitaro supported it." Fainaru-Wada also admitted, "Most of these stories don't come off without some level of conflict because of all the relationships, but in the end, they all seem to run" (personal communication, 2019).

Another story and *OTL* investigation documents a former Olympian and track-and-field coach, Conrad Montgomery Avondale Mainwaring, and his alleged abuse of 41 men across two continents and four states while employed by elite institutions such as UCLA, Syracuse University, Colgate, and others. Fainaru-Wada spent nearly a year working on this investigation with reporter Mike Kessler. They traveled, shot some interviews, and talked to people about their experiences. Meanwhile, Mainwaring was arrested, and the case is slowing working itself through the courts. The *OTL* piece included 15 accounts on record and expanded to a multipart episode podcast in 2020.

Given Fainaru-Wada's vast experience in print, electronic, and digital media, he encourages students to "read and watch good journalism." It is also important to be versatile, he said. "The more diverse a student can make himself or herself, the better opportunities they will have." Nevertheless, Fainaru-Wada still considers reporting to be the most important skill. "If you're a really good reporter developing stories that matter, someone will find a spot for you," he said.

CHAPTER WRAP-UP

Summary

This chapter covers the first two segments of the second component of the Strategic Sport Communication Model (SSCM): sport publishing and print sport communication, as well as electronic and visual sport communication. Though distinct, these two sectors have largely converged in 21st-century sport journalism. Sport publishing is the business or profession of the commercial production and dissemination of information related to sport. Print communication encompasses any medium that disseminates printed matter related to sport. Newspapers are the primary print-delivery system examined here, and they remain by far the biggest and most influential of print sport media. Even so, they have been struggling financially for three decades, due in large part to the advent of the Internet and social media. Newspaper sports sections, first established in 1895 by William Randolph Hearst, now employ thousands of professional journalists who gather, select, process, and present sport for newspapers. Sport publishing involves sport books, sport news delivered through wire services, sport on the Internet (examined further in chapter 8), and sport magazines.

As technology evolved beyond newspaper and magazine to radio, television, film, cable, and new technologies, sport coverage also evolved, as did the ways in which fans perceive sport. These changes made one thing clear: Sport remains a pastime, a passion, and a vital marketing tool with expansive reach and infinite potential in the economic, social, cultural, legal, and political arenas. This chapter builds on the preceding chapters, which set the historical context and foundation for sport communication's development. Like the other chapters, it reinforces the symbiotic nature of sport and the media, which is especially evident with electronic media. Athletes, teams, and leagues use these media to promote their sports, products, and brands. Meanwhile, electronic media use sport's popularity to gain advertising revenue and high ratings. Thus, it is evident that both sides work together in a mutually beneficial manner.

The golden age of radio started where the golden age of sport left off in 1930. Radio enabled listeners to connect with each other in their homes and in public places. Radio still used the words of print journalism but added sound to the mix. This addition meant that fans could hear live commentary from sport announcers, interviews with their favorite players, and crowd noise that enlivened their experience. Today, radio still includes those features but has also adapted to new technology in consumers' content preferences. Two examples are sport radio and satellite radio.

Although print journalism and radio have singular strengths, it is television more than any other medium that has catapulted sport into the mainstream of U.S. culture. As noted in chapter 3, Pete Rozelle and Roone Arledge's roles in developing sport as entertainment and television as a vehicle for showcasing sport cannot be overstated. Their contributions to sport television are enormous. It is difficult to fathom, for example, a culture without *Monday Night Football* or the Super Bowl, as well as the technology, spectacle, and celebrity that come with these events. The "big three" networks of NBC, ABC, and CBS dominated the airwaves until the advent of cable sport coverage with ESPN and HBO in the late 1970s and early 1980s. Today, thousands of stations are available through cable television and satellite services, which highlights how the electronic media have evolved and matured as times have changed and fans' preferences have fluctuated. ESPN single-handedly made sport a 24-hour addiction, and *SportsCenter* has a cult following among men and women alike. The network also offers films, reality shows, game shows, and a wide array of other programming.

Monday Night Football first appeared on cable television in 2006 on ESPN, which, like many sport communication outlets, recognizes the importance of technology (as is discussed further in chapter 8). Radio, television, cable, and technology are used by all segments of sport communication organizations to inform, protect, persuade, and justify. More than any other entity of sport communication, the electronic media have the power to reach the greatest number of people and influence their perceptions.

Because individuals can experience only a finite number of events, they rely on the media—especially radio, television, and cable—to inform them about important people and events in the world. This is also true in the particular arena of sport because we can attend only to a finite number of games and events. From the Biogenesis scandal in baseball to the FIFA World Cup, the media transmit moving pictures and set the agenda for what we see and hear. To be informed citizens, we need to obtain information from diverse sources to gain extensive insight and overcome or balance out potential media biases. Today's information-rich society enables us to be as informed, or as uninformed, as we choose. In this environment, it is obvious that fans, sport communication practitioners, and others continue to follow sport passionately and obsessively, a pattern that will only escalate with the continued expansion of sport at the local, regional, national, and international levels.

Review Questions

1. What is meant by the convergence of media in this era?

2. What is corporate media consolidation, and how has it affected modern sport journalism?

3. How does the phrase "symbiotic relationship" apply to sport and the mass media?

4. Why are sports editors, directors, and other managers in the sport media known as gatekeepers?

5. How has sport on television evolved from the mid-20th century to the present?

Individual Exercises

1. Examine the websites of local newspapers and television stations. How much sport coverage is included? How much convergence of media is evident in the content? How does the content differ from that of the outlet's traditional means of communication?

2. Examine newspaper websites to determine their coverage of men's and women's sport. Your content analysis can include a determination of what sports are covered, how much focus is placed on women's sport compared to men's sport, what links are provided, and the types of photos that appear for female and male athletes.

3. Watch *SportsCenter*, and observe the content of the show and the anchors' verbal and nonverbal gestures. What makes the show so popular?

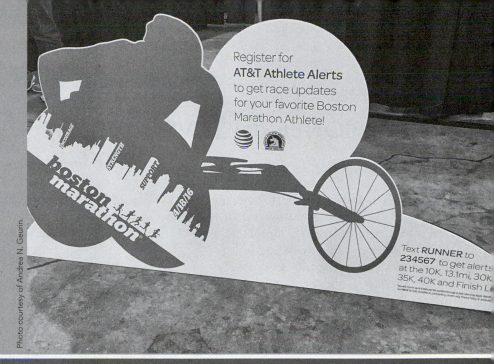

Photo courtesy of Andrea N. Geurin.

CHAPTER 8

Digital, Mobile, and Social Media in Sport

LEARNING OBJECTIVES

- To become acquainted with the Model for Online Sport Communication
- To understand the Internet's impact on new and emerging media and sport communication channels
- To be cognizant of the factors influencing online sport communication
- To understand the components of effective online sport communication
- To become aware of new and emerging media in sport communication
- To understand how sport organizations can best utilize digital media platforms

KEY TERMS

analytical search

augmented reality

browsing

customer relationship management

e-commerce

heuristic search

over-the-top

searching

second screen

video on demand

virtual reality

PIONEERING EVENT VENUE SOCIAL MEDIA USE

Kassie Epstein

As a psychology, theology, and behavioral studies major at Boston College (BC), Kassie Epstein never imagined she would eventually make a career out of managing social media for the largest sport and entertainment venue in Massachusetts. Epstein became interested in marketing when she took courses focused on the psychology of marketing and consumer behavior and pursued her newfound interest through an internship with the NFL's New England Patriots and MLS's New England Revolution during her junior year. From there, she completed another internship with the two teams' home venue, Gillette Stadium, and was hired into a full-time business development role for the Kraft Sports Group/Gillette Stadium after graduating from BC in 2008.

Epstein now serves as the social media manager for Gillette Stadium in the business development and external affairs department, a role she helped to develop. "When I graduated in 2008, social media wasn't seen in the way it is today—businesses were still finding their footing and figuring out how social media could be used and monetized," Epstein said. "I started our accounts for Gillette Stadium around 2009 or 2010 and have been growing with them ever since. I've been lucky to work for an organization and within a department that saw the value in social media and allowed me to learn and grow with this emerging platform as it became more and more integral to our event marketing and promotional campaigns."

Gillette Stadium hosts a wide range of events beyond the Patriots' football games and Revolution's soccer games, such as concerts, monster truck rallies, and supercross races. Epstein says the main challenge of her job is engaging all the different fan bases and demographics that

Kassie Epstein, social media manager for Gillette Stadium.

Photo courtesy of David Silverman Photography.

follow the Gillette Stadium social media accounts. "It's crucial to keep each fan group engaged, while also not posting too much as to turn off the other fan bases," explains Epstein. "A 50-year-old Patriots fan doesn't necessarily want to see 10 tweets a day about Taylor Swift and all the records she's breaking, nor does a 20-year-old Swiftie [Taylor Swift fan] want to see endless posts about football trades and draft predictions." Epstein said that she manages this by carefully planning the content that is posted in relation to when an event will take place. She said, "The closer I get to each event, the more I'll target my content to ensure I'm touching base with each fan group—I want each of our fan bases to feel like they're the most important. As long as each fan group feels like their event is the biggest focus here, I'm doing my job well."

Epstein says that Gillette Stadium's goals for its social media use are to communicate directly with fans while also providing interesting content. "We are here to entertain and engage with fans while also driving business goals," said Epstein. "We want to be a platform where fans can come to share their excitement, but also find valuable information and customer service support when needed." She works closely with the social media teams for all events that come to Gillette Stadium to jointly develop content and promotional ideas.

In the future, Epstein believes that social media will become increasingly important as a customer relations tool for sport organizations. She noted the ever-increasing amount of communication the Gillette Stadium accounts receive regarding customer issues and questions, which has led to having more staff on hand during events to respond to these queries. Epstein views this as a positive development: "Rather than a fan potentially leaving our venue with a small issue creating a negative overall experience, we now have the ability to hear of issues in real time, address them immediately, and turn a fan's experience completely around before they leave our property."

This chapter introduces you to the digital media that have drastically altered and continue to change the way sport-focused organizations and sport media outlets communicate with their key publics. The opening profile featuring Kassie Epstein and her work at Gillette Stadium provides one example of a sport organization that has embraced new communication methods; additional examples are provided in the rest of this chapter. In the mid-1990s, sport fans followed the progress of their favorite sport entities by reading the sports section of the newspaper, listening to sports-talk radio, or watching a segment on the evening news. Today, sport fans are much more sophisticated in charting the progress of their favorite sport entities by logging on to various websites, downloading video clips and podcasts, watching live streams of sporting events online, engaging with sport organizations and other fans via social media, and partaking in online discussions with others who share their sport interests. Online videos have become increasingly popular because they allow sport consumers to watch highlights of their favorite teams or athletes, see replays of key events, and engage in online conversations either in comment sections or via social media. Thus, technology has dramatically influenced the growth of digital and social sport media.

Some, however, believe that new technology often does more harm than good. For example, when Major League Baseball player Josh Thole was a catcher for the Toronto Blue Jays, he was driven to deactivate his Twitter account based on the negative messages he received on the social media platform, where anonymous users can criticize athletes or sport organizations. "Every time you opened your phone up, you had all these Twitter notifications, and it was, 'You stink,' 'You suck,' 'You should jump off the bridge.' I don't need that," said Thole (Brady & Ortiz, 2013, para. 11).

Although there have been many abuses of new technology in sport, for the most part the advances in the Internet and social media have been positive. For example, technological advancements continue to enable increasingly sophisticated levels of communication and affect the way sport-related organizations disseminate information. Whether it be email, live video streaming, real-time sport scores, podcasting, web logs (blogs), or social media interactions, technology provides the foundation for the growth of digital sport media. These technologies and media will continue to influence sport communication through their ability to provide innovative links between sport-focused organizations and their publics. Advances in communication technology allow for instantaneous retrieval and delivery of information anytime and anyplace. As recently as the early 2000s, it was often difficult to stay in contact if one was on the road; that is no longer the case. For example, even when a sport media professional is on an international vacation, she would be expected to remain active on social media and, at a minimum, use her smartphone to stay connected with sources, editors, producers, and colleagues in the event that a story broke involving the players, teams, organizations, or leagues that she routinely covers (Rule, 2017).

This chapter begins by examining the use of the Internet and digital media in sport communication. This examination is followed by a discussion of the Model for Online Sport Communication (MOSC), which highlights key components of effective online sport communication with particular focus on seven aspects that are central to sport websites. The final section of the chapter discusses technological advances that are affecting sport communication, such as mobile devices, social media, digital video, and emerging media such as **virtual reality** and **augmented reality**.

DIGITAL SPORT MEDIA: INTERACTIVITY AND THE INTERNET

This section examines the application of digital media in sport communication, and figure 8.1 illustrates where digital media fit in the Strategic

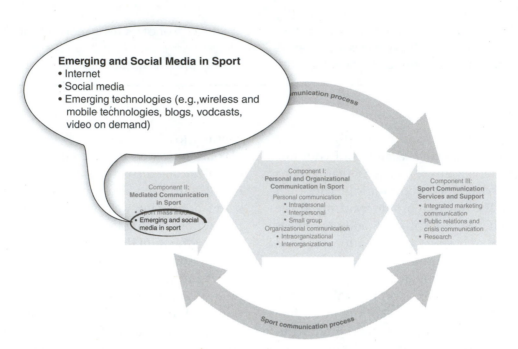

Figure 8.1 The second segment of the second component of the SSCM is emerging and social media in sport, including the Internet, social media, and emerging technologies such as vodcasts and **video on demand**.

Sport Communication Model (SSCM). Kian, Schultz, Clavio, and Sheffer (2019) defined *digital sport media* as "Sports media content that can be created, modified, viewed and distributed through digital, electronic platforms (e.g., Internet, social media)" (p. 210).

Many people, including millions of sport fans and consumers, have transitioned from reliance on traditional mass media to use of the more interactive communication and commercial interfaces provided by the Internet (Mitchell, 2015). Although the Internet has been around for three decades, we still consider it a new medium because it is different from the traditional media, dramatically affects communication at all levels, and continues to influence the way organizations and individuals communicate. When compared with traditional sport media, the Internet is immediate and instantaneous. It is a complex medium that provides an additional communication channel, thus serving as an alternative mechanism to establish communication (Karlsson, 2011). According to Mitchell (2015), media consumers are increasingly turning to the Internet and other digital platforms such as social media sites and podcasts to receive their news. Some of these platforms also allow consumers to connect with each other, whereas traditional media does not allow for such connectivity and interaction.

The immediacy, instantaneousness, and connectivity of the Internet are often best illustrated in the sport industry. For example, on the official Super Bowl website (www.superbowl.com), sport consumers can obtain information such as game recaps and game stats for all past Super Bowls, as well as access their National Football League (NFL) fantasy teams. The site also provides lists of award winners, all-time standings, national anthem singers, halftime performers, Hall of Fame players in the Super Bowl, Super Bowl records, and regular-season statistics for each team ever to play in the Super Bowl (as well as similar information for playoff games). This information is easily accessed, usually within one or two clicks of a mouse, from anywhere in the world with Internet access.

The Internet allows consumers to be interactive, which makes it a unique communication channel (Karlsson, 2011). By going beyond the interactivity limits of traditional media, the Internet provides unique tools that help organizations strengthen their relationships with consumers (Kiesler, 2014). For instance, this interactivity provides opportunities to access a product without having to experience it in person (Kiesler, 2014). On sport websites, this kind of opportunity means that individuals can be particularly active in the communication process by selecting which sections of the site to visit, determining what game clips to download, and even choosing to vote for specific players in competitions such as all-star games.

INTERNET USAGE IN SPORT

The Internet is now a part of everyday life for most Americans; in fact, most students who read this book cannot remember a time when they did not regularly use the web. A 2019 Pew Research Center survey showed that 90 percent of U.S. adults used the Internet, as compared with just 14 percent when Pew first began surveying web usage in 1995 and 52 percent in 2000 (Anderson, Perrin, Jiang, & Kumar, 2019; Berman, 2014). The affordability and availability of high-speed Internet access have enhanced the quality of the Internet and the experiences of Internet users, and the advent of Web 2.0 technology has enabled more interconnectivity and interactivity among Internet and social media users. *Web 2.0* is a term commonly used to describe the advancement of the web from stand-alone screens with limited features (i.e., Web 1.0) to the accessible networks and platforms that now dominate the Internet (Butler, Zimmerman, & Hutton, 2013).

Nearly all professional and college sport organizations and teams rely on the Internet and social media platforms to communicate their key messages. Online communication via the web or social media enables sport entities to essentially eliminate gatekeepers from the media-message process. When sport entities disseminate messages through traditional media, they are often edited, meaning that the narratives and framing desired by a sport entity are changed before the content is published by the independent media outlet. However, sport entities are now able to craft and shape their key messages and disseminate them directly to the sporting public through the Internet and social media. In other words, sport entities are attempting to shape their own agenda rather than having the media shape it for them (Stoldt, Noble, Ross, Richardson, & Bonsall, 2013).

According to the agenda-setting theory (discussed in chapter 4), media outlets use their ability as gatekeepers to shape public opinion by choosing to cover and report on specific issues. This process creates the perception that certain topics deserve more dialogue than others. However, when sport entities use their own websites and social media accounts to communicate with the masses, they essentially become the gatekeepers, thus diminishing the power and influence of much of the traditional media (Suggs, 2015). Therefore, they can influence the perceptions of their key publics based on the way they craft and disseminate their online messages.

Who Uses the Internet?

Initially, the web was used primarily by young, tech-savvy white men and teenage boys, but now it is used heavily by every demographic in the United States, including 97 percent of adults living in a household that earns at least $75,000 per year, 98 percent of individuals with a college degree, and 100 percent of men and women between the ages of 18 and 29 ("Internet/Broadband Fact Sheet," 2019). Whereas the use of the Internet is widespread in Western societies, only an estimated 57 percent of the world's 7.7 billion people used the Internet in 2019, although that number is growing quickly as more than one million new people used the Internet for the first time on each day of 2018 (Kemp, 2019).

Internet access is especially desired by ardent sport fans, many of whom use the web daily to find up-to-the-minute information and statistics related to their favorite sports, leagues, teams, athletes, and coaches. Television remains the most-used medium among sport fans, which should not be surprising because sport fans like to *watch* games (Moses, 2013). However, a 2010 survey revealed that a slight majority of self-identified sport fans cited the Internet as the best source for sport-related news, slightly outpacing national television programming (Burst Media, 2010).

Only 9 percent of sport fans said they had paid for online sport content, and only 11 percent said they were willing to do so (Burst Media, 2010). This finding points to one of the challenges faced by traditional media outlets trying to implement paywalls for accessing their content or stand-alone websites that rely largely on subscriber fees for revenues (Moses, 2013). That challenge may be changing, though. Despite their generation being accustomed to accessing free content online, 39 percent of millennial sport fans said they are willing to pay for online sport content ("New Research Reveals," 2019). Moreover, some websites (e.g., Rivals.com, Scout.com) have attained financial success, popularity, and influence despite requiring paid subscriptions to access most of their content and to post on their message boards (Kian, Lee, Gregg, & Kane, 2014).

Table 8.1 provides an overview of the most popular U.S. sport websites and the number of monthly unique visitors attracted by each site. As the table illustrates, each of the top 15 sites brings in millions of visitors per month ("Top 15 Most Popular Sports Websites," 2020).

The rise of social media has made sport fans' use of the Internet even more prevalent. An estimated 91 percent of U.S. television watchers in 2017 simultaneously used a **second screen** (e.g., smartphone, tablet, desktop, laptop), and 50 percent of all tweets about U.S. television programming in 2013 were related to sport (Friedman, 2014; Wytrwal, 2018). One study (Burns, 2014) showed that sport fans were 67 percent more likely than nonfans to use Twitter as a second medium (e.g., tweeting while watching or listening to a

game). The Internet and social media have become so popular among sport fans that sport teams and leagues have been forced to make the web more accessible to spectators attending their games for fear of losing revenues due to fans staying home to watch games on television while following online—especially the many fans who participate in fantasy sport leagues.

Online Fantasy Sport Games and Online Sport Gambling

The advent of the Internet has also enabled widespread participation in fantasy or rotisserie sport leagues, in part because the web makes it easier to organize and participate from locations around the world. Online fantasy sport leagues often help participants maintain or even build new friendships through interaction and camaraderie (Billings & Ruihley, 2014). In 2017, there were an estimated 59.3 million people in the United States or Canada in at least one fantasy sport league per year, with an average annual spending on fantasy sports of $653 per participant ("Industry Demographics," n.d.).

According to the Fantasy Sports Trade Association (FSTA), fantasy sport participants have an average age of 34, about 50 percent are unmarried, 80 percent hold at least one college degree, 80 percent are male, and 90 percent are white (Goff, 2013). However, the number of female and minority participants has increased across all demographics (Billings & Ruihley, 2014). Roughly 40 percent of participants plan to participate in fantasy sport until they die (Subramanian, 2013). It should not be surprising, then, that fantasy sport participants are highly coveted by advertisers and marketers. They are easily reached since they spend an average of nearly nine hours per week on fantasy sport and twice that many hours consuming sport through some type of media (Goff, 2013). In response to this interest, major sport websites (e.g., ESPN, Yahoo! Sports) employ multiple, full-time fantasy sport experts, and several networks dedicate television shows specifically to fantasy sport. The extent of fantasy sport's popularity can be seen in *The League*, a television sitcom popular among sport fans and young adults that focused primarily on the lives of a group of adult friends and relatives who compete against each other in a fantasy football league.

Table 8.1 Most Popular U.S. Sport Websites

Site	Estimated monthly unique visitors (in millions)
1. Yahoo! Sports	125
2. ESPN	80
3. Bleacher Report	40
4. CBS Sports	30
5. Sports Illustrated	20
6. NBC Sports	19.5
7. SB Nation	19
8. Fox Sports	18
9. RantSports	13
10. Deadspin	12.5
11. ThePostGame	11
12. Sporting News	10
13. Scout	5.5
14. FanSided	5
15. Yardbarker	4

Note: Ranking as of February 2020 by eBizMBA Rank, which is based on the *Alexa* Global Traffic Rank and U.S. Traffic Rank from both Compete and Quantcast.

Whereas many fantasy sport leagues have long included betting pools, fantasy sport gambling has grown into a mainstream business in recent years with the advent of websites such as DraftKings and FanDuel. These sites advertise on national television during major sporting events and offer a variety of "cash prize" contests, including one-day draft leagues in which participants pick players on Sunday morning for that day's NFL games and either win or lose based on their statistical performance that day. Combined, DraftKings and FanDuel, the largest fantasy sport sites focused on betting, reached nearly $3 billion in player entry fees in 2015 (Woodward, 2016). However, since 2018 when the Supreme Court struck down a federal law that mostly prohibited sport gambling in the United States outside of Las Vegas, DraftKings has partnered with states that have initiated legal sport gambling. Specifically, DraftKings opened legal sport betting operations in New Jersey, New York, West Virginia, Iowa, Indiana, Mississippi, and Pennsylvania by 2019 and joined FanDuel, MGM Resorts, and the Stars Group to serve as authorized betting operators for the NBA, which was the first of the major U.S. professional team sport leagues to embrace legal sport gambling (Cohen, 2019). Sport gambling has long been a lucrative industry, but most betting was done through offshore websites or with illegal local bookmakers. The American Gaming Association estimated that Americans illegally wager $150 billion on sport gambling per year (Mayshayekhi, 2019). However, only a year after the 2018 Supreme Court ruling, American gamblers placed more than $10 billion in legal sport bets in just seven states that had implemented legal sport gambling systems, with continued growth likely in states that allow online sport betting (Ramsey, 2019).

As evidenced by the rise of online fantasy sport leagues and now legal, online sport gambling—along with sport analytics sites and the influence of Twitter on sport—the Internet has laid the framework for new and emerging media in sport communication. More than any other medium, the Internet has allowed sport consumers to feed their craving for information about their favorite sport products. New technology has also enabled sport-focused organizations and sport media entities to provide content almost instantaneously through the Internet. Although

Photo courtesy of Paul M. Pedersen.

DraftKings, who up until 2019 had a jersey sponsorship deal with the New York Liberty (worn by guard Brittany Boyd in this photo), offers daily fantasy opportunities for WNBA games as well as contests in other leagues (e.g., NFL, NBA, NHL, MLB) and sports (e.g., esports, mixed martial arts, golf, college football, soccer).

this instantaneous distribution of information can be advantageous, the means by which it is achieved are often complex; therefore, the way sport information is relayed becomes paramount.

What Makes a Good Sport Website?

Sport organizations rely on websites to provide immediate communication with both internal and external publics and key stakeholders. Meân (2014) noted that consumers now widely access information about sport on websites, and other forms of digital media and websites "have themselves become naturalized as central, familiar, and routine sites of sport-media consumption, progressively influencing and guiding sport fan practices" (p. 331). More recently, interconnectivity has become as important as interactivity on team and sport organization websites. Teams that can effectively use the Internet and social media gain a competitive advantage over those sport organizations that rely on traditional print communication. A sport website should reflect the mission and values of the sport organization and provide a high-quality online atmosphere and experience for key publics. It should also serve the organization's business objectives—for example, selling season or group tickets, educating consumers about products, fulfilling key components of a sponsorship package, providing a resource for the sport media, or cross-marketing the organization's other online and social media platforms—all while promoting, reinforcing, and maintaining a favorable image of the organization.

To a large extent, sport organizations rely on service when promoting and selling their products, and an effective website can serve as a supplementary service for sport consumers. For example, an appealing website allows a professional sport franchise to reinforce its image among fans while also creating a sense of identification between consumers and the team. It also creates a social network for fans through message boards, blogs, live chats (including with players and coaches), and embedding social media (e.g., tweets from the team's official feed and from star players). In addition, a sport organization's website provides essential information for both casual fans (who may log on to check game time, parking restrictions, or other game-night policies) and fans who consume the product more heavily (who may desire information about specific players, statistics, or general franchise news). Because most fans love sport at least in part for the action, sport websites should strike an action-oriented tone, which often means using bright backgrounds, plenty of action photos, and embedded videos. At the same time, all sites should be easy to navigate by means of clear menu items at the top and a search tool.

To use the unique capabilities of the Internet to maximum potential, sport entities must understand the key aspects of online sport communication. These aspects are examined in the next section of the chapter, which presents a model outlining the primary focal points for establishing effective online sport communication.

MODEL FOR ONLINE SPORT COMMUNICATION

To fully grasp the nature and scope of online sport communication, the key factors that influence it, as well as the components that are instrumental for success, must be understood. The following subsections address these factors and components by means of the Model for Online Sport Communication (MOSC), which was conceptualized by Kim Miloch of Texas Woman's University during the research for the first edition of this textbook (Pedersen, Miloch, & Laucella, 2007). Miloch's original vision for the MOSC revolved around sport organizations' websites, but today the scope is broader and includes all online components of an organization, including its social media accounts, mobile apps, and digital video content. Online sport communication is influenced by a myriad of factors, and the MOSC highlights the seven factors considered most pertinent:

1. Individuals' level of involvement with the respective sport entity
2. Individuals' motives for Internet use
3. Content of the sport entity's online media (e.g., website, social media accounts)
4. Design of the sport entity's online media
5. Performance of the sport entity's online media
6. Usability of the sport entity's online media
7. Commerce of the sport entity's online media

The first and second components of the MOSC illustrate the role of people's involvement with the sport entity and their motives for using the Internet. These components are presented first because they form the basis for individuals' desires, needs, and expectations when visiting a sport entity's online platforms. In other words, depending on the person's needs, one of the remaining components may influence the effectiveness of the entity's communication more than another component. For example, if someone desires to download a podcast, the performance and usability components of the model may be most pertinent to that person. If the podcast takes too long to download, the individual will not be satisfied, and the opportunity for effective and enhanced communication will be lost. In contrast, if someone visits a sport entity's website to retrieve game statistics for a specific player, then the site's content, design, and usability components are likely to be most important in the online communication process. This person will want the content quickly, and the website should easily lead him or her to the desired content through its design and usability.

Therefore, the influence of individual motives in the online sport communication process should not be overlooked. These motives influence people's needs, and online sport communication should address those needs. The remaining five components of the model—that is, the third through seventh components—address the online needs of sport consumers. These five factors are not limited to websites; rather, in today's ever-expanding technological environment, they also apply to other forms of online communication such as social media, digital videos, podcasts, and smartphone apps.

The first of these five components—which is the third component of the MOSC—focuses on content. A sport entity's digital communication should deliver content that not only meets users' needs but also reflects positively on the mission and values of the organization. That said, users desire a range of content, and the sport entity should provide it quickly.

The fourth component of the model reflects the importance of design in online sport communication. Whereas sport entities are bound by the design and interactivity features of social media platforms such as Facebook or Twitter, the design of their own website can influence user interaction. Interactivity differentiates online sport communication from other media and, when well enabled, can greatly enhance communication with sport consumers.

The fifth component of the MOSC focuses on the performance of online sport communication platforms and the importance of enabling users to access and download certain features in a timely manner. When sport entities rely on third parties to deliver their messages, it is incumbent upon the organization to choose partners that provide a consistent and reliable service. For example, if an organization has its own podcast, it may choose to make it available for download via its own website as well as through third-party applications such as iTunes or Stitcher. The organization must select these third-party applications carefully.

The sixth component involves usability—that is, people's ability to use the features of the site to gather the desired sport information. If a sport entity's communication mechanisms are not readily usable, communication becomes much more challenging, and the sport entity struggles to get its messages out to its publics.

The seventh and final component of the model focuses on commerce. The Internet is not only a highly effective communication tool but also one with great potential to promote and market products; the role of online sport communication in marketing the entity is examined as part of this component.

The components of the Model for Online Sport Communication are instrumental in cultivating high-quality communication and helping the sport entity develop an effective online presence. These components are very much interrelated; each affects the others. To illustrate these components, the MOSC is presented in figure 8.2.

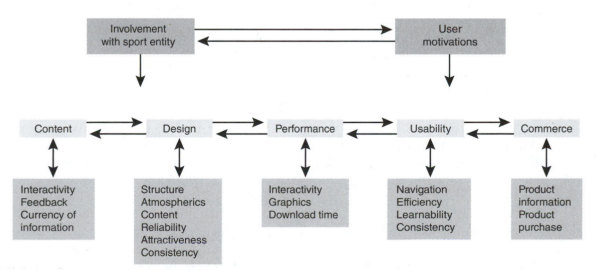

Figure 8.2   The Model for Online Sport Communication.

Involvement With the Sport Entity and User Motivations

Because the Internet is used widely by the masses, we need to examine the variety of motivations for that use. Just as sport fans' motivations vary for attending a specific sporting event or for purchasing a certain sport product, people's motives also vary for acquiring sport-related information online. It is often people's level of involvement that affects their motivations, perceived needs, and desires when using the Internet. Therefore, when identifying and discussing sport consumers' motives, one must consider their level of involvement with the particular sport entity in question. This dynamic is linked to Blumler and Katz's (1974) uses and gratifications theory, a well-known communication theory explained in greater depth in chapter 4. This theory asserts that individuals use the media to satisfy certain needs and wants. Therefore, when people visit a specific sport organization's online communication platform, they are usually doing so with a specific goal in mind, and this goal varies based on their involvement with the sport entity.

For example, someone who has an interest in the National Hockey League's Chicago Blackhawks might visit the franchise's website to examine the team's game schedule and purchase tickets to an upcoming game. However, a season-ticket holder might go directly to the Blackhawks' YouTube page to watch game highlights, visit the Blackhawks' smartphone app to access his or her tickets to the next game, or visit the Blackhawks' Facebook page to interact with the team's content and with other Blackhawks fans. Although these two online users both have an interest in the franchise, the season-ticket holder is much more involved in consumption. Similarly, a sport enthusiast might log on to the French Open's website during the event to see if a well-known player (e.g., Serena Williams, Rafael Nadal) has advanced to the next round. However, an avid tennis fan might log on to the site to watch video highlights of the day's matches, review match statistics, view a live feed of the event's Twitter account, or read a player's blog. In other words, people with different levels of involvement visit online sport communication platforms for varying reasons. Based on that involvement, they each have their own goals

and motives for visiting the platforms; therefore, their online needs and desires vary.

Although the Internet is ever changing, the factors motivating individuals to log on have remained consistent since its inception. A study of over 55,000 global Internet users found that individuals have a variety of reasons for using the Internet, including to be inspired (20 percent), to improve their mood or relax (19 percent), to stay updated socially (17 percent), to be entertained (15 percent), to seek answers or advice (9 percent), to be in the know (8 percent), to connect with others (7 percent), and to seek support or insight (6 percent) (Shanmugham, 2016). To effectively communicate their messages online, sport entities must understand the motives of their key publics when designing, developing, and maintaining online sport communication.

Just as motives influence people's strategies for acquiring desired information, they also influence people's specific online needs. For example, a marathon runner looking for new running shoes might log on to the websites of three manufacturers to compare shoes. The runner's motive is to gain information about the shoes to determine which pair is the best option for purchase. To gather the needed information, the runner seeks to find certain content about each pair of shoes; access this content with navigational ease; perhaps view the shoes from various angles; read other runners' reviews; and determine the cost, color options, and places to purchase. If any of these components is missing, the sport entity has failed to communicate effectively. Therefore, sport entities must understand not only the motivations of their publics but also the method by which individuals seek to obtain information.

Methods and Approaches Used in Seeking Information

People have traditionally used two key methods for obtaining information via the Internet: **searching** and **browsing** (Ackermann & Hartman, 2014). With either method, the user types a query into a search engine, whereupon links related to that query appear on the screen. *Browsing* is characterized by more simplistic queries in which several documents are returned and people browse through the documents to find the ones that are most pertinent to the desired information.

Browsing has been characterized as "navigating through linked chains of hyperlinked documents" (Sandvig & Bajwa, 2004, p. 14). *Searching*, on the other hand, refers to a more detailed and strategic process that is often facilitated by professionals who serve as liaisons between users and the database being searched (Ackermann & Hartman, 2014).

Users choose their information-seeking method based on several factors. Most searchers, however, are influenced by their previous searching experiences (either on the current website or others), the information being sought, the formulation of search terms, and search-feature accessibility. Internet users tend to prefer seeking information by browsing because it is perceived as being less difficult than searching. In addition, Internet users who navigate sport websites are typically more successful at obtaining the desired information by the browsing method than by the searching method (Sandvig & Bajwa, 2004).

In recent years, the rapid growth of social media use has made this technology a primary way of obtaining information (Kim, Sin, & Tsai, 2014). For example, an individual might browse through various social media posts on sites such as Facebook and Twitter to learn about topics of interest; they might also view photographs on Instagram to learn more about specific people, places, or events. In recent years, Internet users have also gained information by posting questions on social media sites for others to answer. As Kassie Epstein illustrated in the opening profile, consumers are increasingly turning to sport organizations via social media to answer customer service questions. For example, a fan preparing to attend his or her first New England Revolution game might be unfamiliar with transportation logistics at the team's venue, Gillette Stadium. Therefore, this user might tweet at the Gillette Stadium account to say, "I'm getting ready to attend my first Revolution game! What are my options for parking at the stadium?" In this method, the user relies on the organization or other social media contacts instead of actively searching for information via a search engine or on the team's website.

The approaches that people use to acquire information when they go online can also be categorized into two groups in another way. These approaches—described by Ylikoski (2005)—are characterized by the reason for the search: heuristic or analytical. A **heuristic search** is conducted with low deliberation, meaning that the individual uses hyperlinks to navigate the web. In contrast, an **analytical search** involves an element of planning and relies heavily on search engines. Heuristic searches are based on trial and error, whereas analytical searches are more focused or more strategic and therefore often require more cognitive effort.

Expectations and Needs of Online Users

As noted earlier, online users' expectations and needs vary widely as a result of their level of involvement and their diverse motives for logging on and surfing the web. As with the level of involvement, expectations and needs can also be tied to individuals' uses and gratifications. For example, a sport reporter may log on to a team website to obtain up-to-date player statistics, injury reports, or press releases. In contrast, a consumer with interest in a specific team may read the sports section of the daily newspaper for information about the same franchise. Both people are making choices based on their information needs and their assessment of which medium best addresses those needs. Their satisfaction is linked to how well the chosen medium provides the information that addresses their needs.

Pedersen (2013) noted that individuals have motivations for using a specific medium and these motivations relate to their own goals (e.g., the specific information an individual hopes to find). Additionally, some scholars (Cutler & Danowski, 1980; Stafford & Stafford, 1996; Stafford et al., 2004) have noted that motivations for using a specific medium usually stem from one of two broad reasons. The first reason is to access content available on a certain medium (e.g., specific information, entertainment). The second reason is to gain the experience of using the specific medium, including exploring the dimensions of the technology provided by the medium. These two reasons have been defined, respectively, as *content gratification* and *process gratification*. Content gratifications involve messages carried by a specific medium, whereas process gratifications involve the sheer use of the medium. In other words, content gratifications focus on the message, and process gratifications focus on the features and technology of the medium itself. For example, one sport fan might log on to a website to gain information about an upcoming game or a community relations event hosted by a specific sport entity. Another fan, however, might log on to the site to download a podcast; this user is specifically interested in using the technology provided on the site.

Along with websites, sport fans also have different motivations for using specific social media platforms. Witkemper, Lim, and Waldburger (2012) examined sport fans' motivations for using a specific medium, in this case Twitter. Their findings revealed that the fans had four primary motivations for using Twitter, including "to gain information, as a form of entertainment, to enhance their fan experience, and simply as a way to pass time" (p. 179). Sport consumers have different motivations for using other social media platforms as well. For example, Billings, Qiao, Conlin, and Nie (2017) studied sport fans' use of Snapchat and found that although fans found other social media platforms to be better for information seeking, relaxation, and overall interaction, fans still chose Snapchat for sport-related media consumption because it is "perceived to be superior for socialization, creativity, and for experiencing a moment in a given point in time" (p. 22).

Several general expectations and needs are apparent in most consumers. Papacharissi and Rubin (2000) were two of the first scholars to classify individuals' motives for using the Internet. They noted that the motivations include using the Internet for its interpersonal utility, as a pastime, for information seeking, for convenience, and for entertainment; in addition, online users expect sport websites to offer both visual and emotional appeal. With regard to sport sites, Seo and Green (2008) developed the Motivation Scale for Sport Online Consumption (MSSOC), which identifies 10 motivational dimensions for consumption of sport websites: fanship, interpersonal communication, technical knowledge, fan expression, entertainment, economic, passing time, information, escape, and support. The fanship, fan expression, and support dimensions speak to the emotional appeal that motivates many sport fans. More generally, when taken together, these 10 dimensions can be used by sport organizations to obtain a sense of their users' website consump-

tion motives (Seo & Green, 2008). Kang, Ha, and Hambrick (2015) also uncovered sport fans' primary motivations for using sport-related mobile device apps, which were fanship, convenience, and information.

Most consumers expect to receive an enjoyable and high-quality experience when they visit an online sport communication platform, just as they would if they attended a live sporting event. This expectation necessarily means that most consumers anticipate a certain level of quality in terms of content, graphics, and performance. Consumers' expectations of online quality are raised as they become more sophisticated in their use of technology. Therefore, sport communicators must become more sophisticated in meeting the needs and demands of online consumers while also positively conveying the key messages of their organization. To do so, sport communicators must first understand the general needs and motivations of their online sport consumers.

Content

Content is, of course, a primary component of any sport entity's website or other digital media platforms, and it is considered a major factor in an individual's decision to return to a website (Rosen & Purinton, 2004). Sport communication content should be selected based on the mission of the sport entity as well as the needs of its key publics. To put it more sharply, the content should reflect the entity's objectives and meet sport consumers' demands by giving them information that they value and find appealing (Yang, Ahmed, Ghingold, & Boon, 2003).

Content can take many forms, and it is important to note that it is not limited to written words on a website or social media post. Exciting photographs, digital videos, infographics, and even humorous memes are all examples of content that sport organizations share on their websites or social media accounts to engage with their followers. For example, fans now have the option to watch some of their favorite teams' full-game broadcasts on social media (e.g., Major League Baseball broadcast 26 of its regular season games on Facebook during the 2018 season), and social media features such as Instagram and Facebook "stories" allow sport organizations to post behind-the-scenes videos or game highlights that are available to fans on these platforms for 24 hours after they are posted.

Nielsen Sports (2018) identified the top five trends in commercial sport, one of which was labeled "Content Rules," highlighting the importance of sport organizations' content in online spaces. In their report, Nielsen Sports also identified three trends that are shaping sport organizations' content decisions. The first two trends include sport consumers' attention spans becoming shorter and having more entertainment options competing for their attention. These trends highlight the need for interesting content that can be consumed quickly, such as short video clips or infographics that can get a point across in a matter of seconds. The National Basketball Association (NBA) adapted its content in 2018 as a result of these trends by offering fans the opportunity to watch only the fourth quarter of a game for only $1.99 via NBA League Pass, which can be accessed on a smartphone; tablet; laptop; PC; or cable, satellite, or streaming television service. Later, the league also unveiled options to purchase the final three quarters of a game or the second half of a game (Rovell, 2018).

The third trend influencing content decisions by sport organizations is the increase in mobile media consumption (Nielsen Sports, 2018). Sport fans are no longer limited to consuming content from home on their televisions or computers; now fans can stay connected to their favorite teams and leagues no matter where they are in the world. Sport organizations can reach fans via their mobile devices through social media platforms, the organization's website, and organization-specific mobile apps. Whereas this myriad of options for consumers means that fans can stay connected to their favorite teams 24-7, it also places great pressure on sport organizations to continually develop new and engaging content to be posted on these platforms. Organizations must choose their content strategically, however, as Craig (2018) warned against creating content just for the sake of creating content. Instead, sport organizations should focus on the quality of the content to provide meaningful information that helps to create a conversation with consumers.

Along with the importance of organizations developing content strategies based on current consumer trends, the interactivity of an online communication platform is also important for attracting and engaging consumers. The interactivity of a medium allows consumers to form social networks, which can be especially important in sport, where the social aspect is thought to influence sport consumption. One of the means for facilitating the social aspect among sport consumers is to provide message boards on an organization's website. Sport news websites also provide live chats to discuss a myriad of sport-related issues. Many websites also allow consumers to write comments about the content (e.g., written stories or videos) to engage in conversations with other consumers. Another way to facilitate interactivity between fans and the sport organization is via social media platforms such as Twitter and Facebook. These platforms allow two-way communication between the fans and the sport organization. Often, a member of the organization's communication staff responds to fan comments and questions, as evidenced in the opening vignette on Kassie Epstein from Gillette Stadium, and organizations also coordinate Twitter or Facebook chats between fans and members of their staff or their athletes. These interactions help build loyalty among fans and increase fans' identification with the sport organization. Clavio and Walsh (2014) examined sport organizations' use of websites and social media to facilitate engagement with fans and found that sport fans were most likely to engage in activities such as watching an embedded YouTube video or interacting with a sport organization or other fans on Facebook.

The content an organization posts must be purposeful and offer some form of value to the consumer rather than posting content for the sake of posting content. Any sport-related communication platform should also offer practical benefits to visitors by providing them with content that meets their needs. The perceived practical value of sport communication platforms is integral in people's decision to use the medium; it also affects their frequency of use (Bei et al., 2004). Filo, Funk, and Hornby (2009) revealed that the information a consumer retrieves from a sport website can enhance his or her experience with the organization and foster a more favorable attitude toward the organization. In addition to using a wide variety of content (e.g., text, images, video), Tandoc (2014) stated that providing search engines and site maps on an organization's website is important as it helps consumers obtain information quickly.

Sport entities should also provide direct links to specific people within the organization for feedback purposes. Doing so establishes a more effective means of communication between the organization and sport consumers. Many sport websites fail to provide phone numbers or email addresses, which can be problematic if consumers desire more personal interaction. In addition, as more sport entities use their websites to obtain data about their consumers, those same consumers should be made aware of each site's privacy policy and how data provided to the sport entity may be used (Migala, 2004).

Design

Another equally important factor is website design, which is influenced by numerous elements. While sport organizations do not have control over the design elements of existing communication platforms such as Facebook, Twitter, or Instagram, they do have control over the design of their organizational website and mobile app. As with every aspect of the MOSC, when a sport entity designs or modifies a website, it must consider the motivations and needs of its consumers. Eide (2018) illustrated the need for an attractive website design that appeals to consumers, citing research that found if a website layout is considered unattractive, 38 percent of consumers will stop engaging with it, and 88 percent will not return to a website after having a bad experience with it. Additionally, 75 percent of consumers indicated that they judge the organization's overall credibility on its website design. Therefore, if a sport entity's website is not designed in a manner that easily communicates key content in a visually pleasing manner, the entity will have difficulty in communicating its message and retaining fans or consumers as repeat visitors. The design process includes determining the placement of links, as well as choosing colors, graphics, and interactive features. Whereas written content was previously a key to a website's success, consumers are now increasingly drawn to strong visual elements such as photographs, videos, or infographics when they first visit a site (Gillett, 2014).

Relating the concept of design to the previous section, the graphic design elements of a sport website can greatly assist in providing content (Rosen & Purinton, 2004). To name just a few, design factors include "elements of space, use of images, size of images, use of animation and/or audio, number of words per line, color and size of characters," (Rosen & Purinton, 2004, p. 788). In addition, as noted by Rosen and Purinton, effective content design involves purposefully determining the placement of these elements. Doing so allows the sport entity to communicate with site visitors in the most effective manner. According to Carlson and O'Cass (2012), a sport organization's website design is related to the organization's brand and can build trust when consumers consider it to be a high-quality website.

Recognizing the Importance of Structure

One of the most important elements of website design is the concept of structure. Developing a sound structure enables sport entities to both incorporate necessary elements into the website and enhance the other components of the MOSC. Proper design is an integral aspect of any website because it affects user interaction, the primary feature that establishes online communication as unique (Garrett, 2010). Interaction is also the feature that enables sport entities to communicate more effectively and enhance the online experience for sport consumers. Site design is also instrumental both in encouraging individuals to visit the entity's website and in fostering repeat visits. The website presents a unique opportunity for the sport entity to grasp the user's attention and communicate its message. However, just as a poorly designed storefront influences a person's decision about whether to enter the store (Auger, 2005), a poorly designed website influences a sport consumer's decisions about whether to visit or return to a specific website.

Given many individuals' preference to browse rather than search, a website should include distinct and concise paths to the information that most users seek (Sandvig & Bajwa, 2004). Therefore, sport entities should understand what information is most desired by visitors to their websites and point the way toward this information with ease. For example, a season-ticket holder should not have to spend much time surfing a franchise's website to find information about parking options or game time. Similarly, an individual desiring to purchase single-game tickets should be prominently directed to the franchise's schedule and ticket prices without having to search the entire site. A website should strive to provide consumers not with an overload of information but with easy access to key information (Weatherhead, 2014).

The key to all of this is structure. A website without an effective structure is like a book with unnumbered and unbound pages (Hackos & Stevens, 1997). To help develop good website structure, sport entities should develop a well-organized menu with easy-to-find information, links to their social media pages and other useful external links, and up-to-date relevant content such as news items and videos featuring exclusive content. The website itself should be developed with the organization's goals in mind and should be designed to appeal to the sport organization's key target markets.

Evaluating Well-Designed Websites

To assess the quality of its website design, a sport entity should continuously evaluate the design as it relates to each component of the MOSC. In an extensive review of **e-commerce** websites, Goi (2012) found that scholars "do not have any commonly agreed-upon standards or techniques for Web site evaluation" (p. 7). Even so, evaluation is crucial to maintaining effective online sport communication. Fortunately, in research conducted outside the sport industry, Akincilar and Dagdeviren (2014) provided a model for website evaluation that can be applied to sport organizations. These authors' analysis of websites involves five main criteria and multiple subcriteria (dimensions). The main criteria (with examples of subcriteria in parentheses) are: the degree to which the website is oriented toward customers (e.g., fulfillment, personalization, playfulness, feedback, contact information), technology (e.g., usability, accessibility, navigability), marketing (e.g., advertising, promotion, customer service), security (e.g., privacy, trust), and other factors (e.g., visual appearance, interactivity, multimedia content).

In addition, Cox and Dale (2002) argued that navigational menus should be simple and should appear in the same place on each page of a given

site. This consistency increases consumers' satisfaction with a site because it allows them to find their way quickly and without incident. McNeil (2015) reports that when Internet users engage with a navigational menu, it is an opportunity for the organization to "steer them towards what you want them to do" (para. 11), and therefore organizations should be strategic in the way in which they design their website menus. A website should also avoid deviating greatly from the design of other websites of its kind. Many consumers, according to Nielsen (2004), form their perceptions of websites based on their experiences with other sites. Therefore, any deviation from general design norms may create frustration and confusion among consumers. For example, the uniformity of the websites associated with Major League Soccer (MLS) (www.mlssoccer.com) and the league's individual teams provides online consumers with consistency and increased design usability. There are no surprises, and frustration and confusion are limited by this approach.

Performance

The fifth component of the MOSC focuses on a sport communication platform's performance, which is related to content and design and closely related to usability. For example, if a video clip does not load for a user within a reasonable amount of time—or if the user cannot navigate the site in an acceptable time span—then the medium is judged to perform poorly. Website performance also hinges on level of interactivity; sport consumers have come to expect sport websites to be both interactive and fast.

The manner of evaluating website performance has changed from determining a site's number of hits to evaluating its interactivity and the amount of time it takes to complete certain tasks, such as downloading a file. Multimedia content most often has a positive effect on consumers when a site performs well; in contrast, consumers may become frustrated and agitated if downloading takes several seconds and tasks cannot be completed in a timely manner.

Sport websites are also expected to be interactive, and interactivity affects a website's performance by enhancing its value to consumers and the organization (Hood, Shanahan, Hopkins, & Lindsey, 2015). Interactivity improves communication options as it provides consumers with an additional avenue of communicating directly with the organization, and vice-versa. This additional communication channel allows the organization to better understand its consumers and meet their needs. Interactivity may prove particularly useful when communicating with consumers in dynamic settings or in settings that change or evolve on a regular basis, such as a social media platform like Twitter, where content and information is constantly updated. This benefit holds significant meaning for sport entities because the nature of sport consumers and sport products can vary dramatically (Auger, 2005).

Although content is a key component of any online sport communication platform, interactive qualities help attract and retain visitors who may not be particularly attracted to the medium's content. Hood and colleagues (2015) noted that it has become increasingly more difficult to make online consumers' experiences with websites unique, but the interactive elements of a site have the ability to make up for this and lead to customer behaviors such as more frequent visits and purchases. This relates to consumers who are less loyal to the sport product, as the entertaining interactive elements of a website may help lure these consumers to the site. Of course, interactivity and entertainment features exert a positive influence on more loyal sport consumers as well. Regular consumers of a sport product tend to be information seekers, and research indicates that entertainment enhances their online experience as well (Richard, 2003).

In sum, the key aspects of an online sport communication platform's performance include speed and interactivity. These elements relate to each component of the MOSC, especially usability. Sport website performance also relates to commerce; when an individual (i.e., potential consumer) wants to purchase or obtain information about a product, the website must perform accordingly.

Photo courtesy of Paul M. Pedersen.

Sport organizations offer a variety of online components (e.g., smartphone apps, social media accounts) to reach, inform, and interact with stakeholders. The promotion featured here directs fans to the organization's website where they can secure free tickets to the NFL Combine Experience.

Usability

When sport consumers visit a website, they expect to find the desired information easily and quickly, which means within two or three mouse clicks or finger taps via a mobile device. Therefore, usability is a key element of any website, yet the word *usability* is a broad term with varying definitions (Hassan & Li, 2005). Nielsen (2012a) characterized usability both as an attribute that determines ease of use and as the way user interfaces are improved when a website is designed. Nielsen (2012a) indicated that the term *utility* refers to the functionality of a system, whereas *usability* refers to how usable that functionality is for consumers. In other words, for a website to be usable, it must fulfill the following actions:

- Serve a distinct purpose
- Be functional
- Enable consumers to use its features with ease

Therefore, *usability* refers to the relationship between a specific tool and its users. For the tool to perform its intended function, users must be able to operate it effectively. This means that a person logging on to a certain website must be able to use it in a way that satisfies her needs and wants; the website should enable consumers to achieve their goals without experiencing frustration. Nielsen (2012a), one of the world's leading experts on usability and the Internet, noted that a website's usability is more than important—it is *essential* if the website is to survive. Usable websites present few navigation problems and are easy to use, thus encouraging individuals to remain on the site to acquire information and enhancing their perceptions of the site (Richard, 2003). In contrast, if a website is confusing or difficult to use, fails to state what the entity offers, or is hard to read, it impedes information searches and causes consumers to look elsewhere (Nielsen, 2012a; Richard, 2003).

Principles of Website Usability

The principles of website usability are grounded in engineering principles pertaining to human interaction with machines (Palmer, 2002). According to Nielsen (2012a), the five key dimensions of website usability are as follows:

1. Learnability
2. Efficiency
3. Memorability
4. Error management
5. Satisfaction

The learnability dimension addresses consumers' ability to accomplish basic tasks during their initial visit to the site, whereas the efficiency dimension addresses their ability to perform tasks quickly once they have learned the site's design. The memorability dimension characterizes consumers' ability to perform tasks effectively and accurately when returning to the site after a period of inactivity. Error management refers to the number and severity of errors made by consumers on a site, as well as their ability to recover from these errors. The satisfaction dimension addresses the appeal of the website's design.

The way these five elements are addressed on a specific website affects consumers' ability to seek and discover information about the sport organization and its products. Therefore, these elements influence the quality of an organization's online communication with its publics. Because communication is a two-way process, websites must be usable if the sport media outlet or sport organization is to convey its messages effectively. If sport consumers leave the site, the flow of communication is interrupted, and the sport-focused organization misses out on the potential advantages associated with online communication.

Importance of Navigability

One of the most important aspects of website usability is navigability, which ensures that visitors can peruse the site with ease. Navigability on a sport website is just as important as a sport franchise's game plan. Proper navigability provides a road map to help both frequent and infrequent visitors acquire the information they desire. For example, suppose that a Los Angeles Kings fan in Brisbane, Australia, plans a business trip to Southern California. The fan logs on to the franchise's website to determine whether the team will be playing at home at that time. To find out, the fan looks for directions to the desired information, which likely includes the team's home schedule, ticket availability and prices, and purchase information. Without proper navigability, the fan may not get the needed information. To enable easy navigation, Nielsen (1997) asserted that users should be able to ascertain at any given moment where they are on the site, where they have been on the site, and where they are able to go on the site. Meân (2014) pointed out that navigational menus on a sport organization's website are extremely important and that the positioning of such a menu on a site has significance for how well a consumer can find information on the site.

When establishing a website with good navigability, sport entities should always include a feature that allows site visitors to find their way back to a certain point on the site. More specifically, Hackos and Stevens (1997) suggested that a website should provide a home base, which serves as consumers' point of entry to the site. A consumer should be able to access that point of entry, or home page, by clicking on a "home" button or other menu option anytime while visiting the site. This option allows consumers a means to escape if they become lost while trying to access information on the site. Additionally, Johnson (2003) pointed out that navigability can be strengthened by minimizing the number of navigation schemes presented on a website; one suggestion for achieving this goal is to provide a navigation bar across the top of the page listing the major content areas of the site.

Commerce

The final component of the model focuses on commerce. The use of the Internet as an effective tool of commerce is now widely accepted. Mualla (2019) reported that *e-commerce*, or the buying or selling products and services online via the Internet, accounted for $2.7 billion of the National Hockey League's (NHL) revenue, $3.8 billion of the NBA's revenue, $7 billion of Major League Baseball's (MLB) revenue, and $9 billion of the NFL's revenue. Clearly, online space can be utilized by sport organizations for more than communication purposes. Seok Kang, a communication scholar, said, "Fans who are more engaged online buy more team product merchandise and have a higher fan loyalty for the sports teams or players they are interacting with on social media" (University of Texas at San Antonio, 2017, para. 5). In combination, the advantages of online com-

munication and the mass appeal of sport make an ideal match for succeeding in e-commerce (Carlson & O'Cass, 2012).

Along with e-commerce from desktop devices, sport consumers are increasingly engaging in commerce via mobile devices. These devices now allow consumers to purchase tickets and merchandise through a smartphone or tablet while eliminating the need for printed event tickets. Team or venue-specific smartphone apps also allow for in-game e-commerce transactions when fans are attending an event. For example, Levi's Stadium, home of the NFL's San Francisco 49ers, has an app that allows fans to purchase tickets, manage their tickets (the app can be used for entry to the stadium), order food and beverages for in-seat delivery or concession stand pickup, and purchase add-on experiences such as a personalized message on the 49ers scoreboard during the game or postgame field access to enhance the user's game day experience. As e-commerce is becoming increasingly popular among sport organizations and an extremely important source of revenue, sport organizations must be able to ensure effective sales and delivery methods for consumers.

The advent of legal sport gambling in an increasing number of states provides another opportunity for significant growth in e-commerce as related to sport communication. However, much of the potential revenue growth in this area for sport organizations is not directly from fees or direct revenues via wagering but instead due to increased fan engagement with those organizations, their teams, athletes, and products since those who gamble are more likely to intensely follow teams and root for those they bet to win (Mashayekhi, 2019). After the 2018 Supreme Court decision opened the door for states beyond Nevada to implement legal sport gambling, Mark Cuban, the outspoken owner of the NBA's Dallas Mavericks, told CNBC, "I think everybody who owns a top four professional sports team just basically saw the value of their team double, at least," (Kilgore, 2018, para. 5).

A study by the American Gaming Association found that fully legalized sport gambling in the United States could result in an additional $4.2 billion in annual revenues for the NFL, NBA, MLB, and NHL, with the vast majority of these new revenues from increased fan engagement via gambling (Mashayekhi, 2019). Fans attending New Jersey Devils hockey games can visit a lounge in the Prudential Center, where they can view online screens listing betting odds and then place bets by simply downloading an app on their phones (Mayshayekhi, 2019). In addition to paying to attend games, these same fans are often purchasing merchandise, food, and beverages at games while gambling on those same contests. Beyond the most popular professional team sport leagues, other sport organizations (e.g., NASCAR, Arena Football League, etc.) have already formed partnerships with sport gambling sites to try to capitalize on fan engagement with sport gambling (Mann, 2018). Mayshayekhi (2019) concluded, "Despite opposition from state gaming lobbies across the country, most people in the sports betting industry agree that mobile sports betting is the way of the future, if not the present" (para. 38).

Internet's Role in Positioning the Sport Product

A sport entity's website or other digital platforms can be used to create a "virtual fan experience" and provide a high-quality service experience for key audiences. Many entities use websites to enhance customer service efforts and to foster more positive and mutually beneficial relations with consumers (O'Shea & Alonso, 2012). The Internet possesses considerable capacity to help organizations provide information and enhance customer relations; therefore, it gives organizations the ability to dramatically improve business and organizational performance (Thompson, Martin, Gee, & Eagleman, 2014). Brown (2003) suggested that sport entities "must focus on the online seller/consumer relationship. Without this focus, business may be lost to [other] organizations [that are] effectively implementing forms of e-commerce" (p. 54). He noted that other forms of entertainment effectively use the Internet to engage consumers and enhance commerce; if sport entities fail to recognize this value, they will lose money. To avoid this pitfall, they can "focus on selling merchandise and tickets online and on generating sales leads through web activities" (Brown, 2003, p. 53).

To enhance the commerce aspect of a website or digital platform, an organization must gear the site's content and design to meet the expectations, needs, and desires of its potential consumers. Accurate knowledge of consumers' desires and motives for using the Internet provides businesses with a more efficient means of serving them (Stafford et al., 2004). Websites that do not provide a satisfactory online experience are less likely to draw visitors or encourage repeat visits. According to Carlson and O'Cass (2012), when consumers develop trust in a sport organization's website, they are more likely to both visit that site and purchase from it more frequently. Additionally, they found that consumers who trusted a website were also less likely to switch to a competitor's site to make purchases. Therefore, sport organizations must develop their websites in ways that elicit trust. Carlson and O'Cass (2012) stated that this can be accomplished through projecting an online image that is consistent with the brand's off-line image, as well as providing a high level of online service quality for consumers.

The design and content of a sport website should also attend to the consumer's sensory shopping experience. As Rosen and Purinton (2004) explained, a sensory shopping experience facilitates sales and helps build relationships with customers. "For the e-retailer, the sensory shopping experience must be played out on the template of the web page" (p. 788). Specifically, music, color, and lighting have been known to influence customer purchases.

Internet's Role in Acquiring Consumer Data

Privacy concerns and issues related to building the organization's database must also be considered when discussing the commerce aspect of a sport website. Ensuring the privacy of site visitors establishes a sense of trust between the sport entity and its key publics and enhances relations with customers (Carlson & O'Cass, 2012). At the same time, using database mining technologies allows sport entities to track consumers' needs and desires, which also enhances the value and benefits associated with their products (Pernice & Caya, 2014). **Customer relationship management** (CRM), or the use of technology to manage interactions and data about current and potential customers, is incredibly important for sport organizations.

CRM systems can be used by sport organizations to build detailed profiles of their customers. Customer data is gathered anytime a purchase is made. For example, when a fan purchases tickets to a Chicago Cubs versus Houston Astros MLB game via the Cubs' website, the Cubs organization can then begin to collect data on the purchaser. Information such as the person's name, address, phone number, email address, type of payment method used, number of tickets purchased, amount spent on tickets, and section of the stadium in which they chose seats all help the organization develop a unique profile for this customer. Most e-commerce platforms encourage customers to create an account with the organization when they make a purchase. Organizations do this for a few different reasons. For the customer, creating an account makes future purchases easier, as the e-commerce platform will be able to fill in details such as the customer's contact information when he reaches the checkout stage of a purchase. From the sport organization's perspective, when a customer creates an account, it assists in developing a more intricate and detailed profile of all his purchasing habits. Sport organizations can use this data to develop more targeted marketing and communication efforts for that specific consumer. For example, if the customer buys tickets to other Chicago Cubs games, the Cubs can look at the customer's data to understand patterns and more effectively target ticket deals and promotions to that customer. If the customer regularly attends weekday games that take place during the afternoon, for example, the Cubs may decide not to send this particular consumer messages about weekend night games, as the customer probably will not be as interested in attending those. Another example may be that the Cubs notice this customer only buys tickets to games when Jon Lester is the starting pitcher. This likely means the customer is a big fan of Lester, and the Cubs can use that information to target the customer for future games where Lester is pitching or special offers for paid meet-and-greet opportunities with the players.

CRM systems offer sport organizations a wide range of other data points that can help the organization target and cater to its customers. For example, MailChimp, an email CRM system, allows organizations to see data such as which customers opened their emails, if they clicked on any links in the email, or if they simply deleted the email without ever opening it. Another example is the data that organizations can collect when customers use a team or league's smartphone app for purchases. Many of these apps allow fans to purchase tickets, merchandise, and even in-game food and beverage, as illustrated in the previous example about Levi's Stadium. When organizations collect all of this data, they have a better understanding of how much money each customer spent on food and beverage at the game, as well as their food and drink preferences. This information can assist the organization in better targeting the needs and wants of individual consumers. According to Scott (2018), CRM is important for sport organizations because "the financial success of a team — whether it's football, soccer, baseball or another sport — is about more than how it plays the game. It's about keeping fans engaged" (para. 4).

In addition to the use of CRM systems via an organization's website or mobile app, online sport communication platforms also provide an efficient means of gauging feedback about various aspects of the sport product. For example, many sport organizations allow customers to write reviews of merchandise they have purchased from the team's website, such as apparel or gifts. These reviews provide valuable feedback for the organization as it determines which products should be updated in some way or which products to continue selling. Additionally, social media allows customers to comment on all aspects of their experience at a sporting event, which organizations can use to enhance the customer experience at their events. As you can see, this feedback can be invaluable when positioning the sport product and addressing the needs and concerns of key publics.

DIGITAL SPORT MEDIA COMMUNICATION CHANNELS

Advances in technology will continue to enhance communication channels and alter the way sport entities communicate with both internal and external publics. Whereas the previous sections briefly touched on some of the digital sport media communication channels beyond websites (e.g., social media, apps, digital videos), this section describes these technological advances in greater depth and provides an overview of technologies predicted to affect sport organizations in the future. These include mobile technology, social media, digital video platforms, and other new developments.

Mobile Technology

Mobile technology in the form of smartphones and tablet devices has enabled people to remain in contact with friends, family, and business colleagues from almost anywhere in the world. The same technology now allows sport entities to communicate with sport consumers 24-7. Sport consumers can access information about their favorite sport entities anytime using mobile and wireless technologies. Sport fans typically seek content such as game highlights, exclusive commentary on athletes or teams, interviews, and feature stories.

Mobile technology allows sport fans to visit their favorite sport websites; interact with sport organizations, athletes, and other fans via social media outlets (e.g., Twitter, Facebook, YouTube, Instagram); download and listen to sport-related podcasts; watch live video streams and video clips; interact through team- and league-specific apps; purchase tickets, merchandise, and in-game items such as food; and perform many other functions. In a global survey of sport fans, two out of five respondents reported watching sport on a mobile device ("The Changing Profile," 2019). The same report stated that use of a mobile device to watch sport has overtaken PCs and laptops, with 3 percent more consumers preferring mobile devices than computers. Another study revealed that sport fans who use smartphones for sport consumption are primarily motivated by a desire to gather information and that the convenience of smartphones allows consumers to do so more quickly than on other communication platforms (Ball, 2019). For sport organizations to keep up with fans' demands for mobile content, they must understand their consumers' needs, stay on top of trends in sport communication, and hire employees who understand new technologies and how to implement them.

A related trend in sport communication is the use of a second screen while watching a live sporting event. According to Martinolich (2012), a *second screen* is counted as "any connected visual media device that can be used alongside the traditional broadcast television, or first screen" (p. 27). Facebook Business reported that among global sport fans, 90 percent said they use a second screen while consuming sport; of those, mobile devices are the preferred second screen of 79 percent of fans ("The Changing Profile," 2019). Fans use such devices to connect with other fans during games via social media, view updated game statistics, view replays or highlight videos, and search for more information about teams and athletes.

Photo courtesy of Paul M. Pedersen.

Fans attending the Winter Youth Olympic Games in Lillehammer, Norway, had the opportunity to enter one of three Samsung Galaxy studios to experience virtual reality (VR) smartphone technology.

Sport organizations have begun to seize the opportunity to become involved in second screen usage. Many have done so by creating event-specific or organization-specific hashtags that fans can use when posting content or engaging in online conversations about a sporting event. For example, during the 2019 FIFA Women's World Cup, the U.S. women's national team used the hashtag #USWNT and encouraged fans to use it as well. This allowed the U.S. women's national team to follow the conversations and content being posted about the team, as well as allowed fans to engage with other like-minded fans in online spaces while watching the games on TV or another device. Additionally, sport organizations often contribute to fans' second screen experiences by posting live game updates and commentary on social media during games and getting involved in fans' social media conversations themselves by responding to fan comments about specific plays or occurrences in the game.

Sport fans also want opportunities to engage with mobile devices and social media while attending sporting events in person. Sport organizations can capitalize on fans' mobile device usage at the event to enhance the overall fan experience, as illustrated through the previous example about the Levi's Stadium app and all the options it provides fans who attend San Francisco 49ers' home games. In addition to the e-commerce aspects of the app, it also provides content such as on-demand video replays from the game, live game video, up-to-date statistics, guides to the shortest bathroom lines, parking and seat location maps, and opportunities to connect virtually with other fans (Bajarin, 2014). Another example of optimizing fans' in-stadium experience via mobile technology is the MLB, which has the Major League Ballpark app that can be used in any MLB stadium. The app allows fans to check in at games, receive targeted offers for merchandise or other items to purchase, upgrade their seats on game day, purchase players' entrance music via iTunes, and share photos with other fans ("5 Sports Stadiums That Score Big," 2016). To compete with the information and interactivity options that sport consumers enjoy while watching from the comfort of home, sport organizations and facilities must continue to develop innovative mobile communication options for fans who watch events in person.

Social Media

Social media is a form of digital media that involves interaction between users. Since the inception of social media sites such as Facebook and Twitter, sport organizations and athletes have adopted this new technology at a rapid pace. In addition to official league, team, and athlete websites, most sport entities also maintain an official presence on social media outlets such as Twitter, Facebook, YouTube, Instagram, and Snapchat. DeMers (2014) indicated that 92 percent of business owners reported that they felt social media was important to their business; indeed, it is difficult to find a sport organization without a presence on social media.

Of the many social media outlets, Facebook is the most popular with nearly 2.4 billion global users as of July 2019 (Clement, 2019). Following Facebook is YouTube (2 billion), WhatsApp (1.6 billion), Facebook Messenger (1.3 billion), WeChat (1.1 billion), Instagram (1 billion), and QQ (823 million). Twitter ranks 12th among worldwide active users with 330 million, and Snapchat ranks 15th with 294 million. The benefits of social media for sport organizations include cost-effectiveness, enhanced identification among fans, and the opportunity to communicate directly to fans instead of relying on traditional media such as newspapers, television, or even news websites (Eagleman, 2013). The drawbacks of social media must also be considered. For example, to engage in social media, a sport organization must have ample staff to consistently update, monitor, and respond on social media accounts. In addition, organizations must consider the potential loss of message control due to inappropriate or negative comments about the organization's posts.

In terms of specific social media outlets, Twitter is arguably one of the most influential and popular social media outlets for sport organizations, athletes, and fans. In 2007, the Sacramento Kings of the NBA became the first professional team to join Twitter (Langer, 2014). It took nearly five years before the next team, the NFL's Arizona Cardinals, joined the microblogging site, but now it is difficult to find a team, sport organization, or athlete without a Twitter presence. Twitter allows users to post updates of up to 280 characters while also offering the ability to post links, images, videos,

Photo courtesy of Paul M. Pedersen.

Fans often post the photos and videos taken on their smartphones to various social media platforms (Instagram, Snapchat, etc.). Here, fans interact with former player and coach Allen Iverson at a Big3 (three-on-three professional basketball) event.

Twitter is also a popular medium for breaking news and making official announcements, which athletes, sport journalists, and sport organizations do on a regular basis. Another example of Twitter's usefulness for sport organizations and fans can be seen in the prevalence of esports-related content on the platform. In 2017, Twitter identified 218 million tweets about gaming ("Gaming and Esports Are Happening on Twitter," 2018). This prompted Twitter to take a greater interest in esports; in 2018, it live-streamed several esports competitions on its platform and began hosting a weekly 30-minute live show covering highlights and behind-the-scenes content for esports fans. Twitter has also assisted in maintaining integrity in the sport, as De Guzman (2014) pointed out that the platform helps to expose fraud and eliminate rumors in the esports industry.

polls, gifs, and emojis. In terms of interactivity, Twitter users can respond directly to others' tweets, as well as retweet an original tweet to one's own followers or "like" a tweet.

Sport fans often take to Twitter during events to provide commentary and thoughts and to engage in conversations with others who are also consuming the event, whether in person or via television. For example, during the 2018 FIFA World Cup, over 76 million tweets mentioned the global soccer tournament throughout the duration of the event, making it the most tweeted-about sporting event in 2018 (Guzzo, 2019). Even though the U.S. men's team failed to qualify for the tournament, it was still the second-most tweeted-about sporting event in U.S. history, behind Super Bowl LII. As previously mentioned, research shows that sport consumers use Twitter to get information, be entertained, pass the time, and indulge their fandom (Witkemper, Lim, & Waldburger, 2012). Therefore, Witkemper and colleagues (2012) suggested that sport organizations should make their tweets both informative and entertaining to best engage their audiences.

Athletes and sport organizations also commonly use Facebook, a platform that allows account owners to create business accounts, which are different from individual users' accounts in that they offer the ability to customize the page with business-specific information (e.g., hours of operation). They also provide the account owner with page analytics that monitor page traffic, engagement levels with each individual post or picture, and demographic information about the page's visitors. Sport organizations often use Facebook to post more in-depth information than they could post on Twitter due to Twitter's character restrictions. Facebook posts also allow users to indicate their reaction to a post by clicking on one of six emoji responses—like, love, laugh, wow, sad, or angry. Facebook users can comment directly on a post or share a post with their own friends on the site.

Sharing content from a sport organization or athlete assists in increasing the visibility of such posts beyond the organization or athlete's core audience of followers. As mentioned earlier in the chapter, Facebook also offers sport organizations a platform on which to stream live content to fans, as it exclusively streamed 25 MLB games in 2018. Research has shown that live videos on Facebook are effective in generating six times more discussion than videos that are recorded and then posted to the site (Kaufman, 2018), indicating the power that live video has on this platform and offering new opportunities for sport brands that have not yet capitalized on this feature.

Instagram is another social media outlet that is popular among sport organizations and athletes. Functioning primarily as a mobile app on users' smartphones, Instagram began as a photo sharing platform but in recent years has integrated a variety of features allowing for both photographic and video content. For example, users can post up to 60-second videos in the main posting area; photo or video stories available on the site for 24 hours; and longer-form live videos, which are then archivable for future watching. Users can include captions and hashtags, tag other Instagram users in their posts, and receive likes and comments. Of the world's top 100 brands, 90 percent have an Instagram account, and 80 percent of Instagram users follow at least one brand on the platform (Smith, 2019). One-third of Instagram users follow a sport-related account ("Insights," 2018). Additionally, Smith (2019) reports that 60 percent of Instagram users have discovered new products or brands on the social media site, and engagement levels with brands on Instagram is 10 times higher than on Facebook and 84 times higher than on Twitter.

Instagram is poised to provide a wide variety of benefits for sport brands, and research that the platform itself has conducted on sport fans revealed three different types of fans who consume content on Instagram. The first type, labeled "Matchday Maniacs," is described as fans who organize their lives around sporting events and who want constant content from their favorite teams and athletes. They tend to engage with Instagram content during breaks in game action (e.g., halftime, time-outs). "Homeland Heroes," the second type of fans, identify strongly with their favorite teams and enjoy Instagram content that allows them to share their allegiance to a specific team with others. Finally, "Social Supporters" are those who enjoy the social media aspects of sporting events more than the event itself. They are highly active on social media and very engaged in sport-related content posted on Instagram ("Insights, 2018). Understanding the various types of sport consumers on different social media platforms can help teams create content and strategies that will best engage each group of fans.

New social media outlets emerge quite frequently; if a sport organization tried to develop a presence on every available social media platform, it would likely spread itself too thin in terms of resources. Therefore, an organization must understand how each social media platform operates, as well as its benefits and drawbacks. The organization must also determine which outlets are most popular with its current customers and target markets.

Digital Video Platforms

Digital video is changing the way consumers watch sport and offers fans more flexibility in terms of how, where, and when they watch sporting events and content. Whereas many sport fans still watch live sport via traditional paid cable TV subscriptions, many consumers, especially those from younger generations, are now consuming sport video content in vastly different ways, including **over-the-top** (OTT) streaming and video on demand (VOD).

OTT refers to the streaming of video content to consumers via the Internet. For example, popular services such as Netflix, Hulu, YouTube TV, Sling TV, and Amazon Prime Video are all examples of OTT services and can be accessed with an Internet connection via a PC, laptop, smartphone, tablet, or smart TV. According to Impey (2019), the number of sport fans who consume sport via OTT platforms now surpasses the number who consume via traditional cable or satellite TV, with 60 percent of fans reporting that they watch using an OTT platform and only 50 percent reporting that they watch via cable or satellite. Based on these numbers, some fans clearly use both methods.

Sport organizations have begun to realize the importance of embracing OTT for content delivery, as 82.4 percent of sport industry executives identified OTT as an important opportunity for increasing revenue, while 65.6 percent also indicated that consumers' shift away from traditional TV consumption represented a top threat to their bottom line (PwC, 2019). Whereas sport organizations' broadcast deals were traditionally held by large sport media TV broadcasters such as NBC, CBS, FOX, ABC, or ESPN, organizations are now diversifying their rights and incorporating more OTT companies in the mix. For example, in an effort to reach fans outside of the United States, MLS sold the rights to its broadcasts to global OTT company DAZN for exclusive broadcasts in Germany, Austria, Switzerland, Italy, and Spain and nonexclusive broadcasts in Brazil from 2019 to 2022 (SportBusiness Media staff, 2019). Additionally, within its domestic market, some MLS teams began exclusive rights deals with OTT platforms in the United States. For example, teams in Los Angeles, Seattle, and Orlando all partnered with YouTube TV in 2019, and OTT platform ESPN+ partnered with the Chicago Fire (Jerde, 2019).

One sport that has greatly benefited from the use of OTT is esports. An Amazon-owned OTT platform, Twitch, focused almost exclusively on streaming esports when it was first founded in 2011. The platform has since expanded to content such as music and talk shows but attracts 15 million unique viewers every day, largely because of its esports content (Iqbal, 2019; Stephenson, 2019). Esports players can host their own streaming channel on Twitch, which allows them to stream their games, speak directly to their fans, and even solicit donations from their followers (Miceli, 2019). With the help of Twitch, the number of annual global esports tournaments grew from 10 in 2000 to over 4,000 in 2018 (Fox, 2019; Popper, 2013), illustrating the influence that streaming can have on the growth of a new sport.

Another form of digital video is video on demand (VOD), which provides sport consumers with the ability to select and watch video by simply pushing a button. This technology can be accessed as part of an interactive television system, via the Internet, or on a smartphone or tablet. Whereas OTT platforms are often consumed live as the sporting event is actually happening, VOD allows consumers to watch content whenever they want, whether it is live or not. An NCAA wrestling meet that a user recorded on YouTube TV and then watched two days after the broadcast aired would

be considered both VOD and OTT since it was consumed at the fan's leisure via an Internet-based platform. Additionally, VOD does not have to be consumed via an OTT platform; many traditional cable or satellite TV services offer consumers the option to record broadcast content and then watch it later when it is convenient.

Some streaming services such as Netflix and Amazon Prime have begun to develop exclusive sport-related VOD content in the form of television series or documentaries. For example, Amazon Prime users can watch a variety of sport-focused docuseries under the name "All or Nothing," which follow sport teams for an entire season and provide "character-driven storytelling and compelling visuals" (Ramos, 2018, para. 2). For example, one edition of the show followed the University of Michigan college football team during its 2017 season, and subsequent series have focused on teams such as the New Zealand All Blacks rugby team and UK-based Manchester City Football Club. When sport organizations partner with filmmakers and content providers for these types of programs, it allows fans to develop a deeper connection with the organization and consume exclusive content they would not be able to access otherwise.

Emerging Technologies

Along with mobile technology, social media, and digital video, other new technologies such as virtual reality (VR) and augmented reality (AR) are beginning to make their way into the lives of sport fans as sport organizations learn how to best utilize them. Virtual reality involves a person (e.g., sport consumer or athlete) wearing a headset with a screen that places them into a simulated environment. The NBA has been at the forefront of VR in terms of major global sport organizations, embracing the technology as far back as 2014. Since 2016, the league has offered one game a week during which fans can use a VR device to watch the NBA game as though they are sitting in courtside seats (Sprung 2019). Aside from using VR for fans, some teams and leagues also use it as a training method for their athletes. For example, the NFL's New England Patriots use the technology to put players into simulated game situations in which they must make decisions on

DIGITAL MEDIA ALLOWS JOURNALIST TO LIVE HIS IDEAL LIFESTYLE

Ryan Wilson
NFL writer, blogger, and podcaster
CBSSports.com

The Internet and social media have radically transformed most of the sport communication profession. Some current job duties were unimaginable as recently as the early 1990s, and the backgrounds of the individuals who fulfill these duties vary far more than in previous eras. Few people better fit this new genre of sport communication professional than Ryan Wilson, a blogger, writer, and podcaster for CBSSports.com, whose primary job duty involves year-round reporting on the NFL and the NFL Draft. Although he loves his job, works many hours, and takes his career seriously, Wilson said his primary goal in life is to spend time with his two children. The fact that nearly all his work is done via computer from his home in upstate New York makes the job ideal for him and provides him with a daily routine that was unheard of prior to the rise of the Internet.

"My job is perfect," said Wilson. "A typical weekday for me starts by getting the kids to school, although I used to take care of them full-time during the day before they went to school, while mostly working at night after my wife returned home from her job. By 8 a.m., I see what's going on by looking at Twitter, my RSS feed, and various websites to figure out what fans will have an interest in and the implications of this news. Then I check in with my boss and our other bloggers to see what I am going to write about that day, although as breaking news happens, you have to react and churn out copy quickly. For example, we will put out little boxes on 3, 4, 5, or 10 things to know about what happened on a new story. That seems to work really well in the shortened attention span of today's culture, but we have to get it out fast."

Photo courtesy of Ryan Wilson.

Spending extra time with his sons while working almost entirely from home is one of the many perks that Ryan Wilson cites about his job with CBSSports.com.

The way in which Wilson landed such a "comfy" job—reporting from home on the most popular sport league in the United States—would have been unfathomable in the predigital age. Wilson was seemingly primed for a business career after earning master's degrees from both the University of Arizona and Carnegie Mellon University. At 29, his career prospects and networking potential reached a pinnacle after he landed a position in the White House Office of Management and Budget in 2003. To pass the time during his daily train commute into Washington, D.C., from his Maryland residence, Wilson began writing about his three favorite sport teams—the University of North Carolina men's basketball team, the Boston Red Sox of MLB, and the Pittsburgh Steelers of the NFL. To do so, he set up a blog (HeelsSoxSteelers) in 2004 to share his fandom with friends and family.

Initially, Wilson had no designs on making money from this venture or expanding beyond the blog, which he did not advertise and did not circulate publicly other than through emails with friends. After all, he had no classroom or practical experience in any realm of journalism. "In grad school, you always have something with school work and your work hours are basically what you make them, other than when you have to go to class," Wilson said. "But after grad school, I didn't know what to do after the workday was over, especially on those long train rides home. So I basically set that blog up to pass time and have something to do. I had no idea what I was doing and never thought about someone actually paying to read my writing." Wilson's readership, however, started growing slowly but steadily, and he enjoyed writing for the blog. As a result, he inquired about freelance writing opportunities with Aaron Schatz, then head of the relatively new start-up website FootballOutsiders, which now provides advanced statistical analysis for ESPN Insider and is frequently visited by most serious NFL followers. Wilson started freelancing for Football Outsiders and other sites, which led to his being recruited by Jamie Mottram, who at that time was charged with building a network of bloggers to launch America Online (AOL) FanHouse. Mottram has since directed digital content for Yahoo! Sports and the USA Today Sports Media Group.

In Wilson's off time from his White House job, he began churning out copy for AOL for a whopping $8 per blog in the summer of 2006. A year later, his family decided to move to upstate New York, and Wilson decided to dedicate himself to a full-time career in sport blogging, even though he was still making less than $10 per blog from AOL. Of course, he was churning out 200 to 400 blog posts per month as one of AOL's lead NFL bloggers and a lead golf blogger. "I was able to make a living and care for my newborn every day at that time while living in a house near where my wife was from," Wilson said. "It was a pretty sweet deal. All of my friends were saying, 'You are getting paid to do what?' They couldn't believe that I was making money for writing about sports from home."

Four years later, as AOL was shutting down FanHouse for financial reasons and thus laying off many sport bloggers and writers, Wilson quickly secured a similar job with CBS Sports without having to leave his living room. However, it wasn't until 2014 that CBS Sports made him a full-time employee with health benefits for the first time in his sport communication career. Wilson had become indispensable to one of the country's larger sport media outlets, in part because, like most other top sport communication professionals, he continually improved his writing skills. He also expanded his media skills to account for the technological changes highlighted throughout this chapter.

"I know I am not going to win a Pulitzer, but I am capable of doing a bunch of things," said Wilson. "I would argue that I am pretty Internet savvy, probably more Internet savvy than most. I realize I am never going to be anywhere near as good as [ESPN's] Wright Thompson as a writer. But I am guessing Wright Thompson can't upload a podcast. Wright Thompson probably doesn't need to with how great a writer he is. But there's only one Wright Thompson, and most of us in this field now have to be able to do a little bit of everything, which is what I do."

Wilson said that social media impressions, or the number of views a particular post receives, are now a primary emphasis from his superiors at CBS Sports. "Social media is the topic our bosses now begin and end every conversation with. So much of what we do now is geared toward social media, like Twitter and Facebook."

A large part of Wilson's job, however, is following up on a story broken by another reporter. Depending on the story, Wilson may provide analysis or commentary or do follow-up reporting. This new-age form of *news aggregation* (where many reporters from different outlets produce content

(continued)

(continued)

providing different angles from a story broken by another reporter) has drawn criticism from some older journalists, with much of their critiques directed at digital-age bloggers like Wilson. "[Fox Sports'] Jay Glazer and [ESPN's] Adam Schefter are breaking most of the NFL news. Newspapers for years have been reporting other people's news. The only thing that changed is it is now on the Internet. I can't imagine a situation where, if the

New York Daily News broke a story, no one else is allowed to write about [it]. We have to write the story when there is major news. We're happy to credit Jay Glazer if he breaks the news. We make it a point to credit people who break the story. Some outlets do not, but we always do. We do hyperlink all the time, too. The old-school newspaper reporters are not happy, but the Internet and social media have changed everything."

---

where to run or pass the ball. This allows them to practice their analytical skills without being physically affected, as they would if they practiced each of these scenarios with other players (Zorowitz, n.d.).

Different from VR, augmented reality superimposes computer-generated images, sounds, or other data on a user's view of the real world, thus providing a composite view. Once again, the NBA has been a pioneer in its use of AR in sport. The league has an AR app that allows fans to feel as though they have an up-close-and-personal experience with NBA players and teams behind the scenes of the game (Sprung, 2019). Other uses of AR in sport

include MLB's At Bat app, which allows MLB fans who are physically present at games to point their smartphone at the field and receive "individual player profiles, including arm strength and catch probability in addition to staples like, on base percentage and batting averages" (Medal, 2017, para. 6). Through the app, fans can also follow the speed and trajectory of every hit during the game. VR and AR are currently not widely used in sport; however, many sport communication experts predict that teams and leagues will continue to explore ways to incorporate these cutting-edge technologies into all aspects of their businesses, especially to enhance fan engagement and experiences.

CHAPTER WRAP-UP

Summary

This chapter introduces you to digital and social media that are drastically altering the way sport-focused organizations and sport media outlets communicate with their key publics. More than ever before, sport fans are using the Internet to research and follow their favorite sport entities. Sport fans' use of the Internet has increased dramatically since its inception, and sport enthusiasts now rely less on traditional media. Today, sport fans are much more sophisticated in charting the progress of their favorite sport entities by logging on to various websites; downloading video clips and podcasts; taking part in online chats with others who share their interests; and interacting with sport organizations, athletes, and fans via social media.

Technology has dramatically influenced the growth of new sport media. Advancements in technology continue to spur a more sophisticated level of communication and affect the way sport-related organizations disseminate information. Whether it be email, live video streaming, mobile applications, social media apps, or video on demand, technology provides the foundation for the growth of digital sport media. These technologies and media forms will continue to affect sport communication through their ability to provide an instantaneous link between sport-focused organizations and their publics.

This chapter begins by examining the use of the Internet in sport communication, followed by a discussion of the Model for Online Sport Communication. The MOSC highlights the key components of effective online sport communication and focuses on seven key aspects of sport websites. The final section of the chapter discusses technological advances affecting sport communication, such as wireless technology and social media.

Review Questions

1. What are the general needs of consumers when logging on to a sport website?
2. What factors affect online sport communication?
3. What factors contribute to a successful sport website?
4. How does the Internet differ from traditional media?
5. What differentiates searching online and browsing online?

Individual Exercises

1. Attend a sporting event. While in attendance, note the many ways in which new technologies affect communication mechanisms, as well as your overall experience of the event.
2. Visit three of your favorite sport teams' official websites. Pick three teams from three different sports. Note the similarities and differences between the three sites in organization, presentation, and type of content offered.

CHAPTER 9

Integrated Marketing Communication in Sport

LEARNING OBJECTIVES

- To understand the concept of integrated marketing communication
- To appreciate the unique challenges of marketing sport products
- To become acquainted with the historical context of advertising in sport
- To understand the use of sport as a means to advertise to mass and diverse audiences
- To comprehend the role of sport sponsorship in sport advertising
- To understand the role of celebrity athlete endorsers in advertising
- To comprehend emerging communication and marketing trends, such as customer-centric marketing, influencer marketing, and the use of business analytics in marketing

KEY TERMS

advertising
athlete endorsements
brand equity
branding
customer-centric marketing

customer relationship
  management (CRM)
influencer
integrated marketing
  communication

lifestyle marketing
sponsorship
sport product

ADAPTABILITY IN AN EVER-CHANGING MARKETING COMMUNICATION LANDSCAPE

Dylan Leslie

As an account director for Endeavor, a global sport marketing agency, Dylan Leslie is responsible for managing Visa's global soccer **sponsorship** portfolio, including its partnerships with FIFA, UEFA Women's Football, CAF Africa Cup of Nations, and the U.S. Soccer Federation, among others. Leslie has been with Endeavor since completing his education at Saint Mary's College of California, where he earned a BA in sport and recreation management and an MBA with a sport management concentration and also competed on the university's Division I men's soccer team. He began his career at Endeavor as an intern and has steadily worked his way up the organizational hierarchy, from account executive to account manager, senior account manager, and currently account director.

Over the course of his career, Leslie has witnessed great changes in the marketing industry, especially related to sponsorship. According to Leslie, "Brands and properties are taking more ownership to be experts in their own space rather than relying on traditional agency support. Agencies intersect more and more—roles aren't clearly defined from advertising to media to digital to consulting. Everyone does a bit of everything! Also, the world of football (soccer) is uncontrollable, and continues to play a unique role geo-politically. Politics and football are inevitably intertwined. Managing those scenarios is the biggest challenge."

The 2018 FIFA World Cup in Russia marked Leslie's first

Photo courtesy of Dylan Leslie.

Dylan Leslie at the 2018 FIFA World Cup, where he was instrumental in activating Visa's sponsorship of the tournament.

time overseeing the entire plan and management of Visa's sponsorship activation strategy, and he was instrumental in leading Visa to its most successful sponsorship event in history. Visa's marketing campaign for the World Cup focused on a narrative to combat World Cup FOMO (fear of missing out) as three billion people around the globe watched the tournament, but only a fraction of those were able to attend in person. To accomplish the goal, Leslie first helped Visa identify a global ambassador, Zlatan Ibrahimović. Ibrahimović had a relevant story to tell regarding the concept of FOMO, as he famously missed out on qualifying for the 2014 FIFA World Cup and was teamed with a roster of global influencers to help fight FOMO with Visa. According to Leslie, "The content and storytelling were relevant, timed right, and came to life in ways that Visa could only provide. Zlatan was legitimately the very first person to step on the field in Luzhniki Stadium—to be clear, before both the Russian and Saudi Arabian national teams." As part of the activation strategy, Visa hosted viewing parties around the world for those fans who were unable to travel to Russia, executed soccer clinics at FIFA World Cup training sites, and took fans on match day experiences.

Leslie feels that the two biggest keys to success in integrated marketing communication are knowing one's audience and requiring tangible results from marketing communication efforts. "Knowing your audience is vital to delivering something that people will care about and buy. Having tangible results allows you to truly measure success," explains Leslie. "Marketing and budgets are more scrutinized than ever, so proof points are crucial to celebrating success and winning new business." Additionally, Leslie noted that traditional advertising is no longer effective in capturing consumers, and building a direct relationship with consumers is crucial. When it comes to organizations competing for consumers' attention, Leslie says, "Whoever can deliver the most desirable content and on a technologically advanced platform to make every individual end user feel like they are the only one watching will win the race."

When asked what advice he has for students wishing to pursue a career in marketing communication, Leslie stressed the importance of gaining real-world experience. "With the practical experience, find what sets you apart and develop it, nurture it. In my case, it wasn't a skill but the love and passion for football," said Leslie. "Know what you want to do but balance that with being picky. Not every path is straight, so you need to be willing to gain valuable experience while keeping your eye on what you want. Lastly, be patient."

Marketing communication is defined by the American Marketing Association (n.d.) as an all-encompassing term that covers aspects of marketing and communication such as **advertising**, **branding**, graphic design, publicity, and public relations. Beyond that definition, **integrated marketing communication** (IMC) refers to the integration of these various marketing and communication methods into a cohesive, consistent message conveyed by an organization to its consumers, fans, and other stakeholder groups. For example, at its most basic form, integrated marketing communication can be displayed by an organization using the same font, colors, design elements, and logo on all its communication and marketing pieces (e.g., letterhead, business cards, website, advertisements, newsletters). In this way, the organization communicates a consistent identity, which often results in greater awareness of the organization among stakeholder groups and helps create brand associations and equity.

In a more complex example, a sport team might use a wide variety of marketing communication methods, such as traditional newspaper and television advertising, social media posts, videos shared on its organizational smartphone app, and personalized emails to its customers. In this example, all the communication presented in these various outlets should be uniform and deliver a consistent message or theme. An even more complex approach might involve using multiple platforms to work together to achieve a goal.

For example, Sport England, a governmental organization that seeks to increase sport participation in England, launched a campaign called "This Girl Can" in 2015. The organization found that 40 percent of English women age 16 and over were not active, so it developed an ad campaign showing women of all shapes, sizes, races, ages, and ability levels participating in various sport and fitness activities. The 90-second video ad was set to Missy Elliott's catchy song "Get Ur Freak On" and aired on television as well as online. Complementing the ad was a specific "This Girl Can" website where women could learn about different ways to get active. The site currently features 94 different forms of exercise, ranging from swimming to ballet to kickboxing to Disney dance-alongs. The website also features inspiring stories about women whose lives were changed by getting active, and women can share their own stories via Instagram, which then appear on the website. The content from the website is complemented on the "This Girl Can" social media pages—such as Facebook, which shares short inspirational video stories, presents opportunities to be active, and posts inspirational quotes—or on Twitter where women are encouraged to tag their posts with #thisgirlcan. By creating a consistent inspirational message that reaches women using several different media outlets, "This Girl Can" is now in its fifth year, and 2.8 million women in England report that they have become more physically active as a result of the campaign (Roderick, 2017; Sport England, n.d.).

Nike provides another example of a complex IMC strategy with its 2017 "Breaking2" campaign, which was used to promote and sell a new running shoe, the Zoom Vaporfly Elite. The Zoom Vaporfly Elite was designed to give athletes a 4 percent improvement in their running economy, leading to faster race times. To communicate this and market the shoe to runners around the globe, Nike devised the idea to host a race in which three elite distance runners would attempt to break two hours in the marathon (26.2 miles). The three runners, Eliud Kipchoge, Zersenay Tadese, and Lelisa Desisa, all wore the Zoom Vaporfly Elite shoes, and the event was live streamed via Facebook and Twitter all over the world, with 13.1 million viewers tuning in to watch it live. Viewers used the hashtag #breaking2 to engage in discussions on social media while watching the race, and Nike even created a unique Zoom Vaporfly Elite emoji. Additionally, Nike used Instagram to provide exclusive photos throughout the event. While all three runners fell short of the sub-two-hour marathon mark (Kipchoge came closest in 2:00:25), the campaign was hugely successful for Nike, with the #breaking2 hashtag used over 400,000 times during the race, garnering 2 trillion impressions. Research showed that 87 percent of the 584,000 social media mentions were positive in sentiment, and Nike effectively turned a product launch into a must-watch event for runners (Digital Marketing Institute, 2018; Hobbs, 2017).

The remainder of this chapter provides an overview of the unique nature of the sport product and marketing the sport product then introduces you to the concept of branding, as well as many of the common elements that make up both traditional and contemporary integrated marketing communication strategies and campaigns. IMC elements such as advertising, sponsorships, endorsements, digital media, and social media are presented, as well as emerging trends such as a customer-centric approach to IMC and the use of analytics in IMC decision making. Figure 9.1 illustrates where IMC and its elements fit within the Strategic Sport Communication Model (SSCM).

CHARACTERISTICS OF THE SPORT PRODUCT

Before we can fully understand the tools used in IMC to market sport products and services, it is important to understand the unique nature of the **sport product** when compared to other products. Constantinescu (2011) defined the *sport product* as "the sport good or service, offered to the consumer in order to satisfy his need for sport, be it spectator, viewer, active participant or sponsor" (p. 71). As many sport marketing scholars have illustrated (e.g., Mullin, Hardy, & Sutton, 2014; Pitts & Stotlar, 2002), marketing a sport product is challenging for several key reasons. Specifically, the sport product is

- intangible,
- heterogeneous,
- perishable, and
- simultaneous.

The intangibility of the sport product essentially means the sport consumer cannot judge the quality of the product until it is purchased. This reality is linked directly to the simultaneous nature of sport—that is, the fact that the sport product is consumed while it is distributed. In

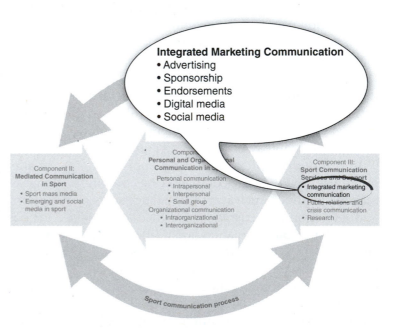

Figure 9.1 Integrated marketing communication within the SSCM.

other words, one must purchase a ticket and attend a sport product (event) to judge the quality of it; in contrast, in more traditional industries, products are not consumed at the time of distribution. The intangible and simultaneous nature of sport emphasizes the quality of the entertainment experience, which falls within the marketer's control. The simultaneous nature of the product also places heightened emphasis on the interaction between the service provider and the consumer.

The heterogeneity of a sport product consists of its ever-changing nature, which means that sport consumers' perceptions of the product can change over time. Numerous factors make a sport product heterogeneous—for example, player injuries, weather, facility amenities, and team performance. As such factors cause changes in the sport product, so do consumers' perceptions of it. These changes in the product and in consumer perceptions affect how marketers communicate, persuade, and formulate advertising strategies.

Another unique aspect of the sport product (regarding live events) is its perishability. It cannot be stored, and it has no shelf life. Because it is consumed while it is produced, it is perishable. Here again, sport marketers must place a great deal of emphasis on the quality of the consumers' experience because it may be a one-time interaction. The quality of this interaction affects the consumers' experience, which in turn shapes the consumers' perception. For example, if consumers have poor interactions with game or event staff—or if they must wait in long concession lines—those interactions may reduce the quality of consumers' experience and thus affect their decision about whether to return. Therefore, sport entities must focus on developing and maintaining a high-quality experience for sport consumers.

Key Distinctions

The sport product has several key distinctions in comparison with more traditional industries. These distinctions are highlighted in the work of sport management scholar William Sutton. According to Mullin and colleagues (2014), demand for the sport product can fluctuate dramatically based on a myriad of factors. For one thing, sport products rarely have inventory (the exception is sponsorship inventory, which is dis-

cussed later in the chapter). In contrast, in most industries, products and supplies can be replenished. In service industries such as sport, however, the product must be used now or it is lost forever (Mullin et al., 2014). For example, if a family of four purchases tickets to a collegiate football game and cannot attend the game, the experience is lost because it cannot be captured and reproduced.

Sport products are most often consumed publicly, which means that consumers' satisfaction is affected by social stimulation and often depends on others' enjoyment. Again, this differs from products in traditional industries, where someone's experience of a product is much less likely to be affected by other consumers' perceptions of it. The sport product is also inconsistent and unpredictable—a state of affairs unlikely to be tolerated in other industries. In the case of sport, however, it is likely that this very volatility appeals to the masses. Even so, it still means that sport marketers have little control over the on-field product, which hinges on factors such as performance, rules, and penalties. They do, however, play a central role in crafting the entertainment experience associated with a sporting event.

As mentioned earlier, the interface between service provider and client is of the utmost importance in sport. The ability of the sport marketer to control the fan experience allows for a focus on high-quality customer service. Service quality is typically categorized into two main groups—technical and functional—where technical quality involves the core service and functional quality addresses service delivery (Gronroos, 1991; Kelley & Turley, 2001). As illustrated by Kelley and Turley, sport managers possess minimal ability to control and influence the technical quality of the sport product (team performance), but they can exert great influence on the functional quality (event experience).

The functional quality of sport involves the fans' perceptions of all facets of the event experience, including accessibility to parking, pre- and postgame activities, arena and on-field promotions, concessions and merchandise, in-game public address announcements and music selection, interaction with game operations staff, venue amenities, technology integrated into the stadium such as Wi-Fi and stadium-specific mobile phone apps, and other aspects of the event experience (Halicka, 2016; Kelley & Turley, 2001; Westerbeek

& Shilbury, 2003). These aspects help create what Wakefield, Blodgett, and Sloan (1996) referred to as the *sportscape*, which can add value to a fan's entertainment experience (Chelladurai & Chang, 2000). Because sport fans consume the sport product while it is produced, providing a high-quality experience is a most effective form of advertising for the sport organization.

When sport-focused organizations advertise their products, they must identify consumers' purchase motivations. Individuals consume products for various reasons, which may vary dramatically. In identifying consumer expectations, sport marketers must face the challenge posed by the intangibles associated with sport (Miloch, 2005). Therefore, marketing strategies should focus on consumer satisfaction and identification with the sport entity (Arnett & Laverie, 2000; Chelladurai & Chang, 2000; Gladden, Milne, & Sutton, 1998; Kelley & Turley, 2001; Pritchard, Havitz, & Howard, 1999; Van Leeuwen, Quick, & Daniel, 2002; Wann & Branscombe, 1993; Zhang, Lam, & Connaughton, 2003). Later in the chapter we will discuss the increasing importance of **customer-centric marketing** for sport organizations.

Individuals purchase products to satisfy personal desires and needs. In other words, a product must serve some purpose for the consumer, and the consumer must gain a perceived benefit from purchasing the product. Consumers' purchase decisions are also affected by various environmental and individual factors (Mullin et al., 2014). Environmental factors include a consumer's demographics and psychographics. Demographics include aspects such as personal relationships, socioeconomic class, ethnicity, gender, age, and income. Psychographics include elements such as one's cultural norms, beliefs, values, and lifestyle. Consumers' choices about purchasing are also affected by their stage in the life or family cycle, which can be assigned to one of three periods (Mullin et al., 2014):

1. Preparation
2. Establishment
3. Reintegration

In the preparation period, individuals are most influenced by peers. In the establishment period, they are typically classified as single, married, or with a life partner, and they usually engage in an active lifestyle. Couples may begin to have children, whereupon their life priorities change, thus altering their personal needs and desires. This change in lifestyle affects their purchase motivations, which in turn influence their decisions to purchase certain products. After their children enter college or leave home, people have more time; once again, their purchase motivations and decisions change. Finally, people enter the reintegration period, characteristic of retirement, in which individuals have much more free time but typically less income. Individuals in this stage of life may also become single again because of the death of a spouse or life partner (Mullin et al., 2014). When sport organizations advertise their products, they must consider a person's stage in the life or family cycle to most effectively formulate marketing strategies.

Branding

One of the most important benefits for sport organizations that implement a cohesive IMC strategy is the development of a strong brand. The process of branding involves developing and cultivating a specific brand image for an organization and its products. Consumers are more likely to purchase products with a well-respected or well-known brand name because specific organizations and products elicit certain associations or perceptions in consumers' minds. Brand associations can include anything in a consumer's memory that is linked to a specific brand, and these associations ultimately create the overall brand image of the product. When the various marketing communication tools involved in IMC are well aligned in terms of their visual elements, tone, and message, a strong, unified brand message is communicated to consumers.

A key goal of branding is to develop **brand equity**, which is achieved when a brand's attributes add value to the brand in the minds of consumers (Gladden, 2014). In other words, brand equity is the premium that a consumer will pay for a branded good or service as compared with the amount that he or she will pay for an identical unbranded version of the same item (Keller, 1998). To achieve brand equity, sport organizations must be able to create strong, positive images of their brands, and IMC activities such as advertising, sponsorship, and social media posts all contribute to these images. Building brand equity provides several advantages to the sport organization, such as helping the entity enhance its image, generate revenue, charge price premiums, attract corporate partners, and cultivate loyalty and repeat purchasing among consumers (Gladden, 2014).

While the sport organization can affect its brand equity through its own communication and marketing efforts, leading to a strong brand image and positive brand associations, media coverage and consumers' reviews or comments about the organization on social media also contribute to brand equity, as do the public opinions and decisions of sport organizations' employees. For example, the National Basketball Association (NBA) worked hard to develop a strong brand image in China, a country in which 300 million people play basketball recreationally and where half a billion people reported watching at least one NBA game during the 2018-2019 season (Blank, 2019). As far back as the 1980s, the NBA sent videos of its games to China's state-run television station, CCTV, and allowed them to air the games for free. In 1992, the NBA opened an office in China; by 2004, teams played exhibition games in China (Zillgitt & Medina, 2019). The league's revenues in China are estimated to be $4 billion annually. Despite the NBA's efforts to build its brand equity in China through its carefully crafted IMC strategy, a politically controversial tweet by an NBA team owner, Daryl Morey, made news headlines around the globe and resulted in CCTV refusing to broadcast NBA games and Chinese businesses cutting ties with the NBA (Tan, 2019). Morey's controversial tweet contributed to the NBA's diminished brand equity in China.

ADVERTISING

Advertising has long been associated with communication and is closely related to public relations and marketing in its intent to persuade. It is a paid form of nonpersonal communication typically disseminated to large audiences. Traditional advertising methods include ads in print news sources such as newspapers and magazines, video ads on television, and audio ads on radio. It also includes placement in towns and cities, such as billboards, ads on public transportation such as buses or subways, or banners and posters on light posts along the street. Placement can also occur inside venues, such as signage surrounding the athletic field or scoreboard, posters on the back of bathroom stall doors, or public address announcements during breaks in the game.

Because of its appeal to both mainstream and niche audiences, sport is an effective means for communicating with and persuading the masses. In this vein, Messner, Dunbar, and Hunt (2000) described sport as including "the huge network of multi-billion-dollar automobile, snack food, entertainment, and other corporate entities that sponsor sport events and broadcasts" (p. 391). Advertising in sport takes many forms and includes not only advertising of sport products but also using sport as the vehicle for nonsport entities to advertise. For example, a college athletics department might develop various pricing strategies to sell more tickets; it might also sell advertising space on video screens around its sport facilities to companies who want to use sport to reach fans attending the games. Other examples of nonsport entities advertising through sport include gymnast Simone Biles appearing in commercials for Lego, as well as sport sponsorship, which is discussed in greater detail in later sections of this chapter. As a product in itself, sport is distinguished by unique characteristics that can make it challenging to market; these same characteristics, however, are what make sport so appealing.

To truly understand the challenges and benefits associated with advertising through sport and advertising for sport, one must understand the historical context of advertising, as well as the application of advertising principles in sport. One should also understand the unique characteristics of sport and how they are used to advertise and market sport as a product.

Understanding Historical Perspectives

Advertisers began using sport in the late 1800s to reach the masses, and early advertisements featuring sport included tobacco ads that showed boxing, hunting, and horse racing. In the 1920s, marketers used broadcasts of boxing to drive the sale of radios, and some suggest that this was the beginning of the symbiotic relationship between sport and the media. Sports such as boxing and football were instrumental in encouraging consumers to purchase new radios or vacuum tubes to maintain quality and clarity. In the 1930s, however, advertisers began to use sport in earnest. Examples include Ford Motor Company's advertisements during the World Series, Chevrolet's purchase of advertising during a series of college football games, and the Brown & Williamson tobacco company's advertisements during the Kentucky Derby. Sport appealed to these advertisers because it allowed them to differentiate their products from those of the competition. With the invention of television in the 1940s, advertisers realized that sport broadcasts offered an effective means of directly reaching a more mainstream audience—specifically, a male audience.

General Mills began to capitalize on the mass appeal of sport by contracting real-life sport figures as spokespeople to endorse Wheaties cereal. Through an ad agency, General Mills first contracted with Babe Ruth in the 1930s and coined the slogan "Breakfast of Champions." Over the years, the company has become known for featuring the faces of famous athletes on its cereal boxes. Among others, Wheaties has featured Michael Jordan, Walter Payton, John Elway, Mary Lou Retton, Tiger Woods, and the 1980 U.S. men's Olympic hockey team.

In addition, many companies in the hygiene, transportation, and electronics industries began to use sport to spark interest in their products. Barbasol shaving cream regularly depicted various sports (e.g., football, fencing, fishing, cricket, archery) in its ads, which featured females admiring clean-shaven men. Hertz, the rental car agency, portrayed individuals renting vehicles to travel for participation in winter sports. Greyhound (bus) Lines and American Airlines also featured sports (e.g., football, hockey) in their advertisements, and the New York Central Railroad used football to promote sleeping options on its Dreamliner. In addition, General Electric, Motorola, and Magnavox used the desire for high picture quality and comfortable viewing of sporting events to entice consumers to purchase their television sets.

Advertisements using sport have made a mark, both on the masses and on advertising agencies. In fact, three sport advertising campaigns were named in the *Advertising Age* list of top 100 advertising campaigns. Nike's "Just Do It" campaign was ranked number 4, followed by Wheaties' "Breakfast of Champions" at number 52 and ESPN *SportsCenter*'s "This Is SportsCenter" at number 77. In addition, both "Just Do It" and "Breakfast of Champions" were included in the *Advertising Age* list of top 10 slogans of the century.

The yearly broadcast of the Super Bowl provides a premier venue for unveiling creative advertising and reaching a mass audience. While the number of people who watch traditional broadcasts on television is steadily decreasing due to new technologies and broadcasting models such as over-the-top (OTT) delivery, one of the unique draws of the Super Bowl is that many consumers watch it primarily to see the innovative advertisements. Indeed, 78 percent of viewers said they view the ads as entertainment (Gough, 2019). This phenomenon serves as a perfect example of a sporting event whose broadcaster consistently demands (and receives) a high price for advertising time. In 2019, the average 30-second Super Bowl ad cost $5.25 million, up from $5 million in 2016, 2017, and 2018 (Gough, 2019). The ability for consumers to watch video content on their laptops, smartphones, or tablet devices also provides an opportunity for businesses who choose to advertise during the Super Bowl. The 2019 Super Bowl resulted in 641,000 hours of Super Bowl ads being consumed on YouTube following the event (Gough, 2019).

Along with widespread exposure for the brand, other benefits of advertising during the Super Bowl include reaching global audiences, introducing new products or services, and increased sales. Hartmann and Klapper (2018) found brands that advertise during the Super Bowl experienced increased sales for several months beyond the game itself. Although some view Super Bowl advertising as a waste of money or question the return on investment companies receive, this advertising has doubled over the past decades, and broadcasters continue to successfully attract advertisers.

Contemporary Advertising

As sport fans' preferences continue to evolve in terms of where they choose to consume sport content, advertisers must be increasingly innovative and savvy in their efforts to reach audiences. A report by Nielsen Sports (2018) showed that global sport fans' use of tablets, smartphones, and PCs for sport consumption contributed to a 55 percent increase in content consumption of sport. Fans are increasingly using social media while they watch sport, whether in person, on traditional television, or via streaming, engaging in behaviors such as interacting with others about the sporting event, sharing photos and videos, and participating in online contests. Younger generations are less likely to watch full games or live broadcasts and instead prefer to consume sport through highlight clips or short videos about their favorite teams or athletes (Newland et al., 2019). Because fans no longer solely focus on the on-screen production of a sporting event, or even the product appearing before them in person, advertisers now have new opportunities to reach consumers both on television and in places such as social media, on team or league smartphone apps, or through team-produced videos and content.

One example of a brand that took advantage of the advertising opportunities afforded by both television and new technologies is Procter and Gamble (P&G). The consumer goods corporation aired television ads during the 2018 PyeongChang Winter Olympics with a theme of "Love Over Bias." The ads honored mothers of Olympic athletes who stood up for their children in the face of prejudice, discrimination, and bias after a survey of Olympians found that 55 percent reported facing prejudice in their lifetime. In addition to airing on television, the ads were also available online and were widely shared on social media. P&G began using the hashtag #LoveOverBias on Twitter, along with links to a special "Love Over Bias" website created in conjunction with the ad campaign, sparking social media conversations about an important social issue (Shayon, 2017).

Identifying the Characteristics and Challenges of Sport

While the P&G example in the last section highlighted a nonsport brand using sport as an adver-

Generational Differences Shaping Sport Marketing Strategies

Sport organizations currently find themselves in a unique position as they attempt to effectively market to sport consumers of vastly different generations. The four primary generations include Boomers (born between 1946 and 1964), Generation X (born between 1965 and 1980), Millennials (born between 1981 and 1996), and Generation Z (born after 1997) (Dimock, 2019). One of the biggest challenges these generations present is their media usage differences. Gen Z are considered "digital natives," growing up in an age where they have always had access to the Internet, smartphones, and social media, and they are technologically savvy. Gen Z is an important consumer segment as well; by 2020, they will comprise 40 percent of the U.S. population and spend $140 billion each year, irrespective of what their parents spend on them (Lefton, 2019). Meanwhile, many Boomers still utilize traditional media such as newspapers and broadcast television and have incredible purchasing power, spending $3.2 trillion annually (Geller, 2019). With sport fans drawn to so many different media, sport organizations must implement increasingly complex marketing strategies to reach all their target segments. Research conducted on generational fandom differences found, for example, that when it came to consumption of the NFL, 55.9 percent of Boomer fans primarily consumed the league's games on traditional television, whereas 61.3 percent of Gen Z fans consumed it using a mobile device (Newland, Geurin, Brown, Gennaro, & Valenta, 2019). Additionally, those in Gen Z do not seem to be affected by traditional marketing and instead "want to be the marketers themselves," according to Mark Zablow of Cogent Entertainment Marketing (as quoted in Lefton, 2019). Being able to experience products and services firsthand and then share their experiences with others via social media is one of Gen Z's unique preferences. While traditional marketing efforts will still assist sport organizations in reaching fans of previous generations, it is incumbent upon them to employ new methods that will reach Gen Z as well.

tising vehicle, marketing the sport product itself presents unique challenges for sport managers, largely because of the unique nature of sport. When sport managers advertise and market a sport product, they are essentially marketing three key elements: the competition between two teams, or the on-field product; the entertainment or fan experience associated with consumption of the sport product; and the benefits gained through that consumption. Although the on-field product lies largely outside the control of marketers, the entertainment or fan experience and the benefits associated with the product fall within marketers' control.

Requirements for Effective Sport Advertising

When formulating an advertising campaign, sport managers should establish clear objectives so they can develop effective strategies for implementation. Advertisements should also be developed to either create or reinforce a specific brand image; that means, of course, that the sport organization must be clear as to what brand image it desires. Once clear objectives have been defined, all elements of the advertising campaign must be formulated to support those objectives.

In part, the campaign should illustrate the merits and benefits associated with the sport product in a way that supports the consumer in deciding to purchase the product. The typical consumer has numerous entertainment options but limited discretionary income. Sport entities are competing for this income with many other options, including other sport teams in the same geographic region, as well as restaurants, theaters, and other recreational activities. Therefore, when formulating advertising campaigns, sport entities must focus on how the benefits associated with consumption of their product outweigh the benefits associated with the purchase of other (perhaps related) products. In other words, why should consumers spend their money on your sport product rather than something else? Advertising campaigns should also feature the sport product in use, if possible, because this imagery helps potential consumers relate to the product and creates a visual sales point.

In addition, advertisements should be straightforward, clear, and consistent in both design and message to build and maintain a brand image for the sport product. Repetition reinforces the messages that the sport entity wants to send to its key audiences.

Target Markets and Segmentation

A target market consists of a segment of consumers with similar characteristics who have purchasing power and are willing to purchase the product. Advertising and marketing strategies should center on reaching a target market. In determining target markets, sport organizations must begin with segmentation to identify groups of potential consumers. Consumers can be segmented in numerous ways—for example, demographics, psychographics, lifestyle, geographic region, and frequency of product usage. Understanding the characteristics of segments and target markets is crucial in advertising. Without this understanding, a sport organization cannot effectively communicate its core messages to consumers. With it, however, the organization can communicate the features of its products in different ways based on the characteristics of each target market.

Sport organizations often use consumers' lifestyles as a basis for reaching them. Reaching consumers through lifestyle requires understanding cultural trends and attitudes and how they influence purchase intentions. To reach consumers via their lifestyle, sport organizations must become involved with the beliefs and culture of their target audiences. As Miloch and Lambrecht (2006) explained, a sport organization should become involved with the activities that "mean the most to its target consumers" (p. 147). Because it is increasingly unprofitable to advertise and market to a mass audience due to the amount of marketing messages consumers are exposed to every day, which is estimated to be at least 5,000 messages per day (Holmes, 2019), and because consumers increasingly ignore or tune out these messages, **lifestyle marketing** has become more prominent.

To advertise and market effectively based on consumers' lifestyles, sport organizations must understand the attitude and activity patterns of their target consumers. Organizations can then tailor their products and promotional strategies to fit these patterns, which represent a person's lifestyle. Within these patterns, sport organizations should examine the target market's psychographics, product and media usage, and demographics.

Customer-Centric Marketing

Today's sport fans have evolved from passive spectators to those who want a more engaging and immersive experience. To achieve this, Bashford (2017) noted that "generating constant, captivating, exclusive content has become a modern marketer's priority" (para. 32). Therefore, it is increasingly important for marketers to adopt a customer-centric approach to marketing, meaning that the individual consumer must be at the center of the design and delivery of marketing strategies. Customer-centric marketing is related to lifestyle marketing in that the needs and interests of customers are considered when designing these methods. According to Bruhn and Schnebelen (2017), "dialogic communication is crucially important" (p. 476) in successful customer-centric marketing. Using one message to market to the masses is no longer sufficient, and organizations must instead be open to co-creation of marketing messages that involve consumers in the process. Illustrating this notion, a study of running brands' Instagram accounts found that when brands reposted photos taken by their fans and customers, these posts elicited significantly greater engagement from the brand's Instagram followers than the posts featuring the brand's original content (Geurin & Burch, 2017).

Successful customer-centric marketing should be relationship-oriented, meaning that organizations must work to maintain and manage their relationships through their marketing activities. It should also be content-oriented, focusing on providing engaging and relevant content that allows customers to take part in a storytelling process (Bruhn & Schnebelen, 2017). For example, in the previous example of P&G's advertising during the 2018 Olympic Games, the brand also set up a website that allowed customers to create content thanking their own mom for her role in helping them achieve or overcome something. Shifting from a marketing mindset that is focused on communication channels to one focused on relationships and content requires brands to keep a close eye on stakeholder communication about the brand, such as customers' brand-related sentiments and photographs in social media posts and online reviews of the brand's products and services. Bruhn and Schnebelen (2017) caution that "the customer centricity has to ultimately be harmonized with the objectives of the brand communication as well as with the strategic objectives and positioning of a company" (p. 480).

SPONSORSHIP

Sponsorship is another very important piece of integrated marketing communication for sport organizations. Defined by Mullin, Hardy, and Sutton (2014) as "the acquisition of rights to affiliate or directly associate with a product, person, organization, team, league, or event" (p. 231), many sport businesses have begun referring to sponsorships as partnerships due to their mutually beneficial nature. Companies have recognized the value of sport as a vehicle for communicating to the masses, and many consistently use sport to advertise their products. Sport entities have also recognized the value of partnering with companies to help them reach mass audiences. The most common means for doing so is sport sponsorship, which helps companies build and support their brand identity. It also is an excellent way for sport entities to increase revenue, enhance their consumers' experiences, and sometimes enhance their own brand image.

In the past, sponsoring companies often gave sport organizations large sums of money in exchange for having their company logo displayed at the team's games or even on the team's jerseys. Because many sponsoring companies were more concerned with the perks that came from being affiliated with a professional sport team and not as much with their return on investment, sponsorships were often seen as being more favorable for the sport organization. In recent years, however, sponsorship has become more strategic from the perspective of both entities. It now often involves an equal partnership between the sponsoring organization and the sport organization, with both seeking mutually beneficial outcomes from the relationship.

For example, the NFL's Seattle Seahawks developed a partnership with another Seattle-based business, Starbucks Coffee. The two businesses worked together to design a co-branded coffee sleeve designed to look like a Seahawks jersey.

Photo courtesy of Andrea N. Geurin.

Many sponsors of the New York Yankees are on display on the scoreboard at Yankee Stadium. How many different corporate sponsors can you identify in this photo?

Knowing that most coffee drinkers also tend to have their smartphones nearby, the sleeve also featured a Snapchat code that fans could scan to view exclusive content about the Seahawks. Additionally, they designed Seahawks-branded Starbucks gift cards, which they knew many fans would want as a souvenir of their favorite team. The sponsorship helped Starbucks boost its coffee and gift card sales while also providing exposure to the Seahawks brand and access to content that couldn't be viewed any other way. Additionally, since both Starbucks and the Seahawks franchise are based in Seattle, it showed unity between two local businesses.

Challenges of Sponsorship

At its most basic level, sponsorship involves a marketing exchange between the sport entity and the sponsoring company. As mentioned previously, sport entities benefit from sponsorship as a revenue generator, as a means to offset expenses, and as a means of promotion. On the other side of the equation, when companies began engaging in sport sponsorship, they viewed it as a means of product differentiation. Now, countless companies use sport to reach the masses. However, because so many companies use sport in this way, they must make their products stand out when compared with those of other advertisers who also seek to capitalize on sport's mass appeal. The number of companies using sport sponsorship to enhance their brands has dramatically increased; because of this increase, sport entities face numerous challenges when soliciting sponsors. Due to the high number of companies wishing to sponsor an organization, sport entities must make strategic decisions as to which companies are best aligned with the organization's mission and values and which will ultimately lead to the most beneficial outcomes for the sport organization. To meet these challenges, sport entities must focus on the following factors:

- Differentiation
- Research
- Sponsors' needs and desires

Sport entities must be creative in differentiating sport sponsorships, especially when multiple sponsoring companies occupy the same sponsorship category. Sponsors are usually classified according to the product or service they provide. For example, Coca-Cola and Pepsi are classified in the beverage category, whereas Ford and Chevrolet are classified in the automobile category. Understandably, these companies want to distinguish their products and services from those of their competitors. Therefore, the sport entity must ensure differentiation by designing sponsorship packages that meet the specific motives of each corporate partner.

In addition to differentiating sponsorships, sport entities must conduct research about their consumers. Sponsoring companies often want to tap into the sport entity's demographics, psychographics, and consumption habits. Therefore, it is in the sport entity's best interest to gather this information to better identify potential corporate partners and develop sponsorship packages to meet the needs and objectives of potential sponsors. Sport entities must also be cognizant of a sponsoring company's rationale for engaging in sport sponsorship. Companies do so for a variety of reasons. IEG, a global agency specializing in partnership strategy, evaluation, and measurement, identified several reasons for which companies partner with sport entities (IEG, 2017). These reasons include a desire to

- heighten visibility,
- increase brand loyalty,
- reinforce the brand's existing image,
- communicate commitment to a particular lifestyle,
- entertain clients,
- stimulate sales, trials, or usage of their products or services,
- develop content that can be used on digital or social media,
- showcase their organization's social responsibility,
- develop leads via the sport property's customer database,
- sell products to the sponsored property, and
- access a platform for experiential branding.

Sporting events provide a wide range of publicity opportunities for sponsoring companies, thus allowing them to increase the visibility of their products. Companies with high-recall and high-recognition brands use sport sponsorship to shape consumer attitudes toward their products and associate their product with a particular lifestyle. As evidenced by the list above, some sponsoring brands are also focused on providing opportunities for customers to sample their products and services or offer an experience with their brand at events. An example of this is Samuel Adams, a beer company based in Boston that sponsors the Boston Marathon. At the Boston Marathon expo where runners pick up their race numbers, Samuel Adams has a booth where runners can sample the brewery's standard line of beers as well as its signature "26.2 Brew," a beer developed specifically for the race. Samuel Adams also sells running and beer-themed merchandise, and the 26.2 brew is available for purchase at the postrace party that all runners and their families are invited to attend.

A sign by the Samuel Adams booth at the Boston Marathon Expo promoting 26.2 Brew.

As mentioned earlier, sport sponsorship can also be used to differentiate an organization's products from the products of its competitors. This possibility is especially pertinent for companies in the service industry, such as banking and insurance, who sell intangible services that consumers must select based on the company's promises about the service. Some sport sponsorships offer opportunities for category exclusivity, thus providing service-oriented companies with a chance to create particular currency with their consumers. Category exclusivity means that the sport entity will not engage in a sponsorship with another company in the same category. For example, if McDonald's were an exclusive sponsor of a minor-league franchise, the franchise would not be able to enter into a sponsorship with a competing company, such as Burger King or Wendy's. Sport sponsorships also provide companies with merchandising opportunities. This option can be appealing because 80 percent of product choices are made in-store and sponsorship allows companies to develop unique and exciting "pop-up" displays at the point of purchase.

When developing sponsorships, sport organizations should focus on the sponsoring company's objectives. If a sponsoring company wants opportunities to make on-site sales and expose consumers to the features of a specific product, the sponsorship agreement should be designed specifically to facilitate these goals. For example, if a car dealership wants to increase awareness of its vehicles and expose consumers to a specific vehicle's features, a sport franchise might allow the vehicles to be displayed during events and allow the dealer's salespeople to be on hand to answer questions from potential consumers. In addition, the sport entity might develop a contest that consumers enter to win a vehicle; the vehicle might also be incorporated into various social media, on-field, or in-arena promotions. This approach would allow the dealer to expose the features of the vehicle while also building a database of potential target consumers.

Sponsors' objectives vary, and the effectiveness of each sponsorship should be measured against its specific objectives. Sport sponsors reported that "the most valuable service a property can provide to its partners is help in evaluating whether the sponsorship is meeting its goals"

(IEG, 2018, para. 1). Therefore, it is critical for sport organizations to assist their sponsors in measuring their objectives. The two parties must work closely together to achieve this, as the objectives must be set in a measurable manner from the beginning of the partnership. Once these objectives are set and both parties understand them, the sport property should develop a plan for monitoring and measuring the objectives. They must ask questions such as what the time period is for the objective to be met. What data do they need to collect? How will the data be analyzed? What resources are necessary to do this evaluation? How will the results be communicated to the sponsor? Ongoing communication between the sponsor and the sport property is important, and the two should work together to continually update objectives and develop strategies to address situations when goals are met and when they are not.

Activation Strategies

Because of the drastic changes in consumer behavior over the past few years, largely driven by technological changes, it is now incumbent upon sport marketers and corporations to become more innovative and creative when designing and activating sport sponsorships. Sport sponsors report that assessing their return on investment in sponsorships was one of their top challenges (IEG, 2017). As previously mentioned, sport organizations are looked to for assistance with this task and must pay closer attention to the needs and objectives of their corporate partners. *Activation* refers to the sponsoring entity's promotion of its sponsorship; in other words, the sponsoring company promotes its association with the sport entity through the fact that it is a sponsor.

For an excellent example of activation, consider sponsors of the 2018 NBA Playoffs and Finals. Different sponsors developed innovative activation methods that helped them achieve their sponsorship objectives. For example, American Express unveiled five NBA-themed flip videos that were posted on the credit card company's social media accounts. The campaign complemented American Express's broader global brand marketing campaign, which launched just before the NBA playoffs began.

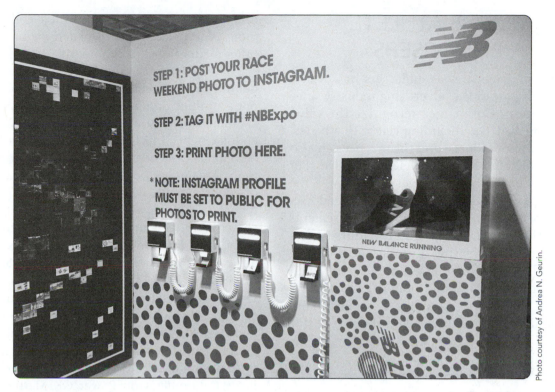

STEP 1: POST YOUR RACE WEEKEND PHOTO TO INSTAGRAM.

STEP 2: TAG IT WITH #NBExpo

STEP 3: PRINT PHOTO HERE.

*NOTE: INSTAGRAM PROFILE MUST BE SET TO PUBLIC FOR PHOTOS TO PRINT.

NEW BALANCE RUNNING

Photo courtesy of Andrea N. Geurin.

New Balance utilizes Instagram in a unique activation strategy at road races the company sponsors.

Another example is Taco Bell, which ran a campaign called "Steal a Game, Steal a Taco." It gave NBA fans all over the United States the opportunity to win (steal) a free taco no matter which team they were cheering for in the playoffs. When the road team stole a win from the home team, Taco Bell ran ads announcing when fans could "steal" their free taco. It provided fans with an extra incentive to pay attention to the games, as well as provided a free sampling experience for Taco Bell's food and kept fans interested in the brand throughout the playoffs.

Finally, automaker Kia developed a program called "Kia Who Ya Got," which allowed fans to predict on Instagram and Twitter which team would win. Some of the fans who guessed correctly were selected as winners of the promotion and received prizes such as free televisions, gaming consoles, video games, and NBA merchandise.

As illustrated by these examples, the way sponsors activate their sponsorships can influence their effectiveness. Therefore, sport entities should strive to include activation strategies as part of the overall sponsorship package. This approach, along with providing suggestions to sponsoring companies, helps both parties reap the maximum benefit from sponsorship.

For every $1 sponsors spent on the sponsorship itself, IEG (a research sponsorship firm) reported that they would spend an average of $2.20 on activations in 2018. Further, 40 percent of sponsor organizations reported that this was an increase in activation spending over their 2017 figures (IEG, 2017). Considering this research, sport managers should develop sponsorship packages that enhance opportunities for sponsors to activate or leverage the sponsorship. Doing so helps sport consumers identify with the sponsor's products and associate the sponsoring company with the sport entity. Sponsoring companies have indicated that, in their view, preferred forms of activation include social media as their top method, followed by public relations, hospitality, on-site or experiential, internal communication, digital or mobile promotions, traditional advertising, business to business, sales promotion offers, and direct marketing. Therefore, sport entities should include these elements as potential inventory pieces when developing packages to meet sponsors' objectives.

USE OF ATHLETE ENDORSERS

The use of celebrities as endorsers has been a significant part of the advertising industry since its inception. Companies recognize the value of having athletes, including celebrity athletes, endorse their products, and the practice can also be quite lucrative for the athletes themselves. For example, tennis player Roger Federer was the highest-paid athlete in 2018 in terms of endorsements, bringing in $65 million in endorsements alone (The *SI* Staff, 2018). **Athlete endorsements** can range from wearing a product to speaking on behalf of a product. Brooks and Harris (1998) identified four key classifications of endorsement: explicit ("I endorse this product"), implicit ("I use this product"), imperative ("You should use this product"), and co-presentation (endorser appears with the product).

In some cases, athlete endorsement deals bump up against team or league policies (or endorsement deals). For example, former Chicago Bears quarterback Jim McMahon was involved in one of the most famous advertising kerfuffles in the history of sport advertising. After McMahon endorsed adidas by wearing a headband with the company's logo, NFL commissioner Pete Rozelle informed McMahon that he was violating the league's strict uniform policy against unlicensed logos and signs. McMahon's response was to wear a headband bearing the word *Rozelle*.

Trends in the Use of Athlete Endorsers

Research indicates that the most popular athletes are the most likely to endorse products and that these athletes usually come from highly visible sports, such as basketball, football, tennis, golf, auto racing, and the Olympic Games (Jones & Schumann, 2000). The use of athlete endorsements has increased since the 1920s (Jones & Schumann, 2000), although as recently as the 1960s there were still relatively few athlete endorsers (Stotlar, 2005). This state of affairs changed in particularly dramatic fashion in the 1980s when shoe companies began using athletes to endorse their products. Before the 1980s were over, one of every five ads featured a sport celebrity. As you might well expect, the use of athlete endorsers is more widespread in sport-related media than in other media (Jones & Schumann, 2000).

Historically, female athletes have lagged behind male athletes in terms of endorsement opportunities. Some tennis players such as Serena Williams and Maria Sharapova earned lucrative endorsements, but few other females ever made it on top 50 lists of athlete endorsements. Slowly, more females are beginning to reap the benefits of endorsements. For example, Nielsen's (2019) report on athletes as endorsers highlighted U.S. soccer national team member Rose Lavelle, who is endorsed by shoe and apparel brand New Balance. Additionally, the report featured U.S. tennis player and 2018 U.S. Open champion Naomi Osaka, who has deals with high-end brands such as Nike, Nissan, Mastercard, Citizen, Shiseido, and Bare Minerals, among others. Finally, U.S. gymnast and five-time Olympic medalist Simone Biles was highlighted for her endorsements with Beats, Caboodles, Core Power, GK, Mattress Firm, and Spieth America. The number of women who identify as sport fans is currently on an upward trajectory, and women control 70 percent to 80 percent of the purchasing power in households (Nelson, 2019). Female athletes are uniquely positioned to connect with female consumers who experience a sense of familiarity with these sportswomen, which allows marketers to reach and influence different markets than when they use male athlete endorsers (Peetz, 2019).

The selection of an athlete as an endorser is not a decision to be made lightly. Similarly, athletes must choose carefully which products or companies to endorse. As with sponsorship, endorsement involves a marketing exchange, and the parties must select each other based on their respective brand images. According to Nielsen (2019), "Relationships between athletes and brands are becoming more meaningful, more integrated and more measurable, in many cases moving far beyond the traditional and straightforward product endorsement" (p. 12). Just as sponsorships have become more focused on a partnership between the sponsoring brand and the sport property, the same is true for athlete endorsements. The alignment of a brand's values with an athlete's values is an important aspect of athlete endorsements. With the prevalence of

Photo courtesy of Andrea N. Geurin.

The England women's national soccer team appeared as endorsers on Budweiser packaging during the 2019 FIFA Women's World Cup.

athlete social media use, brands now have the opportunity to carefully examine the content an athlete posts (and therefore the personal brand that athlete has created for him or herself), which is helpful in selecting athlete endorsers who will align well with the endorsing brand.

The Rise of Influencers

Research shows that consumers are increasingly questioning the authenticity of many brands, which has led to a decrease in brand loyalty (Burmann & Arnhold, 2009). At the same time, consumers have become more empowered as a result of advanced information technology and interactive media. This shift in the power dynamics between brands and consumers has led brands to encourage consumers to create brand-related content in both

online and off-line spaces. This strategy can harm a brand, however, because not all content posted by consumers is positive. Therefore, several brands have begun employing programs and strategies in which they select consumers to become "joint creators of brand meaning" (Burmann & Arnhold, 2009, p. 13). To use content created by people viewed by others as everyday users of a brand, many companies are now turning to **influencers**, or people who are not traditional celebrities but have been able to build a strong online following on social media and have a captive online audience. According to Influencer Marketing Hub (2019), "Influencers, unlike celebrities, can be anywhere. They can be anyone. What makes them influential is their large followings on the web and social media. An influencer can be a popular fashion photographer on Instagram, or a well-read cybersecurity blogger who tweets, or a respected marketing executive on LinkedIn."

Influencer marketing programs vary in structure but often involve a contract between the sport brand and the influencer specifying the terms of the relationship. They also often involve free products and monetary payments for the influencer in exchange for promoting the brand via social media and at events. Influencers are also sometimes referred to as brand ambassadors. Regardless of the term used to describe them, they are attractive to sport brands because they have a large, dedicated following and do not demand the same high price tag as star athletes.

Along with the benefits listed above, additional positive impacts of influencer marketing on companies include the ability to trace consumer contact and the ability to receive immediate feedback about the brand (Burmann, 2010). Some scholars view ambassador programs as more effective for brands than traditional advertising (e.g., Andersson & Ekman, 2009). Schouten, Janssen, and Verspaget (2019) studied consumers' perceptions of the use of celebrity endorsers compared to their use of influencers and found that consumers preferred the communication featuring influencers, as they reported feeling more connected to influencers and trusting them more than celebrities.

One example of a sport organization that has employed an influencer strategy is the United States Tennis Association (USTA). USTA employees wanted more young people to play tennis (i.e.,

Millennials and Gen Z) and made the decision to hire influencers to help promote the sport to these segments. In 2018, USTA officials developed partnerships with 100 youth ambassadors who were tasked with sharing their stories about tennis on social media to generate interest in the sport and encourage more young people to give tennis a try. The organization won an award for its influencer campaign at the 10th Annual Shorty Awards (Keyhole, 2018).

DIGITAL MEDIA

The recent rise of digital media provides a plethora of options for sport organizations to use for IMC purposes. As previously mentioned in this chapter, consumers are increasingly tech savvy and seek content about their favorite teams and athletes outside of game day broadcasts. Sport teams have begun capitalizing on this with digital media options such as video series posted to their website or social media that provides exclusive content, the development of team-specific or venue-specific smartphone apps, virtual reality (VR), and augmented reality (AR). These digital media platforms allow fans to feel a sense of closeness and affiliation with the organization that traditional marketing methods may not elicit.

Chelsea FC in the English Premier League has embraced original video content as a way of reaching fans and deepening their attachments. The Chelsea website features a series called "Ask Frank" in which head coach Frank Lampard answers a wide range of questions about topics from the team's performance to his own shopping preferences. Additionally, the website contains several highlight clips after every match, interviews with the players, and videos focused on historical moments in the club.

Regarding smartphone apps, the NBA's Golden State Warriors moved into a new stadium in 2019, the Chase Center in San Francisco. Together, the Warriors and Chase Center share an app that allows fans to view live game updates and stats, as well as information about the venue if they are attending in person. Venue information includes a ticket management system, events calendar, interactive maps of the arena, assistance with planning transportation to and from the arena, food and beverage ordering, and access to the Warriors' team shop for apparel and merchandise.

At the 2018 PyeongChang Winter Olympics, global e-commerce, retail, and technology company Alibaba demonstrated its facial recognition capabilities in an interactive display for fans to try.

The NBA is currently leading the way in terms of sport leagues' use of VR and AR to engage with consumers. The NBA AR app allows fans around the globe to see up-close-and-personal footage of their favorite teams and players. Additionally, the league's games are broadcast via VR each week. The league refers to this connection strategy as immersive media. Because they are a trailblazer in terms of using AR and VR from a sport organization perspective, the league also understands that the use of AR and VR is a learning experience and they will have to adjust along the way to ensure the fan experience is optimized.

Sport organizations can also use these digital platforms to highlight their sponsorships. For example, Wembley Stadium in London showcased

Photo courtesy of Andrea N. Geurin.

EE signage lines the walkway to Wembley Stadium in London, promoting the mobile provider's 5G capabilities.

its sponsorship from mobile company EE by hosting a game called the Wembley Cup between two teams made up mostly of YouTube influencers, but they also included some famous soccer players such as Steven Gerrard. To promote the game, Wembley and EE joined forces to produce an eight-part series of programs broadcast on YouTube using the influencers who would play in the game. In the end, over 34,000 fans attended the game, rivaling the numbers of many Premier League games.

USE OF DATA ANALYTICS IN IMC

While many organizations use data analytics to fuel decisions about on-field aspects of the business (i.e., athlete analytics), sport organizations can also use analytics about customers to make business decisions. Organizations now have access to more data about their consum-ers than ever before, and many organizations take advantage of this data by using it to make business decisions. Referred to as *customer relationship management*, Kulpa (2017) defines it as "all of the activities, strategies and technologies that companies use to manage their interactions with their current and potential customers" (para. 1).

Using customer relationship management (CRM) provides sport organizations with several opportunities. Customer data can be used to understand drivers of demand for tickets and set ticket prices that will optimize attendance, understand consumers' behavior in terms of concession and merchandise purchases, understand which sections of the stadium customers prefer and how many tickets they typically purchase, and understand consumers' media preferences. This data helps sport organizations to identify the ideal methods by which to target specific consumers. While data can be incredibly useful for organizations, it is important for organizations to understand how to properly use their data to make meaningful business decisions. As Mondello and Kamke (2014) note, the key to using data effectively is identifying which data is actionable, which will allow organizations to adopt and implement data-driven strategies.

The NHL's Tampa Bay Lightning organization has embraced CRM. The Lightning focus on making data-driven decisions, such as identifying individuals who would be promising sales prospects. Using customer data and modeling, the Lightning can predict how likely a past customer is to buy a ticket again in the future, as well as how much the customer is expected to spend on tickets, which allows the Lightning to determine where to focus its sales efforts (Mondello & Kamke, 2014). According to Mumcu (2019), the use of business analytics in women's professional sport organizations lags behind men's leagues,

ENGAGING NATIONAL RUGBY LEAGUE FANS IN AUSTRALIA WITH IMC

Rita Khouri
Marketing manager for premiership and consumer business
National Rugby League (NRL)

Rita Khouri realized her passion for the sport industry when she was 18 and worked as a casual staff member showing people to their seats at the home games for her favorite Australian Football League (AFL) team, the West Coast Eagles. Upon receiving her bachelor's degree in law and commerce from the University of Western Australia, complete with two study abroad exchanges at Indiana University and the City University of Hong Kong, Khouri then worked as an advertising executive for the *West Australian* newspaper, where she received the advice, "If you don't ask, you don't get," which has become her personal philosophy. It was this mindset that led her to the National Rugby League (NRL), the governing body for one of Australia's most beloved sport leagues. Based in Sydney, Khouri has worked in the NRL's marketing department for the past five years.

In her role as marketing manager for premiership and consumer business, Khouri is heavily involved in developing the marketing strategy for the league. Among her many job duties, Khouri develops and implements IMC campaigns, which requires her to manage and coordinate the creative process and media buying activities. For example, she manages the internal production processes for marketing campaigns, briefing photography and video content for broadcast, social media, and online communication. Additionally, Khouri works closely with the NRL's 16 clubs on their marketing and digital strategy to ensure they communicate a consistent message on all platforms and consults with their marketing staffs to assist in achieving their objectives related to membership, attendance, hospitality, merchandise sales, and sponsorship targets.

Khouri likens working for the league to working *for* the sport, whereas she classifies working for a club (team) to working *in* the sport. "As part of my role works closely with the clubs, it's really important to understand their challenges and competing/different objectives with administrative compared to football department's key objectives of playing the actual game," Khouri explains. "On the other hand, working for the league body you get the opportunity to see the big picture and understand how the business works as a whole. It's future facing as you are part of the journey of safeguarding the game and making those adjustments to keep it relevant."

In terms of successful integrated marketing communication, Khouri stresses that the creative marketing materials and messages must fit the

Photo courtesy of Rita Khouri.

On set for the 2019 NRL Telstra Premiership season launch campaign film, Rita Khouri briefs North Queensland Cowboys player Jason Taumalolo on his scene in the film.

organization's purpose, although the way that message is communicated may vary depending on the target audience. Khouri also notes that changing media preferences, such as a shift toward watching highlights and snackable content over watching full games, has affected how the NRL approaches its marketing. "The power of storytelling has ensured our fans are closer to the game than ever before and there are now more channels for them to consume the sport they know and love. It now means that my role as a 'marketer' is very different, as the days of only producing a TV commercial are long dead and I am now tasked with developing and producing a suite of content to effectively achieve a campaign's objectives," said Khouri. She also notes that the NRL views all entertainment options as their competitors, including OTT platforms such as Netflix or Amazon Prime. Khouri identified major challenges for the NRL as being how to get more people to play, watch, and attend rugby games given the plethora of other options people have from an entertainment perspective.

Khouri has been involved in designing and implementing several IMC campaigns during her time with the NRL, and one that proved challenging, yet successful, was the 2019 Telstra Premiership season launch "New Era" campaign. After several high-profile NRL players retired after the 2018 season, the league took the opportunity to promote new players to generate excitement among fans for the new era of NRL. Featuring 26 players, including players from the NRL's women's league, 90-second video spots were developed to help fans learn more about these players. Khouri noted that a challenge to this campaign was having several variables out of the league's control, such as featuring 26 individual players in one piece of content. She pointed out that the league could not control each player's performance on the field, nor could it control whether some of the players were traded midseason. Despite these uncertainties, the campaign was considered a success based on the strong engagement it elicited from fans, as well as increased recognition of the new players featured in the videos. As a result, the league's goals for memberships and attendance were achieved.

In 2019, Khouri was tasked with serving as the project manager for all marketing of the 2019 Grand Final, which is the NRL's version of the Super Bowl or World Series. Khouri's key objective was to generate excitement for the event around the city of Sydney and to create content and activities that would allow all fans to get involved in the Grand Final even if they were not able to attend the event live. Khouri took inspiration from other sport organizations' festivals and events surrounding their year-end championships and developed a theme of "Celebrate the Season," which was brought to life around the city of Sydney with a kickoff ceremony for the media in town to cover the event; a photo exhibition of the season's greatest moments on the iconic Harbour Bridge; and taking over the center of Sydney's central business district with AstroTurf for a three-day Fan Fest, which gave fans an opportunity to meet over 100 NRL players from different clubs. Khouri described the experience as one of her most challenging but rewarding projects in her career. Of the success of the campaign, Khouri said, "The success is in the positive media feedback that showed I successfully created the hype in Sydney, the attendance and engagement from our fans across all clubs, and one of my proudest moments was seeing a full Fan Fest crowd to see the Grand Final teams presented on stage. It was quite an emotional moment for me, as I looked around the crowd and realized that I made that happen."

Khouri encourages students who wish to work in the sport industry to gain experience while they're still in school. "You have to learn how to walk before you run, so be prepared to do the mundane tasks and don't complain," Khouri advises. She also stresses the importance of demonstrating a willingness to help with different tasks and to be a "doer" rather than a "sitter." Additionally, she encourages students to never stop learning and to always follow what other sports and clubs are doing to gather inspiration and better understand what works and what does not.

but leagues such as the Ladies Professional Golf Association (LPGA), Women's Tennis Association (WTA), Women's National Basketball Association (WNBA), and National Women's Soccer League (NWSL) are increasingly adopting analytics strategies to assist in areas such as ticket sales and pricing, consumer insights and marketing, content and media performance, sponsorship sales and evaluations, and branding.

CHAPTER WRAP-UP

Summary

Integrated marketing communication (IMC) is a strategic approach to communicating with and marketing to consumers. It is heavily linked to advertising but also includes other aspects, such as sponsorship, endorsements, broadcasting and digital media, influencers, and social media. Regardless of which elements an organization chooses to use in its IMC efforts, it must communicate a consistent message across its various platforms.

The sport product has many unique characteristics that can make it challenging to market, yet these same factors—intangibility, heterogeneity, simultaneity, and perishability—are also what consumers find most appealing about sport. Changing consumption patterns based largely on technological advancements are forcing sport businesses to refine their IMC efforts to capture their target markets. Adopting a more personalized customer-centric approach to marketing, developing mutually beneficial partnerships with sponsors, and using data analytics in marketing decisions are some of the major shifts taking place in the IMC landscape in the sport industry. This chapter highlights the challenges and benefits associated with IMC for sport; provides the historical context of advertising; and stresses the importance of delivering clear, consistent messages.

Review Questions

1. How can IMC methods communicate a consistent message, and why is this important?

2. What makes the sport product unique and challenging to market?

3. How can sport organizations help their sponsors in evaluating the effectiveness of the sponsorship?

4. Describe the concept of an influencer and why organizations might choose to use influencers in their marketing strategy.

5. Based on what you've read in this chapter, how are consumer preferences changing, and why has this led to sport organizations using more digital media to market to and communicate with fans?

Individual Exercises

1. Attend a sporting event, and examine the manner in which sponsorship is used at the venue. How do the sponsorships seem effective or ineffective?

2. Download the app for one of your favorite sport teams. What information is included on the app? Explain how the content and information on the app could appeal to different segments of fans.

Photo courtesy of Andrea N. Geurin

Public Relations and Crisis Communication in Sport

LEARNING OBJECTIVES

- To understand the value of public relations to sport-focused organizations
- To recognize effective techniques for managing media relationships
- To understand the role of digital media in shaping contemporary public relations practices
- To become acquainted with and understand the key components of crisis management
- To comprehend the breadth and scope of sport public relations
- To appreciate the role of community relations in sport public relations

KEY TERMS

press agentry–publicity model

public information model

public relations

two-way asymmetrical model

two-way symmetrical model

IMPACTING INTERNAL CULTURE AND WORKING THROUGH CRISES VIA PUBLIC RELATIONS

Jodie Hawkins

Jodie Hawkins' first foray into the sport industry was covering for someone on maternity leave in an entry-level position with an Australian National Rugby League (NRL) team, the Parramatta Eels. "While my parents didn't think it was a good idea [since] it was only a fixed term, I knew it was the start of what I wanted to do," explains Hawkins. "The moral of the story is to back yourself when the opportunity arises, because you never know where it will take you." Since that time, she has gone on to work as the public relations and marketing manager for the Eels, the media and public relations manager for the NRL's Sydney Roosters, and the marketing and communications manager for a Big Bash League cricket club, the Sydney Sixers; she now serves as the general manager of the Sixers.

Over the course of her career, Hawkins has witnessed drastic changes in the sport communication and PR landscape, one of which is the increased use of technology by sport organizations. The Sixers are currently working on a chatbot that will allow their fans to engage with the organization and ask questions while also sharing relevant information with the club. Along with fan engagement strategies, Hawkins has also focused heavily on internal public relations in the Sixers organization. One of her proudest achievements as general manager is the positive internal culture she helped to create with the actual team as well as with the business office staff. "Influencing recruitment decisions based not just on the players' ability but also their personality is critical for culture, but can be a hard conversation

Jodie Hawkins, general manager of the Sydney Sixers Big Bash League cricket club based in Australia.

Photo courtesy of Jodie Hawkins.

with the relevant coach. I am extremely proud of the fact that players want to play for us because they enjoy the atmosphere," said Hawkins. "We have also had on-field success within that culture that has been a great reward. Personally, I am most proud of the leader I am becoming and the lessons that I have worked through to get here. I had a leadership style previously where I held a lot of the power, at least that was the perception. I have worked really hard to lead my team but not dictate to them. I want our team to feel empowered and inspired, and I feel I am working towards that."

One major aspect to Hawkins' work in all her PR positions has been handling crises, most often those centered on athletes' off-field behavior. From DUIs to assaults, drunk and disorderly conduct charges, and one player defecating in the hallway of a hotel, Hawkins says she has seen it all. Through every crisis situation, her biggest piece of advice is: "NEVER lie—ever! You will be found out; it's a fact. Always keep the details of the journalists who have been in contact handy and update them hourly, even if it's just to say, 'I don't have anything yet but I haven't forgotten about you.' There's nothing worse than silence for them." During her time as a PR manager, Hawkins insisted on being part of the team that discussed the communication strategy revolving around the crisis so that she was well informed and able to communicate honestly with journalists and help to influence the ways in which each situation was communicated to the public. Hawkins explained, "Too many media managers are left in the dark until the media release needs to be issued, but by then it's too late to influence the way things are communicated."

For students pursuing careers in sport PR, Hawkins stresses the importance of being able to build relationships, saying, "Relationships are key to the work, so keep a black book and keep every contact you make because you never know when you will need to reach out to someone."

This chapter focuses primarily on using the media to the sport entity's advantage and implementing strategies to enhance **public relations** (PR). The chapter-opening vignette about the Sydney Sixers' Jodie Hawkins highlights many of the key aspects of public relations that are discussed in the chapter. From persuading the public and managing the media to interacting with the community and training for interviews, public relations professionals play an important role in communicating a sport entity's messages to its key constituents, especially when it wants to influence public opinion. To maintain a positive organizational image and communicate effectively, communication professionals must understand the organization's key publics, develop appropriate messages, and deliver them in a way that is effective for each of the identified publics. They must also develop proactive communication strategies for dealing with crisis situations. Figure 10.1 indicates how public relations and crisis communication fit into the Strategic Sport Communication Model.

The chapter begins by discussing sport public relations with a special focus on message development and image building through effective management of the sport media. Strategies are presented for effectively managing the media through traditional media relations techniques (e.g., press releases, press conferences, media kits, fact sheets), digital public relations techniques (e.g., social media, digital videos, influencers), and building community relations efforts. The chapter concludes with an examination of crisis communication for sport organizations and outlines strategies for managing crisis situations both internally and externally. Typical crisis situations in sport are presented along with standard protocols and operating procedures for each situation.

Public relations is defined by the Public Relations Society of America (PRSA, 2019) as "a strategic communication process that builds mutually beneficial relationships between organizations and their publics" (para. 4). *Sport public relations* in particular may be best defined as the management of information flow between a sport entity and its key publics, both internal and external, to present the sport organization in the most favorable manner possible and to establish mutually beneficial relationships. At the heart of sport public relations is the image of the sport entity. To create favorable public opinion, the sport entity must understand the perceptions of its sporting publics. The PRSA notes that public relations helps an organization and its publics adapt to each other, thus implying that communication is a continuing process.

This characterization is also found in the work of several public relations scholars. For example,

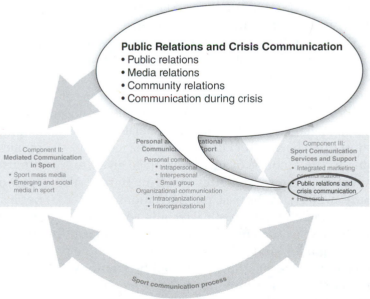

Public Relations and Crisis Communication
- Public relations
- Media relations
- Community relations
- Communication during crisis

Component II:
Mediated Communication in Sport
- Sport mass media
- Emerging and social media in sport

Personal and Organizational Communication in Sport
Personal communication
- Intrapersonal
- Interpersonal
- Small group
Organizational communication
- Intraorganizational
- Interorganizational

Component III:
Sport Communication Services and Support
- Integrated marketing communication
- Public relations and crisis communication
- Research

Sport communication process

Figure 10.1   Public relations and crisis communication in the Strategic Sport Communication Model.

Bronzan (1977) emphasized that public relations is a function of management that focuses on examining the public's attitudes, identifying organizational policies in light of public opinion, and implementing plans designed to earn positive public support. Similarly, Cutlip, Center, and Broom (2000) wrote that public relations is a management function that establishes and maintains mutually beneficial relationships on behalf of the organization and the publics that are integral to the organization's sustained success. And Davis (2004) stressed that the growth and sophistication of the field warrant a more modern definition: "public relations is a communication with people who matter to the communicator, in order to gain their attention and collaboration in ways that are advantageous to the furtherance of his or her interests or those of whoever or whatever is represented" (p. 4).

In the sport industry, this collaboration with publics has traditionally occurred through the media, but as the industry has grown, so has the need for more sophisticated methods of communicating with the public and shaping public perception in a manner that is favorable to the franchise. The proliferation of websites, social media, and smartphone apps in the digital age has shifted public relations from the old reliance on the mass media to a new paradigm in which organizations communicate more directly with their publics (Stoldt, Dittmore, & Pedersen, 2019). Sport-focused organizations collaborate with a variety of publics in numerous ways, and this collaboration may take the form of media relations; community relations; and, in some instances, crisis communication.

As a still-emerging discipline within the realm of sport management, sport public relations has most often been associated with media relations due to the amount of media coverage given to sport in Western societies (Mullin, Hardy, & Sutton, 2014). In the past, public relations professionals maintained statistical records, wrote press releases, scheduled press conferences, developed media guides, and scheduled interviews. More recently, however, the role of public relations in sport organizations has been expanded to better address the complex issues facing franchises and to keep up with emerging new media trends. "These days, the main public relations

tool . . . [consists of] all the social media outlets available," observed Tucker and Wrench (2016, p. 152). Furthermore, Sherwood, Nicholson, and Marjoribanks (2017) noted that some sport organizations have begun to severely limit access for outside media sources, instead choosing to serve as the primary news source for all organization-related information themselves.

Sport public relations professionals are also responsible for identifying the concerns and expectations of the organization's publics and explaining them to the organization's management team. According to the PRSA (2019), the best public relations efforts tell the organization's story to its publics; they also help shape the organization and the way in which it performs. Sport entities depend on their public relations professionals not only to tell the organization's story in a variety of communication outlets but also to help the organization respond to any crises that arise. In all these ways, sport public relations professionals play an integral role in supporting the sport entity's overall objectives by building the organization's desired brand image in the minds of its stakeholders (Stoldt, Dittmore, Ross, & Branvold, 2021).

HISTORICAL PERSPECTIVES AND TRENDS IN PUBLIC RELATIONS

The growth of sport public relations has been influenced by several key trends, including business growth and the continuous availability of information thanks to technological developments such as the Internet (Seitel, 2014). As sport has evolved into a multidimensional industry, it has developed a need for improved communication with key publics. Regardless of a sport entity's size or scope, it must assess and manage public perceptions to sustain its success. Public perception is paramount because the public's image of a sport entity can influence product purchases, ticket sales, media coverage, and even organizational policies. Influencing sport consumers' perceptions is particularly challenging because, unlike traditional industry, sport elicits strong emotions. Whether supporting or criticizing a particular sport product or franchise, sport consumers often attach great meaning to sport. This emotional investment should be remembered as an organization develops strategies to persuade and influence the perceptions of the sporting public.

Sport has often been considered a microcosm of society, and many social issues have played out in the realm of sport. For example, sport has long been considered the domain of males, with few females entering and advancing in the field; in addition, sport has often been criticized for its lack of minorities in management positions. In fact, various incidents of discrimination and harassment have occurred in sport, sparking widespread controversy and dialogue. Such occurrences have led sport entities to place greater emphasis on managing public perception. Take, for instance, the Houston Astros, a Major League Baseball (MLB) team. During the 2019 season as the Astros celebrated winning the American League pennant and advancing to the World Series, Astros assistant general manager Brandon Taubman yelled at three female sport journalists, "Thank God we got Osuna! I'm so (expletive) glad we got Osuna." Taubman was referring to relief pitcher Roberto Osuna, who was previously suspended from 75 games under MLB's domestic violence policy. Additionally, Osuna almost lost the game for the Astros that night, allowing a two-run homer in the ninth inning to tie the game (Apstein, 2019). One of the journalists Taubman yelled at was known for being outspoken about the issue of domestic violence in sport and was wearing a wristband to raise awareness of domestic violence at the time of the incident. The Astros were criticized for their response, as Taubman released a statement saying, "I am sorry if anyone was offended by my actions," but he never directly apologized to the reporters involved for the specific hurtful comments he made. Team officials voiced their public support for Taubman, and the Astros owner, Jim Crane, released a statement highlighting the Astros' charitable work regarding domestic violence but did not address the issue at hand (Folkenflik, 2019). Finally, after increased public scrutiny and criticism, the organization fired Taubman four days later, stating, "His conduct does not reflect the values of our organization and we believe this is the most appropriate course of action" (Mangan, 2019, para. 18).

The increased emphasis on sport public relations is heightened by the globalization and

After clinching their county's Premier Division title, this English cricket team is careful to celebrate in a manner respectful to their organization and sponsors.

Photo courtesy of Andrea N. Geurin.

expansion of sport. As sport becomes an industry without borders, sport entities must carefully manage worldwide perceptions of their organizations. This challenge means that they must pay close attention to the various cultures and demographics that have become part of the sporting public. Sport globalization and expansion have been spurred and enhanced by technology such as the Internet (covered in detail in chapter 8), which, along with new media (e.g., mobile technologies, podcasts, vodcasts, and social media), has created an instantaneous link between sport organizations and their consumers. Sport consumers can now access information about sport products from almost anywhere in the world and interact with sport organizations and personnel more easily than in the past. This access and interactivity emphasize the need to effectively manage public perception, and new technologies are instrumental in crafting and reshaping public opinion as an instantaneous communication channel.

The need for sport entities to focus on effective public relations has been highlighted by recent exposés about sport entities and athletes, as well as controversial incidents, such as the sexual abuse scandal associated with former USA Gymnastics national team doctor and Michigan State University athletics department doctor Larry Nassar, rape charges against athletes (e.g., Stanford University swimmer Brock Turner, Juventus soccer star Cristiano Ronaldo), and cheating scandals (e.g., that of the Australian national cricket team). Along with these high-profile cases, many athletes have found themselves heavily scrutinized for content that they posted on their social media accounts. For example, Josh Allen, a standout quarterback from the University of Wyoming, was set to be selected as the first pick in the 2018 NFL Draft. Shortly before the draft, however, offensive and racist tweets from Allen's high school days surfaced. Instead of being selected first in the draft, he went seventh to the Buffalo Bills and was forced to apologize for his insensitive tweets. The NFL now has an annual Rookie Transition Program, which educates new NFL players on professionalism and includes a section on social media (Bird, 2018).

In another incident, U.S. national gymnastics team member MyKayla Skinner was named an alternate for the 2016 Olympic team, a decision many gymnastics fans disagreed with. Skinner retweeted several inappropriate tweets by fans who were upset that she was not named to the team, including one that photoshopped her face over that of Gabby Douglas, a black gymnast, accompanied by racist emojis. Skinner went on to have a stellar collegiate gymnastics career at the University of Utah, but her tarnished reputation as a result of this Twitter incident followed her long after the 2016 Olympics, even prompting one website to write an article titled "The Most Hated Gymnast in the NCAA" (Schuman, 2019).

Along with athletes posting inappropriate content on social media, some athletes also violate their team's or league's rules regarding social media use. For example, many intercollegiate athletics departments have social media rules and guidelines for their athletes to follow. When Georgia State University student-athlete Natalia Martinez used the *n*-word in an Instagram post, the athletics department suspended her from the university's soccer team. She eventually withdrew her enrollment from the university as a result of the incident (Hawkins & Terrell, 2018). Such incidents can tarnish the image of individual athletes, affect their career prospects, and affect perceptions of the associated sport entity. Therefore, it is crucial for organizations to manage public perception regarding such issues.

Two primary influences on sport public relations are the nature and scope of the player–media relationship. As trends in journalism have changed, so have the manner in which athletes are portrayed in the media. Journalists no longer limit their critiques and analyses of players solely to their on-field performance; instead, they now incorporate elements of athletes' personal lives into stories. In addition, new technology has created more competition among journalists to attract viewers, listeners, and readers. This shift in reporting has caused sport entities to emphasize and increase public relations efforts. One of the keys to enhancing public relations efforts is to maintain effective media relations, which is discussed at length later in this chapter.

Many factors have influenced the growth of sport public relations as a discipline, which—in combination with the growth and expansion of the sport industry—has caused sport entities to recognize the value of cultivating and maintaining favorable public opinion. As a microcosm of soci-

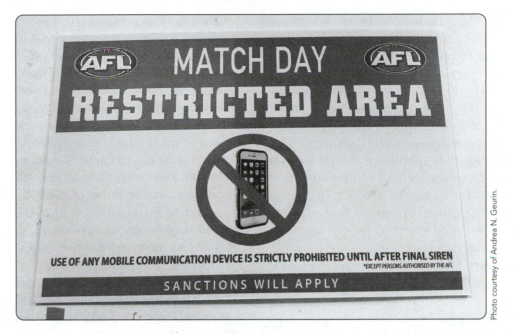

This sign outside the locker room for the Sydney Swans Australian Football League team warns players against using their cell phones on game day until the match is over.

ety, sport brings to the surface many sociocultural issues present in mainstream culture—another reason for sport entities to be cognizant of managing public perceptions. As sport becomes more global and communication technologies continue to advance, sport entities also understand the need not only to reach diverse audiences via a variety of media outlets but also to relate purposefully to these audiences. Because sport garners widespread media coverage in both the sporting press and the mainstream media, it is paramount for sport entities to purposefully manage public perception. This is most often achieved through media interaction with athletes and other high-profile members of the sport entity.

In managing public perception, public relations professionals often rely on four key models for guidance. These models, and their application to sport public relations, are discussed in the next section.

EFFECTIVE PUBLIC RELATIONS

Cultivating positive relations with, and perceptions among, members of the public is a challenging endeavor. Sport entities serve a number of key constituents, each with varying needs, concerns, and desires. To serve their constituents most effectively, sport entities should focus on transferring information, shaping perceptions, and maintaining and facilitating favorable relationships. Doing so means practicing effective public relations. Bernays (1952) posited three main elements of public relations: informing the people, persuading the people, and integrating the people with the people. The manner in which these elements are applied varies based on the sport entity and the constituents the entity wants to reach. For example, in persuading young adults to participate in tennis, the United States Tennis Association (USTA) might use prominent spokespeople, such as Sloane Stephens, Serena Williams, Madison Keys, and John Isner. This approach could influence members of the younger generation to learn the sport because they can relate to and identify with these players. On the other hand, to encourage older adults to participate, the USTA might rely on a spokesperson such as the legendary Pete Sampras.

Four Models of Public Relations

To establish effective and favorable relations with publics, public relations scholars have suggested four key models of public relations: press agentry–publicity, public information, two-way asymmetrical, and two-way symmetrical (Grunig & Grunig, 1992; Guth & Marsh, 2003; Hunt & Grunig, 1994). These four are the most widely accepted and widely practiced models of public relations. Each model has evolved based on the needs of sport entities and their constituents.

The **press agentry–publicity model** focuses primarily on receiving media attention in almost any situation. For example, a coach or athlete might make pregame comments that provoke their opponent in an effort to receive attention from the media. This is the model used most frequently in sport. The sport industry receives more coverage in the media than any other, so sport entities have become quite proficient at providing the media with key information, such as statistics and injury reports, while also understanding how to drum up interest in a story based on the things they say or do. Much communication in sport occurs through the press agentry–publicity model.

The **public information model** is also used often in sport. A key element of this model is the distribution of unbiased and accurate information about the sport entity; in fact, practitioners using this model are often considered by the organization to be journalists in residence. This approach is illustrated in sport by the use of sports information directors (SIDs) and media relations directors (MRDs) at professional franchises. These individuals are primarily responsible for disseminating facts about the organization to members of the media as quickly and as efficiently as possible. Although SIDs and MRDs are concerned with enhancing the sport entity's image, the primary concern is providing the media with the desired information.

The two-way asymmetrical and two-way symmetrical models focus more on shaping and influencing perceptions rather than simply disseminating information. As their names indicate, these models require two-way communication between a sport entity and its publics rather than one-way communication from the sport entity to the public. These two models emphasize the fact that feedback from constituents is integral to the process of establishing effective and favorable relations; therefore, one way to implement these two-way communication efforts is by means of social media platforms.

The **two-way asymmetrical model** is intended to persuade an organization's key publics through message development. Essentially, the organization shapes its messages with the intent of persuading its publics to behave in a manner that the organization desires. This model is effective when conflict with the public is minimal. It is pertinent to sport in that a sport entity can research its consumer base to determine consumers' level of satisfaction with various aspects of the sport product. However, rather than use this knowledge to facilitate further communication, the organization may simply modify the manner in which it sends its messages or alter message content to achieve the desired result.

The **two-way symmetrical model**, in contrast, is often considered the most appropriate model in establishing positive relations with constituents. This model is grounded in research and advocates conflict resolution through the facilitation of mutual understanding between an organization and its key publics. Application of this model is seen in sport in a myriad of ways—for example, when a professional league enters into negotiations with a player union and when a professional franchise or collegiate athletics department seeks public funding for the construction of a new facility.

In recent years, sport public relations has drastically transitioned from reliance on the press agentry–publicity model of public relations to an emphasis on the two-way symmetrical model of public relations. For example, sport entities are more cognizant of the role of public relations in enhancing brand image. To effectively enhance its image, a sport entity must understand the needs and desires of its key publics, and it must seek and obtain feedback from constituents to better address their needs. Because feedback cannot be obtained through the models that focus on one-way communication, two-way communication is a must in today's sport industry.

When practicing either one-way or two-way communication, sport entities are concerned with persuading the public. An examination of persuasion techniques is provided in the next section.

Elements of Persuasion

To truly influence public perception, sport entities must understand the fundamental elements involved in persuasion and use them in conjunction with the four models of public relations just discussed. *Persuasion* has been defined as "getting another person to do something through advice, reasoning, or just plain arm twisting" (Seitel, 2001, p. 56). Seitel, who provides the framework for this section, suggested that most individuals do not have particularly strong opinions in general. This means that a sport entity can, through strategic public relations, influence the perceptions of many sport consumers. Some people, however, do possess strong beliefs and opinions, and changing their minds presents a challenge for any organization. This reality is especially impactful in sport, where consumers may already hold strong beliefs on certain issues, such as stadium financing, franchise expansion or relocation, and free agency.

To persuade individuals, organizations must give them evidence that coincides with their existing beliefs, emotions, and expectations. Some effective methods by which to persuade individuals include

- presenting them with facts and figures,
- appealing to their emotions,
- personalizing the information they receive, and
- focusing on their specific needs.

In the realm of facts and figures, for example, numbers can be misleading, but they tend to be persuasive. This power can be seen in the sport world in the various ranking systems (e.g., NFL power rankings, AP rankings of top collegiate basketball teams, and the Rolex Women's World Golf rankings). Using these rankings, sport consumers formulate their perceptions of the best and most talented athletes and teams at the professional and collegiate levels.

Regarding the second item in the list, emotions run high in sport, and emotional appeals can be quite persuasive. Sport itself is often used to persuade the masses, and sport entities often use additional emotional appeals when trying to shape public perception. Examples include framing the Dallas Cowboys as "America's team" and baseball as the "national pastime." These emotional appeals use patriotism to enhance perceptions among sport consumers. Personalization, the third item, is also used often in sport. For example, retired Olympic gold medal-winning skier Lindsey Vonn established her own foundation to empower young girls, wrote a best-selling book titled *Strong Is the New Beautiful*, and has her own cosmetic line for active women. She now uses her experiences and message of empowerment as a public speaker.

Lindsey Vonn is interviewed about her message of empowerment for young girls in front of a live studio audience at the Build Series Studio in New York City.

Photo courtesy of Andrea N. Geurin.

The fourth way to persuade is to appeal to consumers by focusing on what's in it for them. Sport entities that use this mechanism often succeed, because the focus is placed on the benefits to the consumer rather than on the benefits to the sport entity. Many sport equipment and apparel companies are quite proficient at touting the benefits of wearing certain apparel and using specific products to achieve maximal sport performance. For example, since their initial release in 1985, Nike's Air Jordan basketball shoes have engaged players with images of jumping high and playing the game like Michael Jordan. Today, Air Jordan sneakers continue to top the charts of best-selling basketball shoes in the United States, illustrated by the fact that three of the shoes on a list of the top 10 best-selling sneakers of 2019 were versions of the Air Jordan (Ciment, 2019).

Factors That Influence Perception

A variety of factors influence the perceptions of sporting publics and, in turn, sport organizations' ability to persuade those publics (see figure 10.2). These factors include one's motives for sport product affiliation, as well as sport product performance, level of involvement with the sport product, frequency of sport media exposure, and demographic and sociocultural influences. The first factor, motives for sport product affiliation, influences individuals' frequency of consumption and loyalty to a sport product. Loyalty may lead to repeat purchasing or followership; at the same time, an individual may be a loyal fan yet not purchase tickets regularly. Instead, this fan may loyally follow the franchise by watching its games via online streaming, purchasing franchise merchandise, and engaging in online discussions on social media.

Motives for sport affiliation vary from individual to individual and can be either extrinsic or intrinsic. Extrinsic motivations result in some outward display of the benefit. For example, a fan who wishes to wear the jersey of the U.S. women's national team, the 2019 FIFA Women's World Cup champions, might be motivated by the prospect that others will associate him or her with the most dominant women's soccer team in the world. In contrast, intrinsic motivations are internal benefits that an individual experiences through his or her fandom—for example, feelings of happiness and excitement after a favorite team wins an important game.

Funk, Beaton, and Alexandris (2012) identified five motivations that drive sport consumers: socialization, performance, excitement, esteem, and diversion. Socialization motives involve opportunities to enhance relationships with others through sport consumption. This socialization may take place in person or could also happen in online settings such as social

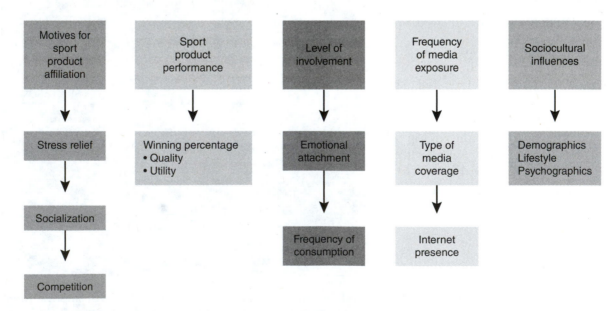

Figure 10.2 Key influences that shape public perceptions of a sport product.

media. Performance motives involve the desire to witness the grace, skill, and artistry of sport performances. Excitement motives involve an individual's desire to take part in the stimulating or dramatic aspects of sport. Esteem motives involve the desire to obtain personal benefits from the act of watching the sporting event. For example, when a fan's favorite team wins a game, it has the ability to positively affect that fan's self-esteem because he identifies with the team and its victory. Finally, diversion motives involve the desire to escape from everyday life by consuming a sporting event (Funk et al., 2012). Motives are integral in shaping people's perceptions and should be considered carefully by sport public relations professionals who work to shape the opinions of sporting publics.

Motives are also linked to perception of sport product performance—that is, the utility of the sport product or the attributes that make it capable of meeting individuals' needs and desires (Mullin et al., 2014). In other words, a sport product's ability to satisfy the desires of sport consumers affects their perception of the product, which in turn affects persuasion.

A sport entity's ability to influence consumers' opinions is also affected by their level of involvement with the sport product. As discussed earlier, sport elicits high levels of emotion. The more involved a consumer is with a sport product, the less likely it is that his or her opinions of the product can be changed. However, those who are highly involved typically have more favorable opinions of the product.

Consumers' perceptions are also affected by the frequency and type of sport media exposure. Favorable coverage in the sport media can enhance public opinion by reinforcing existing positive beliefs or encouraging a shift toward more favorable views. Similarly, negative coverage can reinforce negative opinions and create negative perceptions in the minds of the sporting public.

Finally, demographics and sociocultural factors must not be overlooked when managing perceptions of a sport entity. Demographic factors include characteristics such as gender, household income, education level, and number of children living in the home. Sociocultural factors include aspects pertinent to one's culture and lifestyle, such as religion, political affiliation, or belonging to certain community groups or clubs. All these factors help shape individuals' perceptions and should be considered when formulating strategies to manage perceptions. In managing public perceptions, sport public relations professionals often focus on media relations, which is covered in the next section.

MEDIA RELATIONS

Sport receives tremendous coverage in the media. Entire sections of newspapers, segments on the evening news, cable or streaming television channels, and a wide variety of websites are devoted to covering sport. Therefore, the media provide a powerful way to promote a business and gain exposure (Lontos, 2004). Most companies strategize regarding how to obtain more media coverage, and public relations professionals in sport-focused organizations concentrate on how to use this coverage to their full advantage. Although SIDs and MRDs perform a variety of tasks and serve a myriad of functions, the ultimate goal of the position is to "generate favorable publicity and minimize unfavorable publicity" (Stoldt et al., 2021, p. 15). In seeking to do so, the sport-focused organization must pay close attention to the manner in which it cultivates and manages media relationships. This section highlights the key elements in media relations and provides strategies for enhancing media relationships while presenting the sport-focused organization in the most favorable manner possible.

Strategies for Developing Positive Relationships With the Media

The media should be treated as a direct link to the sport organization's consumers. Sport consumers now have instantaneous access to myriad media sources, which in itself is sufficient reason for sport public relations professionals to cultivate positive relations with the media. The mass media shape public opinion, and the media's perception of a sport-focused organization is often the public's perception as well. As Kline (1996) emphasized, "A good relationship with the media is important for the success of any business. A good relationship will not insure that the media will present only good news about the business; however, it will insure good communication between the two, which is the foundation for effective public relations" (p. 55).

According to sport media scholar Lawrence Wenner (1998), public opinion is shaped both by sports information departments and by the sport mass media. In college athletics departments and in sport franchises, the professionals who work in sports information and media relations are tasked primarily with creating and maintaining a positive image in the community. To do this, professionals must provide the media with much-needed "scoops" about their respective entities. The media's portrayal of the sport entity exerts tremendous influence on public perception; more specifically, the mass media possess the power to "shape the content of the message generated by a news release, a postgame interview, or another form of indirect public relations" (Nichols, Moynahan, Hall, & Taylor, 2002, p. 63).

Connors (2014) identified three styles of media relations: reactive, proactive, and interactive. Reactive media relations involve responding to inquiries and providing information requested from media or other interested parties. In proactive media relations, SIDs and MRDs contact sport media outlets directly to pitch story ideas and distribute information such as player biographies and media guides. Although reactive media relations will always exist, "the primary activity should be proactive—to take the initiative in providing information and creating publicity to enhance the perception of the entity" (Connors, 2014, p. 388). In proactive PR, SIDs and MRDs must take time to carefully craft their pitch, which involves researching media outlets that may be interested in publishing a story on their topic, understanding the reporting style of the news outlet to which one is pitching, and finding third-party data points (e.g., statistics, trends, other insights) that supplement the story to be pitched (Grossman, 2015).

Finally, interactive media relations involves developing a mutually beneficial relationship between the sport entity and a media outlet. In this form of media relations, which can be initiated from either side, the focus is on building a long-term relationship between the two parties. According to Brewer (2014), members of the media depend on trustworthy contacts; therefore, SIDs and MRDs must place prime emphasis on fostering favorable working relationships with local, regional, national, and international media.

Media relations professionals view cultivating positive and mutually beneficial relationships with the media as an integral part of shaping the image of their organization (Grossman, 2015). The relationship between the sport public relations professional and the media may appear basic in nature, but it can be challenging to foster and nurture that relationship. If the relationship is not properly maintained, an adversarial relationship can develop quite rapidly. Echoing Connors' (2014) assertions about the importance of interactive media relations, Miloch and Pedersen (2006) indicated that fostering a positive and mutually beneficial relationship with the media is a necessity. Keeping this relationship positive is thought to enhance coverage of the sport organization.

In today's sport media landscape, the definition of *media* is broader than ever before. It is not limited only to newspapers or sport-specific outlets such as television channels, magazines, or websites but also includes media such as podcasts, social media influencers (see chapter 9), or bloggers. With so many outlets available, it is difficult for media relations professionals to know with which outlets to build relationships. Salzman (2016) reported that to help overcome this challenge, SIDs and MRDs must ask questions like, "Who is media and who is an influencer? Who helps spread the news and who drives actual buying decisions?" (para. 9). Once these questions are answered, PR professionals must understand what the goal of their communication is and match it to the most appropriate outlets. For example, if a sport league wants to draw attention to its new line of apparel for young women, pitching this story to social media influencers who are influential among female sport fans in the millennial and Gen Z generations would likely be more effective and appropriate than pitching it to newspaper sport reporters. The next section expands on this concept by explaining more about the environments in which journalists operate.

Understanding the Journalistic Environment

To foster positive relations with media entities, sport public relations professionals should understand the environment in which journalists work, know what is considered newsworthy, and strive to provide this information in a timely and appropriate fashion. Newsworthy items include "anything significant that relates to the main news priorities at the time . . . conflict . . . controversy, anything that affects the community, human-interest stories . . . the unusual or the different . . . interesting data, statistics or research results, interesting 'firsts,' anything that links up with famous or infamous people, success in major or prestigious awards, or any other significant recognition" (Frangi & Fletcher, 2002, pp. 19-20).

The media will initiate contact with the sport organization for information such as facts, figures, statistics, and attendance figures. They will also want confirmation or disconfirmation of rumors and will seek the sport entity's reaction to rumors. For example, reporters will contact the sport franchise to obtain quotes or official statements if it is rumored that a player may be traded or released or that a head coach may be hired or fired. They may also contact the sport organization to inquire about rumors of athletes', coaches', or staff's off-field behavior, as evidenced in Jodie Hawkins' profile at the beginning of the chapter. Members of the media will also initiate contact when seeking reactions to reports, policies, and major events. For example, player associations may be contacted for a response to a league's stance on a particular issue pertaining to renegotiation of a collective bargaining agreement.

Anticipating Contact

Sport-focused organizations should always anticipate being contacted by the media after a major announcement, such as the suspension of a player, the hiring or firing of a head coach or general manager, or the sale or relocation of a franchise. Sport-focused organizations may also be contacted when the media need more explanation of certain policies or programs. In addition, the media will often want clarification on legal issues associated with operating the sport franchise, such as stadium financing and player contract negotiations. Knowing when to contact the media and when to anticipate that the media will initiate contact with the organization allows public relations professionals to carefully craft statements and responses that reinforce the overall mission and image of the sport-focused

organization. This preparation also allows the organization to provide the media with the information it needs in a timely and efficient manner. Members of the media have different deadlines; to foster mutually beneficial relationships, sport public relations professionals must be timely in providing the media with requested information.

Tools for Maintaining Contact With the Media

Sport public relations professionals use several methods when communicating with the media. This section provides an overview of traditional tools, while a later section in the chapter describes more contemporary digital PR tools. While digital PR tools are increasingly used by sport organizations, the traditional tools described in the section below are also still highly relevant for many organizations.

Sport Press Release

To initiate contact with the media, most sport public relations professionals write and distribute a press release (sometimes referred to as a *news release* or *media release*). Press release content must be relevant to the intended audience's interests and tightly focused (Skerik, 2012). The press release allows the sport organization to notify the media of specific news in a timely fashion. It also allows the organization to notify all media at once so as not to give the impression that certain members of the media take precedence over others. Indeed, it is of the utmost importance that sport public relations professionals do not play favorites with the media. Doing so undermines the organization's credibility and can lead to unfavorable coverage. Despite the widespread use of the press release, Skerik reports that in today's ever-crowded information and news environment, it is becoming increasingly difficult for organizations' press releases to generate news stories in the media, although these are still useful tools for releasing information directly from an organization and are often posted on the organization's website or social media accounts.

Newsworthy Press Releases

Sport entities should not release information to the media unless it is newsworthy and holds general interest for the public. Newsworthiness may take the form of a new development within the sport entity, such as a change in franchise ownership, the retirement of a legendary athlete, or the groundbreaking for a new stadium. Press releases can also provide information about a dramatic element or present an issue of human interest. Human-interest stories take a variety of forms—for example, a popular athlete returning after a serious injury or illness, athletes working with various charitable organizations, or members of the same family competing against each other in a high-profile competition. Press releases with local flavor are also considered newsworthy; this angle might involve, for example, a hometown athlete earning a high-profile award or competing on a national or international level. As mentioned earlier, sport public relations professionals must be cognizant of what constitutes newsworthy information and take great care to notify the media when appropriate.

Characteristics of Well-Written Press Releases

Press releases should follow specific guidelines and should be written in Associated Press (AP) style, which is used by members of the media when formulating stories. Communicating with the media in this format helps build the sport organization's credibility and helps members of the media perform their duties efficiently. Sport public relations professionals must also understand journalists' deadlines and send releases at appropriate times that allow journalists to formulate their stories; doing so may enhance the coverage of the sport entity.

The press release should be written using the inverted pyramid style, which essentially puts the most important information first—that is, in the lede (first) sentence of the release. The lead sentence should provide a clear and concise idea of what the organization is conveying by clearly outlining the five Ws: who, what, when, where, and why. The lead sentence should also summarize the contents of the release and encourage journalists to continue reading. The body of the press release provides more in-depth information and may include quotes from key figures in the organization. The end of the release may include "fluff" information that is not necessarily pertinent to the information being relayed but touts the organization in some way. An example

for a sport franchise includes information about ticket sales or upcoming promotions. The end of the release may also describe the sport entity or its products. Because it is now quite common to distribute press releases via email or other online methods, the release should include a photo or video that the media can use if they choose to cover the story (Skerik, 2012).

A press release should not be distributed to members of the media without the organization being prepared for the information to be made immediately available to the public. Therefore, the release should always include a date and indicate that the information being distributed is for immediate release. These three words—*FOR IMMEDIATE RELEASE*—should appear in all-capital letters in the upper section of the release before the headline and contact information. It is *not* considered best practice for sport-focused organizations to send a press release in advance of when it would like the information to become public. The media should not be expected to withhold information from the public once they receive it.

Press releases should always include a headline, which should clearly convey the subject matter and be written in bold or all-capital letters (or both). The headline should be concise; should stimulate reader interest; and, if possible, should not exceed one line. Keniston (2018) suggested that to ensure people read headlines and to optimize them for posting on social media, headlines should be short and to the point while conveying the message in a way that makes people want to read it.

Here are a few more key characteristics of a good press release: The release should always include the contact information for the public relations professional, including office and mobile phone numbers, email address, web address for the organization, and potentially the PR professional's social media handles on sites such as Twitter. Typically, press releases should be short and concise (no more than two pages). When press releases exceed one page, page numbers should be included. In accordance with AP style, the writer of the release should indicate in the release when no more information will follow. This has usually been indicated by the ### symbol. Recently, however, sport entities have become more creative and often end a release with the organization's name or slogan.

The better a press release is written, the more likely the media is to convey the organization's desired message to the masses. In fact, a well-written press release that uses proper AP style often appears in print exactly as it was written by the sport public relations professional. This result is ideal, of course, because it directly links the sport organization to the public. Sport public relations professionals often craft lede sentences to boost the credibility of their organization. For example, an organization that has recently won a league championship might craft the lede as, "Team A, XYZ League champions, announced today that . . ." This approach allows the organization to remind its publics that the organization is of championship caliber.

It is quite common for sport-focused organizations to email press releases or post them on the organization's website or social media accounts. Doing so allows journalists to easily access a wealth of information in addition to the press release. In addition, posting a release on social media sites allows it to be shared by the organization's fans and other stakeholders, thus resulting in greater distribution to key audiences in an organic fashion rather than relying solely on the media to do the distributing.

Best Practices for Press Releases

When developing a press release, sport public relations professionals should be aware of the following to avoid making several common mistakes:

- The press release should be clear and concise and provide only the necessary background for the journalist.

- Quantity does not equate with quality when writing a press release, and sport public relations professionals should always be cognizant of journalists' time constraints and deadlines.

- Sport public relations professionals should ensure the newsworthiness of the information contained in the press release. If it is not newsworthy, it should not be distributed to the media.

- Press releases should not be used as attempts to generate publicity for the sport-focused organization. The media should be contacted only when the information to be distributed warrants communication.

- Similarly, quotations from key personnel should center on the newsworthiness of the information being conveyed. The quotes included in press releases are often used by the media and should be pertinent to the information contained in the release.

Sport Press Conference

In many cases, a sport organization has information of such high importance that it schedules a press conference. Like a press release, a press conference allows the organization to disseminate information to all members of the media at once. A press conference, however, allows members of the media to interact with key personnel to ask questions and obtain quotes to better develop their stories and broadcasts. Press conferences are warranted when releasing extremely important information such as the hiring or firing of a coach or the relocation of a franchise. In such situations, the sport public relations professional should anticipate that most members of the media will want access to key individuals. The press conference allows the organization to grant this access to all media entities in a timely, convenient, and efficient manner.

As with the distribution of a press release, press conferences should not be scheduled on a regular basis. There are, however, some exceptions. For example, many sport entities host weekly press conferences or press luncheons, especially during the competition season. This approach allows the sport entity to cultivate relationships with the media and provide media members with desired information. Hosting these events regularly during a sport entity's season also serves as an effective tool for disseminating key information in a timely manner. Aside from such exceptions, press conferences should be conducted only when warranted by the importance or urgency of the information.

The conference should be scheduled with consideration of the media's various deadlines and of any other newsworthy items that may require the media's attention that day. In other words, schedule the conference at a time when it is less likely to compete with other entities for coverage. The organization should also provide the media with some measure of advance notice, depending on the nature of the announcement. It is also possible to conduct online or virtual press conferences via streamed video and communication services such as Skype or Google Hangouts.

The press conference should be scripted and coordinated by the organization's sport public relations professionals, and usually it should not exceed 30 minutes. If possible, senior staff members should always speak. Speakers should test microphones and wear dark or neutral clothing because it photographs well. Speakers should be well prepared to make the announcement, and they should always be prepared to respond to the media's questions. Anyone associated with the organization should be prepared to field questions from the media even if they are not speaking during the press conference. Many of the key points discussed in the section on interview preparation (a bit later in this chapter) should be applied when preparing individuals to speak and anticipate questions at a media conference.

Media Kit and Media Guide

Media kits and media guides are often used to showcase the sport entity. These publications may be online or may appear in print. Today, most sport organizations make both versions of the media kits and media guides available to members of the media. While many members of the media still prefer to have a hard copy of a media kit or media guide, the benefit of online publications is that they can be easily updated throughout the sport entity's season with new or changing information. These two media relations tools vary in their content based on the needs and focus of the sport entity. Media kits typically include press releases, selected statistics (e.g., franchise "firsts"), fact sheets, answers to frequently asked questions, feature story ideas, biographical sketches of key figures in the organization, photos, and perhaps video footage that can be used by members of the media. Media guides are much more extensive than media kits and provide a wealth of information about the sport entity, including statistics, player rosters, and historical perspectives.

Fact Sheet

A fact sheet is similar to a press release in that it provides the media with concise information regarding a specific issue or event. Fact sheets typically do not exceed one page, and they often serve as key points of reference for members of the media. Fact sheets tend to answer the five Ws (who, what, where, when, why), as well as H (how). They may also provide background information about the organization, quotes, and other useful information for the media (Smith, 2012). General fact sheets may serve as "fluff" pieces for the organization and may tout its accomplishments, legendary athletes and coaches, or role within the community. Sport-focused organizations may provide fact sheets to the media for specific purposes or to supplement announcements. Fact sheets are written in bulleted format and highlight key points associated with an announcement or issue (Smith, 2012).

Interviews

Interviewing is integral to the process of managing media relationships and presenting the sport entity in a favorable manner. Members of sport entities are interviewed on a regular basis, which can work to the advantage of the sport entity if the interviewees are well trained and well prepared. Positive interviews can both cultivate positive media relations and shape public perceptions of the sport entity. In contrast, poor interviews can result in negative perceptions and create negative relationships. Professional athletes have come to understand the importance of interviewing skills and recognize that developing strong communication skills can be as important to their career as their on-field performance. Developing excellent communication skills through media training can help an athlete build a personal brand, which can increase the athlete's marketability even after retirement (Hill, 2011). Most important, knowing how to communicate effectively and appropriately can prevent athletes from inciting controversy and tarnishing their image, as well as that of their team or organization.

When preparing individuals to interact with the media or be interviewed, sport public relations professionals should address several key elements. The first step is to brainstorm with the interviewee regarding all potential questions that might be asked in an interview. Knowing the context and purpose of the interview is of the utmost importance because it helps the interviewee anticipate questions and formulate appropriate responses. Interviewees should establish credibility not only with the audience but also with the journalist. To do so, they can prepare for the interview by determining three or four key points that reinforce the overall message to be disseminated to the public. Once these key points have been determined, interviewees can articulate the best way to convey them regardless of the questions asked by the journalist. Interviewees should view interviews as an opportunity to relay the sport entity's message to the public, but they should *not* expect interviewers to provide them with the opportunity to do so; rather, they should take steps on their own to integrate the desired messages into their responses.

If possible, the interviewee should personalize the interview by allowing his or her personality to show. Doing so helps the interviewee feel more in control, implies confidence, and lends a conversational tone to the interview. If the interviewee does not understand a question or has difficulty hearing a question, he or she should ask the journalist to repeat it. Interviewees should maintain eye contact with the interviewer to convey confidence to the audience. Interviewees should not chew gum or candy when being interviewed, and they should use simple sentences. Long, technical sentences may confuse the journalist and, more important, the audience. In preparing for the interview, the interviewee should practice summarizing technical or complicated answers and strive to paint a mental picture for the audience.

Individuals should always be honest and straightforward with interviewers and should avoid speculating when responding to questions. Interviewees should also be aware of their posture and use a strong voice. They should make the interaction pleasant for the journalist and for the audience; at the end of the interview, they should thank the journalist for his or her time.

Preparing members of the sport organization for interviews enhances the quality of the interview and fosters favorable public sentiment. The sport organization's image is enhanced by engaging in positive interviews, practicing positive media relations, and communicating effectively with the media.

DIGITAL PUBLIC RELATIONS TOOLS

The rise of digital media allows sport organizations to create their own content and publish messages for their various audiences themselves, meaning they have less reliance on the media to deliver their messages as they once did. Sherwood, Nicholson, and Marjoribanks (2017) called this a "potential paradigm shift in the once symbiotic relationship between sport organisations and the media that cover them" (p. 513) but also noted that social and digital platforms have not dramatically altered public relations practices, as many sport organizations still develop and maintain strong relationships with media outlets in an effort to reach their various publics. Still, the shifting dynamic means that in addition to employing sport PR professionals who possess the skills to communicate with and develop relationships with sport media outlets, sport organizations also have a greater need for tech-savvy employees whose jobs focus on content creation. Although sport organizations can deliver their messages to key publics more easily than ever before, sport public relations professionals must still possess strong people and relationship-building skills, as they must be able to develop engaging content that sparks a conversation with and among publics. Raabe (2017) stated that it is incumbent upon PR professionals to "engage with the public to facilitate discussion and bring influence to the table via the new digital channels" (para. 9).

Social media is one tool that PR professionals use to deliver messages directly to audiences. For example, in November 2019, U.S. women's national soccer team star Megan Rapinoe and her partner, WNBA star Sue Bird, visited the NBA's Golden State Warriors to speak on the issue of inclusion and also to watch the Warriors play in their new stadium, the Chase Center. Before the advent of social media, this would have been a prime opportunity to contact members of the media via a press release with the hope that newspapers or television news stations would cover the event. Instead, the Warriors used their own media team to produce a high-quality highlight video from the day, which was posted on their Facebook page. Teams, leagues, and athletes themselves often use social media platforms such as Facebook, Twitter, Instagram, Snapchat, and YouTube to share news and information directly with stakeholders, and journalists also use these social media platforms to learn about newsworthy stories and to share their own stories about sport organizations and athletes.

As illustrated in the Golden State Warriors Facebook example, the use of high-quality digital video is another method by which sport organizations can directly communicate with their publics, and these videos are most often delivered via the organization's social media accounts or on its website. Today's sport fans are interested in short bites of information, and digital videos allow sport organizations to achieve this. For example, when English Premier League team Manchester City beat its rival Manchester United in a 2018 game, Manchester City uploaded a one-minute highlight video set to dramatic music to its Instagram account, which allowed fans who were unable to watch the full game to quickly understand the key moments in the victory and allowed fans who did watch the full game to relive the excitement. Because Manchester City produced the video in-house, they were able to highlight the moments of the game they deemed most exciting or important rather than relying on journalists to do so. The visual excitement and music element of the video also provided a sensory experience that reading an article about the game would not provide.

Along with the increasing use of social media and digital videos to communicate directly with publics, sport organizations are also beginning to use influencers as part of their public relations strategies to get their messages out to key publics. Discussed in chapter 9, influencers are those people who are not traditional celebrities but have built a strong social media following with a captive audience. Raabe (2017) cautions that influence does not necessarily equate to popularity. In other words, someone with a great number of social media followers but who receives low levels of engagement (e.g., likes, comments, retweets) is not the best choice for an influencer. Sport orga-

nizations should seek influencers whose engagement levels are high, demonstrating a true interest from their followers. For example, MLB's Boston Red Sox wanted to expand its reach with mothers and enlisted the help of local mom bloggers and women who had written books about family travel. By asking these women to write about the Red Sox on their blogs and social media accounts, the Red Sox were able to deliver their messages to a different demographic than their typical fans and do so in a way that felt authentic to the content receivers. In exchange for sharing content about the Red Sox, the women were able to take VIP tours of the Red Sox's stadium, Fenway Park, and attend special meet-and-greet sessions with the team's players.

COMMUNITY RELATIONS

One of the most overlooked elements of sport public relations is community relations, which helps sport-focused organizations cultivate mutually beneficial relationships with key constituents and audiences in the community. Community relations activities can serve as an invaluable public relations tool, yet most sport organizations do not use them to the fullest benefit. These activities should be included in any public relations strategy because they benefit the sport entity as well as the local and regional community.

Stoldt and colleagues (2021) defined *community relations* as an "organizational activity designed to foster desirable relationships between the sport organization and the communities in which it is either located or has strategic interests" (p. 19). Sport organizations engage in a variety of community relations activities, including food drives, reading programs, and involvement with charitable organizations. For example, the WNBA's Chicago Sky team has a #RedefinePossible platform designed to inspire and empower women in leadership positions in the Chicago area. Their Leadership Brunch, Women's Leadership Awards Series, Mentorship Initiative, and Fireside Chats reach over 600 Chicagoland executives, philanthropists, and key influencers. These programs offer women valuable information and knowledge on furthering their careers and progressing as leaders.

Photo courtesy of Andrea N. Geurin.

Allowing stakeholders to take stadium or facility tours, such as this tour of the Sydney Cricket Ground, is one way to foster positive relationships with fans and the community.

Other sport entities have also implemented numerous and diverse community relations efforts. These efforts reinforce and communicate the sport entity's image and values to its constituents. For example, English Premier League team Chelsea FC began a campaign called "Say No to Antisemitism" in 2018, which aims to raise awareness of and educate the Chelsea players, staff, fans, and community about antisemitism in the sport of soccer. Chelsea's owner, Roman Abramovich, is Jewish and was bothered by the number of recent antisemitic incidents that took place in Europe, along with historic accounts of antisemitic chants at Chelsea games in the past. The campaign has several initiatives to help tackle the issue of antisemitism, including educational trips to Holocaust concentration camps in Auschwitz-Birkenau for the athletes and some Chelsea supporters, inviting Holocaust survivors to visit the players and staff at Chelsea's headquarters, and hosting workshops at schools in London. Additionally, the club offers educational courses for Chelsea fans who have been banned from attending games due to antisemitic behavior.

In another example, USA Swimming, the national governing body of swimming in the United States, started a program called "Make a Splash" in 2007 to help spread awareness of the importance of knowing how to swim to cut the number of drowning deaths, as drowning is the second leading cause of death for people under the age of 14. In 2018, the program helped provide swimming lessons for over 1.3 million children; since the inception of Make a Splash, nearly 8 million children have benefited from the program. Make a Splash has over 1,000 partner organizations in all 50 U.S. states, which offer free or low-cost swim lessons to local children.

Beyond these examples, numerous other community-oriented programs help sport entities reinforce and enhance their image while communicating their values and missions to the public. These programs allow sport entities to engage with their communities while emphasizing the key aspects of their organization. Therefore, community relations programs should be included as part of an organization's overall public relations and marketing strategy as a way to manage public perception. This is particularly important in sport because the nature of the sport product is unpredictable, and that unpredictability can influence public perception. Community relations provides an avenue that sport entities can use to maintain a consistent and favorable public perception.

COMMUNICATION DURING A CRISIS

Sport entities are sometimes faced with crises that could tarnish their image by creating unfavorable perceptions in the minds of the media and key constituents. Any threat to a sport entity's image or reputation constitutes a crisis because an entity's reputation is one of its major assets (Saia, 2016). Responding to a crisis often means more than simply responding to media inquiries; it sometimes requires a concerted organizational response.

Examples of Crises in Sport

Crises can arise from something as simple as comments made during an interview. For example, at the 2016 BNP Paribas Open tennis tournament, the CEO and tournament director Raymond Moore said in an interview that the women tennis players "ride on the coattails of the men" (ESPN. com News Service, 2016, para. 3). Moore went on to say, "They are very, very lucky. If I was a lady player, I'd go down every night on my knees and thank God that Roger Federer and Rafa Nadal were born because they have carried this sport. They really have." (para. 3). Moore's comments sparked outrage from prominent female tennis players such as Billie Jean King, who was instrumental in gaining equal pay for women tennis players, as well as Serena Williams, Venus Williams, and Martina Navratilova. Moore eventually apologized, saying his comments were "in extremely poor taste and erroneous" (para. 13), but the damage was done. Just one day later, Moore resigned from his position, which Larry Ellison, the owner of the site of the tournament, Indian Wells, said was the right decision. Ellison went on to thank the four previously mentioned female tennis players for their leadership in the sport.

Crises can also result from posts made on social media, as was the case in 2014 when Paul George, an all-star player for the NBA's Indiana Pacers, tweeted out his support for an NFL player, Ray Rice, who was suspended in a highly publicized domestic violence incident. George's tweet read, "I don't condone hittin women or think it's coo BUT if SHE ain't trippin then I ain't trippin. Lets keep it movin lol let that man play!" (Sims, 2014, para. 3). Thousands of NBA fans took to Twitter to chastise George for his insensitive comment.

Although George deleted the tweet within an hour of posting it, he continued to tweet about the issue, claiming his words had been taken out of context, and to discuss relationships in which women are violent toward men. The president of basketball operations for the Pacers at the time, Larry Bird, issued a statement about the tweets, which said, "Paul George's tweets from earlier were thoughtless and without regard to the subject of domestic violence and its seriousness in society. We have talked to Paul to strongly express our displeasure and made it clear that the NBA and the Pacers' organization will not condone or tolerate remarks of this nature. Paul understands that he was wrong and why his tweets were so inappropriate and is very apologetic" (Sims, 2014, para. 6). Despite this statement from Bird, most fans who continued to discuss the situation did not believe George was sincere in his apology.

Sometimes crises arise from volatile situations or from incidents that happen during a sporting event. One example of this stems from the NFL. In 2016, then-San Francisco 49ers quarterback Colin Kaepernick began kneeling during the pregame playing of the national anthem. Kaepernick said that he did so to protest police brutality of black people in America and racial injustices that exist in society. He had spoken with military veterans to ask about a respectful way to protest, and they suggested taking a knee. NFL fans were drastically divided in their reaction to Kaepernick, with his detractors saying that he was being disrespectful and un-American and was bringing politics into the game of football. It became a national controversy, with everyone from other athletes to celebrities to President Barack Obama weighing in. In March of 2017, amid the controversy, Kaepernick opted out of his contract, and no NFL team has since signed him to a contract. Other players followed Kaepernick's lead and also began to kneel; in 2018, the NFL enacted a policy requiring players to stand during the national anthem, although it allowed them to stay in the locker room during the national anthem if they chose to do so. Teams of players who knelt were to be fined, according to the policy. The new policy was widely viewed in a negative light, with popular news outlets such as *Sports Illustrated*, the *New York Times*, the *Washington Post*, and the *Chicago Tribune* blasting the NFL's move. Public relations expert and *Forbes* columnist Robert Wynne called it "a PR nightmare" (Wynne,

2018, para. 1). The issue is still not resolved, with NFL fans still sharply divided, and NFL television ratings have declined since the incident began.

Interestingly, the way that another sport organization, Nike, handled the Kaepernick national anthem situation was viewed as one of the best responses to a crisis situation by some PR experts (Prezly, 2018). In 2018, Nike developed a campaign featuring Kaepernick with the tagline, "Believe in something. Even if it means sacrificing everything." Much like the kneeling incident itself, the video ad that went along with Nike's campaign was highly controversial. In the days following the ad's release, Nike's stock dropped 3 percent, and some consumers were publicly cutting Nike logos off their shoes or clothes or using black Sharpie markers to cover Nike logos on their apparel. Through it all, Nike and Kaepernick stood their ground and did not apologize for the ad. It turned out to be an excellent strategy for the company, as Nike's sales increased 31 percent and their stock also reached an all-time high. The ad was viewed most favorably by young people in the 18 to 34 age group. Both the NFL and Nike's handling of the crisis illustrate the importance of crisis communication (and specifically the planning, cooperation, and teamwork) that must exist within a sport organization to achieve positive results.

Case Study in Crisis Communication: Deeper Issues in the BNP Paribas Crisis

In addition to the details given in this chapter about the BNP Paribas crisis centered on tournament director Raymond Moore's sexist comments, the following case study provides necessary context to further examine the crisis from a critical perspective.

The history of professional women's tennis has long been steeped in sexism. The Women's Tennis Association (WTA) was formed in 1973 by tennis legend Billie Jean King with the goal of providing equal opportunity to women in the sport. Until then, women were paid far less than their male counterparts and at tournaments were often cast to the outside courts that did not draw nearly as much attention from fans. Through the hard work and dedication of women like King, women finally won the battle to earn equal prize money in all four tennis Grand Slam tournaments in 2007, 34 years after the WTA was formed.

Despite receiving equal pay, sexism is still alive in the sport, as evidenced by Moore's comments at the BNP Paribas. Some critics drew comparisons between Moore and former male tennis player Bobby Riggs, who famously challenged King to a "Battle of the Sexes" tennis tournament in 1973, which King won. Riggs later said, "Billie and I did wonders for women's tennis. They owe me a piece of their checks." Many felt that Moore's comments were reminiscent of Riggs' back in the 1970s.

Unfortunately, Moore was not alone in displaying sexism at the BNP Paribas tournament. When asked to comment on Moore's words, the men's tournament winner, Serbian athlete Novak Djokovic, displayed his own sexist views. With regard to equal prize money, Djokovic said, "I think that our men's tennis world, ATP world, should fight for more because the stats are showing that we have much more spectators on the men's tennis matches. I think that's one of the reasons why maybe we should get awarded more."

Adding insult to injury, Djokovic went on to offend women around the world by talking about their hormones, casting women as the "other" or as delicate inferior beings, saying, "I have tremendous respect for what women in global sport are doing and achieving. Their bodies are much different to men's bodies. They have to go through a lot of different things that we don't have to go through. You know, the hormones and different stuff, we don't need to go into details."

These incidents at the 2016 BNP Paribas tournament reflected poorly on the tournament's reputation as well as on Djokovic's, highlighting that despite the progress made for equality in women's tennis, sexism is still very much an issue. League officials, tournament directors, and athletes' managers must be prepared to deal with these crisis situations.

Guidelines for Responding to Crises

The scenarios described here exemplify the crises that can face sport entities. Crises in sport can take many shapes and forms and involve issues such as player eligibility, player arrest, player death, incidents on the field of play, and the firing of a coach. The public usually forms its perception of a crisis situation within the first 24 hours of the crisis (Nichols et al., 2002). Due to the news being reported on various communication outlets 24 hours a day, sport organizations are under more intense media scrutiny than ever before, and the increasing prevalence of social media use means that sport public relations professionals must be ready to respond to crisis situations more quickly than in the past (Stoldt et al., 2021). First impressions are often the most difficult perceptions to change, and the manner in which an organization initially responds to a crisis often exerts a dramatic effect on the public's perception of the crisis.

To prepare for crisis situations, sport public relations professionals should, with other staff members, brainstorm possible situations that may occur throughout the course of a season (or year) that could threaten the organization's image. Possible situations can be categorized as either unexpected threats or continuous threats. Unexpected threats might include, for example, a player arrest, the firing of a head coach, or a serious injury to a fan or group of fans. Continuous threats may involve various organizational policies that can affect relations with key constituents, such as ticket sales policies, game day operational issues, and even locker room policies.

The organization must put specific plans in place to address crises as they arise. Without proper preparation for a crisis, public perception will usually be negative. Preparation procedures should be kept as simple and straightforward as possible to establish early and regular communication during a crisis. The main objective of any crisis plan should be to quickly and accurately communicate information that can minimize damage to the sport organization's reputation. To begin preparing for a crisis, sport public relations professionals should follow several key steps (see figure 10.3).

To begin, sport public relations professionals should conduct research within the organization.

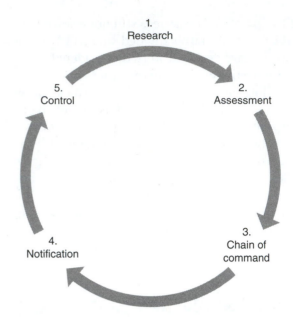

Figure 10.3 Steps in crisis management.

The organization's philosophy for managing the crisis and the makeup of a crisis team should be determined through consultations at all levels of management. The crisis team is instrumental in managing any crisis situation, and its assessment efforts should include predicting and analyzing crisis situations that could arise (crises vary based on the nature of the sport entity). To guide personnel during the crisis, the organization should establish a clear chain of command that specifies roles for leaders and others. Procedures should also be outlined for notifying the crisis team when a crisis occurs. Staff should make any necessary modifications in standard operating procedure to control for any issues or risks that might occur.

Crisis Kit

Sport public relations professionals should prepare a crisis kit. Key components of the kit include a media relations checklist (including guidelines for dealing with the media), a synopsis of policies and procedures, the crisis strategy, and contact information for key personnel. All information in the kit should be checked regularly for accuracy.

Sport public relations personnel should prepare key members of the crisis team to interact with the media; for example, key personnel should rehearse the crisis plan. Public relations professionals should also work diligently to create a cooperative environment with the media during

A LIFETIME OF PR AND CRISIS COMMUNICATION EXPERIENCE

David Cooper
Owner
MVP Communications

Since his freshman year at the University of Arizona nearly three decades ago, David Cooper has worked in sport PR roles. He started as a student intern in the athletics department's sports information office; then interned for the NFL's Arizona Cardinals (which were known as the Phoenix Cardinals at the time); and then worked as a media relations intern for the NBA's Phoenix Suns, where he was fortunate enough to experience the Suns playing in the NBA Finals against legendary Michael Jordan's Chicago Bulls. Through these experiences, Cooper said that he learned to "roll up your sleeves and do the job nobody else wants to do. I learned more about sports business from clipping newspaper articles, making copies, running errands, and staying late to get the job done; it all paid off. This advice stands the test of time. Also, some great advice [I received at the time] was to treat the security guards and concession workers as you would the star athlete. This, too, is relevant in PR as it is *all* about relationships. Understanding 'relations' in public relations is critical."

Now the owner of his own New York City-based PR consultancy firm, MVP Communications, Cooper's path in the sport PR industry has been quite varied. Following his internship with the Suns, he took on a media relations assistant role with the team and spent the 1996 off-season serving as a publicist for the Lithuanian Olympic basketball team on a tour through the United States. At age 25, he took on the role of vice president of communications for the Arena Football League (AFL), which was still a fairly new league looking to gain public attention and legitimacy at the time.

David Cooper, owner of MVP Communications.

Photo courtesy of David Cooper.

According to Cooper, "Representing a niche league fighting to gain relevancy, I learned that credibility is more valuable than temporary hype. My PR efforts were based in that principle—I ended up getting first-ever feature stories across media as the league itself secured a number of credibility-building firsts: ABC national TV contract, NFL ownership, and former player turned NFL MVP and Super Bowl champion in Kurt Warner." Cooper described old-school pitching tactics such as sending pitch letters and media materials via FedEx next-day delivery to outlets such as *Sports Illustrated* and *USA Today*. His efforts to gain mainstream media attention for the league were successful, placing stories in outlets such as the two previously mentioned as well as *Businessweek* and NBC's *Dateline* program.

He then moved on to another league, the NBA, serving as the senior director of marketing communications for the league. During this time, Cooper dealt with many crisis situations, one being when NBA referee Tim Donaghy was involved in a gambling scandal in which he bet on games he was officiating. Cooper said that instead of freezing up or providing minimal information about the situation, as some sport organizations do during crises, the NBA used its commissioner, David Stern, to move fast and get in front of the crisis. Cooper's personal crisis communication philosophy is: "Be swift, tell the truth, and make it count," which he had an opportunity to demonstrate in this situation. Cooper explains, "We called a press conference in New York City and told dozens of media and all those watching

(continued)

(continued)

that the situation involved a rogue individual, the league was on top of the situation, investigating, cooperating with all federal authorities, and that there would be no interruption. He [Stern] divulged information about the history of this referee and the league's handling of prior situations, he addressed the league's policy around gambling, and he debunked speculative commentary in the media. The game was intact. This was a very serious situation, but a lesson in PR crisis is to be present and accessible. This allows for less fear and speculation. He demonstrated strength and how the values of the league demanded such action and attention. He took questions and gave clear answers."

Along with his work handling crises such as the Tim Donaghy gambling scandal, Cooper was also instrumental in some of the NBA's community relations efforts. He was part of the group that launched the NBA Cares program, which highlights players' impact in their communities. For example, the Phoenix Suns run a "Back to School Backpack Drive" that donates backpacks and school supplies for Phoenix-area children in need. Cooper said that his involvement with NBA Cares taught him "the power of purpose over profit."

Cooper's next move was to join high-profile PR firm Coyne Communications as its vice president of sports and media. Of this experience, Cooper said, "Here I found the value in partnership, bringing people and companies together for a common cause. I also learned what it was like to work in an agency environment. At the end of the day in PR you're always serving someone's agenda, so we are all serving clients whether you're in house or at an agency." He also said that he learned the value of building relationships across media genres and platforms such as sport, business, tech, lifestyle media, bloggers, influencers, and social media. According to Cooper, "In today's new media world, a PR practitioner is best served as a generalist when it comes to media—adept at working with all different kinds."

With regard to influencers, Cooper assisted two sport properties, the U.S. Golf Association (USGA) and Ironman, develop their own influencer programs. He was successful in engaging nongolf personalities such as WWE superstar The Miz and NFL Hall of Famer Joe Montana to serve as ambassadors for the USGA. "Both celebrity athlete influencers took to social media in a big way posting videos and images on Twitter, Instagram, and Facebook, to their more than 7 million combined followers, and engagement was extremely high compared to similar posts in the past," said Cooper.

Over the course of his career, Cooper has witnessed massive changes in sport PR and media. He cites the most significant changes as the 24-7 media cycle; the death (or downsizing) of many traditional media outlets in favor of bloggers, social media, podcasts, influencers, and freelancers; and the speed with which media outlets choose to report stories instead of waiting to learn all the facts. He also cites the need for content creation as a major change for sport PR professionals in the digital age, stating that it "has changed the way PR professionals conduct strategy and tactical business. We have to be more creative with how we cut through clutter, and social media allows PR practitioners new avenues to distribute [content]. In order to build on a story, it is important to look at all avenues."

In addition to running his own PR consultancy firm, Cooper also serves as an adjunct professor at New York University, where he teaches several sport PR courses at both the undergraduate and graduate level. His biggest piece of advice to students who hope to pursue a career in sport PR is being able to write efficiently and effectively. "Unfortunately, in this day, when 140+ characters has replaced the five paragraph essay, students are ill-equipped, and I hope that changes," said Cooper. "Writing is a fundamental PR skill. There is real importance in our words, and in a PR sense, using them to build the messages that motivate people to action, inspire, and influence them around a cause or initiative." He also strongly encourages students to gain experience through volunteering or internships, to network, and to invest in themselves by gaining the necessary skills to succeed in the industry.

a crisis. Existing media relationships may be key in managing the crisis, and personnel should be responsive and accessible to the media. In contrast, failing to return phone calls or using statements such as "no comment" may intensify the situation. Sport public relations professionals should strive to meet the demands of the organization while also providing the media with needed information.

Sport entities sometimes face crises that could tarnish their image by creating unfavorable perceptions in the minds of the media and key constituents. In this context, a crisis is anything that threatens a sport entity's image. Crises can arise anytime as the result of various factors. Sport public relations professionals must be prepared to manage a crisis situation when it occurs to maintain a favorable image among key constituents.

CHAPTER WRAP-UP

Summary

This chapter examines the public relations aspect of sport communication and details the central role that it plays in the field; it also provides an analysis of crisis communication in sport. Public relations centers on managing the information flow between an organization and its key publics. The value of public relations to a sport entity should not be overlooked, especially when it is trying to sway public opinion in a favorable manner. As this chapter illustrates, public opinion is instrumental in cultivating favorable relationships with key constituents; for example, it has been instrumental for numerous sport entities in securing financing for new stadium ventures. Public opinion has also played a key role in causing entities to implement certain organizational policies to maintain favorable relationships. For example, concerns over different forms of abuse in sport (e.g., psychological, physical, sexual) led to the creation of the U.S. Center for SafeSport, which is a nonprofit organization offering resources and training to help recognize and prevent abuse in sport as well as reporting mechanisms for those who experienced or witnessed abuse.

In more specific terms, this chapter details the theory and practice of sport public relations. It provides special focus on persuasion, message development, and image building through effective management of sport media. It also addresses strategies for effectively managing the media by using traditional media relations techniques (e.g., press releases, press conferences, media kits, fact sheets), applying digital public relations techniques (e.g., social media, digital videos, and online influencers), and implementing community relations initiatives. The chapter concludes with an examination of crisis communication for sport organizations and outlines strategies for managing crisis situations both internally and externally. Effective public relations is central to the success of a sport entity, and maintaining positive relations with key constituents should be a primary public relations goal.

Review Questions

1. How should sport public relations professionals cultivate relationships with the media?

2. How should a press release be written, and what information needs to be given?

3. How should organizations develop a crisis management plan? Why is a crisis management plan integral to protecting the overall image of a sport-focused organization?

4. What are the models of public relations, and how are they illustrated in the sport industry?

5. What changes to traditional sport public relations have occurred due to digital media?

Individual Exercises

1. Select a sport entity, and conduct a brief analysis of its presence on social media (e.g., Twitter, Facebook, Instagram). What type of content is posted? What target audiences appear to be addressed? What do the posts say about the organization's public relations strategies?

2. Select two sport teams from the same league (e.g., two NFL teams), and visit each team's website. Find the section of their website dedicated to community relations, and study the types of community programs each team offers. How are these programs similar? Different? How do you think the characteristics and needs of each team's community contribute to the types of community relations programs offered?

Photo courtesy of Paul M. Pedersen.

CHAPTER 11

Sport Communication Research

LEARNING OBJECTIVES

- To recognize the functions of sport communication research in the practical and theoretical arenas
- To learn about the historical growth and expansion of research in industry and academia
- To consider the uses of ratings, analytics, and other forms of research in the media and sport communication industries
- To consider diverse options for researchers in sport communication and understand the steps in the research process
- To understand the significance of research in the evolving field of sport communication

KEY TERMS

academic research

audience research

industry research

qualitative document analysis

rhetorical criticism

semiotics

sport communication research

textual analysis

RESEARCHER AND LEADER IN ACADEMIC SPORT COMMUNICATION

Marie Hardin

Marie Hardin is a leading researcher in the field of sport communication who has done pioneering work on Title IX and women in sport. Currently dean of the Penn State College of Communications, she is also a renowned force in administration and makes key decisions about the future of journalism education. With Hardin's leadership, Penn State's College of Communications offers five undergraduate majors and two graduate programs, as well as a certificate in sports journalism, and online programs.

Hardin's longstanding and exemplary experience in sport communication is evident in her publications, awards, and reputation. She has authored more than 80 journal articles and book chapters and coedited the *Routledge Handbook of Sport and New Media* (Billings & Hardin, 2014). In 2013, the University of Georgia Grady College of Journalism and Mass Communication named her a distinguished alumni scholar for her work on issues of diversity, ethics, and professionalism in sport journalism and media. Hardin has also won numerous research awards at national and international academic conferences.

According to Hardin, "sport communication research has both progressed and evolved." In particular, she attributes the "remarkable" progress made in the last decade to the "birth of the new sport-focused journals, the development of new sport-focused groups within our largest academic organizations, and the general movement of our research into a great deal

Marie Hardin.

Photo courtesy of Penn State.

more respectability within the larger communication realm." She observed that research has expanded from using "simple content analyses and surveys . . . to more sophisticated and useful theoretically driven research that connects much more powerfully across the fields of communication, sociology, and psychology." She suggested that students reflect on areas of interest, including fandom, production, or content. "The questions should drive method," she said. "When we allow our attachment to certain methods to drive our questions, we limit what we can do." As far as gender research goes, Hardin said that the field needs fewer content analyses and "a much better handle on the intersection between gender norms, fandom, and sport consumption."

Like many scholars in sport communication, Hardin recognizes the practical importance of interdisciplinary research, which informs industry. "Sport communication, for its producers and consumers, has always occupied a room that is unique in many ways," she said. "The growth of research in this field is important because it addresses key issues that intersect with many areas. The research is, we hope, useful to the professions as they seek to create more positive impact, and, of course, to the academy, where future practitioners are being taught." The scholarly work that Hardin has done over the years in the field of sport communication relates to many of the areas covered in this chapter.

This chapter addresses research from two perspectives—that of industry practitioners and that of academic researchers. Both are important to the sport industry. Knowledge is power, and research enables sport communication practitioners to do their jobs better to meet or surpass their goals. Research enables investigators in more theoretical arenas to provoke inquiry and to bolster sport communication's legitimacy in academia. Together, industry practitioners and academic researchers can work to promote sport communication and establish it as one of the most important fields in sport, communication, and culture. See figure 11.1 for an illustration of how research fits into the Strategic Sport Communication Model (SSCM).

As previous chapters have indicated, sport influences and intersects with all aspects of American life. From politics and business to legal and social issues, sport reflects, reinforces, and shapes cultural values. Because sport is a microcosm of society, it is important to study both the practical arena of industry and the theoretical arena of research, which studies various components of sport communication from sociocultural, historical, and political perspectives. In addition to studying sport from a broad, macroscopic point of view, we should also focus on the media because of their powerful effect on sport and society. Today's fragmented and digital media landscape and increased range of choices have led to greater pressure on the media to capture a targeted audience for advertisers and for overall sustainability. Today, individuals can read sports sections and magazines; listen to sport radio and podcasts; watch nightly sportscasts or shows; stream global sporting events; and check the Internet via a tablet or mobile device for scores, supplemental sport information, and event highlights.

In such a transitory landscape, research can elucidate factors and implications relevant to the media, to media workers, and to the audience. Because of the extensive scope of research, it is most effective to use a broad definition of it. Jones (2015) defined *research* as "a systematic process of discovery and advancement of human knowledge" (p. 3). The definition we use here goes one step further by applying it to sport communication. **Sport communication research**, then, is the process by which sport communication practitioners and scholars initiate, discover, and expand knowledge of sport communication texts, audiences, and institutions (see figure 11.2). This definition is appropriate for both industry and academia because it applies to the media industry, sport organizations, academics, and students.

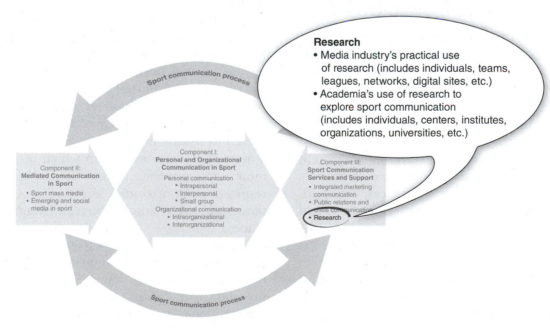

Figure 11.1   Research fits into the Strategic Sport Communication Model.

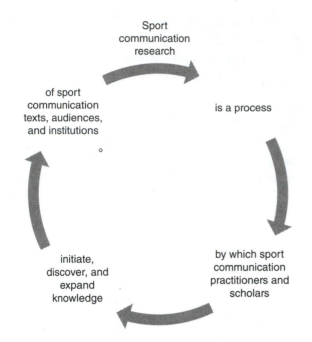

Figure 11.2   Definition of sport communication research and components to study.

This chapter begins with a discussion of how both the media and sport industries use research. It then discusses the uses of research in academia and the specifics of writing research and choosing methodologies in sport communication.

PRACTICAL RESEARCH IN THE MEDIA INDUSTRY

Industry practitioners use research in a wide variety of ways, many of which have been detailed by Folkerts and Lacy (2004). As they and other scholars have indicated, the uses and opportunities for media research are practically infinite, especially for media institutions, advertising agencies, and corporations that use the media as a vehicle to reach targeted audiences. Media management uses research in various ways, such as determining audiences' programming preferences, determining advertising costs, and deciding what news and information choices to offer to audiences.

For example, research shows what advertisers will spend in a specific medium. The Alliance for Audited Media, founded as the Audit Bureau of Circulations in 1914, offers cross-media verification across web, mobile, email, and print platforms ("Alliance for Audited Media," n.d.). It is a nonprofit organization consisting of publishers, advertisers, advertising agencies, and advertising technology providers that delivers audited cross-media metrics, digital consulting, and information services to media companies. AAM provides "independently verified data and information critical to evaluating and purchasing media" ("Alliance for Audited Media," n.d.). Such information serves what Meyer (2002) referred to as *the need for precision journalism*, or the importance of social-scientific research methods in creating news stories.

In addition, most newspapers use computer-assisted reporting (CAR), which uses statistics from existing databases to determine specific patterns. In the current age of "big data," the long-standing practice of CAR has hit the mainstream due to its powerful results. Prominent newspapers such as the *New York Times* have CAR teams, which began as a practice even before the web appeared. Indeed, for decades, media researchers have recognized the importance of social science and data analysis in their use of spreadsheets, database software, and online resources.

In recent years, however, journalists' jobs have come to involve new patterns and elements, such as data journalism, computational journalism, news apps, and data visualization. News apps and data visualization involve publishing formats that combine graphics and information from databases. They share processes with CAR, data journalism, and computational journalism, which use computers and their processing power for reporting and storytelling. Even as technology has affected both the conceptualization and the execution of journalism content, it has also propelled a fervent passion for understanding the audience (McGregor, 2013). Advocates of data-driven decisions believe that metrics promote a more democratic system in which readers are more important than editors (Fitts, 2015). As a result, newsroom culture and decision-making processes have changed across the digital landscape.

Today, media outlets seek to analyze individuals' changing news consumption habits, which influence gatekeepers' decisions about producing and disseminating the news and, in turn, the maintenance of an informed society (Mitchell, 2015). As more and more users find stories through search engines and social media rather than home pages, news organizations increase their efforts to track users' habits and to personalize news delivery (Colhoun, 2015). Google, Facebook, and Amazon have long collected data about users through demographic targeting. Now, newsrooms are catching up by using tools such as Chartbeat, Visual Revenue, and Google Analytics to target readers.

In fact, sociologist Caitlin Petre, who spent months at the *New York Times* and Gawker, suggests that newsrooms increasingly behave more like advertisers by targeting content for readers (Colhoun, 2015, para. 6): "Where did they [readers] come from? Do they stick around on our site? Do they look at other articles? How long do they spend looking at our stuff? When they come back, do they come back directly to us or do they come back through Drudge again? It's that sort of mapping the flow of the users behavior." This way, journalists and editors can measure impact and tailor content through technology. While some believe this approach creates a more democratic news process, others worry that "demographically targeted news" creates a new set of journalistic biases (Colhoun, 2015).

Newspapers continue to work out how to use digital subscriptions, paywalls, and marketing plans. The *Wall Street Journal* began charging readers for digital content in 1996, and the *New York Times* did so in 2011. Because the *Times* was viewed by many as the "nation's premier newspaper," its move to charge for access carried massive implications (Shapiro, Hiatt, & Hoyt, 2015). With the hybrid "metered" model, readers can read a certain number of articles per month for free but then must pay to access additional content. To entice paying readers, news organizations have sought to instill a sense of value in the premium content by filling it with new and particularly interesting stories. By August 2019, the *Times* had more than 3.8 million digital subscribers (4.7 million in all) and seeks to have more than 10 million total subscriptions by 2025 (Tracy, 2019). Operating profits, though, declined to $37.9 million from $40 million the year prior. Hundreds of other newspapers have also adopted paywalls to boost profitability and readership; examples include the *Los Angeles Times*, the *Houston Chronicle*, the *Philadelphia Inquirer*, and the *Star Tribune* of Minneapolis (Shapiro et al., 2015).

Organizations such as the Pew Research Center help newspapers and other outlets understand key issues, trends, and preferences. The Pew center tracks the diversifying news industry longitudinally and monitors variations and trends in media consumption and use. As noted on its website ("About Pew Research Center," n.d.), the center is a "nonpartisan [and nonprofit] fact tank that informs the public about the issues, attitudes, and trends shaping America and the world." Its mission is to "generate a foundation of facts that enriches the public dialogue and supports sound decision making" through "public opinion polling, demographic research, content analysis, and other data-driven social science research." More specifically, the organization studies "politics and policy; journalism and media; [the] Internet; science and technology; religion and public life; Hispanic trends; global attitudes and trends; and U.S. social and demographic trends."

The Pew Center's annual study, *State of the News Media*, enables researchers to analyze questions about the interrelationship of information and democracy (Mitchell, 2015). The center studies both legacy platforms (e.g., newspapers, local television) and new forms of media (e.g., podcasting, digital media, alternative outlets). For instance, the 2018 version of the study reported 8 percent and 9 percent losses, respectively, in U.S. newspaper circulations for weekday and Sunday editions, the lowest levels since 1940. Conversely, there was an 8 percent increase for cable TV's prime-time news' combined average audience. Revenue increased 4 percent for Fox News, CNN, and MSNBC combined. Only cable news saw its audience increase in 2018. The average audience for local TV news dropped that year, down 10 percent for morning news and 14 percent for late night and evening news time slots (Barthel, 2019). The study also investigates the revenue picture for U.S. journalism and the importance of advertising and audience revenue.

The U.S. news industry generates $63 billion to $65 billion annually in revenue (Holcomb & Mitchell, 2014), and the landscape is dominated increasingly by digital reporting. Organizations such as Vice, the *Huffington Post*, Politico, BuzzFeed, Gawker, Bleacher Report, and Vox have expanded the industry and cultivated new forms of storytelling and documentary styles, as well as crowdsourcing (Jurkowitz, 2014). Although some think of the content on Buzzfeed as "frivolous click bait," Pew found that smaller digital outlets are filling gaps in local news and investigative journalism and that larger digital outlets are investing in global coverage (Jurkowitz, 2014).

Digital organizations hire both legacy and non-legacy journalists; for example, 80 percent of journalists at the Institute for Nonprofit News transferred from legacy media. Editors at digital outlets are also hiring younger reporters with digital skills and experience. Solvency at these outlets is in flux until a reliable digital news business model is put in place (Jurkowitz, 2014); however, digital advertising continues to grow, especially in mobile advertising spending, which benefits social media and technology companies such as Google, Facebook, Microsoft, Yahoo!, and AOL. In Pew's 2018 report, revenue from advertising on all digital platforms rose 23 percent from the prior year and comprised nearly half of all ad revenue in the United States. Overall, digital ad revenue has tripled since 2011, the first year it was tracked, according to research firm eMarketer (Barthel, 2019).

Such industry trends are studied by many organizations. For example, the Poynter Institute for Media Studies conducted an EyeTrack study of tablet storytelling, which revealed how people interacted with news when using an iPad. Poynter's study, titled *Core Skills for the Future of Journalism* and conducted by Finberg and Klinger (2014), posed questions to educators, practitioners, and students. It identified 37 key skills for journalists in the digital and mobile age. The research was based on the Future of Journalism Competencies survey, which received more than 2,900 responses. The top-rated skill overall was accuracy, followed by curiosity. Discrepancies appeared between practitioners and academics in regard to knowledge, attitudes, and personal features; a number of factors, however, were valued by both groups, including grammar, ability to meet deadlines, news judgment, ethics, and knowledge of current events. The researchers synthesized tips, techniques, and resources for teaching the identified core skills, thus advancing the conversation about qualifications for success in the future of digital journalism.

SNL Kagan, an offering of S&P Global Market Intelligence, also studies trends in media and communication and offers insight into broadcast, wireless, Internet, film, and global programming (SNL Kagan, n.d.). In addition, a variety of other companies—including Nielsen, comScore, Adobe Analytics, Chartbeat, and Experian Hitwise—compute digital traffic to help organizations understand audience behavior (Sasseen, Olmstead, & Mitchell, 2013). Nielsen provides statistics for television, radio, and digital media and studies consumers in more than 100 countries to assess trends and habits in viewing and buying ("About Nielsen," n.d.). Former CEO Mitch Barns (David Kenny is current CEO) inaugurated the Nielsen News Center, which addresses themes such as population shifts; the rise of the middle class; media and retail fragmentation; and marketing, privacy, and security in the age of big data ("Nielsen Total Audience," 2015).

Another example is comScore, which measures individuals' use of digital space and provides audience, advertising, and enterprise analytics (comScore, 2016); according to the firm's website, it measures more than 1.9 trillion global interactions monthly ("comScore Facts at a Glance," n.d.). It uses Unified Digital Measurement (UDM) methodology to study the size of audiences and Media Metrix to reveal consumption habits. These and other means give organizations an analytics advantage in a competitive arena. Each month, comScore ranks top websites according to unique visitors, and the list usually includes sport sites such as ESPN, Yahoo! Sports, NBC Sports Network, Bleacher Report, Turner Sports Network, Fox Sports Digital, Sporting News Media, CBS Sports, USA Today Sports Media, SB Nation, and Deadspin. For instance, in March 2019, ESPN topped the list with 95.4 million unique visitors ("Sports Video Group Staff," 2019).

Television news stations also distribute recordings of anchors to determine audience preferences. Even movie companies use **audience research** when they test different endings to determine audience preferences (Folkerts & Lacy, 2004; Meyer, 2002).

Companies seek audience research for many reasons, mostly related to money. Although the media originally viewed themselves as public servants, they now emphasize profit. As the late Ben Bagdikian (2004) discussed in *The New Media Monopoly*, contemporary media corporations and

The broadcast of live sporting events came to a halt with the COVID-19 pandemic. With traditional sports programming, advertisers and networks seek information about audience demographics and statistics because advertising prices depend on the number of households watching or listening to particular shows.

conglomerates tend to care about profit first and foremost. In radio and television, local stations and national networks focus on ratings to lure advertisers seeking to reach coveted target demographics. In newspapers, the focus is on circulation and readers' disposable income. Newspapers seek to sell print copies and digital subscriptions to boost circulation numbers, and readers' income is important because of newspapers' reliance on advertisers, who seek to sell products to individuals at certain income levels. In new media, the emphasis falls on the number of unique visitors, as well as money spent online.

Sports readers, listeners, and audiences are especially coveted because they tend to be very loyal to certain sports, teams, and athletes and because they enable advertisers to reach the coveted 18- to 34-year-old male demographic (coveted because it has been reported that these are the ages in which males form brand loyalties). To gain information about readers, viewers, and web surfers, organizations and companies have perfected research techniques, which have evolved over the years. One of the largest trends in the sport industry has been the influence of analytics (Jensen, 2015). As mentioned earlier, media analytics is a crucial component of helping the media understand circulation, advertising, audience engagement, and targeting. When they understand what readers consume and how they consume it, the media can target content and deliver it effectively in today's fast-paced digital environment (Cherubini, 2014).

In addition to analyzing page views and unique visits, attention must also be given to qualitative metrics such as attention, engagement, and time. Publishers seek to increase the time that visitors spend reading their articles and reduce the "bounce" rate—that is, the frequency of readers disappearing after looking at one article (Marsh, 2015). Attention in today's digital universe is a precious resource (Cherubini, 2014), and the "attention web" is less about clicks per se and more about what users do once they click on a link and how they engage with the content. Such technology-driven changes have caused the media to modify the ways in which they produce, report, and disseminate the news. It is still important to build a strong brand with credibility, but the needs of sustaining profitability and keeping pace with technological advancements present their own challenges.

Even in the midst of these cultural pressures, editors and other media gatekeepers must understand that data do not replace news judgment, values, and ethics. Fortunately, newsrooms are learning how to use data efficiently and effectively in various ways. According to Andrea Iannuzzi, former executive editor of national content for the daily newspaper network at Gruppo Expresso, "Today's journalist—and more widely, anybody who produces content—who refuses to use data analytics to assess in real time the level of interaction he or she is having with the readers is someone who has decided not to turn on the light . . . [but instead to] stay in the dark room" (Cherubini, 2014).

The next section discusses how interest in ratings, circulation data, and web use developed, as well as the methods used for studying these issues in sport and media organizations.

The Nielsen Company (Nielsen Holdings, PLC)

Nielsen's mission is to "provide clients with the most complete understanding of what consumers watch and buy" ("Corporate Profile," 2016). Nielsen's Buy segment provides measurement and analytics on sales, market share, and consumer goods to retailers, whereas Nielsen's Watch segment provides media and advertising clients with audience measurement across television, radio, online, and mobile ("Corporate Profile," 2016). As the "global leader in both television and digital measurement," Nielsen helps its clients "reach" the "most desirable consumers"; measure the "resonance" of messages; and "quantify consumer 'reaction' in terms of sales impact" ("Corporate Profile," 2016). Nielsen Media Research, a subsidiary of Nielsen Holdings PLC, specifically provides "television audience measurement, target rating point analysis, industry survey, reporting, and media consulting services. Additionally, it offers product placement and business intelligence services" ("Company Overview," 2016). One example of Nielsen's research is "The Year in Sports Media Report: 2017." People 18 years and older consumed over 79 hours, on average, of sport content weekly, an increase of 55 percent from 2002. This increase was due largely to the increase in tablets, smartphones, and computers, further reinforcing the expansive scope of opportunities for sport across all media ("Nielsen Sports' The Year in Sports Media Report," 2017). The next section will show Nielsen's and other organizations' sampling techniques.

Sampling Techniques

In national ratings studies, Nielsen researchers conduct a representative sample. Everyone in the population possesses an equal chance of being selected for the study—a technique known as *random sampling*, which is often viewed as delivering the most representative sample. In other words, the sample represents the overall popula-

tion, and anyone in the general population could be selected to participate. In this way, random samples are intended to ensure that a study is free from bias. Other common sampling techniques in research include the following methods:

- Stratified random sampling within subgroups.
- Convenience sampling, which is based on physical and organizational proximity of respondents.
- Cluster sampling, which randomly chooses groups (not individuals).
- Systematic sampling, where every kth case is studied. Kth refers to the given interval in a population (Bostrom, 1998; Rothenbuhler, 2005). For instance, if the population is the number of students at a university (20,000) and a researcher wants to have a sample of 500, he would make a random start and choose every 40th student (Bostrom, 1998).

Stratified samples enable researchers to see if a certain attribute occurs throughout a sample. This approach is sometimes referred to as *quota sampling*, and a researcher who wants to learn about certain elements of the population must ensure that the distribution of the chosen attribute is consistent.

Convenience samples are biased in that they are affected by proximity; imagine, for instance, a researcher who wants to study sport viewing habits among 18- to 24-year-olds and tries to do so by simply using names from the Indianapolis phonebook rather than using a more regional or national sample.

Cluster samples examine certain elements of the population—for example, female collegiate athletes' perspectives toward gender equity. In this approach, the researcher could decide that each sport at a university represents one cluster and then select a small number from each team to interview. This basic cluster sample requires one step. Systematic samples can be taken once a population is determined. For instance, you might want to examine the preferences of New York Rangers season-ticket holders. To do so, you would select a random number as a starting point then select ticket holders at certain intervals for your survey or poll. One in 50 might be chosen or one in 100, depending on the sample size needed. Some researchers use the telephone book in systematic samples; however, because some individuals' numbers are unlisted, this approach may or may not work, depending on what is being studied. These are a few examples of sample techniques used in research, and the most effective method will depend on the researcher and the object of study (Bostrom, 1998).

Nielsen's Research Approach

The Nielsen firm has conducted measurement studies since 1923 and began studying television audiences in 1950. It studies the amount of TV and audio use in sample households and provides television and advertising companies with information about homes, televisions, programs, and commercials. Its consumer measurements are conducted with the use of tools that include panels, databases, certain methodologies, and technology. Meters measure engagement, panelists use in-home scanners to record purchases, and surveys are used in evaluating topics such as retail markets or the digital landscape. In 2013, Nielsen acquired Arbitron, a research firm that specialized in radio and audio. Rebranded as Nielsen Audio, this service reveals information about listeners' radio and lifestyle choices and helps radio stations tailor programs to target consumers' preferences.

Nielsen studies 40 percent of the world's viewing behavior—channels, programs, and viewers. Through this information, Nielsen's clients can maximize programs' and advertisements' efficacy with audiences. In the United States alone, $80 billion is spent on television advertising ("Television," 2016).

Uche Onyewu, Nielsen's director of data science, understands why people may be skeptical about Nielsen's ability to measure media engagement and shopping habits without engaging each of the 325 million people living in the United States. He believes that Nielsen's panels offer insight into consumer behavior of the greater population due to Nielsen's rigorous data science and statistical sampling methods on panels and surveys. Simplistically, he defines *sampling* as a statistical means of measuring a given population with the intent to accurately extend the measurement to represent a larger population (2019). The two methods, probability and nonprobability-based sampling, are described as follows: In the former, everyone in a population has an equal chance of being selected to participate; in the latter, some people have a greater or lesser chance. The integrity of a sample relies on the level of detail that was used in preparing it. In Nielsen's radio measurement, more than 100 critical processes are part of Nielsen's Portable People Meter (PPM) and Audio Diary measurement services, which are performed daily, weekly, monthly, quarterly, and annually to have the most representative sample possible. According to Onyewu, "It's true that we're living in a world in which technology, cookies, return-path data, likes, playlist algorithms and myriad other digital markers leave 'footprints' wherever our online lives take us. But much of that data isn't complete. Much of that data carries bias. Much of that data wasn't meant to be used for measurement. Personal-level information, however, remains the definitive source for true measurement. And sampling is the key to unlocking person-level, representative measurement" (2019).

In the 2019-2020 TV season, Nielsen estimates there are 120.6 million TV homes, according to Nielsen's National Television Household Universe Estimates ("Nielsen Estimates," 2019). Nielsen studies viewing habits of a cross section of households across the United States with the use of national and local People Meters (LPM) and the collection of more than 2 million paper diaries during sweeps periods in February, May, July, and November. The People Meter is a box equipped with buttons and lights for each household member and a remote control for easy use; viewers push a button when they begin watching a program, and the box records which shows are watched and who is watching them. Unlike the People Meter, of course, diaries measure only what viewers write in their logs.

Nielsen also uses set-tuning meters inserted into the back of televisions in 49 of the largest television markets to record what viewers watch. Television meters in local markets monitor when televisions are on, as well as which stations are chosen, and send that information to a computer and modem in the form of a central black box. The data are then transferred daily to Nielsen's central computers, which store the information and use it to generate research findings. Nielsen researchers cross-check information from national and local studies and conduct audits and quality checks to maximize the accuracy of their procedures. They compare information from the national People Meter audience with information from television diaries in all local markets. Nielsen also conducts telephone coincidentals, which involves calling randomly selected numbers to ask individuals if they are watching television and, if so, who in the household is watching. Nielsen reports its results in terms of both ratings and shares, which indicate how viewership is divided between channels and markets.

In recent years, Nielsen has modified and updated its procedures and equipment. It uses electronic and proprietary meter technology to study viewing habits. This includes time-shifted viewing, which is viewing recorded programs up to seven days after original broadcast dates. Nielsen also studies video content on mobile devices through panels, which use census-style data from third parties to examine consumer use. Tuning behavior during programs and ads also informs companies about audience engagement, impact, efficiency, and returns on investment as far as commercial blocks and markets are concerned.

To improve accuracy in a fragmented media world, Nielsen increased sample sizes in local television markets and introduced electronic capabilities in other markets. It used ratings stabilization in LPM markets to "mitigate ratings fluctuations that are caused by panel variability, as opposed to true differences in viewing behavior" (Baumgartner, 2015), which boosted the quality similar to the way doubling a panel size would. These enhancements and others diminish the number of zero cells, or network time slots where no viewers were recorded. Nielsen also introduced the "unidentified audience," which occurs when the television is on but no viewer has checked in using the People Meter. Nielsen uses a person's data where the data is complete and a "new viewer assignment" to fill in data that is missing. In markets with ratings stabilization, demographic viewing is based on viewer assignment, a statistical technique that assigns which household members are watching specific programs. These replaced handwritten diaries and are much more accurate.

In addition to electronic measurement using code readers, Nielsen doubled the sample size of the Nielsen People Meter panel from 12,500 homes to more than 25,000 homes with a gross sample size of more than 35,000. The larger sample size decreased zero cells and thereby improved ratings stability. Additionally, it enabled measurement of targeted sales demos, networks, programs, and platforms with more precision. According to Sara Erichson, Nielsen's executive vice president, the multiprong strategy with increased panels, statistical techniques, and big data "will ensure the continued really solid, highly representative accuracy of the foundation of our TV ratings data" (Baumgartner, 2015).

More recently, Nielsen overhauled the way it measures viewing in the 208 local U.S. markets. Panels, new meters, and return path data from 2 million households replaced paper diaries, and Nielsen measured 15 million homes through return path data alone as of 2019. Catherine Herkovic, executive VP and managing director of Nielsen Local TV, said to *Broadcasting & Cable*, "We have built a business on trust, integrity and transparency. Our local TV measurement solutions reflect this with innovative technology and big data, validated by scientifically designed panels for TV and cross platform measurement" (Lafayette, 2019). This local viewing information helps local stations sell advertising and facilitates a transition from ratings to impressions as the foundation of Nielsen's data calculations.

In other developments, Nielsen launched Total Audience in 2015, which measures all video content and advertising across linear and digital platforms. Nielsen Digital Audio Ratings, a component of Total Audience, measures over-the-air radio listening across mobile apps and web players, smartphones, tablets, and computers ("Nielsen Launches Digital Audio Ratings," 2016). The service collects data on over 2,500 station streams across all 48 PPM (Portable People Meter) markets and measures the extension of broadcast radio into streaming markets. Measurement for custom-curated and on-demand audio arose in 2016 ("Nielsen Launches Digital Audio Ratings," 2016).

In 2019, Nielsen launched continuous diary measurement, CDM, in 46 of its audio markets. CDM puts radio in a comparative field with digital and television and allows clients to maintain an edge with the capacity to react to market changes. It also helps minimize bounce in ratings with its rolling samples and their consistent view of the market ("Continuous Diary Measurement," 2019). Brian Kaminsky, president of revenue and data operations at iHeartMedia, said, "With monthly Nielsen ratings in these diary markets, radio is giving its advertisers the most timely and relevant information possible and will have more stable and actionable insights for how audiences are engaging with our content" ("Continuous Diary Measurement," 2019). Digital advertising offers close to real-time metrics; television is moving to a year-round model, so audio must stay relevant ("Nielsen Audio," 2018).

Nielsen also launched its Podcast Listener Buying Power Service in 2019. Clients can profile shows by programs' titles that are gathered from subscribers, connecting specific listeners with advertisers and program information and insights. This service from Nielsen Scarborough has a sample of more than 30,000 respondents and has insights on podcasts across 18 genres, over 2,000 retail categories, and hundreds of brand-name advertisers. The data helps clients, advertisers, and agencies all maximize financial growth ("Audioboom Reaches," 2019).

Nielsen also studies social TV, which includes the digital dialogue about TV. Nielsen Social tracks more than 250 TV channels in the United States and uses a web-based platform and Twitter TV application programming interfaces to measure and analyze Twitter TV conversation and other consumer experiences ("Social TV," 2015). Nielsen Twitter TV ratings measure Twitter activity addressing TV shows, as well as the number of people viewing the tweets. Nielsen has found a strong correlation between Twitter TV engagement and engagement with programming among the viewing audience (Flomenbaum, 2015). In Nielsen's study, changes in Twitter TV activity were 80 percent correlated with neurological engagement—that is, emotion, memory, and attention were all tied to Twitter TV activity—which suggests that advertising could have better memorability and sales outcomes (Flomenbaum, 2015). Nielsen studied tweeting around eight cable television shows that historically had shown different levels of Twitter activity and television ratings. Meanwhile, Nielsen Neuro measured

emotion, memory, and attention to track engagement with the shows (Flomenbaum, 2015). As a result, agencies and advertisers can use Twitter data when making purchasing decisions ("Social TV," 2015). In 2016, Nielsen launched Social Content Ratings, which measures program-related activities across Twitter, Facebook, and Instagram ("Nielsen Social," 2016).

Despite these efforts, Nielsen has been the subject of criticism over the years. According to the *Wall Street Journal*'s Steven Perlberg (2015), Nielsen is the "TV industry's favorite scapegoat." For example, former Viacom CEO Philippe Dauman said that Nielsen has "not caught up to the marketplace" in measuring usage on devices such as gaming systems, mobile phones, and digital technology (Perlberg). Nielsen, however, maintains that "its comprehensive and innovative online methodologies analyze consumer behavior and trends, advertising effectiveness, brand advocacy, social media buzz, and more to provide a 360-degree view of how consumers engage with online media" ("Online," 2015). In the United States alone, Nielsen's online panel measures the actions of more than 200,000 Internet users across 30,000 sites; worldwide, it studies 500,000 panelists. This Total Internet Audience metric studies digital media across all devices and locations, both in the United States and worldwide ("Online," 2015); the hybrid audience measurement includes a representative panel across diverse demographics. Nielsen's tags on publishers' web pages offer measurement of content, and a statistical process then matches demographic attributes with behavior across all studied sites. This process provides information about page-level actions and audience data based on the panel and thus promotes keen analysis ("Online," 2015).

To improve efficiency, Nielsen measures streaming services (e.g., Netflix, Amazon Prime's Instant Video) by analyzing the audio file of programs to report viewing results back to networks (Perlberg, 2015). Nielsen and Roku, Inc. also joined forces so Nielsen can measure video advertising delivered to Roku streaming players and TV models ("Friends With Benefits," 2015). In other deals, Nielsen's initiative with Dish Network helped improve its ratings systems. In the 2016 deal to license set-top-box data from Dish,

Nielsen paired the data with its traditional panel measurements. This helped silence criticisms of its methods, sample size, and capacity to measure smaller markets. Nielsen previously had not reported data for programs with less than 10,000 viewers; however, Dish's data changed this. It also enabled Nielsen to compete with rival comScore's Rentrak in smaller markets, where Rentrak has lower prices and more precise set-top-box data (Gottfried, 2016).

In 2018, Dish chose Nielsen for digital ad measurement for Dish television and Sling TV, its streaming service. Dish adds this to its use of Nielsen's TV Ratings Service and Nielsen Digital in TV ratings for Sling's audience measurement (Aycock, 2018). Nielsen's ratings system has been the "gold standard" and the "currency upon which ads are bought and sold largely because of the company's unique ability to directly collect detailed demographic information on viewers" (Gottfried, 2016).

Uses for Data

Nielsen offers programmers, advertisers, and agencies crucial information about television audiences. Regardless of whether ratings companies use the diary, interview, meter, or other methods, Nielsen integrates the data to determine circulation, or the number of people watching or listening to a show at a certain time. Media buyers use this information to work with advertising agencies in formulating media strategy. The amount that advertisers charge is generally a "negotiated rate per thousand viewers multiplied by the Nielsen . . . audience estimate (in thousands)" ("What TV," 2006). *Cost per thousand* (CPM) refers to the amount that an advertiser must spend to reach a thousand audience members. Noncommercial stations also use Nielsen research to make programming decisions (Turow, 1997). To serve a similar purpose in regard to print publica-

Photo courtesy of Robby General.

Here, Clemson coach Dabo Swinney poses with the national championship trophy after defeating Alabama in the College Football Playoff National Championship. Despite the 44-16 lopsided win, the game had massive TV ratings according to Nielsen's final numbers. Out-of-home viewing and computer and mobile streaming were also high.

tions, quantitative research from MediaMark or Simmons Market Research Bureau provides the "pass-along rate" or "average number of people who read an issue" of a given periodical (Turow, 1997, p. 133). *Sports Business Journal* and other publications regularly share information about sports programming and websites with their subscribers, telling readers which sport shows, networks, and websites score highest during each month or quarter.

Although Nielsen has a long-standing presence and reputation, the competition is increasing for this type of service. Challengers include Rentrak, the audience research company that created President Barack Obama's 2012 media strategy. It launched a sport division in 2015 to compete with Nielsen in the sport measurement business. Rentrak executives want a share of the sport marketing research sector, which they believe is worth $60 million per year. By way of comparison, in 2014, more than $20 billion was spent on sport sponsorships and $10 billion on sport media rights, according to *Sports Business Journal* (Ourand, 2015). Price Waterhouse Coopers' annual PwC Sports Outlook projects that the sport market in North America (college and professional—media rights, gate revenues, sponsorships, and merchandising) will grow to $80.3 billion in 2022, with media rights as the highest revenue stream at close to $24 billion annually ("PWC Sports Outlook," 2018). Rentrak's early clients included the NFL Network, the NHL Network, World Wrestling Entertainment (WWE), IMG, Repucom, and the Canadian Basketball League. "The audience that is watching live sports is incredibly valuable," said Rentrak's CEO Bill Livek. "Ads placed in stadiums or on TV have enormous value, but only when accurately measured" (Ourand, 2015).

Rentrak, "one of America's fastest growing research companies," studies the entertainment, advertising, and television industries with precision. It measures 125,000 screens in 25,000 theaters in 64 countries; television viewing on more than 37 million TVs; and 100 percent of the top multichannel video programming distributors ("Who We Are," 2016).

Rentrak acquired Sponsorhub in 2015, an analytics platform that offers sponsors and advertisers unique insights into sport and entertainment on social media. It tracks fans' emotions during games and tracks and measures athletes' endorsements, as well as teams and leagues' sponsorships. In entertainment, it tracks product placements in television shows and film. If a company is endorsed by a certain athlete, for instance, Sponsorhub shows how he or she trends in specific cities or parts of the country (Probasco, 2015).

Rentrak and comScore merged in January 2016 to form a cross-platform measurement company. Both companies study and unify billions of pieces of "census" data—digital, TV set-top box, movie screens, and demographic information—with the actions of millions of consumers in more than 75 countries.

In the United States, comScore measures behavior on more than 260 million desktop screens, 160 million mobile phone screens, 95 million tablet screens, 40 million television screens, 120 million video-on-demand screens, and 40,000 movie theater screens representing well over a hundred million moviegoers. "The cross-platform world is changing rapidly and this change demands relentless inventiveness, agility, and collaborative intelligence," added Serge Matta, CEO of comScore. "These are qualities on which both companies have built their success. This proven ability to precisely measure extremely fragmented, dynamic audiences in dramatic, innovative ways—and to quickly report on it—has provided the insights that allow our clients to act with great competitive advantages" ("comScore and Rentrak Complete Merger," 2016).

Rentrak collects data on what people watch by means of set-top boxes in 15 million homes. It has deals with DirecTV, Dish Network, Charter, Cox, and AT&T U-verse and will extend its business to teams and leagues with data about fans attending games (Ourand, 2015). For example, Rentrak can tell company executives how many Jeep owners live in a certain area and what programs they watch on TV (Ourand, 2015). Rentrak's Advanced Demographics enables users to target audiences. For example, the Exact-Commercial Ratings data metric gives advertisers and ad agencies valuable information on how specific commercials perform. When used within the TV Essentials service, the ratings divulge how many viewers were exposed to specific commercials in a campaign. comScore has the capacity, then, to analyze a single ad's efficacy over a campaign or longer period of time. Single commercials, networks, dayparts, duration, pods, and pod positions can all be studied and analyzed, providing companies with more in-depth information on both audiences and ads' performance levels ("Exact Commercial Ratings," 2016).

ComScore survived an earlier scandal of misreported revenue from 2013 to 2015; however, 2019 also brought instability when Bryan Wiener and Sarah Hofstetter resigned as CEO and president, respectively. The company's board demanded cuts that the executives thought would minimize their strategy to create a cross-platform measurement currency, and Rentrak appears to be overtaking comScore postmerger. In August 2019, comScore laid off 8 percent of its employees, including employees on the digital side of its business. com-Score was originally Nielsen's biggest competitor, yet today its commitment to cross-platform and digital measurement are more of a long-term, not short-term, strategy. Linear and television measurement, meanwhile, are the short-term priorities (Peterson, 2019).

Research Challenges

As mentioned earlier, increasing audience fragmentation makes research vital for local stations, networks, and cable systems and operators. Despite the need for research, however, it is difficult to measure across media, and each of the methods just discussed has limitations. Media measurement systems from comScore Media Metrix, Relevant Knowledge, Jupiter Research, and Nielsen/NetRatings all study web usage, and opinion varies on which method is most effective. The picture is also complicated by individuals' varying uses of the Internet. Whereas radio and television are used mostly for entertainment, people use the web for research, email, e-commerce, and many other reasons besides entertainment. Recognizing the need to measure more than simply the number of visitors to a website, Nielsen issues the Global Digital Landscape Report, which provides statistics about global consumers' overall digital attitudes and behaviors. As Nielsen reported, 53 percent of global respondents keep up with shows so they can join the conversation and engage on social media ("Screen Wars," 2015). Among the 2019 findings, 63 percent globally think the biggest screen is the best screen for watching video programming. Fifty-nine percent say watching programming on their mobile devices is convenient, while 53 percent say watching on a tablet is just as good as a laptop or personal computer (PC). Sixty-five percent still prefer to watch programming live. It is evident that consumers have the power to watch how, when, and where what they want ("Screen Wars," 2015).

Among the strengths of Internet research, online surveys are cheaper and quicker than traditional surveys (sent through postal mail). The Internet is also more anonymous, which generally leads participants to provide more candid and inclusive responses to delicate questions. In addition, online survey data can be collected 24-7 from individuals not reachable by mail or phone.

Effect of Television Ratings on Sport Communication

Television delivers results like no other media outlet (Shank, 2002). As Shank aptly put it, when television is "used in the right way, it can be a marketer's dream, harnessing the thrill of top-level competition for a targeted mass audience of interested and involved consumers" (p. 338). In addition, even in the midst of digital advances, TV remains at the center of U.S. media consumption ("The U.S. Digital," 2014). The reasons that companies continue to spend millions of dollars yearly on sport programming are its expansive reach and powerful influence. Sport enables a company to center its message on the audience that it wants to persuade. According to Plunkett Research (2015), annual company spending for sport advertising in 2015 totaled nearly $35 billion in the United States.

Importance of Ratings

When talking about audience, size counts. As mentioned earlier, networks and advertisers value advertising in terms of cost per thousand, or CPM, which is the cost that an advertiser must pay in to reach a thousand viewers. They also calculate cost per point (CPP), which is the cost to reach 1 percent of the entire audience. In addition to audience size, another important factor is the aggregate of houses and viewers tuning in to a program over time—that is, the reach, or "cume" (cumulative audience), which is used to indicate the "true audience for sports broadcasts" (Mullin, Hardy, & Sutton, 2000, p. 304). Sponsors look at this last factor before agreeing to long-term advertising contracts. Advertisers also care about an audience's composition or demographics. Younger males are traditionally hard to reach, and sport content of all types—from sports-talk radio to television programs—draws them in and sustains their interest (Mullin et al., 2000).

Super Bowl Ratings, the NFL, and Other Research

The Super Bowl remains the top sporting event in the United States in terms of consistently high ratings and advertising revenue. While the Kansas City Chiefs' 31-20 victory over the San Francisco

49ers in Super Bowl LIV was only the 10th most-watched Super Bowl in history with 102 million viewers across channels and streaming outlets, the Super Bowl is still the most-watched television program in the United States, according to CNN Business' Frank Pallotta. The Super Bowl had 41.6/69 household rating/share, according to Fox Sports ("Super Bowl LIV on FOX," 2020). The NFL's television viewership for the 2019 season was up approximately five percent from 2018 and it was the most-watched season in three years (Pallotta, 2020). Ratings indicate the percentage of *all* televisions tuned in to a certain show in a given market. A share, in contrast, indicates the percentage of televisions that are *on* at a certain time and tuned in to a certain show in a given market. Generally, audiences peak during the prime-time hours of the evening. Streaming coverage of the game on Foxsports.com, the Fox Sports app, FoxDeportes.com, the Fox Deportes app, the Fox NOW app, NFL Digital Properties (including NFL app, NFL Fantasy mobile app, NFL.com, the Kansas City Chiefs, and San Francisco 49ers mobile properties) and Verizon Media Mobile properties (including Yahoo! Sports mobile app) made it the most live-streamed Super Bowl to that date in history. It delivered an average minute audience of 3.4 million, up more than 30 percent from the New England Patriots' 13-3 victory over the Los Angeles Rams in Super Bowl LIII ("Super Bowl LIV on FOX," 2020).

In addition to following ratings, the NFL also seeks and values other practical communication research in a variety of areas. For instance, the league chose Sportradar, a European data company (which also has a deal with NASCAR), to serve as the league's statistics distributor. The company pays about $5 million each year for four years for the service, and the NFL now holds an equity stake in the company (Kaplan & Fisher, 2015). In 2019, the league and Sportradar agreed to a multiyear partnership in which Sportradar has exclusive rights to distribute official NFL data to legal sport betting operators in the United States and beyond (Novy-Williams, 2019). Sportradar also can distribute live NFL game videos along with odds to gambling houses outside the United States and will closely watch betting activity to preserve the integrity of the sport.

In other deals with Sportradar, the league's "next-generation stats" can indicate, for example, how fast a player runs over certain distances, which areas of the field he prefers, and how far the ball travels on a pass. These analytics supplement traditional statistics, such as yards gained or lost (Kaplan & Fisher, 2015). As part of the arrangement, Zebra Technologies produces the transmitters and tracks the data, and Sportradar sells the data. Sportradar acquired SportsData Inc. in 2014 to enter the U.S. market, rebranded as Sportradar U.S. (Kaplan & Fisher, 2015).

Armchair Analysis also has worked on NFL statistics and analysis since 2001, calling its data "NFL stats on steroids" ("NFL Stats on Steroids," n.d.). Its data has been used in stories on FiveThirtyEight.com and Sloane Sports Conference. The Ringer's Kevin Clark notes that the NFL is still behind the NBA and MLB in advanced metrics, but "football's analytics moment has arrived" (2018). He says it's partly the younger coaches and general managers in the league but also says it's the spread of NFL player-tracking data through Next Gen Stats, shared throughout the league for the first time during the 2018-2019 season. There are chips placed in players' shoulder pads that track the speed of a player's movements, whether he sprints or jogs, and the average separation between an offensive player and a defensive player (Clark, 2018). It allows teams to build models to evaluate players and plays differently and to understand the sport and game more. A team in the market for a linebacker, for example, can figure out the closing speed needed for tacklers. Zebra Technologies can provide game day data through its MotionWorks service to share information on players such as the Cowboys' Leighton Vander Esch, who reaches 16 to 17 miles per hour on plays (Clark, 2018). The Eagles have had an analytics department for over 20 years and used data on play calling to help the team win Super Bowl LII. The Vikings have an analytics hub at their practice facility. While all 32 NFL teams want to keep their strategies confidential, all use analytics. These are just a few examples of how leagues are obtaining and disseminating more precise and sophisticated information.

The league has tried to combat the perception of its coverup of brain injuries in its players as documented in *League of Denial: The NFL's Concussion Crisis*, discussed in chapter 7. It has funded research in this area, as seen in its $17 million in funding for research into concussions, and the effects of brain injuries in its current and former players. This commitment was funded for research done by the Department of Defense, TRACK-TBI (funded by NIH), and the National Institute on Aging (branch of NIH) ("NFL Allocates," 2018).

The NFL also conducts fan research and has partnered with academic researchers to explore this subject. One area is on women fans, who make up 45 percent of the league's fanbase (Baier, 2018). One such study, focused on female fans, revealed that more than 70 percent of the 1,600 women who participated in the study felt that they were "valued participants" in the NFL or in a specific NFL team. The survey also found that women want more variety in team apparel; specifically, nearly 40 percent indicated that there was not enough variety of apparel at sporting events (Broughton, 2013).

In another study of NFL fans and their game day experiences, the league commissioned in-game analyses of fans for all 32 teams throughout the season. To conduct the study, LRA Worldwide, an experiential customer service consulting and research firm, visited stadiums. The NFL has sought to improve the in-game experience for fans, and the study provided information about what worked and what did not. To do so, it studied arrivals, safety and security, game day staff, in-game enhancements and technology, game entertainment, concessions, and departures.

In yet another study, the league hired Turnkey Intelligence to poll season-ticket holders via email after four games for each team (Kaplan, 2014). Turnkey Intelligence performs research for more than 70 North American major league teams, offices, and brands. The Turnkey Intelligence survey on NFL sponsor awareness found that nearly 28 percent of respondents correctly identified Verizon as the league's official wireless sponsor; however, AT&T enjoyed the biggest increase in awareness among the 66 sponsors. This could be due in part to AT&T Stadium, home of the Dallas Cowboys, or coverage of AT&T's 2014 $48.5 billion purchase of DirecTV (Broughton, 2015).

Other research not funded by the league includes Mike Lewis' NFL Fandom Report at Emory Marketing Analytics Center and Taylor Digital sports director Samantha Baier's NFL Fan Insights Study. These are just a few examples that reveal how the NFL recognizes the importance of research for the league, its teams, key sponsors, and fans.

Photo courtesy of Robby General.

Teams seek research and vital statistics about players before drafting or trading for them. Here, Kevin Pritchard, president of basketball operations for the Indiana Pacers, and coach Nate McMillan congratulate Malcolm Brogdon as he joins the team after the Milwaukee Bucks agreed to a sign-and-trade deal, sending Brogdon to the Pacers for three future draft picks.

The NBA is another league that values research. For instance, for its annual sponsorship-loyalty study, the league aligned with Turnkey Intelligence for *Sports Business Journal's* study. The annual NBA survey sampled 400 members of a Toluna online panel who were 18 years of age or older to study recognition and impact of the NBA's corporate sponsors. Verizon was identified by 29 percent of respondents as the league's wireless provider, while State Farm had a 24 percent recognition rate in its eighth year as an NBA sponsor (Broughton, 2017).

The NBA's focus on data analytics proves its commitment to technology and progress. The league holds a yearly Hackathon with basketball and business analytics tracks and actively seeks new, talented data analysts. Teams have full-time staff working as data analysts who help identify trends that potentially improve on-court strategies and practice patterns and help general managers obtain crucial information on players and fans. For fans, they have new ways to discuss their players and teams. The NBA has a search engine powered by SAP's HANA platform that can manage 4.5 quadrillion combinations of data (Beck, 2013, as cited in Millington & Millington, 2018). The search engine includes every statistic in its history.

The boundaries between consumer and sport professional have become more obfuscated. There are CCTV cameras for fan surveillance at sporting events and market research in every area of sport culture. Cisco's StadiumVision Mobile in select American and European sport facilities delivers video and data feeds to fans throughout games in exchange for fans' information, which goes into branding and marketing decisions as well as promotions. Dataveillance, the monitoring and analyzing of consumer-produced data, enables teams to understand the demographics of their fan bases (Dorsey, 2013; Millington & Millington, 2018).

Focusing on specific teams, the Houston Rockets' general manager, Daryl Morey, is a statistician, and the team's play is data driven. The Golden State Warriors have partnered with Accenture, Adobe, Google Cloud, SAP, and others for help. The Warriors monitored decibel levels at Oracle Arena to measure fans' preferences about in-game entertainment such as T-shirt tosses and dance team performances. This measurement can help teams figure out in-game entertainment and promotions. The Orlando Magic's senior vice president of strategy, Jay Riola, said the team has spent several million dollars on customer relationship management and marketing automation software, hardware, and systems since the team moved into Amway Center. Real-time information helps teams understand preferences and buying patterns of fans, and they can then segment and target certain demographics. The more they know about patterns, the more they can successfully maintain or add corporate partners (Spanberg, 2019). The style of play and focus on three-point shots comes as a result of data analytics. An analysis revealed that many long-range two-point shots were inefficient. Analysts and coaches then began focusing more on three-pointers.

Technology also helps collect and visualize data. The league partnered with STATS to install six cameras in all the teams' arenas to track players and referees at 25 frames per second, data that teams and the league analyze and use. Coaches can modify offensive and defensive strategies based on the data, and players can adjust their efforts based on opponents and figure out where they shoot their best shots on the court (Abbas, n.d.). Players also use devices that measure their sleep and fatigue levels, ultimately helping them train better and hopefully avoid injury (McLaughlin, 2019).

MLB and its teams are leaders in analytics, as shown in Michael Lewis' book, *Moneyball: The Art of Winning an Unfair Game*, about the Oakland A's and the subsequent movie, *Moneyball*. MLB, like the NBA and professional soccer teams, uses motion capture technology, which tracks movement on the field to a 100th of a second. Teams recognize the importance of analytics, as evident in the Phillies' hiring of Joe Girardi. Managing partner John Middleton noted that he wanted a manager who added structure to the clubhouse and a "leader who is literate in analytics but unafraid to push back against the deluge of data" ("MLB Franchise Notes," 2019). Similarly, Angels' owner Arte Moreno drove the hiring of Joe Maddon, who had spent 31 years in the organization before managing the Chicago Cubs. The *Los Angeles Times'* Bill Plaschke wrote that the hiring should help bring the Angels stability after the death of Tyler Skaggs and subsequent revelations about the team's culture. He wrote that Maddon also "embraces cutting-edge analytics, preaches hardball philosophy, and pushes fun" ("Arte Moreno," 2019). This shows that knowledge and application of analytics count in all levels of teams. Additionally, the Red Sox hired chief baseball officer Chaim Bloom due to his baseball acumen and ability to connect with people. Bloom is a Yale graduate who worked his way up from intern at the Tampa Bay Rays to senior VP of baseball operations. He is considered forward-thinking and able to win within the margins of a team with a low payroll. Additionally, the chairman of the Red Sox, Tom Werner, noted the team's strong analytics department and the need to improve on the communication of information ("Red Sox Hope," 2019).

As these examples indicate, research, including analytics, gives leagues and other sport organizations knowledge they can use to improve the efficiency, efficacy, profitability, and reputations of their products and services. These organizations study fan preferences at games and during television broadcasts. Although the NFL continually tops the ratings charts for single games, especially the Super Bowl, other sport programs also garner high shares.

Networks and Research

ESPN and ABC both agree that "sports is big, big numbers, big impact, big passion, and most important, big return on objective (ROO)" (Whitney, 2005, p. 17). In addition to ratings, ROO is an important factor in the advertising business. It is based on the client's objectives, articulated in an agreement with the network. The two then use "sports polls, Internet measurement, focus groups, customized research and data from measurement companies such as Joyce Julius and Nielsen Sports to assess the impact of sponsorship in sports" (Whitney, 2005, p. 17).

ESPN is so committed to such research that it frequently posts job openings in analytics, digital platforms, research and insights, and stats and information. ESPN conducts a wide variety of research across platforms. Former ESPN president

Photo courtesy of Paul M. Pedersen.

ESPN uses a variety of research approaches and techniques to gather data on the demographics, preferences, and patterns of sport fans and media consumers. Here, an attendee at an ESPN fan experience event completes a survey before gaining admittance to the festivities.

and executive chairman George Bodenheimer discussed ESPN's evolving quest to strengthen and expand its brand through collaborations between its marketing and research departments. First, to bolster ESPN's priority of integrating its brand into key decisions, the marketing department distributed "Brand Baseballs" to every employee with the following values: "The ESPN brand isn't kept in a box, or a safe, or owned by some crazy sports collector. Like this ball, it's owned by you and is in your hands. Respect a sports fan's knowledge. Surprise them, entertain them, and always give them something to talk about. Our brand is the FAN's perception of us—It's what they think or feel when they see the letters ESPN—Everything we do—whether it's a program, a movie, a commercial, a product, a service, a press release—can alter or reinforce the FAN's perception of who we are. ESPN: The world's biggest sports FAN" (Bodenheimer & Phillips, 2015, pp. 222-223).

According to Bodenheimer, "A company's brand is critical in an environment with rapid technological innovation, because such change constantly alters how fans can access the product" (Bodenheimer & Phillips, 2015, p. 223). In a second collaboration between the marketing and research departments, marketing personnel brought together ESPN employees from various units to define the company's brand. In 2006, ESPN's "Brand Promise" read "Sports (what we do) with Authority (how we do it) and Personality (what sets us apart)" (Bodenheimer & Phillips, 2015, p. 223). This concise phrase established ESPN's global reach, brand, expertise, and passion across platforms and its desire to connect sport fans across all demographics.

ESPN has an analytics drop-down menu on its main website and uses the College Basketball Power Index (BPI), a quantitative model that rates Division I college basketball teams based on four factors: quantity of experience on a team's roster, quality of that experience, incoming freshmen's recruiting ranking (stress on five-star recruits), and coaches' past performances and successes. Then, it uses the ratings to simulate the rest of the season through the Final Four. Teams in the top four in ESPN's preseason BPI have won the national championship in 10 of the last 12 years (Walder & Sabin, 2019). ESPN Analytics also has the NFL Football Power Index (FPI), NFL Total Quarterback Rating (QBR), College Football Power Index (FPI), College Football QBR, NBA Basketball Power Index (BPI), and other predictive measurements within ESPN Analytics.

In other research, the ESPN Sports Poll has, for more than 20 years, predicted sport fan behavior by using measures of avidity or fan "bigness" (Luker, 2015). Sport fan avidity comprises two dimensions. Quantity (breadth) measures the amount of activity, and quality (depth) measures the relationship the fan has with teams and players. Many sport fans enjoy many sports and feel many loyalties; at the other end of the spectrum, some fans are devoted to one team in one sport. Fan attachments can also be passed down across generations, especially in the case of professional teams. The ESPN study conducts more than 18,000 interviews of U.S. sport fans age 12 or older (Luker, 2015).

In 2011, ESPN sought to increase its female audience by launching espnW. The site grew out of a 2010 blog and focuses on women's sport, recreational athletes, and general content about men's sport that is geared toward female fans. ESPN calls it the "online destination for female sports fans and athletes" (McBride, 2011). The average woman between 35 and 49 years of age spends 92 hours per year watching sport on television, as compared with 227 hours for men in the same age group. The network has researched the female audience and recognizes that women tend to have a different relationship to sport than do men. It continues to conduct research across demographics and platforms to improve its content and reach.

ESPN Lab conducted a "Valuing Video" study that explored the effectiveness of video advertising across television, over-the-top (OTT), PC, and mobile platforms. ESPN tested spots from eight advertisers by showing ads to respondents in four ESPN video scenarios. ESPN recognizes that digital platforms expand TV's brand-building power; according to the network, TV was the greatest contributor to brand awareness between 2013 and 2014, but the potential for digital video advertising continues to increase. Different screens offer advertisers larger audience impact. TV advertising drives awareness and discussion, but digital screens are more personal and therefore lead to more direct engagement with targeted content (McClellan, 2015).

ESPN also partnered with Global Strategy Group (GSG) to conduct tracking studies of ESPN's live online video offerings over the course of five years. GSG helped ESPN with transitioning through name changes (e.g., ESPN3.com), as well as the WatchESPN.com website and the WatchESPN mobile app. By tracking awareness and understanding across sport fans, ESPN can learn more about fans' connections to the brand and tweak its marketing efforts and products accordingly. GSG measured public opinion through surveys about high-profile news stories (e.g., the Penn State sex abuse scandal) and concussions in the NFL and youth sport. The results were shared on the network's website and on programs such as *SportsCenter* and *Outside the Lines*. In other projects, GSG studied ESPN's local media markets in New York, Los Angeles, Chicago, Dallas, and Boston by means of surveys and interviews. It also surveyed fans about ESPN's fantasy sport products (baseball, football, and March Madness) to evaluate user experiences (Global Strategy Group, 2015).

ESPN's Stats and Information Group (SIG) creates and delivers statistics to ESPN employees and fans. In 2016, it launched ESPN.com/Analytics, which provides analytics content and rankings as well as content from SIG writers, Football Outsiders, Hockey Prospectus, Fangraphs, and others. It connects with SIG's Twitter feed, @ ESPNStatsInfo, and features ESPN's Stats & Info blog. Additionally, the site cross-promotes FiveThirty-Eight.com. "Sports analytics are an important part of our storytelling," said Noel Nash, vice president of ESPN's Stats & Information Group. "This new section will serve our most avid followers with all of ESPN's statistics, data, tools and rankings in one easily accessible destination" (as quoted in Adler, 2016, para. 5).

ESPN invested in esports with a new online vertical in 2016. League of Legends, Dota 2, and Counter-Strike: Global Offensive were part of ESPN's coverage along with the major sport leagues and global events (Gaudiosi, 2016). Esports revenues were expected to exceed $1 billion in 2019 with nearly 100 million viewers globally for the League of Legends championship. Video Game Entertainment and News Network (VENN) is set to launch in 2020 and is a venture co-founded by producer Ariel Horn and entrepreneur Ben Kusin and backed by Twitch, Riot Games, and Blizzard Entertainment. The studios in Los Angeles and New York will have 55 hours of original programming ("The ESPN of eSports," 2019). The popularity of esports came to collegiate sports in 2014 when Robert Morris University was the first university to have esports as a varsity sport within the athletics department. The university offered $500,000 in athletics scholarships to its gamers (Jenny, Manning, Keiper, & Olrich, 2018). Esports fans tend to be young, tech savvy, and affluent, and competitive video game advertising revenues are expected to surpass $200 million by 2020. Newzoo, a gaming analytics firm, predicted global revenue would be $1.1 billion in 2019 from media rights, advertising, and sponsorships. That year, eMarketer said 30.3 million viewers will watch esports at least once a month in the United States, and viewership (mostly on YouTube and Twitch) is expected to reach 46.2 million by 2023. eMarketer's Paul Verna told Reuters' Hilary Russ that esports is a "multi-million dollar business in the U.S., with implications for game developers, players, leagues, teams, live venues, streaming platforms, TV networks, audiences, and marketers" (2019).

ESPN continues to invest in investigative reporting, which takes resources and time. Chris Buckle, executive editor of the ESPN investigative and new enterprise unit, still stresses the importance of certain skills that transcend technology and time. He included the following tips (personal communication, 2019):

- Be accurate and objective (I'm old-school that way).

- Find subject matters of interest and become an expert in them—and then write and report; your work will get noticed.

- Be honest, ethical, and responsible with your sources—it will pay dividends in the long run.

- If you're not innately curious, figure out a way to get curious—it's a key trait and guiding light you should have.

- Similarly, be very skeptical. And I don't mean in the standard journo ways—"if your mom says she's lying, check it out." That's not deep enough. Examine everything, every decision, every happening from 360 degrees until you're sure you're understanding how and why X is happening. Don't take someone's word for it—or anything, really.

- Documents and data—get them whenever possible, and use them.

- Don't be a "sports-head" who can spout rosters and positions but doesn't know how a stadium gets built, or what businesses the team owner is in, or how many agents control players on a team, or what influences are really affecting college sports, for example. (The vast majority of the people in our unit have non-sports backgrounds prior to joining ESPN. I worked 18 years in covering/managing news, politics and government journalism before joining ESPN.)

- Public records—they are your friend. You must learn how the police and courts systems work; you must learn how to file public records requests, even if you see yourself as a feature writer or beat reporter.

- Investigative stories start with very basic questions, so find the basic question and work from there. Example: A Division I, University of Maryland player dies on a field during a workout. Question: How is it possible that a player can die under medical supervision, at a school that has an athletic department budget in the tens of millions of dollars? Those simple questions drive all of your reporting.

As far as other networks, Fox Sports 1 (FS1) challenges ESPN's sole dominance in the 24-hour sport network market. For four years, Fox researched the marketplace to learn how to differentiate itself and create effective personality and branding. Former Fox Sports' CEO David Hill referred to the resulting concept as *jockularity* (Greenfeld, 2013). The network wanted to be viewed as the "funny, irreverent, less serious sports channel" and sought to reinvent the format of ESPN's *SportsCenter*. Through focus groups and interviews, Fox found that fans wanted a more fun and entertaining approach to sport news. As a result, *Fox Sports Live* featured highlights with props and bloopers, guests, and analysis, along with Jay Onrait and Dan O'Toole, who previously hosted Canada's *SportsCentre* on the Sports Network (Greenfeld, 2013). The show only lasted a couple of years, but Fox Sports now has *First Things First*; *Speak for Yourself*; *The Herd*; and *Undisputed*. As mentioned in chapter 7, FS1 aired many of the World Cup soccer matches and has integrated football, basketball, baseball, and other sports into its lineup. Fox Sports partnered with Nielsen for "The 5th Network: Regional Sports Network Passion Index" to ask more than 1,500 pay TV subscribers who identify as sport fans their perceptions of regional sport networks. The Nielsen Media Analytics Primary Research study found that sport fans rate the RSNs as the most essential channels in their television packages after the four broadcast networks ("Fox Sports and Nielsen Study," 2016).

DATA, TECHNOLOGY, AND SOCIAL MEDIA

Today, there's "the datafication of everything" (Millington & Millington, 2018). The "Age of Big Data" has propelled the quest for measurement in new and different ways and can be collected in all aspects of life and crunched at lightning speed. Big Data signifies progress and is relevant in sport. A series of "V" terms constitute Big Data: volume to denote the massive quantities that are collected and evaluated; variety to signify that

Photo courtesy of Robby General.

Sport organizations seek to elevate the fan experience through data and research, whether the facility is over 100 years old like Indianapolis Motor Speedway, home to the Indianapolis 500, or a newer facility. IMS has 240,000 permanent seats and holds many more fans on race day.

data are varied and heterogeneous; and velocity to show that data are exchanged and analyzed with lightning speed. boyd and Crawford (2012) use a more sociological approach, saying Big Data relies on the interplay of technology, analysis, and mythology and that Big Data offers a high level of intelligence, knowledge, and meaning with objectivity and accuracy (boyd & Crawford, 2012).

Technology impacts athletes' training regimes and competitions; fans' engagement and consumption of content; and the construction of venues such as AT&T Stadium and the Chase Center. Whether its fan engagement technologies such as live streaming, esports, gambling, and content platforms; athlete performance technologies such as wearables and coaching platforms; or stadium experience technologies such as in-stadium services, ticketing, and analytics and biometrics, all will impact sport in the future (Proman, 2019). Key trends include the arrival of video-assisted referees in soccer. After goal line technology (GLT) was implemented in soccer, the call for video review got louder. VAR was used at the 2018 World Cup, and the Premier League used it in the 2019-2020 season. Sport streaming services such as DAZN and Eleven Sports are challenging broadcasters. DAZN invested over $1 billion into boxing and combat sports. In the United Kingdom, Eleven Sports holds broadcasting rights for Italian and Spanish soccer, and Amazon had the U.S. Open in tennis and Premier League matches in 2019-2020. The International Olympic Committee is monitoring esports development for the future. Real-time data is common in the United States, as is evident in the NFL's use of Microsoft's Surface tablets on the sidelines. In Europe, the International Football Association Board (IFAB) approved the use of handheld devices during games. At the 2018 World Cup, all 32 teams had access to a tablet-based system from FIFA (McCaskill, 2018).

Social media has revolutionized the sport industry, and its impact will continue to evolve. Global social media rose by 13 percent in 2018, and 61 percent of sport viewers follow sport accounts on social media platforms such as Twitter, Facebook, and Instagram. As a result, social media will continue to be important in marketing strategies for sport organizations, brands, and media in coming years. Companies

will dedicate time and resources to improving content and engaging and growing fanbases. Balancing creativity and content will increase even more in importance. And according to Jeff O'Keefe, senior manager with Golin for Toyota Racing, "The 'story' platform is going to continue to evolve, especially now that we've seen YouTube jump into the fray," he said. "Additionally, creators must continue to come up with content specifically built for the platform" (Londergan, 2019).

Social media platforms offer unique ways for engagement with teams, players, and coaches engaging in new and different ways. From the beginning of 2017 through 2018, MLB, MLS, NFL, NBA, and NHL posted more than 6.3 million social posts and resulted in 16.7 billion engagements. Nineteen percent of the social posts were branded, which equates to $2.1 billion in attributed value for the brands in that content (Nelson, 2018). In addition to engagement, the culture of sport consumption has changed from individual to group or community activities. Fans have immediate and real-time information on Twitter, which is a valuable resource for leagues, teams, players, fans, and reporters. With hashtags, gifs, audio and visual content, and more, the platforms are part of everyone's lives 24-7. Twitter fosters engagement between teams and fans as well as fans interacting with fans in a community. Sport is more accessible and pervasive today and will continue to be even more so as technology evolves. As discussed in chapters 7 and 8, social media has changed the way sport is reported. ESPN, Barstool Sports, and Bleacher Report all constantly share content with mass audiences. This challenges reporters since it's harder to present unique and cohesive messages with so many avenues disseminating information (Swarm, 2018).

A few of the ways social media have influenced sport include live streaming of games, races, and matches; club pages of teams such as Real Madrid and the Dallas Cowboys; the presence, participation, and posts from sport stars such as LeBron James, Steph Curry, and others; content including match clips, interviews, pre- and postgame footage; forums for fans' comments; and sport campaigns such as #ThisGirlCan from 2015, which had over eight million views (Wardini, 2017).

While the Internet offers opportunities for additional coverage, especially of women's sport, there are still disparities in coverage that is inequitable and incommensurate, according to Creedon (2014).

This section of the chapter elucidates the role of ratings and research in various sport communication entities' daily functions. Companies, leagues, teams, and networks all recognize that research helps them plan better, spend better, run better, and generally function better in the sport communication market.

Whereas practitioners have used research over the years, academics have recently begun exploring the intersecting worlds of sport and communication from many perspectives, ranging from the sociological to the journalistic to the political. All research areas—from the practical industry-oriented end of the field to the theoretical academic end—are vital to sport communication's acceptance and progression as a burgeoning and provocative field of inquiry.

ACADEMIC RESEARCH IN SPORT COMMUNICATION

Sport has surfaced relatively recently as a topic of academic inquiry, yet research in this area is crucial to fully understanding how sport intersects the social, cultural, economic, and political arenas. Earlier in this book, you learned about sport communication theory, and theory and research are inextricably linked; in fact, they should be viewed not as separate entities but as forming a continuum. As Salwen and Stacks (1996) succinctly put it, "One cannot conduct good research without theory, and good theory development requires good verification" (p. 4). Bostrom (1998) concurred: "Research is the process of first discovering and then examining theories formally and objectively" (p. 19).

Research Types and Approaches

Research includes the following types (Jones, 2015; Salwen & Stacks, 1996):

- **Exploratory research** sets a foundation for knowledge in an unexplored area of inquiry. For example, an exploratory study in sport communication might analyze athletes' and coaches' perceptions of digital sport reporters as compared with newspaper sportswriters and television sport reporters. This would be a pioneering study and therefore would set a foundation for new academic inquiry.

- **Descriptive research** describes a phenomenon, focusing on *what* occurs rather than *why* it occurs. For example, a descriptive study might analyze how sport reporters integrate stand-ups (appearances at the scene of a current event) into their daily sport reports.

- **Explanatory research** expounds on why something occurs and measures causal relationships. For example, explanatory research might be used to explain why sport companies need to be proactive in their marketing strategies.

- **Predictive research** anticipates phenomena based on explanatory research and its findings. For example, a predictive research study might anticipate how the Internet will continue to change sport coverage and content, as well as the media's attention to sport.

Before undertaking research and expanding knowledge about sport communication, researchers need to understand certain philosophical approaches to research, as well as the nature of knowledge and data collection. The philosophy known as *positivism* considers scientific knowledge, obtained by the methods of the natural sciences, to be the only veritable type of knowledge. In this view, by observing behavior, the researcher can measure facts to articulate "laws" or theories that anticipate future behavior. Early researchers (e.g., the Chicago School of sociologists) often viewed quantitative and qualitative methods as complementary and used both statistics and case studies; however, the positivist philosophy generally focuses on statistics. Positivists use the physical science experiment as a model for research and value what they can observe directly. They believe that universal laws govern relationships between variables and that findings are generalizable. Positivists base validity and reliability on the testing and replication of theories. They have often dismissed qualitative research as lacking scientific rigor because of subjective data and findings (Hammersley & Atkinson, 2002).

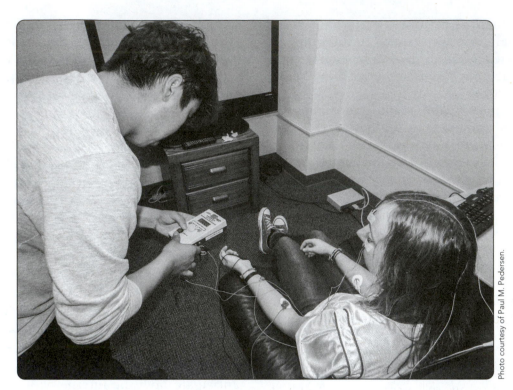

Photo courtesy of Paul M. Pedersen.

The experimental methodology used here is an example of a positivist approach to sport communication research. This sport communication researcher created a mixed-method experimental design that uses psychophysiological measurements to test how study subjects react to TV commercials following sporting contests that end in close scores, lopsided scores, and so forth.

In contrast, an interpretive approach is taken by researchers who view sport more as a social phenomenon. Accordingly, interpretive researchers study words and other nonnumerical measures to delve into meanings and values (Jones, 2015). Also referred to as *naturalists*, interpretive researchers study the social world in its "natural" state rather than in the artificial setting of a lab. Respect for the subject is paramount, and they do not believe that individuals' actions are open to the "causal analysis and manipulation of variables" that characterize the quantitative research valued by positivism (Hammersley & Atkinson, 2002, p. 8). Instead, they hold that researchers must have access to the meanings that direct individuals' actions. In this view, by studying individuals' social worlds, we can understand and interpret the world similarly and learn social processes. In naturalism, the description of cultures is paramount (Jones, 2015; Hammersley & Atkinson, 2002).

Thus, whereas positivists prefer a more quantitative approach to research, interpretivists and naturalists prefer qualitative research because of the depth and breadth of its results. In addition to using different types of measurement, qualitative research and quantitative research vary in their uses of data. Specifically, the quantitative approach uses "numerical measurement and analysis" and involves "measurable 'quantities'" (Gratton & Jones, 2004, p. 21). With this approach, researchers study data that can be evaluated statistically to see if a relationship exists between variables. In contrast, qualitative research seeks to "capture qualities that are not quantifiable" or not "reducible to numbers, such as feelings, thoughts, experiences . . . concepts associated with interpretive approaches to knowledge" (p. 22).

Ultimately, then, the terms *qualitative research* and *quantitative research* apply to methodologies, or the "structured sets of procedures and instruments by which empirical phenomena of mass communication are registered, documented, and interpreted" (Jensen & Jankowski, 1991, p. 8). To be a solid researcher, you should engage with both approaches because both are useful in social research. By using triangulation—that is, combining qualitative and quantitative methods—researchers can gain both depth of meaning and quantification of results (Gratton & Jones, 2004, 2010; Jensen & Jankowski, 1991).

Quantitative research and qualitative research also differ in terms of the categories they utilize (McCracken, 1988). Quantitative research defines and labels categories rigidly before the study begins to evaluate the relationships between them. In contrast, in qualitative research, categories evolve during the process of research. As McCracken (1988) put it, precise categories are the *"means* of [quantitative] research" but "the *object* of [qualitative] research" (p. 16, emphases added). Qualitative research also seeks interrelationships between many categories, whereas quantitative generally looks for a "sharply delineated relationship between a limited set of them" (p. 16). In accordance with these different conceptualizations of the research project, quantitative research "uses a lens that brings a narrow strip of the field of vision into very precise focus," whereas qualitative research "uses a lens that permits a much less precise vision of a much broader strip" (p. 16).

The two approaches also differ in their reporting abilities. In quantitative research, the participant responds quickly to closed questions, whereas qualitative research uses broader, imprecise questions that warrant a more considered response. Finally, another difference involves sampling. In quantitative work, the researcher creates a sample and generalizes it to the general population, whereas in qualitative work, access to culture is an issue. In this sense, "it is the categories and assumptions, not those who hold them, that matter" in qualitative research, which is "more intensive than extensive in its objectives" (McCracken, 1988, p. 17).

Example of the Research Process

Once you understand the approaches to research, the research process can begin (see figure 11.3). To illuminate that process, this section applies the work of Gratton and Jones (2010) to sport. The first step in the research process is to choose a topic of study. To do so, the researcher should consider the literature in the field, current events, social issues, and personal interests. For example,

one potential topic would be the media coverage of the Larry Nassar sex abuse scandal and survivors' victim impact statements during his final Michigan sentencings. Next, the researcher discusses and synthesizes existing literature on the subject and related topics and identifies a gap in the research that justifies further study. In the Nassar example, the researcher would need to start with broad consideration of sex abuse and sport. Next, the researcher can include specific cases of sex abuse such as Penn State, Ohio State, and USA Swimming. The researcher would then need to discuss portrayals in print, electronic, and online media of sex abuse of athletes in various sports. Now the researcher can focus on gymnastics, where stud-

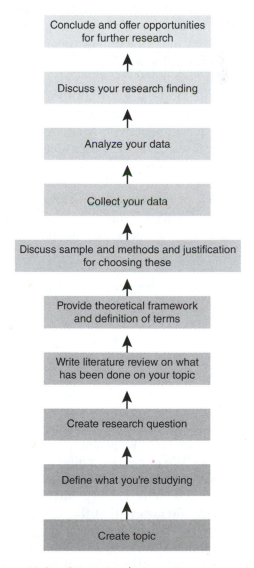

Figure 11.3 Steps in the sport communication research process.

ies have discussed the insular nature of the sport and the culture that potentially enables grooming, abuse, and sex crimes to occur. If studying the survivors' victim impact statements at the sentencings, the importance of them within the U.S. criminal justice system must also be included and discussed as well as the power of media in communicating stories of abuse within society.

The researcher then creates a theoretical framework that defines terms and concepts and presents the study's theoretical foundations. Here, the researcher should define sex abuse for this specific study and could also define other relevant concepts, such as authority figures, power relationships, and grooming. To bolster the study's legitimacy, the researcher could also use theories from communication, mass communication, and sport. Relevant types of theory might include the agenda-setting, attachment theory, feminist theory, or critical theory.

Next, the research develops a clear, coherent research question—a vital component of all research. The researcher then develops the theory behind the question, or hypothesis, which in turn expands the research in the chosen area of inquiry. Research questions result from either the inductive process, in which questions are derived from assumptions, or the deductive process, in which questions are derived from rational observation. Viewed another way, deductive reasoning (often associated with quantitative research) moves from the general to the specific, whereas inductive reasoning (often associated with qualitative research) moves from the specific to the general.

When a researcher contemplates a question, the "so what" factor must come into play. In other words, it is crucial to identify the question's social significance (Bostrom, 1998). Why do we care? Research is conducted to solve problems, whether they are theoretical or practical. Therefore, before a research question is finalized, the researcher should make sure that he or she can answer queries such as, "What are you going to research? Why is this topic of interest? How are you going to conduct your research?" (Stokes, 2003, p. 29). The researcher should ensure that the research question is focused, refined, realistic, and significant.

The researcher should also consider time constraints and accessibility issues. The data must be reasonably available, and the researcher must

be able to conduct the research and deal with all issues related to it. Returning to the Larry Nassar sex abuse example, one possible research question would be, "How did the media frame the survivors during the Michigan sentencings of Larry Nassar?" Another possibility would be, "How did the media frame Larry Nassar during the Michigan sentencings of Larry Nassar?" If the researcher wants to study more of the organizational aspects at USA Gymnastics (USAG), Michigan State University (MSU), or the United States Olympic Committee (USOC), a potential question would be, "How did the media frame USAG, MSU, and USOC during the Michigan sentencings of Larry Nassar? That would require more background information in the literature review about crisis communication strategies and image restoration, but the study can progress any number of ways depending on the researcher's interests and objectives. In any case, the research question must be specific, refined, focused, and doable; it must be sufficiently narrow yet compelling enough to study. After the research question is determined, the researcher must still accomplish the following parts of the project: research design (sampling and methodological procedures), data collection, analysis and discussion of research findings, development of conclusions, and identification of any weaknesses of the study and of opportunities for further research.

In addition, communication researchers should address the following considerations: "Who communicates to whom? (sources and receivers) Why communicate? (functions and purposes) How does communication take place? (channels, languages, codes) What about? (content, references, types of information) What are the consequences of communication (intended or unintended)?" (McQuail, 1996, 2010, p. 9). To create a compelling and significant study, researchers must consider all phases and elements of the communication process.

There are also a few different approaches to studying the communication process:

- Structural approach, which studies media systems (e.g., ESPN, cable television) and how they relate to society
- Behavioral approach, which studies human behavior in the communication process (e.g., job functions specific to sport marketers)

- Cultural approach, which focuses on meaning, language, and cultural context (e.g., textual analysis of sport journalists' writings)

Research Procedures

Approaches to communication research can be divided very generally into two camps: the dominant and the alternative. The dominant paradigm perceives the mass media as powerful and often uses social science and methods such as surveys, statistical analyses, and experiments to study communication in an empirical way. Thus, the dominant paradigm often uses more quantitative methods of research—for example, survey responses, which can be counted and categorized to make general observations about a population. The alternative paradigm, on the other hand, rejects the transmission or linear model of communication, deploys a critical view of society, and uses a more cultural approach and more qualitative methods (McQuail, 2010). Thus, this paradigm uses deeper and more meaningful methods such as in-depth interviewing and textual analysis. This type of study usually uses a smaller sample size than those used in surveys (which can be distributed to hundreds or even thousands of people) but takes a more ritualistic and deeper approach to issues.

When conducting a study, maximize your strengths. If interpersonal skills are your strength, you enjoy observing and talking with people, and you're a good listener, then the alternative paradigm would work well for you. If, on the other hand, you enjoy numbers and seek to generalize your results more easily to the general population, then the dominant paradigm would be most effective for you. Clear and refined research questions and goals are fundamental to the research process.

After determining the research question, the researcher defines and operationalizes terms and concepts (Bostrom, 1998). *Operationalism*, according to Bostrom, is "specifying the operations that you will perform to provide an instance of the theoretical term" (p. 20). It is a way to objectify data; once the operation is agreed to, the definition is communal rather than personal. Credible sources are the foundation of any research, and primary and secondary sources are both needed to explore topics. Primary sources are those that comprise the researcher's "object of analysis," whereas secondary sources are work done by others, which are used as background information or in the literature review (Stokes, 2003, p. 31). For the study listed previously on the Nassar sex abuse scandal, the researcher would define any relevant terms and justify the research and its significance. Research begins with solving problems, which are theoretical or practical in nature.

The researcher then engages in a literature review, which involves studying all literature in the field that pertains to the research question. This body of research both propels future studies and helps determine what is missing in the field's current knowledge; therefore, it enables the researcher to develop a justification for doing his or her study. The literature review has several purposes, according to Jones (2015). First, it should show the researcher's comprehensive knowledge of the topic and outline relevant theories, concepts, and past work. It should also further focus the research question. In addition, it should show the scope of past research while framing the hypothesis for the current research, which is the predicted outcome based on logic or existing evidence. This section should show methodologies used in the past and identify and define all concepts and variables, as well as showing how the researcher's work expands on past research. The literature review must therefore provide a critical synthesis rather than a mere summation of past work. It should address relevant academic journal articles, library books, trade publications, conference papers, doctoral dissertations, government documents, and other secondary sources.

As mentioned, the researcher cannot simply summarize past work but rather needs to organize and synthesize scholars' contributions in a systematic manner that shows how his or her study adds to the existing body of knowledge in this area of inquiry. The researcher knows that the literature review is complete if sources repeat themselves in bibliographies and reference lists. Viable methods for the Nassar study described earlier could include textual analysis or framing analysis, just to name a couple. Textual research and analysis studies language and the way words are used and arranged within narratives (Bostrom, 1998). The most traditional analysis of texts is called *content analysis*, which began as an objective technique for examining newspapers (Krippendorf, 1980). According to Berelson (1952), content analysis is the "objective, systematic, and quantitative description of the manifest content of communication" (p. 18). It can be a quantitative assessment of the amount of content devoted to a subject, or it can also be a qualitative assessment of language and meaning within the narratives. Content analysis is further discussed later in this chapter.

Goffman (1974) used framing analysis to describe individuals' ways of defining events in accordance to the organization of social events and their subjective involvement in those situations. As a "window of the world" (Tuchman, 1978, p. 1), news is like a picture or window frame. News frames offer a selective vista of a scene and a lens for the exploration and understanding of events (p. 29). Framing defines events and issues and lays out terms for deliberation (Tankard, 2001). Communicators use framing judgments in word choice and selection decisions (Entman, 1993). As Pan and Kosicki (1993) said, "Choices of words and their organization into news stories are no trivial matters. They hold great power in setting the context for debate, defining issues under consideration, summoning a variety of mental representations, and providing the basic tools to discuss the issues at hand" (p. 70). How the media cover an event or an issue affects how the public perceives it (Hardin & Zuegner, 2003). Facts take on meaning by being rooted in a frame or story that organizes them in a cohesive way (Gamson, 1989). The researcher would need to investigate how to implement the chosen method, as well as the pioneers who created the method and key scholars who have used it.

Generally, researchers write a proposal or outline to guide their research. A proposal includes the research question, a definition of the object of analysis, a description of primary sources, an overview of secondary sources, a literature review, a time frame for the work, a sample instrument (e.g., survey), an explanation of anticipated findings, and a bibliography (Stokes, 2003).

History of Academic Research on Sport

Sport communication research began as early as the 1930s; however, it is a relatively new discipline in academia. As the media gained prominence and power in the United States with the maturation of television as a medium, more academics focused on the media and sport. Scholars have increasingly recognized the importance of understanding the history and sociology of the institutional relationship between the mass media and sport (Rowe, 2004). As Whannel (2002) summarized, "The growth of television as a significant cultural form during the 1960s put the relationship between sport and the media on the public agenda" (p. 291).

Today, many studies critically analyze television sport coverage in the "sociological and semiological [study of signs] traditions" (Whannel, 2002, p. 291). These studies look at the production of media messages either through the media workers' perspectives and practices or through the perspectives of organizational and cultural-media institutions, legal limitations, and economic pressures. They also examine media content in an age of spectacle, sport media audiences, and the influence of media messages on attendance and participation. Examples of specific topics being considered in the ongoing research include the commercialization of sport, portrayals of women in the sport media, masculinity in media sport, race and media sport, globalization, and sport and the body (Whannel, 2002). Today, many researchers study esports, social media, and technology. In addition to studies on sport mass media, studies are also conducted about personal and organizational communication in both sport and ancillary sport communication (Abeza, O'Reilly, & Nadeau, 2014).

Here is a bit more detail about the history of publishing in this field of inquiry. Communication scholars have published articles about sport in *Journalism & Mass Communication Quarterly* since 1934, when an article appeared on slang in newspaper sportswriting (Trujillo, 2003). In 1975, the *Journal of Communication* published Michael Real's seminal work on the Super Bowl, and it devoted an entire issue to the study of sport in 1977. In the 1980s, sport articles were published in the *Journal of Broadcasting*, *Critical Studies in Mass Communication*, and the *Quarterly Journal of Speech*.

Until the early to mid-1980s, however, sport was not an expansive and developed area in communication and media studies, but today it is one of the main areas of research in these fields. In fact, it brings together sociology, communication, and media studies, thus offering opportunities to further understand both the power of the media in U.S. culture and the effect of sport in U.S. society. From sport institutions to texts and audiences, each subject of study enables scholars to better understand the meaning and significance of sport in terms of cultural values and relationships of power and prestige. As Wenner (1998) observed, "The meanings associated with mediated sport texts often extend well beyond the archetypal heroic myths of the playing field to offer lessons about cultural priorities and the current state of power relations" (p. 5). Wenner's *MediaSport* (1998) set the agenda for research in this field by expanding on his earlier text, *Media, Sports, and Society* (1989). Wenner (1998) explored "sport as communication" and defined *MediaSport* as "the cultural fusing of sport with communication" (p. xiii).

By the turn of the 21st century, sport communication became a formalized field of inquiry, and it was addressed in at least 22 textbooks and edited volumes from 2003 to 2013 (Abeza et al., 2014; Billings, Butterworth, & Turman, 2012). It was also the subject of seven academic conferences from 2002 to 2014, as well as growth in academic programs offered at universities, academic journals (e.g., *Journal of Sports Media*, *International Journal of Sport Communication*, *Communication & Sport*), and academic groups (e.g., International Association for Communication and Sport [IACS] and groups within Association for Education in Journalism and Mass Communication [AEJMC], National Communication Association [NCA], International Communication Association [ICA], North American Society for Sport Management [NASSM]). While over the past few years there have been numerous publications and significant advancements in the scholarly work related to sport communication, Thompson (2016) noted that, "additional research and scholarly inquiry are necessary to further advance the field of sport communication" (p. 125). Thompson added that there have been calls for "advancements in the methodological approaches used in sport communication research" (p. 125). The following section provides an overview of some common methodologies used in sport communication research.

Overview of Research Methodologies

Today, all journalism and communication journals include articles on sport, and work in this area can be conducted from diverse theoretical and methodological perspectives. Examples of work in the field are shared in various books (e.g., *Routledge Handbook of Sport Communication* [Pedersen, 2013b], *Routledge Handbook of Sport and New Media* [Billings & Hardin, 2014]), which reveal the importance of continuing scholarly inquiry and contributions. When considering types of studies, the researcher can study texts, the media industry, audience analysis, and organizations (Trujillo, 2003; Wenner, 1998). The researcher can also study newspapers, magazines, online outlets, television audiences, or workers at the NCAA or other organizations. Indeed, the options are nearly infinite in a world mesmerized by sport and the media. In addition, there is a need for more research in all facets of sport communication, including marketing, advertising, public relations, law, print media, electronic media, and emerging technologies, to name just a few. As Pedersen (2013a) noted, "communication's influence on the sport industry as a whole—and the management and marketing of the industry in particular—is significant, and sport scholars are increasingly aware of its impact on the field" (p. 62). Pedersen (2013a) added that scholars will publish more research "examining communication's involvement in the strategy, management, and marketing of sport organizations, and the stakeholders in the sport industry" (pp. 62-63).

Kinkema and Harris (1998) analyzed the needs and differences of the various types of sport communication research. They noted that more research is needed on production; audience; and the "political and economic dimensions at local, national, and global levels" (p. 53). In textual analysis, more work is needed on sport advertising, the commercialization of sport, drugs and athletes, and teamwork. There is also a need for work on emerging technologies, as well as sports-talk radio, and for research reports aimed at making policy recommendations in sport media.

More recently, in a reflective study, Abeza and colleagues (2014) concluded that more work is needed to develop sport communication theory and to explore personal and organizational communication, which accounted for less than 4 percent of work found in their sample (as compared with more than 20 percent on ancillary sport communication and 49 percent on sport mass media). The research has included an abundance of work using the perspectives of agenda setting, framing, parasocial interaction, disposition, uses and gratifications, and cultivation theory, among others. Content analysis (discussed later in this chapter) is also amply used (Marie Hardin, personal communication) compared to mixed methods (usually qualitative and quantitative to maximize efficacy). Additional work needs to be done on the global sport communication arena, and "the field's future research should address these [growing] 'pains'" (Abeza et al., p. 308). Marie Hardin, profiled earlier in the chapter, said, "I'm happy to see that the research has evolved to be more inclusive of multiple methods and to integrate a wider array of theoretical perspectives as they relate to the psychology of users/consumers and the sociology of production. . . . We need to move beyond simplistic explanations or methodological lenses that have not, over time, led to a deeper understanding and substantive response to the deeply rooted patterns of employment, engagement and coverage of sport" (personal communication).

Among the more fertile fields within sport, social media impacts athletes, coaches, athletics administrators, fans, reporters, media organizations, and others. It is a vibrant area of inquiry, yet it needs to be studied in meaningful ways. According to Jimmy Sanderson (2018), "To date, much of the qualitative research into sport and social media research has been content-focused and descriptive; and while that is not inherently problematic, there is a need for more diversity. Qualitative research into sport and social media should be more thoughtful in topic selection, more compelling in the sample sizes used, and more diverse in the methodological and theoretical frameworks used to guide analysis" (p. 89). Sanderson (2018) recommends that if researchers choose a singular case study, it must be distinctive and should provide information beyond sport and social media and contribute to the field in new ways. Using multiple case studies and creating typologies that explain sport across multiple platforms would also be beneficial; being more theoretically flexible would add rigor and depth, as well as adding critical theory. Researchers have focused on Twitter the most, so investigating other platforms would be useful (Sanderson, 2018).

This section of the chapter offers a sampling of the many methodologies available in sport communication and addresses the strengths and weaknesses of each option presented; in addition, table 11.1 provides brief information about a wider range of options. As noted earlier, the efficacy of a study can be maximized through the process of triangulation if different methods are integrated. Of course, the researcher needs to choose a method based on his or her interests, passions, and objectives, but integrating both quantitative and qualitative methods can optimize the generalizability of research results. The following three subsections discuss research on texts, the media industry, and audiences. Each approach has its strengths, and each furthers understanding of the sport industry and, more specifically, sport communication.

Table 11.1 Commonly Employed Research Methods in Sport Communication

Research method	Types	Key characteristics
Quantitative	Survey Content analysis Polling Social network analysis	Replicable Systematic and structured Statistical Objective
Qualitative	Media analysis Narrative analysis Rhetorical analysis Framing Observation Participant observation In-depth interview Oral history	In-depth (research, meaning) Analytical (words, pictures, meanings) Flexible, adaptable Interpretive Descriptive

Research on Media Texts

This section focuses on methods used in studying texts. These methods, such as content analysis and narrative analysis, enable the researcher to delve into language, meaning, and media content.

Content Analysis

Textual study offers multiple benefits. One is accessibility, due to the many search engines, research databases, and interlibrary loans that facilitate this type of research. In addition, texts are social phenomena—part of our ordinary life at work, at school, and in our personal lives. However, even though texts are often readily available, researchers must consider the time-consuming nature of this type of research, as well as the meticulous detail it requires.

Andrew, Pedersen, and McEvoy (2020) noted that content analysis "is simply the unobtrusive and nonreactive examination of communication" (p. 127) that is used either as a quantitative or qualitative methodology "to examine words, posts, tweets, texts, and discourses in systematic and replicable ways" (p. 127). This method can be used to examine social media posts, sport podcasts, newspaper articles, sport organization press releases, sport documentaries, academic journals, personal diaries, sport television broadcasts, and most any other form of sport communication. For instance, you might hypothesize that The Athletic includes more coverage of men's sport than women's sport. To investigate, you could compare the numbers of articles on each topic since its inception by selecting a representative sample. The factual evidence you find will either support or refute your hypothesis.

Despite providing such straightforward evidence, content analysis does not give you an argument; that is your responsibility. The strength of content analysis lies in its generation of reliable and replicable facts (Andrew et al., 2020). It is also relatively easy to conduct, even for beginning researchers. In terms of challenges and drawbacks, content analysis requires good categories to provide meaningful results. It can also be insensitive and very time consuming, and the researcher must collect a representative sample of the selected texts.

Here is an overview of the steps involved in content analysis. After naming and choosing the text, the researcher specifically identifies the data set (which newspapers or online sites, which editions, how many, and so forth) then establishes a hypothesis or research question. The researcher must articulate a clear vision of what she wants to find out or learn from analyzing the texts. Next, to refine and justify the planned work, the researcher reads widely in the field of study. The next step is to define the object of analysis, whether it is a book, magazine, newspaper, television show, or digital media. The sample should be representative yet realistic. The researcher must also establish clear categories of analysis, or codes, into which data will be placed. The researcher develops a coding sheet, which is a grid indicating the categories and objects of analysis. The researcher uses the grid to record the findings; the more specific it is, the better. Next, the researcher tests the categories on a small sample to determine whether they need refining or revising. If so, the researcher includes the changes and the reasons for them in the methods section of the research proposal.

After the categories are set, the researcher collects the data and writes down the texts to be analyzed on another sheet of paper. If something does not fall into a category, that discrepancy must be noted appropriately. The researcher can list findings on a second log sheet, convert raw data to percentages, and identify any patterns that either support or refute the hypothesis. Even if the hypothesis is not supported, the research is still useful. The researcher then presents the results in the form of tables, charts, and text, which detail how he or she conducted the research and what was found. A researcher can study frequencies of occurrence and other variables like prominence (where a concept appears in a text), space devoted to a concept, and context. As mentioned earlier, content analysis is effective in studying quantities and in making "facts about content" explicit (Stokes, 2003, p. 66). A researcher should always strive for a method that is valid and reliable. In other words, the measure must accurately reflect that the phenomenon and results would be the same if the research were replicated (Jones, 2015).

Narrative Analysis

Narrative analysis is a qualitative methodology centered on the structure of a story, whether it takes the form of a novel, film, television show, or article. Through narratives, the researcher can study and further understand cultural values and ideologies. Narratives contain events that are active or communicate a state or condition; they involve the temporal arrangement of a series of events, as well as causal relationships and a coherent topic. In this method, the researcher selects a limited number of texts because this is in-depth research (Stokes, 2003); for example, one feature film or one news topic in five days would suffice.

Next, the researcher must become acquainted with the text and define the hypothesis accordingly. Foss (2004) identified a number of elements in analyzing the text, or artifact—for example, settings, characters, narrator, events, temporal relations, causal relations, audience, and themes. By exploring the text, the researcher can determine the most significant and valuable parts of the narrative. Although it is not always obvious, "a narrative, as a frame upon experience, functions as an argument to view and understand the world in a particular way" (Foss, 2004, p. 339). A narrative can be judged according to the following questions provided by Foss (pp. 338-340):

- Does the narrative embody and advocate values that you see as desirable and worthwhile?
- What ethical standards does the narrative suggest?
- How readily can the narrative be refuted?
- Is the narrative coherent?
- Does the narrative demonstrate fidelity to life?
- Does the narrative fulfill the purpose of its creators?
- Does the narrative provide useful ideas for living your life?

The researcher can use these questions to formulate a research question that addresses what the narrative shows about cultural values or about an individual or how it controls the understanding of an event. Narrative analysis is an open-ended and creative methodology, thus providing the researcher with much leeway.

After analyzing the text, the researcher should include the basic elements of the narrative analysis in the final paper. The introduction presents the central question or problem, explains its contribution to communication research, and describes its overarching significance. Next, the researcher elaborates on the narrative or artifact, describing it fully, then describes the project's methodology. The next step is to elucidate the findings, which are followed by a conclusion in which the researcher discusses the project's contribution to communication research and theory (Foss, 2004; Stokes, 2003). As an example, one could use this process in sport communication to conduct a narrative analysis of the *Washington Post*'s coverage of the Washington Nationals and the *Houston Chronicle*'s coverage of the Houston Astros during the 2018-2019 MLB season, which culminated in the two teams facing off in the World Series.

Other Methodologies Used to Study Texts

The approaches just described are only two of the various methodologies used to study media texts. Others, shown in the list that follows, include rhetorical criticism, semiotics, textual analysis, quantitative document analysis, and critical discourse analysis:

- **Rhetorical criticism** is based on rhetoric, or individuals' "use of symbols to communicate" (Foss, 2004, p. 4). Rhetorical criticism is a method created to enable "systematic investigation and explanation of symbolic acts and artifacts for the purpose of understanding rhetorical processes" (p. 6). In sport communication, for example, one might study rhetorical strategies used by sport journalists when describing athletes who have a disability.

- **Semiotics**, or the study of signs, was developed from Ferdinand de Saussure's *Course in General Linguistics* (1983). Semiotics studies the meanings of artifacts and is especially valuable in analyzing visual texts.

- **Textual analysis** (sometimes called *media analysis*) involves systematic study of films, television shows, sportscasts, newspaper articles, or any other type of document. Textual analysis, like all qualitative research, is flexible and open ended. Depending on who conducts the research and the model used, there are different steps and measures.

- **Qualitative document analysis** enables researchers to develop categories and protocols after analyzing documents. It emphasizes "process, context, and significance and how the document helps define the situation and clarify meaning for the audience member" (Altheide, 1996, p. 12).

- Critical discourse analysis (CDA) is an interdisciplinary methodology where critical theories are applied to analyze "the opaque relationship of causality and determine between a. discursive practices, events, and texts, and b. wider social and cultural structures, relations and processes" (Fairclough, 1995, p. 132, as quoted in Ramanathan & Tan, 2015).

These approaches are just a few of the possibilities for researchers who are interested in media texts. Whether you choose qualitative or quantitative research, texts enable you to study culture and its artifacts.

Research on the Media Industry

Media **industry research** enables you to learn about media workers, stations, networks, and the overall industry. Methods used to study the media industry include (to name only a few) archival research; participant observation, in which the researcher studies behavior firsthand by becoming part of the study; and interviews, in which the researcher asks subjects open-ended questions to gain insight into their worlds (Altheide, 1996; Foss, 2004; Stokes, 2003).

Archival Research

Research on the media industry develops knowledge of how newspapers, magazines, television stations, cable networks, sport websites, and other forms of media work to produce sport communication content. This section describes some viable methods for studying people and organizations in the sport media industry. The most valuable research in this area is qualitative in nature because the most compelling research questions deal with processes. Whether the research is intended to find out about how sport reporters work or how sport fans experience the media, qualitative research elicits more depth than does content analysis.

In studying the media, access is a key concern. Whether the researcher studies the history of a certain network or the evolution of a certain technology, the primary means of conducting the research are people and documentary evi-

dence, or written sources. One method focused on documents is archival research, whereas methods focused on people include interviewing, participant observation, and oral history. In the archival approach, the researcher obtains original documents and uses them as the primary basis for research. Whether the researcher is studying the history of women's athletics at the University of North Carolina or the history of public relations in the WNBA, he or she must gain access to relevant documents.

As with other forms of research, an archival researcher first defines the object of analysis, creates a research question grounded in the literature of the field, identifies primary sources, and (if necessary) refines the question. The researcher must also ensure that she or he has access to the needed documents. The researcher then gathers data from the documents and synthesizes it, referring back to the hypothesis and expounding on the findings. Archival research is compelling if the researcher has an interest in a certain time period or historical topic. The researcher can uncover nuances from primary sources and thus enliven our understanding of history (Gans, 1979; Gitlin, 1983; Stokes, 2003; Tuchman, 1991).

Interviewing, Participant Observation, and Oral History

Another good methodology for historical research (and for contemporary work) is the interview. Interviews enable sport communication researchers to gain intimate information about experiences in the media industry. In this way, scholars can learn about the perspectives and attitudes of either the audience or media workers themselves. Whether the researcher uses a structured interview, a semistructured interview, an unstructured interview, or a focus group, interviewing provides insightful, meaningful, and sometimes surprising information. As McCracken (1988) vividly described it, "The long interview gives us the opportunity to step into the mind of another person, to see and experience the world as they do themselves" (p. 9). In this type of research, language is vital as both a "tool and the object of analysis" (Jensen, 1991, p. 32). To maximize the work's value, the researcher must interview more than one person and must choose interviewees selectively. The researcher can conduct interviews in person, on the phone, or via email. The researcher should write the questions beforehand using mostly open-ended questions that elicit more than a mere yes or no answer.

Next, the researcher records the interview, takes notes, transcribes it word for word, and determines whether it supports or refutes the research hypothesis. As in other studies, the researcher must offer a detailed account of the process in the methods section of the study write-up, followed by findings in the results and discussion sections. Qualitative research does have limitations, including "time scarcity and concern for privacy," but the long interview overcomes these downsides by giving the researcher data without "participant observation, unobtrusive observation, or prolonged contact" (McCracken, 1988, p. 11). Other challenges include the risk that the researcher's presence could add bias, the fact that data analysis involving interviews is complicated, and the result that the quality of the study relies in part on the interviewees (Gratton & Jones, 2010). Even so, because of their powerful benefits and results, interviews and surveys are the dominant methodologies used in sport research today.

Participant observation involves interviews but goes further because the researcher immerses himself in the actions of a specific group of individuals. This type of research is considered the "most neglected research in sport" (Gratton & Jones, 2010, p. 177). Whereas nonparticipant observation requires the researcher to observe phenomena with no interaction between the researcher, activity, and subjects, participant observation enables the researcher to participate actively in the topic of the research. According to Jankowski and Wester (1991), "The primary purpose of participant-observation research . . . is to describe in fundamental terms, various events, situations, and actions that occur in a particular social setting" (p. 61). For instance, MacGregor and Evanitsky (2005) experienced NASCAR firsthand for an entire season and documented

their results in a book with the racy title *Sunday Money: Speed! Lust! Madness! Death! A Hot Lap Around America With NASCAR*. Similarly, John U. Bacon (2013) studied Big Ten football by embedding himself in the Penn State, Ohio State, Michigan, and Northwestern programs for the 2012 season to produce his book *Fourth and Long: The Fight for the Soul of College Football*. Similarly, Bacon embedded himself in the University of Michigan's

Photo courtesy of Paul M. Pedersen.

Options for conducting research into crowd interactions include nonparticipant observation (in which the researcher observes but does not interact with the crowd) and participant observation (in which the researcher observes and interacts with the crowd). If you were investigating the communication activities of highly identified fans attending a soccer match, why would you choose nonparticipant observation or participant observation as your preferred qualitative research approach?

football program in *Overtime: Jim Harbaugh and the Michigan Wolverines at the Crossroads of College Football* (2019).

In participant observation, researchers use their expertise and experience to gain access to a group of people. They prepare for the experience by reading fully about the industry, company, league, or team that they will observe. They then write a plan and develop a schedule, making sure that the work can fully answer the research question. When conducting fieldwork, they fit in and talk to people discreetly, taking notes and being as unobtrusive as possible; along the way, they monitor their field notes and seek to fill gaps as needed. Once they have completed the fieldwork, they reflect on the experience and write up their thoughts during the observation phase. Next, they write their findings, which detail what they did and did not find; this section also addresses any shortcomings in the work. The researcher reflects not only on whether the findings supported the research question but also on their own actions and methods. Although most of what they write is included in the analysis section, field notes can be provided in an appendix. As in all research, researchers using this method refer to theories, existing literature in the field, and the research question.

This type of research offers many positives, including the direct and candid reporting of events and phenomena. Whereas researchers using other methods generally rely on other people, in this method they engage actively in the process. In addition, the research occurs in a natural environment rather than an artificial one, as is the case with surveys and experiments; therefore, researchers using this method can observe behavior both directly and naturally. In contrast, when researchers use surveys, respondents may not admit certain things and may be generally less forthcoming. Weaknesses of this approach include the researcher's potential inability to fully understand some phenomena experienced, missing observations, and influencing subjects (Gans, 1979; Jones, 2015; Jankowski & Wester, 1991; MacGregor & Evanitsky, 2005).

Oral history is one of the oldest methodologies, fostering seminal and pioneering studies as well as archival research. Oral history involves interviewing individuals about past experiences; therefore, it allows the researcher to collect "memories and personal commentaries of historical significance" (Ritchie, 2003, p. 19). The researcher then transcribes and summarizes the interviews and uses them for research. To use this approach, of course, the researcher must have access to relevant individuals for interviews and must prepare well before each interview. It is best to begin an interview with simple, clear questions about the interviewee's background and then progress to more difficult and provocative questions. Respect for the interviewee is paramount. Ask good questions, and let the subject do most of the talking. It is also vital to adequately document the interview (Ritchie, 2003; Stokes, 2003), record it (for later transcription), and take notes about nonverbal gestures and other relevant information.

Oral history research in sport communication might involve, for example, in-depth interviews of Negro league baseball players. Researchers could document their experiences in segregated baseball before Jackie Robinson's integration of professional baseball in 1947. This project would not only enable contemporary society to better understand the experiences of black players before integration but would also provide insight into U.S. cultural history. A recent example of oral history in industry includes *Basketball: A Love Story* by Jackie MacMullan, Rafe Bartholomew, and Dan Klores (2018), inspired by ESPN's documentary film series of the same name. The authors investigated the entire history and evolution of the game, offering firsthand testimony from players, coaches, executives, journalists, and others.

Research on Audiences

The study of audiences is equally as important as studying the sport media industry; in sport, the audience is especially important for ratings, sponsors, and corporations. When studying audiences, the most effective methodologies use surveys, interviews, focus groups, and oral histories. Communication research on audiences includes studies of the effects of the media on audiences, as was especially evident in the "all-powerful effects" (or hypodermic needle) media theory of the 1930s (see chapter 4 for more on this and other theories mentioned here). The "limited effects era" began in the 1940s with Paul Lazersfeld's work and, later, Joseph Klapper's work

(Creedon, 1994, pp. 9-10).

The "powerful but contingent" era beginning in the 1970s was based on Carl Hovland's World War II research about a "hierarchy of media effects," as well as Maxwell McCombs and Donald Shaw's legendary agenda-setting research (Creedon, 1994, pp. 10-11). Theories during this era focused on the knowledge gap and on uses and gratifications. In the late 1980s, the "powerful content and contextual effects" era began, acknowledging that "the media are powerful *and* that the power is contingent *and* contextual" (Creedon, 1994, p. 12). Media-effects and sport communication research has often focused on "motivations for viewing, locus of exposure, and effects of exposure" (Creedon, 1994, p. 13). One example is Kozman's (2013) study of the Tiger Woods scandal in the media and public opinion toward Woods (Abeza et al., 2014). Media-effects research can use different methods, including experiments.

Survey Research

Experimental research is replicable; that is, it can be repeated by others with identical findings. The survey process proceeds in a similar manner. It begins with a statement of objectives and a clear and coherent proposition or hypothesis to be tested. In social-scientific research, causal hypotheses are most important—that is, those that study the "causes of phenomena" (Weisberg, Krosnick, & Bowen, 1996, pp. 29-30). Next, the researcher states how the concepts will be operationalized or "defined in such a way that they can be measured" (p. 30). The researcher also determines the target population then collects survey data via interview, telephone, mailed questionnaires, or email. Next, the researcher determines whether the study requires a panel study with follow-up surveys or is a typical cross-sectional survey with respondents participating only once.

The strengths and weaknesses of survey research were examined by Babbie (1998), who found that surveys work well when the researcher seeks to describe a large population. They are also flexible in one sense because they allow the researcher to ask different questions on the same topic. Weaknesses include the inability to adequately study complicated issues or engage the "context of social life" (p. 273). Survey research is also inflexible in the sense that the study design remains rigid, whereas in qualitative research the

design can be modified throughout the process. As with scientific experiments, survey research is also somewhat artificial because it does not "measure social action" (p. 274) but addresses only past or hypothetical actions of respondents. In sport communication, this type of research could be used to survey sport fans' consumption patterns through various questions about media use and buying habits (Babbie, 1998; Weisberg et al., 1996).

The Internet is a valuable tool for data collection, especially with tools such as SurveyMonkey and Google Docs. Online surveys' benefits include access to certain populations and groups of people (teams' fans) globally. As a result, a larger sample size can be attained with cleaner data and fewer missing values. Online surveys also are more efficient as far as timing (quicker to send out, quicker to analyze with database or statistical applications such as SPSS). Online surveys are often more cost effective since they don't require postage and printing.

A researcher still must be aware of the challenges and disadvantages. There can be sampling bias since they do not involve random samples from the population being studied. For example, during a survey of fans of the New York Yankees, not everyone will post in the NYYFans.com forum. Younger, more passionate fans may post more than older ones. To combat this, the researcher can combine online and paper surveys, comparing results of both. Online surveys can potentially have low response rates since respondents may not open emails due to the large number of spam emails today. If there is an incentive for respondents, they also may fill in multiple responses to maximize their chances to win. And finally, there can be access issues within an online community where people ignore the message, a moderator deletes it, or the community members respond negatively or abusively since the researcher is viewed as an outsider (Jones, 2015; Wright, 2005).

Ethnographic Research

Ethnography, which is anthropological in nature, is a qualitative method that captures depth of experience. It is based on cultural forms and includes the "everyday" life (Jankowski & Wester, 1991, p. 54). An ethnographer participates in individuals' lives over time—observing, asking questions, and collecting data that elucidate what she is studying. Ethnography is used to study a specific group or subculture and most often uses observation, participant observation, and in-depth interviews. The researcher endeavors to take the emic perspective (that of the individuals being studied) rather than the etic perspective (that of a researcher) (Gratton & Jones, 2010). For example, if you were interested in the Minnesota Lynx of the WNBA, you could follow the team for part of a season, documenting media coverage of athletes at press conferences and interviews.

Focus groups also enable researchers to study complicated issues and individuals' opinions and perceptions of them (Babbie, 1998). For subjects, students can use friends or fellow students; however, unlike participant observation and ethnography, focus-group subjects are in a laboratory setting. The groups typically consist of 12 to 15 people who are convened for a discussion about a predetermined topic relevant to the researcher's work. Generally, the researcher uses more than one group to increase the generalizability of the study. Focus groups are considered social research with real-life data. Other strengths include flexibility, high validity, quick results, and low cost. Disadvantages include the fact that focus groups provide less control than individual interviews; in addition, it is difficult to analyze data singularly and among groups. It is also difficult to convene groups, and the environment must be right to facilitate effective discussion (Babbie, 1998). In sport communication, this method could be used to study fans' perceptions of a team's treatment of season-ticket holders.

Today's digital sport landscape creates vibrant opportunities for sport researchers. Online newspapers can be studied the same way as texts through content or textual analyses. Analysis of social media such as blogs and Twitter, social news networking sites (Digg, Reddit), content communities (YouTube), and social networking sites (Facebook) have text, photographs, videos, and highly interactive data. A researcher can perform a content analysis of NBA clubs' Twitter use (Wang & Zhou, 2015) or spectators' tweets during the Super Bowl (Chang, 2019). The researcher can conduct an online survey as Billings, Qiao, Conlin, and Nie (2017) did

when studying 125 respondents and their uses of Snapchat for following various sports, contrasting their motivations with Facebook, Twitter, Instagram, and Pinterest. A researcher can also immerse himself within a community to develop a descriptive, fertile, and illuminating view of online behavior in a "netnography" such as Abeza, Seguin, O'Reilly, and Nzindukiyimana's (2017) study of data from the official Twitter accounts of 20 professional sport teams from the NBA, NFL, MLB, and NHL. As Jones (2015) discussed in his book on research methods for sport studies, netnography takes principles of ethnography and applies them to online behavior to further understand a community through an immersive and naturalistic approach and flexible methods.

Kozinets (2010, as cited in Jones, 2015) listed steps for a netnography. First, define the research question. Make sure netnography is appropriate for what is being studied, and assess whether there is sufficient online presence as far as communities, interaction, and engagement. Second, identify a site for the study. It must be diverse, data rich, and interactive. Before entering a community or group, get to know the group. Third, make sure ethical considerations and issues are addressed before embarking on the research. Four, join and gain entry to the community and online group. Do not overload members with excessive information at the outset. Only provide essential details and information, yet be clear about project information and goals. Next, collect data from all sources and maintain field notes. Data can be archival (existing data that the researcher did not create), elicited (created through interactions with the community), or field note data (the researcher's records of research, observations, and reflections of the group, including decisions made during data collection and the researcher's own experiences). Then, conduct data analysis manually or with software. Finally, leave the group once conclusions are shared, and keep all commitments made to the group (Jones, 2015).

Some appropriate methods for studying digital content include participant observation, interviews and focus groups, online surveys, and examination of online documents. The quality of data is vital. Anonymity is an issue with online

USING DATA ANALYTICS TO HELP AN NHL TEAM

Mike Peterson
Director of hockey analytics
Tampa Bay Lightning

By the end of Mike Peterson's internship interview with the Tampa Bay Lightning in 2009, he knew it was a great fit for him. More than a decade later, he still feels the same way. "I still feel it is the place I want to be, even more so now since we have great ownership and leadership," he said. "I enjoy working there because everyone is so supportive. I also get to design our own projects for ways we think can help."

Peterson's serendipitous path into hockey began in football country. He was born and raised in Midland, Texas, *Friday Night Lights* country, where football fandom reigns. He earned BS degrees in computer science and mathematics and a master's degree in mathematics—all from Texas Tech University.

Peterson originally planned on working in cryptography and cryptanalysis and aspired to earn a PhD in mathematics. That all changed, however, when he found out about University of Central Florida's DeVos Program, a top-five graduate program in sport business.

During graduate school at UCF, Peterson worked on attendance prediction projects for MLB teams, specifically the Pittsburgh Pirates, Cleveland Indians, and Tampa Bay Rays. It was his second year at UCF, though, when he discovered his passion for another sport. "I felt that working in hockey would be much more exciting and trailblazing as there has been much less work done in that sport," he said, adding, "I did not grow up watching hockey but knew that the same types of analysis and sabermetrics done in baseball could be applied to hockey."

Bill Sutton, former DeVos professor, and former director and founder of the Vinik sport and

Mike Peterson, director of hockey analytics.

Photo courtesy of Mike Peterson.

entertainment management program at the University of South Florida, calls Peterson "the proverbial smartest guy in the room." According to Sutton, "There are a significant number of talented sports analytics people in the sport industry but Mike is the rare person that can help everyone understand the numbers and what they mean without making them feel inadequate in any way. . . . Mike provides intelligence that makes everyone feel better and perform better."

Part of Devos' requirements included an internship. "As fate may have it, the Lightning were looking for an intern in hockey analytics, someone who could explore new ideas and methods of evaluation, ideas prominent in the book *Moneyball* by Michael Lewis," said Peterson. "There is something to be said about being in the right place at the right time."

Peterson submitted his résumé through TeamWork Online and emailed Imran Khan, the director of hockey operations. He heard back within an hour, interviewed, and then interned there for a semester. By the end of his internship, Peterson became the first person with a technical background to be a full-time employee in hockey analytics for an NHL team. That was five years prior to the "summer of analytics," when there was more attention on NHL teams that were first exploring hockey analytics.

Now, Peterson is director of hockey analytics and is in charge of projects and questions that management or the coaching staff have regarding player statistics. For Peterson, a typical week—"there are not enough hours in the day to get everything done that we would like to," he admits—includes managing both short-term and long-term projects as well as updates to reports. "No two days are alike as far as work and there are always new questions and projects," he said. He also enjoys attending research-based and hockey analytics conferences such as NESSIS, the New England Symposium on Statistics in Sports. "I think everyone gets a lot more out of it when the presenters can discuss their work without having to be careful what they say," he admits.

The Lightning also has a business analytics group that invests in data and storytelling. According to Brendan Russell, director of analytics for the Lightning, "The main objective will always be to learn more about our business and our fans and create value." One way to do that is real-time web scraping through Python, which allows teams to constantly monitor trends and react, thereby increasing competition and delivering value to fans.

Data analytics revolutionizes sport by answering questions via patterns that professionals such as Peterson and Russell can measure—whether they're about customer behavior, points, or scoring in different sports. It is integral because it provides ways to put concrete numbers to theories for evaluation and is a way to objectively answer questions via empirical evidence. According to Peterson, "Analytics is necessary on both the business and player side of each sport for these reasons. Questions may pertain to 'How can we sell more tickets, sponsorships, etc.?' or 'What players can we get to help us win more games?'"

Leagues and teams continue their exploration and application of analytics. "MLB (Red Sox, Indians) was a trailblazer on the sports side, so naturally they were the first to enter the business analytics world because they already had people and systems," Russell said. "The NFL (Falcons, 49ers) is a close second thanks to their deep pockets. I'd say the NBA (Magic, Mavericks) has caught up with them, and the NHL (Kings, Lightning) is close behind."

As far as areas of expansion within data analytics, spatial data analysis will continue to grow. "All sports will have locational data for players for all games at the highest pro levels," Peterson said. "Baseball and basketball have had this available to teams for many years. Football recently provided it to all teams to analyze. Hockey has been publicly talking about a system to track similar data and showcased this at the 2019 NHL All-Star game."

Basketball provided shot charts that no longer had to be tracked by hand. "This revealed to them the value of the corner-three, what that did to defenses, and led them to the conclusion that three-pointers should be attempted more than the current rates," Peterson said. "Each year you see a new record for the total number of three-pointers attempted across the league. In baseball, we're seeing more teams shifting than ever before and there has been an increase in the total number of batters shifted on across the league each season. Similar changes may come to football and hockey."

A recent revolution in hockey was the discovery of how much more important controlling the puck in the zone is compared to dumping it in (i.e., releasing control of it and forechecking to get it back). This decision happens when a team is trying to enter the offensive zone at the blue line and must decide if players have enough room to control it in via carrying it over the line; passing to another teammate entering; or dumping it in to avoid turning it over at the line and hoping to regain it deep in the zone (Tulsky, 2011; as quoted from Peterson, personal communication, 2019).

As a result of such progress, more analysts are needed to determine value from such data. While it's difficult to get a job in sport analytics, more teams want to create and add to both the business and player sides of all sports. According to Peterson, "The advice I'd give students is to work hard, try to specialize in one or two areas, whether that is R, Python, or SQL, data visualization, analytics, communication."

Peterson also stresses the importance of experiential learning. "One of the best things you can do is get experience while you are in school," he said. "This may be formal internships or it could be just doing projects on your own using skills and methods you learned in school."

Peterson epitomizes the importance of internships and experience and their ability to jumpstart and sustain careers. He's well on his way to a long, successful career in hockey analytics.

sources of data, but the researcher should not be discouraged. The criteria for evaluating data is similar to any other qualitative research.

The researcher also has to consider informed consent, which is not always possible. With data on closed sites or those that require registration or logins for access, the researcher must have informed consent. It is also necessary with elicited data and can be secured via email or written documentation. With archival data, the data could be viewed as being in the public domain and accessible to the researcher. If there are any doubts about any ethical issues, the researcher should rework and reconsider the approach to the study.

With regards to anonymity, Jones (2015) believes online pseudonyms should be treated as real names and the researcher should use alternative pseudonyms to names adopted by the study's participants.

These methodologies are only a few of the choices available to researchers. Sport communication researchers should select the best method for their specific studies and gear it toward their strengths. For creative individuals with a background in reporting, in-depth interviewing would be a good choice. For those interested in storytelling, narrative analysis would work. For those interested in a more scientific approach, methods that use numbers, such as surveys and content analysis, might work best. The main considerations should be ensuring accuracy, adhering to ethical guidelines, and furthering the discipline of sport communication through significant and thought-provoking topics of inquiry.

CHAPTER WRAP-UP

Summary

This chapter expands on previous chapters by showing how important research is to athletes, teams, leagues, companies, broadcasting stations and networks, newspapers, digital outlets, and other industry practitioners, as well as sport communication academics. It discusses how companies have used research and ratings and offers suggestions for conducting research studies. In today's transitory media environment, it is especially important to be proactive in getting and staying informed. Information and power enable a sport entity to function more effectively and to reach its goals. In industry, this proactive approach includes knowing an entity's place in the sport communication arena, being aware of the competition, and recognizing possible challenges and opportunities for growth.

Research techniques that can be used in both industry and **academic research** include mail, telephone, and computer-based surveys; interviews in an informal or focus-group setting; and textual analysis of newspapers, magazines, and other publications. Academic researchers can also conduct ethnographic research, such as observation and participant observation, in which researchers become part of a culture or subculture and immerse themselves in the sport communication world. Many can work with online studies and data, too. Each method and each technique has its strengths and weaknesses, but all are valuable to sport communication's growth. For sport communication to reach its potential as an academic and industry discipline, thought-provoking research must expand awareness and spark dialogue and debate. An ever-changing sport communication environment challenges both professionals and academics to be resilient, flexible, and innovative.

This chapter also serves as a segue to the next chapter, which addresses sociological dimensions of sport communication. Indeed, research provides a commonality among all the book's chapters because it stresses the requisite components of vision, expanded knowledge, and commitment.

Review Questions

1. What is research, and why is it important in the practical and theoretical arenas of sport communication?

2. What are the four types of research? Define and describe each one.

3. What are the primary differences between quantitative and qualitative research in sport communication?

4. Why is a literature review important in sport communication research?

Individual Exercises

1. List several potential sport communication studies. What methodology would work best for each one? Why?

2. Attend a sporting event, and observe the media, the team, the fans, and other sport communication components. For each component, brainstorm and record research topics and potential research questions.

3. Compile a list of sport communication books, trade publications, online resources, and research databases. How would you use these resources in your research?

Photos courtesy of Paul M. Pedersen.

PART III

Addressing Issues in Sport Communication

Now that you are familiar with the background and components of sport communication, the final section of this book covers ancillary components— that is, the sociocultural and legal aspects. Chapter 12 explores how and where sport communication intersects with sociological and cultural issues. Discussions in this analysis address the emergence, role, function, diffusion, effect, and meaning of sport communication across time and societies. Many aspects of society are reflected and sustained through sport communication. The chapter examines many of these aspects, including the ways in which sport communication often facilitates and maintains culture, societal structures, myths (e.g., in the form of heroes and villains), socialization, cultural values, social policies, norms (e.g., through commentary), and power relationships (e.g., in the form of racism, sexism, and ageism). Key cultural and sociological issues analyzed include enjoyment, gender and sexuality, race and ethnicity, nationalism, and the marketability of violence. Because of the sport media's effect on sociocultural issues, this chapter also examines gatekeepers' ability to reflect, create, shape, reinforce, and sustain myths, values, perceptions, power structures, and societal beliefs.

Finally, chapter 13 examines legal issues in sport communication. Covered areas include freedom of the press, privacy rights, freedom of speech, and the right of publicity in the sport industry. Furthermore, the chapter explores broadcast rights, copyright and trademark, and legal aspects of gender equity and sexual harassment in sport communication.

Photo courtesy of Paul M. Pedersen.

Sociological Aspects of Sport Communication

KEY TERMS

ethnicity	hegemony	race
gender	nationalism	sexual orientation

PROFILE OF AN ADVOCACY GROUP

Association for Women in Sports Media (AWSM)

The Association for Women in Sports Media (AWSM) epitomizes the power of agency, advocacy, and activism. This international, nonprofit organization has more than 1,000 female and male members in industry and academia who support the "advancement and growth of women—both student and professional—in sports media" (AWSM, 2019). It not only serves as a support network for aspiring sport communication professionals but also provides funding, grants, and career development opportunities.

AWSM was founded in 1987 by Nancy Cooney, Susan Fornoff, Michele Himmelberg, and Kristin Huckshorn; in its early years, the organization helped women gain access to locker rooms. Now, according to Vicki Michaelis, John Huland Carmical Chair in sports journalism and society at the University of Georgia, "AWSM has an even more formidable task: to ensure that women have equal access to jobs in sport media" (personal communication).

Marie Hardin, dean of Penn State's College of Communications, has been an AWSM member since 2004 and credits the organization with creating more accountability on gender equity in media organizations: "AWSM has raised the visibility of women in the sports-media workplace and has voiced the need for diversity and equity in sports departments, bringing these issues to the attention of managers and others in hiring positions" (personal communication).

AWSM commemorates pioneering women and honors them with the Mary Garber Pioneer Award. In 2019, columnist, author, and broadcaster Jackie MacMullan won the honor for her longstanding work at the *Boston Globe*, *Sports Illustrated*, and ESPN. She is also the only woman who has won the Naismith Basketball Hall of Fame's Curt Gowdy Award for her basketball writing and reporting ("AWSM Past Pioneers," 2019). Additionally, AWSM's Ann Miller Service Award honors individuals for their contributions to the organization. In 2019, charter member Celeste Wil-

Photo courtesy of Nicola Ferris.

Joining professional organizations provides career networking opportunities. Here, University of Virginia's student chapter of AWSM convened to interview *SB Nation's* Caroline Darney (back row, second from left), other sport professionals from Virginia athletics, and local sport affiliates who spoke to the campus chapter.

liams was honored ("Ann Miller Award Recipients," 2019). Through this award and other efforts, AWSM brings pioneers in the field together with aspiring sport communication professionals.

AWSM places female college students in paid internships and offers career development and mentoring. For instance, Michaelis got her job at *USA Today* after meeting a deputy sports editor at an AWSM convention. In 2019, AWSM placed seven women in paid internships at *USA Today*, *Sports Illustrated*, MLB.com, ESPN, USA Softball, CNN Sports, and *Sporting News* ("AWSM Internships and Scholarships," 2019). The Sports Journalism Institute also hosts one AWSM scholar each summer at its summer workshop. In addition to AWSM's national events and programs, individual chapters also support and mentor members.

AWSM's first collegiate chapter was located at Oklahoma State University (OSU); as of 2019, there are 21 chapters at universities nationwide. Nicola Ferris is co-president of AWSM's chapter at University of Virginia and says, "Having an AWSM chapter at the University of Virginia is incredibly important because it provides its members with various opportunities to excel in a niche career area that is not necessarily emphasized at the University of Virginia, especially not for women. AWSM gives members an ability to explore different areas of sports media and establish relationships with professionals that can provide opportunity and advice."

For sport communicators, AWSM is an invaluable resource. Its website is located at http://awsmonline.org.

Taken as a whole, the media possess the power to make social myths into realities by shaping our perceptions of individuals, events, and places. More specifically, the sport media affect the sport culture in the same manner. As Billings (2018) suggested, differences in coverage and characterization mold the manner in which both the sporting public and society in general perceive the myths of sport. In this process, myths serve a positive function in preserving transcendent athletes and championships in our memories, yet they can also conceal problems such as concussions in football and hockey by mythologizing games and sport. Myths can bind and challenge communities. When myths simplify and dramatize situations, such as race, crime, and other important issues, these myths become reality, and media bias becomes society's bias. As gatekeepers, the media select which stories to report as news; in doing so, they sometimes create and fortify stereotypes because of the public's limited exposure to these issues. Individuals can only experience a finite number of events, so much of their reality is based upon what the media select and present.

In a seminal study of media power in presidential campaigns, McCombs and Shaw (1972) determined that the issues characterized by the public as significant political matters were those that were discussed most often in the mass media. These two scholars developed the agenda-setting theory, which illustrates that even though the media, acting as gatekeepers of information, may not tell the audience *what* to think, they still tell audiences what to think *about*. In doing so, they create the perception that certain topics are more important than others (McCombs & Shaw, 1972). Whereas first-level agenda setting deals with the transmission of object salience, second-level agenda setting is concerned with the transmission of attribute salience; that is, "the media also tell us *how to think* about some objects," (McCombs & Ghanem, 2001, p. 69, emphasis in original).

The media's power and effects are illuminated by other theories, such as framing, uses and gratifications, and cultivation. Through this power, the media shape beliefs and values and therefore society; more specifically, they shape the dynamics of sport entities, sport culture, and public perceptions of sport. This chapter explores the relationships and intersections between sport communication and sociocultural issues such as **gender**, **ethnicity**, **sexual orientation**, violence, **nationalism**, and popular culture. The discussions presented here address the emergence, role, function, diffusion, effect, and meaning of sport communication across time and societies. The chapter examines how sport communication facilitates culture, structure, myths, socialization, values, social policies, norms, and power relationships. The first key cultural theme pertains to **race** and ethnicity.

RACE AND ETHNICITY

The sport media are often scrutinized and criticized both for their coverage and portrayals of minorities and for not hiring and promoting minorities in large enough numbers. Discussions of both of these criticisms are increasingly complex due to the growing number of people who are of mixed race or do not identify with any particular racial group (Billings, Butterworth, & Turman, 2018). As a result, sport communication professionals sometimes find it difficult to discuss race. As we have seen in various scandals involving athletes, coaches, and sport professionals alike, it is important for all to be diligently respectful in choosing language and communicating about multicultural issues.

Race is not the same thing as ethnicity. Ethnicity denotes "a cultural heritage that people use to identify a particular population," whereas race indicates a "population of people . . . believed to be naturally or biologically distinct from other populations" (Coakley, 2016, p. 216). In addition, racial categories are often applied in ways that do not represent an individual's true or full background. For example, individuals of mixed background are often referred to as *black* by the media, as is the case for golfer Tiger Woods, whose background is Caucasian, African American, Indian, and Asian. The sport media, like much of human society, rely on the visual, which sometimes simplifies and limits perspectives on race. Skin pigment substitutes for the complexity of individuals' backgrounds (Billings, Butterworth, & Turman, 2018). As this chapter will show, when addressing issues of race and ethnicity, sport reflects the dominant ideologies and power relations of mainstream society (Coakley, 2016) regarding participation, media coverage, hiring, and other issues.

Media Coverage of African Americans

African Americans have participated in sport since the 16th century and the settling of the "New World" (Whitaker, 2008, p. xviii). However, when professional sport leagues were organized in the United States in the 19th and early 20th centuries, African Americans were mostly barred from participating. As a result, they formed their own leagues—for example, the Negro baseball leagues, which featured stars such as Josh Gibson, Satchel Paige, Cool Papa Bell, Buck Leonard, and many others. After Jackie Robinson integrated Major League Baseball (MLB) in 1947, Negro baseball could not survive in the long term. Other all-black teams remained, however, at historically black colleges and universities, such as Grambling State University with its legendary coach Eddie Robinson (Whitaker, 2008).

After MLB integrated, other leagues and sports followed suit. The National Football League (NFL) was integrated in 1946 by Bill Willis and Marion Motley of the Cleveland Browns and Kenny Washington and Woody Strode of the Los Angeles Rams, who were the NFL's first black players since 1932 ("Senate Marks," 2006). The National Basketball Association (NBA) was desegregated in 1949 by the New York Knicks' Nat "Sweetwater" Clifton, the first black player signed in the NBA. Clifton and other pioneers such as Earl Lloyd paved the way for later stars such as Bill Russell, Kareem Abdul-Jabbar, Michael Jordan, Shaquille O'Neal, Kobe Bryant, and LeBron James (Whitaker, 2008). In the National Hockey League (NHL), the Boston Bruins' Willie O'Ree became the first black player in a 1958 match against the Montreal Canadiens ("NHL," n.d.). Althea Gibson and Arthur Ashe helped integrate tennis by becoming the first African Americans to win grand slam tournaments in 1956 and 1968, respectively (Laucella, 2009). Although these and other pioneering athletes set records and left their legacies, the media did not always accurately and substantively document and report their feats.

According to Stuart Hall (2003), the mainstream media are more than a powerful source for racial ideas. Rather, they promote ideologies by articulating and constructing a definition of race and by organizing representations and frames for understanding our social world and how it works. Until the mid-1970s, African Americans received very limited coverage in the sport media. Today, although that coverage has increased, it often focuses on a few sports, typically football, basketball, and baseball. This lack of coverage, and the manner in which African American athletes are portrayed, often places them in secondary or "entertainment" roles. This combination—insufficient and secondary coverage—marginalizes, minimizes, and devalues the many accomplishments and contributions to sport made by minority athletes (Bernstein & Blain, 2002).

The marginalization of minority athletes occurs in various ways. As black athletes gained success and dominated sport, whites conveniently viewed their success as the result of a purported biological advantage. In this way, sport media serve to naturalize certain conceptions of race through discourse that creates black persons as natural athletes (Birrell & McDonald, 2000). There is a fascination with the alleged natural physicality of the African American "other," and this view of superior athleticism keeps black people in the confines of the physical while downplaying their intellect (Hoberman, 1997). Therefore, black men are often stereotyped as strong, swift, and agile yet dumb or noncerebral (Rhoden, 2006).

In a related issue, the Anglocentric hypothesis offers one perspective on why black and other minority athletes are "over-represented at certain positions" in sport (Entine, 2000, p. 275). This practice, known as *stacking*, is based on the idea that while black athletes excel in sports and positions that require speed and quick reflexes, white athletes are suited to "strategic positions" that demand "decision-making skills" (Entine, 2000, p. 275). For example, in baseball, black athletes are more likely to play outfield positions, Latino athletes to play in the middle infield, and white athletes to play catcher and corner-infield positions (Billings et al., 2018). Stacking can also involve self-selection, as athletes are told that certain sports are not for them, a view that is reinforced by media coverage in which white journalists cover sports played by mostly white athletes (e.g., lacrosse) and black reporters cover sports played largely by black athletes (e.g., football and basketball) (Billings et al., 2018).

Furthermore, the sport media tend to focus on the central roles played by European American athletes and highlight their contributions on the field as integral to the outcome of the competition. For example, the media stressed Peyton Manning's intellect, leadership, preparation, and hard work throughout his 18-year career with the Indianapolis Colts and Denver Broncos (Billings et al., 2018). By focusing on the cerebral or "thinking" abilities of white players, the sport media potentially create the impression that minority athletes make poor team leaders, coaches, or administrators because they lack the necessary knowledge and thinking skills to succeed in these roles. As a result, the sport media encourage society to view African American athletes as dumb jocks while considering European Americans as mentally astute.

The dumb jock stereotype dates back to 500 BC, when Greek athletes were disparaged for spending time preparing to perform rather than spending time enhancing their mental development (Sailes, 2017). Philosophers of the time often portrayed these athletes as inadequate and uninformed citizens with inept minds (Coakley, 2016). Sailes (1993) suggested that today's sport media coverage has helped create a similar perception of athletes in modern society. For example, many college students perceive student-athletes as "dumb jocks," and they perceive African American student-athletes as the most inadequate.

The media also tend to portray black athletes as deviant, violent, and hypermasculine. They are sometimes characterized or stereotyped as "thugs" who are uncontrollable, excessive in their habits, and addicted to drugs and gambling. This tendency fosters the idea that black athletes are overly aggressive or "animal-like" (Coakley, 2016).

This type of media portrayal was particularly evident in the struggles and triumphs of boxer Jack Johnson in the early 20th century. "At a time when whites ran everything in America, he took orders from no one and resolved to live always as if color did not exist," wrote Geoffrey C. Ward (2004, p. 4), author of *Unforgivable Blackness: The Rise and Fall of Jack Johnson*. Boxing was a means for blacks to show skill, gain social status, and earn respect (Gems, 2006). However, when Johnson defeated Caucasian Tommy Burns in Australia to become the first black heavyweight champion of the world, the "press reacted as if Armageddon was here. That this may be the moment when it all starts to fall apart for white society" (Burns, 2005). Many in the press suggested that Johnson did not earn the title because he had not beaten longtime heavyweight champion Jim Jeffries.

Members of the boxing community coerced Jeffries out of retirement, whereupon Johnson knocked him out. In response, the U.S. Congress passed legislation forbidding the transport of films depicting the victory. There would not be another black heavyweight titleholder until Joe Louis defeated Jim Braddock in 1937 ("Louis Becomes Champ," n.d.).

Whites and some blacks viewed Johnson as "profligate, arrogant, amoral, a dark menace, and a danger to the natural order of things" (Ward, 2004, p. 4). Many in the press referred to Johnson with derogatory language for dating white females. He was eventually arrested and jailed for a bogus violation of the Mann Act, which prohibited the transport of females in interstate commerce for the purpose of prostitution or for immoral purposes (Burns, 2005). The portrayal of Johnson exemplifies the "hypersexual brute" stereotype, which has also been applied to contemporary athletes such as the late Kobe Bryant (Leonard, 2004, p. 296), who was charged with sexual assault in 2003. Even though the case was ultimately dropped, and Bryant rebounded from it to continue his career successfully until his tragic death in 2020, it was another example of the "larger dynamics of racialized sports celebrity" (Leonard, 2004, p. 286).

NFL quarterback Michael Vick also weathered controversy, scandal, public fallout, and redemption. As Giardina and Magnusen (2013) wrote, Vick was viewed as a "threat" and fell from grace long before he was convicted of being involved in a dog-fighting ring. The media portrayed him as a "troubled *Black athlete*." (Denzin, 1996, p. 321 as cited in Giardina & Magnusen).

Media treatment of Vick during the dog-fighting case reinforced biased societal discourse about race, sport, and crime. It did little to dispel stereotypes of black athletes (Laucella, 2010a).

These examples reinforce research findings of Cynthia Frisby, professor of strategic communication at the University of Missouri School of Journalism. In her examination of online and print news articles about male athletes, stories on African American athletes focused on criminal actions compared to more positive stories about white athletes. Specifically, 66 percent of crime stories involved black athletes compared to 22 percent on white athletes. Seventy percent of

domestic violence stories involved black athletes compared to 17 percent of white athletes. And 53 percent of stories about black athletes had a negative tone compared to 27 percent of stories about white athletes. "True cultural sensitivity requires the eradication of racial and ethnic stereotyping; thus, journalists and reporters must reflect on how their own unfounded beliefs about race differences in sport likely contribute to the stereotyping of black athletes as engaged in more criminal activity and innately physically gifted yet lacking in intelligence and strong work ethics," Frisby said. "Not only does negative media coverage serve to legitimize social power inequalities, but also it is likely to undermine black athletes' achievements and contribute to stereotype threat" (as quoted in Hurst, 2015).

Media Coverage of Other Minorities

Native American, Latin American, and Asian American athletes also experience stereotypical media characterizations. For example, much discussion has centered on the use of Native American mascots by sport entities; in 2005, the NCAA instituted a ban on the use of such mascots, which affected institutions including the University of Illinois and the University of North Dakota. Chief Illiniwek and the Fighting Sioux, respectively, were retired. The University of Illinois still had not selected a new mascot as of 2019, and North Dakota's athletics teams are now called the Fighting Hawks (Billings et al., 2018). Such mascots are also used by some professional franchises, including the Washington Redskins, Cleveland Indians, Chicago Blackhawks, and Atlanta Braves. Many people argue that these mascots make a mockery of Native Americans, their culture, and their contributions to society. As sport management scholar Ellen Staurowsky (2004) explained, "The manufactured images of American Indians that serve to mark and market athletic teams in the United States contribute to the relegation of American Indians to the past, casting them in limited and limiting social roles" (p. 12). This view was detailed by Strong (2004): "The use of Indian sports mascots, logos, and rituals are just such normalized everyday activities; they exclude contemporary Native Americans from full citizenship by treating them as signs rather than as speakers, as caricatures rather than as players and consumers, as commodities rather than as citizens" (p. 83).

Others suggest that criticisms are simply part of another attempt to own and control the role of Native Americans in U.S. society. "Because members of the dominant culture 'identify' with the invented tradition of Indianness embodied in mascots, they believe that their intention to honor the Indian warrior tradition carries more weight than the dishonor and disrespect experienced by many Native Americans" (Strong, 2004, p. 82). This stance is largely attributable to what King (2004) characterized as an attempt on behalf of white-centered society to "lay claim to Indianness as well as the authority to delimit how it enters into public culture" (p. 5). Not surprisingly, research has found that Native Americans are more offended than the general public by such imagery and are more supportive of changing it (Laveay, Callison, & Rodriguez, 2009). As Billings and Black (2018) noted in *Mascot Nation: The Controversy Over Native American Representations in Sports*, "The Native American debate has evolved from one largely about two entities, sport and indigenous peoples, to one that some perceive to be a struggle over American identity, liberalism versus conservatism, and how agency is determined" (p. 5). Agency is embraced or rescinded, according to the authors, as people seek agency only when they believe they have the power to do what they think is right, along with a perception that they will be rewarded for asserting this power. Native Americans and their allies continue to work toward the eradication of misrepresentation and abuses of Native Americans, their images, names, spirituality, and culture (Billings & Black, 2018).

Nonetheless, some maintain that the use of these mascots honors Native Americans. For example, in a letter to fans, Washington Redskins owner Daniel Snyder wrote, "Our past isn't just where we came from—it's who we are" ("Letter," 2013). However, while other team mascots reference Native Americans, spotlighting skin color is particularly offensive to many people. According to historians and researchers of Native American issues, the very word *redskin* was born out of hatred and referenced the long and

troubled history between Native American people and European colonizers (Martinez, 2013). In 2014, six federal trademarks affiliated with the Redskins (granted between 1967 and 1990) were canceled by the U.S. Patent and Trademark Office, which ruled that the term *Redskins* denigrated "a substantial composite" of American Indians (Brady & Finnerty, 2014). Although the team appealed the ruling, the move reflects the fervor surrounding the issue, which has prompted national campaigns—such as "Change the Mascot," launched by the Oneida Indian Nation—to end the use of "r*dskins" ("Change," n.d.).

Members of other minority groups have also had to combat stereotypes in media portrayals, including past professional baseball players (e.g., Roberto Clemente, Joe DiMaggio) and current and recent stars (e.g., Yu Darvish, Masahiro Tanaka, Yasiel Puig). Latin American athletes are often portrayed in the sport media as "hot tempered," whereas Asian American athletes are often viewed as the "model minority." Though ostensibly positive, the model-minority label suggests that Asian American athletes are obsessive conformers, rigorously self-disciplined people, and excessively hard workers (Mayeda, 1999; Wong, Lai, Nagasawa, & Lin, 1998). In addition, the influx of Asian nationals into Major League Baseball has often been characterized as an "Asian invasion," which some see as a stereotype portraying Asians as hostile foreigners (Mayeda, 1999; Wong et al., 1998).

Andrea Eagleman (2011) found that such biases and stereotypes were perpetuated by *Sports Illustrated* and *ESPN The Magazine*. For example, U.S.-born white athletes were viewed as successful due to a strong work ethic, whereas U.S.-born black athletes were portrayed as having physical talents. U.S.-born Latino athletes were also perceived as hard workers who achieved success on the field as a result. For international Latino athletes, however, the main frame was overcoming a tragedy or obstacle; in addition, as with black athletes, the media framed them as naturally athletic and powerful. International Asian players were portrayed as "other," and the media stressed physical appearance (small stature), nationality (country of origin), and language (use of interpreter, insufficient language skills). Eagleman's study shows the importance of equitable coverage, as well as the intersections of race, ethnicity, and nationality in sport, especially in America's national game.

Employment Opportunities for Minorities

A diverse workplace is one that embraces and practices inclusion and equal opportunity in terms of hiring, treatment, and advancement at all levels. In the 2018 newsroom census conducted by the American Society of News Editors (ASNE), the number of minority journalists employed in daily newsrooms was 22.6 percent, despite the loss of 505 journalism jobs that year among survey respondents. While the response rate was just 17 percent, lead researcher Meredith Clark wrote, "In *these* newsrooms, journalists from underrepresented groups are closing the gap, and women of all racial and ethnic backgrounds make up a big part of those gains" ("The Survey," 2018). Specifically, in online-only organizations, people of color working as managers and full-time journalists made up 25.6 percent of the workforce, up from 24.3 percent the previous year. Additionally, 79.3 percent of the responding organizations had at least one woman among their top three editors, and 32.7 percent had at least one minority journalist in the top three positions ("The Survey," 2018). Other findings showed that women made up more than a third of newsroom employees overall, 41.2 percent of daily newspaper employees, and 47.8 percent of online-only employees. By 2025, ASNE seeks to achieve a percentage of minorities in newsrooms that reflects the percentage of minorities in the United States ("2015 ASNE," 2015).

As for sport organizations in particular, Richard E. Lapchick has been an activist and watchdog for diversity hiring for many years. His studies at the University of Central Florida's Institute for Diversity and Ethics in Sport (TIDES) have set the benchmark for equitable and transparent hiring processes. In 2017-2018, the TIDES report on athletics leadership positions among the 130 Football Bowl Subdivision Schools (FBS) revealed that 89.2 percent of presidents, 83.1 percent of athletics directors, and 100 percent of conference commissioners were white (Lapchick et al., 2017). In all, whites held 86.6 percent

of the 395 campus leadership positions at the schools. One positive, however, was the hiring of Desiree Reed-Francois and Carla Williams at UNLV and UVA, respectively. Reed-Francois was the first Latina woman and Williams the first African American woman to lead FBS athletics departments. Whites also dominated the coaching ranks, accounting for 86.2 percent, 87.4 percent, and 91.4 percent of men's head coaching positions in Divisions I, II, and III, respectively (Lapchick, 2019).

In addition to abysmal grades for racial hiring in collegiate sport, gender hiring was disappointing. According to Kane and LaVoi (2018), the percentage of female coaches in women's sports has declined from 90 percent in the early 1970s to 43 percent in 2018. Only 13.4 percent of campus leadership positions were held by people of color, and only 17.7 percent were held by women, according to Lapchick's study. White women held 5.4 percent of athletics director positions at FBS schools (Lapchick et al., 2017). Similar to Kane and LaVoi's findings, women held only 40.1 percent of head coaching jobs for women's teams in Division I and only 4.0 percent of coaching jobs in Division I for men's teams (Lapchick, 2019). In Division II, women's teams held 35.8 percent of coaching jobs for women's teams and only 4.0 for men's teams. Women held 44.3 percent of head coaching jobs for women in Division III and 6.8 percent for men's teams (Lapchick, 2019). As TIDES reported, women held 40.8 percent of head coaching jobs for women at all three levels combined and 5.2 percent of head coaching positions for men's sport combined in all three divisions. Having women in leadership positions such as coaching is important since it not only influences young girls and women, but also men's perception of women as competent leaders (Kane & LaVoi, 2018).

To help combat poor records, the NCAA adopted *The Pledge and Commitment to Promoting Diversity and Gender Equity in Intercollegiate Athletics* in 2016 for schools. It is not binding, and its impact, so far, has been minimal, according to Lapchick et al. (2017).

On the positive side, the Tucker Center for Research on Girls & Women in Sport documented a slight increase and net gain in women head coaches of women's teams (0.2 percent) in

2018-2019 for the sixth year in a row; even so, however, males were hired to fill 53.6 percent of all head coaching vacancies (LaVoi, 2019). *Forbes'* Kim Elsesser (2019) observed that women NCAA coaches are still losing ground and dealing with gender bias post Title IX. As she explained, "The truth is men dominate coaching for the same reason that they run most of our Fortune 500 companies and our country. When we think of leaders, we tend to think of men. We want someone to lead our team, our company or our country, then our experience and unconscious bias makes us gravitate toward men. There's plenty of scientific evidence that when women who are equally qualified present themselves, they seem deficient compared to the man. Prior to Title IX women did not have to compete with men for these jobs. When the power, prestige and pay for these jobs increased, women were left behind" (Elsesser, 2019)

These observations reinforce Wright, Eagleman, and Pedersen's (2011) findings that until changes are made in the hegemonic masculine culture of sport organizations, athletics administration will not achieve gender fairness and equality in hiring and retention. In addition, inequity in hiring for top management positions has a trickle-down effect on other hiring decisions, as documented in Kanter's (1977) homologous reproduction. Kanter argued that persons in positions of power tend to gravitate toward those who are socially similar to them. Thus, through hiring practices, "men reproduce themselves in their own image" (Kanter, p. 48). This practice has been used to explain the lack of female coaches and female sports information directors in intercollegiate athletics (Laucella, Hardin, Bien-Aime, & Antunovic, 2017).

The work of TIDES is vital to providing a transparent and equitable hiring process in professional leagues and at the collegiate level. Along with stereotypes of minorities in the sport media, the lack of equitable representation of minorities in the sport media and in sport organizations limits opportunities for minorities to obtain high-quality endorsements, play particular sport positions, and become sport leaders. The job of improving media coverage, hiring, and other opportunities requires education, awareness, advocacy, and activism.

MUTUAL INFLUENCE OF SOCIOCULTURAL ISSUES AND SPORT

This section discusses several events and individuals covered by the media in the United States and worldwide, as well as the ambivalence and variances in that coverage. According to sociologist Herman Gray (qtd. in Bruton, 1996), "Black athletes are viewed with a combination of adoration and menace" (Gray, 1995, pp. 12-13). This has been true historically and remains the case today. In one dramatic example, racial issues were covered by the media during the 1968 Olympics, which was broadcast on a large scale, as ABC provided 44 hours of programming that attracted an estimated worldwide audience of 400 million. The particular event—the Black Power salute by U.S. sprinters Tommie Smith and John Carlos on the medal stand—provides an example of sport as a vehicle for highlighting political and nationalistic issues.

The athletes gave the salute, commonly referred to as the *Fist of Freedom*, in response to the social and political unrest occurring in the United States. The two wore black gloves and black stockings with no shoes; Smith also wore a black scarf on his neck. They raised their clinched fists in the air and bowed their heads as the U.S. national anthem played during the awards ceremony for the 200-meter race. The two had planned their nonviolent protest in lieu of the boycott proposed by sociologist Harry Edwards, and the incident is one of the most memorable medal ceremonies in Olympic history. The silver medalist, the late Peter Norman of Australia, who was white, supported the protest and wore a human rights badge on the medal podium ("Salute," 2008). Initially, public reaction was caustic. International Olympic Committee (IOC) president Avery Brundage suspended Smith and Carlos from the U.S. team, and they were ostracized. Now, however, they are viewed as activists and sport heroes; in fact, in 2008, the duo won the Arthur Ashe Courage Award at the ESPY Awards ("Salute," 2008).

Another elite athlete during this era was boxer Cassius Clay, who has been characterized as a "flawed rebel with a cause" (Early, 2006, p. 263). This tumultuous period included the Vietnam

War, the civil rights movement, urban riots, and the Watergate political scandal. Clay won the light heavyweight title at the 1960 Rome Olympics then boxed professionally. After his defeat of Sonny Liston for the heavyweight title in 1964, Clay joined the Nation of Islam and changed his name to Muhammad Ali, for which he was condemned by the boxing world, the press, and the white public. He was viewed as a pariah (Montville, 2017). According to Early, "Never was an athlete so pilloried by the public as Ali was. Most sport journalists ridiculed his religion and refused to call him by his new name" (p. 269). Even so, Ali's ethnic pride and confidence were reflected in his self-proclaimed title, "the greatest," and in his signature phrase, "Float like a butterfly, sting like a bee" ("Muhammad Ali to Receive," 2012). In 1967, Ali was stripped of his title when, citing his religion, he refused to enter the military during the Vietnam War. This decision prompted a draft-evasion conviction and a long legal battle that lasted until 1971, when the U.S. Supreme Court ruled in Ali's favor ("Muhammad Ali to Receive," 2012). Ali suffered from Parkinson's disease for more than three decades and passed away in 2016 due to septic shock (Tinker, 2016). His death put his hometown of Louisville in the national and international spotlight. World leaders, celebrities, athletes, and fans mourned and celebrated the icon's extraordinary life during a memorial service, funeral, and procession. Former boxers Mike Tyson and Lennox Lewis were pallbearers, along with actor Will Smith, who portrayed "The Greatest" in the Hollywood movie *Ali* (Aulbach, 2019; "Celebrities Flock to Muhammad Ali's Memorial Service," 2016). Ali has won numerous awards, including the 2005 Presidential Medal of Freedom, as well as *Sports Illustrated*'s Sportsman of the Century award ("Muhammad Ali to Receive," 2012).

Whereas Ali fought injustice with intensity and fervor, tennis pioneer Arthur Ashe was perceived as "the quiet militant" (Thomas, 2006, p. 279). As the first black man to win the U.S. Open, Wimbledon, the Australian Open, and the NCAA men's tennis singles championship (at UCLA), Ashe used his social platform to address apartheid, mistreatment of Haitian refugees, and the low graduation rates of black athletes (Laucella, 2009). In 1992, Ashe was forced to

Photo courtesy of Paul M. Pedersen.

Covering sport as a media professional often involves writing about much more than just the sporting contest or event. For instance, William C. Rhoden (right), a writer and podcaster for The Undefeated and former sports columnist for the *New York Times*, interviews an individual holding a war protest poster during the grand opening celebration of the Muhammad Ali Center in Louisville, Kentucky.

disclose that he had contracted the HIV virus through a blood transfusion; Magic Johnson had disclosed his HIV-positive status in 1991. Journalists framed Ashe as a victim, a pioneer, a role model, and a hero; he increased dialogue and awareness about HIV and AIDS and donated considerable resources through foundations and advocacy (Laucella, 2009).

After Ashe, other athletes such as Michael Jordan and Tiger Woods have transcended sport and gained universal appeal (Thomas, 2006). Sportswriters have canonized Jordan as a demigod who was the "embodiment of the sports spectacle" with his six NBA championships and his endorsements with Nike, Gatorade, Hanes, Wheaties, Coca-Cola, McDonald's, and others

Arthur Ashe Boulevard, A Tribute to Richmond's Pioneering Athlete and Activist

In 2019, Ashe's home city of Richmond, Virginia renamed a street to honor him after two failed attempts in 1993 and 2003 (Robinson, 2019). Arthur Ashe Boulevard was once a place where Ashe was banned from playing tennis. *Richmond Times-Dispatch* columnist Michael Paul Williams wrote that the renaming "paves way for progress" in the former capital of the Confederacy and signifies a "transformation that goes beyond street signs" (2019, para. 9). U.S. Representative John Lewis of Georgia was the keynote speaker at the street's dedication, and thousands participated in the city's embrace of its African American history. Leaders called it a long overdue honor for Ashe and "a significant milestone in Virginia's commemoration of the 400th anniversary of the arrival of the first enslaved Africans in 1619" (Robinson, 2019). Raymond Arsenault, author of *Arthur Ashe: A Life*, believes Ashe made peace with his hometown and "it paves the way for better days ahead" (as quoted in Williams, 2019, para. 36). Richmond Mayor Levar Stoney echoed these comments and said, "By naming the boulevard after Arthur Ashe, we're once again parting with our darker past and embracing

Photo courtesy of Alex W. Edlund and the *Richmond Times-Dispatch*.

Richmond Mayor Levar Stoney was one of the officials who paid tribute to Ashe, honoring his athletic accomplishments and his commitment to social justice and equality.

our brighter future" (Robinson, para. 9). U.S. Senator Tim Kaine of Virginia called the name "an act of healing" (para. 10).

(Andrews, 2000; Kellner, 2001). Even today, years after his retirement, he remains one of the top sport celebrities, according to the *Forbes* annual ranking of athletes and celebrities.

Throughout his career as a player, and later as majority owner of the Charlotte Hornets, Jordan refrained from publicly discussing politics and social justice. This stance has been addressed by critics such as *New York Times* columnist William C. Rhoden (2006), who discussed what he referred to as the "dilemma of neutrality" (p. 197): "As it is, black athletes like Jordan have abdicated their responsibility to the community with an apathy that borders on treason" (p. 200). Jordan

is not alone in taking this approach. In Rhoden's view, many of today's black athletes—unlike Jack Johnson, Jesse Owens, Jackie Robinson, and Muhammad Ali—do not feel a collective identity and connection with the black community. In a similar vein, David Andrews (2000) wrote that Jordan's charisma popularized the NBA to corporate and middle America but constitutes not an example of transcendence but a "case of complicitous racial avoidance" (p. 177).

Over time, though, Jordan has selectively supported and spoken out on some issues. In fact, he wrote a piece for ESPN's The Undefeated entitled, "I Can No Longer Stay Silent." According to Jordan, "We need to find solutions that ensure people of color receive fair and equal treatment AND that police officers—who put their lives on the line every day to protect us all—are respected and supported" (2016, para. 2). He contributed $1 million each to the International Association of Chiefs of Police's Institute for Community-Police Relations and the NCAACP Legal Defense Fund (Jordan, 2016).

A 2017 *Washington Post* article noted that Jordan is no longer "sitting out" on political and social issues after he spoke out against former Los Angeles Clippers owner Donald Sterling, the killing of blacks by police, and supported athletes making statements during national anthems (Boren, 2017). In 2018, Jordan also supported LeBron James through a statement his spokesperson made to NBC News. President Trump criticized LeBron James, saying he likes Mike (2018). Jordan sided with James, saying he's doing a lot for his community (Thompson, 2018).

There is also a sort of "color blindness" associated with Tiger Woods, who has called himself "Cablinasian," a mix of Caucasian, black, Indian, and Asian (Billings, 2013, p. 52). Woods has drawn attention since he first appeared on the *Mike Douglas Show* in 1978. After he grew up, his Nike "Hello World" announcement in 1996 officially introduced him to marketers and fans worldwide, and he joined Michael Jordan and golfer Arnold Palmer as transformative global sport celebrities and marketing icons (Laucella, 2018). In the following years, Woods gained unrivaled name recognition and influence as he boosted tournament broadcast ratings, newspaper and magazine sales, sales of Nike golf merchandise, and Q Scores (measuring brand recognition) and public opinion polls; he also became sport's first billion-dollar athlete (Laucella, 2018).

In 2009, however, Woods' marital-infidelity scandal greatly affected his game, his endorsements, and his media coverage. The scandal ended up costing Woods his marriage to Elin Nordegren, as well as endorsements with Accenture, AT&T, PepsiCo, Gillette, Tag Heuer, and Electronic Arts. Nevertheless, the media still covered him daily, especially as he regained his winning form ("PGA Tour," 2015). Woods won his 15th major title, the Masters, for the fifth time

in 2019, sealing one of the greatest comeback stories over his scandal and back injury. At that time, Woods had not won a major tournament in 11 years. "As a nation stood witness to the golf brilliance of the man who is perhaps the biggest unifier in this country today—who else can get the president, Candace Owens, Barack Obama, Serena Williams and Stephen Curry on the same page?" wrote The Undefeated's Jerry Bembry (2019).

There are some current athletes, however, that leverage their sport celebrity and power to fight for racial equality. The University of Missouri's black football players vowed to boycott games unless Timothy M. Wolfe resigned as president for failing to address racist incidents at the school (Freedman, 2015). Many of these players were from nearby St. Louis, where racial tensions escalated after the fatal shooting of Michael Brown in Ferguson by Darren Wilson, a white police officer who was never indicted. Black Lives Matter, a grassroots activist movement, has been embraced by the NBA's LeBron James and Derrick Rose, who both wore "I Can't Breathe" shirts in pregame warm-ups to honor Eric Garner. The shirts reference Garner's final words before dying as a result of being held in a chokehold by a New York City police officer (Adande, 2014).

LeBron James, Chris Paul, Carmelo Anthony, and Dwyane Wade opened the 2016 ESPY Awards with a powerful call for social change and justice. LeBron's statement set the tone. "It's not about being a role model, it's not about our responsibility to the tradition of activism," James said. "I know tonight we're honoring Muhammad Ali, the GOAT, but to do his legacy any justice, let's use this moment as call to action for all professional athletes to educate ourselves, explore these issues, speak up, use our influence and renounce all violence." (Mandell, 2016).

In contrast to media coverage of male black athletes, the sport media have generally provided only limited coverage of female black athletes. Historically, the combination of racism and sexism has "meant that stories of people of color and women are far less known" than those of white men (Lapchick, 2009, p. 1). When the media do cover black female athletes, they tend to marginalize these women's performances. As with black men, black women's athletic achievements have often been viewed as a natural result of their alleged closeness to animals, nature, and masculinity. For example, Olympic gold medalist Wilma Rudolph received contradictory coverage by the media, which portrayed her as both attractive, charming, and athletic yet also comparable to a wild animal such as a gazelle (Cahn, 2004).

Female black athletes endure great stigma, both in the sport media and in society, due to their status as both female and black. They are forced to function in two worlds, one in which they are oppressed and one in which they are exploited. In addition, images of female sexuality and femininity have created an ideal of white womanhood versus a supposedly inferior (and "other") black womanhood; more pointedly, black women athletes' sexuality has been viewed as "lascivious and apelike" and the black female body as "virile or mannish" (Cahn, 2004, pp. 220-221). Black female athletes have been, and still are, often characterized as possessing more natural physicality with a different kind of femininity.

This view has been evidenced in numerous instances, including the Williams' sisters, who arrived as the top two tennis players on the women's tour by 2002 (Douglas, 2005). Despite their lofty accomplishments and ongoing successes, they have received ambivalent and sometimes aggressive reactions from fans and the media. Their presence in an elite, white sport has been interpreted by some as the "absence of racism rather than the privileging of whiteness" (Douglas, 2005, p. 259). However, according to Schultz (2005), "The success and visibility of Serena and Venus Williams, in tennis and consumer culture, obscures their racialized exceptionality, extending the myths of color blindness and equal opportunity in U.S. sport and society" (p. 340). They have been rooted against and jeered by fans at some tournaments, especially early in their careers (Schultz), and the mainstream sport media positioned their bodies as "simultaneously sexually grotesque and pornographically erotic" (Cooky Wachs, Messner, & Dworkin, 2010, p. 142).

A recent example occurred during Serena Williams' 2018 U.S. Open finals loss to Naomi Osaka, who won her first grand slam title. Williams was fined $17,000 for three code violations and penalized one game for escalating disputes with chair umpire Carlos Ramos. Williams had previous run-ins with U.S. Open officials in 2009 over a foot-fault call in the semifinal match against Kim Clijsters and a hindrance call in the 2011 final against Sam Stosur. In response to Ramos' rulings, "To lose a game for saying that is not fair," Williams said. "There's a lot of men out here that have said a lot of things, and because they are men, that doesn't happen" ("Naomi Osaka Captures," 2018, para.21). Australia's *Herald Sun* published a controversial cartoon showing Williams throwing a tantrum and, some say, reducing her to a racist and sexist prop ("Cartoon Depicting," para. 4). Retired U.S. men's players James Blake and Andy Roddick came to Williams' defense, calling the penalty sexist and admitting that they said worse things on the court during their playing careers (Yaptangco, 2018). Nevertheless, The Undefeated's Jerry Bembry believed Williams deserved a share of the blame for her actions, calling the meltdown "not a good look" (2018). While there was criticism toward Williams, she did not want to take away from Osaka's special moment. She wrote an apology to Osaka, who idolizes the 23-time major champion.

Osaka's response brought Williams to tears. "People can misunderstand anger for strength because they can't differentiate between the two," Osaka replied, according to Williams. "No one has stood up for themselves the way you have and you need to continue trailblazing" (Martin, 2019, para. 8).

The combination of problematic and sometimes absent media coverage dramatically limits society's awareness and acceptance of black female athletes. It also suggests that "white America, for the most part, is unaware [of] and perhaps even uninterested in the realities of the sport experience for the African American sportswoman" (Corbett & Johnson, 2000, p. 207). As noted by Bonilla-Silva (2003), racial issues shade nearly everything in the United States, where whites often amend "racial reality to legitimize notions of colorblindness, freedom, equality, democracy, and America," especially in sport (Leonard, 2004, p. 287). Celebrity black athletes are often used to make a case for equal opportunity, yet they are still exploited since few hold positions of power (Rhoden, 2006). In the words of the late Arthur

Ashe, without opportunities for advancement and empowerment beyond their roles as athletes, an "incomplete and misleading image" persists of black athletes (Ashe, 1991, p. B7). This also holds true regarding media treatment of other minorities.

GENDER AND SPORT MEDIA

The sport media have traditionally been predominantly white and predominantly male. Just as the sport media have been criticized for their coverage of minorities, they are equally scrutinized for their coverage of female athletes. Many perceive that the media—through commentary as well as amount and type of coverage—devalue and downplay the accomplishments and contributions of females in sport. The sport media tend to characterize females differently than males, focusing on their familial relationships and their physical attractiveness rather than their strength, power, and performances on the fields of play. Similarly, the working environment for women in the sport media is often challenging. Female sport reporters sometimes face the same type of marginalization experienced by women on the field. Even after Title IX opened doors for women in sport, there remains a dearth of coverage and of women working in sports departments (Laucella et al., 2017). This section of the chapter addresses coverage of female athletes and sport, as well as hiring and career opportunities and experiences for women in sport communication.

Coverage of Female Athletes

The development of women's sport has been complex and contradictory (Kristiansen, Broch, & Pedersen, 2014). Since the 1972 enactment of Title IX, a U.S. law prohibiting discrimination based on sex at educational institutions, women's participation in sport has grown more than 900 percent (Women's Sports Foundation, 2012). However, this growth in participation rates is not matched in media representation of female athletes or in employment opportunities for female sport journalists (Cooky & LaVoi, 2012; Laucella et al., 2017).

Considered one of the last bastions of male dominance, the sport media have consistently neglected to provide equitable coverage of female athletics; in fact, females are dramatically underrepresented and underreported at all levels (Lavelle, 2014; Messner & Cooky, 2010). This disparity creates the perception that female athletics are less worthy, lack competitiveness, and lack quality for sport viewers. The sport media's marginalization of women's sport "denies them the status, power, and prestige that are routinely given to male athletes" (Kane, 2002, p. 115). The next few subsections address the quantity and quality of women's sport coverage, as well as hiring issues for women in sport communication and media.

Overall Women's Sport Coverage

Historically, the media have contributed to the marginalization, oppression, and invisibility of women's sport and female athletes. The media tend to reinforce "natural" sex differences by representing a masculine sport **hegemony** that privileges men over women (Daddario, 1998). Female athletes receive less coverage, and the coverage they do receive is often biased. Research literature has focused on quantity and quality of women's sport media coverage and the variances between men's and women's coverage in traditional and online media outlets, consistently finding an underrepresentation of women (Burch, Eagleman, & Pedersen, 2012; Eastman & Billings, 1999; Messner & Cooky, 2010). Thus, female athletes' representations, even decades after Title IX, do little to advance the cultural acceptance of women who participate in sport (Duncan, 2006).

The 2012 Olympiad in London was the first edition of the Games in which women athletes received more overall coverage (55 percent) than men, due in part to the successes of U.S. women in the competition itself (Andrew Billings, 2015, personal communication). The women made up 44 percent of the athletes but won 63 percent of U.S. gold medals and 56 percent of all U.S. medals. The Olympics broadcast reached 3.6 billion unique viewers in 220 territories and countries, and NBC's prime-time telecast averaged more than 31 million viewers, an increase of 12 percent over the 2008 Beijing Olympics (Billings, Angelini, MacArthur, Bissell, & Smith, 2014). The global magnitude of the Games makes it an

Photo courtesy of Paul M. Pedersen.

With the mass media's limited and marginalized coverage of female athletes, sport organizations (such as the Utah Royals of the National Women's Soccer League featured in this photo) often rely on source publicity (through team websites, social media platforms, etc.) to promote their games and inform their fans and stakeholders.

need for a closer examination of comments since the findings from his and his coauthors' longstanding previous research were not consistently replicated in the Olympic telecasts from 2000 to 2010. The researchers concluded that NBC's programming decisions may not have resulted in gender parity, yet there was a "significant tilt in coverage toward female athletes" (Billings et al., 2014, p. 53). Eagleman, Burch, and Vooris (2014) also found more equitable coverage during the 2012 London Olympics. In another study, which looked at websites spanning seven countries and six continents, fewer biases were found in terms of gender and nationalism. At the same time, the Olympics are viewed as a "relative anomaly" in terms of both participation levels and coverage (Billings et al., 2014, p. 38).

NBC touted Rio 2016 as the "most successful media event in history" due to its extensive coverage across broadcast networks, online, and the NBC Sports app (Coche and Tuggle, 2018, p. 200). The network has been criticized for its sexism, yet for the second consecutive summer Olympics, NBC gave more airtime to women's sport. This airtime, however, was given to certain sports—mainly socially acceptable ones. Specifically, prime-time coverage devoted more than 98 percent to gymnastics, track and field, swimming, diving, and beach volleyball. As a result, Coche and Tuggle (2018) found no evidence of sexism in their quantitative analysis of NBC's prime-time coverage of the 2016 Rio Olympics; however, they also did not find diversity in the sports covered. NBC primarily focused on superstars Michael Phelps; Simone Biles; Usain Bolt; Kerri Walsh; and compelling stories and personalities such as Lochtegate and 74-year-old South African coach Anna Sofia Botha, who coached gold medalist Wayde van Niekerk. According to the researchers,

important media event to study, and the increases in female participation and coverage show progress. A paradox exists, however, because men and women were still described differently, although not always in ways that involved sexism or bias. For instance, women's inexperience can be a function of their youth, especially in gymnastics (Billings, 2015, personal communication). Similarly, Eagleman (2015) found that the media portrayed female gymnasts as strong and powerful—much in control of their performances at the London Olympics—even as their language choices and commentaries infantilized and objectified the competitors.

In other differences, women athletes received more comments about emotions and appearance than did men (Billings et al., 2014). In addition, NBC gave the largest amount of airtime to gymnastics and beach volleyball, two sports that have been deemed gender appropriate by societal custom. Billings and colleagues (2014) noted the

NBC's coverage follows a "great man/great woman syndrome" rather than including profiles of lesser-known athletes and their accomplishments. Overall, the findings indicated that NBC did not necessarily treat male and female athletes differently; however, it treated them differently based on their sport and athletic status. On a side note, Coche and Tuggle noted that there was a dearth of women as NBC anchors, commentators, analysts, and reporters.

The differentiation in media coverage for males and females is defined by the manner in which they are portrayed in the sports pages. Males are most often characterized in terms of their physical and athletic abilities; in contrast, females are often depicted in terms of their femininity and physical attractiveness (Dafferner, Campagna, & Rodgers, 2019). This "sexualization" of female athletes "trivializes them and robs them of athletic legitimacy" (Bernstein & Blain, 2002, p. 8). According to Kane (2011), this "sex sells" strategy regarding women's sport is deeply ingrained in sport journalists and marketers. For example, athletes such as Amanda Beard, Gabrielle Reece, Danica Patrick, Hope Solo, Ronda Rousey, Alex Morgan, and Caroline Wozniacki have posed for images that showcase their beauty and athleticism. While the resulting media attention may not necessarily lead to more attention to their athletic performances (or past performances), it can lead to more sponsorships.

Olympic gold medalist and sport journalist Donna de Varona said she is not critical of the athletes but of "a media culture consumed with pushing images of the impossibly perfect woman" (Billings et al., 2015). This tendency extends beyond traditional media. Clavio and Eagleman (2011) found that 71 percent of images on sport blogs featured a male as the primary subject as compared with just 9 percent for women (the remainder focused on both or neither); in addition, the female portrayals were far more likely than the male portrayals to be sexually suggestive.

Billings and colleagues (2018) discussed gendered language in sport—specifically, the media practices that introduce bias and differentiate between men and women in dialogue and commentary. The media often attribute male athletes' success to exceptional power, courage, experience, skill, and composure (Eastman & Billings, 1999; Halbert & Latimer, 1994), whereas female athletes' achievements are often linked to interpersonal relationships, signifying their dependency on significant others. Examples of attributions to male athletes include powerful, fearless, and conquering compared to talented, dedicated, and emotional attributions for women. Men are called "best in the world" and women are called "best women in the world" (Billings et al., 2018, p. 112). They are also the subject of misguided and limiting comments about emotion, compassion, beauty, and luck. Other categories of differentiation include gender marking, naming practices, and sexual disparagement.

Gender Marking

Sport media coverage and acceptance of female athletes depends on their ability to manage traditional feminine roles while pursuing a career in athletics. If this balance is not achieved, female athletes do not gain acceptance (Hilliard, 1983). This process often takes place through a practice known as *gender marking*. Whereas male athletes are described as affecting the sport through their performance—for example, having the best rebounding skills in basketball—female athletes are gender marked by commentators noting that their performance is outstanding but only in relation to other women's performances.

In another example, women are gender marked when media outlets refer to a men's sport simply as the sport itself (e.g., basketball) but to a woman's sport by means of a gender tag (e.g., women's basketball). This type of marking is even built into the names of the premier U.S. professional basketball leagues—the NBA, or National Basketball Association, and the WNBA, or Women's National Basketball Association (Billings et al., 2018). Similarly, Kian, Vincent, and Mondello (2008) analyzed media coverage of March Madness, including online sport publications, and found that men's basketball was framed as the standard, women's basketball was marginalized as "the other," and portrayals reinforced dominant notions of the gender order in sport. Gender marking supports and strengthens bias against female athletes by qualifying their abilities (Halbert & Latimer, 1994).

Naming Practices

Naming practices also are problematic in the coverage of women's sport. Female athletes are often referred to by their first names, whereas male athletes are generally referred to by their last names (Billings et al., 2018; Halbert & Latimer, 1994). It is theorized that using athletes' last names distances them from viewers and that this distance assists in creating the perception that the athletes are first class and heroic (Billings et al., 2018). In addition, some schools use an added feminine qualifier in naming their women's teams. For example, the men's basketball team at Old Dominion University is called the Monarchs, whereas the women's team is called the Lady Monarchs.

Sexual Disparagement

Women athletes are often labeled as "butch" or lesbian, which can both mislabel and denounce one's sexual orientation (Billings et al., 2018). Gay athletes such as Brittney Griner and Gus Kenworthy have helped spark dialogue, as has the website OutSports, but misperceptions (and sometimes silence) persist, especially in terms of women athletes. According to Lavelle (2014), however, Griner's successes have changed the discourse. In 2012, Griner won the ESPY Awards' Female Athlete of the Year and Female College Athlete of the Year (Lavelle, 2014). Her height (6 feet 8 inches), wingspan, and dunking ability are often discussed in the media. Yet in media coverage of Griner's 2012 undefeated national-championship season at Baylor, Lavelle (2014) found that comparisons to Yao Ming, references to gender identity, and physical appearance reinforced the oppositional ways in which male and female athletes are generally covered.

Further information also emerged about Griner's experience at Baylor. She said that everyone knew she was gay but that an unspoken rule imposed by Baylor coach Kim Mulkey prevented players from discussing sexuality. Griner, who now plays for the WNBA's Phoenix Mercury, came out to journalist Maggie Gray in an SI.com article ("Griner, Delle Donne, Diggins," 2013). Since then, more and more media members and sport figures have portrayed Griner as an "unstoppable" and "revolution-ary figure in sport," including coaching legends Bob Knight and Geno Auriemma on SB Nation's basketball blog SwishAppeal (Fetters, 2013). This development was lauded by the *Atlantic*'s Ashley Fetters (2013), who wrote, "The way fans, coaches, and the mainstream media talk about Griner is a subtly radical, relatively new, and pretty damn great way to talk about women in sports: as an athlete."

Women in sport careers want to be valued for their intellect, talents, and leadership skills. Former WNBA All-Star Becky Hammon was

The NBA has taken a proactive approach in hiring women. Commissioner Adam Silver, team executives, and coaches like Gregg Popovich hire the most qualified candidates, and Becky Hammon, Nancy Lieberman, Jenny Boucek, Kara Lawson, and others are working at the league's teams.

Photo courtesy of Paul M. Pedersen.

hired as the first female assistant NBA coach in 2014-2015 and became the first female NBA All-Star assistant coach in 2016 (Mandell, 2016). She is just one example of the talented women working in sport. As of September 2019, the NBA had 11 female assistant coaches. These include Brittni Donaldson, who was promoted from a data analyst to an assistant coach on the Toronto Raptors; Teresa Weatherspoon (New Orleans Pelicans), who joined Swin Cash, the Pelicans' vice president of basketball operations; Jenny Boucek (Dallas Mavericks); Kristi Toliver (Washington Wizards); Lindsay Gottlieb (Cleveland Cavaliers); and Kara Lawson (Boston Celtics) (Matange, 2019). Both the NBA and WNBA have showcased diversity efforts, including their partnership with leanin.org, #LeanInTogether. This public service campaign encourages men and women to work together to embrace equality in the workplace and home ("NBA and WNBA Partner With LeanIn. Org," 2015). As discussed in the opening vignette, AWSM is another organization that mentors, supports, and empowers women. Upcoming sections of this chapter discuss the need for more women in the sport communication industry, both as gatekeepers of content and as decision and policy makers.

Hegemony and Sport

The term *hegemony* refers to a dominant group's ability to establish and maintain power over other groups (Pedersen, 2002); its origins go back to Italian theorist and Marxist Antonio Gramsci. According to the theory of hegemony, females threaten the hegemonic structure of the male domain of sport (Whisenant & Pedersen, 2004). Furthermore, this threat would be reinforced by increased coverage of women's sport or by changes in media characterizations of female athletes. In the meantime, one recent study found that women's sport received only 3.2 percent of the media coverage at local network affiliates (Cooky, Messner, & Musto, 2015)—with few changes over the 25-year longitudinal study. More specifically, ESPN's *SportCenter* devoted only 2.0 percent of airtime to women's sport (Cooky et al., 2015). The authors suggest three policy benchmarks for producers, commentators, and sport anchors. They include presenting a roughly equitable quantity of coverage of women's sport, specifically 12 percent to 18 percent of broadcast coverage. They also stress the need for a wider range of men's sports beyond the big three—men's college and professional football, basketball, and baseball. The second suggested benchmark is presenting women's stories in ways "roughly equivalent" with the presentation of men's sport, including both technical quality and quality of the anchor's verbal description and presentation. Third, the authors suggest hiring and retaining on-camera anchors who are willing to do the prior benchmarks and are supportive and knowledgeable about women's sport (Cooky et al., 2015). Through such decisions, the news media influence audience members' interest in and perceptions of women's sport.

Historically, sports editors have argued that audiences are not interested in women's sport, so they are not obligated to cover it. However, a recent follow-up to Hardin's 2005 study of newspaper sports editors found a shift in the attitudes, values, and beliefs of sports editors (Laucella et al., 2017). If sustained, this shift could lead to more opportunities for women as journalists and to improvements in the coverage of female athletes and women's sport. In the follow-up survey, more editors than in the past disagreed with the notion that Title IX has "hurt" men's sport; in addition, although attitudes about the obligation to cover women's sport had not changed much, a higher percentage of editors—20 percentage points higher—said that they see hiring women as an ethical obligation (Laucella et al., 2017). When editors commit to hiring women, they find women who can move up and become leaders in their organizations. This hiring is especially needed to combat the patriarchal structure of male superiority and bias often found in sport journalism departments.

Working Environment for Females in Sport

The sport media landscape has been conceptualized as "ideological terrain" in which meanings of gender are "contested and reconstructed" (Messner, 2002, p. 93). The sport media promote patriarchal ideologies that permeate U.S. culture and reinforce perceptions of identity that both reflect and mold the status quo (Messner, 2002).

Female athletes and coaches receive less media coverage than their male colleagues, and female sport journalists consistently struggle to find opportunities and advance in sport journalism careers.

Female sport journalists strive to legitimize their role in sport journalism, and they face numerous barriers to doing so. As discussed earlier, women's entrance into this traditionally male domain threatens the hegemonic masculinity associated with sport. The challenges faced by female sport journalists have been depicted in an episode of ESPN's *Nine for IX* series titled "Let Them Wear Towels: The Women Who Changed American Sports Forever," which covers pioneering sport journalists such as Lisa Olson, Robin Herman, Melissa Ludtke, Claire Smith, Paola Boivin, and Lesley Visser. Professional sport leagues now have policies allowing women in the locker room thanks to Olson and other pioneers who forged a new frontier despite mistreatment, intimidation, and harassment.

Although attitudes are changing and there are now many opportunities for women in the sport media, challenges remain. Hegemonic masculinity is still upheld through discriminatory hiring practices, as well as limited opportunities for women in terms of advancement, payment, and recognition. Just as women are underrepresented in administrative roles in athletics departments and professional sport organizations, they remain underrepresented in the sport media across the United States, where males still tend to dominate both supervisory roles and sport reporting (Miloch, Pedersen, Smucker, & Whisenant, 2005).

In a 2018 TIDES study of 75 Associated Press Sports Editors (APSE) newspapers and websites, hiring practices were given a grade of B in terms of race and a grade of F for the fifth consecutive time in terms of gender. More specifically, whites made up 85 percent of sports editors, 76.4 percent assistant sports editors, 80.3 percent of columnists, 82.1 percent of reporters, and 77.7 percent of copy editor and designers (Lapchick et al., 2018). Similarly, the proportion of men is about 90 percent in the editor positions, 69.9 among assistant sports editors, more than 83 percent among columnists, 88.5 percent of reporters, and 79.6 percent of copy editors and designers. There

was an increase in all categories for women except for reporters, which decreased from 12.6 percent to 11.4 percent from 2014 to 2018 (Lapchick et al., 2018).

On the positive side, the proportion of female sports editors rose from 9.8 percent in 2014 to 30.9 percent in 2018, and the proportion of female columnists rose from 12.4 percent to 16.8 percent, while reporters dropped from 12.6 percent to 11.4 percent. There was improvement in all five categories for people of color. The improvements can be attributed, in part, to former ESPN president John Skipper's commitment to diversity (Lapchick et al., 2018). In fact, without ESPN, the numbers would drop in the categories for editors, assistant sports editors, and columnists; for example, ESPN employed 2 of the 12 people of color who were sports editors; without them, the proportion of female editors would fall from 15 percent to 12.8 percent. ESPN employed 75 of the 89 assistant sports editors. That percentage would drop from 30.1 percent to 6.3 percent if the ESPN staffers were taken out of the sample. ESPN also employed 38 of 44 women who were columnists at the highest circulation newspapers and websites; if they were removed, the proportion would plummet from 18.6 percent to 2.9 percent. Since the 2018 TIDES Report, ESPN has endured rounds of layoffs, and Lapchick notes the need for APSE to adopt the Ralph Wiley Rule, similar to the Rooney Rule in the NFL, which calls for a diverse pool of candidates for each vacant position in these five categories (Lapchick et al., 2018).

Although much work remains to be done in improving the coverage of female athletes and the working environment for women in the sport media, females who are interested in sport communication should not hesitate to pursue this career ambition. According to Marie Hardin (introduced in the chapter-opening vignette in chapter 11), "Universities and educators can play a strong role as advocates for our students—male and female—by teaching students about the opportunities and barriers and by doing research that highlights the progress (or lack thereof) in the sports-media workplace" (personal communication).

As discussed in chapters 1 and 2, sport communication's expansion in both academic programs and professional positions provides openings and opportunities for women and minorities. Students should maximize their potential through the classroom and experiential opportunities offered by Michaelis, Hardin, and other academic and industry leaders.

NATIONALISM AND SPORT MEDIA

Nationalism can best be defined as identification with the life and aspirations of the fellow members of a nation, even when we do not know these citizens or have not seen the boundaries of the nation in its entirety (Wenner, 1998). Nationalism is a type of national mythmaking that uses stereotypes signifying the ethical and cultural norms that shape, generate, or reinforce habits among the nation's citizens. Nationalism is reinforced through the media and, specifically, the sport media. In fact, the more that a country's national–political, economic, and military sovereignty is undermined, the greater its need to construct a potent cultural nation. Because of the power of sport in society, sport is the most appropriate means of creating an imagery of national unity through shared experiences and "collective consciousness" (Rowe, 1999, p. 22, as cited in Billings et al., 2018, p. 146).

Nationalistic images can be seen in sport media throughout history, and these images have often reflected the tenor of the society in which they occurred. Such images are particularly visible during the Olympics, as was certainly the case with the 1936 Games. Referred to as the Nazi Games, the 1936 Olympics were used by Adolf Hitler as a forum to push his agenda. Specifically, he exploited the attention given to the Games in an attempt to create the perception that Germany was a tolerant and peaceful nation. Anti-Semitic propaganda was removed, and some 20 transmitting vans and 300 microphones were provided to the foreign media to encourage radio broadcasts, which were given in 28 languages. Hitler perceived hosting the Games as a way to prove to the world that Nazi Germany was the most efficient and superior race in the world. In promoting the Games, Germany used posters and magazine ads that linked Nazi Germany to ancient Greece. The ads depicted what Hitler believed to be the ideal race: blue-eyed, blonde-haired, marked by distinctive features, and heroic. After the Games, Germany dramatically advanced its Nazi agenda, resulting in an invasion of Poland and, ultimately, World War II and the Holocaust.

Hitler's plans for the Olympics were disrupted when American track athlete Jesse Owens won four gold medals, thus dramatically debunking the Aryan myth of racial superiority. Pamela C. Laucella (2016) found that sport journalists at mainstream newspapers respected Owens' talent yet were descriptive, stylistic, and evasive in dealing with the racial and political issues associated with the event. They referred to Owens and other African American athletes as either African or Ethiopian and discussed alleged genetic variances between the races, focusing on African Americans' speed and agility and downplaying their intelligence. Journalists of the African American press remained passive yet resolute in emphasizing Owens' place in history while denouncing Adolph Hitler and Nazism. They touted U.S. athletes' accomplishments and treated all athletes equitably while deriding Hitler. The journalists at the American Communist press were forthright and forceful in promoting equal rights and opportunities for all Americans. They deprecated Hitler and the Nazis and everything for which they stood, including their propaganda, myth of racial supremacy, and ideologies (Laucella, 2016).

The 1972 Munich Games will always be remembered for the tragic massacre of Israeli athletes by the Palestinian terrorist group Black September. The Games also made news for the controversial men's basketball gold-medal game between the United States and the Soviet Union. The "quasi-professional" Soviets won the game 51-50 after the questionable resetting of the clock in the last minute of play (Saraceno, 2004, para. 4). The U.S. team filed a complaint with the International Basketball Federation, but a five-member panel voted in favor of the Soviets. As *Sports Illustrated* wrote, "Everything progressed according to strictly Cold War politics" (Saraceno, 2004, para. 23).

Conversely, the U.S. media characterized the 1980 U.S. Olympic hockey team's victory over the Soviets at Lake Placid as a "miracle on ice." The political context was fraught: Americans had been

Sporting events often reveal and promote international aspects (such as the displayed country flags from a golf tournament in Crans-sur-Sierre GC, Crans Montana, Switzerland). With the globalization of sport, these events are frequently covered by sport media members from around the globe.

taken hostage in Iran, the end of the Vietnam War was still fresh on the minds of many Americans, the Soviet Union had invaded Afghanistan, the United States had endured the Watergate scandal and was facing an energy crisis and increasing unemployment numbers, and many Americans believed that the country was facing its toughest challenges in years. The upset of the Soviets in the semifinals gave such a boost to the American psyche that even sport reporters often erroneously forget about the team's subsequent gold-medal victory over Finland. Many even argue that this victory gave Americans a reason to believe in their country again.

The achievement was recounted in various forms, including an HBO documentary and the movie *Miracle*. Many of these stories characterize the U.S. team's quest for the gold medal as a "Herculean" task. In contrast, most portray the Soviet players and coaches as focused on their work ethic, framing them as robots who showed little emotion and never smiled—even after scoring goals. In interviews, Soviet team members discussed playing hockey as their job,

which required separation from their families. These characterizations symbolized the Soviet team as the antithesis to American values and beliefs, setting the tone for a "good versus evil" theme. In fact, members of the American team received many telegraphs before the game indicating American disdain for the Soviet Union and illustrating that the hockey match represented much more to the American public than a sporting competition. U.S. head coach Herb Brooks was framed as a magical character who inspired his team to defeat the Soviets and later capture the gold medal; he was also framed as a family man who, in stark contrast to the Soviets, balanced his familial obligations with his quest for the gold medal.

A sense of nationalism, or nation building through sport, is often seen in sport media. U.S. athletes are often portrayed differently than their foreign counterparts, and these portrayals typically reflect American culture, tending to reinforce stereotypes of certain nations and bonding Americans together in these beliefs. For example, Brazil is often depicted as synonymous with soccer, New Zealand with rugby, and Canada with hockey. In this way, sport often builds and reinforces the values, beliefs, and character of nations or regions and, in doing so, unifies its citizens.

The soccer World Cup also epitomizes the global nature of sport and the fervor surrounding sport megaevents. During the 2002 World Cup, South Korean fans watched their team's matches on public television screens (Mahoney, 2006). As a nation seeking to increase its economic power in Asia, its passion was evident in its collective rooting interest in its team. In the United States, fans' excitement resulted in viewing parties, record attendance, and social media interactions. Globally, the World Cup is one of the most-watched and most-followed sporting events. Brazil has won five World Cups, and Germany and Italy have each won four (Hackett, 2018).

There is a fine line between celebrating national unity and fostering perceptions that potentially stereotype or devalue other identities (Billings et al., 2018). Former San Francisco 49ers quarterback Colin Kaepernick challenged sport's nationalism and its rituals by sitting and kneeling during the national anthem in 2016, while he was still playing in the NFL. He admitted that he felt uncomfortable honoring the symbol of the United States, a country "that oppresses black people and people of color," and was protesting racial injustice, oppression, and police brutality (quoted in Blackistone, 2016, para. 4). Kaepernick's concerns were similar to Smith, Carlos, and other racial advocates, as well as the mission statement of the #BlackLivesMatter movement (Blackistone, 2016). The message created controversy, and its means of dissemination sparked outrage. After all, Kaepernick protested in the athletics space, which has usually exuded patriotism and political conformity. ESPN's Kevin Blackistone wrote, "if sport is also a boost for societal and political change, as has been touted most prominently by the story of Jackie Robinson (the part where he turns the other cheek to racial slights rather than confronts it head-on as he did in the army), then what Kaepernick is saying is to be listened to rather than ignored" (Blackistone, 2016, para. 18).

In March 2017, Kaepernick opted out of the last year of his contract with San Francisco and became a free agent. He filed a grievance against the NFL later that year, alleging that teams were colluding to deny him another opportunity to

Fans celebrate the World Cup champion French team near the Arc de Triomphe.

Photo courtesy of Hallie S. Pedersen.

play. Eric Reid also had a collusion case against the league (Reid was one of the many players who joined him in the anthem protests), and both were settled in February 2019. As of April 2020, Kaepernick still has not had another opportunity to play in the NFL, and many believe he is being blackballed, including Reid, former safety for the Carolina Panthers ("Kaepernick Tweets," 2019; Kasabian, 2019).

ESPN's Howard Bryant writes about black activism in sport, a tradition he calls "The Heritage." In his book, *The Heritage: Black Athletes, a Divided America, and the Politics of Patriotism*, he discussed pioneers such as Paul Robeson, Jackie Robinson, Muhammad Ali, and contemporary athletes who use "the black body" to advocate for "the black mind" (p. 238). There is a collision today between post-9/11 patriotism and black reality, white escapism and black activism, and white leadership of sport and black athletes.

Activism, justice, equality, and oppression have all come to the forefront of discussions about Kaepernick, who has endorsed Nike since 2011. To commemorate the 30th anniversary of Nike's "Just do it" slogan, Kaepernick starred in the campaign along with LeBron James, Serena Williams, Odell Beckham Jr., Shaquem Griffin, and Lacey Baker (Coaston, 2018). In 2019, Kaepernick still has a powerful voice and influence. Nike pulled its Betsy Ross sneaker, created to commemorate Independence Day, after Kaepernick said the shoe's symbol was offensive to some. The flag with 13 white stars in a circle was created during a time when slavery was still legal in the United States. Nike saw a 2 percent stock increase and added almost $3 billion in market value since cancelling the shoes (Hale, 2019).

In 2019, the NFL continues to navigate social issues. It announced a longtime partnership with Shawn "Jay-Z" Carter and his entertainment company, Roc Nation. The partnership began as the NFL celebrated its 100th season. The league especially can benefit from the initiative due to the ramifications of the anthem controversies and protests. African Americans are still skeptical of the league due to the Colin Kaepernick situation. This includes some of its players; nearly 70 percent of the league is African American. Jay-Z is an activist and has supported Kaepernick, even wearing a Kaepernick jersey when he performed on *Saturday Night Live* in 2017. Jay-Z co-founded REFORM Alliance with hip-hop artist Meek Mill and seeks to change laws, policies, and practices in the criminal justice system (Baskin, 2019; Reid, 2019).

The NBA also has dealt with recent controversy. In 2019, the NBA and commissioner Adam Silver had to do damage control after Houston Rockets' GM Daryl Morey tweeted in support of Hong Kong's protest movement, leading to dramatic economic and other consequences for the league from China. Morey tweeted, "Fight for Freedom. Stand with Hong Kong" about Hong Kong's civil rights protests about judicial independence, proposed extradition rules, and other issues (Shea, 2019). The Rockets have ties to China due to Yao Ming's tenure with the team. Following Morey's tweet, the Chinese Basketball Association; sportwear brand Li-Ning; Tencent's online sport channel; and Shanghai Pudong Development Bank, a sponsor of the team, all ceased partnerships with the team. Additionally, CCTV Sports announced it would no longer broadcast the Rockets' games ("NBA, Silver, Try," 2019). After LeBron James criticized Morey, calling him misinformed, other players such as Enes Kanter derided James' comments, supporting free speech and freedom of expression (Bumbaca, 2019). Hong Kong was promised rights when China gained control of the territory from the United Kingdom. The NBA had just signed a reported five-year, $1.5-billion extension of its digital broadcast rights with Tencent earlier in 2019 (Shea, 2019). How this affects the league long term remains to be seen.

CURRENT SOCIOLOGICAL ISSUES AFFECTING SPORT MEDIA

The mass media are intertwined with numerous sociological aspects of sport and often reinforce cultural values and public perceptions of sport. Even so, the media can also catalyze change in sport and in society at large, sometimes even prompting new legislation. In addition to the sociological issues covered thus far in the chapter, other relevant current issues include violence, head trauma, doping and steroids, sex abuse, disability, and homophobia in sport.

Violence

One of the U.S. Surgeon General's top objectives for 2020 was to reduce the burden of violence, with a specific focus on understanding date-related and sexual violence (Healthy People, 2013). Statistically, women bear the greatest burden of violence. In the United States, one in five women has experienced (completed or attempted) rape during her life. One in 14 men was made to penetrate someone (completed or attempted) during his life, according to the National Center for Injury Prevention and Control and the Center for Disease Control's National Intimate Partner and Sexual Violence Survey (Smith, Zhang, Basile, Merrick, Wang, Kresnow, & Chen, 2018). The disproportionately high rate among women has received considerable scholarly attention and is framed within the greater context of hegemonic masculinity and its relationship with sexual and physical aggression.

One institution that has been observed to perpetuate traditional masculine values is sport. As explained by David Rowe (1998), "Sport is a crucial site for the reproduction of patriarchal structures and values, a male-dominated secular religion that has celebrated the physically aggressive and often violent deeds of men. Sport has been an integral element of self-sustaining forms of exclusivist male culture, lubricating a closed system of male bonding and female denigration" (p. 246). Hypermasculine sports—such as football, basketball, baseball, hockey, wrestling, and lacrosse—are characterized as such due to their rough nature, in which physical domination of an opponent is necessary for success (Stevens, 2012). The two most relevant signifiers in violence research are aggression and violence, according to Kevin Young in *Sport, Violence and Society* (2012). Coakley and Donnelly define *aggression* as "verbal or physical actions grounded in an intent to dominate, control, or do harm to another person" (2009, pp. 187-188), while *violence* refers to the "use of excessive physical force, which causes or has the potential to cause harm or destruction" (as cited in Young, 2012, p. 2). Aggression is viewed as a more general term, while violence is perceived as a more hurtful, physical form of aggression (Young, 2012).

Domestic violence has been the number one crime perpetrated by athletes for decades (Benedict & Yaeger, 1998). Cultural spillover theory is one perspective that has been used to explain how on-field violent behavior could lead to off-field violent behavior (Bloom & Smith, 1996). When violence and aggression in one environment is accepted, usage might carry over into other areas of life (Brown, Sumner, & Nocera, 2002). In almost every case involving an elite athlete, domestic violence involves a male athlete in a violent sport who physically abuses his wife or girlfriend. Leonard (2006) argues that a subculture of entitlement facilitates and encourages criminal activity against women while often protecting the perpetrators from prosecution and accountability. The escape from punishment by male athletes and other role models has "dulled public consciousness of their increasing levels of deviance" (Benedict, 1997, p. viv). Men whose identities derive exclusively from athletic success can be susceptible to fears that their manhood is being challenged (Benedict, 1997). Researchers have studied violence, abuse, and aggression at all levels of sport—high school, college, and the professional ranks—and found an overrepresentation of male athletes in reports of violence against women (Young, 2019).

Other sex abuse cases include Ohio State University, USA Swimming, and former Olympic figure skater Ashley Wagner. Wagner alleges she was sexually abused when she was 17 years old by the late John Coughlin, a two-time U.S. pairs champion who committed suicide a day after the U.S. Center for SafeSport suspended him as a result of three reports of sexual assault brought against him (Brennan, 2019). The U.S. Center for SafeSport also declared longtime U.S. figure skating coach Richard Callaghan "permanently ineligible" due to violations including sexual misconduct with a minor, according to *USA Today's* Christine Brennan (2019). Allegations from more than 20 years ago led to an initial suspension, and the harsher penalty came after a former figure skating student, Adam Schmidt, filed a lawsuit alleging he was sexually abused by Callaghan from 1999 to 2001 (Abdeldaiem, 2019a). The FBI and U.S. Attorney's Office in Manhattan have investigated USA Swimming over allegations that it mishandled and suppressed

Larry Nassar and the USA Gymnastics Sex Abuse Scandal

Male athletes are not the only perpetrators, however, as authority figures such as coaches and medical personnel also have abused and exploited others. One of the largest sex abuse scandals in sport history involved former Michigan State and USA Gymnastics Olympic team doctor Larry Nassar, who abused hundreds of young women and girls from Michigan State University and gymnasts nationwide, including members of the 2012 Olympics' gold-medal-winning "Fierce Five" and 2016 individual all-around gold medalist Simone Biles. Organizations such as the United States Olympic Committee (USOC), USA Gymnastics (USAG), and Michigan State University (MSU) all bore legal fallout in their failures to report incidents, to remove perpetrators and enablers, and to protect women. Michigan State alone paid a $500 million settlement to more than 300 victims (Kirby, 2018).

Nassar will likely spend the rest of his life in prison. He was sentenced to 60 years in federal prison on child pornography charges and two Michigan state sentences he's serving concurrently—40 to 175 years in Ingham County and 40 to 125 years in Eaton County (Joseph, 2019). Nassar used his position and stature to assault and molest girls under the guise of medical treatments for more than two decades (Levenson, 2018a). *Indianapolis Star* reporters Marisa Kwiatkowski, Mark Alesia, and Tim Evans and photojournalist Robert Scheer broke the story in 2016 with their "Out of Balance" series, and outrage increased in January 2018 with the coverage of statements in Judge Rosemarie Aquilina's Lansing (Ingham County) courtroom. There, over 150 women shared emotional and empowering victim impact statements (VIS)

during the sentencing; attorney John Manley, who represents many of the women in civil lawsuits, called the event a "watershed moment in our country" (Levenson, 2018a). The athletes' voices sparked outrage nationally about decades of sex abuse ignored while empowering an "army of survivors" to promote dialogue, change, and healing (Levenson, 2018a).

In 2018, 141 women accepted the ESPY's Arthur Ashe Courage Award, and Olympic gold *medalist* Aly Raisman was on the cover of *ESPN The Magazine*'s Heroes Issue ("141 Women Accept," 2018). According to Raisman, "We have to change the way our society views women" ("The Heroes Issue," 2018).

USA Gymnastics, under the leadership of president and CEO Li Li Leung, its fourth in two years, must restore the organization and sport's image. At the 2019 U.S. championships, Simone Biles won her sixth U.S. all-around title and discussed the lasting trauma. She admitted she still does not trust USAG to protect its athletes. "They couldn't do one damn job. You had one job. You literally had one job and you couldn't protect us," she said.

In a statement to NBC News, Leung acknowledged that the organization has more work to do to earn back the trust of its athletes. "Simone Biles is undoubtedly the best gymnast in the world and possibly of all time. She is an outstanding representative for gymnastics and the United States," Leung said. "We will continue to work hard to demonstrate to Simone and all of our athletes, members, community and fans that we are working to foster a safe, positive and encouraging environment where athlete voices are heard" (Kesslen, 2019).

athletes' sex-abuse claims and had improper business practices, including hundreds of thousands of dollars in rebates from its in-house insurance agency (Bengel, 2019).

In other cases, a former Ohio State University doctor who committed suicide in 2005, Richard Strauss, was accused of sexually abusing nearly

300 men over a 17-year period. A wrestling referee says he reported misconduct to Representative Jim Jordan (R-Ohio), who was a former assistant wrestling coach at OSU. Jordan, however, has denied knowing about the abuse. In May 2019, OSU paid for an independent investigation and identified more than 177 male students who alleged sexual

abuse by Strauss between 1979 and 1996 (Maese & DeBonis, 2019).

Physical and mental abuse takes many forms. The Nike Oregon Project came under scrutiny when runner Mary Cain claimed there was an abusive and toxic culture under coach Alberto Salazar, which other members confirmed. This Portland-based elite, professional training group was owned and operated by Nike from 2001 to October 2019. Cain revealed to *Sports Illustrated* that she suffered five broken bones, missed her period for years, and endured suicidal thoughts as a result of the extreme training measures Salazar and other authority figures took, including those without proper certifications (Chavez, 2019). Changes at Nike included a new CEO as of January 2020, when John Donahoe succeeded Mark Parker. While Nike said this change was not due to the scandal, other events also affected Nike's image. In 2018, multiple lawsuits over gender discrimination led to a shakeup in other leadership positions. In spring 2019, track athletes Kara Goucher and Alison Felix discussed the company's treatment of pregnant athletes and contract reductions with the *New York Times*, and Nike opted to no longer apply those reductions (Chavez, 2019).

The media increasingly cover cases of violence involving athletes and coaches. The NFL dominates such coverage, and even a partial list of those charged or convicted includes plenty of names, such as O.J. Simpson, Aaron Hernandez, Jovan Belcher, Rae Carruth, Ray Rice, Adrian Peterson, Ray McDonald, Brandon Marshall, Jonathan Dwyer, Darren Sharper, Josh Brown, Quincy Enunwa, and Greg Hardy and more recently Desmond Harrison, Kam Moore, Tyrel Dodson, Mark Walton, and Trevor Bates, all listed on *USA Today's* "NFL Player Arrest Database" (2019). According to Todd Crosset (1999), media discourse has shaped public opinions of athletes' violence. The "brutal truth" of the TMZ video of former Baltimore Ravens' player Ray Rice punching his then-fiancée Janay Palmer (now his wife Janay Rice) in an Atlantic City hotel elevator forced NFL commissioner Roger Goodell to acknowledge moral responsibility and accountability in handling players' incidents of violence (Taylor, 2014). After an initial two-game ban, Goodell admitted later that he "got it wrong"

(Taylor, 2014). The Ravens ultimately cut Rice, and he has not returned to the field.

In other examples, Deadspin published pictures of battered Nicole Holder, ex-girlfriend of former Carolina Panthers and Dallas Cowboys player Greg Hardy. Holder stopped cooperating with prosecutors, and the case was ultimately dropped (Waldron, 2015). TMZ Sports released video of Kareem Hunt in a physical altercation with a woman at a Cleveland hotel in November 2018 (Chiari, 2018). The Kansas City Chiefs released him shortly thereafter, but the NFL did not announce his punishment until March 2019. Now with the Browns, the running back was suspended eight games for violating its personal conduct policy (Patra, 2019). Although the media covered these and other NFL cases extensively, problems have existed for decades, as is evident in Benedict and Yaeger's *Pros and Cons: The Criminals Who Play in the NFL* (1998). Until a new NFL personal conduct policy was unveiled in December 2014, the league as a whole, and NFL commissioner Roger Goodell, had a "major blind spot" when it came to domestic violence cases (Pennington & Eder, 2014). As disclosed by Mark Fainaru-Wada and Steve Fainaru on ESPN's *Outside the Lines*, the league issued no suspensions after domestic violence convictions until 2000; furthermore, of 48 players considered guilty under the policy between 2000 and 2014, the NFL suspended players for one game or none in 88 percent of the cases (Fainaru-Wada & Fainaru, 2014). Even after the policy was modified, questions remain about various components and language, including "sexual assault involving physical force." For instance, quarterback Jameis Winston escaped a six-game suspension after touching an Uber driver in a sexual and inappropriate way without consent. He was suspended three games and was sued by the Uber driver (Smith, 2018). If violent offenders are not punished, sport, its athletes, and its coaches will lose credibility and more importantly, victims will continue to suffer and endure violence and abuse (Moser, 2004).

There have been incidents in college sport, too, as is evident in Stanford swimmer Brock Turner's sexual assault case. The case captured national attention after the victim, known as *Emily Doe*, read an emotional letter to Turner at his sentencing on three counts of sexual assault.

In 2015, two Stanford graduate students saw Turner raping an unconscious woman behind a dumpster at a campus party (Pallotta, 2016). Prosecutors asked for a six-year sentence for the victim, but Judge Aaron Persky sentenced Turner to only six months in a county jail. He served only three months and had three years' probation (Park, 2018).

In 2019, Chanel Miller put a face and name to "Emily Doe" by coming forward in a *60 Minutes* interview. "Know my name," her victim impact statement, captured global attention, and Stanford's campus now has two plaques with quotes from the statement in the same location where she was sexually assaulted. *Time* included Miller on its 2019 "Time 100 Next List" celebrating tomorrow's leaders (Mansoor, 2019).

At Ohio State, football coach Urban Meyer temporarily lost his job after a scandal involving assistant coach Zach Smith. Smith's ex-wife, Courtney Smith, filed a temporary restraining order and a trespassing charge against Smith, which was later dropped when Smith pled guilty to disorderly conduct. While Meyer downplayed his knowledge of Smith's domestic violence incidents, he said he was familiar with a 2009 incident when Smith battered his then-pregnant wife. Ohio State's investigation led to a three-game suspension of Meyer and athletics director Gene Smith. The investigation revealed that Meyer did not notify the athletics director of Smith's past incidents when he was hired in 2012. The university's sexual misconduct policy and Meyer's contract had specifications about handling such matters, and he failed to follow proper protocol. In December 2018, Meyer stepped down as head coach, citing health issues. There was documentation that other football staff members and Meyer's wife, Shelley, had raised concerns about Smith in writing or texts (McCann, 2019).

The "toxic culture at Maryland football" was evident in another Big Ten university's program (Dinich, Rittenberg, & VanHaaren, 2018). Head coach D.J. Durkin instituted a culture based on fear and intimidation that led offensive lineman Jordan McNair to die of heatstroke after a football workout in June 2018. Verbal abuse, including humiliation and belittling of players, was common, as were grueling workouts and coaches using food punitively, according to people who spoke to ESPN after McNair's death. While the school's Board of Regents reinstated Durkin after suspending him during an investigation, outrage ensued, and University of Maryland president Wallace Loh subsequently fired him (Broadwater, Richman, & Barker, 2018).

Media coverage and crisis communication strategies are vital in informing the public accurately; promoting fairness; and, ultimately, inducing social justice and change. As Lapchick (2015) stated in a *Sports Business Daily* column, sport has the power to heal communities and influence decisions and social change through sport media and sport communication practitioners. In a 24-7 media environment dominated by technology and social media, words still matter, both privately and publicly. This reality was brought home to Donald Sterling, then-owner of the Los Angeles Clippers, when social media exposed his racist statements recorded by a former employee. The response by NBA commissioner Adam Silver was decisive and swift, reinforcing the need for accountability. He banned Sterling from the league for life; forced him to sell his part of the team; and levied a $2.5 million fine, which was donated to antidiscrimination organizations. The Clippers were bought by former Microsoft CEO Steve Ballmer for a record $2 billion (Martinez & Hall, 2014).

Another example in the NBA includes the Dallas Mavericks. The team's toxic workplace environment was first disclosed by *Sports Illustrated*'s Jon Wertheim and journalist Jessica Luther (2018), who interviewed more than 12 current and former employees about the sexual harassment, domestic violence, threats, and misogynistic and predatory behavior. After the disclosure, owner Mark Cuban was proactive and did not make excuses.

An independent investigation cleared Cuban of being personally involved, and he donated $10 million to women's organizations as suggested by NBA commissioner Adam Silver (MacMahon, 2018). Silver opted not to suspend Cuban due to the Mavericks' transparency and cooperation with the investigation. Cuban was quick to fire and suspend perpetrators, launched his own investigation, and hired AT&T executive Cynthia Marshall as the team's new CEO. The NBA constitution and bylaws enable Silver to fine owners up to $2.5 million. Silver recommended $10 million to Cuban, who willingly paid the fine by another name, helping women in the sport industry and promoting education around domestic violence and other social issues (Zillgitt, 2018).

The decisions, actions, and consequences made and experienced by athletes, coaches, and sport administrators are important, and it is the media's responsibility to inform the public with accurate and substantive information. This need can clearly be seen in the work of investigative reporters such as Mark Fainaru-Wada, whose work on steroids and concussions has brought about changes in the NFL and MLB.

Head Trauma

Concussions have been addressed in many sports, but football receives the most media coverage on this topic. Journalists, medical doctors, and industry and personal advocates are using traditional and social media to publicize the danger of head trauma in football (Hull & Schmittel, 2015).

ESPN investigative reporters (and brothers) Mark Fainaru-Wada and Steve Fainaru broke the story of the NFL's long denial of the debilitating neurological effects of playing football under commissioners Paul Tagliabue and Roger Goodell (Van Natta Jr., 2013). Their award-winning book *League of Denial: The NFL, Concussions, and the Battle for Truth* and its companion Frontline documentary, *League of Denial: The NFL's Concussion Crisis* have changed the way football is viewed and played. Since the untimely deaths of former NFL players Mike Webster, Junior Seau, Dave Duerson, and others, the sport's dangerous consequences have now been examined at all levels, including Pop Warner football. Between 2010 and 2012, Pop Warner participation dropped 9.5 percent, which many believe was due to the NFL's head-trauma crisis brought to light by *League of Denial* (Belson, 2015; Fainaru & Fainaru-Wada, 2013).

Jeanne Marie Laskas' book, *Concussion*, continued the narrative and inspired a motion picture starring Will Smith. Both focused on Bennet Omalu's important contributions to research on chronic traumatic encephalopathy (CTE), which he discovered while performing an autopsy on the

Media coverage of head trauma in sport has increased dramatically over the past few years, and the coverage has affected sport (e.g., players in photo wearing padded covers on their helmets to reduce impact and concussions). Although football, and especially the NFL, has received the most attention in this area, the media have covered the subject across many sports, including ice hockey, soccer, rugby, boxing, skiing, and snowboarding.

Photo courtesy of Paul M. Pedersen.

brain of the late Mike Webster, a former center for the Pittsburgh Steelers.

Doping and Steroids

Sport centers on competition, and those who compete want to win. When combined with the pressures of high-profile sport, that desire often leads athletes, coaches, and administrators to seek dubious means to achieve the goal of winning. In addition, sporting society often turns a blind eye to the use of performance-enhancing drugs. In the 1988 Seoul Olympic trials, American Carl Lewis tested positive for using three stimulants banned by the International Olympic Committee and the U.S. Olympic Committee. Rather than go public with the results, however, the U.S. Track and Field Federation hid the results from officials and the public (Todd, 2005). Similarly, many sport reporters, and even members of the U.S. Congress, allege that Major League Baseball consistently ignored the fact that many of its players reportedly had used performance-enhancing drugs. Even tennis player Maria Sharapova admitted to taking Meldonium for 10 years, which was permissible until the World Anti-Doping Agency banned the drug as of January 1, 2016 (Brennan, 2016).

Steroids and doping are among the most serious issues plaguing sport, and the 1988 Seoul Olympics set what has been characterized as a benchmark in doping history (Todd, 2005). During the Games, Canadian Ben Johnson, considered the fastest man alive, won the 100-meter race with a time of 9.79 seconds. Two days later, he tested positive for Stanozolol, a steroid similar to testosterone, and was stripped of his gold medal, which was then awarded instead to American Carl Lewis. Britain's Linford Christie was awarded the silver medal, but years later he also tested positive. American Dennis Mitchell, who finished fourth in the race, would also test positive later in his career. Johnson's positive tests and the revocation of his gold medal created much debate. Canadians began referring to him as "the Jamaican-born Ben Johnson" instead of the "great Canadian runner," hoping to distance the country from the controversy (Todd, 2005).

Johnson's time in the 100-meter sprint was not surpassed until 2002, when American Tim Montgomery posted a time of 9.78. Montgomery himself was later banned from the sport for ste-

roid use and for his link to the infamous BALCO (Bay Area Lab Co-Operative) scandal. His partner, Marion Jones, was also linked to BALCO. In addition, Jones' former husband, C.J. Hunter, a retired shot putter, tested positive for steroids four times before the 2000 Sydney Olympic Games (Gaines, 2004). These stories and others, including that of Barry Bonds, were covered in *Game of Shadows: Barry Bonds, BALCO, and the Steroids Scandal That Rocked Professional Sports* by Lance Williams and Mark Fainaru-Wada. The book sent shock waves through baseball and beyond about the prevalence of performance-enhancing drugs in track and field and baseball.

Another major scandal rocked MLB and some of its star players in 2012 when the *Miami New Times* broke the Biogenesis story by exposing records from the South Florida antiaging clinic owned by Anthony Bosch, who supplied drugs to professional ballplayers. The scandal led to the suspension of 14 total players, including the New York Yankees' Alex Rodriguez and former National League MVP Ryan Braun (Garcia-Roberts, 2014). Whistleblower and former Biogenesis employee Porter Fischer said that professional baseball and basketball players, boxers, soccer players, collegiate athletes, police officers, lawyers, and a judge all spent money at the clinic (Brown, 2013). As a result of the scandal, the Major League Baseball Players Association and the league agreed to adopt a stronger policy, under which players are required to submit two urine samples during the season. In addition, 400 random blood collections are conducted to test for human growth hormone, and 1,200 mandatory tests are administered in spring training (Nightengale, 2014). For a first violation, the penalty was increased from 50 to 80 games; for a second violation, the punishment went from 100 games to 162 games (a full season), and a third violation still draws a lifetime ban from the league ("MLB," 2014). In 2016, New York Mets pitcher Jerry Mejia became the first player to receive a permanent ban from Major League Baseball for a third positive test (Rubin, 2016). In 2018, Robinson Cano was suspended for 80 games for violating the league's drug's policy. In the offseason, he tested positive for a diuretic, furosemide (Nightengale, 2018). The death of Angels pitcher Tyler Skaggs in 2019 brought into question the use of opiates in baseball, specifically within the Angels organization. Skaggs was found unresponsive and died in his Texas hotel room before his team was set to play the Rangers. The toxicology report indicated that he had fentanyl, oxycodone, and alcohol in his system. ESPN's T.J. Quinn reported that Eric Kay, director of communications for the Angels, told federal agents that he had used and abused drugs with Skaggs for several years. The U.S. Drug Enforcement Administration interviewed several Angels players about the possible prevalence of opiates within the team and clubhouse (Abdeldaiem, 2019b).

In other sports, Lance Armstrong fought testicular cancer and won the Tour de France seven times. However, after admitting that he doped after years of adamant denial, he is now one of the most polarizing figures in sport (Majendie, 2014). The report on the doping from the U.S. Anti-Doping Agency (USADA) led to Armstrong's loss of sponsors, credibility, and respect. Others that contributed to Armstrong's ultimate fall include former teammate Frankie Andreu and his wife Betsy, three-time Tour de France winner Greg LeMond, and Irish journalist David Walsh (Majendie, 2014).

For years, Armstrong denied that he had ever used performance-enhancing drugs. Many allegations stemmed from the French media and were linked to his nine-year association with Italian physician Michele Ferrari. An Italian court convicted Ferrari of "sporting fraud" in 2004, and Armstrong immediately ended the association. Armstrong engaged in several legal battles stemming from confrontations with another cyclist during the 2004 event and from various allegations and reports, as well as Walsh's book *LA Confidential: The Secrets of Lance Armstrong.* The French newspaper *L'Equipe* reported that Armstrong had tested positive for erythropoietin (EPO), a performance enhancer designed to increase the production of red blood cells. Armstrong denied the claims and accused the French media, as well as Tour de France officials, of engaging in a "witch hunt" (Kroichick, 2005).

One of Armstrong's former teammates, Floyd Landis, winner of the 2006 Tour de France, finally came clean and admitted doping in 2010. Andreu, another of Armstrong's teammates and close friends, had disclosed publicly that he used performance enhancers during the 1999 Tour de France, a race that Armstrong won (Buckner, 2006;

"One Cyclist's Brave Candor," 2006; Robertson, 2006). Andreu and his wife were in Armstrong's hospital room in 1996 when Armstrong admitted using performance-enhancing drugs to a doctor as he battled cancer. Now, Andreu views him as a "lying bully" (Majendie, 2014).

On an episode of Oprah Winfrey's television show in January 2013, Armstrong finally admitted to using testosterone, human growth hormone, and EPO. He also had blood transfusions to excel and keep a competitive edge over other competitors. In addition, Armstrong said that he would probably use them again if he found himself in the same situation. He was stripped of his seven consecutive Tour de France victories (1999 through 2005) and banned for life from cycling. He lost endorsement deals and has endured public shame, humiliation, and censure (Botello & Levs, 2013).

While working as a sport journalist at the *Sunday Times*, Walsh later wrote a book, *Seven Deadly Sins: My Pursuit of Lance Armstrong*, about his long battle to expose the cyclist's use of performance-enhancing drugs. Armstrong sued the newspaper for $1.5 million. Armstrong settled with Walsh and the *Sunday Times* for an undisclosed settlement (MacMichael, 2013). The journalist had this to say about Armstrong: "He was an iconic figure. That's gone. I'd like him to get on with his life and move forward, to spend time with his kids, have an enjoyable personal life and play golf. But he should stay away from public life—there's too much baggage" (Majendie, 2014). If there is a silver lining, Armstrong's fall helped put doping at the forefront of media coverage.

Doping can affect individuals, as seen with Armstrong and others; however, it can be much more widespread, as it was with the Russian national team. A World Anti-Doping Agency (WADA) report documented pervasive doping by the Russians and cheating at all levels for the Sochi Olympics. The report's update noted there was a state-sponsored doping program in place for four years starting in 2011, and the systemic cover-up of positive drug tests benefited more than 1,000 athletes in 30 summer and winter sports. The IOC announced that 271 athletes of 389 could compete in Rio, while 118 were banned. In 2017, the IOC banned Russia from participating in the 2018 Olympics. Russia's

Olympic Committee also had to pay the IOC $15 million both for the cost of the investigation and to create a new Independent Testing Authority, making it the most widespread punishment ever instituted to a country. Subsequently, the IOC allowed 169 Russian athletes to participate in the 2018 Olympics, but they did not carry the Russian flag nor wore uniforms identifying them as Russian. They were called "Olympic athletes from Russia" ("Performance Enhancing Drugs," 2019; Price, 2016). On the day of the closing ceremonies of the 2018 Olympics, the IOC reinstated Russia into the Olympics. In December 2019, WADA unanimously agreed to ban Russia from both the 2020 Olympics (postponed to 2021) and 2022 World Cup due to doping noncompliance (Church & Morse, 2019).

Corruption

Corruption occurs in many forms and affects sport in the United States and globally. The 2002 Salt Lake City Olympics, and specifically the Salt Lake City bid committee, endured a bidding scandal involving illicit payments, gifts, and other bribery and ethical breaches. The scandal led to the expulsion of six members from the IOC, resignations from four, and warnings for others. The IOC's 50-point reform came as a result and included a ban on visits to bid cities, the institution of an ethics committee, and term limits for members (McCombs, 2018).

Additionally, a figuring skating scandal rocked the pairs competition that same Olympics. French judge Marie-Reine Le Gougne was part of a vote-trading plot within the competition. She voted for Russian figure skaters Yelena Berezhnaya and Anton Sikharulidze to win the gold, leaving Canadians Jamie Sale and David Pelletier with the silver for their superior performance. The Russian mafia was accused of fixing a victory for the Russian pair, and the judge and head of the French skating federation were both suspended three years (Pilon, Lehren, Gosk, Siegel, & Abou-Sabe, 2018). After the competition, the Canadians received a second, duplicate gold medal. Reforms of the point system from this event still stand today.

Sepp Blatter became president of FIFA in 1998, the same year the IOC became entangled in the Salt Lake City bidding scandal. As with the IOC, there is a long history of bribery at FIFA. Buzzfeed's Ken Bensinger wrote an exposé, *Red Card: How the U.S. Blew the Whistle on the World's Biggest Sports Scandal*, about the evolution of corruption in soccer beginning in the 1980s. The current FIFA president, Gianni Infantino, insists he banished corruption, bribery, and scandal from the soccer body after the downfall of Blatter and leaders in North and South America. Prosecutors from both the United States and Switzerland focused on financial corruption and payouts linked to the sport's governing bodies ("Infantino Says FIFA Scandals Gone," 2019).

MLB investigated a sign-stealing scandal involving the Houston Astros in 2019, and The Athletic's Ken Rosenthal believed the investigation should not stop with the 2017 World Series champions. Rosenthal does not think electronic sign stealing is a single-game issue in MLB, nor does he believe the 2017 season was a singular case. "How far does baseball want to go?" he wrote (2019). "The league should not stop with 2017, the only season in which The Athletic confirmed rule breaking by the Astros. It should probe more deeply into the actions of the Astros and other clubs in '18 and especially '19, the first season in which baseball enacted more comprehensive measures to clamp down on electronic sign stealing" (Rosenthal, 2019). In January 2020, the Astros fired general manager Jeff Luhnow and manager A.J. Hinch. The Red Sox cut ties with manager Alex Cora, formerly the Astros' bench coach, and the Mets parted with Carlos Beltran before he even managed one game. Beltran, as a player on the 2017 Astros, was integral in executing the plan ("Everything you need to know," 2020).

In other sports, the FBI indicted 10 people in 2017 for bribery and fraud in men's college basketball. Coaches allegedly partnered with an executive from an apparel manufacturer and other individuals to deal high-cost bribes to sway athletes' school selections, shoe sponsors, agents, and an array of other services. A former assistant coach from South Carolina and Oklahoma State, Lamont Evans, was sentenced to three months in jail. James Gatto, Christian Dawkins, and Merl Code were all convicted of conspiring to commit wire fraud so recruits would attend Louisville, Kansas, and North Carolina State. The NCAA announced that six schools would face allegations of Level I violations in 2019, which includes punishments such as scholarship reductions, postseason bans, and show-cause orders against coaches ("At Least Six Men's Basketball Programs," 2019). As of August 2019, North Carolina State was the first to receive punishment—four Level I violations and two Level II infractions for the program and two former head coaches Mark Gottfried and assistant coach Orlando Early (Forde, Thamel, & Wetzel, 2019a). Kansas received multiple Level I infractions in September 2019. Yahoo! first reported that the NCAA charged KU with lack of institutional control, three Level I violations in men's basketball, and a charge against head coach Bill Self. There were also Level II violations against the football team (Forde, Thamel, & Wetzel, 2019). More allegations will likely come for other schools.

Mental Health

Athletes such as Michael Phelps, Kevin Love, and Liz Cambage have spoken out about mental health issues. As high-profile athletes, they have a platform for reducing stigmas and helping others cope and understand their own battles with depression, bipolar disorder, anxiety, addiction, and other issues. Teams and leagues have taken notice.

The Aces' Liz Cambage (2019) penned a powerful essay for *The Players' Tribune* in 2019. In it, she shared that she had requested a trade from the Dallas Wings to be closer to her family. Cambage battles anxiety and depression and believes the WNBA, like the NBA, should put policies into place for its athletes. The NBA expanded its mental health program after advocating from Kevin Love, DeMar DeRozan, Keyon Dooling, and others. The league issued a memo to all 30 teams about the changes that took effect before the 2019-2020 season. All teams must have one or two mental health professionals for players; identify a licensed MD or DO to be available for players; have a written plan for mental health emergencies; have policies for communicating its practices to players and team staff with privacy; and attend a health and wellness meeting. In this era of player empowerment, athletes' voices have made a difference (Amick, 2019).

In college sports, former UVA guard Kyle Guy was the subject of many stories prior to the Cavaliers' national championship. After UVA lost to UMBC the prior year, the first time an overall number 1 seed had lost to a number 16 seed, Guy battled anxiety. He overcame it and was even stronger in his personal growth and redemption.

Other athletes who have spoken out include 23-time Olympic gold medalist Michael Phelps. He first publicly addressed his depression, anxiety, and suicidal thoughts after his second drunken-driving arrest. He partners with Talkspace, which connects individuals with therapists online through a computer, tablet, or smartphone. Phelps said mental issues are important today due to rising suicide rates and mass shootings in the United States. He hopes to make an impact now that he's in a much better place as a married father of sons Boomer, Beckett, and Maverick (Newberry, 2018).

Community Health Issues

In 2020, the global coronavirus disease 2019 (COVID-19) pandemic had a life-changing impact on sports and all of society. "Thursday [March 12] will be forever remembered as the day sports went dark, turning off its lights, nailing plywood over its windows, bolting its doors to the insidious approach of the coronavirus," wrote *Los Angeles Times* columnist Bill Plaschke. "The one thing that has long helped America endure a national crisis was its games and, now, suddenly, just as this health crisis is peaking, the games have disappeared, poof, vanished." The blackout included college sports, professional sports, and major events like March Madness, the Masters, and the Boston Marathon as of March 2020. Athletes like the NBA's Rudy Gobert and Donovan Mitchell, both on the Utah Jazz, were two of the first athletes to test positive. COVID-19's impact could also be felt by media members and other sport professionals whose lives were profoundly altered (Plaschke, 2020).

Disability

As discussed earlier, sport both reflects society and, in some instances, can spur social change. This is certainly true of sport in its portrayal and integration of people with disability. Athletes with disability face the same challenges as other minority groups in the realm of sport; that is, they struggle to garner much media coverage; when coverage is provided, it characterizes disability in differing ways. Over the last 25 years, the media have provided more coverage of disabled athletes competing with and against nondisabled athletes (Nixon, 2000). This coverage has highlighted, for example, the participation and prowess of one-armed major leaguer pitcher Jim Abbott and outfielder Pete Gray. Other athletes with disabilities have received coverage for their participation in sports such as boxing, triathlon, basketball, gymnastics, cycling, sailing, wrestling, swimming, karate, and many others (Nixon, 2000). These athletes include IMTC (International Muay Thai Council) World Super Welterweight Champion Baxter Humby; five-time handcyclist world champion Oz Sanchez; Paralympic gold medalist Alana Nichols (wheelchair basketball and alpine skiing); and professional surfer Bethany Hamilton, who was featured in the movie *Soul Surfer* (Marie, 2013).

Nixon (2000) pointed out that the word *disability* can have a different meaning in the context of sport, in which athletes are sometimes placed on the "disabled list." Of course, placement on that list simply indicates that an athlete is temporarily unable to participate in competition. In contrast, society views "disability" as meaning that a person has a permanent disability, whether mental or physical, that prevents participation in specific activities but does not necessarily prevent playing and competing in sport. "Thus, a person can be disabled in society, but not be disabled in certain kinds of sports or sports roles" (Nixon, 2000, p. 422).

In 2011, one-legged wrestler Anthony Robles of Arizona State University won the NCAA Division I championship in his weight class. David Merrill's Deadspin article, included in *The Best American Sports Writing 2014*, documented Robles' strength, resolve, and power (Merrill, 2014). This and many other stories of disability need to be told because, as emphasized throughout this chapter, the frequency with which an issue is discussed, as well as the way in which it is reported, can influence public perception. Disabled athletes should be covered with dignity, respect, and equality. As NPR's Joe Shapiro said, "The hardest part of having a disability is not physical or mental—it's the reactions of others, lack of access, and pity" (Njuguna, 2004).

In 2018, the Seattle Seahawks Shaquem Griffin made history as the first one-handed player to play in the NFL in the modern era. He and brother Shaquill played together at University of Central Florida and then the Seahawks after Shaquem joined his brother on the team. The twins made a childhood pact that they would always live together, marry twins, have children, and raise them in the same house. The pact also included playing on the same football team, which so far has come to fruition (Farmer, 2018).

In 2019, high school football coach Rob Mendez was on the cover of *ESPN The Magazine*'s Heroes Issue. Mendez was born with a rare disorder, tetra-amelia syndrome, and does not have arms or legs. He learned football through Madden video games; after working 12 years as an assistant football coach, he became Prospect High School's (CA) junior varsity head coach. ESPN awarded Mendez the Jimmy V Award for Perseverance at the 2019 ESPY Awards (Christie, 2019).

Sexual Orientation, Intersex, and Transgender Issues

Athletes' sexual orientation is often characterized in the media in a manner that reinforces certain hegemonic ideologies (Nylund, 2004). As Nylund explained in some depth, "At this historical moment when hegemonic masculinity has been partially destabilized by global economic changes and by gay liberation and feminist movements, the sport media industry seemingly provides a stable and specific view of masculinity grounded in heterosexuality, aggression, individuality, and the objectification of women" (p. 160). For example, as illustrated by Spencer (2003), media depictions of tennis stars Chris Evert and Martina Navratilova were quite different during the heyday of their rivalry and remain different today. Whereas Navratilova has faced a coding of lesbianism, Evert has been portrayed as "America's sweetheart."

Another athlete who endured difficulties was transgender pioneer Renée Richards, whose story was documented in ESPN's *30 for 30* episode titled "Renée." Richards finally gained access to tennis tournaments as a woman and was able to play in the 1977 U.S. Open after the U.S. Supreme Court ruled in her favor (Zeigler, 2011). She made the final in the doubles competition, and her professional career lasted about five years. She became friends with Navratilova, as well as tennis star and activist Billie Jean King (Weinreb, 2011). Just four years earlier, King had defeated former top men's player Bobby Riggs in straight sets (6-4, 6-3, 6-3) in a nationally televised megaevent from the Houston Astrodome called Battle of the Sexes (Billings et al., 2015). Although King had not yet come out as a lesbian, the event challenged gender inequity just as Richards had pioneered on LGBTQ+ issues.

A modern-day activist and fighter for racial, gender, and LGBTQ+ rights is USWNT co-captain and midfielder Megan Rapinoe. She won the World Cup Golden Ball for the best player in the 2019 World Cup and Golden Boot for being the top scorer. She has said that gay rights, equal pay,

Ten years before Rapinoe (far right) won the World Cup Golden Ball in 2019, she was the second player selected in the Women's Professional Soccer (WPS) league and played for the Chicago Red Stars in the inaugural season of the WPS.

Photo courtesy of Paul M. Pedersen.

and racial inequality are inextricably linked. She is among the 28 members of the U.S. team that filed a federal class-action lawsuit against the United States' soccer federation, and will appeal a federal judge's April 2020 ruling in favor of U.S. soccer. She has kneeled during the national anthem and is open about her sexuality. In fact, she and girlfriend Sue Bird of the WNBA were the first openly gay couple to be included in *ESPN The Magazine*'s Body Issue (Lewis, 2019).

Sex, gender, and identity are still in the news with the discourse about South African middle-distance runner Caster Semenya. At the 2009 world championship, 18-year-old Semenya won the 800 meters, but track and field's governing body tested her for gender verification. The media disclosed her personal details to the world—that she was intersex and had both male and female sexual characteristics. In the aftermath, gender-testing practices were changed in 2012 to measure testosterone levels of females rather than DNA (Curley, 2012).

Semenya discussed the experience with the British Broadcasting Corporation's (BBC's) Ben Smith. "It was upsetting, you feel humiliated," she said. Now, though, she wants to focus on the future. "When I am in that lane and I hear 'Caster Semenya from South Africa,' I always know I am doing it for my people. They love and support me and I will always do them proud, I will always put them first. Without them, I am nothing." Among her goals was to win an Olympic gold medal in the 2016 Rio Olympics. "I am a dreamer. And what I dream of is to become Olympic champion, world champion, world record holder—I can't stop running because of people" (Smith, 2015).

Semenya won a gold medal in the 800-meter final in the 2016 Rio Olympics. Still, she has had to fight to continue competing. In 2018, the International Association of Athletics Federations (IAAF) ruled that runners with higher testosterone levels would now be required to take medication to lower the levels if they wanted to compete against women in the 400-, 800-, and 1,500-meter events (North,

2019). Human Rights Watch sent a letter to IAFF president Sebastian Coe, saying this new ruling on testosterone regulation is discriminatory toward women. The letter said it was worried the rules "encourage violations of internationally-protected human rights, including the rights to privacy, health, bodily integrity, dignity and non-discrimination" (Carroll, 2018, para. 4). Even though IAFF claims the rules will not prevent any women from participating, Human Rights Watch disputes this, writing, "They do effectively force some women with intersex traits (or differences of sex development) to choose between undergoing medically unnecessary intervention to lower their testosterone levels or be precluded from participating in international sport" (Carroll, 2018, para. 5). IAFF did not revoke the regulations, and Semenya has pursued legal action against the rule, which came into effect in November 2018 (Carroll, 2018).

In 2019, the Court of Arbitration for Sport ruled against Semenya's appeal. Semenya has been scrutinized since 2009, and her story demonstrates the consequences when athletes do not conform to others' perceptions about womanhood and gender norms. As more openly trans and intersex athletes compete, this issue needs more understanding and clarity.

In 2018, trans cyclist Rachel McKinnon was the recipient of criticism from other athletes and online harassment on Twitter, Facebook, and Instagram after she broke the 200-meter sprint final world record, the first time a trans woman won a world championship in any sport. Since 2004, the IOC has allowed trans athletes to compete in the gender on their legal documents; however, trans women must prove their testosterone is below a certain level for 12 months before their first competitions (Shilton, 2019). McKinnon says the IOC deemed sport a human right and denying her access to sport is stripping away a fundamental human right.

Misleading characterizations and bullying are not limited to females. Many times, portrayals of male athletes also reinforce hegemonic ideologies. There are few openly gay athletes in team sports in the United States, although the tide is turning, due in part to former University of Missouri standout football player Michael Sam, who proclaimed that he was gay before the NFL combine in 2014.

Although he is currently not playing football (he played briefly for the St. Louis Rams and Dallas Cowboys), the discussions following his announcement created much buzz. When the Rams drafted Sam, his kiss with then-boyfriend Vito Cammisano on ESPN caused a stir on social media, including homophobic responses from Miami Dolphins safety Don Jones, former New York Giants and Houston Texans player Derrick Ward, and others (Yan & Alsup, 2014).

A second incident involving Sam occurred when reporter Josina Anderson reported on *SportsCenter* that Sam had not been seen showering in the locker room with teammates (Scarry, 2014). The report highlighted the uninformed and differentiated coverage of gay athletes that focuses on nonathletic and trivial aspects rather than athletic skills. Deadspin's Tom Ley, however, argued that Sam's showering habits did matter and compared the situation to Jackie Robinson's plight. Ley wrote that the discussion was missing the depth of the story—that of an "openly gay man integrating a straight man's space" (Ley, 2014). Outsports co-founder Jim Buzinski also believed that it could be a legitimate story if handled with good sources and reporting. "Don't rush to judgment and assumptions," Buzinski said in an interview with *Sport Illustrated*'s Richard Deitsch. "Ask direct and detailed questions and listen for nuance. Avoid looking for an angle and instead report the facts. This is tough in our Internet-driven, click-bait, talking-head world, but it is the only way to deal with this issue fairly and professionally. For gay athletes, coming out publicly is fraught with anxiety, so be sensitive to that, but at the same time don't be afraid to inquire so as to learn" (Deitsch, 2014).

The pressure to adhere to cultural norms and expectations can lead athletes to compromise their voices. Ryan O'Callaghan hid his true self for decades. He played in the NFL for six years and came out as gay in 2017 after retiring from football in 2011. He grew addicted to painkillers and had suicidal thoughts through his journey. He admits in his memoir, *My Life on the Line*, that Ellen DeGeneres' coming out helped him figure out who he was (O'Callaghan & Zeigler, 2019). His family and close friends, including Aaron Rodgers, were supportive of him.

A SPORTSWRITER'S DETERMINATION, RESILIENCE, AND DESIRE TO "PAY IT FORWARD"

Dana O'Neil
Senior writer
The Athletic

Dana O'Neil has worked on different platforms throughout her career in sport yet remains true to herself. "I always wanted to be a writer," she said. "That's all I ever wanted to be."

She credits her father, a former college baseball player at West Virginia Wesleyan, for drawing her into sport. "I can remember as a kid, he drafted me to keep score for his beer league softball team and computing averages and ERAs and stuff," she said. O'Neil played basketball and field hockey at South Hunterdon High School in New Jersey.

Dana O'Neil, senior writer at The Athletic.

O'Neil continued to keep baseball and football statistics but never thought of sport as a potential career path until college at Penn State. Her freshman RA wrote for the *Daily Collegian* and told her about the paper. O'Neil did not have journalism experience but took a preliminary test to see if she could join the staff. "At the end of the test it asked which section you'd prefer to work for and I thought sports would be fun," she said. "'Maybe I'll meet Joe Paterno.' I had no idea what I was doing."

Nonetheless, O'Neil came home that Thanksgiving and told her parents she aspired to be a sport journalist. "Looking back, it made sense," she said. "My mother was an English teacher and my father was a sports fan. I had a really good English teacher, but on my own I never put them together."

In addition to writing and reporting for the student-run newspaper, she also edited Penn State's weekly football magazine. Her first student internship was at the *Trentonian*, which led to her first job covering Rider, Princeton, and Rutgers sports. From there, she went to the *Florida Times-Union*; the *Bucks County Courier Times*; and the *Philadelphia Daily News*, where she worked from 2000 to 2007. She covered La Salle and Villanova basketball and was a backup writer for the Phillies and Eagles. There, she met Dick Jerardi, who still covers basketball and horse racing for the *Daily News* and the *Philadelphia Inquirer*. According to Jerardi, O'Neil is "relentless, passionate and knowledgeable." The duo rode to many events together and still live near each other. "I could see very early that she was a unique talent with a unique voice, so I wanted to help in any way I could," said Jerardi.

O'Neil credits Jerardi with career advice and guidance. "He vouched for me to get a job at the *Daily News*," she said, "and he knows more about writing, basketball, and journalism than I will ever know. He is always first and foremost my sounding board on every move I make to this day."

At the *Daily News*, O'Neil also met ESPN basketball reporter Andy Katz, who was the company's only full-time college basketball writer at the time. That all changed, however, after a phone call from David Albright, ESPN's former college editor. "He called me about the job and asked me a couple of questions and that was the end of the conversation," she said. "I never went to Bristol. I never did an interview. I got a contract in my email and I said, 'OK, that's my offer.'"

O'Neil worked at ESPN for 10 years on all platforms. When she was laid off in 2017, she posted 11 heartfelt Tweets and admitted that day was a bit like attending her own funeral. She especially credited Andy Katz and Pat Forde for their support. Neither is still with ESPN; Katz does work for NCAA.com, the Big Ten Network, and other outlets. Forde writes for *Sports Illustrated*.

O'Neil is grateful for her time there, yet admits she was "a cog in a very large wheel." "When you're catering to clicks and advertising, you have to write differently," she said. "We got told all the time that people don't read long-form. They read lists." While ESPN is "chronically trying to reinvent" itself, according to O'Neil, The Athletic staff believes, "This is who we are, and if you like us, you'll subscribe, and if you don't, you won't."

From the time she first talked to co-founder Alex Mather, O'Neil viewed The Athletic as a good fit. "I remember hanging up, thinking, if this is true, I just talked to my journalistic fairy godfather," she said. "It sounds like heaven and I will say it's been phenomenal." The Athletic values creativity and out-of-the-box thinking. One example was the men's 2019 national semifinal basketball game between Virginia and Auburn. O'Neil told her boss, executive editor Hugh Kellenberger, that she wanted to sit in the parents' section. She pitched the story because she gets nervous watching her son Kieran play JV lacrosse. "What would it be like to be a parent in the stands?" she asked. "That was exactly my thought process." When UVA guard Kyle Guy sank game-winning free throws with less than a second remaining, she saw his family's excitement firsthand. She was sitting behind Guy's two sets of parents, then-fiancée Alexa (now wife), and grandparents.

Kellenberger attributes O'Neil's access to "top-shelf reporting" and trust. "They [sources and subjects] believe she will tell their story the right way, because history suggests she will," he said. "It's also why even at major events like the NCAA Tournament, with hordes of reporters all looking for something different, you consistently see Dana in a corner with a coach or staff member, getting that exclusive quote or a lead on a story no one else has."

O'Neil credits Kellenberger and others for their encouragement. "Journalists tend to be insecure, so we like to be told we're doing a good job and they're happy to do that," she said. "To be part of something from the beginning is really fun."

O'Neil is an award-winning journalist yet is modest when asked about her stories. She felt privileged and "terrified" to write about Austin Hatch, a former Michigan basketball player who survived two airplane crashes and tragically lost his family in one. She never comes home to Kieran and Madigan (her daughter) and suggests that they meet anyone, but this story was different. She said, "I hope someday you get to meet Austin Hatch because he's the kind of person you need to be around. He's a gamechanger." And that day came when Hatch Skyped into Kieran's middle-school class.

She wrote oral histories of the Big East tournament while at ESPN and one of NBA star Kevin Durant's college career for The Athletic. She also profiled a Princeton field hockey player, Annabeth Donovan, who has two children and competed as a Division I athlete. O'Neil has covered every Final Four since 2003, including Villanova's first national championship win on Chris Jenkins' buzzer beater in 2016. The Olympics are still on her bucket list, and she'd like to cover Wimbledon "just because it's Wimbledon."

As a woman with a longstanding career, O'Neil has worked with many great people, mostly men. "I've been the only woman at a lot of places," she said, "and everyone has been supportive and more disinterested in my gender. . . . I think that's important to stress. There are a lot of horror stories, but I've been fortunate not to have them. I've been blessed to work with really great people." She does not want to be known as a "good female sportswriter" but rather as "a good sportswriter." She helps other young women pursue careers just as others helped her, including former *Los Angeles Times* reporter Robin Norwood. "There aren't a lot of women in this profession and she's been really kind to me as I've gone up," O'Neil said.

When it comes to women's sport coverage, O'Neil believes the more attention given to it by all journalists, the better. "It's important and it should be across gender. It's not required. It's deserved because it merits coverage."

As far as advice, she urges students to get involved in student media and to network. "When you're sitting at games, go talk to someone like me, introduce yourself," she suggested. "We've all been there before. Say, 'Hey, I'm a student journalist, I like your work. Do you have five minutes?'"

According to O'Neil, work ethic and attitude make a big difference. She covered Little League baseball when she started and views all

(continued)

experiences as valuable. "Don't think anything is beneath you or too small. . . . It is your work. Treat it seriously," she advised. "Go eagerly into any opportunity you're given because opportunities are hard to get, and once you get a job opportunity, then it's on you. If you do it well, then you'll get another one and another one and another one, hopefully."

As discussed earlier, Brittney Griner needed to hide her true self while in college at Baylor. Bruce Jenner hid his desire to be a woman until 2015, when he first discussed it with Diane Sawyer on a *20/20* television special and later introduced Caitlyn Jenner in a *Vanity Fair* cover article. The media are integral to telling authentic stories about all individuals in sport and society. As this chapter and others have shown, their power extends far beyond a newscast, article, or blog.

CHAPTER WRAP-UP

Summary

Scholars have long suggested that the media have a pervasive effect on society in their power to create social myths and reinforce existing beliefs. The sport media affect sport culture in the same manner. Through their power as gatekeepers, the media mold our beliefs and values and, in turn, shape our society, the dynamics of sport entities, the sport culture, and public perceptions of sport. As technologies evolve and progress, there are more opportunities and more space for dialogue, discussion, and coverage. Although research has not always shown variances between traditional media and new media, such outlets as The Undefeated, The Athletic, Outsports, espnW, and others have highlighted the talents, accomplishments, and personalities of diverse athletes who deserve equity and respect. Diverse voices in newsrooms, team organizations, leagues, and other sport and media entities will increase the efficacy and vibrancy of sport communication organizations.

Much of the media's portrayal of sport is influenced by the lack of diversity in media entities and sport organizations. These groups have become more diverse, but minorities consistently remain underrepresented in all roles. This chapter explores the intersection of and relationship between sport communication and sociocultural issues such as gender, ethnicity, violence, nationalism, activism, and popular culture. The analysis includes discussions related to the emergence, role, function, diffusion, effects, and meaning of sport communication across time and societies. The chapter also addresses the ways in which culture, structure, myths (e.g., heroes and villains), socialization, values, social policies, norms (e.g., commentary), and power relationships (e.g., race, minorities) are facilitated through sport communication.

Review Questions

1. What are the ramifications of biased media coverage?

2. What is nationalism, and how is it evident in the sport media?

3. Identify five athlete-activists and pioneers and their contributions to sport and society.

4. How do media stereotypes of minorities and females affect sport participation and sport coverage?

5. What are five current sociological issues in sport communication, and how have they been characterized in the media?

Individual Exercises

1. Think about two or three key sociocultural issues prevalent in today's society. Examine how these issues are characterized in the sport media. How do the sport media shape society's beliefs and values in regard to these issues? What are the similarities and differences between characterizations? How would you rate the coverage of these issues? Why?

2. Select a specific sport medium, and examine its sport coverage for one week. Examine the amount and type of coverage of women's sport as compared with coverage of men's sport. Think about the amount of coverage given to each sex. How are female athletes characterized? How are male athletes characterized? How are these characterizations similar, and how do they differ?

Photo courtesy of Barbara Osborne.

CHAPTER 13

Legal Issues in Sport Communication

Barbara Osborne, JD

University of North Carolina at Chapel Hill

LEARNING OBJECTIVES

- To identify the many legal issues related to sport communication
- To understand the role of the First Amendment in protecting sport media
- To identify the limitations placed on free speech
- To comprehend the privacy rights of athletes and other sport personnel
- To examine the rights of entities (e.g., leagues, schools, teams) and individuals (e.g., athletes) related to social media
- To explore the rapidly evolving athlete's right of publicity
- To recognize legal issues related to gender equity and sexual harassment in sport media

KEY TERMS

actual malice	expressive speech	right of privacy
commercial speech	fair-use doctrine	right of publicity
copyright	freedom of speech	state action
defamation	public domain	trademark

INTEGRATING EFFECTIVE SPORT COMMUNICATION AND LEGAL ADVICE

Laura Warren

Having spent much of her life immersed in the world of sport, senior associate general counsel Laura Warren knows how influential effective sport communication can be to promoting competition. As an attorney for a major collegiate athletics program, Warren also knows how damaging it can be when it runs afoul of the law.

A former student-athlete and coach, Warren currently serves as in-house athletics counsel for DePaul University in Chicago, Illinois, the nation's largest Catholic university serving over 22,000 students and 3,400 employees. After law school, Warren completed a judicial clerkship and worked at a large Chicago law firm with a higher education practice. Warren now serves as the primary legal advisor to DePaul's NCAA Division I athletics department with 13 varsity intercollegiate athletics teams participating in the Big East Conference. Warren advises on a host of athletics legal issues including conduct, health, and safety; personnel matters; NCAA compliance and litigation; facility operations; and sponsorships. Warren also serves as the co-chair of the American Bar Association's sports division.

Sport communication is interwoven into most, if not all, of Warren's legal practice. Like any good play caller, Warren relies on a comprehensive rulebook of local, state, and federal laws to inform the University's decision making in matters such as the following:

- *Information privacy and security.* To start, Warren must ensure that sharing student-athlete information abides by various information privacy and security laws. Students in kindergarten through college are governed by a federal law known as the Family Education Rights and Privacy Act (FERPA) that prevents disclosure of their education records except in limited circumstances, such as when approved by the student or when necessary to respond to a health or safety emergency. Because college athletics departments also provide medical care and mental health services to

Laura Warren, senior associate general counsel, DePaul University.

Photo courtesy of Laura Warren.

student-athletes, schools must likewise follow stringent health privacy laws including the Health Information Portability and Accountability Act (HIPAA). University counsel routinely advise athletics staff regarding what information is permissible to share with other school officials or report to sport media outlets who may, for example, be inquiring about ongoing disciplinary matters or injuries.

- *Free speech and social activism.* University attorneys must also advise their campus on policies governing free speech for students and faculty alike. For athletics, this involves managing growing demonstrations from socially active players who may take a knee during the national anthem, wear protest apparel, or even refuse to play. In such instances, university counsel will coordinate with executives and athletics to assess governing legal standards (which differ for private versus public colleges, the latter considered to be government actors) and develop policies and procedures for managing speech and expression in competition. Many schools opt to permit such expression as consistent with their educational mission of fostering open dialogue—so long as the activism does not disrupt athletics operations. Relatedly, legal counsel may work with college athletics departments to craft policies for student-athletes' use of social media, setting expectations that posts in violation of school policy or displaying unlawful or dangerous conduct may trigger team discipline.

- *Crisis communication.* Lastly, university counsel partner closely with athletics and public relations officials to coordinate internal and external communication as crises rapidly develop on campus. This can include assessing what information, if any, about individual student or staff misconduct can be shared publicly or with law enforcement or how public statements impact pending litigation, such as recent legal challenges to NCAA amateurism rules. Finally, university counsel also support governance communication, often drafting and delivering updates to the university's Board of Trustees on high-profile athletics and other matters.

Lawyering at the intersection of sport and communication is quite challenging, as illustrated in the description of Laura Warren's typical duties, but lawyers are not the only ones managing challenges in sport communication. As you will read in this chapter, knowledge of legal issues helps all sport industry professionals assess risk and avoid liability.

Sport and the media have enjoyed a symbiotic relationship: Sport benefits from the interest generated by various media sources, and the media reap the benefits of additional consumers as fans seek more sport content. Thus, neither industry would flourish without the support of the other. As a result, Laucella and Osborne (2002) have suggested that building professional trust and respect between sport personnel and the media would benefit both sides. In the early years of professional sport, journalists reported primarily on athletes' performance on the field (Craig, 1994). For example, in 1928, baseball writers covering the New York Yankees were sitting in a train's club car, playing poker. Suddenly, the door to the club car burst open, and Babe Ruth ran down the aisle, chased by a knife-wielding woman who was screaming, "I'll kill you, you son of a bitch!" The writers all looked at each other, and one commented, "That'd make a helluva story." They laughed and resumed playing, and no one reported the incident until 1976. Writer Fred Lieb explained that journalists at the time "were in the business of creating heroes, not tearing them down" (Telander, 1984, p. 5).

Over time, the relationship between sport personnel and the media has become more critical and increasingly adversarial. Simply reporting on games is no longer enough because anyone with a cell phone or tablet can stream the event live, access real-time statistics, and watch video highlights. The 24-7-365 news cycle—along with the desire to be first in reporting information to a seemingly insatiable public—forces print journalists, broadcasters, and digital media companies alike to continually dig for personal information about athletes, coaches, managers, and owners. Because media is a business, sport journalists often sensationalize headlines and stories to attract larger audiences (and therefore bring in more advertising revenue). This race to break stories is potentially fraught, however, with journalistic inaccuracies, misquotes, quotes delivered out of context, use of off-the-record information, and disclosure of intimate details of the private lives of athletes and coaches. As a result, some individual sport figures are leery of interacting with the media (Laucella & Osborne, 2002).

In contrast, sport leagues and teams generally understand the value they gain by maintaining a cooperative relationship with the media. However, this goal can pit an individual athlete's desire for privacy against league policy. In 2014, for example, Seattle Seahawks running back Marshawn Lynch deliberately avoided the media by arriving late and departing early via a side door to the stadium. In 2015, Lynch was required by the league to attend media-day interviews. Maintaining his insistence on privacy during Super Bowl week, Lynch provided the same answer to all media questions: "I'm just here so I won't get fined." Interviews were less than five minutes, he did not get fined, and he subsequently registered the phrase as a **trademark**!

Athletes, owners, and even team and league officials' cooperation with the media, or their own use of social media, can have significant unintended consequences. For example, in October 2019, the general manager of the Houston Rockets, Daryl Morey, expressed his support for protestors in Hong Kong with a short tweet. The Chinese government was unhappy with this message and responded by canceling all NBA games scheduled to run on state-sponsored networks. NBA commissioner Adam Silver apologized for offending the Chinese, but all the NBA's Chinese partners and sponsors either ended or suspended their agreements, potentially costing the NBA billions of dollars in revenues. Since that time, players have generally been silent or nonresponsive when asked by the media about the situation; some of these players may have been advised to avoid the issue rather than risk endorsement deals (Young, 2019).

Should athletes be required to cooperate with the media? Do the media have a right to publish every detail of a sport figure's private life? This chapter examines the relationships between sport personnel and the media from a legal perspective. First, the chapter introduces constitutional law issues stemming from the First Amendment and the right to privacy. The emergence of social media requires consideration of the rights of entities (e.g., leagues, schools, teams) and individuals (e.g., athletes) in regard to **freedom of speech** and disciplinary measures. The discussion also explores the evolution of the **right of publicity** and its effect on media promotions and broadcast rights. Finally, the chapter examines issues of gender equity and sexual harassment in the hypermasculine culture of sport and male dominance in sport media. As with the broad variety of activities under the umbrella of sport communication, legal issues in sport communication reach across a wide spectrum of laws and regulations, including issues of constitutional law, torts, contracts,

and agency. This chapter is intended simply to introduce these legal concepts and should not be construed as legal advice.

CONSTITUTIONAL LAW TENSION: FREEDOM OF THE PRESS VERSUS PRIVACY RIGHTS

The First Amendment of the U.S. Constitution states, "Congress shall make no law respecting an establishment of religion, or prohibiting the free exercise thereof; or abridging the freedom of speech, or of the press; or the right of the people peaceably to assemble, and to petition the government for a redress of grievances." The United States prides itself on allowing people the freedom to express their opinion, to engage in debate, and to be informed. Freedom of the press is necessary to advance these values, and it has been rigorously protected by the courts.

On the other hand, an individual's **right of privacy** is not explicitly stated in the Constitution, yet it is also protected by the courts (see *Griswold v. Connecticut*, 1965). The right of privacy is generally viewed as the right to be free of unnecessary public scrutiny, or to be let alone. However, if a person is a public figure or is involved in newsworthy events, the right to privacy may be precluded by the freedom of the press to publish truthful information of public concern (see *New York Times v. Sullivan*, 1964; *Rosenbloom v. Metromedia, Inc.*, 1971).

Balance between the press' freedom to provide information to the public and an individual's right to be let alone is provided by **defamation** law. *Defamation* consists of communication so harmful that it significantly tarnishes an individual's reputation, exposing the person to public ridicule, contempt, embarrassment, or disassociation. To be considered defamatory, a statement must be communicated to a third party; more specifically, defamatory oral communication is referred to as *slander*, and defamatory written communication is referred to as *libel*. If an individual believes that her or his right of privacy has been violated by the media, six elements must be proven to win a defamation claim: (1) a defamatory statement; (2) identification of the individual; (3) publication or distribution of the statement; (4) fault of the publisher for negligently, recklessly, or maliciously publishing the information; (5) falsity of the published information; and (6) personal harm. In libel, damages are assumed, but actual damages must be proven for slander (*Restatement of Torts [3rd]*, 1998). The media can defend against a defamation claim either by proving that the published information was true or by asserting consent or a privilege (e.g., editorial or opinion) that allows for hyperbole or figurative language.

Elements of Defamation
- Defamatory statement
- Identification of an individual
- Publication
- Fault
- Falsity
- Personal harm

Defenses Against Defamation Claims
- Truth
- Editorial or opinion
- Exaggeration, hyperbole, figurative language
- Totality of circumstances
- Consent
- Absolute privilege for government officials
- Qualified privilege for journalists

Courts also balance the freedom of the press with an individual's right of privacy based on whether the person is a private or public figure. Private individuals are those who do not seek public attention and are not engaged in activity that is of public concern. Public figures, on the other hand, are those whose fame or notoriety put them in the public eye—for example, politicians and entertainers. Individuals may also be considered public figures if they engage in community affairs or are involved in activities of public interest, as are CEOs of major corporations and leaders of charitable or community organizations.

The U.S. Supreme Court made the distinction between public and private figures in its 1964 decision in *New York Times v. Sullivan* (1964). In an opinion written by Justice William Brennan, the court held that a public official may not be awarded damages for a defamatory falsehood related to his or her official conduct unless it is proven that the published statement was made with **actual malice**—that is, with knowledge of its falsity or reckless disregard of whether it was true or false. In the 1964 case, even though the published advertisement contained factual errors and the content could harm the public official's reputation, the evidence was insufficient to prove that the newspaper had knowledge that the statements were false or that it recklessly disregarded the truth. The Supreme Court ruling balances the right of privacy with freedom of the press by requiring the media to verify information that may be perceived as negative; as long as the media makes reasonable professional attempts to verify the statement, a public figure is not able to recover, even if the statements are inaccurate.

In terms of sport, another landmark Supreme Court decision, *Curtis Publishing Co. v. Butts* (1967), established that a university athletics director is a public figure. In 1962, the *Saturday Evening Post* published an article accusing the University of Georgia athletics director, Wally Butts, of attempting to "fix" a football game between the Bulldogs and the University of Alabama. By divided opinion, the Supreme Court held that Butts was a public figure by virtue of his position as athletics director and applied the actual malice test. Although it is extremely difficult for a public figure to meet this legal burden of proof—reckless disregard with full knowledge of the harm that is likely to result—Butts prevailed by showing that the *Saturday Evening Post* published an unreliable informant's false description without interviewing any other sources that would have access to the same facts; nor did they look at game film to corroborate supposed illicit acts. Other cases indicate that athletes, coaches, athletics administrators, and sport management personnel may all be considered public figures.

In *Bilney v. The Evening Star Newspaper Co.* (1979), six University of Maryland men's basketball players sued the *Washington Star*, the *Diamondback* (a student newspaper), and various writers and editors for invasion of privacy for publishing information claiming that four of the players were "on academic probation and in danger of flunking" (p. 563). The other two players were identified as having been "academically dismissed" (p. 564) the previous semester. The athletes were identified by name, and their grade point averages were published. The players claimed that the publishers "wil[l]fully, wrongfully, and maliciously" (p. 564) invaded their privacy by publishing private and privileged facts that were unlawfully obtained from confidential academic records. The players conceded that they were public figures based on the popularity of the University of Maryland basketball program. The court reasoned that the scholastic standing of other students in the general student body may be of only private concern but that student-athletes' eligibility to play basketball is of legitimate interest to the general public. The court was decidedly unsympathetic to the players' situation, finding that they "sought and basked in the limelight" as members of the basketball team and therefore cannot complain when that same "light focuses on their potentially imminent withdrawal from the team" (p. 573).

At the same time, the *Warford v. The Lexington Herald-Leader Company* (1990) case illustrates that sport-related figures are not automatically classified as public figures. The *Lexington Herald Leader* reprinted a story alleging that Reggie Warford, the assistant men's basketball coach at the University of Pittsburgh, had violated NCAA rules by offering a prominent high school recruit money to sign with the team. The trial court considered Warford a private figure, but the appellate court ruled that Warford was a public figure based on his roles as coach and recruiter for a Big East Conference university. The Kentucky Supreme Court reversed again, finding that Warford was a private person at the time that the defamatory statement was published. The court held that his status as a recruiter was not a matter of public concern, nor did it automatically put him in the public eye.

As shown by the rulings of the various courts in Kentucky in the *Warford* case, an individual's status as a public or private figure is determined on a case-by-case basis. In addition, some courts have recognized a limited-purpose public figure category. A limited-purpose public figure may not be well known or notorious but is still considered a public figure because

he or she is distinguished in a particular field or has inserted him- or herself into a particular controversy. A four-step analysis can be used to determine an individual's status (Laucella & Osborne, 2002, p. 197):

1. Isolation of the controversy and determination of the scope of the public's interest

2. An examination of the plaintiff's role in the controversy

3. A determination of whether the defamatory statement is germane to the plaintiff's role in the controversy

Photo courtesy of Paul M. Pedersen.

As illustrated in the opening profile on Laura Warren and in numerous examples throughout this chapter, various legal issues in sport communication (e.g., the McNair and Butts defamation cases, using student-athletes' likenesses in video games) have involved stakeholders (e.g., student-athletes, broadcast partners) of the National Collegiate Athletic Association (NCAA), the sport governing body located in Indianapolis.

4. An analysis of the extent of the plaintiff's access to channels of communication

Todd McNair was an assistant football coach at the University of Southern California (USC) during the Reggie Bush scandal that resulted in major infractions from the NCAA. The NCAA Committee on Infractions found that McNair violated ethical conduct and recruiting rules and imposed sanctions on McNair, which resulted in USC not renewing his contract. When McNair failed to find other coaching employment, he filed a lawsuit against the NCAA claiming defamation; McNair claimed the NCAA published falsehoods in the COI and Appeals Committee reports and committed slander in oral statements made by NCAA officials. The case was finally heard in the Los Angeles County Superior Court in May 2018; the jury found 9 to 3 in favor of the NCAA. The court identified McNair as a limited purpose public figure, and the jury was not sufficiently convinced the NCAA's findings were false or that they acted with "actual malice" in issuing the COI report (McCann, 2018).

It is highly unlikely that sport figures will ever win an invasion-of-privacy claim based on truthful-information grounds. Even athletes' most personal information—relationships, sexual orientation, and medical information—is headline news. Sport figures pursue occupations that are high profile because the public is interested, and freedom of the press gives the media the right to publish truthful information, no matter how publicly embarrassing it may be.

CONSTITUTIONAL RIGHTS: FREEDOM OF SPEECH

If the media have the freedom to publish almost any bit of truthful information, do sport figures also have unfettered ability to share their thoughts and opinions? The First Amendment of the U.S. Constitution guarantees freedom of speech, which has been expanded by the courts to include freedom of expression. This section examines the rights of entities (e.g., leagues, schools, teams) and individuals (e.g., athletes) related to freedom of speech.

Freedom of speech is not unlimited. Constitutional rights are protected only from infringe-

ment by the government; therefore, for a claim to go forward, some type of **state action** must be involved. Purely private entities, such as professional leagues, are relatively free to establish policies that limit employees' speech to some degree. However, state actors, such as public high schools and universities, must be vigilant to establish policies that do not inhibit free speech.

State actors are generally allowed to restrict the time, place, and manner of speech, but they are not allowed to prohibit speech content. However, public schools may restrict speech that could cause a "substantial disruption or material interference with school activities" (*Tinker v. Des Moines Indep. Cmty. School Dist.*, 1969, p. 514). Similarly, public schools can censor student publications when doing so advances legitimate pedagogical concerns (*Hazelwood School Dist. v. Kuhlmeier*, 1988). In *Crue v. Aiken* (2004), students wanted to contact prospective student-athletes to inform them about the controversy surrounding the University of Illinois' use of a Native American mascot. The court ruled that the university was justified in prohibiting the students from doing so.

Coaches and athletes sometimes argue that their free-speech rights are violated when they are disciplined for comments made publicly. However, freedom of speech does not guarantee that a person will not be accountable for making comments; in fact, if a statement is not political speech or of public concern, there is little legal protection. In addition, in school-based sport programs, participation in athletics is viewed as a privilege, not a right. When a student-athlete makes comments that contain offensive language or statements that could disrupt team order or discipline, courts have given coaches and athletics administrators broad latitude to punish that student-athlete. For example, when a wrestler at Kent State University tweeted antigay remarks in response to football player Michael Sam's announcement that he is gay, an immediate uproar arose on campus, and the athletics department suspended the wrestler from the team (Nichols, 2014). Schools have also completely banned student-athletes from posting on social media—a policy that is acceptable as a "time, place, and manner" restriction.

Private leagues are not state actors, which means that professional leagues and teams are free to impose conduct standards that limit free-

Just because you can say it doesn't mean you should. During the 2019 NBA Finals between the Toronto Raptors and the Golden State Warriors, the league released a statement noting that the action of an individual who has minority stake ownership of the Warriors "was beyond unacceptable and has no place in our league." The individual—who was banned from NBA games for one year and given a $500,000 fine by NBA commissioner Adam Silver—issued a statement accepting "full responsibility" for his actions after it was revealed that he had shoved and shouted obscenities at the Raptors' Kyle Lowry from his courtside seat.

dom of speech or expression and to punish those who violate those standards. Such standards are generally negotiated between management and the players' union in collective bargaining. The saga of former San Francisco 49ers quarterback Colin Kaepernick illustrates the consequences of exercising free speech rights for an employee of a private league. At the start of the 2016 NFL season, Kaepernick refused to stand for the playing of the national anthem, stating that he could not "show pride in a flag for a country that oppresses black people and people of color" (Vera, 2018). While fans had a lot to say about the protest—both positive and negative—the NFL policy at the time encouraged, but did not require, players to stand for the anthem. Throughout the season, other NFL players, NBA players, WNBA players, national team members, and dozens of college and high school teams knelt or locked arms during the anthem in solidarity with Kaepernick. At the start of the 2017 NFL season, Kaepernick was an

unsigned free agent, and the number of player demonstrations dwindled. However, President Donald Trump tweeted his displeasure at NFL players who did not stand as well as the NFL owners for not requiring them to stand. While the remarks prompted more protests, with some owners standing in solidarity with their players, public backlash prompted the NFL commissioner, Roger Goodell, to issue a league policy requiring all personnel on the field to stand for the national anthem. Some players and teams responded by remaining in the locker room, and the policy was rolled back when the NFL Players Association filed a grievance. Kaepernick also filed a grievance against the NFL and the team owners for colluding to deprive him of employment in retaliation for his social justice advocacy. Ultimately, the NFL pledged to contribute over $89 million over the next seven years to social justice causes, and Kaepernick agreed to a confidential settlement with the NFL in February 2019.

Political Message Earns Bedoya MLS Player of the Week

Major League Soccer (MLS) struggled through the 2019 season to find the right balance between supporting free speech while eliminating hate speech and fan misconduct in stadiums. The MLS Code of Conduct prohibits "political, threatening, abusive, insulting, offensive language and/or gestures" (Mather, 2019, p. 21). But on Sunday, August 4, 2019, after scoring the first goal of the game and celebrating with his teammates, Philadelphia Union midfielder Alejandro Bedoya grabbed a television microphone and said, "Congress, do something now. End gun violence. Let's go" (p. 5). MLS rules allowed the league to fine Bedoya, but instead the league chose to issue a statement supporting the right of players to express their opinions. At the same time, fans were showing their support through a successful Twitter campaign for the player of the week voting by writing in #VoteBedoya, even though he was not one of the listed candidates.

Photo courtesy of Paul M. Pedersen.

Fans attending a Major League Soccer (MLS) game in Colorado. During an MLS game between the Philadelphia Union and D.C. United, Union midfielder Alejandro Bedoya grabbed a microphone and expressed his opinion regarding the need for gun legislation. While the MLS could have fined him for such an expression, the league chose not to do so, and fans started a social media campaign in favor of Bedoya.

RAPIDLY EVOLVING RIGHT OF PUBLICITY

Whereas sport figures' constitutional rights related to speech and privacy may be somewhat limited, a right related to their interest in protecting the commercial value of a name, image, or likeness is rapidly evolving. A right of publicity can be established either through the common law (i.e., recognized in decisions by the court) or by state legislation. It is generally accepted that the notion of a right of publicity stems from an 1890 article by Louis Brandeis and Samuel Warren (1890), who advocated that the courts should recognize a cause of action for an invasion of privacy. In

1960, William L. Prosser (1960) expounded on this right to privacy by defining what it protects against and when protection is warranted. Prosser identified four invasion-of-privacy torts (legal wrongs) (p. 389):

1. Intrusion upon the plaintiff's seclusion or solitude, or into his or her private affairs
2. Public disclosure of embarrassing private facts about the plaintiff
3. Publicity that places the plaintiff in a false light in the public eye
4. Appropriation, for the defendant's advantage, of the plaintiff's name or likeness

The first tort reflects our typical understanding of the constitutional right to privacy, whereas the second and third torts are addressed by defamation law. The fourth tort, dealing with appropriation, arises when the defendant uses the plaintiff's name or likeness for his or her own benefit without the plaintiff's permission (Prosser, 1960). Prosser wrote that for the courts to determine appropriation, they must first decide "whether there has been appropriation of an aspect of the plaintiff's identity" and then "whether the defendant has appropriated the name or likeness for his [or her] own advantage" (p. 404). Prosser's ideas about the four invasion-of-privacy torts were later adopted in the *Restatement (Second) of Torts*, a universally recognized legal treatise with significant influential authority (Hanlon & Yasser, 2008).

Although the four privacy torts were widely accepted by the courts, it was unclear whether commercial injuries, such as those experienced by celebrities and athletes, were covered under the appropriation tort. One of the first cases involved Davey O'Brien, a famous college football player at Texas Christian University. Without obtaining permission, Pabst Sales Company used a picture of O'Brien in his uniform on a promotional calendar for Pabst Blue Ribbon beer (*O'Brien v. Pabst Sales Co.*, 1941). O'Brien was a member of an organization that encouraged U.S. youth to stay away from alcohol, and he claimed that the use of his photograph to promote alcohol sales was an invasion of his right of privacy and that he had been damaged by it. The court held that O'Brien's status as a famous college football player made him a public person and that his claim would have been actionable only for a private person. Pabst was allowed to continue using O'Brien's picture in its promotional beer campaign (*O'Brien*, 1941). The court's reluctance to extend the appropriation tort to famous people paved the way for the creation of a new right that would protect the economic value of celebrities' names and likenesses, now commonly referred to as the right of publicity.

As explained by Cook (1999, p. 310), "The right of publicity signifies the right of an individual, especially a public figure or celebrity, to control the commercial value and exploitation of his (or her) name and picture or likeness and to prevent others from unfairly appropriating this value for commercial benefit." In 1953, the U.S. Court of Appeals for the Second Circuit was the first court to recognize that an athlete had a "right of publicity." The case, *Haelan Labs., Inc. v. Topps Chewing Gum Inc.* (1953), essentially involved a contract dispute to determine which company could use a player's photograph to promote sales of gum. The court found that the player did own a right of publicity "to grant the exclusive privilege of publishing his picture" (p. 868). In addition, the court ruled that celebrities have the right to receive compensation damages done by the unauthorized use of their persona or likeness and that without this right, celebrities would "feel sorely deprived" for not being compensated (p. 868).

The U.S. Constitution delineates certain rights to the federal government, while state governments retain primary rights to legislate for the health, safety, and welfare of their citizens. Under federalism, the right of celebrities (including sport figures) to be compensated for the use of their name, image, or likeness is a right recognized by the state, so the law in this area has evolved haphazardly across the United States under various legal theories, including invasion of privacy, misappropriation, and right of publicity. These theories are illustrated by the following cases.

The unauthorized use of a professional athlete's likeness in a game was considered in *Palmer v. Schonhorn Enterprises, Inc.* (1967). Schonhorn Enterprises, Inc. created a boxed game that included cards with biographical profiles of 23 professional golfers, including Arnold Palmer, Gary Player, Doug Sanders, and Jack Nicklaus. These players did not give authorization to Schonhorn to use their likenesses or career data in the game; in fact, they expressly requested that the company cease using their "Profile and Playing Charts" (p. 74). When Schonhorn continued to use the players' images and career information in the game, the players sued for invasion of privacy—specifically, for "unfair exploitation and commercialization of their names and reputations" under New Jersey common law (p. 75). The Superior Court of New Jersey acknowledged that publication of celebrities' biographical information was not an invasion of privacy per se but held that it was unfair to use that data to exploit a player's name, reputation, or accomplishment for commercial purposes.

The distinction between a misappropriation-of-name tort and the right of publicity was clarified by the Supreme Court of Missouri in *Doe v. TCI Cablevision* (2003). Tony Twist was a former professional hockey player who had earned a reputation as an enforcer. He was a fan favorite and had parlayed that popularity into lucrative endorsements, a television talk show, and involvement in children's charities. Because he had carefully created a positive personal image in the community, he had serious concerns when a character named Anthony "Tony Twist" Twistelli appeared in the dark comic series *Spawn*. In response to a fan letter published in the September 1994 issue of the comic (and in a trade-magazine interview two years later), *Spawn* creator Todd McFarlane admitted that he had named the character after Tony Twist the professional hockey player. Twist sued McFarlane and others associated with the comic book, seeking an injunction and damages for misappropriation of name among other claims.

The case involved subtle differences between a misappropriation-of-name claim and a right-of-publicity claim, which are often used interchangeably. As defined in the *Twist* case by the Supreme Court of Missouri, a *misappropriation-of-name tort* provides protection against intrusion on an individual's private self-esteem and dignity, thus allowing for recovery of monetary losses and emotional distress. This protection is distinguished from the right of publicity, which protects against commercial loss caused by appropriation of an individual's identity for commercial exploitation and provides damages not just for monetary loss to the plaintiff but also for unjust gain by the defendant (*Doe v. TCI Cablevision*, 2003). The court

also identified a subtle difference in the elements of the two claims. For the misappropriation tort, the "plaintiff must prove that the defendant used the plaintiff's name without consent to obtain some advantage" (*Doe*, 2003, p. 368), whereas "the elements of a right of publicity action include: (1) that defendant used plaintiff's name as a symbol of his identity (2) without consent (3) and with the intent to obtain a commercial advantage" (p. 369). Although Tony Twist had proven that his name was used as a symbol of his identity, the case was remanded (sent back) to the lower court to rule on the other elements of the claim.

Right of Publicity and the First Amendment

In many cases, establishing the elements for a right-of-publicity claim may not be enough to win the case, particularly when the situation also involves freedom of the press or freedom of speech. In *Zacchini v. Scripps-Howard Broadcasting Company* (1977), the Supreme Court addressed the constraints of the First Amendment on the right of publicity. The plaintiff, a circus performer, was filmed by a local news station being shot from a cannon during his circus act. This footage was later shown on the local news without the performer's permission. The Supreme Court ruled that the First Amendment did not protect the television station and that it had violated Zacchini's right of publicity because people may be less likely to pay to see his show if they can see it on television (*Zacchini*, 1977). Thus, although the media may enjoy the right to broadcast news of public interest, the court would not allow the performer to be deprived of the value of his performance.

Freedom of speech also intersected with the right of publicity in *Cardtoons, L.C. v. Major League Baseball Players Association* (1996). Cardtoons produced a line of trading cards that featured artists' caricatures of Major League Baseball (MLB) players and humorous summaries of the players' careers on the back side. The Major League Baseball Players Association (MLBPA) sent a cease-and-desist letter to Cardtoons because it did not have authorization or a licensing agreement to produce the trading cards with the images of active MLB players. Cardtoons filed suit seeking declaratory judgment that the trading cards did not violate the rights of publicity or other property rights of the players or of MLBPA. The court analyzed MLBPA's property rights under the Oklahoma right-of-publicity statute and balanced those rights against Cardtoons' First Amendment rights. The case established that although baseball trading cards are not a traditional medium of expression, they nonetheless contain protected speech. The court also addressed the conflict between protected First Amendment speech and **commercial speech**, finding that parody was protected even if the baseball trading cards were manufactured for a commercial purpose. This case was also important because it placed a limitation on MLBPA's ability to protect the proprietary right of publicity of its players.

The California Court of Appeals further examined the intersection of rights of publicity, First Amendment protection of speech, and commercial speech applications in *Gionfriddo v. MLB* (2001). In the case, four retired baseball players sued Major League Baseball Properties, Inc., for unauthorized use of their names, photographic images, video images, and statistics in media guides, game programs, and print and video publications and on the MLB website (p. 405). The trial court granted summary judgment to Major League Baseball Properties, finding that the use of the retired players' images and statistics were matters of public interest that were protected by the First Amendment and by sport-news exemptions in the California Civil Code.

The decision was affirmed by the California Court of Appeals, which found that the players' images were "mere bits of baseball's history" that were protected by the First Amendment (p. 410). The court recognized that MLB was packaging this history for commercial profit by selling written and video programs; however, the use of the data for profit did not render that as commercial speech. The court applied a "relatedness test" and clarified that commercial speech violates the right of publicity when the plaintiff's identity is used without consent to propose a commercial transaction of an unrelated product. In this case, the retired players' identities and statistics were being used to promote and enhance the game of baseball. In balancing the players' commercial interest in the value of their likenesses and statistics against the public interest in access to information regarding baseball's history, the court found that the retired players' economic interests were not harmed and may even have been enhanced.

In the *Doe v. TCI Cablevision* (2003) case described earlier, the Supreme Court of Missouri also examined the intersection between Tony Twist's right of publicity and the comic-book creator's First Amendment rights. Historically, courts have focused on whether the use of a person's name or identity is "expressive" or "commercial" to determine whether the use is protected by the First Amendment. The court in the Twist case analyzed several approaches that had been used to identify a work as either expressive or commercial speech. The **relatedness test**, used by the court in *Gionfriddo v. MLB* (2001), applies if the person's name, likeness, or identity is used in a way that is "related to that person" (*Doe*, 2003, p. 373). Related uses include the use of a person's name or likeness in news reporting; in entertainment and other creative works, including both fiction and nonfiction; as part of an article published in a fan magazine or a feature story broadcast on an entertainment program; as part of dissemination of an unauthorized print or broadcast biography; and in a novel, play, or motion picture.

The court in the Twist case also examined the **transformative test**, applied in the California courts, which measures whether the creative elements employed in the use of the celebrity likeness transform the character into something with a separate identity beyond the celebrity imitation, thus warranting First Amendment protection. The court found both the relatedness test and the transformative test inadequate, as they each lacked acknowledgement that uses of a person's name, identity, or likeness could have both expressive and commercial purposes. The court instead favored the **predominant use test** to balance the expressive and commercial interests in speech:

If a product is being sold that predominantly exploits the commercial value of an individual's identity, that product should be held to violate the right of publicity and not be protected by the First Amendment, even if there is some "expressive" content in it that might qualify as "speech" in other circumstances. If, on the other hand, the predominant purpose of the product is to make an expressive comment on or about a celebrity, the expressive values could be given greater weight. (Doe v. TCI Cablevision, *2003, p. 374*)

Although the court recognized an expressive component in the use of "Tony Twist" as a "metaphorical reference to tough-guy 'enforcers'" in the Twist case, the literary value was deemed insignificant as compared with the commercial value of using Twist's name and identity to sell comic books (*Doe v. TCI Cablevision*, 2003).

C.B.C. Distrib. & Mktg. v. Major League Baseball Advanced Media, L.P. (2007) was the first opportunity for a court to directly address the right of publicity in another commercial industry—fantasy sport. From 1995 through 2004, CBC enjoyed a licensing relationship with the Major League Baseball Players Association, which granted CBC the right to use "the names, nicknames, likenesses, signatures, pictures, playing records, and/or biographical data of each player" in association with its fantasy sport games (p. 1080). In January 2005, MLBPA granted Major League Baseball Advanced Media, L.P. (MLBAM), the exclusive rights to use and sublicense player names and statistics in interactive media. CBC sued MLBAM for a declaratory judgment establishing "its right to use, without license, the names of and information about major league baseball players in connection with its fantasy baseball products" (p. 820).

The U.S. Court of Appeals for the Eighth Circuit ultimately found that the players had a valid right of publicity under Missouri law and that CBC's commercial use of the names and statistics in its fantasy baseball products was sufficient to infringe on that right. However, CBC ultimately won the case because "it would be strange law that a person would not have a first amendment right to use information that is available to everyone" (*C.B.C.*, 2007, p. 823). Thus, the court concluded that the First Amendment trumped the right of publicity by finding that the players' names and statistics are not owned by the individual players or the leagues but instead are facts in the public domain. Although CBC used the players' statistics for a commercial purpose, that use was deemed speech with an entertainment purpose, which was entitled to full First Amendment protection.

In intellectual property law, the term *public domain* generally refers to ideas and expressions such as facts and dates that cannot be copyrighted, patented, or propertized (Landes & Posner, 2003). Things that lie outside of **copyright** and trademark

Legal issues in sport communication reach across a wide spectrum of laws and regulations, including the various aspects related to the recent approval and growth of legalized sport gambling in many states. Player statistics and game results are all in the **public domain**, allowing gaming sites and establishments to use this data for their own profit without the player or league's permission. The gambling industry also benefits from the use of communication technology, and states rushing to legislate are regulating advertising channels and mandating content, as well as use of online and handheld devices to place bets.

protection include ideas, facts, statutes, judicial opinions, basic scientific principles, discoveries, procedures, processes, unoriginal works, methods and systems of operation, information that is in the public domain, and government documents (Mitten, Davis, Shropshire, Osborne, & Smith, 2013). Content in the public domain is free for use in speech. The court in the CBC case (*C.B.C.*, 2007) helped clarify the relationship between the exclusive rights to use information that is in the public domain and the First Amendment. The Eighth Circuit findings strengthened the public-domain doctrine by identifying a presumptive First Amendment right to freely use baseball statistics or other information provided for use in the public domain.

With the high level of fan interest in college sport, it seemed inevitable that fantasy operators would use the precedent established by the CBC case to offer fantasy college sport. Indeed, it took only three months for the NCAA's broadcasting partner, CBS, to use the names and statistics of college players in its fantasy college football league. The reasoning behind this move was that the athletes' names and statistics are part of the public domain and therefore free to use. However, the ruling in *C.B.C.* specifically addressed professional athletes, thus leaving the door open for college athletes to claim violation of their rights of publicity.

Ryan Hart was the quarterback for the Rutgers University NCAA Men's Division I football team from 2002 to 2005. Meanwhile, Electronic Arts (EA) sold a video game called NCAA Football that included more than 100 virtual teams comprised of digital avatars that resembled real-life players on those teams. In 2004, 2005, and 2006, the Rutgers quarterback in the game wore uniform number 13, stood 6 feet 2 inches, and weighed 197 pounds—all of which resembled Hart—and included his biographical and career statistics. In addition, EA promoted sales of the game with footage from the Rutgers bowl game against Arizona State University showing Hart throwing a pass. Hart sued EA for violation of his right of publicity (*Hart v. Electronic Arts, Inc.*, 2013).

In considering the case, the Third Circuit recognized that video games are protected as **expressive speech** under the First Amendment while also applying the transformative-use test

to determine "whether the product containing a celebrity's likeness is so transformed that it has become primarily the defendant's own expression rather than the celebrity's likeness" (*Hart*, 2013, p. 160). For guidance, the court turned to a similar case involving the Band Hero video game and its use of avatars of real-life musicians, including Gwen Stefani and the band No Doubt. In that case, the California Court of Appeals had found that even though the avatars appear in the context of a video game containing many other creative elements, they were not transformed into anything other than exact depictions of the band members. Similarly, the Third Circuit found that the digitized "sights and sounds in the [football] video game" did not significantly "alter or transform" Hart's identity and that EA's avatars failed to satisfy the transformative-use test. Even so, the use of Ryan's image to promote the game was shielded by the First Amendment because it was only a "fleeting component part of the montage" (*Hart*, 2013, p. 170).

In 2009, former University of Nebraska quarterback Sam Keller filed a class-action lawsuit in federal court against the NCAA, Electronic Arts Inc., and the Collegiate Licensing Company (CLC) (*Keller v. Elec. Arts, Inc.*, 2010). Keller's claim was similar to Hart's in regard to the use of former student-athletes' likenesses as avatars in video games, but it also complained about the use of likenesses in archival broadcast footage, photographs, and promotions. Several other former student-athletes, including Ed O'Bannon, Oscar Robertson, Ray Ellis, and Bill Russell, also filed complaints, which were consolidated in 2010 as *In re: NCAA Student-Athlete Likeness Licensing Litigation* (2014).

The consolidated case added a unique twist to the litigation by making an antitrust claim. Specifically, it argued that NCAA rules against student-athletes profiting from the use of their name, image, or likeness (on penalty of losing their NCAA eligibility to compete) violated the Sherman Antitrust Act (1890). This act prohibits businesses and organizations from engaging in practices that would restrain interstate commerce. The case was eventually settled in 2013 for $60 million ($20 million from the NCAA and $40 million from EA). Former student-athletes who opted into the class action will receive distribu-

Photo courtesy of Paul M. Pedersen.

NCAA Football 14 was the last college sports video game produced by EA Sports as a result of the *In re: NCAA Student-Athlete Likeness Licensing Litigation* consolidated cases.

EA advanced one additional First Amendment defense—that the use of the former professional athletes' likenesses was "incidental" as compared with the whole. In California, the incidental-use test is measured according to the following considerations (*Davis*, 2015, p. 1180):

- Whether the use has a unique quality or value that would result in commercial profit to the defendant
- Whether the use contributes something of significance
- The relationship between the reference to the plaintiff and the purpose and subject of the work
- The duration, prominence, or repetition of the name or likeness relative to the rest of the publication

tion payments, with the majority of the settlement going to Keller and the other named plaintiffs from the consolidated cases.

Sam Keller was also a plaintiff in a lawsuit filed by Michael "Tony" Davis against EA Sports in California; other plaintiffs include Vince Ferragamo and Billy Joe Dupree, representing a class of former professional athletes whose likenesses were used in EA's popular Madden NFL game (*Davis v. Elec. Arts, Inc.*, 2015). EA pays National Football Players, Inc. millions of dollars in annual licensing fees to use the likenesses of current players for all 32 NFL teams, along with player names and team logos, colors, and uniforms. From 2001 to 2009, Madden NFL also included avatars of about 6,000 former NFL players on more than 100 "historic teams" without authorization. EA filed a motion to dismiss the lawsuit under California's Anti-SLAPP statute, which protects against meritless and harassing claims aimed at limiting protected speech. The district court rejected the motion, and EA appealed. The Ninth Circuit Court of Appeals affirmed the lower court's decision after analyzing EA's First Amendment defenses and applying the transformative-use test, as well as precedent from *Keller v. NCAA* (2013).

Because Madden NFL relies on its ability to simulate the experiences of a real NFL game, the creation of realistic avatars of players on the field is closely aligned with the core experience of the game. Therefore, the Ninth Circuit held that EA would not likely prevail using the incidental-use test under the common law. EA then filed a motion for summary judgement under California's right of publicity statute, which requires that a likeness be readily identifiable (*Davis v. Elec. Arts Inc.*, 2018). Because the avatars in the Madden games required additional context from the game to be identifiable, EA won its motion for summary judgement regarding claims made under the right of publicity statute. However, the case is still currently pending litigation of the common law claims.

One area of the law that is quite clear is that use of players' performance statistics is protected by the First Amendment, which allows use of information that is in the public domain even if it is used for a commercial purpose. This use of a player's performance data contrasts with the use of a player's personal physical likeness and actual game performances, which violates the player's right of publicity if such use is not authorized. However, the question of whether former players should be compensated for rebroadcasts of actual game footage remains a hotly disputed legal issue that continues to evolve.

Right of Publicity and Broadcast Rights

Broadcasts of sporting events have been a media staple since the creation of each medium. A play-by-play broadcast of a professional hockey game was transmitted via telegraph from Montreal to Winnipeg in 1896. In 1921, KDKA broadcast a boxing match on the radio. The 1936 Olympic Games in Berlin were the first live televised sporting event. The invention of cable television spawned ESPN and revolutionized sport broadcasting. Satellite, digital cable, and the Internet have all expanded fans' ability to access live sport content.

As broadcast revenues skyrocketed in the 1990s and 2000s, professional athletes in the major leagues negotiated a share of the broadcast fees through collective bargaining. However, a group of former NFL players filed a class-action lawsuit against the NFL in 2010, claiming that the use of their names, images, and likenesses in video footage used in NFL Films productions violated their publicity rights, caused consumer confusion, and unjustly enriched the NFL (*Dryer v. NFL*, 2010). The players in the *Dryer* case played in the NFL from the late 1960s to the mid-1980s. The lawsuit was settled in 2013, and the settlement provided a fund to distribute payments to former players and permission for a licensing agency to market former players' publicity rights (*Dryer v. NFL*, 2013). However, several former players opted out of the settlement and chose to pursue their own individual claims (*Dryer v. NFL*, 2014).

NFL Films creates original content portraying famous seasons, games, and players by compiling clips of game footage and cameo interviews with the players and others associated with the film's subject. The *Dryer* plaintiffs' claim—that use of the game clips violated their rights of publicity—failed because the content is protected speech under the First Amendment. Similarly, the NFL's right to use its copyrighted film in other productions is protected by the Copyright Act (1976),

which preempts a right-of-publicity claim. The former players' claim of false endorsement failed because the use of historic game footage that is not altered in any way cannot be false or misleading. Summary judgment was granted to the NFL because it has the right to exploit copyrighted game footage in expressive works (*Dryer v. NFL*, 2014).

The Middle District Court in Tennessee followed the *Dryer* precedent in dismissing a case filed by former college student-athletes against several Division I athletics conferences as well as various television networks and licensing agencies (*Marshall v. ESPN Inc.*, 2015). The former players claimed that the defendants profited from broadcasts that used their names, images, and likenesses without permission and alleged both statutory and common-law right-of-publicity violations under Tennessee law, among other claims. The district court found that participants in sporting events have no right of publicity under the common law: "An athlete who takes the field before 100,000 fans at Neyland Stadium can hardly claim that a broadcast of the game threatens any constitutionally protected 'privacy right'" (Docket No. 269, p. 7). Without an underlying cause of action that could be protected by statute, all the statutory claims were rendered moot.

The decisions in the *Dryer* and *Marshall* cases indicate that former players have no compensable right of publicity in game-broadcast footage. Although leagues and broadcasters control the right to broadcast, distribute, and redistribute games and derivative works, professional football players may have found a new way to generate broadcast revenues. The NFL Players Association launched Athlete Content & Entertainment, aka ACE Media, in 2015 to create original content and programming opportunities for current and former players. Since that time, ACE media has produced content across all media platforms featuring more than 350 athletes from the NFL, NBA, NHL, and U.S. Soccer.

COPYRIGHT AND TRADEMARK

As sport has evolved into big business, sport organizations, event organizers, and athletes have realized the importance of protecting their brand images. The U.S. Constitution gives Congress the power to "promote the Progress of Science and useful Arts, by securing for limited Times to Authors and Inventors the exclusive Right to their respective Writings and Discoveries" (Art. 1, Sec. 8). The Copyright Act of 1976 (Title 17 of the U.S. Code) includes all rules of copyright protection. Copyright law protects the works of artists and authors by giving them the exclusive right to publish, copy, reproduce, distribute, perform, or display their works. A work must be original and exist in a tangible form that can be reproduced to receive copyright protection, which lasts for 28 years with a right to renew for 67 years (for a total of 95 years). The following lists indicate what may and may not receive copyright protection:

Protected by Copyright

- Literary works
- Dramatic works
- Pantomime and choreographic works
- Pictorial, graphic, and sculptural works
- Motion pictures and other audiovisual works
- Sound recordings
- Architectural works

Not Protected by Copyright

- Ideas
- Procedures and processes
- Systems and methods of operation
- Concepts, principles, and discoveries
- Government documents
- Works in the public domain
- Works that are not original (e.g., calendars, charts, tape measures)
- Competitions
- Slogans, titles, and names
- Variation, lettering, and coloring
- Facts and raw data

There are limited exceptions when the public can use copyright-protected material without the owner's permission. The **fair-use doctrine** allows the use of copyrighted material for criticism, comment, news reporting, teaching, scholarship, or research. In such cases, the court examines whether the purpose and nature of the use is commercial or not for profit, as well as the nature of the work used, the amount of material used in comparison with the whole, and the effect of the use on the potential market value of the original work.

Many copyright cases in sport involve broadcast rights. For example, the NFL and NBA sued TvRadioNow Corporation for video streaming copyrighted live broadcasts of games to Canada (*NFL v. TvRadioNow Corp.*, 2000). TvRadioNow would capture games and other popular programs from television stations in New York, convert the television signals into computerized data, insert their own advertisements, and stream them through an Internet website called iCraveTV.com. The public could access the site by entering a three-digit Canadian area code and then clicking two additional buttons. The broadcasts were all copyright-protected works, and TvRadioNow was not authorized to use them; therefore, the court issued an injunction to prevent the company from streaming the broadcasts.

The unauthorized commercial usage of recorded broadcasts of sporting events also constitutes copyright infringement, as does reporting of real-time game accounts that are not authorized. For example, one case addressed the PGA's requirement that media organizations obtain free press credentials to access real-time scores as a tour event progressed (*Morris Communications Corporation v. PGA Tour, Inc.*, 2004). Through the use of a spectator at the event, Morris Communications Corporation was able to publish the scores on its website before the PGA reported them and used that speed to sell real-time scores to other media. The Eleventh Circuit found that the PGA held a proprietary interest in the information and that Morris was freeloading and profiting from the PGA's investment. Conversely, reporting real-time game statistics, such as the names of the teams playing, time remaining in the game, and scores obtained from television or radio broadcasts, does not constitute copyright infringement under the fair-use exception (*NBA v. Motorola, Inc.*, 1997).

A *trademark* is any word, name, symbol, or device—or any combination thereof—adopted or used by a manufacturer or merchant to identify goods and distinguish them from goods manufactured or sold by others (Trademark Revisions Act, 1988). Trademarks serve an identification function and signify that goods come from a particular source; may also indicate the quality of the product; and act as a symbol of goodwill used by a business in advertising, promoting, and selling goods. Trademark law also includes service marks (which identify and distinguish the services of an entity) and collective marks (which are used by members of a cooperative, association, or other organization to indicate membership). The Federal Trademark Act of 1946, also known as the Lanham Act, governs trademarks, including registration of trademarks and actions to protect trademark infringement.

The University of Alabama was engaged in a trademark infringement and breach-of-licensing-contract lawsuit with artist Daniel Moore and his company, New Life Art, Inc., for nine years (*Univ. of Ala. Bd. of Trs. v. New Life Art, Inc.*, 2013). Moore, an alumnus, had been painting iconic University of Alabama football scenes and reproducing those paintings in prints and other forms (e.g., calendars, mugs). From 1991 to 1999, the parties had a contractual agreement whereby New Life paid the university royalties based on the revenues generated by sales of five "limited edition" prints. New Life continued to sell other merchandise containing reproductions of the paintings, and the University objected, claiming that additional licensing agreements were needed.

Moore contended that the images contained in the paintings were his copyrighted works, whereas the university argued that registered university marks (e.g., uniforms, helmets, crimson and white colors) were depicted in the paintings without permission. Nevertheless, the university continued to sell New Life's unauthorized calendars from 2001 to 2004 in its campus stores and in a museum. The university sued New Life in 2005 for breach of contract, trademark infringement, unfair competition, and unjust enrichment. After nine years of litigation, it was eventually held that Moore's First Amendment rights superseded the University's trademark claims relative to the fine art paintings and reproductions of those works. The court also found that the depiction of the football team's uniforms or logos in the paintings did not infringe on the university's protected trademarks (*Univ. of Ala.*, 2013).

People may typically think of trademarks in terms of logos, team names, names and depictions of mascots, and such symbols. Under the Lanham Act (Federal Trademark Act, 1946), an athlete may use his or her name as a trademark or service mark if it has acquired secondary meaning. Sport figures who have trademarked their names include athletes Michael Jordan, Tiger Woods, and Natalie Gulbis, as well as college football coach Dabo Swinney and former coach and now broadcaster Urban Meyer (Williams, 2012).

Sport figures have become more entrepreneurial and now recognize the need to protect their brand; if a nickname or catchphrase sticks, it

Tiger Woods and many other athletes (as well as celebrities, etc.) have trademarked their name. Here, an advertisement on a taxicab uses the name "Tiger" and a photo of Tiger Woods to promote the BMW Championship.

is important for the individual to secure intellectual property rights so that others cannot profit from it. In addition, a term or phrase may become associated with a sport team (e.g., Evil Empire for the New York Yankees) through public usage or fan recognition, thus conferring trademark rights on the team (*New York Yankees Partnership v. Evil Enterprises, Inc.*, 2013). Table 13.1 includes a list of phrases that sport figures have trademarked.

Trademark infringement is the reproduction, counterfeiting, copying, or imitation in commerce of a registered mark in connection with the unauthorized sale, offering for sale, distribution, or advertising of any goods or services likely to cause confusion, mistake, or deceit. To make a claim under the Lanham Act (Federal Trademark Act, 1946), the plaintiff (trademark owner) must establish (1) a protectable property right in the trademark (typically use and registration) and (2) that the other party's use of a similar mark is likely to cause confusion or mistake or deceive consumers as to who is the true source of the mark. In determining confusion, the court may use the following factors:

- Strength of the mark
- Similarity between marks
- Similarity between products and marketing channels used to sell them
- Likelihood that the trademark owner will expand use of the mark on future products
- Evidence of actual confusion
- Defendant's good-faith intent in adopting the mark
- Quality of the defendant's mark
- Sophistication of consumers

Legal proceedings to prevent and remedy infringement or counterfeiting of federally registered marks may be brought in federal courts to obtain injunctive relief and damages (Mitten et al., 2013).

Much of the litigation in media law is driven by money—determining who owns the rights to capitalize on a broadcast, likeness, copyright, or

Table 13.1 Trademarked Sport-Related Phrases

Phrase	Trademark owner
Beast Mode	Marshawn Lynch
Bolt to the world	Usain Bolt
Fab Five	Jalen Rose
Fear the brow; raise the brow	Anthony Davis
Hit King	Pete Rose
Holla Energy	Kevin Garnett
Invincible	Vince Young
It's go time	Brett Freeman
Johnny Football; JMAN2	Johnny Manziel
Just a Kid from Akron; King James	LeBron James
Kobe Bryant Flight 24	Kobe Bryant
Let's get ready to rumble!	Michael Buffer
Let's play two	Ernie Banks
Linsanity	Jeremy Lin
Lovee	Venus and Serena Williams
Mad Chad	Chad (Ochocinco) Johnson
Man on a mission; M.O.A.M.	Austin Rivers
Money Green	Draymond Green
Refuse to lose	John Calipari
Revis Island	Darrelle Revis
Rice Rocket	Michelle Kwan
Shaq Attaq; ShaqFu; Shaqtacular	Shaquille O'Neal
Sky Hook	Kareem Abdul-Jabbar
Stomp you out	Michael Strahan
Tebowing	Tim Tebow
The Big Unit	Randy Johnson
The Great One	Wayne Gretzky
Thorpedo	Ian Thorpe
Three-peat; 3-peat	Pat Riley
Turn 2	Derek Jeter
You cannot be serious	John McEnroe

trademark. Another area of legal concern in sport media also has monetary implications—the ability to get a job. The next section focuses on barriers that women have faced in sport communication.

GENDER ISSUES IN SPORT MEDIA

ESPN made sport communication history on October 6, 2015, when Jessica Mendoza officially became the first female analyst to call a nationally

Photo courtesy of Paul M. Pedersen.

In addition to her status as a star player in the WNBA, Sue Bird has done color commentary for ESPN. Bird is also a front-office executive with the Denver Nuggets.

televised Major League Baseball postseason game. On September 26, 2018, Andrea Kremer and Hannah Storm became the first all-female broadcast team for an NFL game. These milestones for female sport broadcasters are cause for celebration because women have struggled since the 1970s to achieve equity in sport journalism. Women's success in the field has been hindered through sexual harassment, discrimination in hiring, and limitations on their access to locker rooms.

One of the earliest legal cases in this arena was *Ludtke v. Kuhn* (1978), which illustrates the obstacles that female reporters faced in obtaining access to locker rooms to interview athletes. In 1975, MLB Commissioner Bowie Kuhn sent letters to all the teams' general managers encouraging them to take a unified stand against allowing female sport reporters into the locker room. In 1977, Melissa Ludtke, a reporter for *Sports Illustrated*, was covering a World Series Game between the New York Yankees and the Los Angeles Dodgers. Although Ludtke had previously been allowed access to the Yankees locker room during the American League play-offs, the MLB commissioner's office informed her that she would not be allowed access to either team's locker room during the World Series. Ludtke sued the commissioner, claiming sex discrimination. MLB argued that excluding female reporters from the locker rooms was necessary to protect the privacy of players, to protect the image of baseball as a family sport, and to preserve traditional notions of decency and propriety (*Ludtke v. Kuhn*, p. 16). The court considered these claims "too insubstantial to merit serious consideration" (p. 37). It found that MLB's policy "substantially and directly" interfered with Ludtke's right to "pursue her profession as a sports reporter" and put her at a significant disadvantage as compared with her male peers, who were able to get immediate access to "fresh off the field" remarks from players (p. 37).

Gaining access to locker rooms was only a partial victory because female sport reporters were often harassed and degraded while attempting to conduct postgame interviews. In 1990, the *Boston Herald* advanced the progress of women in print journalism by promoting Lisa Olson to NFL beat reporter covering the New England Patriots. Insulted that the *Herald* had assigned a woman to cover his team, Patriots owner Victor Kiam actively discouraged players and other Patriots personnel from cooperating with Olson. Players made vulgar comments and lewd suggestions and even exposed themselves to Olson in the locker room. When Olson lodged a complaint with the NFL, the Patriots orchestrated a cover-up utilizing the media. This sparked a national debate during sport radio talk shows, with callers blasting Olson, and she began receiving threatening phone calls. Vendors at Foxborough Stadium sold inflatable "Lisa dolls," which male fans subjected to various suggestive acts, and Olson's home and car were vandalized. The NFL investigated and fined the Patriots $50,000. Olson was so traumatized by the experience that she moved to Australia (Druzin, 2006; Sharp, 1997).

Pedersen, Osborne, Whisenant, and Lim (2009) studied the extent to which female sport print media professionals (e.g., sports editors, sportswriters, sport columnists) were subjected to sexual harassment in the workplace. Of the women who participated in the study, more than half indicated that they had encountered some form of sexual harassment in the past 12 months. The harassers included their immediate supervisors, sport media co-workers, peers working for other sport media organizations, athletes, and employees of sport organizations. Younger professionals were more likely to encounter sexual harassment, which included verbal harassment, physical harassment, sexual advances, and requests for sexual favors. In a somewhat surprising finding, most female sport journalists attempted to ignore these behaviors rather than report them; a small minority changed jobs.

On a positive note, significantly fewer incidents of sexual harassment occurred when sport media organizations had a sexual harassment policy (Pedersen et al., 2009). Although the #MeToo movement has exposed predatory behavior in business and entertainment, very little has changed in the sport industry; female sport reporters are still hesitant to report harassment for fear of being removed from their assignments (Deitsch, 2017), and female reporters are still targeted for harassment. During the Houston Astros American League Championship Series victory celebration in 2019, an assistant general manager shouted a profane statement directly at female reporters, expressing appreciation for Roberto Osuna, a player the Astros acquired after he had been suspended for violating baseball's domestic violence policy. When a female reporter wrote about the incident, the Astros accused her of fabricating the story. When several other witnesses corroborated the report, Major League Baseball opened an investigation. The Astros then issued an apology and fired the employee (Sheinin, 2019).

Title VII of the Civil Rights Act of 1964 prohibits discrimination on the basis of race, color, religion, sex, or country of national origin; specifically, it is unlawful for organizations with 15 or more employees (1) "to fail or refuse to hire or to discharge any individual, or otherwise to discriminate against any individual with respect to . . . compensation, terms, conditions, or privileges of employment" or (2) "to limit, segregate, or classify employees or applicants for employment in any way which would deprive or tend to deprive any individual of employment opportunities or otherwise adversely affect his [or her] status as an employee, because of such individual's race, color, religion, sex, or national origin." Title VII is administered through the Equal Employment Opportunity Commission (EEOC), which creates guidelines and regulations for interpretation of the law. As an administrative agency, the EEOC also investigates charges of employment discrimination and attempts to conciliate alleged violations. If EEOC does not find reasonable cause to go forward, the employee may proceed with a private Title VII lawsuit alleging sex discrimination. Sexual harassment affects an employee's conditions and privileges of employment and is therefore considered discrimination based on sex, which is also prohibited under Title VII.

Despite legislation and regulations prohibiting sex discrimination, women are still significantly underrepresented in sport media. According to the 2018 Associated Press Sports Editors Racial and Gender Report Card published by the Institute for Ethics and Diversity in Sport, only 17.9 percent of reporters, 19.7 percent of columnists, and 15 percent of sports editors are women (Lapchick, 2018). These figures show improvement from the 2014 report. However, numbers remain relatively stagnant in sports-talk radio, with only 7 women (out of 200) regular hosts. These numbers would be significantly lower if not for ESPN, which has five women in host roles.

NAVIGATING A SUCCESSFUL CAREER IN LAW, SPORT, AND COMMUNICATION

Nichelle Nicholes Levy
Senior counsel, digital and privacy data
NASCAR Digital Media, LLC

Nichelle Nicholes Levy's lifelong goal has been to find a way to integrate her interests in sport and entertainment into a rewarding career. While at the University of Chicago, where Levy received her AB/AM in psychology and social sciences, Levy was able to pursue her interest in sport by serving as the football team manager as well as a sport reporter for the school newspaper; Levy began to realize that there are many ways to be involved in sport and the business of sport in addition to being a star athlete.

Unable to identify a sport-related opportunity upon graduation from college, Levy instead pursued a career in advertising and brand management—initially with Leo Burnett as a research analyst then with Philip Morris as a brand manager. The entertainment world then beckoned with an opportunity for Levy to serve in a strategic marketing role with EMI Music, helping artists across a range of labels with new and innovative marketing approaches. Levy learned that many successful professionals in the sport and entertainment realms off-field and off-stage had law degrees; Levy decided to attend law school and to focus on understanding intellectual property rights (e.g., copyrights and trademarks) and business transactions.

While attending the New York University School of Law, Levy served as a law clerk with the National Hockey League. There Levy had the opportunity to see firsthand the many ways lawyers are involved in sport, including as trademark licensors and rights protectors and negotiating sponsorship deals and labor deals on behalf of the league and the affiliated team owners. Each of these legal transactions provides financial support for the business of sport, without which the action on the field would not be possible. To round out her experiences during law school, Levy also clerked with Loeb & Loeb LLP, an entertainment law firm, in its New York office. While there, Levy gained experience in the litigation, corporate, and entertainment departments.

Upon graduation from law school, Levy joined Loeb & Loeb in its New York entertainment department, representing entertainment clients including New Line/Fine Line Films, the Beastie Boys, and Woody Allen, as well as marketing clients including Visa, Citibank, and Quaker Oats. Levy handled a variety of matters for these clients, including reviewing film promotional rules, drafting website terms and conditions, clearing samples with music publishers and artist representatives, reviewing discovery materials in preparation for litigation, reviewing advertising claims to ensure their accuracy, and advising financial services companies on state advertising laws and restrictions governing their marketing programs. In each of these matters, Levy learned that the most important skill was attention to detail and understanding the law applicable to a particular matter.

Although Levy enjoyed working with clients in a firm setting and the opportunity to learn about a variety of subjects, she yearned to be more closely involved in the entertainment and media business. Levy joined Time Warner as director of business affairs for the global marketing group. In this role, Levy assisted business teams with coordinating deals and licensing content across Time Warner's various entities, which at that time included AOL, Time Inc., Turner Broadcasting Systems, Warner Brothers, Fine Line/New Line Films, and HBO. These deals took advantage of the broad marketing platform that Time Warner could offer to large advertisers who needed one point of contact with Time Warner, rather than having to negotiate deals with each entity individually.

Although this was an ideal opportunity, Levy and her family chose to move to Charlotte, North Carolina, to be closer to family once she and her husband Sid began a family of their own. Levy joined Charlotte-based firm Robinson Bradshaw & Hinson, where she practiced as part of the sports and entertainment and intellectual property practice groups within the corporate department. Robinson Bradshaw is well known in the motorsports industry as counsel to many race teams (large and small), drivers, and other industry participants. During her time with Robinson Bradshaw, Levy registered trademarks for several motorsports teams and drivers; negotiated trademark licenses; and assisted motorsports teams and other clients with entertainment-related opportunities, including reality show production deals. Levy also represented talent management companies and a leading amusement park in the development of talent agreements and other entertainment licensing documentation. At times, a majority of Levy's work was in the burgeoning area of data privacy regulation and technology. Levy advised clients on technology license agreements, including the licensing of hardware and software, technology vendor service agreements, website and mobile application privacy policies, terms of use, and data management practices.

Levy currently serves as senior counsel of digital and privacy data for NASCAR Digital Media, LLC, the NASCAR affiliate that is responsible for the digital distribution of NASCAR content and management of NASCAR's digital presence via nascar.com and NASCAR's associated mobile applications, as well as the provision of digital services to other

Courtesy of Nichelle Nicholes Levy.

Nichelle Nicholes Levy, senior counsel of digital and privacy data for NASCAR Digital Media.

NASCAR industry participants via its NASCAR Digital Media Network. In this role, Levy advises NASCAR Digital Media and other NASCAR affiliates on technology-related agreements and compliance with privacy, data security, advertising, promotion, and other laws. Levy led negotiation of nascar.com's primary e-commerce agreement, content syndication deals that permit NASCAR content to be displayed on other sport websites, real-time data license agreements, partnership agreements with leading technology companies, and social media partnership agreements, and she most recently established legal processes associated with advertising sales operations that were brought in-house. Levy particularly enjoys this work because social media and technology are quickly evolving areas that require creative negotiating skills.

Levy was recognized as a Legal Elite in intellectual property by *Business North Carolina* magazine in 2013 and as an Emerging Legal Leaders finalist by *North Carolina Lawyers Weekly* in 2010. She is a past chair of the sports and entertainment law section of the North Carolina Bar Association. Levy is licensed to practice law in New York, New Jersey, and North Carolina. In addition, Levy is accredited by the International Association of Privacy Professionals as a privacy law specialist (2019), certified information privacy manager (2019), and a certified information privacy professional–United States (2016).

CHAPTER WRAP-UP

Summary

The legal issues involved in sport, communication, and media are intriguing and wide ranging. Often, the parties involved in such litigation have conflicting rights (e.g., freedom of the press, right to privacy) that must be weighed by the court to reach a fair decision. Additional tensions have arisen between freedom of speech and an organization's right to maintain its public image, as well as order and discipline, thanks to new technologies and the expanding ability of the general public to record and publish content. In addition, increased focus on personal branding has escalated conflicts between the right of publicity and the commercial use of one's name, image, or likeness without permission. Similarly, sport figures are increasingly acting to protect their brand by trademarking the names, nicknames, and catchphrases with which they are associated. Conflict also persists in creating opportunities for women to work in sport media, be paid fairly, and be free from harassment. Finally, contract law, a common issue raised in many cases, always presents the potential for legal conflict. As a whole, this chapter helps you recognize the various rights and responsibilities related to sport communication to avoid legal conflict.

Review Questions

1. What is defamation, and how do you prove it? What defenses does the media have?

2. What tests are used to determine whether a company can use an athlete's name, image, or likeness associated with their commercial products?

3. Who owns the rights to broadcasts of sporting events?

4. What is the difference between a copyright and a trademark?

5. What laws protect women from employment discrimination?

Individual Exercises

1. Find a current event related to freedom of the press, free speech, privacy rights, defamation, right of publicity, copyright, or trademark. Summarize and explain how it relates to the legal issues presented in this chapter.

2. Find a case related to any of the legal issues presented in this chapter. Brief the case, and present it to the class.

3. Develop a social media policy for a high school or college athletics department that protects student-athletes' freedom of speech and privacy rights but still maintains order, discipline, and proper public image of the school and athletics program.

Glossary

academic research—Research within academia using quan-titative, qualitative, or mixed methods that is crucial to fully understanding how sport intersects the social, cultural, economic, legal, and political arenas.

actual malice—With knowledge of its falsity or reckless disregard of whether it was true or false.

actuality sound—Sounds heard via electronic media at events that help listeners imagine the event, the players, the fans, and the stadium or arena.

advertising—A paid form of nonpersonal communication typically disseminated to large audiences.

Agricultural Age—Time period from late 18th century through most of the 19th century when sporting journals and newspapers covered sport; the first regular sports pages were created later in this era.

analytical search—A web search that involves an element of planning and relies heavily on search engines.

athlete endorsements—A relationship between an athlete and a brand in which the athlete agrees to promote the brand in exchange for money and/or products.

audience research—Research conducted on sport and media audiences to understand fans' preferences, consumption habits, and the impact on choices they make.

augmented reality—Superimposes computer-generated images, sounds, or other data on a user's view of the real world, thus providing a composite view.

autocratic communication style—An authoritarian approach to leadership in the sport industry when followers are controlled through the strict regulation of policies, procedures, and behaviors.

brand equity—A key goal of branding; achieved when a brand's attributes add value to the brand in the minds of consumers.

branding—Developing and cultivating a specific brand image for an organization and its products.

browsing—Use of the Internet that is characterized by more simplistic queries in which several documents are returned and people browse through the documents to find the ones that are most pertinent to the desired information.

cable television—System of a variety of channels that expanded coverage beyond television by the development of coaxial cable lines. HBO, ESPN, and CNN were early networks.

change-oriented communication—One of the dimensions (in addition to interpersonal-oriented communication and task-oriented communication) that makes up sport leadership communication styles and involves communicative actions that are considered visionary and innovative.

chronemics—A form of nonverbal communication that involves how individuals perceive and use time (e.g., being punctual to express respect, perceiving a person arriving late as an expression of displeasure, finishing a task by a requested deadline to express commitment, keeping a schedule to express respect, responding quickly to an email to express enthusiasm).

commercial speech—Communication with the intent of earning revenue or profit.

consultative communication style—An approach by sport leaders who exhibit a combination of highly supportive (i.e., relationship-oriented) and highly directive (i.e., task-oriented) communication behaviors.

context—The levels, environment, or setting (ranging from the interpersonal, group, organizational, and mediated to relationships, culture, and society) in which communication takes place.

copyright—Legal rights vested in the creator of an original work.

customer-centric marketing—An approach to marketing in which the individual consumer is at the center of the design and delivery of marketing strategies.

customer relationship management—Using activities, strategies, and technology to manage interactions and data about current and potential customers.

defamation—Communication so harmful that it significantly tarnishes an individual's reputation, exposing the person to public ridicule, contempt, embarrassment, or disassociation.

demassification—Breaking down media into specializations to reach and appeal to more specific audiences.

Digital Age—Time period after the Information Age that is usually viewed as the 21st century until today where the innovations in legacy and emerging media impacted the norms and practices of professionals, the consumption of sport by fans, and the interactions and interconnectivity between sport entities. Speed, accessibility, interactivity, and multimedia strategies and choices abound in this era of continuity and change.

e-commerce—The buying or selling of products and services online via the Internet.

emerging and social media in sport—The growing and evolving digital, mobile, and social media and their overall convergence and cutting-edge elements, activities, and innovations in sport communication. These media make up the latter half of the SSCM's second component (Mediated Communication in Sport).

environmental factors—A type of nonverbal communication that involves how the space of a certain area (e.g., a team's front office, the sales department room) is used in terms of its physical setting, layout, architecture, elements, arrangements, and so forth.

ethnicity—Denotes cultural heritage that people use to identify a specific population. Examples include Hispanic or Latino; not Hispanic or Latino.

expressive speech—Nonverbal conduct that communicates a message.

fair-use doctrine—Allows use of copyrighted material for criticism, comment, news reporting, teaching, scholarship, or research without the permission of the creator.

freedom of speech—A fundamental right guaranteed by the First Amendment of the U.S. Constitution.

gender—Socially and culturally constructed attributes of each sex. Gender involves interrelationships between our body, our identity, and how we present our gender to others, according to gender spectrum.

genre—A main group of communication theory upon which sport communication is based. The SSCM is built on several elements, one of which is theory (or communication genres).

haptics—A form of nonverbal communication that involves communicating (e.g., between individuals, with virtual reality) through touch and the sense of touch.

hegemony—A dominant group's ability to establish and maintain power over other groups. The origins go back to Marxist Antonio Gramsci.

heuristic search—A web search conducted with low deliberation, meaning that the individual uses hyperlinks to navigate the web.

Industrial Age—Time period from the late 19th century through the 1980s characterized by technology, urbanization, and advancement of sport communication, especially during the golden age of sport and advent of television.

industry research—Research within industry that offers data about media workers, stations, networks, and the overall industry.

influencer—A person who is not a traditional celebrity but has been able to build a strong online following on social media and has a captive online audience.

Information Age—Time period in the 1990s when sport's focus shifted to spectators and the technological advancements and economics of their consumption habits, communication experiences, and social and cultural changes.

integrated marketing communication in sport—As part of the SSCM's third component (Sport Communication Services and Support), this segment encompasses technological advancements in sport-industry marketing (e.g., mobile payment options at sporting events),

innovative and traditional methods in the advertising of sport (e.g., connecting with potential consumers via their smartwatches), and advertising through sport (e.g., marketing a product through a popular sport media app).

interaction management—A self-monitoring skill involving the ability to facilitate and maintain effective interactions during an interpersonal communication process.

interorganizational sport communication—As part of the first component of the SSCM, this is communication between a sport stakeholder in one entity and a stakeholder in another entity. This is the type of communication that takes place between a sport organization and its external organizational publics, such as boosters, media entities, consumers, and leagues.

interpersonal-oriented communication—Also referred to as relationship-oriented or employee-oriented communication, this is one of the dimensions (in addition to task-oriented communication and change-oriented communication) that makes up sport leadership communication styles. This relations-oriented communication is exemplified by a sport leader who listens and provides an environment of support, trust, and respect.

interpersonal sport communication—Individuals (typically two persons) in sport, in a sport setting, or through a sport endeavor sharing the roles of sender and receiver (two-way flow of information) and creating meaning through their mediated or unmediated personal interactions.

intraorganizational sport communication—As part of the SSCM's first component, this involves communication within a sport-affiliated organization. This type of communication occurs between a sport organization's internal publics. This category includes communication between employees and colleagues of an organization, as well as the organizational culture, staff rituals, traditions, and other organizational influences that affect communication.

intrapersonal sport communication—The most basic, and most often used, communicative act among sport professionals or sport media professionals. This is communicating with oneself, or internal communication.

kinesics—A form of communicating in a nonverbal way through the use of facial expressions and body movements such as communicator's posture, head movement, gestures, and eye contact.

laissez-faire communication style—An approach to sport leadership—characterized as nonleadership or avoiding leadership—in which the sport leader exhibits a combination of low support (i.e., low relationship-oriented) and low directive (i.e., low task-oriented) communication behaviors. A sport leader who adopts this style provides little direction, accepts messages and decisions from subordinates, and conveys to subordinates that they are in charge.

leaders—In the sport communication profession, leaders include owners, publishers, producers, presidents, vice presidents, entrepreneurs, editors, and directors, among other titles. Most oversee the day-to-day sport communication operations of a sport- or media-focused organization and perform a variety of functions.

lifestyle marketing—Marketing based on consumers' lifestyles that requires marketers to understand the attitude and activity patterns of their target consumers and then tailor their promotional strategies to fit these patterns, which represent a person's lifestyle.

mass media—Segment of media focused on reaching the masses—that is, large numbers of people.

media—A variety of means through which communication takes place.

metacommunication—An interpersonal communication skill that involves proficiency in conveying and understanding messages by communicating about the communication.

multimedia convergence—The merging of traditional and new media platforms and delivery systems.

nationalism—Identification with the life and aspirations of the fellow members of a nation, even when we do not know these citizens or have not seen the boundaries of the nation in its entirety.

network television—Most powerful medium in sport communication history that instantly transported viewers to events and began with the Big Three broadcasting networks: ABC, CBS, and NBC. Dominated the 1950s through the 1970s.

new sport media—Sport mass media through the use of digital technologies, specifically the Internet and social media.

organizational communication in sport—The process in which messages are created, exchanged, interpreted, and stored within a system of human relationships in sport. Organizational communication in sport consists of both the communication within (i.e., intraorganizational) and between (i.e., interorganizational) organizations.

other-orientedness—An interpersonal communication skill that refers to the ability to focus on others and communicate interest in what they are saying.

over-the-top—Streaming of video content to consumers via the Internet.

participative communication style—An approach also referred to as a democratic style where the sport leader exhibits a combination of low task-oriented (i.e., low directive) and high relationship-oriented (i.e., high supportive behavior) communication. This communication style is evident when interaction between the leader and followers is both encouraged and achieved through supportive communication.

premium channel—Channels offered through cable and satellite packages for a separate fee.

press agentry–publicity model—A public relations model that focuses primarily on receiving media attention in almost any situation.

process of sport communication—The way in which people in sport, in a sport setting, or through a sport endeavor share symbols as they create meaning through interaction. In addition to providing the various fields of communication (e.g., communicator, message, medium, audience, effect, noise, feedback, context), we can also trace every action, aspect, and activity of sport communication to at least one of the unique components of this definition.

proxemics—A form of nonverbal communication that is constituted by how communicators feel about and perceive space (i.e., distance between communicators) and how they use space in their personal, social, and public interactions.

public domain—Ideas and expressions such as facts and dates that cannot be copyrighted, patented, or propertized.

public information model—A public relations model focused on the distribution of unbiased and accurate information about the sport entity.

public relations—A strategic communication process that builds mutually beneficial relationships between organizations and their publics.

public relations and crisis communication in sport—As part of the SSCM's third component (Sport Communication Services and Support), this segment involves message development and image building through effective management of sport media.

publishing—Producing print publications, such as newspapers, books, journals, newsletters, etc.

qualitative document analysis—Research on documents that emphasizes "process, context, and significance and how the document helps define the situation and clarify meaning for the audience member" (Altheide, 1996, p. 12).

race—Denotes a population of people who are believed to be biologically distinct from other populations. Race usually includes African American, Caucasian, Asian, American Indian and Alaska Native, Native Hawaiian and other Pacific Islander, and other races.

rhetorical criticism—Method created to enable the "systematic investigation and explanation of symbolic acts and artifacts for the purpose of understanding rhetorical processes" (Foss, 2004, p. 6).

right of privacy—The right to be free of unnecessary public scrutiny or to be let alone.

right of publicity—A right related to a person's interest in protecting the commercial value of their name, image, or likeness.

searching—A detailed and strategic web search that is often facilitated by professionals who serve as liaisons between users and the database being searched.

second screen—Any connected visual media device that can be used alongside the traditional broadcast television, or first screen.

semiotics—Study of signs and the meanings of artifacts, especially valuable in analyzing visual texts.

sexual orientation—A person's sexual identity and attraction to individuals of a different gender, the same gender, or multiple genders.

situational supervisory style—The situational supervisory style is the approach a sport leader takes depending on the variation of emphasis (i.e., high or low) devoted to task-oriented and interpersonal-oriented behaviors. The four situational supervisory styles in the communication process in the sport industry are autocratic, consultative, participative, and laissez-faire.

small-group sport communication—As part of the SSCM's first component (Personal and Organizational Communication in Sport), this type of communication involves the flow of information within a limited gathering (typically three or more persons) who are either in a sport environment or involved with a sport-related subject.

source–receiver—As one of the major elements or variables (in addition to message, feedback, channel, etc.) involved in the ongoing process of interpersonal sport communication, this element consists of the interactants (e.g., generally two participants) who continuously send messages (as source) and receive messages (as receiver) during their communication.

speech act—One of the three levels of meaning examined when analyzing language and its structure. This third level of meaning, following the word and the sentence, is known as *pragmatics* and involves the use of words and sentences in interactions.

sponsorship—The acquisition of rights to affiliate or directly associate with a product, person, organization, team, league, or event. Sometimes also referred to as a partnership.

sport administration—Administration of sport, recreation, and physical activity.

sport communication—All communication of sport through verbal and nonverbal messages.

sport communication research—As part of the SSCM's third component (Sport Communication Services and Support), this segment includes scholarship disseminated at academic gatherings (e.g., conferences) and through various academic publications (e.g., journals, textbooks, edited volumes).

sport journalism—The global coverage of events and individuals in sport via a variety of media that has evolved, developed, and expanded as a result of technological, cultural, economic, and other factors.

sport leadership—Leadership in sport, recreation, and physical activity.

sport leadership communication style—The way in which a sport leader behaves toward and interacts and communicates with followers.

sport management—A field of business dealing with sport, recreation, and physical activity.

sport mass media—Within the second component of the SSCM (Mediated Communication in Sport), this segment consists of the traditional areas of mass communication, such as the sport print media and sport broadcast media.

sport media—The coverage and framing of sport by mass media.

sport media buying—This area includes professionals in sport sales and sport marketing who either secure media purchases for sport teams and organizations or work with a private enterprise to secure media purchases through sport media outlets (e.g., sport broadcasts, sport websites).

sport product—The sport good or service designed to satisfy a consumer's need for sport, be it spectator, viewer, active participant, or sponsor.

sports information directors (SIDs)—Directors of media relations and public relations for sport organizations or teams. These professionals work with and provide access to external media, and increasingly produce media content for teams to directly reach their supporters.

state action—Related to the actions of a public or government official (local, state, or federal).

trademark—Any word, name, symbol, or device—or any combination thereof—adopted or used by a manufacturer or merchant to identify goods and distinguish them from goods manufactured or sold by others.

task-oriented communication—Also referred to as production-oriented communication or task behavior, this is one of the dimensions (in addition to change-oriented communication and interpersonal-oriented communication) that makes up sport leadership communication styles. This concern for production communication is exemplified by a sport leader who closely supervises a performance and tells a subordinate what to do.

textual analysis—Systematic study of films, television shows, sportscasts, newspaper articles, or any other type of document.

toy department—A derogatory and mocking term used to describe media sport departments and journalists due to a perception that they do not cover serious news.

two-way asymmetrical model—A public relations model intended to persuade an organization's key publics through message development. This model is effective when conflict with the public is minimal.

two-way symmetrical model—A public relations model grounded in research that advocates conflict resolution through the facilitation of mutual understanding between an organization and its key publics. It is considered the most appropriate in establishing positive relations with constituents.

video on demand—Digital video content that consumers can watch at their leisure; it does not need to be consumed live.

virtual reality—A process that involves a person (e.g., sport consumer or athlete) wearing a headset with a screen that places him into a simulated environment.

web development—Involves planning, creating, and updating sport websites for intercollegiate athletics departments, newspapers, television stations, sport teams, and other sport media outlets and sport organizations.

wire services—Agencies that provide reporting and content to be used and published by media outlets.

Bibliography

Chapter 1

Anderson, D.A. (1994). *Contemporary sports reporting* (2nd ed.). Chicago: Nelson-Hall.

Andrews, P. (2013). *Sports journalism: A practical introduction* (2nd ed.). Thousand Oaks, CA: Sage.

Asher, J. (2012, June 26). Why Chris Christie is right about sports betting. *U.S. News & World Report*. www.usnews.com/opinion/articles/2012/06/26/why-chris-christie-is-right-about-sports-betting

Badenhausen, K. (2018, July 18). The world's 50 most valuable sports teams 2018. *Forbes*. www.forbes.com/sites/kurtbadenhausen/2018/07/18/full-list-the-worlds-50-most-valuable-sports-teams-of-2018/#6edd0dcd6b0e

Beaton, A. (2019, January 7). How much is your college football team worth? *The Wall Street Journal*. www.wsj.com/articles/how-much-is-your-college-football-team-worth-11546875092

Billings, A.C. (Ed.). (2011). *Sports media: Transformation, integration, consumption*. London: Routledge.

Borland, J.F., Kane, G.M., & Burton, L.J. (2014). *Sport leadership in the 21st century*. Burlington, MA: Jones & Bartlett Learning.

Broughton, D., Lee, J., & Nethery, R. (1999). The answer: $213 billion. *Street & Smith's Sports Business Journal, 2*(34), 23, 26.

Commission on Sport Management Accreditation. (2010, June). Accreditation principles and self-study preparation. www.cosmaweb.org/uploads/2/4/9/4/24949946/cosma_accreditation_principles_self_study_preparation_61510.doc

Crosset, T.W., & Hums, M.A. (2005). History of sport management. In L.P. Masteralexis, C.A. Barr, & M.A. Hums (Eds.), *Principles and practice of sport management* (2nd ed., pp. 1–18). Boston: Jones & Bartlett.

Crupi, A. (2019, January 3). Network TV can't survive without the NFL. *AdAge*. https://web.archive.org/web/20190104030953/https://adage.com/article/media/top-50-u-s-broadcasts-2018/316102

DeSensi, J.T., Kelley, D.R., Blanton, M.D., & Beitel, P.A. (1990). Sport management curricular evaluation and needs assessment: A multifaceted approach. *Journal of Sport Management, 4*(1), 31–58.

Diamond, J. (2015, January 12). What's your college team worth? Ohio State overtakes Texas as the most valuable program in college football. *Wall Street Journal*. www.wsj.com/articles/whats-your-college-team-worth-1421081367

Entertainment and Sports Occupations (2019, April 12). United States Department of Labor Bureau of Labor Statistics. www.bls.gov/ooh/entertainment-and-sports/home.htm?view_full

Eschenfelder, M.J., & Li, M. (2007). *Economics of sport* (2nd ed.). Morgantown, WV: Fitness Information Technology.

Flaherty, K. (2019, January 28). College sports' top 25 money-makers by gross revenue. 247 Sports. https://247sports.com/ContentGallery/College-sports-top-25-money-makers-by-gross-revenue-119496046/#119496046_1

Fried, G., DeSchriver, T.D., & Mondello, M. (2013). *Sport finance* (3rd ed.). Champaign, IL: Human Kinetics.

Gillentine, A., & Crow, R.B. (2014). *Foundations of sport management* (3rd ed.). Morgantown, WV: Fitness Information Technology.

Gisondi, J. (2010). *Field guide to covering sports*. Washington, DC: CQ Press.

Glatzer, J. (2006). Interview with Bud Collins. *Absolute Write*. http://archive.today/tMPqo

Gray, D.P., & McEvoy, C.D. (2005). Sport marketing: Strategies and tactics. In B.L. Parkhouse (Ed.), *The management of sport: Its foundation and application* (4th ed., pp. 228–255). New York: McGraw-Hill.

Hedrick, T. (2000). *The art of sportscasting: How to build a successful career*. Lanham, MD: Diamond.

Katowitz, J. (2014, October 1). NFL, DirecTV sign deal report-edly worth $12 billion over 8 years. CBS Sports. www.cbssports.com/nfl/eye-on-football/24733096/nfl-directv-sign-new-deal-reportedly-worth-12-billion-over-8-years

Ketterer, S., McGuire, J., & Murray, R. (2014). Contrasting desired sports journalism skills in a convergent media environment. *Communication & Sport, 2*(3), 282–298.

Kian, E.M., Pedersen, P.M., & Vincent, J. (2008). In demand? Examining sport management faculty openings and hires. *Journal of Contemporary Athletics, 3*(2), 129–138.

Kian, E.M., Schultz, B., Clavio, G., & Sheffer, M.L. (2019). *Multimedia sports journalism: A practitioner's guide for the digital age*. New York: Oxford University Press.

Kirk, J. (2014, June 6). College athletic departments aren't as broke as you think. SB Nation. www.sbnation.com/college-football/2014/6/6/5783394/college-sports-profits-money-schools-revenues-subsidies

Kondolojy, A. (2014, December 19). NFL telecasts make up 23 of 25 most-watched shows this fall. TV by the Numbers. http://tvbythenumbers.zap2it.com/2014/12/19/nfl-telecasts-make-up-23-of-25-most-watched-shows-this-fall/341433

Mason, J.G., & Paul, J. (1988). *Modern sport management.* Englewood Cliffs, NJ: Prentice Hall.

Masteralexis, L.P., Barr, C.A., & Hums, M. (2015). *Principles and practice of sport management* (5th ed.). Sudbury, MA: Jones & Bartlett.

McGowan, A., & Bouris, G. (2005). Sport communications. In L.P. Masteralexis, C. A. Barr, & M. Hums (Eds.), *Principles and practice of sport management* (2nd ed., pp. 340–359). Sudbury, MA: Jones & Bartlett.

Meek, A. (1997). An estimate of the size and supported economic activity of the sports industry in the United States. *Sport Marketing Quarterly, 6*(4), 15–21.

Milano, M., & Chelladurai, P. (2011). Gross domestic sport product: The size of the sport industry in the United States. *Journal of Sport Management, 25*, 24–35.

Mullin, B.J., Hardy, S., & Sutton, W.A. (2014). *Sport marketing* (4th ed.). Champaign, IL: Human Kinetics.

NCAA Finances. (2015, May 26). *USA Today.* http://sports.usatoday.com/ncaa/finances

O'Toole, T. (2010, April 22). NCAA reaches 14-year deal with CBS/Turner for men's basketball tournament, which expands to 68 teams for now. *USA Today.* http://content.usatoday.com/communities/campusrivalry/post/2010/04/ncaa-reaches-14-year-deal-with-cbsturner/1#.VM1-5sYXq3A

Parkhouse, B.L., & Pitts, B.G. (2001). Definition, evolution, and curriculum. In B.L. Parkhouse (Ed.), *The management of sport: Its foundation and application* (pp. 2–14). New York: McGraw Hill.

Pedersen, P.M. (Ed.). (2013). *Routledge handbook of sport communication.* London: Routledge.

Pedersen, P.M., & Schneider, R.G. (2003). Investigating the academic openings in sport management: An analysis of the field's professorial position announcements and hires. *International Sports Journal, 7*(1), 34–46.

Pedersen, P.M., & Thibault, L. (Eds.). (2019). *Contemporary sport management* (6th ed.). Champaign, IL: Human Kinetics.

Penn State News Online. (2005, September 30). Knight Foundation's $1.5 million grant supports Center for Sports Journalism. http://news.psu.edu.story/208095/2005/09/30/knight-foundations-15-million-grant-supports-center-sports-journalism

Pennsylvania State University. (2012). *Schools across country increase focus on sports communication.* http://news.psu.edu/story/152329/2012/01/23/schools-across-country-increase-focus-sports-communication

Pitts, B.G., Fielding, L.F., & Miller, L.K. (1994). Industry segmentation theory and the sport industry: Developing a sport industry segment model. *Sport Marketing Quarterly, 3*(1), 15–24.

Pitts, B.G., & Stotlar, D.K. (2013). *Fundamentals of sport marketing* (4th ed.). Morgantown, WV: Fitness Information Technology.

Pratap, A. (2018, March 20). Nike retail stores domestic and international. Notesmatic. https://notesmatic.com/nike-retail-stores-domestic-and-international

Purdum, D. (2019, May 14). One year into legal sports betting: What have we learned? ESPN. www.espn.com/chalk/story/_/id/26740441/one-year-legal-us-sports-betting-learned

Rovell, D. (2014, October 6). NBA in unique position with TV deal. ESPN. www.espn.go.com/nba/story/_/id/11653435/new-tv-deal-shows-league-unique-position

Rovell, D. (2015, January 21). Forbes: Team values rose 72 percent. ESPN. http://espn.go.com/nba/story/_/id/12204869/forbes-reports-11-nba-teams-now-worth-1b

Sandomir, R. (1988, November 14). The $50-billion sports industry. *Sports Inc.,* 11–23.

Sandomir, R. (2014, May 7). NBC extends Olympic deal into unknown. *New York Times.* www.nytimes.com/2014/05/08/sports/olympics/nbc-extends-olympic-tv-deal-through-2032.html?_r=0

Schultz, B. (2005). *Sports media: Reporting, producing, and planning.* Burlington, MA: Elsevier.

Smith, M.D. (2015, February 2). Super Bowl delivers its highest overnight TV rating ever. NBC Sports. http://profootballtalk.nbcsports.com/2015/02/02/super-bowl-delivers-its-highest-overnight-tv-rating-ever

Solomon, J. (2014, May 30). SEC announces $20.9 million average payout per school. CBS Sports. www.cbssports.com/collegefootball/writer/jon-solomon/24577128/sec-announces-209-million-average-payout-per-school

Sport management program standards and review protocol. (2000). Sport Management Program Review Council. Reston, VA: National Association for Sport and Physical Educators.

Sport Management Programs: United States. (2019). North American Society for Sport Management website. www.nassm.com/Programs/AcademicPrograms/United_States

Sports Industry Overview. (2014). Plunkett Research. www.plunkettresearch.com/sports-recreation-leisure-market-research/industry-statistics

Stier, W.F. (2001). Sport management: The development of sport management. In D. Kluka & G. Schilling (Eds.), *The business of sport* (pp. 39–56). Oxford, UK: Meyer & Meyer Sport.

Stoldt, G.C., Dittmore, S.W., Ross, R.M., & Branvold, S.E. (2021). *Sport public relations* (3rd ed.). Champaign, IL: Human Kinetics.

Travis, C. (2017, March 1). How much do the NFL and TV partners make a year? *Outkick the Coverage*. www.outkickthecoverage.com/how-much-do-the-nfl-and-tv-partners-make-a-year-030117

Wanta, W. (2006). The coverage of sports in print media. In A.A. Raney & J. Bryant (Eds.), *Handbook of sports and media* (pp. 105–115). Mahwah, NJ: Erlbaum.

Wenner, L.A. (2015). Communication and sport, where art thou? Epistemological reflections on the moment and field(s) of play. *Communication & Sport, 3*(3), 247–260.

Wordsman, E. (2014, December 18). Journalism schools add courses in sports, emerging technology. *American Journalism Review.* http://ajr.org/2014/12/18/journalism-schools-add-courses-sports-emerging-technology

Chapter 2

Aamidor, A. (Ed.). (2003). *Real sports reporting*. Bloomington, IN: Indiana University Press.

Abeza, G., O'Reilly, N., & Nadeau, J. (2014). Sport communication: A multidimensional assessment of the field's development. *International Journal of Sport Communication, 7*(3), 289–316.

Anderson, D.A. (1994). *Contemporary sports reporting* (2nd ed.). Chicago: Nelson-Hall.

Andrews, P. (2013). *Sports journalism: A practical introduction* (2nd ed.). Thousand Oaks, CA: Sage.

Bandura, A. (2002). Social cognitive theory of mass communication. In J. Bryant & D. Zillmann (Eds.), *Media effects: Advances in theory and research* (2nd ed., pp. 121–153). Hillsdale, NJ: Erlbaum.

Battenfield, F.L., & Kent, A. (2007). The culture of communication among intercollegiate sport information professionals. *International Journal of Sport Management and Marketing, 2*(3), 236–251.

Benton, J. (2018, September 26). What will happen when newspapers kill print and go online-only? Most of that print audience will just . . . disappear. *Nieman Lab.* www.niemanlab.org/2018/09/what-will-happen-when-newspapers-kill-print-and-go-online-only-most-of-that-print-audience-will-just-disappear

Bernstein, A., & Blain, N. (Eds.). (2003). *Sport, media, culture: Global and local dimensions*. New York: Routledge.

Billings, A.C. (2008). *Olympic media: Inside the biggest show on television*. London: Routledge.

Billings, A.C. (Ed.). (2011). *Sports media: Transformation, integration, consumption*. London: Routledge.

Billings, A.C., & Brown, K.A. (Eds.). (2017). *Evolution of the modern sports fan: Communicative approach*. Lanham, MD: Lexington Books.

Billings, A.C., Butterworth, M.L., & Turman, P.D. (2017). *Communication and sport: Surveying the field* (3rd ed.). Thousand Oaks, CA: Sage.

Billings, A.C., & Hardin, M. (Eds.). (2014). *The Routledge handbook of sport and new media*. London: Routledge.

Billings, A.C., & Ruihley, B.J. (2014). *The fantasy sport industry: Games within games*. London: Routledge.

Bodenheimer, G., & Phillips, D.T. (2015). *Every town is a sports town: Business leadership at ESPN, from the mailroom to the boardroom*. New York: Grand Central.

Boudway, I. (2019, July 29). The Athletic sports news site hits 500,000 subscribers. *Bloomberg.* www.bloomberg.com/news/articles/2019-07-29/the-athletic-sports-news-site-hits-500-000-subscribers

Bower, G.G., & Hums, M.A. (2014). Examining the mentoring relationship of women working in intercollegiate athletic administration. *Mentoring & Tutoring: Partnership in Learning, 22*(1), 4–19.

Boyle, R. (2006). *Sports journalism: Context and issues*. London: Sage.

Boyle, R. (2019). *Changing sports journalism practice in the age of digital media*. London: Routledge.

Boyle, R., & Haynes R. (2009). *Power play: Sport, the media, and popular culture* (2nd ed.). Edinburgh: Edinburgh University Press.

Brennan, C. (2006). *Best seat in the house: A father, a daughter, a journey through sports*. New York: Scribner.

Brennan, E. (2013, July 10). The college basketball video game is dead. ESPN. http://espn.go.com/blog/collegebasketballnation/post/_/id/86183/the-college-basketball-video-game-is-dead

Brookes, R. (2002). *Representing sport*. London: Arnold.

Brown, R.S., & O'Rourke III, D.J. (Eds.). (2003). *Case studies in sport communication*. Westport, CT: Praeger.

Bureau of Labor Statistics. (2019). *Occupational outlook handbook*. U.S. Department of Labor. www.bls.gov/ooh/management/advertising-promotions-and-marketing-managers.htm

Butler, J.G. (1999). *Writing sports stories that sell: How to make money from writing about your favorite pastime*. Oxford: How to Book.

CareerBuilder. (2014, August 28). Sports-related employment is on the rise and creating jobs in other industries, according to new research from CareerBuilder and Economic Modeling Specialists. Careerbuilder.com. www.careerbuilder.com/share/aboutus/pressreleasesdetail.aspx?sd=8%2F28%2F2014&id=pr839&ed=12%2F31%2F2014

Conrad, M. (2011). *The business of sports: A primer for journalists* (2nd ed.). New York: Routledge.

Craig, S. (2002). *Sports writing: A beginner's guide*. Shoreham, VT: Discover Writing.

Creedon, P.J. (1994). *Women, media, and sport: Challenging gender values*. Thousand Oaks, CA: Sage.

Deninger, D. (2012). *Sports on television: The how and why behind what you see.* New York: Routledge.

Eisenstock, A. (2007). *Sports talk: A journey inside the world of sports talk radio* (2nd ed.). New York: Atria.

Farrey, T. (2014, May 31). Players, game makers settle for $40M. ESPN. http://espn.go.com/espn/otl/story/_/id/11010455/college-athletes-reach-40-million-settlement-ea-sports-ncaa-licensing-arm

Favorito, J. (2012). *Sports publicity: A practical approach* (2nd ed.). New York: Routledge.

Finberg, H., & Klinger, L. (2014). Core skills for the future of journalism. *Poynter Institute for Media Studies.* www.newsu.org/course_files/CoreSkills_FutureofJournalism2014v5.pdf

Fischer, S. (2018, October 30). Exclusive: The Athletic raises $40 million in new funding round. *Axios.* www.axios.com/the-athletic-40-million-series-c-round-9585ff32-c007-4212-ae31-913df625aa9a.html

Fuller, L.K. (Ed.). (2006). *Sport, rhetoric, and gender: Historical perspectives and media representations.* London: Palgrave Macmillan.

Fuller, L.K. (2008). *Sportscasters/sportscasting: Principles and practices.* New York: Routledge.

Gardner, T. (2014, August 17). UGA fortunate to have collegiate sports' premier publicist, Claude Felton. *The Fifth Down: The Online Newsletter of the Football Writers Association of America.* http://the5thdown.com/2014/08/17/uga-fortunate-to-have-collegiate-sports-premier-publicist-claude-felton

Garrison, B., & Sabljak, M. (1993). *Sports reporting* (2nd ed.). Ames, IA: Iowa State University.

Gisondi, J. (2017). *Field guide to covering sports* (2nd ed.). Washington, DC: CQ Press.

Hall, A., Nichols, W., Moynahan, P., & Taylor, J. (2006). *Media relations in sport* (2nd ed.). Morgantown, WV: Fitness Information Technology.

Hardin, M. (2005). Stopped at the gate: Women's sports, "reader interest," and decision making by editors. *Journalism & Mass Communication Quarterly, 82*(1), 62–77.

Hardin, M., Whiteside, E., & Ash, E. (2014). Ambivalence on the front lines? Attitudes toward Title IX and women's sports among Division I sports information directors. *International Review for the Sociology of Sport, 49*(1), 42–64.

Hardin, R., & McClung, S. (2002). Collegiate sports information: A profile of the profession. *Public Relations Quarterly, 47*(2), 35–39.

Hawthorne, B. (2001). *The coverage of interscholastic sports.* Austin, TX: Interscholastic League Press Conference.

Hedrick, T. (2000). *The art of sportscasting: How to build a successful career.* Lanham, MD: Diamond.

Helitzer, M. (2001). *The dream job: Sports publicity, promotion, and marketing* (3rd ed.). Athens, OH: University Sports Press.

Hopwood, M., Kitchin, P., & Skinner, J. (2010). *Sport public relations and communications.* Oxford: Elsevier.

Hundley, H.L., & Billings, A.C. (Eds.). (2010). *Examining identity in sports media.* Thousand Oaks, CA: Sage.

Hutchins, B., & Rowe, D. (Eds.). (2012). *Sport beyond television: The Internet, digital media, and the rise of networked media sport.* New York: Routledge.

Hutchins, B., & Rowe, D. (Eds.). (2013). Digital media sport: Technology, power and culture in the network society. New York: Routledge.

Jeanrenaud, C., & Kesenne, S. (Eds.). (2006). *The economics of sport and the media.* Cheltenham, UK: Elgar.

Jewell, R.T. (2006). Sports economics: The state of the discipline. In J. Fizel (Ed.), *Handbook of sports economics research* (pp. 9–20). Armonk, NY: Sharpe.

Kian, E.M., & Murray, R. (2014). Curmudgeons but yet adapters: Impact of Web 2.0 and Twitter on newspaper sport journalists' jobs, responsibilities, and routines. *#ISOJ, 4*(1), 61–77.

Kian, E.M., Schultz, B., Clavio, G., & Sheffer, M.L. (2018). *Multimedia sports journalism: A practitioner's guide for the digital age.* New York: Oxford.

Kian, E.M., & Zimmerman, M.H. (2012). The medium of the future: Top sports writers discuss transitioning from newspapers to online journalism. *International Journal of Sport Communication, 5*(3), 285–304.

King, B. (2018, December 17). Most influential. *Street & Smith's Sports Business Journal.* www.sportsbusinessdaily.com/Journal/Issues/2018/12/17/Most-Influential.aspx

Koppett, L. (1994). *Sports illusion, sports reality: A reporter's view of sports, journalism, and society.* Urbana, IL: University of Illinois Press.

Lambert, C.M. (2018): *Digital sports journalism.* London: Routledge.

L'Etang, J. (2013). *Sports public relations.* London: Sage.

Lowes, M.D. (2000). *Inside the sports pages: Work routines, professional ideologies, and the manufacture of sports news.* Toronto: University of Toronto.

Miller, J.A. (2013, July 30). NFL television pioneer to step down next year. *New York Times.* www.nytimes.com/2013/07/31/sports/football/nfl-television-pioneer-to-step-down-next-year.html?_r=0

Miller, J.A., & Sandomir, R. (2013, October 27). NFL Network's 10-year gains: 13 games and 72 million homes. *New York Times.* www.nytimes.com/2013/10/28/business/media/nfl-networks-10-year-gains-13-games-and-72-million-homes.html?_r=0

Miloch, K.S., & Pedersen, P.M. (2006). Sports information directors and the media: An analysis of a highly symbiotic and professional relationship. *Journal of Contemporary Athletics, 2*(1), 91–103.

Moritz, S. (2014, October 2). DirecTV renews right to air NFL Sunday Ticket for 8 years. *BloombergBusiness.* www.

bloomberg.com/news/articles/2014-10-01/directv-renews-rights-to-air-nfl-sunday-ticket

Murray, J. (1995). *Jim Murray: The autobiography of the Pulitzer Prize winning sports columnist.* New York: Macmillan.

Newman, T., Peck, J.F., Harris, C., & Wilhide, B. (2013). *Social media in sport marketing.* Scottsdale, AZ: Holcomb Hathaway.

Nicholson, M., Kerr, A., & Sherwood, M. (2015). *Sport and the media: Managing the nexus* (2nd ed.). London: Routledge.

Owen, B.M. (2009). *The Internet challenge to television.* Cambridge, MA: Harvard University Press.

Owens, J. (2015). *Television sports production* (5th ed.). New York: Routledge.

Papper, B. (2012). *RTNDA research: Salary survey.* Radio-Television Digital News Association. www.rtnda.org/article/rtnda_research_salary_survey_2017

Pedersen, P.M. (Ed.). (2013). *Routledge handbook of sport communication.* London: Routledge.

Pedersen, P.M., Whisenant, W.A., & Schneider, R.G. (2005). Analyzing the 2001-02 sport management faculty openings. *International Journal of Sport Management, 6*(2), 154.

Peter, J. (2014, April 28). Meet Mel Kiper: Fallible, parodied, relentless, rich, famous, successful. Bleacher Report. http://bleacherreport.com/articles/2036569-meet-mel-kiper-fallible-parodied-relentless-rich-famous-successful

Price, J., & Howard, G.D. (2012, December 11). An update on *Sporting News* for 2013. *Sporting News.* www.sportingnews.com/sport/story/2012-12-11/sporting-news-magazine-ipad-yearbook-2013-ios-android

Raney, A.A., & Bryant, J. (Eds.). (2006). *Handbook of sports and media.* Mahwah, NJ: Erlbaum.

Real, M.R. (1996). *Exploring media culture: A guide.* Thousand Oaks, CA: Sage.

Reinardy, S., & Wanta, W. (2015). *The essentials of sports reporting and writing* (2nd ed.). New York: Routledge.

Robinson, M.J., Hums, M.A., Crow, R.B., & Phillips, D.R. (2001). *Profiles of sport industry professionals: The people who make the games happen.* Gaithersburg, MD: Aspen.

Ross, B. (2010). *Playing ball with the boys: The rise of women in the world of men's sports.* Covington, KY: Clerisy.

Rowe, D. (2004a). *Critical readings: Sport, culture, and the media.* New York: Open University Press.

Rowe, D. (2004b). *Sport, culture, and the media: The unruly trinity* (2nd ed.). New York: Open University Press.

RTNDA survey sees radio salaries on an upswing. (2016, June 29). Inside Radio. www.insideradio.com/free/rtnda-survey-sees-radio-salaries-on-an-upswing/article_2b137d26-3dd0-11e6-997e-876a6b1006f5.html

Sanderson, J., & Yandle, C. (2015). *Developing successful social media plans in sport organizations.* Morgantown, WV: Fitness Information Technology.

Sandomir, R., Miller, J.A., & Eder, S. (2013, August 26). To protect its empire, ESPN stays on offense. *New York Times.* www.nytimes.com/2013/08/27/sports/ncaafootball/to-defend-its-empire-espn-stays-on-offensive.html?pagewanted=all&_r=0

Schultz, B., & Arke, E. (2015). *Sports media: Reporting, producing, and planning* (3rd ed.). New York: Routledge.

Schultz, B., Caskey, P.H., & Esherick, C. (2014). *Media relations in sport* (4th ed.). Morgantown, WV: Fitness Information Technology.

Shoemaker, P.J., & Vos, T.P. (2009). *Gatekeeping theory.* New York: Routledge.

Steen, R. (2014). *Sports journalism: A multimedia primer* (2nd ed.). Oxon, UK: Taylor & Francis.

Stofer, K.T., Schaffer, J.R., & Rosenthal, B.A. (2019). *Sports journalism: An introduction to reporting and writing* (2nd ed.). Lanham, MD: Rowman & Littlefield.

Stoldt, G.C., Dittmore, S.W., Ross, M., & Branvold, S.E. (2021). *Sport public relations* (3rd ed.). Champaign, IL: Human Kinetics.

Stoldt, G.C., Noble, J., Ross, M., Richardson, T., & Bonsall, J. (2013, March). Advantages and disadvantages of social media use: Perceptions of college athletics communicators. College Sports Information Directors of America. *CoSIDA Strategic Communicators for College Athletics March 2013 E-Digest.* www.cosida.com/media/documents/2013/3/March_2013_EDigest.pdf

Suggs, D.W. (2016). Tensions in the press box: Understanding relationships among sports media and source organizations. *Communication & Sport, 4*(3), 261–281.

Trujillo, N. (1994). *The meaning of Nolan Ryan.* College Station: Texas A&M University Press.

Tucker, D., & Wrench, J.S. (Eds.). (2015). *Casing sport communication.* Dubuque, IA: Kendall/Hunt.

Walsh, C.J. (2006). *No time outs: What it's really like to be a sportswriter today.* Lanham, MD: Taylor Trade.

Wenner, L.A. (1998). *MediaSport.* New York: Routledge.

Whiteside, E., & Hardin, M. (2010). Public relations and sports work force demographics in the intersection of two gendered industries. *Journal of Sports Media, 5*(1), 21–52.

Wilstein, S. (2002). *Associated Press sportswriting handbook.* New York: McGraw-Hill.

Wong, G. (2014, June 9). The path to the athletic director's office. *Street & Smith's Sports Business Journal.* www.sportsbusinessdaily.com/Journal/Issues/2014/06/09/In-Depth/Wong-column.aspx

Zumoff, M., & Negin, M. (2014). *Total sportscasting: Performance, production, and career development.* New York: Focal Press.

Chapter 3

Andrews, J. (2011, April). Tackling the digital future of sports journalism: A look at sports journalism in the United Kingdom and United States. University of Canterbury. www.arts.canterbury.ac.nz/journalism/documents/robert_bell_report_april11.pdf

Auter, P.J., & Palmgreen, P. (2000). Development and validation of a parasocial interaction measure: The Audience-Persona Interaction Scale. *Communication Research Reports, 17*(1), 45–56.

Badenhausen, K. (2011, December 14). The NFL signs TV deals worth $27 billion. *Forbes.* www.forbes.com/sites/kurtbadenhausen/2011/12/14/the-nfl-signs-tv-deals-worth-26-billion

Badenhausen, K. (2014, April 29). The value of ESPN surpasses $50 billion. *Forbes.* www.forbes.com/sites/kurtbadenhausen/2014/04/29/the-value-of-espn-surpasses-50-billion

Badenhausen, K. (2016, February 23). Cristiano Ronaldo is first athlete with 200 million social media followers. *Forbes.* www.forbes.com/sites/kurtbadenhausen/2016/02/23/cristiano-ronaldo-is-the-first-athlete-with-200-million-social-media-followers/#463dd7a71129

Badenhausen, K. (2019a, June 11). The world's highest-paid athletes. *Forbes.* www.forbes.com/athletes/#2350b5ee55ae

Badenhausen, K. (2019b, May 22). The world's most valuable brands 2019: Apple on top at $206 billion. *Forbes.* www.forbes.com/sites/kurtbadenhausen/2019/05/22/the-worlds-most-valuable-brands-2019-apple-on-top-at-206-billion/#33764b2437c2

Baker, L.D. (1998). *From savage to Negro: Anthropology and the construction of race, 1896–1954.* Berkeley: University of California Press.

Baranauckas, C. (2013, July 20). "Let them wear towels," said early female sportswriters. *Washington Post.* www.washingtonpost.com/blogs/she-the-people/wp/2013/07/20/let-them-wear-towels-pioneering-female-sportswriters-with-lessons-for-all-of-us

Battaglio, S. (2020, February 3). Super Bowl 2020 scores 99.9 million TV viewers with Chiefs comeback. *Los Angeles Times.* Retrieved from https://www.latimes.com/entertainment-arts/business/story/2020-02-03/super-bowl-2020-scores-99-9-million-tv-viewers-with-chiefs-comeback

Bernstein, A., & Blain, N. (Eds.). (2003). *Sport, media, culture: Global and local dimensions.* London: Cass.

Betts, J.R. (1953a). Sporting journalism in nineteenth-century America. *American Quarterly, 5,* 39–56.

Betts, J.R. (1953b). The technological revolution and the rise of sport: 1850–1900. *Mississippi Historical Review, 40,* 231–256.

Blanchard, M.A. (Ed.). (1998). *History of the mass media in the United States: An encyclopedia.* Chicago: Fitzroy Dearborn.

Bob Ley retires after 40 years as ESPN anchor. (2019, June 27). ESPN.com. www.espn.com/espn/story/_/id/27058914/bob-ley-retires-40-years-espn-anchor

Boss, S.J. (2002). Television pioneer Roone Arledge '52: Spanning the world. *Columbia College Today.* www.college.columbia.edu/cct_archive/win99/18_fr.html

Boyle, R. (2006). *Sports journalism: Context and issues.* London: Sage.

Boyle, R. (2007). Sports journalism and communication: Challenges and opportunities in the digital media age. In *Asia Communication and Media Forum* (pp. 14–16). Beijing, China.

Boynton, R.S. (n.d.). Gay Talese. The New New Journalism. www.newnewjournalism.com/bio.php?last_name=talese

Brennan, C. (2019, July 13). Opinion: Serena Williams will never stop equality fight. Billie Jean King would have it no other way. *USA Today.* www.usatoday.com/story/sports/columnist/brennan/2019/07/13/wimbledon-serena-williams-billie-jean-king-never-stop-fighting-equality/1724107001

Bryant, J., & Holt, A.M. (2006). A historical overview of sports and media in the United States. In A.A. Raney & J. Bryant (Eds.), *Handbook of sports and media* (pp. 21–43). Mahwah, NJ: Erlbaum.

Butler, A. (2019, July 8). Women's World Cup: Equal pay tweets skyrocket after USA win. UPI.com. www.upi.com/Sports_News/2019/07/08/Womens-World-Cup-Equal-pay-tweets-skyrocket-after-USA-win/8571562600464

Caron, E. (2019, January 20). When did the Rams move to Los Angeles? *Sports Illustrated.* www.si.com/nfl/2019/01/20/when-did-rams-move-los-angeles-franchise-history-locations

Carroll, B. (2007). *When to stop the cheering? The black press, the black community, and the integration of professional baseball.* New York: Routledge.

Carter, B. (2000). ESPN Sports Century biography: Rozelle made NFL what it is today. Retrieved March 5, 2016, from http://espn.go.com/classic/biography/s/rozelle_pete.html

Clark, K. (2018, December 1). The Kareem Hunt scandal shows the NFL hasn't learned anything since Ray Rice. The Ringer. www.theringer.com/nfl/2018/12/1/18120220/kareem-hunt-kansas-city-chiefs-nfl-league-office

Covil, E.C. (2005). Radio and its impact on the sports world. American Sportscasters online. www.americansportscastersonline.com/radiohistory.html

Creedon, P.J. (1994). Women in toyland: A look at women in American newspaper sports journalism. In P.J. Creedon (Ed.), *Women, media, and sport: Challenging gender values* (pp. 67–107). Thousand Oaks, CA: Sage.

Danzig, A., & Brandwein, P. (Eds.). (1948). *Sport's golden age: A close-up of the fabulous twenties.* New York: Harper.

Deford, F. (2012). *Over time: My life as a sportswriter*. New York: Atlantic Monthly Press.

DeGaris, L. (2003, December 15). BCS can help itself by helping others. *Street & Smith's Sports Business Journal*, 6(34), 22.

de la Cretaz, B. (2019, February 3). Super Bowl 2019 commercials from Olay, Bumble are a step in the right direction for female fans. NBCNews.com. www.nbcnews.com/think/opinion/super-bowl-2019-commercials-olay-bumble-are-step-right-direction-ncna966096

Deitsch, R. (2018, January 31). What the Fox Thursday Night Football deal means for viewers. *Sports Illustrated*. www.si.com/tech-media/2018/01/31/thursday-night-football-fox-sports-deal-announcers-schedule-possibilities

Digital news fact sheet. (2018, June 6). Pew Research Center State of the News Media. www.journalism.org/fact-sheet/digital-news

Dizard, W., Jr. (2000). *Old media, new media: Mass communications in the information age* (3rd ed.). New York: Longman.

Dyreson, M. (1989). The emergence of consumer culture and the transformation of physical culture: American sport in the 1920s. *Journal of Sport History*, 16(3), 261–281.

Edmonds, R. (2018, January 9). *Sports Illustrated* is now reduced to a biweekly publication. Poynter.org. www.poynter.org/business-work/2018/sports-illustrated-is-now-reduced-to-a-biweekly-publication

Emery, M., Emery, E., & Roberts, N.L. (2000). *The press and America: An interpretive history of the mass media* (9th ed.). Boston: Allyn & Bacon.

Enders, E. (2016, September 23). Scully's smooth sendoff. MLB.com. www.mlb.com/news/vin-scully-retires-from-los-angeles-dodgers/c-202932590

ESPN, about. (2019). ESPN.com. www.worldofespn.com/about

ESPN lands rights to college playoff for $470M per year through 2025. (2012, November 12). CBS Sports. www.cbssports.com/collegefootball/story/21083692/espn-lands-rights-to-college-playoff-for-470m-per-year-through-2025

ESPN's Bob Ley to retire after nearly 40 years at the network. (2019, June 26). ESPN.com. www.espn.com/espn/story/_/id/27058914/bob-ley-retires-40-years-espn-anchor

Evensen, B.J. (1993). Jazz age journalism's battle over professionalism, circulation, and the sports page. *Journal of Sport History*, 20, 229–246.

Fang, K. (2017, July 21). VICE Sports lays off staff as it pivots to video. *Awful Announcing*. https://awfulannouncing.com/online-outlets/vice-sports-lays-off-staff-pivots-video.html

Fay, J. (2012). ESPN's Scott Van Pelt looks back as "SportsCenter" set to air 50,000th episode. *Sports Business Daily*. www.sportsbusinessdaily.com/Daily/Issues/2012/09/13/Media/SportsCenter.asp

Finn, C. (2015, January 2). ESPN finally gets a shot at NFL playoff broadcast. *Boston Globe*. www.bostonglobe.com/sports/2015/01/01/espn-finally-gets-shot-nfl-playoff-broadcast/Yt2uWHWIMLS0VDtgb76OGJ/story.html

Fishcher, B. (2019, July 3). Steelers make mark on Esports with Pittsburgh Knights franchise. *Sports Business Daily*. www.sportsbusinessdaily.com/Daily/Issues/2019/07/03/Esports/Steelers-Esports.aspx

Fisher, E. (2018a, December 20). ESPN continues reign over monthly comScore rankings for November. *Sports Business Daily*. www.sportsbusinessdaily.com/Daily/Issues/2018/12/20/Media/Comscores.aspx

Fisher, E. (2018b, February 20). Digital sports media audience avoids typical January drop off. *Sports Business Daily*. www.sportsbusinessdaily.com/Daily/Issues/2019/02/20/Media/ComScores.aspx

Fisher, E. (2019, February 20). Digital sports media audience avoids typical January drop off. *Sports Business Daily*. www.sportsbusinessdaily.com/Daily/Issues/2019/02/20/Media/ComScores.aspx

Folkerts, J., Lacy, S., & Davenport, L. (1998). *The media in your life: An introduction to mass communication*. Boston: Allyn & Bacon.

Fountain, C. (1993). *Sportswriter: The life and times of Grantland Rice*. Bridgewater, NJ: Replica.

The Four Horsemen. (2019). Notre Dame Fighting Irish Official Athletics site. https://und.com/trads-horse-html

Frankel, D. (2019, July 12). AT&T and NFL to stick with DirecTV 'Sunday Ticket' deal through 2020-21: Report. *Multichannel News*. Retrieved from https://www.multichannel.com/news/att-and-nfl-to-stick-with-current-nfl-sunday-ticket-deal

Freeman, M. (2001). *ESPN: The uncensored history*. Lanham, MD: Taylor.

Fry, J. (2011a, August 29). Thinking about the future: Five changes that may be coming to digital sports and how to meet them. National Sports Journalism Center. http://sportsjournalism.org/sports-media-news/thinking-about-the-future-five-changes-that-may-be-coming-to-digital-sports-and-how-to-meet-them

Fry, J. (2011b, September 15). Rules of the game change as sports journalists compete against teams they cover. Poynter Institute. www.poynter.org/latest-news/top-stories/146069/rules-of-the-game-change-as-sports-journalists-compete-against-teams-they-cover

Furlong, K. (2018, September 20). VU alum Grantland Rice focus of new documentary. *Vanderbilt News*. https://news.vanderbilt.edu/2018/09/20/vu-alum-grantland-rice-focus-of-new documentary

Gallico, P. (1946). *Confessions of a story writer*. New York: Knopf.

Gallico, P. (1965). *Golden People*. Garden City, NY: Doubleday.

Garrison, B., with Sabljak, M. (1993). *Sports reporting* (2nd ed.). Ames: Iowa State University Press.

Giuliano, L.A. (2011, January 5). Next generation TV over the Internet: This revolution will be televised. Network World. www.networkworld.com/article/2198051/tech-primers/next-generation-tv-over-the-internet--this-revolution-will-be-televised.html

Greenfield, K.T. (2012, August 30). ESPN: Everywhere sports profit network. *Bloomberg Business*. www.bloomberg.com/bw/articles/2012-08-30/espn-everywhere-sports-profit-network

Guttmann, A. (2002). *The Olympics: A history of the modern Games* (2nd ed). Urbana: University of Illinois Press.

Halberstam, D., & Stout, G. (Eds.). (1999). *The best American sports writing of the century*. Boston: Houghton Mifflin.

Hale, D.M. (2018, November 30). ACC Network set to launch August 2019. ESPN.com. www.espn.com/college-sports/story/_/id/25419387/acc-network-set-launch-august-2019

Ham, E.L. (2011, October 17). Broadcast 90 years ago was first to help listeners 'see' Series. *Street & Smith's Sports Business Journal, 14*, 15.

Hardy, S. (1997). Sport in urbanizing America: A historical review. *Journal of Urban History, 23*(6), 675–708.

Harper, W.A. (1999). *How you played the game: The life of Grantland Rice*. Columbia: University of Missouri Press.

Harris, J.H. (2002, May 20). Marketing stars and targeting women a winning combination for WNBA. *Street & Smith's Sports Business Journal, 5*, 11.

Hillenbrand, L. (2001). *Seabiscuit: An American legend*. New York: Random House.

Horton, D., & Wohl, R.R. (1956). Mass communication and para-social interaction. *Psychiatry, 19*, 215–229.

Huang, E., Davison, K., Shreve, S., Davis, T., Bettendorf, E., & Nair, A. (2006). Bridging newsrooms and classrooms: Preparing the next generation of journalists for converged media. *Journalism & Communication Monographs, 8*(3), 221–262.

Hunnicutt, B.K. (1996). *Kellogg's six-hour day*. Philadelphia: Temple University Press.

Inabinett, M. (1994). *Grantland Rice and his heroes: The sportswriter as mythmaker in the 1920s*. Knoxville: University of Tennessee Press.

James, M. (2014, September 6). TV networks going far down the financial field with the NFL. *Los Angeles Times*. www.latimes.com/entertainment/envelope/cotown/la-et-ct-tv-networks-nfl-20140906-story.html

Jolee, T. (2019, May 31). Mavericks become first NBA team to host pro-style combine for elite teams. NBA.com. www.mavs.com/mavericks-become-first-nba-team-to-host-pro-style-combine-for-elite-teens

Jordan, L. (1927, July 2). Sports reporting was a scholarly occupation fifty years ago. *Editor & Publisher, 60*, 9.

Kahn, R. (1999). *A flame of pure fire: Jack Dempsey and the roaring '20s*. New York: Harcourt Brace.

Kassing, J.W., & Sanderson, J. (2010). Fan–athlete interaction and Twitter tweeting through Giro: A case study. *International Journal of Sport Communication, 3*, 113–128.

Kidd, R. (2018, July 20). From Brazil to Cristiano Ronaldo, meet World Cup 2018's social media stars. *Forbes*. www.forbes.com/sites/robertkidd/2018/07/20/from-brazil-to-cristiano-ronaldo-meet-world-cup-2018s-social-media-stars/#52c427aa7179

Kindred, D. (2010). The sports beat: A digital reporting mix—With exhaustion built in. *Nieman Reports, 64*(4), 51–53.

King, B. (2005, March 14). Reaching today's fans: Delivery of sports info continues to evolve as fans demand more. *Street & Smith's Sports Business Journal, 7*(44), 8, 17–21.

Know the fan: The global sports media consumption report, 2014. (2014, May). Sport Business Group. www.knowthefan.com/wp-content/uploads/2014/05/KTF_GlobalOverview_2014_WEB.pdf

Kondolojy, A. (2014, November 7). NFL games 26 of 30 most-watched shows this fall. TV by the Numbers. http://tvbythenumbers.zap2it.com/2014/11/07/nfl-games-26-of-30-most-watched-shows-this-fall/325101

Lamb, C. (2012). *Conspiracy of silence: Sportswriters and the long campaign to desegregate baseball*. Lincoln: University of Nebraska Press.

Laucella, P.C. (2004). An analysis of mainstream, black, and communist press coverage of Jesse Owens in the 1936 Berlin Olympic Games (Doctoral dissertation, University of North Carolina at Chapel Hill). Proquest Dissertations and Theses, Document ID 845 70 7401.

Laucella, P.C. (2005). Review of the book *Blackout: The untold story of Jackie Robinson's first spring training. Journalism & Mass Communication Quarterly, 82*(1), 208–209.

Laucella, P.C. (2014). From print to online sports journalism. In A. Billings & M. Hardin (Eds.), *The Routledge handbook of sport and new media* (pp. 89–100). London: Routledge.

Laucella, P.C. (2016). Jesse Owens: A case study of mainstream and alternative press coverage on the 1936 Berlin Olympic Games. In C. Lamb (Ed.), *Jack Johnson to LeBron James: Essays on race, sport, and the media* (pp. 52-85). Lincoln: University of Nebraska Press.

Lefton, T. (2002, April 15). League deals signal change. *Street & Smith's Sports Business Journal, 5*, 23.

Lewis, M. (1998, December 7). High commissioner Pete Rozelle. *Time*. www.time.com/time/time100/profile/rozelle.html

Lipsyte, R. (2014, December 3). Serving sports fans through journalism. ESPN. http://espn.go.com/blog/ombudsman/post/_/id/501/serving-sports-fans-through-journalism

Lipsyte, R.W., & Levine, P. (1995). *Idols of the game: A sporting history of the American century.* Atlanta: Turner.

Litman, L. (2019, July 7). Rapinoe, Lavelle recover to lead USWNT to historic fourth World Cup title. Yahoo! Sports. https://sports.yahoo.com/rapinoe-lavelle-recover-lead-uswnt-184329443.html

Lowery, S.A., & DeFleur, M.L. (1995). *Milestones in mass communication research: Media effects* (3rd ed.). White Plains, NY: Longman.

Lule, J. (2001). *Daily news, eternal stories: The mythological role of journalism.* New York: Guilford Press.

MacCambridge, M. (1997). *The franchise: A history of Sports Illustrated magazine.* New York: Hyperion.

Mavericks to start using high-tech camera system that can turn images 360 degrees. (2014, November 20). *Sports Business Daily.* www.sportsbusinessdaily.com/Daily/Issues/2014/11/20/Facilities/Mavericks.aspx?hl=%22mavericks%20to%20start%20using%20high-tech%22&sc=0

McCarriston, S. (2019, February 3). Super Bowl 53 commercials: How much do ads cost in 2019? *Sporting News.* www.sportingnews.com/us/nfl/news/super-bowl-53-commercials-how-much-do-ads-cost-in-2019/l9ghpuv7kwwq1uhwy9xd35rhm

McChesney, R.W. (1989). Media made sport: A history of sports coverage in the United States. In L.A. Wenner (Ed.), *Media, sports, and society* (pp. 49–69), Newbury Park, CA: Sage.

McCollough, J.B. (2018, October 9). Sports journalists battle for relevancy. *Nieman Reports.* https://niemanreports.org/articles/sports-journalists-battle-for-relevancy

Michaels, A. (2014). *You can't make this up: Miracles, memories, and the perfect marriage of sports and television.* New York: Morrow.

Miller, J.A., & Shales, T. (2011). *Those guys have all the fun: Inside the world of ESPN.* New York: Little, Brown.

Mitchell, A. (2014, March 26). *State of the News Media 2014: Overview.* Pew Research Center. www.journalism.org/2014/03/26/state-of-the-news-media-2014-overview

Mitchell, A. (2015, April 29). *State of the News Media 2015: Overview.* Pew Research Center. www.journalism.org/2015/04/29/state-of-the-news-media-2015

Moses, L. (2014, June 23). How Sports Illustrated is relaunching for the mobile era. Digiday. http://digiday.com/publishers/sports-illustrated-relaunching-site-mobile

National Baseball Hall of Fame. (n.d.). Henry Chadwick. http://baseballhall.org/hof/chadwick-henry

Nauright, J., & Wiggins, D.K. (2010). Race. In S.W. Pope & J. Nauright (Eds.), *Routledge companion to sports history* (pp. 148–161). London: Routledge.

Newspapers fact sheet. (2018, June 13). Pew Research Center State of the News Media. www.journalism.org/fact-sheet/newspapers

NFL expands "Thursday Night Football" package. (2016, February 1). NFL.com. www.nfl.com/news/story/0ap3000000630862/article/nfl-expands-thursday-night-football-package

Nielsen Sports top 5 global sports industry trends 2018. (2018). Nielsen. http://nielsensports.com/wp-content/uploads/2014/09/nielsen-top-5-commercial-sports-trends-2018.pdf

Noverr, D.A., & Ziewacz, L.E. (1983). *The games they played: Sports in American history, 1865–1980.* Chicago: Nelson-Hall.

Oriard, M. (1991). *Sporting with the Gods: The rhetoric of play and game in American culture.* New York: Cambridge University Press.

Ourand, J. (2014, October 27). Like Jeter's site, Vice Sports gives athletes unfiltered outlet. *Street & Smith's Sports Business Daily.* www.sportsbusinessdaily.com/Journal/Issues/2014/10/27/Media/Sports-Media.aspx?hl=vice%20sports%20gives%20athletes%20unfiltered&sc=0

Ourand, J. (2015, January 12). Legacy of ESPN's Scott reaches far beyond the highlights. *Street & Smith's Sports Business Daily.* www.sportsbusinessdaily.com/Journal/Issues/2015/01/12/Media/Sports-Media.aspx

Owens, J., with Neimark, P. (1972). *I have changed.* New York: Morrow.

Ozanian, M. (2015, September 14). The most valuable teams in the NFL. *Forbes.* Retrieved March 5, 2016, from www.forbes.com/sites/mikeozanian/2015/09/14/the-most-valuable-teams-in-the-nfl/#518f32c8326f

Patel, S. (2019, January 25). Bad week for digital media: The Players' Tribune lays off eight. Digiday. https://digiday.com/media/layoffs-hit-the-players-tribune

Pedersen, P.M. (1997). *Build it and they will come: The arrival of the Tampa Bay Devil Rays.* Stuart, FL: Florida Sports Press.

Pope, S.W. (1995). An army of athletes: Playing fields, battlefields, and the American military sporting experience. *Journal of Military History, 59*(3), 435–456.

Putnam, R.D. (2000). *Bowling alone.* New York: Simon & Schuster.

Quillen, I. (2019, July 10). TV ratings show U.S. women's World Cup success good for U.S. men, too. *Forbes.* www.forbes.com/sites/ianquillen/2019/07/10/tv-ratings-show-us-womens-world-cup-success-good-for-us-men-too/#22018ad52bf7

Rader, B.G. (2004). *American sports: From the age of folk games to the age of televised sport* (5th ed.). Upper Saddle River, NJ: Prentice Hall.

Real, M.R. (1975). Super Bowl: Mythic spectacle. *Journal of Communication, 25*(1), 31–43.

Real, M.R. (1998). MediaSport: Technology and the commodification of postmodern sport. In L.A. Wenner (Ed.), *MediaSport* (pp. 14–26). London: Routledge.

Red Sox' free agent signings highlight Twitter's growing impact on sports reporting. (2014, November 26). *Street & Smith's Sports Business Daily.* www.sportsbusinessdaily.com/Daily/Issues/2014/11/26/Media/Twitter-Reporting.aspx?hl=%22Red%20Sox%27%20free%20agent%22&sc=0

ReplyBuy, the technology behind every NCAA Final Four team in 2019. (2019, April 5). *Globe Newswire.* www.globenewswire.com/news-release/2019/04/05/1797615/0/en/The-Technology-Behind-Every-NCAA-Final-Four-Team-in-2019.html

Rice, G. (1924, October 19). Notre Dame's cyclone beats Army, 13 to 7. *New York Herald Tribune,* 1, 15.

Rice, G. (1954). *The tumult and the shouting.* New York: Barnes.

Riess, S.A. (1990). The new sport history. *Reviews in American History, 18,* 311–325.

Roberts, D. (2015, July 6). The real winner of the Women's World Cup: Nike. *Forbes.* http://fortune.com/2015/07/06/womens-world-cup-nike

Roberts, G., & Klibanoff, H. (2006). *The race beat: The press, the Civil Rights struggle, and the awakening of a nation.* New York: Vintage.

Rovell, D. (2014, January 26). NFL most popular for 30th year in row. *ESPN.* http://espn.go.com/nfl/story/_/id/10354114/harris-poll-nfl-most-popular-mlb-2nd

Rusinack, K.E. (1998). Baseball on the radical agenda: The *Daily Worker* and *Sunday Worker* journalistic campaign to desegregate Major League Baseball, 1933–1947. In J. Dorinson & J. Warmund (Eds.), *Jackie Robinson: Race, sports, and the American dream* (pp. 75–85). Armonk, NY: Sharpe.

SB Nation. (n.d.). Vox Media. www.voxmedia.com/brands/sbnation

Scola, N. (2014, November 24). Why Mark Cuban opposes net neutrality: "I want there to be fast lanes." *Washington Post.* www.washingtonpost.com/blogs/the-switch/wp/2014/11/24/why-mark-cuban-opposes-net-neutrality-i-want-there-to-be-fast-lanes

Shaikin, B. (2018, March 28). Vin Scully comes out of retirement for 60 seconds. *Los Angeles Times.* www.latimes.com/sports/mlb/la-sp-dodgers-vin-scully-20180327-story.html

Shapiro, L., & Maske, M. (2005, April 19). "Monday Night Football" changes the channel. *Washington Post,* p. A1.

Sheridan, A. (2014, December 23). App review: The best of '14 from the big four pro sports leagues. *Street & Smith's Sports Business Daily.* www.sportsbusinessdaily.com/Daily/Issues/2014/12/23/Media/App-Review.aspx

Silber, I. (2003). *Press box red: The story of Lester Rodney, the columnist who helped break the color line in American sports.* Philadelphia: Temple University Press.

Smith, A.F., & Hollihan, K. (2009). *ESPN the company: The story and lessons behind the most fanatical brand in sports.* Hoboken, NJ: Wiley.

Solomon, D. (2018, September 24). Sports journalism is as relevant, and important, as ever in 2018. *Texas Monthly.* www.texasmonthly.com/the-culture/sports-journalism-relevant-important-ever-2018

Spangler, T. (2018, April 12). ESPN+ launches with a ton of live sports—and limited ads. *Variety.* https://variety.com/2018/digital/news/espn-plus-subscription-sports-streaming-limited-ads-1202751319

Sports Law: Sports-related laws and legal cases through the years. (2005). *Street & Smith's Sports Business Journal.* www.sportsbusinessdaily.com/Journal/Issues/2002/05/20020506/Special-Report/Sports-Related-Laws-And-Legal-Cases-Through-The-Years.aspx

Starr, M. (1999, October 25). Blood, sweat, and cheers. *Newsweek, 134*(17), 42.

Steinberg, B. (2019, May 27). Meredith sells Sports Illustrated to Authentic Brands Group for $110 million. *Variety.* https://variety.com/2019/biz/news/sports-illustrated-sale-meredith-authentic-brands-1203226481

Strother, T.E. (1978). The race advocacy function of the black press. *Black American Literature Forum, 12*(3), 92–99.

Super Bowl LIII draws 98.2 million TV viewers, 32.3 million social media interactions. Nielsen. www.nielsen.com/us/en/insights/article/2019/super-bowl-liii-draws-98-2-million-tv-viewers-32-3-million-social-media-interactions

Super Bowl XLIX on NBC is most-watched show in U.S. television history. (2015, February 2). NBC Sports Group Press Box. http://nbcsportsgrouppressbox.com/2015/02/02/super-bowl-xlix-on-nbc-is-most-watched-show-in-u-s-television-history

Susman, W.I. (1984). *Culture as history: The transformation of American society in the twentieth century.* New York: Pantheon.

Sweet, D. (2002, November 11). Fabulous Sports Babe still one and only female sports radio host. *Street & Smith's Sports Business Journal,* 5, 21.

Talese, G. (1966, July). Silent Season of a Hero. *Esquire.* www.randomhouse.com/kvpa/talese/essays/dimaggio.html

Tallack, D. (1991). *Twentieth-century America: The intellectual and cultural context.* London: Longman.

Towers, W.M. (1981). World Series coverage in New York City in the 1920s. *Journalism Monographs, 73,* 1–29.

Townsend, B. (2014, November 19). Mark Cuban says Mavericks AAC about to deploy innovative video technology that will make "watching a game crazy." Dallas Sun Times Network. http://dallas.suntimes.com/mavericks/7/75/25261/mark-cuban-says-mavericks-aac-about-to-deploy-innovative-video-technology-that-will-make-watching-a-game-crazy

Tuite, J. (1995, July 2). Backtalk; take a long time to admire Gehrig's lengthy feat. *New York Times,* pp. 8–9.

Walker, M. (2019, November 19). Americans favor mobile devices over desktops and laptops for getting news. *Pew Research.* Retrieved from https://www.pewresearch.org/fact-tank/2019/11/19/americans-favor-mobile-devices-over-desktops-and-laptops-for-getting-news/

Wenner, L.A. (Ed.). (1998). *MediaSport.* London: Routledge.

Wiley, R. (2002, December 9). Arledge's world flowed with ideas. ESPN. http://espn.go.com/page2/s/wiley/021209.html

Wilson, C. C. (n.d.). Overview of the past 182 years of the Black press. *National Newspapers Publishers Association.* https://nnpa.org/black-press-history

Yoder, M. (2018, May 10). The end of ESPN's public editor position completes a disappointing decline in relevancy that could have been avoided. *Awful Announcing.* https://awfulannouncing.com/espn/the-end-of-espns-public-editor-position-completes-a-disappointing-decline-in-relevancy-that-could-have-been-avoided.html

Chapter 4

Abeza, G., O'Reilly, N., & Nadeau, J. (2014). Sport communication: A multidimensional assessment of the field's development. *International Journal of Sport Communication, 7,* 289–316.

Abeza, G., O'Reilly, N., Seguin, B., & Nzindukiyimana, O. (2015). Social media scholarship in sport management research: A critical review. *Journal of Sport Management, 29*(6), 601-618.

Adler, R.B., & Proctor, R.F. (2017). *Looking out/looking in* (15th ed.). Boston: Cengage Learning.

Battenfield, F. (2013). The culture of communication in athletics. In P.M. Pedersen (Ed.), *Routledge handbook of sport communication* (pp. 441–450). London: Routledge.

Beebe, S.A., Beebe, S.J., & Redmond, M.V. (2020). *Interpersonal communication: Relating to others* (9th edition). London: Pearson.

Bodenheimer, G., & Phillips, D.T. (2015). *Every town is a sports town: Business leadership at ESPN, from the mailroom to the boardroom.* New York: Grand Central.

Bryant, J., Thompson, S., & Finklea, B.W. (2013). *Fundamentals of media effects* (2nd ed.). Long Grove, IL: Waveland.

Burton, G. (2002). *More than meets the eye: An introduction to media studies.* New York: Oxford.

Burton, G. (2010). *Media and society: Critical perspectives* (2nd ed.). Berkshire, UK: Open University.

Cobley, P., & Schulz, P.J. (2013). Introduction. In P. Cobley & P.J. Schulz (Eds.), *Theories and models of communication* (pp. 1–15). Berlin/Boston: de Gruyter Mouton.

Craig, R.T. (2013). Constructing theories in communication research. In P. Cobley & P.J. Schulz (Eds.), *Theories and models of communication* (pp. 39–57). Berlin/Boston: de Gruyter Mouton.

DeVito, J.A. (2019). *The interpersonal communication book* (15th ed.). London: Pearson.

Dewey, J. (1916). *Democracy and education.* Project Gutenberg. www.gutenberg.org/files/852/852-h/852-h.htm

Dittmore, S.W., & McCarthy, S.T. (2014). Sports marketing and new media. In A.C. Billings & M. Hardin (Eds.), *Routledge handbook of sport and new media* (pp. 165–176). Abingdon, UK: Routledge.

Evans, O. (2015, June). Social lessons. *Sports Business International, 212,* pp. 16–17.

Fetchko, M.J., Roy, D.P., & Clow, K.E. (2013). *Sports marketing.* Upper Saddle River, NJ: Pearson.

Fitzgerald, B.R. (2014, March 13). Data point: How many hours do millennials eat up a day? *Wall Street Journal.* http://blogs.wsj.com/digits/2014/03/13/data-point-how-many-hours-do-millennials-eat-up-a-day

Godoy-Pressland, A. (2014). "Nothing to report": A semi-longitudinal investigation of the print media coverage of sportswomen in British Sunday newspapers. *Media Culture Society, 36*(5), 595–609.

Greenberg, B.S., & Salwen, M.B. (2009). Mass communication theory and research: Concepts and models. In D.W. Stacks & M.B. Salwen (Eds.), *An integrated approach to communication theory and research* (2nd ed., pp. 61–74). New York: Routledge.

Griffin, C.L. (2018). *Invitation to public speaking* (6th ed.). Boston: Cengage Learning.

Heath, R.L., & Bryant, J. (2000). *Human communication theory and research: Concepts, contexts, and challenges* (2nd ed.). Mahwah, NJ: Taylor & Francis.

How Gen Z is watching TV & video right now, in 5 stats. (2019, August 5). Ypulse: Actionable Research on Gen Z and Millennials. www.ypulse.com/article/2019/08/05/how-gen-z-is-watching-tv-video-right-now-in-5-stats

Inbox. (2016, March 14). *Sports Illustrated, 124*(10), 10.

Kaplan, D. (2016). NFL hallway to $25B goal. *Street & Smith's Sport sBuinsess Journal, 18*(44), 1, 33.

Kassing, J.W., & Sanderson, J. (2015). Playing in the new media game or riding the virtual bench: Confirming and disconfirming membership in the community of sport. *Journal of Sport & Social Issues, 39*(1), 3-18.

Kastrinos, A., Damiani, R., & Treise, D. (2018). Print to podium: Exploring media coverage of 2016 Olympic athletes' perceptions about the Zika virus. *International Journal of Sport Communication, 11*, 447-461.

Kelley, S.W., & Tian, K. (2004). Fanatical consumption: An investigation of the behavior of sports fans through textual data. In L.R. Kahle & C. Riley (Eds.), *Sports marketing and the psychology of marketing communication* (pp. 27–65). Mahwah, NJ: Erlbaum.

Krauskopf, K. (2016, January). At 20, WNBA has chance to embrace its relevance to women. *Street & Smith's Sports Business Journal, 18*(39), 13.

Lanigan, R.L. (2013). Information theories. In P. Cobley & P.J. Schulz (Eds.), *Theories and models of communication* (pp. 59–83). Berlin/Boston: de Gruyter Mouton.

Littlejohn, S.W., Foss, K.A., & Oetzel, J.G. (2017). *Theories of human communication* (11th ed.). Long Grove, IL: Waveland.

Lowery, S.A., & DeFleur, M.L. (1995). *Milestones in mass communication research: Media effects* (3rd ed.). White Plains, NY: Longman.

McCombs, M.E., & Shaw, D.L. (1972). The agenda-setting function of mass media. *Public Opinion Quarterly, 36*(2), 176–187.

McQuail, D., & Windahl, S. (1993). *Communication models for the study of mass communications* (2nd ed.). New York: Longman.

Moore, J.H. (2018). Reading, watching, and tweeting about sports: An analysis of sport-news retention. *International Journal of Sport Communication, 11*(4), 503–528.

Moy, P., & Bosch, B.J. (2013). Theories of public opinion. In P. Cobley & P.J. Schulz (Eds.), *Theories and models of communication* (pp. 289–308). Berlin/Boston: de Gruyter Mouton.

Norman, G. (2016, May 23). Greg Norman shares his secrets to success in business. *Newsweek.* www.newsweek.com/greg-norman-golf-entrepreneurs-462561

Oliver, M.B., Woolley, J.K., & Limperos, A.M. (2013). Effects. In P. Cobley & P.J. Schulz (Eds.), *Theories and models of communication* (pp. 411–423). Berlin/Boston: de Gruyter Mouton.

Our Organization: What is CoSIDA? (2020). College Sports Information Directors of America. https://cosida.com/sports/2013/7/25/general.aspx

Pavlik, J.V., & McIntosh, S. (2019). *Converging media: A new introduction to mass communication* (6th ed.). New York: Oxford University Press.

Pedersen, P.M. (2013). Introduction. In P.M. Pedersen (Ed.), *Routledge handbook of sport communication* (pp. 1–6). London: Routledge.

Pedersen, P.M. (2014). The changing role of sports media producers. In A.C. Billings & M. Hardin (Eds.), *Routledge handbook of sport and new media* (pp. 101–109). Abingdon, UK: Routledge.

Pedersen, P.M., Laucella, P., Miloch, K., & Fielding, L. (2009). The juxtaposition of sport and communication: Defining the field of sport communication. In J. Nauright & S. Pope (Eds.), *The new sport management reader* (pp. 429–444). Morgantown, WV: Fitness Information Technology.

Pegoraro, A. (2013). Sport fandom in the digital world. In P.M. Pedersen (Ed.), *Routledge handbook of sport communication* (pp. 248–258). London: Routledge.

Rodriguez, D. (2016). *Sport communication: An interpersonal approach.* Dubuque, IA: Kendall Hunt.

Shoemaker, P.J., & Reese, S.D. (2014). *Mediating the message in the 21st century: A media sociology perspective* (3rd ed.). New York: Routledge.

Stoldt, G.C., Dittmore, S.W., Ross, M., & Branvold, S.E. (2021). *Sport public relations* (3rd ed.). Champaign, IL: Human Kinetics.

Subtil, F. (2014). James W. Carey's cultural approach of communication. *Intercom: RBCC, 37*(1), 19–44. www.scielo.br/pdf/interc/v37n1/en_a02v37n1.pdf

Thomas, G.F., & Stephens, K.J. (2015). An introduction to strategic communication. *International Journal of Business Communication, 52*(1), 3–11.

Tian, Y., & Yoo, J.H. (2015). Connecting with *The Biggest Loser*: An extended model of parasocial interaction and identification in health-related reality TV shows. *Health Communication, 30*, 1–7.

2022 Global Sports Market Size, Drivers, Trends and Forecast. (2019, May 10). The Business Research Company. www.globenewswire.com/news-release/2019/05/10/1822074/0/en/2022-Global-Sports-Market-Size-Drivers-Trends-and-Forecast.html

Vaughn, M. (1995). Organization symbols: An analysis of their types and functions in a reborn organization. *Management Communication Quarterly, 9*(2), 219-250.

Vote, K. (2018, September 6). The five most savage official football club Twitter accounts. Urban Pitch. https://urbanpitch.com/five-savage-official-football-club-twitter-accounts

White, D.M. (1950). The "gate keeper": A case study in the selection of news. *Journalism Quarterly, 27*(4), 383–390.

Wood, J.T. (2020). *Interpersonal communication: Everyday encounters* (9th ed.). Cengage: Wadsworth.

Yoo, S.K., Smith, L.R., & Kim, D. (2013). Communication theories and sport studies. In P.M. Pedersen (Ed.), *Routledge handbook of sport communication* (pp. 8–19). London: Routledge.

Chapter 5

Adler, R.B., & Proctor, R.F. (2017). *Looking out/looking in* (15th ed.). Boston: Cengage Learning.

Beebe, S.A., Beebe, S.J., & Redmond, M.V. (2020). *Interpersonal communication: Relating to others* (9th edition). London: Pearson.

Benbow, D.H. (2019, February 11). Pacers pro scout: 'You have to be real careful because these guys are like actors.' *Indianapolis Star*. www.indystar.com/story/sports/2019/02/11/pacers-scout-you-have-real-careful-these-guys-like-actors/2833598002

Bradberry, T. (2015, February 26). Your emails are silently enraging your coworkers—Here's how to stop. *Forbes*. www.forbes.com/sites/travisbradberry/2015/02/26/your-emails-are-silently-pissing-off-your-coworkers-heres-how-to-stop

Denhollander, R. (2019). *What is a girl worth? A story of breaking the silence and exposing the truth about Larry Nassar and USA Gymnastics*. Carol Stream, IL: Tyndale Momentum.

DeVito, J.A. (2017). *Interpersonal messages* (4th ed.). Upper Saddle River, NJ: Pearson Education.

DeVito, J.A. (2019). *The interpersonal communication book* (15th ed.). London: Pearson.

Haines, R. (2019). *Abused*. Lanham, MD: Rowman & Littlefield.

Hargie, O. (2011). *Skilled interpersonal communication: Research, theory, and practice* (5th ed.). Hove, East Sussex: Routledge.

Hartley, P. (1999). *Interpersonal communication* (2nd ed.). London: Routledge.

Krzyzewski, M., & Phillips, D.T. (2000). *Leading with the heart: Coach K's successful strategies for basketball, business, and life*. New York: Warner.

Lisanti, J. (2019, July 18). Fashionable 50. *Sports Illustrated*. www.si.com/lifestyle/2019/fashionable-50

Pavlik, J.V., & McIntosh, S. (2019). *Converging media: A new introduction to mass communication* (6th ed.). New York: Oxford University Press.

Rodriguez, D. (2016). *Sport communication: An interpersonal approach*. Dubuque, IA: Kendall Hunt.

Shapiro, R. (2015). How to sell and negotiate more effectively in sports. *Street & Smith's Sports Business Journal, 17*(44), 14.

Trenholm, S. (1986). *Human communication theory*. Englewood Cliffs, NJ: Prentice Hall.

Trenholm, S., & Jensen, A. (2013). Interpersonal communication (7th ed.). Oxford, UK: Oxford University Press.

Wood, J.T. (2020). *Interpersonal communication: Everyday encounters* (9th ed.). Cengage: Wadsworth.

Chapter 6

Adler, R.B., & Proctor, R.F. (2017). *Looking out/looking in* (15th ed.). Boston: Cengage Learning.

Athletics Mission Statement. (2020). Pratt Institute. https://goprattgo.com/sports/2019/1/2/information-articles-mission.aspx

Barnard, C. (1938). *The functions of the executive*. Cambridge, MA: Harvard University Press.

Barrett, D.J. (2014). *Leadership communication* (4th ed.). New York: McGraw-Hill Education.

Barrett, K. (2005, February 22). NCAA names Williams managing director of public and media relations. *Inside Black College Sports*. www.ibcsports.com/ncaa/2005/ncaa_names_williams_managing_dir.htm

Bass, A. (2018). Why is team communication important when in teams? Career Trend. https://careertrend.com/why-is-team-communication-important-when-in-teams-4233172.html

Battan, C. (2015, March). Meet Becky Hammon, the NBA's first female coach. *MarieClaire*. www.marieclaire.com/career-advice/news/a13562/becky-hammon-interview

Belzer, J. (2015, March 2). The best organizations to work for in sports. *Forbes*. www.forbes.com/sites/jasonbelzer/2015/03/02/the-best-organizations-to-work-for-in-sports

Blake, R.R., & McCanse, A.A. (1991). *Leadership dilemmas—Grid solutions*. Houston: Gulf.

Bodenheimer, G., & Phillips, D.T. (2015). *Every town is a sports town: Business leadership at ESPN, from the mailroom to the boardroom*. New York: Grand Central.

Bovee, C.L., & Thill, J.V. (2018). *Business communication today* (14th ed.). New York: Prentice Hall.

Bradberry, T. (2014). Why successful people never bring smartphones into meetings. LinkedIn. www.linkedin.com/pulse/20140922000612-50578967-why-successful-people-never-bring-smartphones-into-meetings?_mSplash=1

Bradberry, T. (2019). 10 communication secrets of great leaders. *TalentSmart*. www.talentsmart.com/articles/10-Communication-Secrets-of-Great-Leaders-2147446607-p-1.html

Carlton, C. (2015, July 16). Carlton: Sources say Texas president told AD Steve Patterson to change personal style. *Dallas Morning News*. www.dallasnews.com/sports/college-sports/columnists/chuck-carlton/20150715-carlton-sources-say-texas-president-told-ad-steve-patterson-to-change-personal-style.ece

Cathy Engelbert named WNBA commissioner. (2019, May 15). WNBA. www.wnba.com/news/cathy-engelbert-named-wnba-commissioner

Chat with NCAA VP Bob Williams. (2015). ESPN SportsNation. http://espn.go.com/sportsnation/chat/_/id/39323/ncaa-vp-bob-williams

Clapp, B. (2015, June 22). The skills needed for sports marketing jobs. Work in Sports. www.workinsports.com/blog/sports-marketing-jobs-the-skills-you-need

Curtis, B. (2015, March 20). Distant Thunder: What did Oklahoma City's media do to piss off Russell Westbrook and Kevin Durant? *Grantland*. http://grantland.com/the-triangle/nba-russell-westbrook-kevin-durant-oklahoma-city-thunder-sports-media

Dreier, F. (2015, April 27). Plugged in: Josh Furlow. *Street & Smith's Sports Business Journal, 18*(3), 3.

Grazer, B., & Fishman, C. (2015, May). The man of many questions. *Fast Company*, pp. 40, 42, 44.

In the office. (2015). FC Bayern Munich's Manhattan office. *Street & Smith's Sports Business Journal, 18*(8), 30.

Johnson, C.E., & Hackman, M.Z. (2018). *Leadership: A communication perspective* (7th ed.). Long Grove, IL: Waveland.

John Wood – Inspirational leadership series. (2020). The Leaders Institute. https://www.leadersinstitute.com/john-wooden-inspirational-leadership-series/

Jordan, J.S., Kent, A., & Walker, M. (2015). Management and leadership in the sport industry. In A. Gillentine & R.B. Crow (Eds.), *Foundations of sport management* (3rd ed., pp. 49–71). Morgantown, WV: Fitness Information Technology.

Kaser, K., & Oelkers, D. (2016). *Sports and entertainment marketing* (4th ed.). Boston: South-Western, Cengage Learning.

Kelly, L., Lederman, L.C., & Phillips, G.M. (1989). *Communicating in the workplace: A guide to business and professional speaking.* New York: Harper & Row.

Lussier, R.N. (2019). *Human relations in organizations: Applications and skill building* (11th ed.). New York: McGraw-Hill Education.

MacMullan, J. (2019). Pat Riley on Magic Johnson: "He's going to speak his mind." ESPN. www.espn.com/nba/story/_/id/26788966/going-speak-mind

Madkour, A.D. (2015). How United uses content, and why being interesting matters. *Street & Smith's Sports Business Journal, 18*(9), 20.

Modaff, D.P., Butler, J.A., & DeWine, S.A. (2017). *Organizational communication: Foundations, challenges, and misunderstandings* (4th ed.). New York: Pearson.

NACE Staff. (2018, December 12). Employers want to see these attributes on students' resumes. National Association of Colleges and Employers. www.naceweb.org/talent-acquisition/candidate-selection/employers-want-to-see-these-attributes-on-students-resumes

O'Boyle, I., Cummins, P., & Murray, D. (2015). Framing leadership in sport. In I. O'Boyle, D. Murray, & P. Cummins (Eds.), *Leadership in sport* (pp. 1–6). New York: Routledge.

Pedersen, P.M. (2020). *Sport communication case studies* (2nd ed.). Champaign, IL: Human Kinetics.

Pepper, G.L. (1995). *Communicating in organizations: A cultural approach.* New York: McGraw-Hill.

Potter, L. (2013). Social media, the new grapevine of employee communication, comes with responsibilities. More with Les. https://lespotter001.wordpress.com/2013/01/24/social-media-the-new-grapevine-of-employee-communication-comes-with-responsibilities

Robbins, S.P., & Judge, T.A. (2019). *Organizational behavior* (18th ed.). New York: Prentice Hall.

Rosenberg, M. (2015, May 18). Maize. Blue. Khaki. *Sports Illustrated, 122*(2), 32–38.

Rotella, B., & Cullen, B. (2015). *How champions think.* New York: Simon & Schuster.

Saxtorff, M. (2018, March 22). Building organizations of gaming and eSports. Tricas. https://tricas.dk/building-organizations-of-gaming-and-esports

Schwartzberg, L. (2015, May). Full-court press. *Fast Company*, p. 60.

Scott, D. (2014). *Contemporary leadership in sport organizations.* Champaign, IL: Human Kinetics.

Shipnuck, A. (2015, February 9). "He lifts us all." *Sports Illustrated, 122*(5), 108–116, 118.

Shockley-Zalabak, P.S. (2016). *Fundamentals of organizational communication: Knowledge, sensitivity, skills, values* (updated 9th ed.). Upper Saddle River, NJ: Pearson.

Spruill, T. (2019, May 15). Protracted trade talks with Dallas Wings impacting Liz Cambage's health. SBNation Swish Appeal. www.swishappeal.com/wnba/2019/5/15/18624467/wnba-protracted-trade-talks-with-dallas-wings-impacting-liz-cambages-health

Stoldt, G.C., Dittmore, S.W., Ross, M., & Branvold, S.E. (2021). *Sport public relations* (3rd ed.). Champaign, IL: Human Kinetics.

Torres, R.T., Preskill, H., & Piontek, M.E. (2005). *Evaluation strategies for communicating and reporting: Enhancing learning in organizations* (2nd ed.). Thousand Oaks, CA: Sage.

Wertheim, L.J. (2015, February 9). The case for . . . Serena Williams, boss. *Sports Illustrated, 122*(5), 15.

Whan's world. (2015, June). *Sports Business International*, 96.

Witherspoon, P.E. (1997). *Communicating leadership: An organizational perspective.* Boston: Allyn & Bacon.

Wong, G.M. (2013). *The comprehensive guide to careers in sports* (2nd ed.). Burlington, MA: Jones & Bartlett.

Vasel, K. (2019, May 24). Should you text with your boss? CNN Business. www.cnn.com/2019/05/24/success/texting-with-your-boss/index.html

Yukl, G.A., & Gardner, W.L. (2020). *Leadership in organizations* (9th ed.). Boston, MA: Pearson Education.

Chapter 7

About the Olympic Channel (n.d.). Olympic Channel Services. https://olympicchannelservices.com/about

ACC Network's female leadership ready for launch this month (2019, August 12). *Sports Business Daily.* www.sportsbusinessdaily.com/Daily/Issues/2019/08/12/Media/ACC-Network.aspx

Ackerman, W.C. (1945). The dimensions of American broadcasting. *Public Opinion Quarterly, 9*(1), 1–18.

Adgate, B. (2013, April 4). Can sports help radio fight disruption the way they help TV? *Ad Age.* http://adage.com/article/media/sports-save-radio-pandora-spotify/240697

Adler, K. (2019, August 23). ESPN Digital records its largest U.S. sports category lead ever for the second consecutive month. ESPN Pressroom. https://espnpressroom.com/us/press-releases/2019/08/espn-digital-records-its-largest-u-s-sports-category-lead-ever-for-the-second-consecutive-month

Andrews, P. (2013). *Sports journalism: A practical introduction* (2nd ed.). Thousand Oaks, CA: Sage.

AOL using original behind-the-scenes content to attract sports fans in lieu of live action. (2015, April 28). *Street & Smith's Sports Business Daily.* www.sportsbusinessdaily.com/Daily/Issues/2015/04/28/Media/AOL.aspx

Antitrust lawsuit revived against NFL, DirecTV over "Sunday Ticket." (2019, August 14). *Sports Business Daily.* www.sportsbusinessdaily.com/Daily/Issues/2019/08/14/Media/Sunday-Ticket.aspx

Arbel, T. (2019, August 5). The country's two largest newspaper chains announce merger as industry struggles. *Huffington Post.* www.huffpost.com/entry/newspaper-chain-gatehouse-buying-gannett-usa-today_n_5d488415e4b0ca604e36ab17

The Athletic grows business model with launch of podcast service. (2019, April 10). *Sports Business Daily.* www.sportsbusinessdaily.com/Daily/Issues/2019/04/10/Media/Athletic-Podcasts.aspx

Atkinson, C. (2019, July 8). Women's World Cup final ratings surpass last year's men's final. NBCnews.com. www.nbcnews.com/business/business-news/women-s-world-cup-final-ratings-surpass-last-year-s-n1027486

Audience analysis: IndyCar up for NBC's first exclusive season. (2019, September 25). *Sports Business Daily.* www.sportsbusinessdaily.com/Daily/Issues/2019/09/25/Media/Audience.aspx?hl=Audience+analysis%3a+IndyCar+up&sc=0

Audio and podcasting fact sheet. (2019, July 9). Pew State of the News Media. www.journalism.org/fact-sheet/audio-and-podcasting

Baccellieri, E. (2018, February 13). Where does the IOC's money go? Deadspin. https://deadspin.com/where-does-the-iocs-money-go-1822983686

Badenhausen, K. (2019, May 22). The world's most valuable brands 2019: Apple on top at $206 billion. *Forbes.* www.forbes.com/sites/kurtbadenhausen/2019/05/22/the-worlds-most-valuable-brands-2019-apple-on-top-at-206-billion/#37d5a85837c2

Bandura, A. (2002). Social cognitive theory of mass communication. In J. Bryant & D. Zillmann (Eds.), *Media effects: Advances in theory and research* (2nd ed., pp. 121–153). Hillsdale, NJ: Erlbaum.

Baran, S.J. (2006). Sports and television. Museum of Broadcast Communicators. www.museum.tv/eotv/sportsandte.htm

Barr, J. (2018, February 20). What the decline in the Olympics' ratings says about the future of TV. Forbes. www.forbes.com/sites/jonathanberr/2018/02/20/what-the-decline-in-the-olympics-ratings-says-about-the-future-of-tv/#7d34154963a5

Battaglio, S. (2019, April 30). ESPN will end publication of its print magazine in September. *Los Angeles Times.* www.latimes.com/la-fi-ct-espn-magazine-20190430-story.html

Bauder, D. (2015, February 2). Another viewership, social media record for Super Bowl. *The Seattle Times.* http://old.seattletimes.com/html/sports/2025604535_apxsuperbowlratings.html

Beaujon, A. (2014, March 4). Sun-Times will rehire 4 photographers. *Poynter.* www.poynter.org/2014/sun-times-will-rehire-4-photographers/242118

Belts, J.R. (1953). Sporting journalism in nineteenth-century America. *American Quarterly, 5*(1), 56.

Benedetto, R. (2018, August 18). Demise of print newspapers may have far-reaching consequences for communities and the nation. *The Hill.* https://thehill.com/opinion/technology/402382-demise-of-print-newspapers-may-have-far-reaching-consequences-for

Bernstein, A., & Blain, N. (2002). Sport and the media: The emergence of a major research field. *Culture, Sport, Society, 5*(3), 1–30.

Biasotti, T. (2015, May 11). Bill Simmons is leaving Grantland. Can the site survive without him? *Columbia Journalism Review.* www.cjr.org/analysis/bill_simmons_is_leaving_grantland_can_the_site_survive_without_him.php.

Bibel, S. (2014, December 23). ESPN's "Monday Night Football" is cable's most watched series for ninth straight year. TV by the Numbers. http://tvbythenumbers.zap2it.com/2014/12/23/espns-monday-night-football-is-cables-most-watched-series-for-ninth-straight-year/343021

Billings, A.C., Butterworth, M.L., & Turman, P.D. (2015). *Communication and sport: Surveying the field* (2nd ed.). Los Angeles: Sage.

Bishop, B. (2019, June 29). Ruper Murdoch's News Corp. completes split from 21st Century Fox entertainment business. The Verge. www.theverge.com/2013/6/29/4476062/rupert-murdochs-news-corp-completes-split-from-21st-century-fox

Blanchard, M.A. (Ed.). (1998). *History of the mass media in the United States: An encyclopedia.* Chicago: Fitzroy Dearborn.

Boyle, R., & Haynes, R. (2003). New media sport. In A. Bernstein & N. Blain (Eds.), *Sports, media, culture: Global and local dimensions* (pp. 95–114). London: Cass.

Brian, D. (2001). *Joseph Pulitzer: A life*. Hoboken, NJ: Wiley.

Brinson, S.L. (2005). From Marconi to Cop Rock: An introduction to broadcasting history. In J.E. Winn, & S.L. Brinson (Eds.), *Transmitting the past: Historical and cultural perspectives on broadcasting* (pp.1–15). Tuscaloosa: University of Alabama Press.

Butler, B., Zimmerman, M.H., & Hutton, S. (2013). Turning the page with newspapers: Influence of the Internet on sports coverage. In P.M. Pedersen (Ed.), *Routledge handbook of sport communication* (pp. 219–227). London: Routledge.

Carpenter, J.W. (2019, February 11). The top 5 companies owned by Disney. Investopedia.com. www.investopedia.com/articles/markets/102915/top-5-companies-owned-disney.asp

Castleman, H., & Podrazik, W.J. (2003). *Watching TV: Six decades of American television* (2nd ed.). Syracuse: Syracuse University Press.

CBS's McManus takes on the Arledge challenge. (2006, January 9). *Street & Smith's Sports Business Journal, 9*, 42.

Chemi, E. (2014, August 27). ESPN pays four times the going rate to air NFL games. Bloomberg News. www.bloomberg.com/bw/articles/2014-08-27/why-does-espn-pay-four-times-more-for-nfl-games-than-nbc-cbs-and-fox

Clavio, G., & Kian, E.M. (2010). Uses and gratifications of a retired female athlete's Twitter followers. *International Journal of Sport Communication, 3*(4), 485–500.

Conaghan, J. (2015, October 9). Newspaper digital audience. Newspaper Association of America. www.naa.org/Trends-and-Numbers/Newspaper-Websites/Newspaper-Web-Audence.aspx

Conlan, N. (2014, April 24). Can you guess what the highest grossing sports movies are? *Sports Illustrated*. www.si.com/extra-mustard/2014/04/24/highest-grossing-sports-movies

Creedon, P. J. (1994). *Women, media and sport: Challenging gender values*. Thousand Oaks, CA: Sage.

Crepeau, R.C. (2005, December 27). Sport & society; ARETE electronic mailing list.

Crupi, A. (2012, August 13). NBC has the last laugh as Olympics strike gold: London Games the most-watched U.S. TV event in history. *Adweek*. www.adweek.com/news/television/nbc-has-last-laugh-olympics-strike-gold-142706

Crupi, A. (2014, May 7). NBCUniversal strikes gold with megawatt Olympics deal. *Adweek*. www.adweek.com/news/television/nbcuniversal-strikes-gold-megawatt-olympics-deal-157522

Deford, F. (2012). *Over time: My life as a sportswriter*. New York: Atlantic Monthly Press.

Deitsch, R. (2015, June 4). Women's World Cup viewer's guide: Inside Fox Sports's coverage plans. *Sports Illustrated*. www.si.com/planet-futbol/2015/06/04/womens-world-cup-tv-guide-uswnt-fox-sports

Dirs, B. (2015, May 21). Mayweather-Pacquiao damaged boxing, says Ricky Hatton. BBC. www.bbc.com/sport/0/boxing/32800798

Disis, J. (2018, February 4). Why Super Bowl ads still matter. CNN.com. https://money.cnn.com/2018/02/01/news/companies/super-bowl-commercials/index.html

Edmonds, R. (2014, June 4). Gannett earnings reports hints at coming problem with paywalls. Poynter. www.poynter.org/news/mediawire/237601/gannett-earnings-report-hints-at-a-coming-problem-with-paywalls

Edmonds, R., Guskin, E., Mitchell, A., & Jurkowitz, M. (2013, July 18). The state of the news media 2013. Pew Research Center's Project for Excellence in Journalism. www.stateofthemedia.org/2013/newspapers-stabilizing-but-still-threatened

ESPN extends broadcast deal with Special Olympics. (2019, September 19). *Sports Business Daily*. www.sportsbusinessdaily.com/Daily/Morning-Buzz/2019/09/19/Special-Oly.aspx

ESPN, NBA, CFP among big winners at 8th annual Sports Business Awards in N.Y. (2015, May 21). *Street & Smith's Sports Business Daily*. www.sportsbusinessdaily.com/Daily/Issues/2015/05/21/Sports-Business-Awards/SBA-Winners.aspx

ESPN's first redesign of its website in six years getting positive reviews. (2015, April 1). *Street & Smith's Sports Business Daily*. www.sportsbusinessdaily.com/Daily/Issues/2015/04/01/Media/ESPN-website.aspx

ESPN's Skipper calls Simmons split "business decision," but not strictly over salary. (2015, May 12). *Street & Smith's Sports Business Daily*. www.sportsbusinessdaily.com/Daily/Issues/2015/05/12/Media/Grantland.aspx

Esquire editors. (2019, August 4). The 15 best sports podcasts of 2019. Esquire. www.esquire.com/entertainment/a28581197/best-sports-podcasts-2019

Exit interview: Shapiro on sports. (2005, October 3). *Street & Smith's Sports Business Journal, 8*, 1.

Fainaru-Wada, M. (2019, February 10). Bob Costas unplugged: From NBC and broadcast icon to dropped from Super Bowl. ESPN.com. www.espn.com/espn/otl/story/_/id/25914913/inside-story-how-legendary-nfl-broadcaster-bob-costas-ended-excised-football-nbc-espn.

2019 FIBA World Cup reached record audience of over 3 billion. (2019, October 2). *Sports Business Daily*. www.sportsbusinessdaily.com/Daily/Global/2019/10/02/FIBA-WC-Viewership.aspx?hl=2019+FIBA+World+CUP+reached+record&sc=0

50 most influential: Introduction. (2014, December 8). *Street & Smith's Sports Business Daily*. www.

sportsbusinessdaily.com/Journal/Issues/2014/12/08/Most-Influential/Intro.aspx

Fischer, B. (2019, September 12). NFL renews deal with Facebook through '20 season. Sports Business Daily. www.sportsbusinessdaily.com/Daily/Issues/2019/09/12/Media/NFL-Facebook.aspx

Fisher, E. (2015a, May 14). ESPN sees drop in unique visitors, but still easily tops April comScore rankings. *Street & Smith's Sports Business Daily*. http://m.sportsbusinessdaily.com/Daily/Issues/2015/05/14/Media/Comscores.aspx

Fisher, E. (2015b, April 30). SI to create film division that will develop documentaries, other features. *Street & Smith's Sports Business Daily*. http://m.sportsbusinessdaily.com/Daily/Issues/2015/04/30/Media/SI.aspx

Fisher, E. (2015c, May 21). StubHub releases new mobile apps that include partnership with ESPN. *Street & Smith's Sports Business Daily*. www.sportsbusinessdaily.com/Daily/Issues/2015/05/21/Media/StubHub.aspx

Fleenor, R. (2019, October 10). Every Apple TV Plus show announced so far, and the latest trailers and teasers. C/NET.com. www.cnet.com/news/every-apple-tv-plus-show-announced-and-latest-trailers-and-teasers-truth-be-told-octavia-spencer

Folkerts, J., & Lacy, S. (2004). *The media in your life: An introduction to mass communication* (3rd ed). Boston: Pearson.

Football Federation Australia signs broadcast deal with ABC. (2019, October 4). *Sports Business Daily*. www.sportsbusinessdaily.com/Daily/Global/2019/10/04/ALeague-ABC.aspx?hl=Football+Federation+Australia+signs+broadcast+deal&sc=0

Friedman, W. (2018, January 19). TV's regional sports networks remain top financial earners. MediaPost.com. www.mediapost.com/publications/article/313199/tvs-regional-sports-networks-remain-top-financial.html

Fung, B. (2014, February 10). NBC single-handedly pays for a fifth of all Olympic Games. *Washington Post*. www.washingtonpost.com/blogs/the-switch/wp/2014/02/10/nbc-single-handedly-pays-for-a-fifth-of-all-olympic-games

Gaines, C. (2015, May 12). The Mayweather-Pacquiao fight numbers are in—they shattered expectations by tens of millions of dollars. *Business Insider*. www.businessinsider.com/floyd-mayweather-manny-pacquiao-revenue-2015-5

Garrison, B., with Sabljak, M. (1993). *Sports reporting* (2nd ed.). Ames: Iowa State University.

Gisondi, J. (2010). *Field guide to covering sports*. Washington, DC: CQ Press.

Greenstein, T. (2019, January 2). NBC Sports Chicago announces multiyear deal with the White Sox, Bulls and Blackhawks. *Chicago Tribune*. www.chicagotribune.com/sports/breaking/ct-spt-nbc-sports-chicago-bulls-blackhawks-white-sox-20190102-story.html

Global Sports Media Consumption Report: US Overview (2014). SportBusiness Group. http://sportsvideo.org/main/files/2014/06/2014-Know-the-Fan-Study_US.pdf

Godfrey, S. (2015, June 5). Longhorn Network doomed? Texas' TV money stacking up fine against SEC's. SB Nation. www.sbnation.com/college-football/2015/6/5/8733131/texas-longhorn-network-money-revenue

Gough, C. (2019, August 9). TV viewership of the Super Bowl in the United States from 1990 to 2019 (in millions). Statista. www.statista.com/statistics/216526/super-bowl-us-tv-viewership

Grossman, A. (2005a, November 7). Sports radio stations take their brand extension into publications, even restaurants. *Street & Smith's Sports Business Journal*, 8, 11.

Grossman, A. (2005b, December 19). Sports stations try to scoop up Stern fans. *Street & Smith's Sports Business Journal*, 8, 9.

Harbord, J.G. (1929). The commercial uses of radio. *Annals of the American Academy of Political and Social Science*, 142, 57–63.

Harper, W.A. (1999). *How you played the game: The life of Grantland Rice*. Columbia: University of Missouri Press.

Hayes, D. (2019a, April 25). Comcast Q1 profit beats estimates but Olympics comparison dings NBCUniversal. Deadline.com. https://deadline.com/2019/04/comcast-q1-profit-beats-estimates-but-olympics-comparison-dings-nbcuniversal-1202601755

Hayes, D. (2019b, August 29). YES Network finalizes $3.5 billion sale to New York Yankees, Sinclair and Amazon. Deadline.com. https://deadline.com/2019/08/yes-network-amazon-new-york-yankees-sinclair-broadcast-group-disney-fox-1202707647

Hayes, D. (2019c, September 12). ESPN chief Jimmy Pitaro tackles NFL rights, streaming strategy, gambling coverage, ACC Network launch and more. Deadline.com. https://deadline.com/2019/09/espn-chief-jimmy-pitaro-tackles-nfl-rights-streaming-strategy-gambling-coverage-acc-network-launch-and-more-1202732529

HBO planning to leave boxing at end of '18 amid viewership decline. (2018, September 28). *Sports Business Daily*. www.sportsbusinessdaily.com/Daily/Issues/2018/09/28/Media/HBO.aspx?hl=HBO+planning+to+leave+boxing&sc=0

Hill, L.A. (2004, September 6). Building a TV sports empire. *Television Week*, 23(36), 11–12.

Hilliard, R.L., & Keith, M.C. (2005). *The broadcast century and beyond: A biography of American broadcasting* (4th ed.). Boston: Focal.

Holloway, D. (2016, August 23). How Rio ratings surprised NBC and will impact future Olympics. Variety. https://variety.com/2016/tv/news/2016-olympics-ratings-rio-nbc-1201843200

How we see it: Big challenges, payoffs in selling the 24/7 fan. (2005, March 7). *Street & Smith's Sports Business Journal, 8,* 38.

Humes, M. (2014, July 14). 2014 World Cup final on ABC: Most-watched men's World Cup championship. ESPN Mediazone. http://espnmediazone.com/us/press-releases/2014/07/2014-world-cup-final-on-abc-most-watched-mens-world-cup-championship-ever

James, M. (2019, October 3). *Sports Illustrated,* under Ross Levinsohn, plans to dramatically cut staff. *Los Angeles Times.* www.latimes.com/entertainment-arts/business/story/2019-10-03/sports-illustrated-maven-ross-levinsohn-layoffs

Kafka, P. (2019, May 30). Jimmy Pitaro moved ESPN away from politics, controversy, and anything else that isn't sports. Vox. www.vox.com/2019/5/30/18644638/espn-jimmy-pitaro-podcast-recode-media-peter-kafka-disney-streaming-sports-bob-iger

Kaplan, D. (2015, March 9). NFL projecting revenue increase of $1B over 2014. *Street & Smith's Sports Business Journal.* www.sportsbusinessdaily.com/Journal/Issues/2015/03/09/Leagues-and-Governing-Bodies/NFL-revenue.aspx

Karp, A. (2012, August 14). NBC wraps up London Games with best Olympic audience since 1996. *Street & Smith's Sports Business Daily.* www.sportsbusinessdaily.com/SB-Blogs/Olympics/London-Olympics/2012/08/finalratings.aspx

Karp, A. (2019a, January 14). Sports maintains dominant viewership. *Sports Business Daily.* www.sportsbusinessdaily.com/Journal/Issues/2019/01/14/Media/Top-100.aspx

Karp, A. (2019b, May 10). Basketball dominates top sports telecasts since Super Bowl. *Sports Business Daily.* www.sportsbusinessdaily.com/Daily/Issues/2019/05/10/Media/Top-Sports-Telecasts.aspx

Kausler, D. (2011, November 1). Alabama football notes: The big game will be well covered; Duron Carter is Jordan Jefferson. Al.com. www.al.com/sports/index.ssf/2011/11/alabama_football_notes_the_big.html

Kellner, D. (1981, January). Network television and American society: Introduction to a critical theory of television. *Theory and Society, 10*(1), 31–62.

Kessler, M., & Fainaru-Wada, M. (2019, August 1). 44 years. 41 allegations. Now the past is catching up. ESPN.com. www.espn.com/espn/feature/story/_/id/27244072/44-years-41-allegations-how-caught-former-olympian

Kian, E.M., Burden, J.W., Jr., & Shaw, S.D. (2011). Internet sport bloggers: Who are these people and where do they come from? *Journal of Sport Administration & Supervision, 3*(1), 30–43.

Kian, E.M., & Murray, R. (2014). Curmudgeons but yet adapters: Impact of Web 2.0 and Twitter on newspaper sport journalists' jobs, responsibilities, and routines. *#ISOJ, 4*(1), 61–77.

Kian, E.M., & Zimmerman, M.H. (2012). The medium of the future: Top sports writers discuss transitioning from newspapers to online journalism. *International Journal of Sport Communication, 5,* 285–304.

King, B. (2005, March 7). World Congress of Sports: The 24/7 fan. *Street & Smith's Sports Business Journal, 8,* 23.

King, B., & Ourand, J. (2014, March 17). The RSN conundrum. *Street & Smith's Sports Business Daily.* www.sportsbusinessdaily.com/Journal/Issues/2014/03/17/In-Depth/RSNs.aspx

Lafayette, J. (2019, May 21). McCarthy tapped to run Sinclair's Cubs network. *Broadcasting & Cable.* www.broadcastingcable.com/news/mccarthy-tapped-to-run-sinclairs-cubs-network

Laucella, P. (2014). The evolution from print to online platforms for sports journalism. In A.C. Billings & M. Hardin (Eds.), *The Routledge handbook of sport and new media* (pp. 342–352). London: Routledge.

Le, V. (2015, May 22). The world's largest media companies of 2015. *Forbes.* www.forbes.com/sites/vannale/2015/05/22/the-worlds-largest-media-companies-of-2015

Lefton, T., & Ourand, J. (2015b, February 9). Super Bowl XLIX: Arizona. *Street & Smith's Sports Business Journal.* www.sportsbusinessdaily.com/Journal/Issues/2015/02/09/Events-and-Attractions/SuperBowl.aspx

Lincoln, R.A. (2019, May 20). 2019 Sports Emmy Awards: ESPN, NBC lead the pack with 6 wins each. *The Wrap.* www.thewrap.com/2019-sports-emmy-awards-espn-nbc-lead-the-pack-with-six-wins-each

Lipsyte, R. (1975). *Sportsworld: An American dreamland.* New York: Quandrangle.

Lisa, A. (2019, August 20). Most valuable sports business brands worldwide. Yahoo! Finance. https://finance.yahoo.com/news/most-valuable-sports-business-brands-090717745.html

Lutz, A. (2012, June 14). These 6 corporations control 90% of the media in America. *BusinessInsider.* www.businessinsider.com/these-6-corporations-control-90-of-the-media-in-america-2012-6

MacCambridge, M. (2018, April 11). "Who can explain the athletic heart?" The past and perilous future of *Sports Illustrated. The Ringer.* www.theringer.com/2018/4/11/17220176/sports-illustrated-future-meredith-sale-history

Madrigal, A.C., Meyer, R. (2018, October 18). How Facebook's chaotic push into video cost hundreds of journalists their jobs. *The Atlantic.* www.theatlantic.com/technology/archive/2018/10/facebook-driven-video-push-may-have-cost-483-journalists-their-jobs/573403

Magowan, A. (2015, June 6). Women's World Cup 2015: One billion TV viewers expected. BBC. www.bbc.com/sport/0/football/33019625

Malcolm, H. (2014, May 1). *USA Today* No. 1 newspaper in daily circulation. *USA Today*. www.usatoday.com/story/money/business/2014/05/01/usa-today-daily-circulation/8573269

Mandese, J. (2005, January 31). Big ticket. *Broadcasting & Cable, 135*(5), 14.

McCann, M. (2019, August 14). Why DirecTV's NFL Sunday Ticket might be illegal under antitrust law. *Sports Illustrated*. www.si.com/nfl/2019/08/14/nfl-sunday-ticket-directv-antitrust-violation-lawsuit

McChesney, R. (1989). Media made sports: A history of sports coverage in the United States. In L.A. Wenner (Ed.), *Media, sports, and society* (pp. 49–69). Newbury Park, CA: Sage.

Media notes. (2015, April 24). *Street & Smith's Sports Business Daily*. www.sportsbusinessdaily.com/Daily/Issues/2015/04/24/Media/Media-Notes.aspx

Megargee, S. (2004, October 25). His idea created magazine giant. *Stuart News*, 1C, 3C.

Memphis latest college hoops program to get ESPN+ series. (2019, September 25). *Sports Business Daily*. www.sportsbusinessdaily.com/Daily/Issues/2019/09/25/Media/Memphis.aspx

Michaels, A. (2014). *You can't make this up: Miracles, memories, and the perfect marriage of sports and television*. New York: Morrow.

Miller, J.A., & Shales, T. (2011). *Those guys have all the fun: Inside the world of ESPN*. New York: Little, Brown.

Mitchell, A. (2015, April 29). State of the News Media 2015. Pew Research Center. www.journalism.org/2015/04/29/state-of-the-news-media-2015

Morales, M. (2004, October 11). The Latino playing field. *Multichannel News, 25*(41), 58.

Mullin, B. (2019a, March 18). ESPN, UFC reach exclusive pay-per-view deal. *Wall Street Journal*. www.wsj.com/articles/espn-ufc-reach-exclusive-pay-per-view-deal-11552939288

Mullin, B. (2019b, July 8). Women's World Cup Final drew higher U.S. ratings than men's Final. *Wall Street Journal*. www.wsj.com/articles/womens-world-cup-final-drew-higher-u-s-ratings-than-mens-final-11562628017

Mullen, L. (2015, February 17). NBC Sports Radio to broadcast all three Triple Crown races for the first time. *Street & Smith's Sports Business Daily*. www.sportsbusinessdaily.com/Daily/Issues/2015/02/17/Media/Triple-Crown-Radio.aspx

Mullis, S. (2012, December 11). After 126 years, 'The Sporting News' stops the presses. NPR. www.npr.org/sections/thetwo-way/2012/12/11/167001870/after-126-years-the-sporting-news-stops-the-presses.

Nagle, D. (2018, December 20). ESPN, Inc.: 2018 in review—Launch of ESPN+ marks year of innovation, storytelling and audience expansion. ESPN Press Room. https://espnpressroom.com/us/press-releases/2018/12/espn-inc-2018-in-review-launch-of-espn-marks-year-of-innovation-storytelling-and-audience-expansion

National Academy of Television Arts and Sciences announces winners of the 36th annual Sports Emmy Awards. (2015, May 5). National Academy of Television Arts and Sciences. http://emmyonline.com/sports_36th_winners

NBC, ESPN take home most Sports Emmy wins; Ernie Johnson honors late Stuart Scott. (2015, May 6). *Street & Smith's Sports Business Daily*. www.sportsbusinessdaily.com/Daily/Issues/2015/05/06/Media/Sports-Emmys.aspx

Newspaper circulation volume. (2012, September 4). Newspaper Association of America. www.naa.org/Trends-and-Numbers/Circulation-Volume/Newspaper-Circulation-Volume.aspx

Nielsen Year in Sports Media report 2014. (2015, February). New York: Nielsen Company.

Nielsen: Sports radio listeners are smart and well-heeled. (2018, February 21). Inside Radio. www.insideradio.com/free/nielsen-sports-radio-listeners-are-smart-and-well-heeled/article_d9142044-16d5-11e8-b47d-af1336a448e0.html

Norman, J. (2018, January 4). Football still Americans favorite sport to watch. Gallup. https://news.gallup.com/poll/224864/football-americans-favorite-sport-watch.aspx

Olympic marketing fact file. (2019). IOC. https://stillmed.olympic.org/media/Document%20Library/OlympicOrg/Documents/IOC-Marketing-and-Broadcasting-General-Files/Olympic-Marketing-Fact-File-2018.pdf

Otterson, J. (2018, February 26). 2018 Winter Olympics close out as least-watched on record, down 7% from Sochi Games. *Variety*. https://variety.com/2018/tv/news/2018-winter-olympics-ratings-2-1202710137

Ourand, J. (2012, February 13). A strong signal. *Street & Smith's Sports Business Journal*. http://m.sportsbusinessdaily.com/Journal/Issues/2012/02/13/In-Depth/Lead.aspx

Ourand, J. (2014a, November 17). NFL Network finds post-"TNF" slot a good launch pad for new shows. *Street & Smith's Sports Business Journal*. www.sportsbusinessdaily.com/Journal/Issues/2014/11/17/Media/NFL-Net-show.aspx

Ourand, J. (2014b, November 3). With major media rights deals done, how will networks grow revenue? *Street & Smith's Sports Business Journal*, p. 1. www.sportsbusinessdaily.com/Journal/Issues/2014/11/03/In-Depth/Networks-main.aspx

Ourand, J. (2015a, February 2). CBS price for Super Bowl 50 spot: $5M? *Street & Smith's Sports Business Journal*. www.sportsbusinessdaily.com/Journal/Issues/2015/02/02/Media/SuperBowlAds.aspx

Ourand, J. (2015b, June 1). Execs signal they may ease up on all-out pursuit of millennials. *Street & Smith's Sports Business Journal*, p. 12. www.sportsbusinessdaily.com/Journal/Issues/2015/06/01/Media/Sports-Media.aspx

Ourand, J. (2015c, March 23). Univision to produce weekly shows as part of new NBA deal. *Street & Smith's Sports Business Journal*. http://corporate.univision.com/2015/03/sports-business-journal-univision-to-produce-weekly-shows-as-part-of-new-nba-deal

Ourand, J. (2015d, January 12). Will Dish's offering kill cable bundle? *Street & Smith's Sports Business Journal*. www.sportsbusinessdaily.com/Journal/Issues/2015/01/12/Media/ESPN-Sling-TV.aspx

Ourand, J. (2015e, January 19). With record-setting year in books, what next for CFP title game? *Street & Smith's Sports Business Journal*. www.sportsbusinessdaily.com/Journal/Issues/2015/01/19/Media/Sports-Media.aspx

Ourand, J. (2015f, June 1). Execs signal they may ease up on all-out pursuit of millennials. *Street & Smith's Sports Business Journal*.

Ourand, J. (2019a, June 11). ESPN Deportes radio operations shutting down in September. *Sports Business Daily*. www.sportsbusinessdaily.com/SB-Blogs/Breaking-News/2019/06/ESPN-Deportes.aspx

Ourand, J. (2019b, August 6). Ryen Russillo leaves ESPN to go exclusive with The Ringer. *Sports Business Daily*. www.sportsbusinessdaily.com/Daily/Morning-Buzz/2019/08/06/Russillo.aspx

Ourand, J. (2019c, September 30). ESPN lands Bundesliga media rights starting in '20. *Sports Business Daily*. www.sportsbusinessdaily.com/Daily/Morning-Buzz/2019/09/30/ESPN-Bundesliga.aspx

Ourand, J., & Smith, M. (2015, January 19). 1st CFP offers Super Bowl-like aura. *Street & Smith's Sports Business Journal*. www.sportsbusinessdaily.com/Journal/Issues/2015/01/19/Events-and-Attractions/CFP-reaction.aspx

Pavlik, J.V., & McIntosh, S. (2015). *Converging media: A new introduction to mass communication* (4th ed.). New York: Oxford University Press.

Pedersen, E. (2019, May 20). Sports Emmys: ESPN & NBC tie for most trophies; Winter Olympics leads programs. Deadline.com. https://deadline.com/2019/05/sports-emmys-espn-nbc-tie-for-most-trophies-winter-olympics-leads-programs-1202619609

Pedersen, P. (2014). The changing role of sports media producers. In A.C. Billings & M. Hardin (Eds.), *Routledge handbook of sport and new media* (pp. 101–109). London: Routledge.

People & Personalities: Katie Nolan getting bigger platform with new FS1 show. (2015, February 24). *Street & Smith's Sports Business Daily*. www.sportsbusinessdaily.com/Daily/Issues/2015/02/24/Media/People-Personalities.aspx

Piecoro, N. (2015, February 19). Diamondbacks' new TV deal believed to be worth more than $1 billion. *Arizona Republic*. www.azcentral.com/story/sports/mlb/diamondbacks/2015/02/18/diamondbacks-new-tv-deal-believed-to-be-worth-more-than-1-billion/23651245

Podcasts quickly become major revenue source for Barstool Sports. (2019, August 22). *Sports Business Daily*. www.sportsbusinessdaily.com/Daily/Issues/2019/08/22/Media/Barstool-Podcasts.aspx

Povich, S. (1995, May 2). Telling it like it was about Howard Cosell. *Washington Post*, p. E2.

Powell, M.K. (2003, January 21). Should limits on broadcast ownership change? Yes. *USA Today*. http://usatoday30.usatoday.com/news/opinion/editorials/2003-01-21-powell_x.htm

Prisbell, E. (2019a, September 30). Fox debuting new tech during MLB postseason, including 4K HDR. *Sports Business Daily*. www.sportsbusinessdaily.com/Daily/Issues/2019/09/30/Media/Fox-Postseason.aspx?hl=Fox+debuting+new+tech+during+MLB+postseason%2c+including+4K+HDR&sc=0

Prisbell, E. (2019b, September 30). MLB touts many metrics in '19 despite attendance drop. *Sports Business Daily*. www.sportsbusinessdaily.com/Daily/Morning-Buzz/2019/09/30/MLB-attendance.aspx?hl=MLB+touts+many+metrics+in+%2719+despite+attendance+drop&sc=0

Real Fan Life. (n.d.). *The Players' Tribune*. www.theplayerstribune.com/en-us/collections/real-fan-life

Relatively cheap sports documentaries growing in popularity as TV programming. (2015, March 23). *Street & Smith's Sports Business Journal*. www.sportsbusinessdaily.com/Daily/Issues/2015/03/23/Media/Sports-Documentary.aspx

Reynolds, M. (2004, November 8). Slicing up a spinoff. *Multichannel News, 25*(45), 18.

The Ringer's Bill Simmons talks podcast advertising, outlet's future. (2019, June 12). *Sports Business Daily*. www.sportsbusinessdaily.com/Daily/Issues/2019/06/12/Media/Bill-Simmons.aspx

Rival networks align as HBO, Showtime co-produce Mayweather-Pacquiao bout. (2015, April 28). *Street & Smith's Sports Business Daily*. http://m.sportsbusinessdaily.com/Daily/Issues/2015/04/28/Media/May-Pac-Media.aspx

Rovell, D. (2014a, January 26). NFL most popular for 30th year in a row. ESPN. http://espn.go.com/nfl/story/_/id/10354114/harris-poll-nfl-most-popular-mlb-2nd

Rumsey, D. (2019, October 14). "Ballers," series finale focuses on potential strike, healthcare proposal. *Sports Business Daily*. www.sportsbusinessdaily.com/Daily/Issues/2019/10/14/People-and-Pop-Culture/Ballers.aspx?hl=%22Ballers%22+series+finale+focuses+on+potential+strike&sc=0

Sanderson, J. (2011). *It's a whole new ball game: How social media is changing sports*. New York: Hampton.

Sandomir, R. (2015, March 21). Documentaries are the go-to players of sports television. *New York Times*. www.nytimes.com/2015/03/22/sports/documentaries-are-the-go-to-players-of-sports-television.html?_r=0

Sarah Spain about. (2019). Sarah Spain website. http://sarahspain.com/about

Schoenherr, S.E. (1999). Television's split personality. Audio Engineering Society. www.aes.org/aeshc/docs/recording.technology.history/television4.html

Schultz, B. (2005). *Sports media: Reporting, producing, and planning*. Burlington, MA: Elsevier.

Schultz, B., & Arke, E. (2015). *Sports media: Reporting, producing, and planning* (3rd ed.). New York: Routledge.

Schultz, B., & Sheffer, M.L. (2007). An exploratory study of how Twitter is affecting sports journalism. *International Journal of Sport Communication, 3*, 226–239.

Schultz, B., & Sheffer, M.L. (2014). Local TV sports and the Internet. In A.C. Billings & M. Hardin (Eds.), *Routledge handbook of sport and new media* (pp. 110–118). London: Routledge.

Schwartz, L. (2000). SportsCentury biography: Billie Jean won for all women. ESPN. https://espn.go.com/sportscentury/features/00016060.html

Settimi, C. (2018, February 8). By the numbers: The 2018 Pyeongchang Winter Olympics. *Forbes*. www.forbes.com/sites/christinasettimi/2018/02/08/by-the-numbers-the-2018-pyeongchang-winter-olympics/#41baa8d97fb4

Shapiro, L. (1995, April 24). Howard Cosell dies at 77: Sportscaster was a magnet for controversy. *Washington Post*, p. A1.

Sheffer, M.L., & Schultz, B. (2010). Paradigm shift or passing fad? Twitter and sports journalism. *International Journal of Sport Communication, 3*, 472–484.

Sherwood, M., & Nicholson, M. (2013). Web 2.0 platforms and the work of newspaper sport journalists. *Journalism, 14*(7), 942–959.

Siltanen, R. (2014, January 29). Yes, a Super Bowl ad really is worth $4 million. *Forbes*. www.forbes.com/sites/onmarketing/2014/01/29/yes-a-super-bowl-ad-really-is-worth-4-million

Simmons' Goodell barb seen as last straw for ESPN, which has controlled narrative so far. (2015, May 11). *Street & Smith's Sports Business Daily*. www.sportsbusinessdaily.com/Daily/Issues/2015/05/11/Media/Simmons.aspx

Smith, A.F., & Hollihan, K. (2009). *ESPN the company: The story and lessons behind the most fanatical brand in sports*. New York: Wiley.

Smith, C. (2015, January 16). Could a Super Bowl commercial really be worth $10 million? Surprisingly, yes. *Forbes*. www.forbes.com/sites/chrissmith/2015/01/16/could-a-super-bowl-commercial-really-be-worth-10-million

Smith, G. (2019a, July 1). Journalism job cuts haven't been this bad since the recession. www.bloomberg.com/news/articles/2019-07-01/journalism-layoffs-are-at-the-highest-level-since-last-recession

Smith, G. (2019b, January 24). Super Bowl ad prices stall after years of relentless increases. Bloomberg.com. www.bloomberg.com/news/articles/2019-01-24/super-bowl-ad-prices-stall-after-years-of-relentless-increases

Smith, M. (2019c, August 26). ACC Network: A decade in the making. *Sports Business Daily*. www.sportsbusinessdaily.com/Journal/Issues/2019/08/26/Media/ACC-Network.aspx

Sowell, M. (2008). The birth of national sports coverage: An examination of the *New York Herald's* use of the telegraph to report America's first "championship" boxing match in 1849. *Journal of Sports Media, 3*(1), 51–75.

Spain, S. (2015, April 3). C'mon, guys. It's time to elevate the conversation on sports talk radio. ESPN. http://espn.go.com/espnw/news-commentary/article/12612828/cmon-guys-time-elevate-conversation-sports-talk-radio

2019 Sports Business Awards. (2019, May 22). *Sports Business Daily*. www.sportsbusinessdaily.com/Conferences-Events/2019/SBA.aspx

Stainer, J., & Master, S. (2018). Nielsen's Year in Sports Media 2017 Report. www.nielsen.com/us/en/insights/report/2018/2017-year-in-sports-media

Stark, P., & Schiffman, M. (2000, May 6). Sports/talk leads in "power ratios." *Billboard, 112*(19), 116–117.

Strupp, J. (2001, June 11). The changing face of sports. *Editor & Publisher, 134*(24), 10–13.

Sutton, K. (2019, July 23). NBCUniversal expects to exceed $1.2 billion in ad sales during 2020 Tokyo Olympics. *Adweek*. www.adweek.com/tv-video/nbcuniversal-expects-to-exceed-1-2-billion-in-ad-sales-during-2020-tokyo-olympics

SVG staff. (2019, January 11). YES Network concludes 2018 as most watched RSN in the nation. Sports Video Group news. www.sportsvideo.org/2019/01/11/yes-network-concludes-2018-as-most-watched-rsn-in-the-nation

Sweet home, Chicago: ESPN, NFL Net take differing approach to NFL draft coverage (2015, April 30). *Street & Smith's Sports Business Daily*. www.sportsbusinessdaily.com/Daily/Issues/2015/04/30/Media/Draft-TV.aspx

Szalai, G. (2019, May 3). Sinclair to buy Fox Regional Sports Networks from Disney for $10.6 billion. *Hollywood Reporter*. www.hollywoodreporter.com/news/sinclair-buy-fox-regional-sports-networks-disney-106-billion-1193249

Team, T. (2019, September 9). Comcast revenues to keep growing? *Forbes*. www.forbes.com/sites/greatspeculations/2019/09/09/comcast-revenues-to-keep-growing/#78c191506af8

Teitelman, R. (2019, March 20). The AT&T-Time Warner merger battle is over. The antitrust battle is just beginning. *Barron's*. www.barrons.com/articles/the-antitrust-battle-after-at-t-time-warner-merger-51553025503

Theories swirling around reason for Simmons' forthcoming exit from ESPN. (2015, May 14). *Street & Smith's Sports Business Daily*. www.sportsbusinessdaily.com/Daily/Issues/2015/05/14/Media/Simmons.aspx

Total Circ. (no date). Alliance for Audited Media. http://abcas3.auditedmedia.com/ecirc/magtitlesearch.asp

Tracy, M., & Draper, K. (2019, April 30). *The New York Times*. www.nytimes.com/2019/04/30/sports/espn-magazine-print-closes.html

Travis, C. (2015a, May 7). The 15 most valuable sports networks. Fox Sports. www.foxsports.com/college-football/outkick-the-coverage/the-15-most-valuable-sports-networks-050715

Travis, C. (2015b, May 11). The Longhorn Network is all hat, no cattle. Fox Sports. www.foxsports.com/college-football/outkick-the-coverage/the-longhorn-network-is-all-hat-no-cattle-051115

Travis, C. (2019, August 7). Cable vs. streaming, how does ESPN navigate the future? *Outkick the Coverage*. www.outkickthecoverage.com/cable-vs-streaming-how-does-espn-navigate-the-future

Tribeca/ESPN Sports film festival kicks off with Tony Gonzalez documentary. (2015, March 11). *Street & Smith's Sports Business Daily*. www.sportsbusinessdaily.com/Daily/Issues/2015/03/11/Media/Films.aspx

Univision finds success appealing to wider soccer TV audience in U.S. (2019, September 23). *Sports Business Daily*. www.sportsbusinessdaily.com/Daily/Issues/2019/09/23/Media/Univision.aspx

U.S. publishing industry's annual survey reveals $28 billion in revenue in 2014. (2015, June 10). Association of American Publishers. http://publishers.org/news/us-publishing-industry's-annual-survey-reveals-28-billion-revenue-2014

Vaillant, D. (2002). "Your voice came in last night . . . but I thought it sounded a little scared": Rural radio listening and "talking back" during the progressive era in Wisconsin, 1920–1932. In M. Hilmes & J. Loviglio (Eds.), *Essays in the cultural history of radio: Radio reader* (pp. 63–88). New York: Routledge.

Vogan, T. (2014). *Keepers of the flame: NFL Films and the rise of sports media*. Champaign: University of Illinois Press.

Vogt, N. (2015a, April 29). State of the news media 2015: Audio fact sheet. Pew Research Center. www.journalism.org/2015/04/29/audio-fact-sheet

Vogt, N. (2015b, April 29). State of the news media 2015: Podcasting fact sheet. Pew Research Center. www.journalism.org/2015/04/29/podcasting-fact-sheet

Watson, A. (2019, August 27). U.S. radio industry—statistics & facts. Statista. www.statista.com/topics/1330/radio

Weprin, A. (2019, August 29). Sinclair, Amazon back $3.5B Yankees deal to take full control of YES Network. *Hollywood Reporter*. www.hollywoodreporter.com/news/sinclair-amazon-back-35b-yankees-deal-take-full-control-yes-network-1193246

White, P. (2019, February 13). Amazon is "dipping its toe in the water" of sports rights, co-TV chief Albert Cheng says at TCA. Deadline.com. https://deadline.com/2019/02/amazon-sports-rights-tca-1202556831

Whitney, D. (2004, September 6). Becoming the place for sports. *TelevisionWeek, 23*(36), 26–27.

Williams, A.T. (2016, February 29). Paying for digital news: The rapid adoption and current landscape of digital subscriptions at U.S. newspapers. *American Press Institute*. www.americanpressinstitute.org/publications/reports/digital-subscriptions/single-page

World's most valuable brands (2019, May 22). #47 ESPN. *Forbes*. www.forbes.com/companies/espn/#5d73ab504331

Yang, A. (2020, February 2). How much does a Super Bowl commercial cost? *Sports Illustrated*. https://www.si.com/nfl/2020/02/02/how-much-does-super-bowl-commercial-cost-history-2020

Yoder, M. (2015, July 7). Women's World Cup final beats NBA finals, World Series and much more. *Awful Announcing*. http://awfulannouncing.com/2015/womens-world-cup-final-beats-nba-finals-world-series-and-much-more.html

Chapter 8

Ackermann, E., & Hartman, K. (2014). *The information specialist's guide to searching and researching on the internet and world wide web* (2nd ed.). New York: Routledge.

Akincilar, A., & Dagdeviren, M. (2014). A hybrid multi-criteria decision model to evaluate hotel websites. *International Journal of Hospitality Management, 36*, 263–271. doi:10.1016/j.ijhm.2013.10.002.

Anderson, M, Perrin, A., Jingjing, J., & Kumar, M. (2019, April 22). 10% of Americans don't use the internet. Who are they? Pew Research Center. www.pewresearch.org/fact-tank/2019/04/22/some-americans-dont-use-the-internet-who-are-they

Auger, P. (2005). The impact of interactivity and design sophistication on the performance of commercial websites for small business. *Journal of Small Business Management, 43*(2), 119–137.

Bajarin, T. (2014, August 18). Meet Levi's Stadium, the most high-tech sports venue yet. *Time*. http://time.com/3136272/levis-stadium-tech

Ball, B. (2019, June 18). Smart phones have significant impact on sports fans' behavior. *University of Florida Research & Insights*. www.jou.ufl.edu/insights/smartphones-have-significant-impact-on-sports-fans-behavior

Bei, L., Chen, Y., & Widdows, R. (2004). Consumers' online information search behavior and the phenomenon of search vs. experience products. *Journal of Family and Economic Issues, 25*(4), 449–467.

Berman, M. (2014, February 27). Thirteen percent of U.S. adults say they don't use the Internet. *Washington Post*. www.washingtonpost.com/news/post-nation/wp/2014/02/27/thirteen-percent-of-u-s-adults-say-they-dont-use-the-internet

Billings, A.C., Qiao, F., Conlin, L., & Nie, T. (2017). Permanently desiring the temporary? Snapchat, social media, and the shifting motivations of sport fans. *Communication & Sport, 5*(1), 10-26. doi:10.1177/2167479515588760

Billings, A.C, & Ruihley, B.J. (2014). *The fantasy sport industry: Games within games*. London: Routledge.

Blumler, J.G., & Katz, E. (1974). *The uses of mass communications: Current perspectives on gratifications research*. Beverly Hills, CA: Sage.

Brady, E., & Ortiz, J.L. (2013, July 31). For athletes, social media not all fun and games. *USA Today*. www.usatoday.com/story/sports/2013/07/31/for-athletes-social-media-not-all-fun-and-games/2606829

Brown, M.T. (2003). An analysis of online marketing in the sport industry: User activity, communication objectives, and perceived benefits. *Sport Marketing Quarterly, 12*(1), 48–55.

Burns, M.J. (2014, July 25). How Twitter is part of the "fabric" of sports in 2014. *Forbes*. www.forbes.com/sites/markjburns/2014/07/25/how-twitter-is-part-of-the-fabric-of-sports-in-2014

Burst Media. (2010, September 9). *The internet scores with sports fans as the best medium for sports news and information*. www.burstmedia.com/about/press_releases/press_09_09_2010.asp

Butler, B., Zimmerman, M.H., & Hutton, S. (2013). Turning the page with newspapers: Influence of the Internet on sports coverage. In P.M. Pedersen (Ed.), *Routledge handbook of sport communication* (pp. 219–227). London: Routledge.

Carlson, J., & O'Cass, A. (2012). Optimizing the online channel in professional sport to create trusting and loyal consumers: The role of the professional sports team brand and service quality. *Journal of Sport Management, 26*, 463–478.

The changing profile of sports fans around the world. (2019, January 29). *Facebook for Business*. www.facebook.com/business/news/insights/the-changing-profile-of-sports-fans-around-the-world

Clavio, G., & Walsh, P. (2014). Dimensions of social media utilization among college sport fans. *Communication & Sport, 2*(3), 261–281.

Clement, J. (2019, September 6). Most famous social network sites worldwide as of July 2019, ranked by number of active users (in millions). *Statista*. www.statista.com/statistics/272014/global-social-networks-ranked-by-number-of-users

Cohen, A. (2019, November 5). DraftKings joins growing list of NBA's authorized sports betting operators. *SportTechie*. www.sporttechie.com/draftkings-nba-authorized-sports-betting-operator-basketball

Cox, J., & Dale, B.G. (2002). Key quality factors in web site design and use: An examination. *International Journal of Quality and Reliability Management, 19*(6/7), 862–889.

Craig, W. (2018, May 8). The importance of quality over quantity in digital content marketing. *Forbes*. www.forbes.com/sites/williamcraig/2018/05/08/the-importance-of-quality-over-quantity-in-digital-content-marketing

Cutler, N., & Danowski, J. (1980). Process gratification in aging cohorts. *Journalism Quarterly, 57*, 269–277.

De Guzman, J.N. (2014, April 30). How social media changed eSports forever. *Red Bull*. www.redbull.com/gb-en/how-social-media-has-changed-esports

DeMers, J. (2014, July 23). The top 7 social media marketing trends dominating 2014. *Forbes*. www.forbes.com/sites/jaysondemers/2014/07/23/the-top-7-social-media-marketing-trends-dominating-2014

Eagleman, A.N. (2013). Acceptance, motivations, and usage of social media as a marketing communications tool amongst employees of sport national governing bodies. *Sport Management Review, 16*, 488–497.

Eide, T. (2018, November 20). 9 stats that prove the importance of website design. *Parqa*. https://parqamarketing.com/blog/why-your-websites-design-is-important-stats-that-prove-it

Filo, K., Funk, D.C., & Hornby, G. (2009). The role of web site content on motive and attitude change for sport events. *Journal of Sport Management, 23*, 21–40.

5 sports stadiums that score big with mobile engagement. (2016, October 13). *Genesys*. www.genesys.com/blog/post/5-sports-stadiums-score-big-cx

Fox, D. (2019, May 10). eSports to break through $1bn barrier in 2020 as it moves from niche to mainstream. *SVG Europe*. www.svgeurope.org/blog/headlines/esports-market-set-to-break-1-billion-in-2020-as-it-moves-from-niche-to-mainstream

Friedman, W. (2014, February 17). Sports TV scores huge gains, dominates TV programming. MediaPost. www.mediapost.com/publications/article/219582/sports-tv-scores-huge-gains-dominates-tv-programm.html

Gaming and esports are happening on Twitter. (2018, February 15). *Twitter*. https://blog.twitter.com/en_us/topics/events/2018/Gaming-and-esports-are-happening-on-Twitter.html

Garrett, J.J. (2010). *The elements of user experience: User-centered design for the web and beyond* (2nd ed.). Berkeley, CA: Pearson Education.

Gillett, R. (2014, September 18). Why we're more likely to remember content with images and video (infographic). *Fast Company*. www.fastcompany.com/3035856/why-were-more-likely-to-remember-content-with-images-and-video-infogr

Goff, B. (2013, August 20). The $70 billion fantasy football market. *Forbes*. www.forbes.com/sites/briangoff/2013/08/20/the-70-billion-fantasy-football-market

Goi, C.-L. (2012). A review of web evaluation criteria for e-commerce web sites. *Journal of Internet Banking and Commerce, 17*(3), 1–10. www.arraydev.com/commerce/JIBC/2012-12/Goi percent20Chai percent20Leev02.pdf

Guzzo, M. (2019, January 3). Year in review: 2018's most mentioned athletes and sporting events. *Taylor Strategy*. https://taylorstrategy.com/2018-most-mentioned-twitter

Hackos, J.T., & Stevens, D.M. (1997). *Standards for online communication: Publishing information for the Internet/World Wide Web/help systems/corporate intranets*. Hoboken: Wiley.

Hassan, S., & Li, F. (2005). Evaluating the usability and content usefulness of websites: A benchmarking approach. *Journal of Electronic Commerce in Organizations, 3*(2), 46–67.

Hood, K.M., Shanahan, K.J., Hopkins, C.D., & Lindsey, K.K. (2015). The influence of interactivity on visit and purchase frequency: The moderating role of website informational features. *Journal of Internet Commerce, 14*(3), 294-315.

Impey, S. (2019, November 12). Study: More fans streaming sport than paying for TV packages. *SportsPro*. www.sportspromedia.com/news/dazn-facebook-youtube-sports-fans-tv-streaming-study

Industry demographics. (n.d.). *Fantasy Sports & Gaming Association*. https://thefsga.org/industry-demographics

Insights: Engaging with sports fans on Instagram. (2018, November 26). *Creative Review*. www.creativereview.co.uk/insights-engaging-with-sports-fans-on-instagram

Internet/broadband fact sheet. (2019, June 12). Pew Research Center. www.pewresearch.org/internet/fact-sheet/internet-broadband/#who-uses-the-internet.

Iqbal, M. (2019, February 27). Twitch revenue and usage statistics (2019). *Business of Apps*. www.businessofapps.com/data/twitch-statistics

Jerde, S. (2019, March 1). Major League Soccer experiments with streaming partners as it eyes next TV rights deal. *AdWeek*. www.adweek.com/tv-video/major-league-soccer-experiments-with-streaming-partners-as-it-eyes-next-tv-rights-deals

Johnson, J. (2003). *Web bloopers: 60 common web design mistakes and how to avoid them*. Cambridge, MA: Kaufmann.

Kang, S.J., Ha, J.P., & Hambrick, M.E. (2015). A mixed-method approach to exploring the motives of sport-related mobile applications among college students. *Journal of Sport Management, 29*(3), 272–290.

Karlsson, M. (2011). The immediacy of online news, the visibility of journalistic processes and a restructuring of journalistic authority. *Journalism, 12*(3), 279-295.

Kaufman, K. (2018, June 15). Will Facebook become the preferred way for fans to watch sports? *Forbes*. www.forbes.com/sites/karlkaufman/2018/06/15/will-facebook-become-the-preferred-way-for-fans-to-watch-sports

Kemp, S. (2019, January 30). Digital 2019: global internet use accelerates. we are social. https://wearesocial.com/blog/2019/01/digital-2019-global-internet-use-accelerates

Kian, E.M., Lee, J.W., Gregg, E., & Kane, J.J. (2014). Rivals.com framing of FBS-FCS football games: Immoral mismatch or just another game. *Journal of Contemporary Athletics, 8*(2), 75–91.

Kian, E.M., Schultz, B., Clavio, G., & Sheffer, M.L. (2019). *Multimedia sports journalism: A practitioner's guide for the digital age*. New York: Oxford University Press.

Kiesler, S. (2014). *Culture of the internet*. New York: Psychology Press.

Kilgore, A. (2018, May 14). For sports leagues, legalized sports betting offers new risks, and massive rewards. *The Washington Post*. www.washingtonpost.com/sports/for-sports-leagues-legalized-sports-betting-offers-new-risks-and-massive-rewards/2018/05/14/5ce4caf4-5790-11e8-858f-12becb4d6067_story.html

Kim, K.S., Sin, S.C., & Tsai, T.I. (2014). Individual differences in social media use for information seeking. *Journal of Academic Librarianship, 40*(2), 171–178.

Langer, E. (2014, May 29). Crowning the most social sports teams in the US. CNBC. www.cnbc.com/id/101714566

Lister, M., Dovey, J., Giddings, S., Grant, I., & Kelly, K. (2009). *New media: A critical introduction* (2nd ed.). London: Routledge.

Mann, R. (2018, October 23). Smaller sports leagues racing for legal sports betting opportunities. *SportsHandle*. https://sportshandle.com/why-smaller-sports-league-want-in-on-legal-sports-betting

Martinolich, J. (2012). The second screen. *Broadcast Engineering, 54*(11), 27–29.

Mashayekhi, R. (2019, April 10). Inside the battle for the future of sports betting. *Fortune*. https://fortune.com/longform/sports-betting-battle

McNeil, P. (2015, January 1). 3 essential navigation trends for 2015. *Web Designer Depot*. www.webdesignerdepot.com/2015/01/3-essential-navigation-trends-for-2015

McQuail, D. (2002). *McQuail's reader in mass communication theory*. Thousand Oaks, CA: Sage.

Meân, L.J. (2014). Sport websites, embedded discursive action, and the gendered reproduction of sport. In A.C. Billings & M. Hardin (Eds.), *Routledge handbook of sport and new media* (pp. 331–341). London: Routledge.

Medal, A. (2017, October 13). Why augmented reality is the next big move for the sports industry. *Inc.* www.inc.com/andrew-medal/why-augmented-reality-is-next-big-move-for-sports-industry.html

Miceli, M. (2019, March 23). How streamers monetize Twitch popularity. *Sports Business Journal: The Esports Observer*. https://esportsobserver.com/essentials-twitch-streamers

Migala, D. (2004, September 13). If your website doesn't have these features, you're losing business. *Street & Smith's Sports Business Journal*, 15.

Mitchell, A. (2015, April 29). State of the news media 2015. Pew Research Center. www.journalism.org/2015/04/29/state-of-the-news-media-2015

Moses, L. (2013, July 24). Sports fans slowly move from TV to the Internet. *AdWeek*. www.adweek.com/news/technology/sports-fans-slowly-move-tv-internet-151329

Mualla, K. (2019, January 16). Ecommerce in the sport industry. *Digital Boutique*. www.digitalboutique.co.uk/ecommerce-in-the-sport-industry

New research reveals Millennial and GenZ sports fans changing the game for leagues, teams and players. (2019, November 4). *Business Wire*. www.businesswire.com/news/home/20191104005245/en/New-Research-Reveals-Millennial-GenZ-Sports-Fans

Nielsen, J. (1997, June 15). Top ten mistakes of web management. Jakob Nielsen's Alertbox. www.nngroup.com/articles/top-10-mistakes-of-web-management

Nielsen, J. (2004, September 13). The need for web design standards. Jakob Nielsen's Alertbox. www.nngroup.com/articles/the-need-for-web-design-standards

Nielsen, J. (2012a, January 4). Usability 101: Introduction to usability. *Nielsen Norman Group*. www.nngroup.com/articles/usability-101-introduction-to-usability

Nielsen, J. (2012b, April 10). Mobile site vs. full site. *Nielsen Norman Group*. www.nngroup.com/articles/mobile-site-vs-full-site

Nielsen Sports. (2018). *Top 5 Global Sports Industry Trends 2018*. http://nielsensports.com/wp-content/uploads/2014/09/nielsen-top-5-commercial-sports-trends-2018.pdf

O'Shea, M., & Alonso, A.D. (2012). Opportunity or obstacle? A preliminary study of sport organisations in the age of social media. *International Journal of Sport Management and Marketing, 10*(3/4), 196-212.

Palmer, J. (2002). Web site usability, design, and performance metrics. *Information Systems Research, 13*(2), 151–169.

Papacharissi, Z., & Rubin, M. (2000). Predictors of Internet use. *Journal of Broadcasting and Electronic Media, 44*(2), 175–196.

Pedersen, P.M. (2013). *Routledge handbook of sport communication*. London: Routledge.

Pedersen, P.M., Miloch, K.S., & Laucella, P. (2007). *Strategic sport communication*. Champaign, IL: Human Kinetics.

Pernice, K., & Caya, P. (2014, June 29). Intranet portals are the hub of the enterprise universe. *Nielsen Norman Group*. www.nngroup.com/articles/intranet-portals

Popper, B. (2013, September 30). Field of streams: How Twitch made video games a spectator sport. *The Verge*. www.theverge.com/2013/9/30/4719766/twitch-raises-20-million-esports-market-booming

PwC. (2019). Sports industry: Time to refocus? *PwC's Sports Survey*. www.pwc.ch/en/insights/sport/sports-survey-2019.html

Ramos, D.R. (2018, March 20). Amazon Prime announces "All or Nothing" sports docuseries. Deadline.com. https://deadline.com/2018/03/amazon-prime-video-all-or-nothing-sports-docuseries-1202346663

Ramsey, E. (2019, September 19). Analysis: Winners and losers from the first $10 billion in legal US sports betting. *Legal Sports Report*. www.legalsportsreport.com/35373/winners-losers-10-billion-us-sports-betting

Richard, M. (2003). Modeling the impact of Internet atmospherics on surfer behavior. *Journal of Business Research, 58*(2005), 1632–1642.

Rosen, D.E., & Purinton, E. (2004). Website design: Viewing the web as a cognitive landscape. *Journal of Business Research, 57*, 787–794.

Rovell, D. (2018, December 10). NBA to start selling league pass by the quarter. *The Action Network*. www.actionnetwork.com/nba/nba-league-pass-selling-by-quarter-2018-19-season

Rule, H. (2017, July 6). How social media has changed the world of sports journalism. *National Institute for Social Media*. https://nismonline.org/how-social-media-has-changed-the-world-of-sports-journalism

Sandvig, J., & Bajwa, D. (2004). Information seeking on university web sites: An exploratory study. *Journal of Computer Information Systems, 45*(1), 13–22.

Scott, G. (2018, November 2). 5 ways sports teams use CRM systems. *BizTech Magazine*. https://biztechmagazine.com/article/2018/11/5-ways-sports-teams-use-crm-systems

Seo, W.J., & Green, B.C. (2008). Development of the motivation scale for sport online consumption. *Journal of Sport Management, 22,* 82–109.

Shanmugham, S. (2016, October 24). Why do you use the internet? *World Economic Forum.* www.weforum.org/agenda/2016/10/why-do-you-use-the-internet.

Smith, K. (2019, May 7). 49 incredible Instagram statistics. *Brand Watch.* www.brandwatch.com/blog/instagram-stats

SportBusiness Media staff. (2019, May 24). DAZN picks up MLS rights in multiple markets. *SportBusiness Media.* https://media.sportbusiness.com/news/dazn-picks-up-mls-rights-in-multiple-markets

Sprung, S. (2019, March 15). How the NBA is using virtual reality and augmented reality to get fans closer to the action. *Forbes.* www.forbes.com/sites/shlomosprung/2019/03/15/behind-the-scenes-how-the-nba-is-using-virtual-reality-to-get-fans-closer-to-the-action

Stafford, M., & Stafford, T. (1996). Mechanical commercial avoidance: A uses and gratifications perspective. *Journal of Current Issues and Research in Advertising, 18,* 27–38.

Stafford, T., Stafford, M., & Schkade, L. (2004). Determining uses and gratifications for the Internet. *Decision Sciences, 35*(2), 259–288.

Stephenson, B. (2019, November 9). Twitch: Everything you need to know. *Lifewire.* www.lifewire.com/what-is-twitch-4143337

Stoldt, C., Noble, J., Ross, M., Richardson, T., & Bonsall, J. (2013, March). Advantages and disadvantages of social media use: Perceptions of college athletics communicators. *CoSIDA Strategic Communicators for College Athletics March 2013 E-Digest.* www.cosida.com/media/documents/2013/3/March_2013_EDigest.pdf

Subramanian, P. (2013, September 4). 5 surprising stats about fantasy sports. Yahoo! Finance. http://finance.yahoo.com/blogs/breakout/5-surprising-stats-fantasy-sports-154356461.html

Suggs, D.W. (2015, April 8). Tensions in the press box: Understanding relationships among sports media and source organizations. *Communication & Sport.* doi:10.1177/2167479515577191

Tandoc, E.C. (2014). Journalism is twerking? How web analytics is changing the process of gatekeeping. *New Media & Society, 16*(4), 559-575. doi:10.1177/1461444814530541

Thompson, A.J., Martin, A.J., Gee, S., & Eagleman, A.N. (2014). Examining the development of a social media strategy for a national sport organization: A case study of Tennis New Zealand. *Journal of Applied Sport Management, 6*(2), 42-63.

Top 15 most popular sports websites. (2020, February). *eBiz.* www.ebizmba.com/articles/sports-websites

University of Texas at San Antonio. (2017, November 28). Research studies how professional sports fans use mobile phones. *Phys.org.* https://phys.org/news/2017-11-professional-sports-fans-mobile.html

Weatherhead, R. (2014, March 1). Say it quick, say it well—the attention span of a modern internet consumer. *The Guardian.* www.theguardian.com/media-network/media-network-blog/2012/mar/19/attention-span-internet-consumer

Witkemper, C., Lim, C.H., & Waldburger, A. (2012). Examining the motivations and constraints of Twitter users. *Sport Marketing Quarterly, 21,* 170–183.

Woodward, C. (2016, February 29). DraftKings, FanDuel collected $3b in entry fees last year, analyst says. *The Boston Globe.* www.bostonglobe.com/business/2016/02/29/fantasy-sports-industry-hits-amid-legal-questions-analyst-says/NKw364kiLjv8XcD54vRr4H/story.html

Wytrwal, L. (2018; September 7). Sports and the second screen: Implications for advertisers. *Mindstream Media.* https://mindstreammedia.com/2018/09/07/sports-and-the-second-screen-implications-for-advertisers

Yang, X., Ahmed, Z., Ghingold, M., & Boon, G. (2003). Consumer preferences for commercial web site design: An Asia-Pacific perspective. *Journal of Consumer Marketing, 20*(1), 10–17.

Ylikoski, T. (2005). A sequence analysis of consumers' online searches. *Internet Research, 15*(2), 181–194.

Zorowitz, J. (n.d.) It just got real. *NBC Sports.* https://sportsworld.nbcsports.com/virtual-reality-sports-arkansas-kentucky

Chapter 9

American Marketing Association. (n.d.). Marcom. www.ama.org/topics/marcom.

Andersson, M., & Ekman, P. (2009). Ambassador networks and place branding. *Journal of Place Management and Development, 2*(1), 41–51. doi:10.1108/17538330910942799

Arnett, D.B., & Laverie, D.A. (2000, September/October). Fan characteristics and sporting event attendance: Examining variance in attendance. *Sports Marketing & Sponsorship,* 219–231.

Bashford, S. (2017, March 6). What you need to know about sports marketing in 2017 and beyond. *Campaign.* www.campaignlive.co.uk/article/need-know-sports-marketing-2017-beyond/1424873.

Blank, J. (2019, October 10). China bends another American institution to its will. *The Atlantic.* www.theatlantic.com/international/archive/2019/10/nba-victim-china-economic-might/599773

Brooks, C.M., & Harris, K.K. (1998). Celebrity athlete endorsement: An overview of the key theoretical issues. *Sport Marketing Quarterly, 7*(2), 34–44.

Bruhn, M., & Schnebelen, S. (2017). Integrated marketing communication—from an instrumental to a customer-centric perspective. *European Journal of Marketing, 51*(3), 464-489. doi:10.1108/EJM-08-2015-0591

Burmann, C. (2010). A call for "user-generated branding." *Journal of Brand Management, 18*(1), 1–4.

Burmann, C., & Arnhold, U. (2009). *User-generated branding: State of the art research*. Wiesbaden, Germany: Gabler Verlag.

Chelladurai, P., & Chang, K. (2000). Targets and standards of quality in sport services. *Sport Management Review, 3*, 1–22.

Constantinescu, M. (2011). The specifics of the sport product and their implications within the marketing activity. *International Journal of Economic Practices and Theories, 1*(2), 71–76.

Digital Marketing Institute. (2018, March 27). Integrated marketing: 7 successful campaigns through the decades. *Digital Marketing Institute.* https://digitalmarketinginstitute.com/en-gb/blog/27-03-18-integrated-marketing-7-successful-campaigns-through-the-decades

Dimock, M. (2019, January 17). Defining generations: Where Millennials end and Generation Z begins. Pew Research Center. www.pewresearch.org/fact-tank/2019/01/17/where-millennials-end-and-generation-z-begins

Geller, G. (2019, May 22). Baby boomers spend more than Millennials—yet are ignored by advertisers. *MediaPost.* www.mediapost.com/publications/article/336177/baby-boomers-spend-more-than-millennials-yet-ar.html

Geurin A.N., & Burch, L.M. (2017). User-generated branding via social media: An examination of six running brands. *Sport Management Review, 20*, 273–284. doi:10.1016/j.smr.2016.09.001

Gladden, J. (2014). Managing sport brands. In B.J. Mullin, S. Hardy, & W.A. Sutton (Eds.), *Sport Marketing* (4th ed., pp. 161–178). Champaign, IL: Human Kinetics.

Gladden, J.M., Milne, G.R., & Sutton, W.A. (1998). A conceptual framework for assessing brand equity in Division I college athletics. *Journal of Sport Management, 12*, 1–19.

Gough, C. (2019, August 9). Super Bowl average costs of a 30-second TV advertisement from 2002 to 2019 (in million U.S. dollars). *Statista.* www.statista.com/statistics/217134/total-advertisement-revenue-of-super-bowls

Gronroos, C. (1991). The marketing strategy continuum: Towards a marketing concept for the 1990s. *Management Decision, 29*(1), 7–13.

Halicka, M. (2016, July 20). The trends that are redefining the match day experience. *Eventbrite.* www.eventbrite.co.uk/blog/trends-redefining-game-day-experience-ds00

Hartmann, W.R., & Klapper, D. (2018). Super Bowl ads. *Marketing Science, 37*(1), 78-96. doi:10.1287/mksc.2017.1055

Hobbs, T. (2017, May 9). Is Nike's "Breaking2" marathon bid more than just a marketing stunt? *Marketing Week.* www.marketingweek.com/nike-dominated-social-media-running-2-marketing-stunt

Holmes, R. (2019, February 19). We now see 5,000 ads a day . . . and it's getting worse. *LinkedIn.* www.linkedin.com/pulse/have-we-reached-peak-ad-social-media-ryan-holmes

IEG. (2017, December 18). Sponsor survey reveals dissatisfaction with property partners. *IEG Sponsorship Report.* www.sponsorship.com/Report/2017/12/18/Sponsor-Survey-Reveals-Dissatisfaction-With-Proper.aspx

IEG. (2018, January 29). Measurement essentials part 1. *IEG Sponsorship Report.* www.sponsorship.com/Report/2018/01/29/Measurement-Essentials-Part-1.aspx

Influencer Marketing Hub. (2019, September 12). What is influencer marketing: An in-depth look at marketing's next big thing. https://influencermarketinghub.com/what-is-influencer-marketing

Jones, M.J., & Schumann, D.W. (2000). The strategic use of celebrity athlete endorsers in *Sports Illustrated*: An historic perspective. *Sport Marketing Quarterly, 9*(2), 65–76.

Keller, K.L. (1998). *Strategic brand management: Building, measuring, and managing brand equity*. Upper Saddle River, NJ: Prentice Hall.

Kelley, S.W., & Turley, L.W. (2001). Consumer perceptions of service quality attributes at sporting events. *Journal of Business Research, 54*, 161–166.

Keyhole. (2018, May 16). How the USTA is leveraging social media to reach the next generation of tennis players. https://keyhole.co/stories/usta-usopen-leverages-social-media-analytics-to-reach-generationz-millenials

Kulpa, J. (2017, October 24). Why is customer relationship management so important? *Forbes.* www.forbes.com/sites/forbesagencycouncil/2017/10/24/why-is-customer-relationship-management-so-important/#363212587dac

Lefton, T. (2019, April 1). Youth movement: Reaching Gen Z. *Sports Business Journal.* www.sportsbusinessdaily.com/Journal/Issues/2019/04/01/In-Depth/Gen-Z.aspx

Messner, M., Dunbar, M., & Hunt, D. (2000) The televised sport manhood formula. *Journal of Sport & Social Issues, 24*, 380–394.

Miloch, K. (2005). Making it in the minors: Seven simple steps to achieving sustained financial health. *SMART Online Journal, 2*(1).

Miloch, K., & Lambrecht, K. (2006). Consumer awareness of sponsorship at grassroots sport events. *Sport Marketing Quarterly, 15*, 147–154.

Mondello, M., & Kamke, C. (2014). The introduction and application of sports analytics in professional sport organizations. *Journal of Applied Sport Management, 6*(2), 1–12.

Mullin, B., Hardy, S., & Sutton, W. (2014). *Sport marketing* (4th ed.). Champaign, IL: Human Kinetics.

Mumcu, C. (2019). Business analytics in women's professional sports. In N. Lough & A.N. Geurin (Eds.), *Routledge handbook of the business of women's sport* (pp. 239–251). London: Routledge.

Nelson, A. (2019, July 17). Women drive majority of consumer purchasing and it's time to meet their needs. *Inc.* www.inc.com/amy-nelson/women-drive-majority-of-consumer-purchasing-its-time-to-meet-their-needs.html

Newland, B., Geurin, A.N., Brown, B., Gennaro, V., & Valenta, B. (2019, May). *The great divide: How younger generations are disrupting the sport consumption landscape.* Paper presented at the 2019 North American Society for Sport Management Conference, New Orleans, LA.

Nielsen Sports. (2018). Year in Sports Media Report: U.S. 2017. https://nielsensports.com/reports/2017-year-sports-media-u-s-report

Nielsen Sports. (2019). Power of one: Athletes as endorsers. http://nielsensports.com/wp-content/uploads/2014/09/nielsen-power-of-one-athletes-as-endorsers.pdf

Peetz, T. (2019). You're just not our type: An examination of the obstacles faced by women athlete endorsers. In N. Lough & A.N. Geurin (Eds.), *Routledge handbook of the business of women's sport* (pp. 429–438). London: Routledge.

Pitts, B.G., & Stotlar, D.K. (2002). *Fundamentals of sport marketing* (2nd ed.). Morgantown, WV: Fitness Information Technology.

Pritchard, M.P., Havitz, M.E., & Howard, D.R. (1999). Analyzing the commitment–loyalty link in service contexts. *Journal of the Academy of Marketing Science, 27*(3), 333–348.

Roderick, L. (2017, January 31). New "This Girl Can" campaign to target "teens, mums and their grandmothers." *Marketing Week.* www.marketingweek.com/new-girl-can-campaign

Schouten, A.P., Janssen, L., & Verspaget, M. (2019). Celebrity vs. influencer endorsements in advertising: The role of identification, credibility, and product-endorser fit. *International Journal of Advertising,* advance online publication. doi:10.1080/02650487.2019.1634898

Shayon, S. (2017, November 2). #LoveOverBias: P&G refreshes "Thank You Mom" with inclusivity them. *Brand Channel.* www.brandchannel.com/2017/11/02/pg-love-over-bias-thank-you-mom-2018-winter-olympics

The SI Staff. (2018, September 19). Ranking the top 10 athletes by endorsement income for 2018. *Sports Illustrated.* www.si.com/sports-illustrated/2018/ranking-top-10-athletes-endorsement-deals-income

Sport England. (n.d.). This girl can. www.sportengland.org/our-work/women/this-girl-can

Stotlar, D. (2005). *Developing successful sports marketing plans.* Morgantown, WV: Fitness Information Technology.

Tan, H. (2019, October 21). China state media: NBA's Silver will face "retribution" for saying Beijing wanted Rockets GM fired. *CNBC.* www.cnbc.com/2019/10/21/china-state-media-on-nba-commissioner-adam-silver-hong-kong-tweet-fallout.html

Van Leeuwen, L., Quick, S., & Daniel, K. (2002). The sport spectator satisfaction model: A conceptual framework for understanding the satisfaction of spectators. *Sport Management Review, 5*(2), 99–128.

Wakefield, K.L., Blodgett, J.G., & Sloan, H.J. (1996). Measurement and management of the sportscape. *Journal of Sport Management, 10*, 15–31.

Wann, D.L., & Branscombe, N.R. (1993). Sports fans: Measuring degree of identification with their team. *International Journal of Sport Psychology, 24*, 1–17.

Westerbeek, H.M., & Shilbury, D. (2003). A conceptual model for sport services marketing research: Integrating quality, value, and satisfaction. *International Journal of Sports Marketing & Sponsorship, 5*(1), 11–27.

Zhang, J., Lam, E., & Connaughton, D. (2003, March/April). General market demand variables associated with professional sport consumption. *International Journal of Sports Marketing and Sponsorship*, 33–55.

Zillgitt, J. & Medina, M. (2019, October 9). As impasse over pro-Hong Kong tweet simmers, what's at stake for the NBA in China? *USA Today.* https://eu.usatoday.com/story/sports/nba/2019/10/09/nba-china-hong-kong-whats-at-stake/3912447002

Chapter 10

Apstein, S. (2019, October 22). Astros staffer's outburst at female reporters illustrates MLB's forgive-and-forget attitude toward domestic violence. *Sports Illustrated.* www.si.com/mlb/2019/10/22/houston-astros-roberto-osuna-suspension

Bernays, E. (1952). *Public relations.* Norman, OK: University of Oklahoma.

Bird, H. (2018, August 8). "It's not tolerable": How offensive tweets are spurring an evolution in sports. *Boston Globe.* www.boston.com/sports/sports-news/2018/08/08/josh-hader-sean-newcomb-tweets

Brewer, D. (2014, August 1). The importance of fact-checking for journalists. *Media Helping Media.* www.mediahelpingmedia.org/training-resources/journalism-basics/640-fact-checking-separates-journalism-from-rumour-and-gossip

Bronzan, R.T. (1977). *Public relations, promotions, and fundraising for athletic and physical education programs.* New York: Wiley.

Ciment, S. (2019, August 2). These are the 10 best-selling sneakers of the year so far. *Business Insider.* www.businessinsider.com/best-selling-sneakers-of-the-year-2019-8?r=US&IR=T

Connors, K. (2014). Public relations. In B.J. Mullin, S. Hardy, & W.A. Sutton (Eds.), *Sport marketing* (4th ed., pp. 311–341). Champaign, IL: Human Kinetics.

Cutlip, S.M., Center, A.H., & Broom, G.M. (2000). *Effective public relations* (8th ed.). Edgewood Cliffs, NJ: Prentice Hall.

Davis, A. (2004). *Mastering public relations.* New York: Macmillan.

ESPN.com News Service. (2016, March 22). Indian Wells CEO Raymond Moore resigns after remarks drew outrage. ESPN. www.espn.co.uk/tennis/story/_/id/15039381/indian-wells-ceo-raymond-moore-resigns-remarks-drew-outrage

Folkenflik, D. (2019, October 22). Astros executive's rant at reporters draws firestorm on eve of series. NPR. www.npr.org/2019/10/22/772368868/astros-executives-rant-at-reporters-draws-firestorm-on-eve-of-series.

Frangi, A., & Fletcher, M. (2002). *So you want media coverage: A simple guide on how to get it and how to handle it.* St. Lucia, Queensland: University of Queensland.

Funk, D.C., Beaton, A., & Alexandris, K. (2012). Sport consumer motivation: Autonomy and control orientations that regulate fan behaviours. *Sport Management Review, 15*(3), 355–367. doi:10.106/j.smr.2011.11.001.

Grossman, A. (2015, September 17). The PR pro's guide to effective media relations. *Adweek.* www.adweek.com/digital/the-pr-pros-guide-to-effective-media-relations

Grunig, J., & Grunig, L. (1992). Models of public relations and communications. In J. Grunig (Ed.), *Excellence in public relations and communication management* (pp. 285–326). Hillsdale, NJ: Erlbaum.

Guth, D., & Marsh, C. (2003). *Public relations: A values-driven approach* (2nd ed.). Boston: Allyn & Bacon.

Hawkins, M., & Terrell, R. (2018, January 24). GSU students speak up about soccer player's racial slur on social media. *WABE.* www.wabe.org/gsu-students-speak-soccer-players-racial-slur-social-media

Hill, M. (2011, February 11). The benefits of media training for athletes. Sports Networker. www.sportsnetworker.com/2011/02/11/media-training-athletes

Hunt, T., & Grunig, J. (1994). *Public relations techniques.* Fort Worth, TX: Harcourt Brace.

Keniston, P. (2018, January 31). How to write press release headlines people actually read. *Marx Communications.* https://b2bprblog.marxcommunications.com/b2bpr/how-to-write-press-release-headlines-that-people-read

Kline, R.S. (1996). Effective public relations—A model for business. *Management Research News, 19*(6), 55–60.

Lontos, P. (2004). Max your relationship with the media. *Consulting to Management, 15*(4), 29–31.

Mangan, D. (2019, October 24). Houston Astros fire assistant general manager Brandon Taubman for taunting female reporters. CNBC. www.cnbc.com/2019/10/24/houston-astros-fire-brandon-taubman-after-he-taunted-female-reporters.html

Miloch, K., & Pedersen, P. (2006). Sport information directors and the media: An analysis of a highly symbiotic relationship. *Journal of Contemporary Athletics, 2*(1), 91–103.

Mullin, B.J., Hardy, S., & Sutton, W.A. (2014). *Sport marketing* (4th ed.). Champaign, IL: Human Kinetics.

Nichols, W., Moynahan, P., Hall, A., & Taylor, J. (2002). *Media relations in sport.* Morgantown, WV: Fitness Information Technology.

Prezly. (2018). The best-managed PR crises of 2018. *Prezly.* www.prezly.com/academy/relationships/crisis-communication/the-best-managed-pr-crises-of-2018

Public Relations Society of America. (2019). About Public Relations. www.prsa.org/about/all-about-pr.

Raabe, S. (2017, September 8). The relationship between social media and PR in the digital age. *Dow Social.* https://dowsocial.com/relationship-social-media-and-pr

Saia, C. (2016, September 7). Reputation: How to protect, preserve and enhance a precious asset. *The Wall Street Journal.* https://deloitte.wsj.com/riskandcompliance/2016/09/07/reputation-how-to-protect-preserve-and-enhance-a-precious-asset-2

Salzman, M. (2016, June 3). Media relations: Still important. *Forbes.* www.forbes.com/sites/mariansalzman/2016/06/03/media-relations-still-important/#525baf3027f0

Schuman, R. (2019, April 17). The most hated gymnast in the NCAA. *Slate.* https://slate.com/culture/2019/04/mykayla-skinner-utah-red-rocks-ncaa-gymnastics-championships.html

Seitel, F.P. (2001). *The practice of public relations* (8th ed.). Upper Saddle River, NJ: Prentice Hall.

Seitel, F.P. (2014). *The practice of public relations* (12th ed.). Upper Saddle River, NJ: Prentice Hall.

Sherwood, M., Nicholson, M., & Marjoribanks, T. (2017). Controlling the message and the medium? *Digital Journalism, 5*(5), 513–531. doi:10.1080/21670811.2016.1239546

Sims, C. (2014, September 23). Pacers' Larry Bird calls Paul George's tweets on Ray Rice, domestic violence "thoughtless." *Indianapolis Star.* https://eu.indystar.com/story/sports/nba/pacers/2014/09/11/pacers-paul-george-talks-ray-rice/15435895

Skerik, S. (2012, August 7). Writing press releases that generate results. PR Newswire. www.prnewswire.com/blog/writing-press-releases-that-generate-results-4495.html

Smith, R.D. (2012). *Becoming a public relations writer: A writing workbook for emerging and established media* (4th ed.). New York: Routledge.

Stoldt, G.C., Dittmore, S.W., Ross, M., & Branvold, S.E. (2021). *Sport public relations* (3rd ed.). Champaign, IL: Human Kinetics.

Stoldt, G.C., Dittmore, S.W., & Pedersen, P.M. (2019). Communication in the sport industry. In P.M. Pedersen & L. Thibault (Eds.), *Contemporary sport management* (6th ed., pp. 292–311). Champaign, IL: Human Kinetics.

Tucker, D.L., & Wrench, J.S. (Eds.). (2016). *Casing sport communication*. Dubuque, IA: Kendall/Hunt.

Wenner, L.A. (1998). Preface. In L.A. Wenner (Ed.), *MediaSport* (pp. xiii–xiv). London: Routledge.

Wynne, R. (2018, May 24). NFL fumbles the national anthem and creates a PR nightmare. *Forbes*. www.forbes.com/sites/robertwynne/2018/05/24/nfl-fumbles-the-national-anthem-and-creates-a-pr-nightmare/#5afb48939e3c

Chapter 11

Abbas, N.M. (2019, August 13). NBA data analytics: Changing the game. Towardsdatascience.com. Retrieved from https://towardsdatascience.com/nba-data-analytics-changing-the-game-a9ad59d1f116

Abeza, G., O'Reilly, N., & Nadeau, J. (2014). Sport communication: A multidimensional assessment of the field's development. *International Journal of Sport Communication, 7*, 289–316.

Abeza, G., Seguin, B., O'Reilly, N., & Nzindukiyimana, O. (2017, September). Social media as a relationship marketing tool in professional sport: A netnographical exploration. International *Journal of Sport Communication, 10*(3), p. 325-334.

About Nielsen. (n.d.). Nielsen. www.nielsen.com/us/en/about-us.html

About Pew Research Center. (n.d.). Pew Research Center. www.pewresearch.org/about

Adler, K.C. (2016, March 11). ESPN. http://espnmediazone.com/us/press-releases/2016/03/espn-stats-information-group-to-power-new-destination-for-analytics-on-espn-com

Alliance for Audited Media. (n.d.). About AAM. http://auditedmedia.com/about

Altheide, D. (1996). Qualitative media analysis. *Qualitative Research Methods, 38*. Thousand Oaks, CA: Sage.

Andrew, D.P.S., Pedersen, P.M., & McEvoy, C.D. (2020). *Research methods and design in sport management* (2nd ed.). Champaign, IL: Human Kinetics.

Arte Moreno makes influence felt in Angels' hiring of Joe Maddon. (2019, October 17). *Sports Business Daily*. Retrieved from https://www.sportsbusinessdaily.com/Daily/Issues/2019/10/17/Franchises/Angels.aspx

Audioboom reaches agreement for Nielsen's podcast listener buying power service. (2019, September 24). Nielsen.com. Retrieved from https://www.nielsen.com/us/en/press-releases/2019/audioboom-reaches-agreement-for-nielsens-podcast-listener-buying-power-service/

Aycock, J. (2018, September 20). Dish taps Nielsen for digital ad measurement. Seekingalpha.com. Retrieved from https://seekingalpha.com/news/3391826-dish-taps-nielsen-digital-ad-measurement

Babbie, E. (1998). *The practice of social research* (8th ed.). Belmont, CA: Wadsworth.

Bacon, J.U. (2013). *Fourth and long: The fight for the soul of college football*. New York: Simon & Schuster.

Bagdikian, B. (2004). *The new media monopoly* (20th ed.). Boston: Beacon.

Baier, S. (2018, September 25). Understanding the female NFL fan: 'Seekers' vs. 'Savors.' *AdAge*. Retrieved from https://adage.com/article/taylor/understanding-female-nfl-fan-seekers-savors/315020

Barthel, M. (2019, July 23). 5 Key takeaways about the state of the news media in 2018. Pewresearch.org. Retrieved from https://www.pewresearch.org/fact-tank/2019/07/23/key-takeaways-state-of-the-news-media-2018/

Baumgartner, J. (2015, February 19). Nielsen moves ahead on TV-ratings upgrades. *Multichannel News*. www.multichannel.com/news/technology/nielsen-moves-ahead-local-tv-improvements/388150

Beck, H. (2013, February 14). Advanced statistics added to revamped NBA site. *The New York Times*. Retrieved from https://www.nytimes.com/2013/02/15/sports/basketball/nbas-site-to-feature-updated-statistics-database.html

Berelson, B. (1952). *Content analysis in communication research*. New York: The Free Press.

Billings, A.C., Butterworth, M.L., & Turman, P.D. (2012). *Communication and sport: Surveying the field*. Thousand Oaks, CA: Sage.

Billings, A.C., & Hardin, M. (Eds.). (2014). *Routledge handbook of sport and new media*. London and New York: Routledge.

Billings, A.C., Qiao, F., Conlin, L., & Nie, T. (2017). Permanently desiring the temporary? Snapchat, social media, and the shifting motivations of sport fans. *Communication & Sport, 5*(1), 10-26. doi:10.1177/2167479515588760

Bodenheimer, G., & Phillips, D.T. (2015). *Every town is a sports town: Business leadership at ESPN, from the mailroom to the boardroom*. New York: Grand Central.

Bostrom, R.N. (1998). *Communication research*. Prospect Heights, IL: Waveland.

boyd, d. & Crawford, K. (2012). Critical questions for Big Data: Provocations for a cultural, technological, and scholarly phenomenon. *Information, Communication & Society, 15*(5), 662-679.

Broughton, D. (2013, October 14). Report spotlights female NFL fans. *Street & Smith's Sports Business Journal*. www.sportsbusinessdaily.com/Journal/Issues/2013/10/14/Leagues-and-Governing-Bodies/NFL-women.aspx

Broughton, D. (2015, March 16). AT&T pushes Verizon for NFL fan awareness. *Sports Business Journal*. www.sportsbusinessdaily.com/Journal/Issues/2015/03/16/Research-and-Ratings/NFL-Sponsor-Loyalty.aspx

Broughton, D. (2017, July 24). Stalwarts thrive; AmEx, Taco Bell struggle in NBA sponsor loyalty survey. *Sports Business Daily*. Retrieved from https://www.sportsbusinessdaily.com/Journal/Issues/2017/07/24/Research-and-Ratings/NBA-sponsor-loyalty.aspx

Chang, Y. (2019). Spectators' emotional responses in tweets during the Super Bowl 50 game. *Sport Management Review, 22*(3), p. 346-362.

Cherubini, F. (2014, August 1). When data drives the news: A look at analytics beyond the page view. Media Analytics Summit. http://mediaanalyticssummit.com/blog/2014/08/06/when-data-drives-the-news-a-look-at-analytics-beyond-the-page-view

Clark, K. (2018, December 1). The Kareem Hunt scandal shows the NFL hasn't learned anything since Ray Rice. The Ringer. www.theringer.com/nfl/2018/12/1/18120220/kareem-hunt-kansas-city-chiefs-nfl-league-office

Colhoun, D. (2015, May 1). Is the news behaving more like advertising? *Columbia Journalism Review*. www.cjr.org/analysis/news_behaving_more_like_advertising.php

Company overview of Nielsen Media Research, Inc. (2016). *Bloomberg Business*. www.bloomberg.com/research/stocks/private/snapshot.asp?privcapId=386044

comScore. (2016). About us. www.comscore.com/About-comScore

comScore and Rentrak complete merger, creating the new model for a dynamic, cross-platform world. (2016, February 1). *Rentrak*. http://investor.rentrak.com/releasedetail.cfm?ReleaseID=952532

comScore facts at a glance. (n.d.). *comScore*. www.comscore.com/About-comScore/comScore-Facts-at-a-Glance

Continuous diary measurement launches in 46 Nielsen audio markets. (2019, August 13). Niesen.com. Retrieved from https://www.nielsen.com/us/en/press-releases/2019/continuous-diary-measurement-launches-in-46-nielsen-audio-markets/

Corporate profile. (2016). Nielsen. http://ir.nielsen.com/investor-relations/Home/corporate-profile/default.aspx

Creedon, P.J. (1994). Women, media and sport: Creating and reflecting gender values. In P.J. Creedon (Ed.), *Women, media and sport: Challenging gender values* (pp. 3–27). Thousand Oaks, CA: Sage.

Creedon, P. (2014). Women, social media, and sport: Global digital communication weaves a web. *Television & New Media*, 15(8), 711-716.

Dorsey, B. (2013). Sports teams grow up with Big Data and predictive analytics. SEAT, Spring, 76-78.

Entman, R.M. (1993). Framing: Toward clarification of a fractured paradigm. *Journal of Communication, 43*(4), 51–58.

Exact commercial ratings (2016). *Rentrak*. www.rentrak.com/downloads/product_info/comScore-Exact-Commercial-Ratings-Infosheet.pdf

Fairclough, N. (1995). *Critical discourse analysis*. London: Longman.

Finberg, H.I., & Klinger, L. (2014, April). *Core skills for the future of journalism*. Poynter Institute for Media Studies. www.newsu.org/course_files/CoreSkills_Futureof-Journalism2014v2.pdf

Fitts, A.S. (2015, May 11). When metrics drive newsroom culture. *Columbia Journalism Review*. www.cjr.org/analysis/how_should_metrics_drive_newsroom_culture.php.

Flomenbaum, A. (2015, March 9). Nielsen study: Strong correlation between Twitter TV activity and general audience engagement. *AdWeek*. www.adweek.com/lostremote/nielsen-study-strong-correlation-between-twitter-tv-activity-and-general-audience-engagement/50824

Folkerts, J., & Lacy, S. (2004). *The media in your life: An introduction to mass communication* (3rd ed). Boston: Pearson.

Foss, S.K. (2004). *Rhetorical criticism: Exploration and practice* (3rd ed.). Long Grove, IL: Waveland.

FOX Sports and Nielsen study, "The 5th network," finds regional sports networks are most essential cable channels to sports fans. (2016, December 14). FOXsports.com. Retrieved from https://www.foxsports.com/presspass/latest-news/2016/12/14/fox-sports-and-nielsen-study-the-5th-network-finds-regional-sports-networks-are-most-essential-cable-channels-to-sports-fans

Friends with benefits: TV-connected devices bring consumers together in the living room. (2015, November 19). Nielsen. www.nielsen.com/us/en/insights/news/2015/friends-with-benefits-tv-connected-devices-bring-consumers-together.html

Gamson, W.A. (1989). News as framing. *American Behavioral Scientist, 33*(2), 157-161.

Gans, H.J. (1979). *Deciding what's news: A study of CBS Evening News, NBC Nightly News, Newsweek, and Time*. New York: Vintage.

Gaudiosi, J. (2016, January 22). Why ESPN is investing in eSports coverage. *Fortune*. Retrieved from https://fortune.com/2016/01/22/espn-invests-in-esports-coverage/

Gitlin, T. (1983). *Inside prime time*. New York: Pantheon Books.

Gitlin, T. (2000). *Inside prime time with a new introduction*. Berkeley: University of California.

Global Strategy Group. (2015). ESPN [case study]. http://globalstrategygroup.com/case-studies/espn

Goffman, E. (1974). *Frame analysis: An essay on the organization of experience*. Boston: Northeastern University Press.

Gottfried, M. (2016, April 4). Why Nielsen's TV data just got harder to beat. *Wall Street Journal*. www.wsj.com/articles/why-nielsens-tv-data-just-got-harder-to-beat-1459799093

Gratton, C., & Jones, I. (200). *Research methods for sport studies*. London: Routledge.

Gratton, C., & Jones, I. (2010). *Research methods for sport studies* (2nd ed.). New York: Taylor & Francis.

Greenfeld, K.T. (2013, July 18). Fox Sports 1's strategy vs. ESPN: "Jockularity." Bloomberg. www.bloomberg.com/bw/articles/2013-07-18/fox-sports-1s-strategy-vs-dot-espn-jockularity

Hammersley, M., & Atkinson, P. (2002). *Ethnography: Principles in practice* (2nd ed.). London: Routledge.

Hardin, R., & Zuegner, C. (2003). Life, liberty, and the pursuit of golf balls. *Journalism History, 29*(2), 82–90.

Holcomb, J., & Mitchell, A. (2014, March 26). The revenue picture for American journalism and how it is changing. Pew Research Center.www.journalism.org/2014/03/26/the-revenue-picture-for-american-journalism-and-how-it-is-changing

How we measure. (2015). Nielsen. www.nielsen.com/us/en/solutions/measurement.html

Jankowski, N.W., & Wester, F. (1991). The qualitative tradition in social science inquiry: Contributions to mass communication research. In K.B. Jensen & N.W. Jankowski (Eds.), *A handbook of qualitative methodologies for mass communication research* (pp. 44–74). London: Routledge.

Jenny, S.E., Manning, R.D., Keiper, M.C., & Olrich, T.W. (2018). Virtual(ly) athletes: Where eSports fit within the definition of "sport." *Quest, 69*(1), 1-18.

Jensen, J.A. (2015, June 22). Advanced analytics create "Moneyball" approach in marketing. *Street & Smith's Sports Business Journal.* www.sportsbusinessdaily.com/Journal/Issues/2015/06/22/Opinion/Jonathan-Jensen.aspx

Jensen, K.B. (1991). Humanistic scholarship as qualitative science: Contributions to mass communication research. In K.B. Jensen & N.W. Jankowski (Eds.), *A handbook of qualitative methodologies for mass communication research* (pp. 17–43). London: Routledge.

Jensen, K.B., & Jankowski, N.W. (1991). *A handbook of qualitative methodologies for mass communication research.* London: Routledge.

Jones, I. (2015). *Research methods for sports studies* (3rd ed.). New York: Routledge.

Jurkowitz, M. (2014, March 26). The growth in digital reporting. Pew Research Center. www.journalism.org/2014/03/26/the-growth-in-digital-reporting

Kaplan, D. (2014, June 16). NFL gives teams expanded fan experience study. *Street & Smith's Sports Business Journal.* www.sportsbusinessdaily.com/Journal/Issues/2014/06/16/Leagues-and-Governing-Bodies/NFL-fans.aspx

Kaplan, D., & Fisher, E. (2015, April 20). NFL buys stake in stats firm. *Street & Smith's Sports Business Journal.* www.sportsbusinessdaily.com/Journal/Issues/2015/04/20/Leagues-and-Governing-Bodies/NFL-sportradar.aspx

Kinkema, K.M., & Harris, J.C. (1998). MediaSport studies: Key research and emerging issues. In L.A. Wenner (Ed.), *MediaSport* (pp. 27–56). London: Routledge.

Kozinets, R. (2010). *Netnography: Doing ethnographic research online.* Los Angeles: Sage.

Kozman, C. (2013, June). The Tiger Woods scandal in the media: Measuring attribute effects on the public. *International Journal of Sport Communication, 6*(2), 214-233.

Krippendorf, K. (1980). *Content analysis.* Beverly Hills: Sage.

Lafayette, J. (2019, May 21). McCarthy tapped to run Sinclair's Cubs network. *Broadcasting & Cable.* www.broadcastingcable.com/news/mccarthy-tapped-to-run-sinclairs-cubs-network

Londergan, J. (2019, January 2). Three predictions for sports digital media in 2019. *PC Magazine.* Retrieved from https://www.pcmag.com/roundup/337820/the-best-social-media-management-analytics-tools

Lowery, S.A., & DeFleur, M.L. (1995). *Milestones in mass communication research: Media effects* (3rd ed.). White Plains, NY: Longman.

Luker, R. (2015, June 29). Study of avidity reveals 2 dimensions of sports fan. *Street & Smith's Sports Business Journal.* www.sportsbusinessdaily.com/Journal/Issues/2015/06/29/Research-and-Ratings/Up-Next-with-Rich-Luker.aspx

MacGregor, J., & Evanitsky, O. (2005). *Sunday money: Speed! Lust! Madness! Death! A hot lap around America with NASCAR.* New York: Harper Collins.

Marie Hardin: Biography. (2019). Penn State College of Communications. http://comm.psu.edu/people/individual/marie-hardin

Marsh, P. (2015, February 22). Research shows ROI of audience, advertising analytics. International News Media Association. www.inma.org/blogs/ahead-of-the-curve/post.cfm/research-shows-roi-of-audience-advertising-analytics.

McBride, K. (2011, December 27). Letter of intent. ESPN. http://espn.go.com/espn/story/_/id/7379853/espn-tries-solve-equation-women-sports-fans

McCaskill, S. (2018, December 31). Sports technology year in review: Five of the biggest trends of 2018. *Forbes.* Retrieved from https://www.forbes.com/sites/stevemccaskill/2018/12/31/sports-technology-year-in-review-five-of-the-biggest-trends-of-2018/#6cf219ce1f38

McClellan, S. (2015, March 25). More screens are better than one: ESPN unveils new cross-screen research at 4As. MediaPost Agency Daily. www.mediapost.com/publications/article/246443/more-screens-are-better-than-one-espn-unveils-new.html

McCracken, G. (1988). *The long interview*: Qualitative research methods, 13. Newbury Park, CA: Sage.

McGregor, S. (2013, March 18). CAR hits the mainstream. *Columbia Journalism Review.* www.cjr.org/data_points/computer_assisted_reporting.php.

McLaughlin, M. (2018, December 13). How data analytics is revolutionizing sports. BizTechmagazine.com.

Retrieved from https://biztechmagazine.com/article/2018/12/how-data-analytics-revolutionizing-sports

McQuail, D. (1996). *Mass communication theory: An introduction*. (3rd ed.). London: Sage.

McQuail, D. (2010). *McQuail's mass communication theory* (6th ed.). Los Angeles: Sage.

Meyer, P. (2002). *Precision journalism: A reporter's introduction to social science methods* (4th ed.). Lanham, MD: Rowman & Littlefield.

Mitchell, A. (2015, April 29). State of the news media 2015. Pew Research Center. www.journalism.org/2015/04/29/state-of-the-news-media-2015

MLB franchise notes: Girardi checks all the boxes for Phillies. (2019, October 25). *Sports Business Daily*. Retrieved from https://www.sportsbusinessdaily.com/Daily/Issues/2019/10/25/Franchises/MLB-Fran-Notes.aspx

Mullin, B.J., Hardy, S., & Sutton, W.A. (2000). *Sport marketing* (2nd ed.). Champaign, IL: Human Kinetics.

Nelson, K. (2018, December 24). 2019 will see a change in how sports are processed over social media. *Adweek*. Retrieved from https://www.adweek.com/brand-marketing/2019-will-see-a-change-in-how-sports-are-processed-over-social-media/

NFL allocates over $17M to three groups to fund concussion, brain health research. (2018, January 8). *Sports Business Daily*. Retrieved from https://www.sportsbusinessdaily.com/Daily/Issues/2018/01/08/Leagues-and-Governing-Bodies/NFL-Research.aspx?hl=NFL+research+study&sc=0

NFL stats on steroids (n.d.). Armchairanalysis.com. Retrieved from https://www.armchairanalysis.com

Nielsen acquires Arbitron. (2013, September 30). Nielsen. www.nielsen.com/us/en/press-room/2013/nielsen-acquires-arbitron.html

Nielsen audio measurement. (2018.). Nielsen. www.nielsen.com/us/en/solutions/measurement/audio.html.

Nielsen announces significant expansion to sample sizes in local television markets. (2014, May 28). Nielsen. www.nielsen.com/us/en/press-room/2014/nielsen-announces-significant-expansion-to-sample-sizes-in-local-tv-markets.html

Nielsen audio measurement. (n.d.). Nielsen. www.nielsen.com/us/en/solutions/measurement/audio.html

Nielsen launches digital audio ratings to quantify broadcast radio's online consumption. (2016, March 17). CBS19. www.cbs19.tv/story/31497702/nielsen-launches-digital-audio-ratings-to-quantify-broadcast-radios-online-consumption

Nielsen social (2016). Nielsen. www.nielsensocial.com

Nielsen Sports' "Year in Sports Media Report: U.S., 2017. (2018). Retrieved from https://radioconnects.ca/wp-content/uploads/2018/02/Nielsen-2017-Year-in-Sports.pdf

Nielsen statement: National and local market TV accreditation status. (2015, December 30). Nielsen. www.nielsen.com/us/en/press-room/2015/nielsen-statement-national-and-local-market-tv-accreditation-status.html

Nielsen Total Audience: Putting TV, radio, and digital on level playing field. (2015, June 26). Nielsen. http://sites.nielsen.com/newscenter/nielsen-total-audience-putting-tv-radio-and-digital-on-level-playing-field

Novy-Williams, E. (2019, August 12). NFL takes first major gambling step with Sportradar data deal. *Bloomberg.com*. Retrieved from https://www.bloomberg.com/news/articles/2019-08-12/nfl-takes-first-major-gambling-step-with-sportradar-data-deal

One-on-one, CBS's research guru says DVRs are good for network TV. (2006). *Street & Smith's Sports Business Journal, 8*(26), 34.

Online. (2015). Nielsen. www.nielsen.com/us/en/solutions/measurement/online.html

Onyewu, U. (2019, July 18). Sampling is the key to representative person-level measurement. Nielsen.com. Retrieved from https://www.nielsen.com/us/en/insights/article/2019/sampling-is-the-key-to-representative-person-level-measurement/

Ourand, J. (2015, July 13). Obama 2012 research firm to battle Nielsen. *Street & Smith's Sports Business Journal*. www.sportsbusinessdaily.com/Journal/Issues/2015/07/13/Media/Rentrak.aspx

Pallotta, F. (2020, February 3). Super Bowl LIV averaged 102 million viewers. CNN.com. Retrieved from https://www.cnn.com/2020/02/03/media/super-bowl-2020-ratings/index.html

Pan, Z, & Kosicki, G.M. (1993). Framing analysis: An approach to news discourse. *Political Communication, 10*, 55–75.

Pedersen, P.M. (2013a). Reflections on communication and sport: On strategic communication and management. *Communication & Sport, 1*(1/2), 55–67.

Pedersen, P.M. (Ed.). (2013b). *Routledge handbook of sport communication*. London: Routledge.

Perlberg, S. (2015, June 25). Nielsen, the TV industry's favorite scapegoat, is fighting back. *Wall Street Journal*. http://blogs.wsj.com/cmo/2015/06/25/nielsen-mitch-barns-tv-networks-netflix

Peterson, T. (2019, August 27). 'A Rentrak takeover': Inside the fallout from Comscore's executive shakeup. Digiday. Retrieved from https://digiday.com/marketing/rentrak-takeover-inside-fallout-comscores-executive-shakeup/

Plunkett Research. (2015). Industry statistics sports industry statistic and market size overview. www.plunkettresearch.com/statistics/Industry-Statistics-Sports-Industry-Statistic-and-Market-Size-Overview

Probasco, J. (2015, October 4). Sponsorhub's acquisition by Rentrak Corporation creates synergy, says CEO. Benzinga.com. Retrieved from https://www.benzinga.com/news/15/10/5884660/sponsorhubs-acquisition-by-rentrak-corporation-creates-synergy-says-ceo

Proman, M. (2019, October 1). The future of sports tech: Here's where investors are placing their bets.

Techcrunch.com. Retrieved from https://techcrunch.com/2019/10/01/the-future-of-sports-tech-heres-where-investors-are-placing-their-bets/

PWC Sports Outlook (2018, October). PWC.com. Retrieved from https://www.pwc.com/us/en/industry/entertainment-media/assets/2018-sports-outlook.pdf

Red Sox hope Bloom hiring brings synergy to baseball operations. (2019, October 29). *Sports Business Daily.* Retrieved from https://www.sportsbusinessdaily.com/Daily/Issues/2019/10/29/Franchises/Red-Sox.aspx

Ritchie, D.A. (2003). *Doing oral history: A practical guide* (2nd ed.). New York: Oxford University Press.

Rothenbuhler, E. (2005). A.C. Nielsen Company: U.S. media market research firm. Museum of Broadcast Communications. www.museum.tv/eotv/acnielsen.htm

Rowe, D. (2004). *Sport, culture, and the media: The unruly trinity* (2nd ed.). New York: Open University Press.

Salwen, M.B., & Stacks, D.W. (1996). *An integrated approach to communication theory and research.* Mahwah, NJ: Erlbaum.

Sanderson, J. (2018). Guarding against quick and easy: Tightening up qualitative sport and social media research. In A. Bundon, (Ed.), *Digital qualitative research in sport and physical activity* (pp. 80-92). New York: Routledge.

Sasseen, J., Olmstead, K., & Mitchell, A. (2013). Digital: As mobile grows rapidly, the pressures on news intensifies. Pew Research Center. www.stateofthemedia.org/2013/digital-as-mobile-grows-rapidly-the-pressures-on-news-intensify

Saussure, F., de. (1983). *Course in general linguistics* (C. Bally & A. Sechehaye, Eds.; R. Harris, Trans.). LaSalle, IL: Open Court.

Screen wars: The battle for eye space in a TV-everywhere world. (2015, April 1). Nielsen. www.nielsen.com/us/en/insights/reports/2015/screen-wars-the-battle-for-eye-space-in-a-tv-everywhere-world.html

Shank, M.D. (2002). *Sports marketing: A strategic perspective* (2nd ed.). Upper Saddle River, NJ: Prentice Hall.

Shapiro, M., Hiatt, A., & Hoyt, M. (2015, April 23). The value of news. *Columbia Journalism Review.* www.cjr.org/analysis/the_value_of_news.php.

SNL Kagan. (n.d.). Media & communications data. www.snl.com/Sectors/Media/MediaCommunicationsOverview.aspx

Social TV. (n.d.). Nielsen. www.nielsen.com/us/en/solutions/measurement/social-tv.html

Spanberg, E. (2019, May 13). Data tells the story. *Sports Business Daily.* Retrieved from https://www.sportsbusinessdaily.com/Journal/Issues/2019/05/13/In-Depth/Main.aspx

Sports Video Group staff. (2019, May 1). ESPN digital posts best March ever; remains No. 1 U.S. digital sports property. SVG News. Retrieved from https://www.sportsvideo.org/2019/05/01/espn-digital-posts-best-march-ever-remains-no-1-us-digital-sports-property/

Stokes, J. (2003). *How to do media and cultural studies.* London: Sage.

Super Bowl LIV on Fox draws viewership of more than 102 million across television and digital platforms. (2020, February 3). Foxsports.com. Retrieved from https://www.foxsports.com/presspass/latest-news/2020/02/03/super-bowl-liv-fox-draws-viewership-102-million-across-television-digital-platforms

Swarm, J. (2018, October 29). The impact of social media on the sports industry. Boston University College of Communications. Retrieved from https://www.bu.edu/prlab/2018/10/29/the-impact-of-social-media-on-the-sports-industry/

Tankard, J.W., Jr. (2001). The empirical approach to the study of media framing. In S.D. Reese, O.H. Gandy, Jr., & A.E. Grant (Eds.), *Perspectives on media and our understanding of the social world* (pp. 95–106). Mahwah, NJ: Lawrence Erlbaum Associates.

Television. (2016). Nielsen. www.nielsen.com/us/en/solutions/measurement/television.html

Television City at the MGM Grand. (2015). TV City Research. http://tvcityresearch.com

The ESPN of eSports? Big names pledge $17 million toward new videogame network. (2019, September 17). Marketwatch.com. Retrieved from https://www.marketwatch.com/story/the-espn-of-esports-big-names-pledge-17-million-toward-new-videogame-network-2019-09-17

Thompson, A.-J. (2016). 23rd Annual European Association of Sport Management Conference, Dublin, Ireland. *International Journal of Sport Communication, 9,* 123–125.

Tracy, M., & Draper, K. (2019, April 30). *The New York Times.* www.nytimes.com/2019/04/30/sports/espn-magazine-print-closes.html

Trujillo, N. (2003). Introduction. In R.S. Brown & D.J. O'Rourke III (Eds.), *Case studies in sport communication* (pp. xi–xv). Westport, CT: Praeger.

Tuchman, G. (1978). *Making news: A study in the construction of reality.* New York: Free Press.

Tuchman, G. (1991). Media institutions: Qualitative methods in the study of news. In K.B. Jensen & N.W. Jankowski (Eds.), *A handbook of qualitative methodologies for mass communication research* (pp. 79–92). London: Routledge.

Turow, J. (1997). *Media systems in society: Understanding industries, strategies, and power* (2nd ed.). New York: Longman.

The U.S. digital consumer report. (2014, February 10). Nielsen. www.nielsen.com/us/en/insights/reports/2014/the-us-digital-consumer-report.html

Walder S., & Sabin, P. (2019, November 1). Preseason BPI rankings like Michigan State, skeptical about Memphis. ESPN.com. Retrieved from https://www.espn.com/mens-college-basketball/story/_/id/27975683/college-basketball-bpi-likes-michigan-state-skeptical-memphis

Wang, Y., & Zhou, S. (2015). How do sports organizations use social media to build relationships? A content analysis of NBA Clubs' Twitter use. *International Journal of Sport Communication, 8*, 133-148.

Wardini, J. (2017, November 2). 6 ways that social media has an influence in sports. National Institute for Social Media. Retrieved from https://nismonline.org/6-ways-that-social-media-has-an-influence-in-sports/

Weisberg, H.F., Krosnick, J.A., & Bowen, B.D. (1996). *An introduction to survey research, polling, and data analysis* (3rd ed.). Thousand Oaks, CA: Sage.

Wenner, L.A. (1989). *Media, sports, and society.* Newbury Park, CA: Sage.

Wenner, L.A. (1998). *MediaSport.* New York: Routledge.

Whannel, G. (2002). Sport and the media. In J. Coakley & E. Dunning (Eds.), *Handbook of sports studies* (pp. 291–308). London: Sage.

What TV ratings really mean. (2006). Nielsenmedia.com. Retrieved November 20, 2006, from www.nielsen-media.ca/English/NMR_U_PDF/What%20TV%20Ratings%20Really%20Mean.pdf

Whitney, D. (2005, March 21). ESPN and ABC Sports woo clients with ROO. *TelevisionWeek, 24*(12), 17.

Who we are. (2016). *Rentrak.* www.rentrak.com/section/about_rentrak/who_we_are.html

Wright, K.B. (2005). 'Researching internet-based populations: Advantages and disadvantages of online survey research, online questionnaire authoring, software packages, and web survey services. *Journal of Computer-Mediated Communication, 10*(3), article 11, available at https://doi-org.proxy.ulib.uits.iu.edu/10.1111/j.1083-6101.2005.tb00259.x

Chapter 12

Abdeldaeim, A. (2019a, August 21). Longtime U.S. figure skating coach Richard Callaghan banned for sexual misconduct. *Sports Illustrated.* www.si.com/olympics/2019/08/21/richard-callaghan-banned-life-sexual-misconduct-us-figure-skating

Abdeldaiem, A. (2019b, October 15). Report: DEA interviews Matt Harvey, current Angels players in Tyler Skaggs investigation. *Sports Illustrated.* www.si.com/mlb/2019/10/16/angels-players-interviewed-tyler-skaggs-death-probe

About AWSM. (2019). AWSM. http://awsmonline.org/we-are-awsm

Adande, J.A. (2014, December 10). Purpose of "I Can't Breathe" t-shirts. ESPN. http://espn.go.com/nba/story/_/id/12010612/nba-stars-making-statement-wearing-breathe-shirts

Amick, S. (2019, August 7). NBA ramps up mental health program, setting new expectations for each team—details from a league memo. The Athletic. https://theathletic.com/1120892/2019/08/07/nba-ramps-up-mental-health-program-setting-new-expectations-for-each-team

Andrews, D.L. (2000). Excavating Michael Jordan's blackness. In S. Birrell & M.G. McDonald (Eds.), *Reading sport: Critical essays on power and representation* (pp. 166–205). Boston: Northeastern University Press.

Ann Miller Award recipients (2019). AWSM. http://awsmonline.org/ann-miller-service-award

Ashe, A. (1991, February 11). It doesn't take an army to discover young blacks' choices of role models. *Washington Post*, p. B7.

ASNE 2018 Survey. (2018). ASNE. www.asne.org/diversity-survey-2018.

Association for Women in Sports Media (AWSM) internships. (2019). http://awsmonline.org/internships-scholarships

Association for Women in Sports Media (AWSM) past pioneers. (2019). http://awsmonline.org/mary-garber-pioneer-award#past-pioneers

At least six men's basketball programs to face NCAA allegations. (2019, June 13). *Cincinnati Enquirer.* www.cincinnati.com/story/sports/college/2019/06/13/college-basketball-corruption-six-programs-face-ncaa-allegations/1447769001

Aulbach, L. (2019, June 3). Looking back on the life of international icon Muhammad Ali, 3 years after his death. *Courier Journal.* www.courier-journal.com/story/news/local/2019/06/03/muhammad-ali-3-years-after-his-death/1275830001

Baskin, B. (2019, August 14). Jay-Z expresses plan to inspire change, but NFL partnership met with skepticism. *Sports Illustrated.* www.si.com/nfl/2019/08/14/jay-z-roc-nation-partnership-roger-goodell-social-justice

Belson, K. (2015, January 29). Concussions are down, NFL says. *New York Times.* www.nytimes.com/2015/01/30/sports/football/concussions-are-down-nfl-says.html?_r=0

Bembry, J. (2018, September 10). Serena Williams deserves share of the blame for her actions. *The Undefeated.* https://theundefeated.com/features/serena-williams-deserves-share-of-blame-for-her-actions

Bembry, J. (2019, April 14). Tiger Woods' victory at the Masters wasn't supposed to happen. *The Undefeated.* https://theundefeated.com/features/tiger-woods-victory-at-the-masters-wasnt-supposed-to-happen

Benedict, J. (1997). *Public heroes, private felons: Athletes and crimes against women.* Boston: Northeastern University Press.

Benedict, J., & Yaeger, D. (1998). *Pros and cons: The criminals who play in the NFL.* New York: Warner.

Bengel, C. (2019, October 2). USA Swimming being investigated by FBI over sexual abuse claims, business practices. CBSSports.com. www.cbssports.com/olympics/news/usa-swimming-being-investigated-by-fbi-over-sexual-abuse-claims-business-practices

Bernstein, A., & Blain, N. (2002). Sport and the media: The emergence of a major research field. *Culture, Sport, Society, 5*(3), 1–30.

Billings, A.C. (2013). Tiger Woods lands in the rough: Golf, apologia, and the heroic limits of privacy. In L. Wenner (Ed.), *Fallen sports heroes, media, & celebrity culture* (pp. 51–63). New York: Lang.

Billings, A. C., Angelini, J. R., MacArthur, P. J., Bissell, K., & Smith, L. R. (2014). (Re)Calling London: The gender frame agenda within NBC's primetime telecast of the 2012 Olympiad. *Journalism and Mass Communication Quarterly, 9*(1), 38–58.

Billings, A.C. & Black, J.E. (2018). *Mascot nation: The controversy over Native American representations in sports.* Urbana: University of Illinois Press

Billings, A.C., Butterworth, M.L., & Turman, P.D. (2015). *Communication and sport: Surveying the field* (2nd ed.). Los Angeles: Sage.

Billings, A.C., Butterworth, M.L., & Turman, P.D. (2018). *Communication and sport: Surveying the field* (3rd ed.). Los Angeles: Sage.

Birrell, S., & McDonald, M.G. (2000). Reading sport, articulating power lines. In S. Birrell & M.G. McDonald (Eds.), *Reading sport: Critical essays on power and representation* (pp. 3–13). Boston: Northeastern University Press.

Blackistone, K.B. (2016, September 4). Colin Kaepernick challenges sport's nationalism, and our notion of it as safe space. *The Washington Post.* www.washingtonpost.com/sports/colin-kaepernick-challenges-sports-nationalism-and-our-notion-of-it-as-safe-space/2016/09/04/7a312dac-71fd-11e6-be4f-3f42f2e5a49e_story.html

Bloom, G.A., & Smith, M.D. (1996). Hockey violence: A test of cultural spillover theory. *Sociology of Sport Journal, 13,* 65–77.

Bonilla-Silva, E. (2003). *Racism without racists: Color-blind racism and the persistence of racial inequality in America.* New York: Rowman & Littlefield.

Bonk, T. (2005, November 4). Martin won't be forgotten. *Los Angeles Times,* p. 8.

Boren, C. (2017, September 26). Michael Jordan isn't sitting out any more, says protesting athletes "shouldn't be demonized." *The Washington Post.* www.washingtonpost.com/news/early-lead/wp/2017/09/26/michael-jordan-isnt-sitting-out-any-more-says-protesting-athletes-shouldnt-be-demonized

Botello, G., & Levs, J. (2013, January 17). "Deeply flawed" Lance Armstrong admits using performance-enhancing drugs. CNN. www.cnn.com/2013/01/17/sport/armstrong-doping

Brady, E., & Finnerty, M. (2014, August 14). Washington Redskins appeal decision to cancel trademark. *USA Today.* www.usatoday.com/story/sports/nfl/redskins/2014/08/14/washington-redskins-appeal-federal-trademark-registrations/14066527

Brennan, C. (2016, March 10). Brennan: Maria Sharapova can't avoid lengthy suspension. *USA Today.* www.usatoday.com/story/sports/columnist/brennan/2016/03/09/maria-sharapova-suspension-positive-drug-test-meldonium/81554818

Brennan, C. (2019, August 1). Olympic figure skater Ashley Wagner says she was sexually assaulted as a 17-year-old. *USA Today.* www.usatoday.com/story/sports/olympics/2019/08/01/ashley-wagner-olympian-figure-skating-sexual-assault-john-coughlin/1876517001

Broadwater, L, Richman, T., & Barker, J. (2018, October 31). University of Maryland president fires football coach DJ Durkin, reversing decision by regents. *Baltimore Sun.* www.baltimoresun.com/sports/terps/bs-md-durkin-gone-20181031-story.html

Brown, J.K. (2013, July 26). Biogenesis whistleblower calls the doping scandal bigger than baseball. *Miami Herald.* www.miamiherald.com/news/local/community/miami-dade/article1953578.html

Brown, T.J., Sumner, K.E., & Nocera, R. (2002, September). Understanding sexual aggression against women: An examination of the role of men's athletic participation and related variables. *Journal of Interpersonal Violence, 17,* 937–952. doi:10.1177/0886260502017009002

Bruton, M. (1996, January 21). Amid racial polarity black athletes star as salesmen they seem to transcend color, endorsing products like never before. Philly.com. http://articles.philly.com/1996-01-21/sports/25652865_1_athletes-black-superstars-audience

Buckner, C. (2006, July 28). Scandal shadows cycling champ. *Knight Ridder Tribune Business News,* p. 1.

Bumbaca, C. (2019, October 15). "Freedom is not free": Celtics' Enes Kanter responds to LeBron James' China, Daryl Morey comments. *USA Today.* www.usatoday.com/story/sports/nba/celtics/2019/10/15/lebron-james-morey-china-comments-enes-kanter-freedom-turkey/3983357002

Burch, L.M., Eagleman, A.N., & Pedersen, P.M. (2012). New media coverage of gender in the 2010 Winter Olympics: An examination of online media content. *International Journal of Sport Management, 13,* 143–159.

Burns, K. (2005). *Unforgivable blackness: The rise and fall of Jack Johnson.* Washington, DC: Florentine Films.

Cahn, S. (2004). "Cinderellas" of sport: Black women in track and field. In P.B. Miller & D.K. Wiggins (Eds.), *Sport and the color line: Black athletes and race relations in twentieth-century America* (pp. 211–232). New York: Routledge.

Cambage, L. (2019, August 11). DNP-Mental Health. *Players Tribune.* www.theplayerstribune.com/en-us/articles/liz-cambage-mental-health

Carroll, C. (2018, July 26). Human Rights Watch says IAAF's new testosterone rule discriminations against some women. *Sports Illustrated.* www.si.com/olympics/2018/07/26/human-rights-watch-says-iaaf-testosterone-rule-discriminates-against-women

Celebrities flock to Muhammad Ali's memorial service. (2016, June 10). *Hollywood Reporter.* www.hollywoodreporter.com/news/muhammad-ali-funeral-celebrities-flock-901555

Centers for Disease Control and Prevention (CDC). 2013. Intimate partner violence: Consequences. www.google.

com/search?q=CDC+INtimate+partner+violence%3 A+consequences&ie=utf-8&oe=utf-8&aq=t&rls=org. mozilla:en-US:official&client=firefox-a&channel=fflb

Change the Mascot. (n.d.). Change the Mascot. www. changethemascot.org

Chavez, C. (2019, November 13). Inside the toxic culture of the Nike Oregon Project "cult." *Sports Illustrated*. www.si.com/track-and-field/2019/11/13/mary-cain-nike-oregon-project-toxic-culture-alberto-salazar-abuse-investigation

Chiari, M. (2018, November 30). TMZ releases video of Kareem Hunt in physical altercation with woman in February. Bleacher Report. https://bleacherreport. com/articles/2808617-tmz-releases-video-of-kareem-hunt-in-physical-altercation-with-woman-in-february

Christie, J.C. (2019, June 18). High school football coach Rob Mendez featured on cover of *ESPN The Magazine*'s Heroes Issue—Hitting newsstands on Friday. ESPNpressroom.com. https://espnpressroom. com/us/press-releases/2019/06/high-school-football-coach-rob-mendez-featured-on-cover-of-espn-the-magazines-heroes-issue-hitting-newsstands-on-friday

Church, B., & Morse, B. (2019, December 9). Russia banned from 2020 Olympics and 2022 World Cup over doping scandal. *CNN.com*. Retrieved from www. cnn.com/2019/12/09/sport/wada-ban-russia-decision-rusada-doping-spt-intl/index.html

Clavio, G., & Eagleman, A.N. (2011). Gender and sexually suggestive images in sports blogs. *Journal of Sport Management, 7*, 295–304.

Coakley, J. (2009). *Sports in society: Issues and controversies* (10th ed.). Boston: McGraw-Hill.

Coakley, J., & Donnelly, P. (2009). *Sports in society: Issues and controversies* (2nd Canadian ed.). Toronto: McGraw-Hill Ryerson.

Coakley, J. (2016). *Sports in society: Issues and controversies* (12 ed.). New York: McGraw-Hill.

Coaston, J. (2018, September 4). Nike reignited the Kaepernick controversy in naming him the face of "Just Do It." Vox.com. www.vox.com/2018/9/4/17818162/nike-kaepernick-controversy-face-of-just-do-it

Coche, R., & Tuggle, C. A. (2018). Men or women, only five Olympic sports matter: A quantitative analysis of NBC's prime-time coverage of the Rio Olympics. *Electronic News, 12* (4), 199–217.

Cooky, C., & LaVoi, N.M. (2012, February 1). Playing but losing: Women's sports after Title IX. *Contexts,* 11(1), pp. 42-46. https://journals.sagepub.com/doi/pdf/10.1177/1536504212436495

Cooky, C., Messner, M., & Musto, M. (2015, June). "It's Dude Time!": A quarter century of excluding women's sports in televised news and highlight shows. *Communication & Sport, 3*, 261-287.

Cooky, C., Messner, M.A., & Hextrum, R.H. (2013). Women play sports, but not on TV: A longitudinal study of televised news media. *Communication & Sport, 1*, 203–230.

Cooky, C., Wachs, F.L., Messner, M., & Dworkin, S.L. (2010). It's not about the game: Don Imus, race, class, gender, and sexuality in contemporary media. *Sociology of Sport Journal, 27*, 139–159.

Corbett, D., & Johnson, W. (2000). The African American female in collegiate sport: Sexism and racism. In D. Brooks & R. Althouse (Eds.), *Racism in college athletics: The African American athlete's experience* (pp. 200–225). Morgantown, WV: Fitness Information Technology.

Crosset, T. (1999). Male athletes' violence against women: A critical assessment of the athletic affiliation, violence against women debate. *Quest, 51*, 244–257.

Crosset, T.W., Benedict, J.R., & McDonald, M.A. (1995). Male student-athletes reported for sexual assault: A survey of campus police departments and judicial affairs offices. *Journal of Sport & Social Issues, 19*, 126–140.

Crosset, T.W., Ptacek, J., McDonald, M.A., & Benedict, J.R. (1996). Male student-athletes and violence against women: A survey of campus judicial affairs officers. *Violence against women, 2*, 163–79.

Curley, A.J. (2012, August 8). Expert: Gender testing "imperfect" for female athletes. CNN. www.cnn. com/2012/08/08/health/athletes-gender-testing

Daddario, G. (1998). *Women's sport and spectacle: Gendered television coverage and the Olympic Games.* Westport, CT: Praeger.

Dafferner, M., Campagna, J., & Rodgers, R.F. (2019, June). Making gains: Hypermascularity and objectification of male and female Olympic athletes in *Sports Illustrated* across 60 years. *Body Image, 29*, pp. 156–160.

Deitsch, R. (2014, September 1). How ESPN erred in its report on Michael Sam's showering habits. *Sports Illustrated*. www.si.com/nfl/2014/09/01/michael-sam-espn-josina-anderson-showering-report

Denzin, N.K. (1996). More rare air: Michael Jordan on Michael Jordan. *Sociology of Sport Journal, 13*(4), 319–324.

Digiovanna, M. (2015, February 9). Hope Solo act may be wearing thin with U.S. soccer. *Los Angeles Times*. www. latimes.com/sports/soccer/la-sp-hope-solo-20150210-story.html#page=1

Dinich, H., Rittenberg, A., & VanHaaren, T. (2018, August 10). The inside story of a toxic culture at Maryland football. ESPN. www.espn.com/college-football/story/_/id/24342005/maryland-terrapins-football-culture-toxic-coach-dj-durkin

Douglas, D.D. (2005). Venus, Serena, and the Women's Tennis Association: When and where "race" enters. *Sociology of Sport Journal, 22*, 256–282.

Duncan, M.C. (2006). Gender warriors in sport: Women and the media. In A.A. Raney & J. Bryant (Eds.), *Handbook of sports and media* (pp. 231-252). Mahwah, NJ: Erlbaum.

Eagleman, A. (2011). Stereotypes of race and nationality: A qualitative analysis of sport magazine coverage of MLB players. *Journal of Sport Management, 25*, 156–168.

Eagleman, A. (2015). Constructing gender differences: Newspaper portrayals of male and female gymnasts at the 2012 Olympic Games. *Sport in Society: Cultures, Commerce, Media, Politics, 18*(2), 234–247.

Eagleman, A., Burch, L.M., & Vooris, R. (2014). A unified version of London 2012: New-media coverage of gender, nationality, and sport for Olympics consumers in six countries. *Journal of Sport Management, 28,* 457–470.

Early, G. (2006). Muhammad Ali: Flawed rebel with a cause. In D.K. Wiggins (Ed.), *Out of the shadows: A biographical history of African American athletes* (pp. 263–278). Fayetteville: University of Arkansas Press.

Eastman, S.T., & Billings, A.C (1999). Gender parity in the Olympics: Hyping women athletes, favoring men athletes. *Journal of Sport & Social Issues, 23*(2), 140–170.

Elsesser, K. (2019, March 1). Here's why women's teams are coached by men. *Forbes.* www.forbes.com/sites/kimelsesser/2019/03/01/heres-why-womens-teams-are-coached-by-men/#700e63dfb3f9

Entine, J. (2000). *Taboo: Why black athletes dominate sports and why we're afraid to talk about it.* New York: Public Affairs.

Everything you need to know about MLB's sign-stealing scandal (2020, February 13). *ESPN.com.* Retrieved from www.espn.com/mlb/story/_/id/28476282/everything-need-know-mlb-sign-stealing-scandal Fainaru, S., & Fainaru-Wada, M. (2013, November 14). Youth football participation drops. ESPN. http://espn.go.com/espn/otl/story/_/page/popwarner/pop-warner-youth-football-participation-drops-nfl-concussion-crisis-seen-causal-factor

Fainaru, S., & Fainaru-Wada, M. (2013, November 14). Youth football participation drops. ESPN.com. http://espn.go.com/espn/otl/story/_/page/popwarner/pop-warner-youth-football-participation-drops-nfl-concussion-crisis-seen-causal-factor.

Fainaru-Wada, M. (2015, October 2). Hope Solo again will face charges after reversal of earlier court decision. ESPN. http://espn.go.com/espn/otl/story/_/id/13793673/hope-solo-again-face-domestic-violence-charges

Fainaru-Wada, M., & Fainaru, S. (2014, November 12). OTL: NFL didn't enforce own policies. ESPN. http://espn.go.com/espn/otl/story/_/id/11849798/outside-lines-most-nfl-players-domestic-violence-cases-never-missed-down

Farmer, B.M. (2018, November 11). Brotherly love: Shaquem and Shaquill Griffin's pact. 60 Minutes Overtime. www.cbsnews.com/news/brotherly-love-seattle-seahawks-shaquem-grffin-and-shaquill-griffin-pact-60-minutes

Fetters, A. (2013, March 26). People talk about Brittney Griner like she's a basketball player, because she is. *The Atlantic.* www.theatlantic.com/sexes/archive/2013/03/people-talk-about-brittney-griner-like-shes-a-basketball-player-because-she-is/274353

Fleming, J. (2018, September 10). Cartoon depicting tantrum-throwing Serena Williams at U.S. Open causes new round of outrage. *USA Today.* www.usatoday.com/story/sports/tennis/2018/09/10/serena-williams-cartoon-outrage-naomi-osaka-us-open-tennis/1256274002

Forde, P., Thamel, P., & Wetzel, D. (2019a, July 10). NCAA hits NC State with notice of allegations tied to hoops corruption investigation. Yahoo! Sports. https://sports.yahoo.com/ncaa-hits-nc-state-with-notice-of-allegations-tied-to-federal-hoops-corruption-case-220117755.html

Forde, P., Thamel, P., & Wetzel, D. (2019b, September 23). Sources: Kansas men's basketball charged with multiple Level I allegations, including lack of institutional control. Yahoo! Sports. https://sports.yahoo.com/sources-kansas-basketball-charged-with-multiple-level-1-violations-including-lack-of-institutional-control-210015300.html

Freedman, S.G. (2015, November 10). The civil rights legacy that led to Mizzou. *Vice Sports.* https://sports.vice.com/en_us/article/the-civil-rights-legacy-that-led-to-mizzou

Gaines, P. (2004, July 31). Doping: Will the Olympic Games in Athens be clean? *The Record,* p. J1.

Garcia-Roberts, G. (2014, November 13). MLB told feds about players' ties to Biogenesis months before story broke. *Newsday.* www.newsday.com/sports/baseball/mlb-told-feds-about-players-ties-to-biogenesis-months-before-story-broke-1.9616225

Gems, G.R. (2006). Jack Johnson and the quest for racial respect. In D.K. Wiggins (Ed.), *Out of the shadows: A biographical history of African American athletes* (pp. 59–77). Fayetteville: University of Arkansas Press.

Giardina, M.D., & Magnusen, M. (2013). Dog bites man? The criminalization and rehabilitation of Michael Vick. In L.A. Wenner (Ed.), *Fallen sport heroes, media, & celebrity culture* (pp. 165–178). New York: Lang.

Gray, H. (1995). *Watching race: Television and the struggle for "blackness."* Minneapolis: University of Minnesota Press.

Griner, Delle Donne, Diggins discuss sports and sexuality. (2013, April 17). *Sports Illustrated.* www.si.com/more-sports/2013/04/17/wnba-griner-delle-donne-diggins-sports-sexuality

Grizzlies name Notre Dame's Niele Ivey the NBA's 9th female assistant coach. (2019, August 5). *Chicago Sun-Times.* https://chicago.suntimes.com/2019/8/5/20755406/grizzlies-nba-notre-dame-niele-ivey-assistant-coach

Hackett, T. (2018, June 11). List of World Cup winners. *Sports Illustrated.* www.si.com/soccer/2018/world-cup-winners-list-past-history-champions-final

Halbert, C., & Latimer, M. (1994). "Battling" gendered language: An analysis of the language used by sports commentators in a televised coed tennis competition. *Sociology of Sport Journal, 11,* 298–308.

Hale, K. (2019, July 8). Colin Kaepernick spurs Nike's stock after it pulled "Betsy Ross Flag" sneaker. *Forbes*. www.forbes.com/sites/korihale/2019/07/08/colin-kaepernick-spurs-nikes-stock-after-it-pulled-betsy-ross-flag-sneaker/#4770d5c27ff6

Hall, S. (2003). The whites of their eyes: Racist ideologies and the media. In G. Dines & J.M. Humez (Eds.), *Gender, race, and class in media: A text-reader* (pp. 89–93). Thousand Oaks, CA: Sage.

Healthy People. 2013. Injury and violence prevention. www.healthypeople.gov/2020/topicsobjectives2020/overview.aspx?topicid=24

Hilliard, D.C. (1983). *If you've come a long way, why do they still call you baby: Magazine profiles of women professional tennis players*. North American Society for the Sociology of Sport Annual meeting. Unpublished paper.

Hoberman, J. (1997). *Darwin's athletes: How sport has damaged black America and preserved the myth of race*. Boston: Houghton Mifflin.

Hull, K., & Schmittel, A. (2015). A fumbled opportunity: A case study of Twitter's role in concussion awareness opportunities during the Super Bowl. *Journal of Sport & Social Issues, 39*(1), 78–94.

Hurst, N. (2015, June 2). Black athletes stereotyped negatively in media compared to white athletes. University of Missouri news bureau. http://munews.missouri.edu/news-releases/2015/0602-black-athletes-stereotyped-negatively-in-media-compared-to-white-athletes

Infantino says FIFA scandals gone, despite corruption cases. (2019, June 5). ESPNupstate.com. https://espnupstate.radio.com/articles/ap-news/infantino-says-fifa-scandals-gone-despite-corruption-cases

Jordan, M. (2016, July 25). Michael Jordan: "I can no longer stay silent." *The Undefeated*. https://theundefeated.com/features/michael-jordan-i-can-no-longer-stay-silent

Joseph, E. (2019, June 21). Michigan State hires law firm to investigate its handling of the Larry Kaepernick tweets he's "still ready" for NFL return. ESPN. www.espn.com/nfl/story/_/id/27341745/kaepernick-tweets-ready-nfl-return

Kane, M.J. (2002). Sociological aspects of sport and physical activity. In J.B. Parks, & J. Quarterman (Eds.), *Contemporary sport management* (2nd ed., pp. 107–126). Champaign, IL: Human Kinetics.

Kane, M.J. (2011, July 27). Sex sells sex, not women's sports. *Nation*. www.thenation.com/article/162390/sex-sells-sex-not-womens-sports

Kane, M.J. & LaVoi, N. (2018). An examination of intercollegiate athletic directors' attributions regarding the underrepresentation of female coaches in women's sports. *Women in Sport and Physical Activity Journal, 26*(1), 3–11.

Kanter, R. M. (1977). *Men and women of the corporation*. New York: Basic Books.

Kaepernick tweets he's 'still ready' for NFL return. (2019, August 7). *ESPN.com*. Retrieved from https://www.espn.com/nfl/story/_/id/27341745/kaepernick-tweets-ready-nfl-return

Kasabian, P. (2019, August 13). Eric Reid discusses Jay-Z, NFL partnership; "blackballing" of Colin Kaepernick. Bleacher Report. https://bleacherreport.com/articles/2849557-eric-reid-discusses-jay-z-nfl-partnership-blackballing-of-colin-kaepernick

Katz, J. (1995). Reconstructing masculinity in the locker room: The Mentors in Violence Prevention Project. *Harvard Educational Review, 65*, 163–174.

Kellner, D. (2001). The sports spectacle, Michael Jordan, and Nike: Unholy alliance? http://pages.gseis.ucla.edu/faculty/kellner/essays/sportsspectaclemichaeljordan.pdf

Kesslen, B. (2019, August 8). "You had one job": Simone Biles on USA Gymnastics' failure to protect athletes in abuse scandal. NBCNews.com. www.nbcnews.com/news/sports/you-had-one-job-simone-biles-usa-gymnastics-failure-protect-n1040296

Kian, E.M., Vincent, J., & Mondello, M. (2008). Masculine hegemonic hoops: An analysis of media coverage of March Madness. *Sociology of Sport Journal, 25*, 223–242.

King, C.R. (2004). This is not an Indian: Situating claims about Indianness in sporting worlds. *Journal of Sport and Social Issues, 28*, 3–10.

Kirby, J. (2018, May 16). The sex abuse scandal surrounding USA Gymnastics team doctor Larry Nassar, explained. Vox. www.vox.com/identities/2018/1/19/16897722/sexual-abuse-usa-gymnastics-larry-nassar-explained

Koss, M.P., & Cleveland, H.H. (1997). Stepping on toes: Social roots of date rape lead to intractability and politicization. In M.D. Schwartz (Ed.), *Researching sexual violence against women: Methodological and personal perspectives* (pp. 4–21). Thousand Oaks: Sage.

Kristiansen, E., Broch, T.B., & Pedersen, P.M. (2014). Negotiating gender in professional soccer: An analysis of female footballers in the United States. *Sports Management International Journal Choregia, 10*(1), 5–27.

Kroichick, R. (2005, August 26). Vicious cycle, the saga: Controversy over doping and lawsuits are nothing new for Armstrong. *San Francisco Chronicle*, A1.

Lapchick, R. (2009). An introduction: Great women athletes who opened doors for future generations. In R. Lapchick (Ed.), *100 trailblazers: Great women athletes who opened doors for future generations* (pp. 1–10). Morgantown, WV: Fitness Information Technology.

Lapchick, R. (2018, May 2). The 2018 Associated Press Sports Editors Racial and Gender Report Card. TIDES. http://nebula.wsimg.com/e1801a8b96d97c40f57cf3bf7cd478a3?AccessKeyId=DAC3A56D8FB782449D2A&disposition=0&alloworigin=1

Lapchick, R. (2019, February 27). The 2018 Racial and Gender Report Card: College sport. TIDES. https://docs.wixstatic.com/ugd/7d86e5_05a980a149c24e69baa5265abc63c3b2.pdf

Lapchick, R. (2015, June 15). Athletes rising to the occasion on issues of social justice. *Sports Business*

Journal. Retrieved from www.sportsbusinessdaily.com/Journal/Issues/2015/06/15/Opinion/Richard-Lapchick.aspx

Lapchick, R.E. (2014, March 3). Minority numbers in coaching, graduation rates unacceptable. *Street & Smith's Sports Business Journal.* www.sportsbusinessdaily.com/Journal/Issues/2014/03/03/Opinion/Richard-Lapchick.aspx

Lapchick, R., et al. (2017, November 8). The 2017 D! FBS Leadership College Racial and Gender Report Card: Collegiate Athletic Leadership Gets a D- as it is still dominated by White men. The Institute for Diversity and Ethics in Sport. https://docs.wixstatic.com/ugd/71e0e0_dc737aeb28644995a539306807dbce1b.pdf

Lapchick, R., et al. (2018, May 2). The 2018 Associated Press Sports Editors Racial and Gender Report Card. The Institute for Diversity and Ethics in Sport. https://43530132-36e9-4f52-811a-182c7a91933b.filesusr.com/ugd/7d86e5_9dca4bc2067241cdba67aa2f1b09fd1b.pdf

Laucella, P.C. (2009). Arthur Ashe, privacy, and the media: An analysis of newspaper journalists' coverage of Ashe's AIDS announcement. *International Journal of Sport Communication, 2,* 56–80.

Laucella, P.C. (2010a). Michael Vick: An analysis of press coverage on federal dogfighting charges. *Journal of Sports Media, 5*(2), 35–76.

Laucella, P.C. (2010b). Tiger Woods: The first billion-dollar athlete. In J.W. Lee (Ed.), *Branded: Branding in sport business* (pp. 257–265). Durham: Carolina Academic.

Laucella, P.C. (2016). Jesse Owens: A case study of mainstream and alternative press coverage on the 1936 Berlin Olympic Games. In C. Lamb (Ed.), *Jack Johnson to LeBron James: Essayson race, sport, and the media* (pp. 52-85). Lincoln: University of Nebraska Press.

Laucella, P.C. (2018). Hope Solo: Sport brand profile. In J.W. Lee (Ed.), *Branded: Branding in sport business* (pp. 293-311). Durham, NC: Carolina Academic Press.

Laucella, P.C. (in progress). Sex abuse survivors and victim impact statements: A framing analysis of media coverage during Larry Nassar's sentencings. Manuscript in progress.

Laucella, P.C., Hardin, M., Bien-Aime, S., Antunovic, D. (2017). Diversifying the sport department and covering women's sports: A survey of sports editors. *Journalism & Mass Communication Quarterly 94*(3), 772-792.

Laveay, F., Callison, C., & Rodriguez, A. (2009). Offensiveness of Native American names, mascots, and logos in sports: A survey of tribal leaders and the general population. *International Journal of Sport Communication, 2,* 81–99.

Lavelle, K.L. (2014). "Plays like a guy": A rhetorical analysis of Brittney Griner in sports media. *Journal of Sports Media, 9*(2), 115–131.

LaVoi, N.M. (2019, April). Head coaches of women's collegiate teams: A report on seven select NCAA Division-I institutions, 2018-19. Minneapolis: The Tucker Center for Research on Girls & Women in Sport. www.cehd.umn.edu/tuckercenter/library/docs/research/WCCRC_Head-Coaches_2018-19_D-I_Select-7.pdf

Leonard, D. (2006). A world of criminals or a media construction? Race, gender, celebrity, and the athlete/criminal discourse. In A.A. Raney & J. Bryant (Eds.), *Handbook of sports and media* (pp. 523–541). Mahwah, NJ: Erlbaum.

Leonard, D.J. (2004). The next M.J. or the next O.J.? Kobe Bryant, race, and the absurdity of colorblind rhetoric. *Journal of Sport & Social Issues, 28*(3), pp. 284–313.

Letter from Washington Redskins owner Dan Snyder to fans. (2013, October 9). *Washington Post.* www.washingtonpost.com/local/letter-from-washington-redskins-owner-dan-snyder-to-fans/2013/10/09/e7670ba0-30fe-11e3-8627-c5d7de0a046b_story.html

Levenson, E. (2018a, January 24). Larry Nassar sentenced to up to 175 years in prison for decades of sexual abuse. *CNN.com.* Retrieved from https://www.cnn.com/2018/01/24/us/larry-nassar-sentencing/index.html

Lewis, A. (2019, July 4). Megan Rapinoe: USWNT captain, World Cup winner and campaigner for social justice. CNN.com. https://edition.cnn.com/2019/06/28/football/megan-rapinoe-donald-trump-uswnt-spt-intl/index.html

Ley, T. (2014, August 28). ESPN was dumb, but Michael Sam's showering habits do matter. Deadspin. http://deadspin.com/espn-was-dumb-but-michael-sams-showering-habits-do-mat-1627600462?utm_campaign=socialflow_deadspin_twitter&utm_source=deadspin_twitter&utm_medium=socialflow

Louis becomes champ. (n.d.). History.com. www.history.com/this-day-in-history/louis-becomes-champ

MacDonald, C.A., & Lafrance, M.E. (2018). "Girls love me, guys wanna be me": Representations of men, masculinity, and junior ice hockey in *Gongshow* magazine. The International Journal of Sport and Society, *10*,1, 1–19.

MacMahon, T. (2018, October 5). NBA are of additional sexual misconduct allegations. ESPN.com. www.espn.com/nba/story/_/id/24900963/nba-monitoring-additional-mavericks-sexual-misconduct-allegations

MacMichael, S. (2013, August 25). Lance Armstrong settles $1 million Sunday Times lawsuit. http://road.cc/content/news/90878-lance-armstrong-settles-£1-million-sunday-times-lawsuit

Maese, R., & DeBonis, M. (2019, November 8). Second person says he told Rep. Jim Jordan about sexual misconduct at Ohio State. *The Washington Post.* www.washingtonpost.com/sports/2019/11/08/second-person-says-he-told-rep-jim-jordan-about-sexual-misconduct-ohio-state

Mansoor, S. (2019, November 14). "We will not let her disappear into the abyss." Chanel Miller on the

Stanford plaques with her victim impact statement. *Time.* https://time.com/5726188/chanel-miller-time-100-next

Mahoney, R. (2006, May 3). Sports and nationalism. PBS. www.pbs.org/pov/borders/2006/talk/ridge_mahoney/000178.html

Majendie, M. (2014, August 20). Lance Armstrong: Can the lies and bullying be forgiven. CNN. http://edition.cnn.com/2014/08/20/sport/lance-armstrong-rehabilitation-cycling

Mandell, N. (2016, February 11). Becky Hammon on being the first female NBA All-Star assistant: "Life just has a funny way of just getting better." *USA Today.* http://ftw.usatoday.com/2016/02/becky-hammon-all-star

Mandell, N. (2016, July 14). The story behind the powerful appearance by LeBron, Chris Paul, Dwyane Wade and Carmelo Anthony at the ESPY Awards. *USA Today.* https://ftw.usatoday.com/2016/07/carmelo-anthony-lebron-james-chris-paul-dwyane-wade-espy-change

Marie, J. (2013, August 21). 12 incredible athletes with disabilities. Bleacher Report. http://bleacherreport.com/articles/1743213-12-incredible-athletes-with-disabilities

Martin, J. (2019, July 9). Serena Williams said she owed Naomi Osaka an apology after the U.S. Open. Osaka's response *brought* her to tears. CNN.com. www.cnn.com/2019/07/09/tennis/serena-williams-opens-up-in-harpers-bazaar-essay-on-us-open-loss-to-naomi-osaka-trnd/index.html

Martinez, M. (2013, October 12). A slur or term of "honor"? Controversy heightens about Washington Redskins. CNN. www.cnn.com/2013/10/12/us/redskins-controversy

Martinez, M., & Hall, L. (2014, August 12). Steve Ballmer now owns NBA's Clippers for record $2 billion. CNN. www.cnn.com/2014/08/12/us/sterling-nba-clippers-ballmer

Matange, Y. (2019, September 26). List of female assistant coaches in the NBA. NBA.com Canada. Retrieved from https://ca.nba.com/news/list-of-female-assistant-coaches-in-the-nba/14oge3l57tj3b1ssx27sidf4fh

Mayeda, D.T. (1999). From model minority to economic threat: Media portrayals of Major League Baseball pitchers Hideo Nomo and Hideki Irabu. *Journal of Sport & Social Issues, 23*(2), 203–217.

McCann, M. (2019, August 2). Five key takeaways from Ohio State's records release involving Urban Meyer, Zach Smith. *Sports Illustrated.* www.si.com/college-football/2019/08/02/ohio-state-records-release-urban-meyer-zach-smith

McCombs, B. (2018, December 18). Salt Lake City's new Olympics bid comes after scandal's lessons. *Las Vegas Review-Journal.* www.reviewjournal.com/news/nation-and-world/salt-lake-citys-new-olympics-bid-comes-after-scandals-lessons-1554309

McCombs, M., & Ghanem, S.I. (2001). The convergence of agenda setting and framing. In S.D. Reese, O.H. Gandy, Jr., & A.E. Grant (Eds.), *Framing public life: Perspectives on media and our understanding of the social world* (pp. 67–81). Mahwah, NJ: Erlbaum.

McCombs, M.E., & Shaw, D.L. (1972). The agenda-setting function of mass media. *Public Opinion Quarterly, 36*(2), 176–187.

Merrill, D. (2014). The one-legged wrestler who conquered his sport, then left it behind. In G. Stout (Ed.), *The best American sports writing 2014* (pp. 19–35). Boston: Houghton Mifflin.

Merrill, E. (2018, July 12). There's no handbook for this. *ESPN The Magazine.* www.espn.com/espn/feature/story/_/id/24052260/marjory-stoneman-douglas-family-looks-answers-tragedy-parkland

Messner, M.A. (2002). *Taking the field: Women and men in sports.* Minneapolis: University of Minnesota Press.

Messner, M.A., & Cooky, C. (2010). *Gender in televised sports: News and highlight shows, 1989-2009.* Los Angeles: USC Center for Feminist Research (Research Report).

Messner, M.A., & Cooky, C. (2010, June). *Women play sport, but not on TV: A longitudinal study of televised news media.* Center for Feminist Research, University of Southern California, Los Angeles.

Miloch, K.S., Pedersen, P.M., Smucker, M.K., & Whisenant, W.A. (2005). The current state of women print journalists: An analysis of the status and careers of females in newspapers sports departments. *Public Organization Review, 5,* 219–232.

MLB ups length of drug use bans. (2014, March 31). ESPN. http://espn.go.com/mlb/story/_/id/10690127/major-league-baseball-union-toughen-drug-agreement-provisions

Montville, L. (2017, May 19). Muhammad Ali knew how to play the villain, but dodging the draft turned him into a pariah. *The Undefeated.* https://theundefeated.com/features/muhammad-ali-knew-sting-like-a-bee

Moser, C.A. (2004). Penalties, fouls, and errors: Professional athletes and violence against women. *Sports Lawyers Journal, 11,* 69–87.

Muhammad Ali to receive medal. (2012, July 5). ESPN. http://espn.go.com/boxing/story/_/id/8132289/muhammad-ali-named-2012-liberty-medal-recipient

Naomi Osaka captures U.S. Open; Serena Williams fined, penalized game for calling chair umpire "a thief." ESPN. www.espn.com/tennis/story/_/id/24617080/naomi-osaka-wins-controversial-2018-us-open-serena-williams

Nassar scandal. CNN. www.cnn.com/2019/06/21/us/msu-hires-investigation-into-larry-nassar/index.html

NBA and WNBA partner with LeanIn.org to encourage men to support equality at work and play. (2015, March 5). Oursportscentral.com. Retrieved from https://www.oursportscentral.com/services/releases/nba-and-wnba-partner-with-leanin-org-to-encourage-men-to-support-equality-at-work-and-play/n-4934171

NBA, Silver try to mitigate damage in China following Morey's tweet. *Sports Business Daily*. www.sportsbusinessdaily.com/Daily/Issues/2019/10/07/Leagues-and-Governing-Bodies/NBA-China-Rockets.aspx

Nelson, M. B. (1994). *The stronger women get, the more men love football*. Orlando, FL: Harcourt Brace.

Neupauer, N.C. (1998). Women in the male-dominated world of sports information directing: Only the strong survive. *Public Relations Quarterly, 43*(1), 27–30.

Newberry, P. (2018, May 22). Michael Phelps opens up about his struggles with mental health. *The Boston Globe*. www.boston.com/sports/olympics/2018/05/22/michael-phelps-depression-mental-health/amp

NHL is integrated. (n.d.). History.com. www.history.com/this-day-in-history/nhl-is-integrated

Nightengale, B. (2018, May 15). Robinson Cano suspended 80 games by MLB for performance-enhancing drug violation. *USA Today*. www.usatoday.com/story/sports/mlb/2018/05/15/robinson-cano-suspended-performance-enhancing-drugs-steroids/612153002

Nightengale, B. (2014, March 28). MLB toughens drug agreement provisions. *USA Today*. www.usatoday.com/story/sports/mlb/2014/03/28/mlb-toughens-drug-agreement-provisions/7023401

Nixon, H.L. (1997). Gender, sport, and aggressive behavior outside sport. *Journal of Sport & Social Issues, 21*, 379–391.

Nixon, H.L. (2000). Sport and disability. In J. Coakley & E. Downing (Eds.), *Handbook of Sports Studies* (pp. 422–438). Thousand Oaks, CA: Sage.

Njuguna, W. (2004, June). Seeking the slot: Media coverage of disability issues. *PVA Magazine*. http://pvamag.com/pn/article/1193/seeking_the_slotmedia_coverage_of_disability_issues

North, A. (2019, May 3). "I am a woman and I am fast"; what Caster Semenya's story says about gender and race in sports. Vox.com. Retrieved from https://www.vox.com/identities/2019/5/3/18526723/caster-semenya-800-gender-race-intersex-athletes

Nylund, D. (2004). When in Rome: Heterosexism, homophobia, and sports talk radio. *Journal of Sport & Social Issues, 28*(2), 136–168.

O'Callaghan, R. with Zeigler, C. (2019). *My life on the line*. New York: Akashic Books.

One cyclist's brave candor. (2006, September 15). *Knight Ridder Tribune Business News*, p. 1.

Pallotta, F. (2016, June 6). Why Ashleigh Banfield read Stanford rape victim's letter on CNN. CNN. https://money.cnn.com/2016/06/06/media/ashleigh-banfield-cnn-stanford-letter

Park, M. (2018, August 9). Brock Turner loses appeal in sexual assault case. CNN. www.cnn.com/2018/08/08/us/brock-turner-appeal-rejected/index.html

Past pioneers. (2019). AWSM. http://awsmonline.org/mary-garber-pioneer-award#past-pioneers

Patra, K. (2019, March 15). NFL suspends RB Kareem Hunt eight games. NFL.com. www.nfl.com/news/story/0ap3000001022826/article/nfl-suspends-browns-rb-kareem-hunt-eight-games

Pedersen, P.M. (2002). Examining equity in newspaper photographs: A content analysis of the print media photographic coverage of interscholastic athletics. *International Review for the Sociology of Sport, 37*(3/4), 303-318.

Pennington, B., & Eder, S. (2014). In domestic violence cases, the NFL has a history of lenience. *New York Times*. www.nytimes.com/2014/09/20/sports/football/in-domestic-violence-cases-nfl-has-a-history-of-lenience.html?_r=0

Performance enhancing drugs in sports fast facts. (2019, June 7). CNN. www.cnn.com/2013/06/06/us/performance-enhancing-drugs-in-sports-fast-facts/index.html

PGA Tour world golf rankings. (2015). CBS Sports. www.cbssports.com/golf/rankings/world-rankings

Pilon, M., Lehren, A.W., Gosk, S., Siegel, E.R., Abou-Sabe, K. (2018, February 6). Think Olympic figure skating judges are biased? The data says they might be. NBC News. www.nbcnews.com/storyline/winter-olympics-2018/think-olympic-figure-skating-judges-are-biased-data-says-they-n844886

Plaschke, B. (2020, March 12). The day sports stopped. *Los Angeles Times*. www.latimes.com/sports/story/2020-03-12/plaschke-day-sports-stopped

Price, S. (2016, July 22). Everything you need to know about the doping scandal rocking the Russian national team. SB Nation. www.sbnation.com/2016/7/22/12258488/russia-doping-scandal-suspensions-rio-olympics-2016

Raisman, A. (2018, July 30). Cover of The Heroes Issue, *ESPN The Magazine*.

Reid, J. (2019, August 13). ROC Nation to lead NFL entertainment endeavors. ESPN. www.espn.com/nfl/story/_/id/27380099/roc-nation-lead-nfl-entertainment-endeavors

Rhoden, W.C. (2006). *Forty-million-dollar slaves: The rise, fall, and redemption of the black athlete*. New York: Crown.

Robertson, L. (2006, July 28). To the sports fan, just another fallen hero. *Knight Ridder Tribune Business News*, p. 1.

Robinson, M. (2019, June 23). "A spectacular and momentous day." *Richmond Times-Dispatch*, p. S4.

Rosenthal, K. (2019, November 19). Rosenthal: MLB's sign-stealing investigation should not stop at the Astros. The Athletic. https://theathletic.com/1393498/2019/11/19/rosenthal-mlbs-sign-stealing-investigation-should-not-stop-at-the-astros

Rowe, C.J. (1998). Aggression and violence in sports. *Psychiatric Annals, 28*, 265–269.

Rowe, D. (1999). *Sport, culture, and the media: The unruly trinity*. Buckingham, UK: Open University Press.

Rubin, A. (2016, February 13). Jenrry Mehia first player to get permanent ban for 3rd positive PED test. ESPN. http://espn.go.com/mlb/story/_/id/14768114/jenrry-mejia-new-york-mets-suspended-permanently-mlb-third-positive-ped-test

Sailes, G. (1993). An investigation of campus typecasts: The myth of black athletic superiority and the dumb jock stereotype. *Sport Sociology Journal, 10,* 88–97.

Sailes, G.A. (2017). The African American athlete: Social myths and stereotypes. In G.A. Sailes (Ed.), *African Americans in Sport* (3rd ed., pp. 183–198). New York: Routledge.

Salute at ESPYs: Smith and Carlos to receive Arthur Ashe Courage Award. (2008, May 29). ESPN. http://sports.espn.go.com/espn/news/story?id=3417048

Saraceno, F. (2004, August 6). Classic 1972 USA vs. USSR basketball game. ESPN Classic. http://espn.go.com/classic/s/Classic_1972_usa_ussr_gold_medal_hoop.html

Scarry, E. (2014, August 27). ESPN: Sorry we covered Michael Sam's locker room showering. Mediaite. www.mediaite.com/tv/espn-sorry-we-covered-michael-sams-locker-room-showering

Schultz, J. (2005). Reading the catsuit: Serena Williams and the production of blackness at the 2002 U.S. Open. *Journal of Sport & Social Issues, 29*(3), 338–357.

Senate marks 60th anniversary of NFL's integration. (2006, July 18). ESPN. http://sports.espn.go.com/nfl/news/story?id=2523315

Shea, B. (2019, October 8). How much does the NBA stand to lose in China over a tweet? The Athletic. https://theathletic.com/1275004/2019/10/08/how-much-does-the-nba-stand-to-lose-in-china-over-a-tweet

Shilton, A.C. (2019, January 4). Transgender track world champion defends her human right—to race. Bicycling.com. www.bicycling.com/culture/a25736012/transgender-world-champion-track-cycling-race

Smith, B. (2015, May 20). Caster Semenya: "What I dream of is to become Olympic champion." BBC. www.bbc.com/sport/athletics/32805695

Smith, M.D. (2018, June 29). NFL shows once again that its six-game suspension policy is meaningless. NBC Sports. https://profootballtalk.nbcsports.com/2018/06/29/nfl-shows-once-again-that-its-six-game-suspension-policy-is-meaningless

Smith, S.G., Zhang, X., Basile, K.C., Merrick, M.T., Wang, J., Kresnow, M., & Chen, J. (2018). The National Intimate Partner and Sexual Violence Survey (NISVS): 2015 Data Brief—Updated release. Atlanta, GA: National Center for Injury Prevention and Control, Centers for Disease Control and Prevention.

Spencer, N. (2003). "America's sweetheart" and "Czech-mate." *Journal of Sport & Social Issues, 27*(1), 18–37.

Staurowsky, E.J. (2004). Privilege at play: On the legal and social actions that sustain American Indian sport imagery. *Journal of Sport and Social Issues, 28,* 11–29.

Stevens, C. (2012). Violence by male athletes. Northeastern University Center for the Study of Sport in Society. www.northeastern.edu/sportinsociety/wp-content/uploads/2012/10/ViolenceByMaleAthletes.pdf

Strong, P.T. (2004). The mascot slot: Cultural citizenship, political correctness, and pseudo-Indian sports symbols. *Journal of Sport and Social Issues, 28,* 79–87.

Student chapters. (2019). AWSM. http://awsmonline.org/student-chapters

Taylor, P. (2014, September 14). The brutal truth. *Sports Illustrated.* www.si.com/vault/2014/09/15/106634562/the-brutal-truth

Tetrault-Farber, G. (2018, January 12). Years after Salt Lake City scandal, French judge finds peace. Reuters. www.reuters.com/article/us-olympics-2018-figs-scandal/years-after-salt-lake-city-scandal-french-judge-finds-peace-idUSKBN1F11L8

Thomas, D. (2006). "The quiet militant": Arthur Ashe and black athletic activism. In D.K. Wiggins (Ed.), *Out of the shadows: A biographical history of African American athletes* (pp. 279–296). Fayetteville: University of Arkansas Press.

Thompson, C. (2018, August 4). Michael Jordan backs away from President Trump with limpest possible statement. Deadspin. https://deadspin.com/michael-jordan-backs-away-from-president-trump-with-lim-1828107458

Tinker, B. (2016, June 9). What killed Muhammad Ali. CNN. www.cnn.com/2016/06/09/health/muhammad-ali-parkinsons-sepsis/index.html

Todd, J. (2005, March 18). Seoul scandal a benchmark in doping history: Ben Johnson is carving out a new career as a clothing designer but he will forever be known as Canada's "disgraced sprinter." *Edmonton Journal,* p. D5.

2015 ASNE Newsroom Census. (2014). American Society of News Editors. http://asne.org/content.asp?pl=121&sl=15&contentid=415

USA Today's NFL Player Arrest Database (2019). *USA Today.* www.usatoday.com/sports/nfl/arrests

Van Natta, D., Jr. (2013, October 2). Book: NFL crusaded against science. ESPN. http://espn.go.com/espn/otl/story/_/id/9745797/new-book-league-denial-says-nfl-used-resources-power-two-decades-deny-football-link-brain-damage

Waldron, T. (2015, November 10). Congressman wants to review NFL domestic violence policies in wake of Greg Hardy photos. *Huffington Post.* www.huffingtonpost.com/entry/greg-hardy-nfl-domestic-violence-congress_us_564222b4e4b0307f2caf1256

Ward, G.C. (2004). *Unforgivable blackness: The rise and fall of Jack Johnson.* New York: Knopf.

Washington state prosecutors drop assault charges against Hope Solo. (2018, May 25). *USA Today.* www.usatoday.com/story/sports/soccer/2018/05/25/authorities-drop-assault-charges-against-hope-solo/35372017

Weinreb, M. (2011, July 7). Renée Richards wants to be left alone. *Grantland*. http://grantland.com/features/reneacutee-richards-wants-left-alone

Wenner, L.A. (1998). Preface. In L.A. Wenner (Ed.), *MediaSport* (pp. xiii–xiv). London: Routledge.

Wertheim, J., & Luther, J. (2018, February 20). Exclusive: Inside the corrosive workplace culture of the Dallas Mavericks. *Sports Illustrated*. www.si.com/nba/2018/02/20/dallas-mavericks-sexual-misconduct-investigation-mark-cuban-response

Whisenant, W.A., & Pedersen, P.M. (2004). Analyzing attitudes regarding quantity and quality of sports page coverage: Athletic director perceptions of newspaper coverage given to interscholastic sports. *International Sports Journal, 8*(1), 54–64.

Whitaker, M.C. (2008). Introduction. In M.C. Whitaker (Ed.), *African American icons of sport: Triumph, courage, and excellence* (pp. xvii–xxi). Westport, CT: Greenwood Press.

Williams, M.P. (2019, June 23). Renaming paves way for progress. *Richmond Times-Dispatch*, p. S3.

141 women accept ESPYs' Arthur Ashe Courage Award for Larry Nassar survivors. (2018, July 18). NBC Sports.com. https://olympics.nbcsports.com/2018/07/18/espys-gymnasts-larry-nassar-aly-raisman

Women's Sports Foundation (2012). A Title IX primer. www.womenssportsfoundation.org/home/advocate/title-ix-and-issues/what-is-title-ix/title-ix-primer

Wong, P., Lai, C., Nagasawa, R., & Lin, T. (1998). Asian Americans as a model minority: Self-perceptions and perceptions by other racial groups. *Sociological Perspectives, 41*(1), 95–118.

Wright, C., Eagleman, A.N., & Pedersen, P.M. (2011). Examining leadership in intercollegiate athletics: A content analysis of NCAA Division I athletic directors. *Sport Management International Journal Choregia, 7*(2), 35–52.

Yan, H., & Alsup, D. (2014, May 13). NFL draft: Reactions heat up after Michael Sam kisses boyfriend on TV. *CNN*. www.cnn.com/2014/05/12/us/michael-sam-nfl-kiss-reaction

Yaptangco, A. (2018, September 9). Male tennis pros confirm Serena Williams' penalty was sexist and admit to saying worse on the court. *Elle*. www.elle.com/culture/a23051870/male-tennis-pros-confirm-serenas-penalty-was-sexist-and-admit-to-saying-worse-on-the-court

Young, K. (2012). *Sport, violence and society*. London: Routledge.

Young, K. (2019). *Sport, violence and society* (2nd ed.). London: Routledge.

Zeigler, C. (2011, October 4). Renee Richards gets ESPN treatment. *Outsports*. www.outsports.com/2011/10/4/4051946/renee-richards-gets-espn-treatment

Zillgitt, J. (2018, September 21). Three reasons the NBA didn't suspend Mavs owner Mark Cuban. *USA Today*. www.usatoday.com/story/sports/nba/2018/09/21/mark-cuban-adam-silver-penalty-not-supsended/1385039002

Chapter 13

Bilney v. The Evening Star Newspaper Co., 43 Md. App. 560 (1979).

Cardtoons, L.C. v. Major League Baseball Players Association, 95 F.3d 959 (10th Cir. 1996).

C.B.C. Distrib. & Mktg. v. Major League Baseball Advanced Media, L.P., 505 F.3d 818 (8th Cir. 2007).

Cook, A.D. (1999). Case note & comment, Should right of publicity protection be extended to actors in the characters which they portray. 9 *DePaul-LCA Journal of Art & Entertainment Law and Policy* 309.

Copyright Act, 17 U.S.C. §301 (1976).

Craig, A. K. (1994). The rise in press criticism of the athlete and the future of libel litigation involving athletes and the press. 4 *Seton Hall J. Sports L.* 527-763.

Crue v. Aiken, 370 F.3d 668 (7th Cir. 2004).

Curtis Publishing Co. v. Butts, 388 U.S. 130 (1967).

Davis v. Elec. Arts, Inc., 775 F.3d 1172 (2015).

Deitsch, R. (2017, November 26). Revisiting sexual harassment of female sports reporters and media members. *Sports Illustrated*. www.si.com/tech-media/2017/11/26/female-sports-reporters-sexual-harassment-media-circus.

Doe v. TCI Cablevision, 110 S.W. 3d 363 (Mo. 2003).

Druzin, R. (2001). Women reporters in the men's locker room: Rugged terrain. Women's Sports Foundation. www.druzin.com/womens-sports-foundation.html

Dryer v. NFL, 689 F.Supp. 2d 1113 (D. Minn., 2010).

Dryer v. NFL, 2013 U.S. Dist. LEXIS 39993 (2013).

Dryer v. NFL, 55 F.Supp. 3d 1181 (D. Minn. 2014).

Federal Trademark Act (Lanham Act), 60 Stat. 427 (1946).

Gionfriddo v. MLB, 94 Cal. App. 4th 400 (Cal. App. 1st Dist., 2001).

Griswold v. Connecticut, 381 U.S. 479 (1965).

Haelan Labs., Inc. v. Topps Chewing Gum Inc., 202 F.2d 866 (2d Cir. N.Y., 1953).

Hanlon, S. & Yasser, R. (2008). "J.J. Morrison" and his right of publicity lawsuit against the NCAA. *Villanova Sports and Entertainment Law Journal, 15*, 241–298.

Hart v. Electronic Arts, Inc., 717 F.3d 141 (2013).

Hazelwood School Dist. v. Kuhlmeier, 484 U.S. 260 (1988).

In re NCAA Student-Athlete Name & Likeness Licensing Litig., 37 F. Supp. 3d 1126 (N.D. Cal, 2013).

Keller v. Electronic Arts, et al., 2013. https://pennstatelaw.psu.edu/_file/Sports%20Law%20Policy%20and%20Research%20Institute/Keller_v_EA-OBannon.pdf

Keller v. Elec. Arts, Inc., 2010 U.S. Dist. LEXIS 10719 (N.D. Cal., 2010).

Landes, W.M., & Posner, R.A. (2003). *The economic structure of intellectual property law*. Cambridge, MA: Harvard University Press.

Lapchick, R. (2018). The 2018 Associated Press Sports Editors racial and gender report card. http://tidesport.org

Laucella, P., & Osborne, B. (2002). Libel and college coaches. *Journal of Legal Aspects of Sport, 12,* 183–204.

Ludtke v. Kuhn, 461 F.Supp. 86 (S.D. N.Y., 1978).

Marshall v. ESPN Inc., 2015 U.S. Dist. LEXIS 72494 (M. D. Tenn., 2015).

Mather, V. (2019, August 5). Alejandro Bedoya spoke out on gun violence. It helped make him M.L.S.'s player of the week. *The New York Times.* www.nytimes.com/2019/08/05/sports/alejandro-bedoya-mls-gun-violence.html

McCann, M. (2018, May 21). Ex-USC coach Todd McNair losing trial to NCAA shows why defamation lawsuits are tricky to win. *Sports Illustrated.* www.si.com/college-football/2018/05/21/todd-mcnair-usc-loses-ncaa-defamation-lawsuit

Mitten, M., Davis, T., Shropshire, K., Osborne, B., & Smith, R. (2013). *Sports law governance and regulation.* New York: Wolters Kluwer Law & Business.

Morris Communications Corporation v. PGA Tour, Inc., 364 F.3d 1288 (11th Cir., 2004).

NBA v. Motorola, Inc., 105 F.3d 841 (2nd Cir., 1997).

New York Times v. Sullivan, 367 U.S. 254 (1964).

New York Yankees Partnership v. Evil Enterprises, Inc., 2013 WL 1305332 (T.T.A.B.) (2013).

NFL v. TvRadioNow Corp., 53 U.S.P.Q.2d 1831 (W.D. Pa. 2000).

Nichols, J.M. (2014, February 13). Sam Wheeler, Kent State wrestler, suspended for anti-gay tweets about Michael Sam. *Huffington Post.* www.huffingtonpost.com/2014/02/11/sam-wheeler-suspended_n_4768838.html

O'Brien v. Pabst Sales Co., 124 F.2d 167 (5th Cir., 1941).

Palmer v. Schonhorn Enterprises, Inc., 96 N.J. Super. 72 (1967).

Pedersen, P.M., Osborne, B., Whisenant, W., & Lim, C.H. (2009). An examination of the perceptions of sexual harassment by newspaper sports journalists. *Journal of Sport Management, 23*(3), 335–360.

Prosser, W.L. (1960). Privacy. *California Law Review, 48*(3)383–423.

Restatement of Torts, 3rd. American Law Institute (1998).

Rosenbloom v. Metromedia, Inc., 403 U.S. 29 (1971).

Sharp, K. (1997). Ex-patriot. *Women's Sports & Fitness, 19*(9), 27–28.

Sherman Antitrust Act, 15 U.S.C. §1 (1890).

Sheinin, D. (2019, October 24). Brandon Taubman fired by Astros in wake of incident with female reporters. *The Washington Post.* www.washingtonpost.com/sports/2019/10/24/brandon-taubman-fired-by-astros-wake-incident-with-female-reporters

Telander, R. (1984). The written word: Player-press relationships in American sports. *Sociology of Sport Journal, 1,* 3–14.

Tinker v. Des Moines Indep. Cmty. School Dist., 393 U.S. 503 (1969).

Title VII of the Civil Rights Act, 42 USCS §2000 (1964).

Trademark Revisions Act, 134 Cong Rec H 10411(1988).

Univ. of Ala. Bd. of Trs. v. New Life Art, Inc., 2013 U.S. Dist. LEXIS 139864 (N.D. Ala., 2013).

Vera, A. (2018, September 4). How National Anthem protests took Colin Kaepernick from star quarterback to unemployment to a bold Nike ad. CNN. www.cnn.com/2018/09/04/us/colin-kaepernick-controversy-q-and-a/index.html

Warford v. Lexington Herald-Leader Co., 789 S.W.2d 758 (Ky. 1990).

Warren, S., & Brandeis, L. (1890). The right to privacy. *Harvard Law Review, 4*(5), 193–220.

Williams, D. (2012, July 24). Athletes trademarking the phrase that pays. http://espn.go.com/blog/playbook/fandom/post/_/id/6108/athlete-trademarks-becoming-commonplace

Young, J. (2019, October 10). Sports agents warn NBA players to avoid China talk as athletes, executives walk "fine line." CNBC. www.cnbc.com/2019/10/10/sports-agents-warn-players-to-avoid-china-talk-as-nba-walks-fine-line.html

Zacchini v. Scripps-Howard Broadcasting Company, 433 U.S. 562 (1977).

Index

Note: The italicized *f* and *t* following page numbers refer to figures and tables, respectively.

About the Authors

Photo courtesy of Jennifer L. Pedersen.

Paul M. Pedersen, PhD, is a professor of sport management in the School of Public Health at Indiana University at Bloomington (IU). In addition to teaching undergraduate and graduate courses at IU, Pedersen has been the doctoral chair of 19 PhD graduates and a committee member of another 22 dissertations. As an extension of his previous work as a sportswriter and sport business columnist, Pedersen's primary areas of scholarly interest and research are the symbiotic relationship between sport and communication as well as the activities and practices of various sport organization personnel.

A research fellow of the North American Society for Sport Management (NASSM), Pedersen has published eight books (including *Contemporary Sport Management*, *Handbook of Sport Communication*, and *Strategic Sport Communication*) and more than 100 articles in peer-reviewed outlets such as the *Journal of Sport Management*, *European Sport Management Quarterly*, *Sport Marketing Quarterly*, *International Journal of Sports Marketing and Sponsorship*, *Sociology of Sport Journal*, *International Review for the Sociology of Sport*, and *Journal of Sports Economics*. He has also been a part of more than 100 refereed presentations at professional conferences and more than 50 invited presentations, including invited addresses in China, Denmark, Hungary, Norway, and South Korea. He has been interviewed and quoted in publications as diverse as the *New York Times* and *China Daily*.

Founder and editor in chief of the *International Journal of Sport Communication*, he serves on the editorial board of nine journals. A 2011 inductee into the Golden Eagle Hall of Fame (East High School in Pueblo, Colorado), Pedersen lives in Bloomington, Indiana, with his wife, Jennifer, and their two youngest children, Brock and Carlie. Their two oldest children, Hallie and Zack, graduated from IU.

Photo courtesy of Pamela C. Laucella.

Pamela C. Laucella, PhD, is the academic director of the sports capital journalism program at Indiana University–Purdue University Indianapolis (IUPUI) as well as an associate professor. She was previously academic director of the National Sports Journalism Center and, along with the former director, helped create and develop the first sport journalism graduate program in the United States. She earned her PhD in journalism and mass communication from the University of North Carolina at Chapel Hill, where she was a Roy H. Park fellow, and received her master's and bachelor degrees from The George Washington University and the University of Virginia, respectively.

Before coming to IUPUI, Laucella was an assistant professor of sport communication at Indiana University and an assistant professor in communication studies at Christopher Newport University.

Laucella's positions integrate academia and industry. She has moderated numerous panels and supervised students at major sporting events like the Women's Final Four and the Indianapolis 500, editing articles for sites such as those of NCAA, Turner Sports, and the *Indianapolis Star*.

Laucella has presented at numerous professional conferences in journalism, sociology, history, and communication and has published in peer-reviewed national and international journals, including *Journalism & Mass Communication Quarterly*, *Journal of Sports Media*, and *International Journal of Sport Communication*. Outside of IUPUI, she has served as head and vice head of the Association for Education in Journalism and Mass Communication's Sports Communication Interest Group. She is active in the North American Society for the Sociology of Sport, the Association for Education in Journalism and Mass Communication, the National Communication Association, and the Association for Women in Sports Media.

Laucella is originally from Richmond, Virginia, and enjoys hiking with her rescue Labrador retriever, doing yoga, playing tennis, and swimming. She also plays the violin, writes creative nonfiction, and roots for her ACC alma maters.

Courtesy of Oklahoma State University.

Edward (Ted) M. Kian, PhD, is a professor and the Welch-Bridgewater Endowed Chair of Sports Media in the School of Media and Strategic Communications at Oklahoma State University. He earned an undergraduate degree in journalism from the University of Georgia, a master's in sport management from the University of Texas at Austin, and a doctorate in sport administration from Florida State University.

Previously, he served on the faculty at the University of Central Florida, where he was founding coordinator of the graduate program in sport leadership and coaching and held the rank of tenured associate professor of sport administration. Kian's research focuses on sport media, examining the framing of gender, sex, and LGBT issues in media coverage and social media content; attitudes and experiences of sport media members; and marketing of sport. He has authored more than 100 journal articles, conference papers, and book chapters, and his work has appeared in top journals from a variety of academic disciplines. Dr. Kian has reviewed more than 110 submissions for 30 different academic journals as an editorial board member or ad hoc reviewer.

Kian's journalism, research, and expertise have been cited by media outlets such as 60 Minutes, the New York Times, and Fox Sports. Dr. Kian has 15 years of professional experience in sport communication, having worked in the newspaper, magazine, and radio industries as well as in media relations. He served as prep sports editor for the *Press-Telegram* (Long Beach), where he was on a team of reporters honored with a national Associated Press sports editors award for investigative journalism. Among his other positions were serving as a full-time sportswriter for the *Pensacola News Journal*, covering University of Texas athletics as editor and website manager for *Horns Illustrated*, and being one of the original contracted bloggers for AOL Fanhouse, where he wrote about University of Georgia and Southeastern Conference football.

Photo courtesy of Andrea N. Geurin.

Andrea N. Geurin, PhD, is a reader and the program director for the master's sport marketing program in the Institute for Sport Business at Loughborough University London. She has published extensively on the topics of sport communication and marketing, focusing on athletes' and sport organizations' use of social media and on media portrayals of athletes with regard to race, gender, and nationality. Her work has appeared in more than 40 peer-reviewed articles in publications such as *Journal of Sport Management*, *Sport Management Review*, *European Sport Management Quarterly*, *Sport Marketing Quarterly*, and *International Journal of Sport Communication*.

She has presented her research at conferences and invited lectures around the world, including the United States, Canada, Mexico, Germany, Spain, Australia, New Zealand, Ireland, Norway, Sweden, and South Korea. In 2015, she was named a North American Society for Sport Management (NASSM) research fellow in recognition of her outstanding contributions to the field of sport management. Additionally, she received the NASSM Janet B. Parks research grant in 2012 and 2015. Geurin is an associate editor of *Managing Sport and Leisure* and *Frontiers in Sports and Active Living*. Additionally, she serves on the editorial boards of six academic journals and is a professional member of the European Association for Sport Management (EASM) and NASSM, where she served on the executive council from 2017 to 2019.

Prior to her appointment at Loughborough University London in 2019, Geurin was an associate professor and served as the academic director of graduate programs in the Tisch Institute for Global Sport at New York University. She also held full-time faculty positions at Griffith University (Australia), Massey University (New Zealand), Indiana University–Purdue University Indianapolis, Indiana University at Bloomington, and Saint Mary's College of California. She earned her undergraduate degree in journalism from Indiana University, where she also received both her master's degree and her PhD in sport management.

Geurin is a former sport public relations professional who held positions with USA Gymnastics and the National Hot Rod Association (NHRA) Top Fuel drag-racing team. Originally from Mount Vernon, Indiana, Geurin was awarded the Mount Vernon Senior High School Outstanding Alumnus Award in 2019 and served as the commencement speaker at the class of 2019 graduation ceremony. In her spare time, she enjoys running; yin yoga; traveling with her partner, Martyn; and spending time with her cat, DC.